this
business of
MUSIC

the definitive guide to the music industry
9th edition

M. William Krasilovsky
and Sidney Shemel

Contributions by John M. Gross

BILLBOARD BOOKS
an imprint of Watson-Guptill Publications, New York

Senior editor: Bob Nirkind
Production manager: Hector Campbell
Cover design by Spencer Drate
Book design by Eric Baker Design Associates

First Published in 2003 by Watson-Guptill Publications,
a division of VNU Business Media, Inc.
770 Broadway, New York, N.Y. 10003
www.watsonguptill.com

ISBN: 0-8230-7728-4

Library of Congress Control Number: 2003103770

Printed in the United States
First printing, 2003
3 4 5 6 7 8 9 / 10 09 08 07 06 05 04

Dedication

In the memory of Donald E. Biederman, an esteemed attorney and friend who made substantial contributions throughout his career in music business education and practice

Acknowledgments

We wish to acknowledge the devoted and expert editorial services of Sylvia Warren, a veteran editor who has worked with us on this as well as the prior eighth edition. She has been a major constructive force in bringing this edition to completion. In doing so, both she and the authors of this edition have worked with the continuing cooperation and supervision of Bob Nirkind, Executive Editor of Billboard Books.

We also wish to acknowledge our special indebtedness for the valuable research and editorial contributions made by Maya Funaro and William Marino. Assistance in specialized areas was generously given by many fellow members of the music industry. Especially deserving of note are Lewis Bachman, Ed Cramer, Pamela M. Golinski, David Grossberg, Elissa Hecker, Carol Hernandez, Ronald S. Kadden, Mike Kissell, Joan McGivern, Gary Roth, Peter Spellman, and Jim Steinblatt.

Table of Contents

In the first edition of *This Business of Music,* published in 1964, we stated our goal as follows:

> This book has been written with a view toward assisting participants in the music and recording industries to understand the workings of the business and their rights and obligations. It is meant to present the economic facts for day-to-day decisions and actions and to act as a simplified guide to common legal concepts underlying business determinations. . . . It is hoped that the participants in the music business may use this volume to increase their understanding of its practices both here and overseas.

We have sought to maintain this goal throughout the book's various updates. This current edition continues to cover copyright revisions, Berne Convention requirements, the dominance of major labels and major music publishers, and new media. This edition also updates sections on government demands for increased regulation, the ongoing search for secure copyright digital initiative, challenges in defining and protecting the public domain, artist dissatisfaction with traditional accounting practices, and the increasing strength of foreign markets. The sheet music industry has been given a new lease on life due to digital methods of distribution, and we have, accordingly, devoted an entire chapter to sheet music. We have also included a new section on the buying and selling of record companies.

In the late 1960s Marshal McLuhan stated: "The medium is the message." In the new millennium print, broadcast, and other performance and mechanical forms of reproduction are no longer discrete entities: as the various media have converged, the message has become dominant. At the same time, content that in the past was mainly available only in tangible, printed form can now be accessed, read, and printed out via a personal computer. Films, videotapes, recordings, and radio programs are now available via that same personal computer, and all of these media but streamed radio broadcasts can also be downloaded and stored on CDs or DVDs that are owned by consumers. In this world of media convergence, music is an essential ingredient. Our goal in this edition, therefore, is not only to educate our readers about the customs and practices of the music business but also to give them useful tools for survival in this new world.

We think it is likely that new forms of financial compensation will develop to meet the challenges of digital distribution, but it is imperative that they remain consistent with the copyright clause of the Constitution: "To promote the progress of science and useful arts, by securing for limited times to authors the exclusive right to their writings and discoveries."

In the 8th edition, a CD-ROM was included which gave readers access to selected contract forms. Some of the contents of that CD-ROM, as well as additional materials, are now available on our Web site: **www.thisbusinessofmusic.info**

—M. William Krasilovsky and John M. Gross

Part One

Music Business Trends and Transformations

1

The Music Industry in the 1990s

The music business is dynamic and ever-changing. Its consumers include amateur and professional performers as well as listeners. A 2002 Gallup poll found that 50 percent of American households included one or more members who played a musical instrument, up from 38 percent in 1997.

But according to a U.S. Department of Labor report,* there were only 240,000 music-related salaried jobs in 2000, and significant numbers of musicians were "between engagements." Median annual earnings of salaried musicians in 2000 were $36,740. Overall employment is expected to grow only as much as other professions between now and 2010, according to the U.S. Department of Labor. "Musicians often must supplement their income with earnings from other sources because they can find only part-time or sporadic employment," the report stated.

On the other hand, the category of "listener" encompasses practically the entire population. The average American listens to about 20.5 hours of radio per week, much of it as background music in restaurants, hotel lobbies, elevators, and factories. People listen to music in airplanes, while playing video games or jogging, or while driving. Car radios alone reach four out of five adults.

Music is big business in the United States. There are about 10,300 commercial radio and 1,550 television stations in operation and an estimated 575 million radios and 219 million television sets in use. Ninety-nine percent of American homes have radios—an average of five or more—and 98 percent have at least one television set, which is on almost 7 hours a day.

Finally, between 2000 and 2001, total sales of prerecorded music video programming on videocassette rose from $281 million to $329 million. The same year, sales of music videos in the digital versatile disc (DVD) format skyrocketed from $80 million to $190 million. Music is also an essential part of most other DVDs such as feature films. By 2002, over 1 billion DVDs had been pro-

*The Department of Labor statistics do not include the large number of independent contractors who work part-time or full-time in the music industry on an unsalaried basis.

duced, making it the fastest recorded medium to reach that mark. In 2001 DVD sales were at $4.6 billion, and by the end of 2002, 31 million players had been sold.

New technology has always had a dramatic effect on the music business, ever since the day Al Jolson sang "Mammy" in the first public demonstration of the "talkies" (motion pictures with sound). The industry has progressed from Edison's cylinder recordings to shellac 78 rpms, long-play 45 rpms and 33¹/₃s, to 8-track tapes and cassettes, to compact discs (CDs) and DVDs. Recording studios are relying more and more on synthesizers, drum machines, and digital equipment for recording, engineering, and mixing. And just as bar coding has made retail inventory control much more efficient, new methods are being developed to identify performance and mechanical rights with greater accuracy.

Industry Growth

For 25 years, beginning in the mid-1950s, sales of sound recordings grew an average of 20 percent a year. The most dramatic growth came in the 1970s when sales (based on manufacturers' suggested list prices) rose from less than $2 billion at the beginning of the decade to over $4 billion in 1978; that year, however, sales began to fall sharply, reflecting in part the American economy as well as the effect of home taping.

Table 1-1

Percent of Market for All Music Genres, 1989, 1993, and 2001

Genre	1989	1993	2001
Rock	41.7%	30.2%	24.4%
Country	7.3	18.7	10.5
R&B	9.5	10.6	10.6
Rap/Hip-Hop	6.4	9.2	11.4
Pop	15.0	11.9	12.1
Religious	3.1	3.2	6.7
Classical	3.6	3.3	3.2
Jazz	4.9	3.1	3.4
Oldies	0.9	1.0	0.8
Soundtracks	0.7	0.7	1.4
New Age	1.4	1.0	1.0
Children's	0.3	0.4	0.5
Other (includes Latin)	4.0	4.6	7.9

Source: Recording Industry Association of America, 1998, 2001 *Consumer Profile.*

But this situation changed in 1984. When CDs entered the consumer market, sales once again exceeded $4 billion. By 1988, the combined dollar volume of record, tape, and CD shipments rose to $6.25 billion, according to the Recording Industry Association of America (RIAA). By 1998 sales figures for combined audio and music video product had risen to $13.7 billion.

Between 1997 and 1998, CDs grew 15.1 percent, while cassette sales decreased 6.8 percent. Sales of CD singles dropped 21.8 percent. Vinyl LPs and singles continued to decline to relatively insignificant sales.

In 1994 the RIAA reported that rock, country, and pop registered as clear favorites among consumers. Country more than doubled in size over the previous five years, rock's share of the market came down from a high of 41.7 to a still impressive 35.1 percent, while rap decreased slightly from the prior year, to 7.9 percent. By 2001 the situation had changed: rock was now at 24.4 percent, country at 10.5 percent, R&B at 10.6 percent, and rap, at 11.4 percent, was catching up with pop, at 12.1 percent (see Table 1-1).

RIAA statistics show that by 2001, record stores had almost been overtaken by other retail outlets such as department stores, electronics retailers, and large chain stores like Wal-Mart and Target as the primary consumer outlets for records and tapes. Record stores slipped from 60 percent of total consumer sales in 1992 to 42.5 percent in 2001. During the same period, other retail outlet stores rose from 24.9 to 42.4 percent, while record clubs declined from 11.4 to 6.1 percent. Finally, Internet sales went from having no share of the market, as late as 1995, to a 2.9 percent share in 2001.

In other areas, aggregate annual sales of sheet music decreased from $433.5 million in 1997 to $328 million in 2001. However, collections by performing rights organizations had climbed in this period. The American Society of Composers, Authors, and Publishers (ASCAP) collected over $635 million on behalf of its members as of end of year 2000. In 1999 ASCAP collected $508 million. As of December 31, 2002, ASCAP writer membership was close to 100,000 and its publisher membership was 48,000.

Broadcast Music Inc. (BMI), which represents about 300,000 writers and publishers combined, collected $540.8 million at the end of fiscal year 2001, up from $455 million in 1998.

The third U.S. performing rights organization, SESAC, would not make recent figures available; in 1983 it collected $5 million. According to SESAC, its membership includes some 8,000 writers and publishers and has a catalog of more than 200,000 compositions.

The figures cited for all three organizations include substantial sums forwarded by foreign affiliates on behalf of songwriter shares.

Factors Relating to Growth

New technology has been responsible for much of the industry's growth. In 1948 the LP was introduced; stereo dominated toward the close of the

1960s. Prerecorded cartridges and cassettes, which were introduced in the mid-1960s,opened an entirely new market for record manufacturers. In 1983, cassettes became the configuration of choice, but by 2000 CDs dominated unit sales, with cassettes constituting only about 35 percent of unit sales and vinyl less than 1 percent.

Today's technology includes digital audio tape (DAT), the tape counterpart to the CD. DAT tapes are smaller than the standard cassette and permit up to 2 hours of programming—more than twice as much as a CD. However, unlike the practically indestructible CD, DAT tape deteriorates. Additionally, DVD audio and Super Audio CD offer even better sound quality and are extremely durable. One of the most dramatic developments has been the surge of MP3 compressed music files and the extensive incursion into conventional marketing.

Videocassettes, videocassette recorders (VCRs), and DVDs have also accounted for considerable growth. By 2001, 95 million American households were equipped with a VCR and 30 million with a DVD player. In 2001 videocassette and DVD rentals and purchases totaled $16.8 billion. Whether the videocassettes or DVDs were full-length films with background or incidental music or musical motion pictures or concerts, the music industry gained substantially from this market.

Industry growth over the last few decades can also be attributed to new marketing methods: rack jobbing, mail-order and record clubs, and, most recently, mail order via the Internet. Rack jobbing was introduced in the mid-1950s; record companies set up and maintained large-scale displays of records and tapes in supermarkets, variety stores, department and discount stores, drugstores, and other retail outlets. Many record stores, including Borders Books & Music, have installed listening stations or "kiosks" that allow consumers to preview albums or help them navigate the inventory of the store.

In the 1950s record companies set up clubs to target older consumers. CBS created the Columbia House club in 1955; in 1991 it was jointly owned by Sony (CBS's successor) and Time Warner. In June 2002 Sony and Time Warner sold a major interest to Blackstone Capital Partners. The RCA Record Club, which was first created in 1958, is now known as BMG Music Service and is an affiliate of Bertelsmann Music Group. As of 2001, record club sales had declined to 6.1 percent of the total U.S. market, supplemented by other direct marketing of another 3 percent. Germany, the United Kingdom, and the Netherlands have higher percentages of total sales through clubs. Market research suggests that aging baby-boomers prefer the convenience of record clubs to the noise and hassle of shopping malls and large retail outlets.

On-line record stores and chains such as CDNow, Tower, and Sam Goody, as well as on-line bookstores such as amazon.com (currently the largest online music retailer) and barnesandnoble.com, are targeting both the older home shopper and the young, college-aged computer browser through the Internet, offering an immense selection of mail-order CDs, DVDs, videocassettes, and tapes.

It is widely believed that there is a long-term benefit to the music industry in the expansion of leisure time in the United States. Older persons have more income upon retirement, and those who continue in the current work force have larger entertainment budgets. In 2001, consumers 45 years and older accounted for 23.7 percent of the record-buying market; this figure represents a total increase of 12.2 percent since 1992.

Demographic shifts have opened up new domestic markets. According to the RIAA, Latin music sales for 2001 were at $582.6 million; this represents an increase of over 100 percent from the $268 million reported in 1996. The U.S. Hispanic market has been steadily increasing since 1993, except for a temporary 12 percent decrease in sales for 1997. It is interesting to note that in 2001, 594 U.S. radio stations were broadcasting full-time in Spanish, up from 454 in 1999. By the end of 2002 the importance of Latin music was such that *The Latin Grammy Show* was featured in prime time on CBS.

The countries that now form the European Union have lowered their trade barriers. This has had profound effects on the music business. It has led to both consolidation and competition among the various European subpublishers, record companies, and performance and mechanical collection societies. In the open-border world of Europe, the legality of exclusivity within any area of the European Union must be called into question. Some "social and cultural" national favoritism is allowed, but with international broadcast programming, deregulation of broadcasting, and joint film production and marketing, a European market which equals the North American market seems possible.

Factors Inhibiting Growth

The RIAA estimates that lost sales due to piracy amounted to over $4 billion in 2001. According to the RIAA , out of the 27, 000 records released in the United States annually about 10 percent are profitable, and it is often the hit records that are the target of commercial pirates.

The music industry has long been concerned about DAT technology. Initially, it opposed the introduction of DAT into the United States because it was afraid that DAT would stunt the CD market and result in mass home duplication of high-quality recordings, with an attendant loss of compensation to record companies, artists, and music publishers. Ultimately, the copyright industries and the manufacturers of DAT equipment reached an agreement, which was officially legislated in the Audio Home Recording Act (AHRA) of 1992.

Much of the industry's attention in the last several years has been focused on controlling new technologies, especially the MP3 format, and the piracy and bootlegging that these new technologies have enabled. Many believe that these new formats are the greatest threat faced by the music industry today; others consider them the greatest opportunity. There has been a parade of legal and commercial developments in response to them. At the time of this writing, the situation is still very much in flux.

Legislative Changes

When he was presiding over the U.S. Patent Office, Thomas Jefferson stated: "Laws and institutions must go hand in hand with the progress of the human mind. As that becomes more developed, more enlightened, as new discoveries are made . . . institutions must advance also to keep pace with the times. We might as well require a man to wear still the coat which fitted him when a boy." Technological advancements necessitate legislative review and changes. Since 1994, significant and timely legislative changes have occurred in rapid succession. This was largely in response to new requirements under the Berne Convention and the General Agreement on Tariffs and Trade (GATT) and to the need for artist digital performance rights. The major recent statutes are:

- ► 1988: Berne Convention Implementation Act
- ► 1992: Audio Home Recording Act
- ► 1994: Uruguay Round Agreements Act passed by the World Trade Organization
- ► 1995: Digital Performance Right in Sound Recordings
- ► 1997: No Electronic Theft Act, which defined criminal acts in digital recording
- ► 1998: Technical correction to 1976 Copyright Act, which amended the definition of *publication* concerning pre-1978 sound recordings ("The La Cienga" clarification)
- ► 1998: Digital Millennium Copyright Act, bringing the United States into compliance with two World Intellectual Property Organization (WIPO) treaties dealing with issues related to copyright in a digital environment
- ► 1998: Copyright Term Extension Act, to conform to copyright duration in other major nations
- ► 1999: Fairness in Music Licensing Act, which exempts small restaurants and shops from performance licensing

Part Two

Record Industry Agreements and Practices

2

Recording Artist Contracts

A lot of kids dream of becoming recording stars, of being the next Linkin Park, Alicia Keys, Britney Spears, Jennifer Lopez, or Garth Brooks. But it's often a long, tough road between the dream and the recording contract. Assuming would-be stars do not wish to launch their careers through their own Web site, or one hosted by others, they must first make contact with a record producer or an A&R (artists and repertoire) executive, usually through a recommendation from a friend, a manager, an attorney, an agent, another artist, or a music publisher. Or they may put a demonstration record into a producer's hands or get a break simply by haunting the offices of the record companies—one of the big five record companies (Sony, Warner, BMG, Universal, EMI); one of the many smaller labels owned by the big five (e.g., Epic, Jive, Interscope); or one of the independents (e.g., Koch, Epitaph, TVT, Fantasy). Assuming that their talent is recognized and they are offered a recording contract, artists must then try to negotiate a fair and reasonable agreement. For this, they need an understanding of the basic elements of a standard recording contract and, preferably, the aid and advice of a knowledgeable representative, such as a manager or an attorney.

The Standard Agreement

Under the standard agreement, the artist is engaged to render his or her personal services as a recording artist on an exclusive basis for the purpose of making recordings from which records can be derived. The term *records* encompasses not only traditional compact discs, cassettes, and other "hard" devices, including videos that contain the artist's recorded performances, but also interactive media (e.g., CD-ROM) and electronic transmissions (e.g., streamed digital audio, whether or not downloadable).

The artist is required to appear at times and places designated by the record company to perform for the purpose of making recordings to be delivered to the record company. These recordings must be acceptable to the record company as being "technically and commercially satisfactory." Although the standard agreement states that the musical selections to be recorded will be selected by the record company, in practice the company may give the artist the right to select compositions to be recorded, subject to the record company's approval.

In the case of record companies which are signatory to agreements with the American Federation of Television and Radio Artists (AFTRA) or the American Federation of Musicians (AFM) (which includes all the "majors"), the artist is required to be a union member or become one within 30 days, and the artist must be paid no less than union scale. Most artists receive advances in excess of union scale.

The record company agrees to pay all recording costs, including artist's advances, fees to the producers and arrangers, copyists, engineers, and musicians, as well as studio and equipment rental charges and mixing and editing costs. Recording costs so paid by the record company are deemed to be advances against (that is, recoupable out of) royalties payable to the artist.

Duration

The standard agreement runs for a term based on the delivery of a minimum number of recordings plus a period of time following acceptance of the recordings (usually 9 months). The minimum number of recordings has traditionally been framed in terms of albums (defined as not less than 10 individual selections totaling not less than 50 to 55 minutes duration). In the Internet era, however, because consumers will likely be able to buy a selection of individual tracks rather than an entire album, this may have to be modified. The record company generally has options to extend the agreement for additional albums. Even when the contract period is stated in years, a contract year is invariably connected with the delivery of a product, since the passage of time without the delivery of recordings is of no interest to a record company.

Most recording contracts are either signed in or made subject to the laws of New York or California. Under California law a personal service contract which lasts more than 7 years cannot be specifically enforced. New York does not have a maximum term for personal service contracts, so it is up to the courts to decide whether the length of an exceptionally long-term commitment violates public policy. Contracts with minors are special situations that may require shorter contract terms (see the discussion in Chapter 5).

If an artist fails to fulfill his or her obligations, most recording contracts permit the record company to suspend the running of the term. In other words, the "clock stops" until such time as the artist cures his or her failure to perform. Theoretically, if the artist continues to fail to perform, he or she could be bound indefinitely. However, courts have generally tended to grant relief to the artist. For example, in *Vanguard Recording Society, Inc. v. Kweskin*, 276 F. Supp. 563 (S.D.N.Y. 1967), a New York federal court refused to enjoin the artist from performing for a different record company where enforcement of a suspension clause for an indefinite period would make the contract "harsh and unreasonable."

In a California case, MCA Records sought to prevent the recording artist Olivia Newton-John from recording for another label after an alleged breach by the artist in the delivery of recordings. The California Court of Appeals stated that the artist could not be prevented from recording for another company for a period longer than the one in which her commitments to MCA could have been fully performed. This was considered to be 5 years (an initial period of 2 years plus three 1-year options). MCA unsuccessfully contended that the term could be extended for up to 7 years by reason of contractual language permitting suspension until the delivery of recordings was completed. As a consequence, record companies usually define the duration of a recording contract in terms of satisfactory delivery of a stipulated number of albums, not in terms of a stated number of years. (See *MCA Records, Inc. v. Newton-John*, 90 Cal. App. 3d 18 [1979].)

Under section 3423 of the California Labor Code, record companies must pay a guaranteed minimum amount per year in order to obtain an injunction against an artist seeking to leave a label while still under exclusive contract. It is important to note that this California statute relates to obtaining a court order barring recording for another company, but does not affect the continuing right to sue for monetary damages should any recording so forbidden be made. The minimum guaranteed payments (subject to further conditions based on actual payments) are as follows:

YEAR 1: $9,000

YEAR 2: $12,000

YEARS 3–7: $15,000

Recording budgets and tour support payments are not part of this guaranteed minimum amount.

These guaranteed payments must be fixed and not merely contingent amounts to be paid under a royalty deal. However, the contingent factor of earned royalties can be used to pay the additional sums required in years 4 and 5 ($15,000) and in years 6 and 7 ($30,000) as long as such sums are actually paid. Any amounts earned in excess of statutory minimums in any particular year can be carried forward as a credit for the next or subsequent years' minimums.

A fail-safe clause in the California law provides that an artist can still be prevented from terminating an agreement, even if it is not in conformity with the requirements of the law, if the record company makes a lump-sum payment to the artist that is 10 times the required minimums. For example, if the first-year guarantee of $9,000 were missing from the agreement, a record company could still make a $90,000 late payment to prevent an artist from terminating by reason of the omission. This is appropriately called the "superstar insurance provision."

Group Artists

A recording contract may cover two or more artists who perform together as a group. In addition to acquiring the exclusive right to the group's recording services, the record company acquires the exclusive right to use the group's name on records during the term of the agreement. If the group has recorded previously on another label, the contract may include a provision recognizing the right of the first record company to continue using the group name on its recordings.

The time may come when, for various reasons, the group members' paths diverge. When a group member drops out, a satisfactory replacement must be found. This may cause problems between the record company and the remaining group members. The record company may wish to select or approve the replacement so as to ensure the continuation of the group's special sound or quality, but the group may fight for the right to select its own replacement.

The record company may also contend that it is entitled to continue to record the dropout artist as a solo artist, especially if the departing member is a standout performer in the group. The terms of an agreement covering a potential solo artist entail separate negotiations when the group is first signed. The provisions ordinarily run the gamut of those commonly contained in a solo artist agreement, including the initial period of the recording contract, renewal options, royalties, advances, and recording and release commitments.

In some instances, an A&R person may propose that two artists under separate agreements perform together on one or more records. A combined recording made by well-known artists, for example, The Three Tenors, may achieve greater sales than records featuring each artist separately. Record contracts anticipate the division of royalties in such cases by providing for the apportionment of the royalties and the recording costs.

Exclusivity

Record companies customarily acquire the exclusive right to record an artist during the term of the recording agreement, although there are exceptions in classical music and jazz. Without exclusivity, different companies could issue competing versions of an artist's recordings, with resultant confusion. Furthermore, a record company would be unwilling to spend the time and money required to develop and promote an artist if the artist were also recording for other labels at the same time.

Many performers make a livelihood performing as *sidemen*. They are not the featured performers on recordings, and they are not prominently highlighted on the album cover, packaging, or advertising. Most exclusive recording artist contracts cover any and all recording services except where specifically waived. Accordingly, it is desirable to specify the terms and conditions under which sideman services can be performed for other record companies. Typical negotiated terms require credit to the artist's regular record company, such as "courtesy of . . .”; limitation of name credit to sideman only and not on the front of the album packaging; a maximum of two or three songs on which the sideman services can be used in any one album; and sometimes a requirement that the artist-sideman not receive royalties.

Artists may wish to be part of a movie soundtrack album distributed by another record company. The artist's own record company may feel that this exception to its exclusivity is worthwhile, since it promotes the exposure of the artist. Much depends on the bargaining position of the parties as well as the concessions made by the distributor of the soundtrack album. These concessions may include proper credit to the artist's label and royalty payments to the artist's record label. Generally, the artist's record company will reserve the right to distribute its artist's recording as a “single” or to include it in the artist's own albums, possibly with the right to refer to the movie itself for added promotional effect.

Recording contracts usually forbid recording the same selection for another company for a minimum period of time. This is known as the *re-recording restriction*. In most contracts the restrictive period is 5 years from the date of delivery of the recording to the record label or 2 years from the expiration of the term of the recording contract, whichever is later. During this period the record company will not be faced with competition by the same artist performing the same material.

Recording and Release Requirements

A recording agreement sets forth the minimum number of sides to be recorded during each contract year. A *side* customarily consists of a single composition with a minimum duration of $2^{1}/_{2}$ minutes. The minimum number of sides for an album is usually 10 to 12. The agreement may also state that the artist will make additional recordings at the company's request. Sometimes the parties agree that an excess over a certain maximum number of recordings must be mutually approved. The agreement may also contain a provision that if the artist exceeds the minimum recording requirement in any one period, at the company's discretion the excess will be credited against the minimum recording requirements in the succeeding period.

Although a recording agreement signifies the company's intention to produce recordings by that artist, this intention is rarely expressed as a contractual commitment. After the initial recordings are made, the record company may become disillusioned and try to avoid further recording obligations to the artist. Thus, recording agreements sometimes state that the artist shall be paid union scale, or another amount reflecting the cost of prior albums, for the agreed-upon minimum number of sides that remain unrecorded.

Artists quickly sense when companies have cooled toward them, and they may request a release from their contract, which the companies may be willing to grant, particularly if they are repaid their recording costs and/or granted an override on the artist's future releases. But where the record company is unwilling, the artist faces the prospect of sitting out the balance of the current contractual period. To avoid this situation, some artists have been able to negotiate a provision which provides that they are free from further recording obligations if the company allows 6 months (or an alternative negotiated period) to elapse between a prior U.S. release date and the next authorized recording session.

Recordings are meaningless unless they are released commercially. However, a record company will not want to absorb the expense of releasing a recording in which it has no confidence. Its position is that it has already made a sizable investment in the recording, and that if the recording has no commercial potential, its release would amount to throwing good money after bad. So as not to be at the mercy of an arbitrary judgment on the part of the company, artists should try to have a release commitment in the contract. If the company fails to comply with that commitment, the artist may end the agreement.

Most record companies have several labels, including a so-called top-line label, a midprice label, a budget label, and possibly other specialty labels. In addition to price points, different labels within the same price category at a major record company may have different marketing and promotion teams. An artist with sufficient negotiating power may request that his or her recordings be initially released only on a top-line label. The record company may grant such a request for the United States, where it has sole control, but may refuse it for other countries where it has no direct control and where flexibility in pricing is necessary. Even where top-line initial release is part of the agreement, the record company may reserve the right to distribute records on midprice or budget labels after a period of time, in order to stimulate additional sales through lower prices.

Artist Royalties

A typical recording contract provides that the artist is to be paid a royalty that is calculated either as a percentage of the suggested retail list price of records sold, or as a percentage of the wholesale price of records sold (usually at least double the royalty rate applied to the suggested retail list price). New artists usually receive 9 to 12 percent of the suggested retail list price for domestic sales and a lesser percent for sales outside the United States, although established artists may obtain a higher royalty rate.

In negotiating royalty rates for foreign sales, artists should try to get not less than 85 percent of the U.S. royalty rate for sales in Canada, 75 percent for Europe, Japan, and Australia, and 50 percent for the "rest of the world." Where the U.S. record company owns and operates foreign subsidiaries, the rates may be higher. If the U.S. company owns its Canadian distributor or ships records directly to customers in Canada, the artist royalty rate for Canadian sales should be the same as those for U.S. sales.

Domestic royalty rates frequently escalate in increments known as *bumps* based on the quantity of sales. For example, there may be a 1 percent increment for U.S. sales of albums over 500,000 and a further 1 percent increment for sales over 1 million units. Bumps are limited to sales after the albums have attained the requisite plateaus. Also, royalty rates are often, though not always, increased when a company decides to exercise its option to extend the term of a recording agreement. Such increases apply only to recordings made in the option period, not to recordings made in earlier contract periods. These two forms of escalation are not mutually exclusive; both may be applicable in an appropriate instance.

Record companies pay a lower royalty rate for singles than for albums, because singles are usually less profitable than albums. For example, an artist may receive a 13 percent album royalty but only 10 percent on singles.

The suggested retail list price in the United States has for some time been $6.98 for singles and $14.98 to $16.98 for compact discs. The suggested retail list prices are either published by the manufacturer or extrapolated from the whole-sale prices charged to dealers. Retailers are constantly offering records for sale at a discount from the suggested retail list price. If these discounts are subsidized by the manufacturer through a reduction in wholesale prices, the artist whose royalties are calculated on the basis of wholesale prices will suffer a reduction in royalties. However, even artists on a retail price royalty basis usually have a clause allowing pro rata reduction when normal wholesale prices are discounted.

The cost of packaging is also deducted from the base amount for computing royalties. Traditionally these deductions have been 15 to 20 percent for cassettes and 25 percent for CDs, even though the actual cost to the manufacturer is generally much less. The packaging deduction is predicated on the theory that the artist should receive a royalty based solely on the recording itself, not on the art-work, wrapping, or sales appeal added on by the packaging. In this regard, it should be noted that the record company generally absorbs the entire cost of creating the artwork and other elements of packaging. Unlike recording costs, these costs are generally not charged back to the artist.

Record companies do not pay artist royalties on records that are given away to distributors for promotional purposes as "free goods" (which are, despite the name, intended to be sold to consumers). The amount of these free goods (not to be confused with bona fide promotional copies distributed free of charge to reviewers, radio stations, etc.) is generally 15 percent of records sold, and more in the case of special promotions. The artist should try to negotiate a maximum on the amount of free goods that is consistent with actual practice.

Under generally accepted industry practice, retailers have the right to return any unsold records to the distributor, who then returns them to the record company. Since artists are not paid royalties on returned (i.e., unsold) records, record companies hold back a portion of an artist's royalties as a reserve against these returns. The artist should endeavor to negotiate a limit on the amount of reserves, such as 35 percent of album sales during a particular accounting period, and a reasonable time limit for liquidation of the reserve, such as in equal installments over four semiannual accounting periods, rather than as one lump sum liquidated at the very last moment.

Once upon a time CDs were considered " new technology," and record companies reduced the artist royalty rate on CDs by 15 to 20 percent, claiming that they needed to be reimbursed for their research and development costs as well as for higher costs of manufacture. Although this is now rarely done in the case of CDs, record companies will continue to take a new-technology reduction on "new media" as soon as they come into existence. For their own protection, artists may endeavor to limit the new media royalty rate reductions to a stipulated period, such as 2 years, or to a stipulated sales level. Alternatively, artists may try to get a so-called "favored nation" clause stating that if in the future the record company changes to a more favorable royalty computation formula for the medium in question, this formula will also be applied to the calculation of the artist's royalty.

An artist may have a so-called *all-in* royalty agreement, which means that the artist must pay the producer's royalty, typically 3 percent, out of his or her royalties. For example, if the artist's royalty is 12 percent of the suggested retail list price, the producer gets 3 percent, leaving a 9 percent net artist royalty.

Here is a typical all-in royalty calculation on a $14.98 CD where the artist's base royalty is 12 percent:

12 percent − 3 percent (producer's royalty) = 9 percent

9 percent × .75 (25 percent reduction for packaging) = 6.75 percent

6.75 percent × .85 (15 percent for free goods) = 5.74 percent

5.74 percent × .65 (35 percent reduction for reserves) = 3.731 percent

3.731 percent of $14.98 = $0.5589

The artist's royalty account will therefore only be credited initially with less than 60 cents for each $14.98 CD distributed by the record company (subject to an increase if the reserve turns out to be greater than the units actually returned). This is a far cry from $1.79 (12 percent of $14.98) per CD.

Note that the calculation of royalties does not take into account items charged against an artist's royalty account, such as a portion (or all) of video production costs or a portion (or all) of independent promotion costs. The cost of the promotion of records by independent parties hired by the record company to obtain radio airplay of records can be substantial, up to $100,000 or more for a release. This should be an important issue during negotiations. Artists should not have to pay such costs out of their royalties; at most, half of such costs should be a charge against artist royalties.

The increasing importance of the Internet, including audio streaming and downloads, has thrown traditional methods of calculating royalties into a state of disarray. For income from Internet-related sources major record companies require artists to take a substantial reduction in the otherwise applicable royalty rate (up to 15 percent) as well as to permit the record company to deduct a distribution fee of between 15 and 25 percent. Alternatively, net income might be divided, but after the same distribution fee has been deducted. The assumption is that the entity providing the on-line service will be able to specifically identify the recordings which are used, either by direct tracking or sampling, which is not always the case where blanket licensing is done. The economic models in this area are very much in flux at the time of this writing, due to the record companies' high start-up costs for going on-line, as well as the effect of unauthorized downloading.

Lest it be assumed that the low royalties payable to artists generally indicate high profits to record companies, bear in mind that, according to the RIAA, most albums fail to recoup their recording and marketing costs. On the other hand, the status of recoupment of an artist's royalty account bears no mathematical relationship to a record company's actual profits on any given release.

In addition to royalties based on records sold, artists should negotiate to receive a share of the record company's income from so-called ancillary uses of their recordings, for example, motion pictures and new media licenses. If they fail to do so, they run the risk of suffering the fate of The Ronettes. In 2002 the New York Court of Appeals ruled against The Ronettes, who were seeking a share of millions of dollars received from synchronization usages of their pre-1973 recordings. The court based its decision on the fact that there was no reference in the The Ronettes' contract to receiving royalties from synchronization uses, and the grant of rights in the contract was sufficiently broad to vest in the record company all rights in their recordings and income derived from all uses.

Recording Costs

An artist generally does not receive any royalties until the record company has recovered all of the recording costs incurred for that artist's records. The cost of making a record depends on many factors, including the size of the project, the cost of bringing in an outside producer, the complexity of the recordings, and the level of perfection desired. Recording costs for relatively new artists can range from $80,000 to $150,000 or more for one album. Established artists have been known to run up costs in excess of $500,000 for an album. Original-cast albums of Broadway shows may cost as much as $100,000 or more, depending on the size of the cast. On the other hand, greatest hits albums entail little or no additional recording costs, since they are assembled from existing recordings—although the addition of one or more new recordings is not unusual and can run up costs.

The record company will recover its costs for *all* recordings made by the artist from *all* artist royalties. Thus, if three of an artist's albums are released and only the last one is successful, no royalties will be payable to the artist until the recording costs for all three albums have been recouped from the royalties earned on the successful record. Obviously, it will take longer to recoup recording costs at a lower royalty rate than at a higher one.

Record companies may liken the system of recoupment of recording costs from royalties to a joint venture in which the production costs and overhead must be repaid before the partners divide any profits. Record companies contend that they are justified in recouping all their costs first because they are the ones taking the large financial risk while the artists invest only their time. They also point out that many artists derive major income from songwriting and personal appearances—income in which the record company does not share, even though the company's recordings may have been essential in building the artist's popularity and generating such income.

Recording Funds

In some instances recording artists are their own producers; more frequently the artist hires an independent producer. It is increasingly common for record companies to provide artists with a recording fund. The artist is then responsible for paying all third parties out of the fund, which is customarily disbursed in three segments: the first upon commencement of recording, the second upon completion of basic tracks, and the balance upon delivery of finished master to the record company. The artist can retain the difference (if any) between the recording fund and the actual recording costs; this gives the artist an incentive to keep within the budget. Recording funds, like recording costs paid directly by the record company, are always treated as advances against artist royalties.

The contract may contain a formula for computing recording funds. This formula may set forth the fund for the first recording and contain parameters for funds for subsequent recordings, generally based on two-thirds of the average royalty earnings on U.S. sales through normal retail channels for the artist's most recent two albums, with stipulated minimum and maximum amounts.

Publishing Rights

Many artists are also successful composers and many record companies are affiliated with music publishing firms. A publishing interest in a composition reduces the risk of the recording company in investing in and exploiting a record of the composition. For this reason, a record company may argue strongly for contract language giving the company the right to acquire through its affiliate a publishing interest in compositions written by the artist and recorded under the recording agreement.

Record companies may claim that, except for a publisher's distribution of printed copies and attempts to secure cover records of the same composition, it is difficult to differentiate between what a record company and a publishing firm will do to exploit a musical composition. A record company sends promotional copies of records to radio and television stations and has its promotional staff or hires independent promoters to call on programmers to encourage the playing of records. It may also advertise its records on the radio and in trade publications.

All of these activities will result in publishing income, since there will be broad-casting performances for which the performing rights organization will pay royalties, sales of records for which the record company will remit mechanical license fees, and sales of sheet music if the composition becomes popular.

In some cases, the artist may agree, believing that the additional interest of the record company, through its affiliated publishing firm, may lead the record company to make greater efforts on the artist's behalf. Alternatively, the artist may be willing to compromise by granting an interest in publishing income only from the particular record issued by that company, or by entering into a copublishing arrangement with the record company's publishing affiliate rather than assigning all of the publishing rights to the record company's publishing affiliate.

Artists who own their own publishing firms are most likely to resist assigning their interest in the copyright or publishing income. Some artists argue that the record company's publishing enterprise is a mere shell and does not offer any publishing services over and above the activities of the record company. A recognized publisher has the staff and budget to supplement that of the record company, and thus effectively promote the artist's work. The artist may be acting in a self-defeating manner, however, if the independent publisher obtains and promotes a cover version of the same composition by a competing recording artist. This is less likely to happen when the publisher is an affiliate of the artist's record company.

If the record company's affiliate does become the artist's publisher or co-publisher, it may attempt to recoup the artist's recording costs from publishing royalties that would otherwise be payable. Artists should negotiate vigorously to disallow this practice, known as *cross-collateralization*.

Controlled Compositions

The term *controlled composition* refers to any composition written, owned, or controlled, in whole or in part, by the artist. The record company may seek a reduced royalty rate for a mechanical license for controlled compositions, commonly 75 percent of the minimum *compulsory* rate (also known as the *statutory* rate) under the Copyright Act. Since the year 2002 the minimum statutory rate (for compositions of 5 minute or less duration) has been 8 cents, making the 75 percent "bargain rate" on controlled compositions only 6 cents.

In addition, although CDs today often contain more than 10 compositions, record companies usually stipulate that they will pay only 10 or 11 times the minimum rate for the CD, no matter how many compositions are included. Further, the contracts with the artists may provide that to the extent mechanical license fees for controlled and noncontrolled compositions exceed the maximum rate the company has agreed to pay, the excess is deductible from monies otherwise payable on controlled compositions and (if not sufficient) from artist royalties or advances. In effect, this places the responsibility on the artist to negotiate favorable mechanical license rates with outside publishers for compositions that the artist proposes to record.

The record company does not usually pay artist royalties on free goods and similarly seeks not to pay mechanical royalties for controlled compositions on free goods. The artist will contend that such royalties should be paid because free goods are merely a form of discount that the record company should absorb. Often a compromise is reached, with the record company agreeing to pay mechanical royalties on 50 percent of the albums distributed as free goods.

Under a controlled composition clause, the record company will fix the reduced mechanical license fee as of a particular date; the applicable rate on that date remains in effect forever and does not change regardless of increases in the compulsory license rate. The artist will attempt to provide for the latest possible date, such as the date of record release, in order to take advantage of any increases in the compulsory license rate. For the same reason, the company will insist on an earlier date, such as the recording or delivery date of the master.

Tour Support

Touring is an excellent means of promoting an artist's album, as sales consistently increase in areas in which the artist performs. However, for most newer artists, the costs of touring exceed the income derived from the engagements.

Record companies sometimes subsidize tours on the theory that the tour will promote sales of the record, which in the long run will provide more income than is disbursed for the tour. But some recording agreements may provide that tour support is recoupable against future artist royalties. The artist should negotiate to make tour support nonrecoupable or only partially recoupable. The development of video as a promotional tool has reduced the importance of conventional tour support.

Video Rights

In most contracts the definition of "records" includes audiovisual devices as well as audio-only records. Record companies will negotiate for the right to control the use of recordings in audiovisual form and to restrict the artist from performing in such media, such as in feature films, for other companies.

A key area in contract negotiations between artists and record companies concerns music videos. Videos are usually visualizations of songs performed by the artist. They are a significant promotional tool, and recording artists will try to get their record companies to produce at least one video for each of their albums. Because videos can be expensive and difficult to place on the various video channels, such as MTV, record companies resist making any firm commitments.

Most recording contracts provide that artist royalties are not payable on videos that are distributed to promote record sales. Royalties should be payable on videos that are distributed commercially. Although the commercial market for videos is still limited, this may change in the future with the increased use of alternative distribution modes, such as DVDs and the Internet.

Generally, 100 percent of the video production costs are recoupable out of artist royalties from the sale or use of videos and 50 percent of any balance due is recoupable out of artist royalties on sale of records.

Under copyright law, a video producer must obtain from a copyright proprietor or its agent a synchronization license to record protected music in synchronization with or timed relation to the pictures in a video. Permission is also necessary to publicly perform, make copies of, and distribute the music as a part of the music videos. With controlled compositions, record companies will demand that the artist provide free video licenses. While artists may agree to this if the video is for promotional purposes, they may balk if the video is being exploited commercially.

Assignment

In certain circumstances, for example, in the event of a sale or merger, a record company may wish to assign its rights to a recording agreement to another entity. In most contracts there is no prohibition against the assignment of the agreement. This unfettered freedom of assignment can be injurious to an artist, particularly when the new owner lacks the same interest in the artist as the original record company.

New artists may not be in a position to quibble about the assignability of their contract, although successful performers will seek to limit such assignability. Sometimes a contract includes a *key man clause,* referring to an individual who has been important in getting an artist to sign on with a particular company. Such a clause may give the artist the right to terminate the agreement if the key man (or woman) leaves the company for any reason. Given the volatile nature of employment in the industry, record companies are understandably reluctant to include key man clauses in their contracts.

Some record companies will agree to limit the possibility of assignment to "successors in interest," that is, to successors who acquire all or substantially all of the assigning record company's stock or assets. This is a way of assuring the artist of the continuing financial viability of the successor, which would be at least as big as the original company. A small company may be financially unsound and unable to invest the same amount in marketing and promotion. An artist may be willing to consent to assignment if the original record company continues to be liable for the fulfillment of all obligations, or if the assignee is an entity owned or controlled by the original company or any company distributed by one of the major labels.

Ownership and Use of Masters

A recording agreement is usually written as an employment contract, and therefore the record company will claim that the results and proceeds of the artist's services belong to the record company as a work for hire. This means that the artist retains no interest in the physical tapes or masters or the copyright in the sound recordings and is restricted to a claim for contractual compensation and royalties. Under the U.S. Copyright Act, exclusive rights in sound recordings are limited to reproduction, the preparation of derivative works, and distribution; the right of public performance is not included for traditional (that is, nondigital) AM and FM broadcasts. Digital broadcasts, including streaming, are now subject to compulsory licensing under the Digital Millennium Copyright Act of 1998 (see Chapter 7, page 67).

Determining whether the artist is an employee producing a work for hire or an independent contractor is a complicated subject that is treated in depth in Chapter 17, "Works for Hire." The answer affects copyright ownership, the duration of copyright, and copyright termination rights.

A record company will jealously guard its ownership rights in masters and copyrights. However, in rare cases with certain highly successful artists, record companies have agreed that the ownership of the masters and copyrights will revert to the artists after a period of years. Artists who desire to transfer to another record company find that the reversion of their recordings is a valuable right that enhances their worth to a new company.

A record company can usually use a recording as it sees fit. It may issue the recording on any label it desires, and it may couple the recording with the recordings of other artists. Established artists will try to restrict a record company's unlimited discretion, especially seeking to limit the time prior to which a record company may (without artist's consent) release the artist's records at less than full price, the use of artist's recordings in advertising, or the number of artist's recordings that can be used in any compilation with other artists.

Coupling

Record companies sometimes issue or authorize others to issue recordings that couple the performances of various artists into a compilation album. Thanks to the Internet explosion, services such as Music Net and Pressplay enable the consumer to listen to and even download custom compilations of personal favorites. Fearing that they may be cheapened and damaged by association with artists of lesser stature, artists will try to negotiate the right to approve such availability for couplings of their recordings. If the artist is of sufficient stature to merit the granting of this type of request, the record company will want contractual protection that the artist's approval will not be unreasonably withheld.

Accountings and Defaults

Artist recording agreements usually provide that the recording company will account to the artist semiannually and that if the artist fails to complain within a certain period, such as within 2 to 3 years from the date the statement is rendered, the artist will be deemed to have waived any objections to any royalty accountings. This is known as the "account stated clause." The artist should not overlook this clause, which is designed to insulate the company from claims arising long after the facts become known to the artist. Note that the courts will generally uphold account stated clauses which reduce the otherwise applicable statute of limitations, so long as the reduction does not result in an unreasonably short period after which the artist cannot object or audit. In the absence of a contractual right to audit the record company's books, an artist may have to sue in court in order to obtain the right to audit.

If a company fails to account for or pay royalties when due, artists may commence legal proceedings against the company. Artists may wish to treat the breach as an excuse for terminating the agreement, freeing them from all further obligations to record for the company. However, unless the original agreement specifically authorizes such termination, a court will have to determine whether the breach is serious enough to justify a cancellation. A slight delay in rendering accounts and payments would not be regarded as material, whereas long delays after many demands might be.

Other defaults may occur. For example, the company may refuse to allow an inspection of books and records, even though the artist has a contractual right to do so. The company may fail to release recordings which they have committed to release or fail to record the artist at given periods as provided by the agreement.

The record company will strongly oppose a default clause that does not require a written notice of default and a sufficient opportunity to remedy any alleged default. No record company will accept a unilateral right of termination by the artist, although some may be willing to agree to an arbitration clause instead of forcing the artist to bear the expense of going to court. Many recording contracts specifically state that the artist's only remedy for any default is monetary damages and that the artist does not have the right to terminate the contract no matter what the circumstances.

Bankruptcy

A normal recording contract, consisting of an initial contract period and subsequent option periods, will potentially continue for an extended period of time. Recordings made during the exclusive term of the agreement will be owned by the record company and will potentially continue to be sold indefinitely, thereby giving rise to an ongoing royalty payment obligation. These relationships between the artist and the record company may, however, be interrupted or revised by a bankruptcy proceeding involving either party.

Several independent record labels—Stax, General Recorded Tapes (Chess), All Platinum, Springboard—filed for bankruptcy in the 1980s. In each instance the debtor's master recordings were sold and the net proceeds were distributed among the debtor's creditors. Delinquent artist royalties are ordinarily general debts with no priority in bankruptcy. Future artist royalties constitute a continuing obligation that is assumed by the party that acquires the master recordings. That party also may take over any unrecouped balance in the artist's royalty account.

In some record contracts there is an attempt to treat bankruptcy as cause for returning the record masters to the artist. Such a reversion of valuable rights would be contrary to the principles of bankruptcy, as it would give an unlawful preferential treatment to the artist at the expense of other legitimate creditors.

At times, recording artists have resorted to the bankruptcy courts to free them from onerous exclusive recording contracts. Robert Noonan (professionally known as Willie Nile), an Arista Records recording artist, had accumulated a deficit royalty recoupment account that required the sale of a large number of records before it would become positive. He also had significant financial obligations for prebankruptcy legal expenses and his manager's $60,000 arbitration award. He had a limited cash flow and insubstantial assets. Arista Records, despite low sales, exercised its options to extend the agreement for 18 months, during which Nile would have been obligated to record two albums, in addition to two already made. Arista refused to give Nile any further advances to help him pay his financial obligations. Nile commenced a Chapter 11 proceeding and sought to terminate all future contractual obligations to Arista as part of a financial reorganization plan. Nile subsequently exercised his right to convert the case to a Chapter 7 ("straight") bankruptcy proceeding, which Arista resisted strongly, since it would have deprived the court of the possibility of affirming Nile's recording contract. In the matter of *Noonan* (17 Bankr. 793 [S.D.N.Y. 1982]), the U.S. district court ruled against Arista, thereby giving Nile the fresh start which he sought.

Record companies may argue that artists who file for bankruptcy do so "in bad faith" for the sole purpose of breaking their recording contract or pressing the record company to renegotiate the agreement. This contention is of dubious merit when a performing artist is in actual financial distress and is evidencing a need for the protection of the Bankruptcy Code.

In a case involving the artist George Jones, then under contract to CBS Records, a bankruptcy court held that the trustee in bankruptcy was vested with the artist's right to receive record royalties on prebankruptcy recordings. The court also decided that CBS could continue to recoup its advances in respect of such recordings from royalties on sales generated by the recordings. It is of interest that Jones's discharge in bankruptcy was ultimately denied for his failure to produce data proving his financial status and business transactions for the year preceding the filing of his petition.

3

Contracts with Minors

Historically, the age of legal maturity was 21, but there has been a marked statutory trend to lower the legal age to 18. Prior to reaching the age of legal maturity, an individual is regarded as an "infant" or a "minor." While still legally considered infants when their professional careers skyrocketed, Elvis Presley, Stevie Wonder, and Bob Dylan earned large amounts of money and had considerable sums invested in them by record companies, managers, and the like in the music business. Today growing numbers of singers, rappers, and musicians—e.g., Brandy, Usher, LeAnn Rimes, and Britney Spears—are breaking into the music industry before the age of legal maturity. The success stories of many teenage celebrities tend to obscure the legal difficulties stemming from their status as minors.

Generally, the common law has regarded minors as not having the maturity of mind or judgment required to make legally binding agreements. Unless a contract involves the necessities of life—food, clothing, housing—a minor can void an agreement within a reasonable period of time after reaching the age of maturity. The other party to the agreement cannot avoid its contractual obligations to the minor.

Contracts with minors contain a financial risk: the minor may disaffirm (i.e., repudiate) their agreement. Even if a minor fraudulently misrepresented his or her age—a common occurrence in the search for employment and a career— this is not sufficient legal ground to enforce a contract or collect damages from the minor for breach of contract. The entire risk in dealing with the minor is placed on the other party. This has greatly discouraged investment in training and promoting young artists.

The statutory age of majority in the key music industry states—California, New York, Tennessee, and Illinois—is now 18 years: a contract signed by a person 18 years or older cannot be disaffirmed on the grounds of infancy. This has significantly eased the problems of the entertainment industry in dealing with artists over age 18.

In recognition of the difficulties involved in contracting with minors, many states have established procedures for the court approval of such agreements.

This formal approval has the effect of preventing disaffirmance and encourages investment in the early careers of deserving young artists under fair terms.

Disaffirmance of an Agreement

A minor's act to disaffirm or void an agreement does not have to follow any particular pattern. Typically, written notice of disaffirmance on the grounds of minor status is sufficient. Other such acts include making contracts that are inconsistent with the agreement in question or pleading infancy as a defense in an action brought under the contract.

Ratification of an Agreement

An agreement that is entered into by a minor becomes fully enforceable if it is ratified after the minor reaches the age of majority. Ratification does not need to be in written form. Silence for a certain period of time after reaching the age of maturity is considered sufficient ratification of a completed transaction. A contract can be deemed legally ratified if the artist performs certain acts indicating an intent to continue with the agreement after reaching the age of majority: for example, coming to a recording session or accepting compensation for future performances.

Statutory Provisions of Contracts with Minors

In many states, statutes deal with the enforceability of contracts with minors. Since New York and California are centers of the music industry, our focus will be on the statutes in those states.

New York has provided a statutory method of ensuring that the agreements in the field of entertainment cannot be disaffirmed on the grounds of infancy. A procedure has been established for court review and approval of record contracts as well as agreements for managerial and agency services. There are three basic requirements for court approval: (1) the contract must be fair to the minor, (2) the term may not extend beyond statutory limits, and (3) the minor's parents or guardian must consent.

A contract with a minor cannot be approved if its term, including any extensions by option or otherwise, extends beyond 3 years from the date of the agreement. However, if the court finds that the minor is represented by qualified counsel experienced in entertainment law and practice, it may approve a term as long as 7 years. Provisions other than duration of term (for example, depositing and holding income in a trust account for the the benefit of the minor) may be approved by the court if they are found to be reasonable.

The New York Law Revision Commission has gone on record as being in favor of permitting an agent's commissions to continue beyond 3 years on royalty-producing property created during the original 3 years of the agreement. It has also recommended that a minor who is a recording artist should be allowed to agree not to re-record a song for a competitor for a period longer than 3 years; the normal clause in the record business restricts such re-recordings for at least 5 years from the date of recording of the record.

The first step for obtaining judicial approval is to file a petition. The petition must include a copy of the agreement, a schedule of estimated earnings, and the consent of the parents.

The next step is a court hearing, at which the minor must be present. The court appoints a legal guardian, sometimes, but not always, a parent of the minor, whose function is to collect and save the earnings on behalf of the minor. The court may also appoint a guardian *ad litem* ("for the suit" or "for the action"), who is usually an attorney knowledgeable on the subject matter of the contract. This guardian reviews the agreement and advocates fairness for the minor, at the expense of the petitioner. Complicated and unfair contracts (ones requiring much negotiation) are the primary reasons for delays in the whole procedure.

If there is a claim that the well-being of the minor is being impaired by performance of the contract, the court may either revoke the approval or suspend approval until an appropriate modification of the questioned conduct has been made.

Under California statutes, court approval can be sought for agreements with minors under 18 that cover the employment of a minor in the entertainment field as an actor, a recording artist, or a writer; the purchase, sale, or licensing of literary, musical, or dramatic properties for entertainment purposes; and service contracts between duly licensed managers or agencies and minors in the entertainment field. Employment or other agreements cannot be disaffirmed by a minor after court approval. Under California law, a term of employment of up to 7 years may be approved. As in New York, a California court may require earnings to be set aside for the benefit of the minor.

Since most new artists disappear from the public eye after one or two recordings are released and since the procedure for seeking approval usually involves attorneys' fees and expenses as well as court appearances of the minor, guardians, and other parties to the agreement, applications for approval of contracts with minors are rarely filed.

Parents' Guarantee of Contract Performance

Those drafting contracts with minors have sometimes insisted that the parents or guardians become a party to or a guarantor of the contract for the minor's performance. This may have strong psychological value in enforcing performance by the minor, although it does not prevent the minor from disaffirming the agreement. Unless protected by statute, parents or guardians who sign such contracts become potentially liable for large sums representing damages for breach of contract by a minor.

4

Independent Record Producers

In the 1950s and 1960s, A&R executives reigned supreme at record companies. They selected the artists, taught, encouraged, and supervised them, and got the credit for nurturing the hits. They were so highly regarded that their substantial salaries were sometimes augmented by special bonuses or small royalties that were rarely charged to the artist royalty accounts.

From the 1970s on, independent producers have assumed more and more of the A&R function. A producer with a good track record is frequently given carte blanche to propose a recording budget (subject to approval by the record company) and to conduct recording sessions and supervise mixing and editing of recordings.

In his autobiography *Rhythm and Blues: A Life in American Music,* Jerry Wexler, renowned producer and former co-owner of Atlantic Records, noted that there are three kinds of producer.

> The first is the documentarian, like Leonard Chess, who took Muddy Waters' Delta blues and recorded them just as Muddy played them— raw, unadorned and real . . . replicated in a studio what he heard in a bar. . . . The second category—the producer as servant of the project . . . an impassioned fan [who] . . . somehow finds himself in charge of the sessions with no special cachet. His job is to enhance: meaning find the right song, the right arranger, the right band, the right studio—in short, do whatever it takes to get the best out of the artist. . . . The third category—producer as star, as artist, as unifying force . . . every item in a record—the rhythm track, strings, background vocal, lead vocal, instrumental solo—was a tile in a mosaic. The design was solely of his making, not the singer's or the songwriter's.

Whether documentarian, project leader, or studio superstar, increasingly the producer is relied on by the record company to deliver hits, remain within budget, and stimulate the artist's productivity.

The growth of the role of the independent producer has largely paralleled the record industry's increasing emphasis on albums rather than singles. Since the latter part of the 1970s, most singles have failed to achieve sufficient sales to recoup production and marketing costs. Singles have been regarded primarily as promotional aids for the sales of albums, which have carried a higher profit margin for the record companies and have thus borne the burden of recovering the substantial investments made by record companies in recording and marketing their products. This is in the process of changing, given the music consumer's ability to download individual tracks via the Internet. In any event, while the artist remains the most important part of the mix, employing an independent producer with a good track record will continue to be considered good business, especially where large recording budgets are involved.

The Role of the Independent Record Producer

Independent record producers perform a number of important functions. They serve as talent scouts; they often choose appropriate musical material and select and supervise arrangers, back-up musicians and vocalists, studios, and engineers. They may also do mixing and remixing, or select the people who will perform those functions They are critical to keeping recording costs within budget.

By the mid-1990s, the independent producer was often assuming the role of arranger as well. This happened primarily when tracks were laid down at an early session and the words and melody were added later, often at a different recording studio. Whether the producer-arranger should be listed as coauthor of the music is unclear under these circumstances, and a potential source of conflict. In practice, the strong role and bargaining position of established producers like Dallas Austin, Jermaine Dupri, Sean "Puffy" Combs, Jimmy Jam, and Terry Lewis—all of whom often write, arrange, and sometimes even perform on a song—ensure that the producer is credited as a writer and that the producer's music publisher may claim copublishing status as well.

The producer also controls the different textures used in a song, such as layered keyboard or harmony vocals. Where samples are used in a recording, the producer frequently is the one who chooses the samples and is responsible for integrating them into the new recording. However, to the extent that a new recording is a cover of a prior recording, the producer has no legal right to intrude on existing writer or publisher credits.

Whatever the role of the producer and whatever type of agreement the producer enters into, the record company will want to ensure, as best it can, that the results of the producer's services belong to the record company, either as a work for hire or by assignment, just as the company would in the case of an artist.

Label Deals and Pressing and Distribution Deals

Independent producers with particularly desirable artists under contract may be able to negotiate a *label deal* with a major record label. A label deal may provide that records will be released under the trade name and label of the producer.

Producers claim that a label deal helps them attract artists to their fold. Such deals may also be advantageous to producers who wish to develop alternative distribution operations in the future.

When negotiating label deals with record companies, producers will seek both fixed and royalty compensation. *Fixed compensation* may be in the form of a weekly overhead payment, other periodic payments, a fee for each recorded master, or a combination of these elements. *Royalty compensation* will be a percentage of the wholesale or retail list price of records sold. The percentage will depend on the bargaining power of the producer, who is usually responsible for paying royalties to recording artists. In some cases the record company, as an accommodation, may undertake this responsibility pursuant to an appropriate letter of direction from the producer. When the producer is responsible for paying royalties to the recording artist, the all-in royalty payable to the producer's label must be sufficiently high to cover both the artist royalty and the producer royalty.

In a label deal, the record company may seek the contractual right to apply the royalties from the hits of one artist to recoup the recording costs of another less successful artist. This practice, an example of cross-collateralization, is a major issue in most label deals. A production company may find itself in financial difficulties if it has to pay royalties to its successful artists at a time when its ready cash has been consumed by the overhead and unrecouped recording costs of less successful artists. As a compromise, a label deal may provide that only the producer's share of the all-in royalty (that is, amounts in excess of the artist royalty) is subject to cross-collateralization, so that artist royalties (payable through the producer) are excluded from cross-collateralization.

In *pressing and distribution* arrangements, the production company relies on profits from distributing the product rather than on royalties. Under such an arrangement, the record company deducts pressing charges, mechanical royalties, and other specified expenses, including a negotiated distribution fee for its services. Distribution fees of 20 to 30 percent of gross dealer prices are common.

Highly successful artists have also been known to contract for so-called superstar labels, under which they can produce artists consistent with their vision. For example, after Mariah Carey's contract with EMI was terminated, for which she received $50 million, she signed with UMG for a $5 to $8 million advance per album plus a $20 dollar investment by UMG in Carey's own record company. Similar superstar labels include Eminem's Shady Records and Madonna's Maverick Recording Company.

Producer Royalties

If an independent producer is hired to supervise an artist already under contract to a record company, the producer's royalty in the United States is usually 3 percent of album sales, with escalations on volume, usually an additional 0.5 percent on each additional 500,000 units, up to a specified maximum.

A highly successful producer may receive a base royalty rate of 4 percent. Packaging deductions, free goods exclusions, and royalty reductions for record club, foreign, and other sales are generally calculated in the same manner as the artist's royalties.

A record company usually does not have to pay the producer royalty until recording costs have been recouped out of the net artist royalty (i.e., gross royalties less the royalties payable to the producer). On rare occasions, recording costs are recouped from the combined artist and producer royalties; this results in faster recoupment and both artist and producer receive royalties sooner. Even when a producer produces less than an entire album and has no control over recording costs incurred by others, costs for the *entire* album are recouped before a record company begins to pay any royalties. Although this practice seems unfair, it works two ways: the producer may benefit from the sales of a single produced by someone else—sales that contribute to the recoupment of the entire album's recording costs.

When recording costs and other charges are fully recouped at the net artist rate, the producer is paid royalties retroactively to the first record sold. However, royalties are subject to further recoupment of any producer fees paid at the time of recording. Where both artist and producer royalties are used for recoupment, there is usually no retroactive producer royalty; instead, royalties are paid only on records sold after the date of full recoupment.

In a producer-artist royalty package, where the producer pays the artist's royalty, gross royalty rates may range from about 10 to 14 percent of the retail list price (or the equivalent royalty based on wholesale); of this, the artist's royalty rate is generally 7 to 10 percent and the producer's rate is 3 to 4 percent, with the usual royalty deductions for packaging, foreign sales, etc. All monies paid by a record company to obtain a recording, whether as payments to the producer or as expenditures for recording costs, are deemed advances against and recoupable from the total royalties payable by the record company.

The recording fund for an important artist or an established producer may be several hundred thousand dollars per album, with a royalty package (based on retail) of 18 percent or higher.

If the independent producer acts as arranger, he or she is entitled to be paid union scale for the arrangements. Arranger's fees are not deducted from producer royalties, but are an additional recording cost ultimately absorbed by the artist.

Recording Funds

When independent producers are hired to make a recording, either by the record company or by the artist, the record company will frequently agree to provide the producer with an agreed-upon recording fund for each project. This fund is in lieu of a recording budget supervised by the record company and is treated as an advance against royalties. The producer retains whatever portion of the fund is not spent on recording costs. Thus, if the recording fund is $200,000 and the actual studio, engineering, musician scale, and other recording costs equal $150,000, the balance of $50,000 remains available as compensation for the producer and the artist. This balance is separate and apart from any royalties payable after the record company has recouped the recording fund, although a portion of the fund may be allocated to a producer fee, which will be treated as an advance against producer royalties.

Determining the amount of the recording fund in the first instance is a matter of negotiation between the producer, the artist, and the record company. A balance must be struck between expected sales on the one hand and adequate compensation for the producer and the artist on the other hand. A $100,000 fund for a recording with limited sales potential might be excessive, whereas a $250,000 recording fund for a potential blockbuster album might be too little if insufficient funds were to remain for marketing and promotion costs. From the standpoint of the producer and the artist, an extremely low recording fund can result in little or no compensation, as all monies will be absorbed in actual recording costs.

Sometimes album recording funds are based on two-thirds of the preceding album's gross royalties (i.e., producer and artist royalties combined, before recoupment) calculated on the basis of U.S. sales during a fixed period, typically 6 to 9 months following the initial release date. When this formula is used, record club, foreign, or other types of sales are customarily not included in the calculation. The resultant calculation is then subject to a so-called minimum-maximum amount. A record company may be unwilling to write a blank check for $1 million simply because the previous album was a blockbuster, so it will fix a maximum amount of the recording fund in order to reduce its risk. On the other hand, the producer or artist will demand a minimum recording fund even if the preceding album is a failure. Typically, minimums are one-half of maximums.

The risk of the producer or artist incurring costs in excess of the agreed-upon fund can sometimes be alleviated by the provision of an overbudget allowance of, say, 10 percent. This protects against unforeseen expenditures such as delays in the arrival of a major guest artist. Alternatively, the budget is simply "reforecast" by the record company to accommodate cost overruns.

Production and Development Deals

Often independent producers and new artists establish a working relationship before either party has a commitment from a record company. In such a situation, they may enter into a joint venture, which delineates their respective rights and obligations, including the sharing of advances and royalties, under any record contract which may ultimately be obtained.

In a development deal, the division of income between a producer and an artist will vary. In a simple arrangement, the producer and the artist may agree to share all receipts on a fixed-ratio basis, at, say, 50-50. It may be in a producer's interests to agree to pay a fixed royalty to the artist. For example, a development deal may provide that the artist will be paid a base royalty of 7 percent, calculated in the same manner as the distribution agreement that the producer hopes to enter. If the record company grants the producer a better base royalty than 14 percent, the producer may do better under a fixed artist royalty arrangement.

If (as is usually the case) the producer makes one or more demonstration recordings in order to generate interest in the part of record companies, the producer may have to absorb the expense of procuring studio facilities and musicians. A producer with a successful track record may be able to obtain a modest demonstration record budget from a record company or music publisher. This is referred to as a *demo deal*. In return, the subsidizing party may acquire the right of first refusal, that is, a first option on signing the artist. Whether or not the artist is signed, the subsidizing party is usually given the right to recoup the demo funds out of the first receipts.

In the absence of a demo deal, the producer may obtain other types of financing. For example, in order to persuade a studio to defer or reduce its charges, the producer may offer the studio a small royalty participation in the resultant recording. This agreement is often referred to as a *spec deal*. The producer and the artist may also seek to have musicians defer or reduce their charges. Thus, payment to a studio or to musicians may be structured as off-the-top deductions from any advances or royalties that are received. The contract may call for certain minimum payments to the artist and the producer as the next off-the-top deductions prior to an ultimate profit sharing between the artist and the producer.

Under a typical development deal, the producer and the artist agree to cooperate in obtaining a recording contract that contains specified minimum terms. In addition to a condition that the record will be produced or distributed by a major company (or a label distributed by a major), the parties may stipulate that the recording contract must contain a minimum recording commitment by the record company and a minimum net artist royalty after deducting the producer's royalty, as well as a minimum per-album advance.

While the producer may assume responsibility for negotiating with the record company, the artist may retain a right of consultation or approval. The artist may also insist on the right to replace the producer or to appoint a coproducer if the resulting recordings do not achieve specified chart action. The producer may have the right to approve the new producer or coproducer, assuming such approval is not unreasonably withheld. Under the contract, the costs of the new producer or coproducer are deductible from the share otherwise due to the first producer. If a record company does not exercise its contract options, the artist-producer contract may grant the producer 3 to 6 months to obtain a new record contract.

Often such contracts have a *pass-through arrangement.* This means that the artist receives the same benefits as the producer from any provisions negotiated by the producer on such complex matters as record club rates, foreign sale rates, premium and budget record rates, rights of audit, and royalty escalations. Often the contract will contain a clause to the effect that if the terms of the distribution agreement (between the record company and the producer) differ from the terms of the artist-producer agreement, then the terms of the distribution agreement take precedence and will be incorporated into the artist-producer agreement.

Producer Fees

Independent record producers rarely produce recordings without a fee in addition to a producer royalty. These fees are usually deemed advances recoupable from the producer royalties, although occasionally they may be deemed nonrecoupable bonuses. Advance payments to independent producers for work with artists on minor labels may be as low as $1,000 or as high as $5,000. On major label deals, it is often the case that the producer, using his or her own studio and engineering services, will command payments of $30,000 to $40,000 per song, with only part of that being a recoupable producer advance.

Producer advances and royalties are accounted separately from mechanical royalties payable to songwriters or publishers. When mechanical license fees are payable to the artist or producer in their capacity as songwriter or publisher, the contract should be scrutinized for cross-collateralization clauses that would make all advances chargeable against payments of *any kind* that may be due to them.

Music Publishing and Follow-up Rights

Producers often control the music publishing rights for original recorded material. They thereby derive additional compensation from performance fees when the record is played and mechanical royalties when records are sold. In some instances, the record company may bargain to acquire some or all of the music publishing rights controlled by the producer. Alternatively, the company may be willing to settle for a controlled-composition rate, which is customarily a minimum of 75 percent of the statutory mechanical rate.

When acquiring a new artist's recordings from a producer, a record company will insist on obtaining rights to subsequent recordings by the artist. It will be the company's position that, having expended time and money in establishing an artist, the company is entitled to continue with an artist.

An independent producer who is engaged to work with an artist under contract to a record company may negotiate to obtain the right to continue as the producer of future recordings. Under such a provision, the record company may not use other producers for the artist unless and until the initial producer declines to produce additional recordings. For example, the producer may request a contractual clause stating that if a certain level of sales is achieved within a specified time period, he or she will be given the right to produce future recordings on the basis of the same or higher fee and royalty. For purposes of calculating the sales plateau, there may be a provision limiting free goods and providing that records in a reserve for returns must be counted. The time period should be short enough to be within the normal production period for a follow-up record and yet long enough for the sales plateau to be achieved. Often the time period is from 6 to 9 months or to the date of commencement of the next studio session, whichever comes earlier.

A record company may be content to have the producer produce and supply further recordings, but usually it will want a recording contract with the artist and a separate agreement with the producer regarding future recordings, fixed compensation, and royalties. Or the record company may take an option to enter into a recording contract with the producer, the artist, or both within a given period of time, for instance, within 120 days of the release of the initial recording, so as to give the record company time to evaluate the market acceptance of the record before exercising its option. For convenience, the company may execute a record agreement with the artist or attach it as an exhibit to an option agreement executed when the contract for the initial recording is signed, which will not become effective unless the option is exercised.

Contractual Safeguards

If the independent producer wishes to preserve the producer-artist contractual relationship and therefore refuses to consent to a recording agreement between the artist and the record company, the record company will insist that its own interest in the artist be protected through an *artist inducement letter* between the record company and the artist. Such an inducement letter usually states, among other provisions, that:

1. The artist is familiar with the agreement between the producer and the record company, including any rights which the producer may have with respect to subsequent recordings by the artist.
2. The artist will abide by the producer agreement insofar as it pertains to his or her personal recording services.
3. The artist will look solely to the producer for royalty statements and payments.
4. A breach of the agreement between the producer and the artist will not relieve the artist of the obligation to render recording services exclusively to the record company.

The record company must protect itself against the possibility that the producer may become unavailable, for any reason, to produce further recordings for the artist. Accordingly, the record company may insist that if this happens, the recording contract between the producer and the artist will be assigned to the record company. As a safeguard against the producer's unwillingness to execute a formal written assignment, most contracts provide that the record company may sign such an assignment on the producer's behalf.

In addition, the record company may insist that the agreement between the artist and producer be in a form satisfactory to the company. In particular, the company may require that the artist-producer agreement provide that it may be enforced by the record company; that the record company receive copies of any notice by artist to producer of any alleged defaults by the producer; that the record company be given an opportunity to cure such defaults; and that if the producer's defaults are incurable, the record company has the right to take over the artist-producer agreement with no responsibility for past defaults by the producer.

For recordings of artists under contract to the producer, the record company will require the producer to make appropriate warranties that the material is original and that the recordings do not infringe on any rights of third parties. The company will also look to the producer for warranties that all recording costs have been paid so that no claims will be made against the company for unpaid bills, and will generally reserve payment of the balance of any recording fund until it is assured that there will be no further recording costs.

A record company which is signatory to the American Federation of Musicians (AFM) and American Federation of Television and Radio Artists (AFTRA) union agreements must procure a warranty from the producer that all union musicians and vocalists who rendered services were paid union scale for their services. This warranty must appear in the agreement which must expressly state that it is for the benefit of the unions. In order to ensure that the record company is not faced with future competition by the artist, it will require the producer (and, through the inducement letter, the artist) to agree not to re-record the same material for a certain period, which is customarily 5 years from date of delivery of the recordings or 2 years from the expiration of the exclusive artist agreement, whichever is longer.

Because the producer is an intermediary between the artist and the record company, the company must obtain from the producer the contractual safe-guards that the company would include in direct agreements with the artist. The company will also seek from the producer provisions (in addition to an artist inducement letter) to protect the company from the effects of default or misunderstanding in the relations between the producer and the artist.

Producers, on the other hand, who stand to some extent in the same position as artists, should try to secure the same contractual clauses that an artist would want to secure. Thus producers should watch for appropriate provisions relating to accountings, audits, renewal of the agreement, prohibitions against re-recordings, guaranteed release of records, etc.

5

Foreign Distribution Agreements

Before the Internet virtually eliminated national boundaries, there were basically two ways for U.S. record companies to distribute their recordings outside of the United States. Multinational companies such as Universal Music Group (resulting from a merger of the PolyGram group of labels and the MCA group of labels), Sony (which includes the Columbia and Epic labels), BMG (which includes the RCA, Jive, Arista, and J labels), the Warner group (which includes the Warner Bros., Atlantic, and Elektra labels, among others), and the EMI group (which includes the Capitol, Angel, Blue Note, and Sparrow labels, among others) own and operate their own subsidiaries in most major territories and distribute their records through them. Smaller U.S. companies generally use licensees to distribute their records in foreign markets, which are either a local affiliate of one of the multinational companies or a local independent record company. There are advantages and disadvantages to either method.

It is simpler to have one multinational company handle the contractual and servicing aspects of foreign distribution. The power of a major multinational concern in distributing product cannot be overlooked, not to mention the fact that a major multinational corporation is in a better position to pay large advances. On the other hand, a smaller U.S. company may get more individualized attention from an independent local representative than would be the case if its catalog were but one of the many catalogs (including its own) distributed by a large multinational company.

Royalty Provisions

In the United States, most record companies base royalties on the wholesale price of records, although a few still use the suggested retail list price. Most record company licensees outside of the United States base royalty payments on the published price to dealers (PPD) fixed by the mechanical rights societies for the computation of copyright royalties. In the past, royalty rates ranged from 8 to 17 percent, based on 90 percent of net sales. Today, royalty rates range from 12 to 26 percent or more and are based on 100 percent of net sales. (Net sales are gross sales less disc jockey and other promotional records, as well as returns and other credits.) There is a reduced rate for midprice and budget product, usually half the rate of the top-line product. With the growing importance of lower-priced product in foreign markets, the reduced rate is vital to most foreign licensees.

If the American licensor has to pay artist royalties that are higher than usual, the licensee may be required to pay a supplemental royalty. Otherwise, the licensor would realize little or no profit. This would occur in the case of superstars who command royalties in excess of customary artist royalties. Albums made with the original Broadway musical cast and certain motion picture soundtrack albums may also command higher royalties. For these special recordings, licensing royalties may rise to 28 percent or more of the PPD, or be governed by a formula that is equivalent to an override of 3 to 5 points on top of the artist royalties payable by the American licensor.

The price used for the royalty base will exclude both a packaging allowance and excise taxes and purchase taxes such as the value-added tax that is common in many countries other than the United States. The foreign licensee's royalty payments must also cover any royalty obligations that the American licensor has to the AFM's Music Performance Trust Fund and Special Payments Fund.

Advances and Guarantees; Term

An American licensor will try to obtain monetary advances and royalty guarantees from the licensee, not only for the immediate financial reward, but also to encourage the licensee to vigorously exploit the licensor's records in order to recover its financial investment.

The minimum term of a licensing agreement is usually 3 years. Where distribution agreements cover an entire catalog, most licensees will insist on a 1-year minimum period to manufacture and exploit recordings that are delivered during the last half-year of the agreement.

As a bargaining point and an incentive to greater efforts by the licensee, licensors may only agree to an extension of the term if royalty earnings have exceeded the guarantee for the original term. They may also require an increase in the advance or guarantee as a condition to an extension.

If the licensee has made substantial guarantees of royalties or releases and the licensor's catalog has failed to meet expectations, the licensee may reserve the right to cancel the agreement at an anniversary date prior to normal expiration of the agreement or to extend the term for an additional period. As a defense against the licensee's lack of effort, the licensor may reserve the right to cancel the agreement if the licensee fails to achieve stated minimum royalty earnings within a certain period.

The licensor will want the licensee to release a minimum amount of product during the term of the agreement. A fairly common clause states that if a licensor's release attains a listing on the *Billboard* Top 100 charts it must be released in the licensed territory. Record companies which control soundtrack albums will insist on the release of these soundtrack albums when the film is shown in the licensed territory (although this would normally happen in any event). American record companies with original Broadway cast albums may demand the release of such albums when a production of the show takes place in the licensed territory, at least in English-speaking countries; but the licensee may negotiate to prevent such a requirement if an album featuring the local cast is available in the licensed territory.

Recording contracts with top artists sometimes require that the artist's recording be released not only in the United States but in certain other territories as well. In these cases, the licensee may be required to release these artists' recordings in its territory.

When artists go on a foreign promotional tour and appear on local radio and television or in concert halls, auditoriums, and nightclubs, it is important that their recordings be readily available where these appearances take place. Distribution agreements may contractually impose this requirement upon licensees and also require them to cooperate and sometimes to give financial support to tour promotion. Agreements may also require the licensee to arrange for artist's videos to be given appropriate exposure in the territory.

Exclusivity

There are presently fifteen members of the European Union (EU): Austria, Belgium, Denmark, Finland, France, Germany, Greece, Ireland, Italy, Luxembourg, the Netherlands, Portugal, Spain, Sweden, and the United Kingdom. Together, these countries comprise a common market allowing people, goods, and services to move more easily among them. In 2000, the EU member nations had a total population of over 377 million (compared to 277 million in the United States that year) and a GDP (gross domestic product) of $7,836.7 billion (compared to $9,896.4 billion in the United States). Import duties do not exist within the EU. It is possible for records and jackets manufactured in one EU country to be shipped to another at no additional expense aside from freight charges. Licensees of the same American licensor can make contractual arrangements to purchase the licensor's product from each other. The result has been centralized manufacturing, which cuts costs and potentially increases the number of items that are released from a licensor's catalog. Centralized manufacturing has also been encouraged by the increasing acceptance of the original packaging, in the language of the country of origin (usually English). The abolition of tariff barriers has accelerated the trend toward licensing arrangements with a single licensee for the entire EU. Centralized manufacturing tends to occur most often where the licensees are affiliated with each other as subsidiaries of a large multinational record company.

At the time of this writing, twelve members of the European Union (all except Denmark, Sweden, and the United Kingdom) participate in the European Monetary

Union (EMU), which adopted a single currency known as the euro on January 1, 1999. Prior to that time, divergent currency valuations made the unified marketing of recordings within the EU countries complex and inefficient. Prices for CDs varied from an equivalent low of U.S.$17.55 in Portugal to an equivalent high of U.S.$23.30 for the same album in Finland. Not a single European country approached the suggested U.S. retail list price of $14.98 to $16.98. In addition, the American practice of widespread discounting was unheard of in Europe. If the euro succeeds, the volume of mass marketing within the EU will increase substantially, since aberrations and disincentives caused by varying prices will have been eliminated. At the same time, there will be more incentive to make arrangements within the EU that encompass all member countries.

Licensees desire exclusivity for their particular territory, especially when they have made substantial guarantees of royalties and releases. Within the EU, exclusivity is severely restricted by the regulations that mandate free competition, the unrestricted transshipment of goods across borders, nondiscrimination, and market unity. In fact, records first sold anywhere within the EU under the authority of the copyright holder or its licensee may be imported into or exported out of any member country. Consequently, if an American record company licenses its Dutch subsidiary to manufacture and sell certain records, a British company may buy them in bulk and export them to England, in contravention of the so-called exclusive rights granted by the licensor to another British company.

Another development that is rapidly bringing an end to traditional exclusivity arrangements is digital distribution. Digital distribution simply ignores national boundaries. While this may speed up and increase the efficiency of distribution, it does raise serious economic problems for record companies attempting to maintain their traditional bottom-line profits based on the distribution of hard copies of phonorecords.

Broadcast Performance Fees

Under the International Convention for the Protection of Performers, Producers, Phonograms, and Broadcasting Organizations—the so-called Rome Convention, which now has over 30 signatories, but not the United States—when a record is used for broadcasting or any communication to the public, the user is required to pay a fee to the performers, the producers, or both, depending on local law. The principal European broadcasting systems, whether owned by the state or privately, pay broadcast fees to the representatives of record companies. Fees are also collected from jukebox proprietors, dance halls, nightclubs, and other users of recordings.

These fees are also collectible for broadcasts and performances of American records released in a foreign territory. In agreements with licensees, licensors are frequently granted an interest in the fees, usually 50 percent. But major licensees may insist on retaining broadcast performance fees until such time as the United States passes legislation requiring that American broadcasters pay similar performance fees. Where fees paid to the licensee are not allocated in direct relation to the broadcasts of particular records, the agreement with the licensee may provide for an allocation to the licensor in the ratio of the licensee's sales of the licensor's records to the total sales of records by the licensee. Although it seems fair that the licensor receive a share of these fees, most licensees are unwilling to take the time and effort to calculate them.

Music Publishing

The licensee customarily assumes the obligation to obtain licenses to reproduce copyrighted musical material contained in the licensor's recordings, as well as in audiovisual devices such as promotional videos. This involves the payment of so-called mechanical royalties based on the number of copies sold.

Labels

Major multinational firms usually have no problem requiring licensees to use the licensor's own label, but less well-known independent companies may have a harder time getting licensees to agree to this. Licensors want to use their own labels in order to gain prestige, name recognition, and acceptance by local dealers and the public. Such recognition makes it easier for a licensor to switch to another licensee, set up its own local enterprise (assuming it is not already part of a multinational structure), and promote its product through unified multinational advertising and other methods. For all these reasons foreign licensees may resist a request for the use of a specific label. They do not wish to build up a potential competitor. They may claim that valuable sales will be lost because the public will not purchase records on unknown labels. As a compromise, a licensor may propose the use of a split label, composed of the licensor's and the licensee's labels.

For their own protection, American companies should register their labels promptly as trademarks in foreign countries. Companies that delay doing so may find that their right to use their labels has been preempted by local registrants.

Release Requirements

A foreign licensee (whether an independent or an affiliate of a multinational) will wish to pick and choose from among a licensor's recordings. Many recordings may never be released by the licensee, either because they are unsuitable to the local market or because the licensee is granting priority to other product. Needless to say, there will be differences of opinion on the question of whether a given recording will sell in a given territory.

To overcome this problem where a licensor has given exclusivity to its entire catalog, a licensor may have the right to seek to place recordings which a licensee fails to release, as well as subsequent recordings by the same artist, with another company. In order to prevent confusion about the licensor's representative in the area, the primary licensee may require that releases by other licensees not give prominent credit to the licensor.

A licensee being asked to commit to substantial financial guarantees may well balk at being deprived of rights in this way. It will demand an exclusive right to all the licensor's recordings whether or not they are released locally, claiming that some recordings may become appropriate for release in the future and that confusion will result if recordings by the same artist are released on different record labels. The licensor may agree, concluding that such releases will skim the cream off its catalog and provide little gain from releases by other licensees.

Record Clubs

There are record clubs in most of the principal markets. Some foreign record companies operate their own record clubs; others have arrangements with third-party record clubs. In either case, licensees will seek the right to release a licensor's recordings through record club channels.

Some licensors may refuse to permit sales through record clubs without prior approval. Licensees frequently request the right to pay reduced royalty rates on club sales, arguing that they receive a reduced licensing royalty from clubs owned and operated by third parties or (where the licensee operates its own club) that the high cost of advertising and large amounts of uncollectable monies mandate a reduced royalty rate. The rates will be the subject of bargaining and are usually one-half of the rates applicable to regular retail sales.

Coupling

The licensee may wish to have the right to couple the performances of various of the licensor's artists, or of the same artist drawn from different releases, into a single package commonly known as a *compilation*. Compilations have for many years been especially popular in Europe, particularly in the dance field.

Previously, many licensors sought to restrict or prohibit licensing (at least without prior consent) for various reasons, including a fear that its image or the image of its artists would be adversely affected by coupling or simply to avoid giving a competitive label any potential commercial advantage. With the advent of the Internet, the ability to prevent consumers from downloading their own cuts, whether illegally or through legitimate subscription services, has significantly reduced the importance of contractual coupling restrictions.

Cover Recordings

A *cover record* is a competing version of the same song made after the original recording has been issued. Cover records may be a great source of friction between a licensor and a licensee. Obviously, a licensor will be hostile to its licensee releasing a cover record and may insist on a clause prohibiting cover records made by the licensee.

If the licensed recording is suitable for the local market, a licensee may be willing to exclude a cover version. This is especially true for instrumental recordings. But if the lyrics of a licensed recording are in English, its release in an area in which English is not the indigenous language may be meaningless. In these instances the licensee may be unwilling to preclude a local-language cover record, pointing out that otherwise its competitors may obtain a great advantage. The two parties may compromise by agreeing that the licensee will not release a local cover version earlier than an agreed-upon interval—for example, 2 to 3 months—after the release of the licensed recording. As a matter of good relations with their licensors, the major multinational record companies with affiliates in many countries generally avoid cover versions.

Samples and Materials

Licensors send out samples to licensees so they can decide which recordings they wish to release in their territory. These samples are usually shipped via overnight mail or digitally so that the licensee may review them quickly. Although there may be no charge for the samples, it is not uncommon to require the licensee to pay for packing and for freight and other transportation costs.

It is usually more cost-effective to manufacture recordings locally than to import finished records from the United States. For the purpose of manufacture, the licensee orders digital audio tapes (DATs)—master tapes from which CDs, cassettes, and vinyl albums can be made locally. For the production of album covers, the licensee may request cover images, either as negatives or in digitized form, or order copies of printed front covers or back liners. The licensee usually pays the licensor's cost for orders of DATs, negatives, and printed covers or liners, as well as the costs of packing and shipping.

Accountings and Auditing

The agreement between the licensee and licensor will require quarterly or semi-annual accountings: licensors prefer quarterly accountings; licensees prefer semiannual accountings. The accountings should set forth in detail the computation of the amounts due, including the number of records sold from each recording, broken down by configuration, as well as the royalty rate and all deductions and other charges.

The U.S. licensor should obtain the right to audit the licensee's books and records, so as to verify the accuracy of the royalty statements which are submitted. Licensees usually require that the cost of the inspection and audit be borne by the licensor and be conducted by a certified or chartered public accountant. The licensee should also agree to furnish its accountings to the mechanical rights society in the licensed territory. This should serve as a simple check on the accuracy of the licensee's royalty reports to the licensor.

Termination Procedure

At the end of a licensing agreement, the licensee will have on hand DATs and an inventory of finished records. To protect its interests and those of a successor licensee, the licensor will want to control the licensee's disposition of these items.

It is common to give the licensee six months following the end of the agreement to sell off any inventory of finished records. Without such a sell-off period, the licensee would have to stop releasing any new product months before the final date of the agreement. This could operate to the detriment of licensee and licensor. To protect itself, the licensor may provide that all sales in the sell-off period shall be in the normal course of business and at regular prices; otherwise the product may be downgraded by severe discounting and other practices.

The licensor may require a written list of the inventory, to be supplied within a short period after the expiration of the licensing agreement. The list provides information useful to the licensor and any new licensee regarding the state of the prior licensee's inventory. The licensor may also have the right at any time after the expiration of the licensing agreement to purchase from the licensee, at the licensee's cost, all or part of the unsold inventory. The new licensee may be interested in purchasing this inventory. Where the old licensee is not trusted, the licensor may wish to acquire the inventory so as to avoid the risk of new pressings continuing to be sold under the guise of inventory.

The licensee is usually required to dispose of materials other than finished records in one of four ways:

1. Deliver them to the licensor in the United States or the licensed territory
2. Transfer them to a new licensee
3. Destroy them under the licensor's supervision
4. Destroy them and supply an appropriate affidavit to that effect

The licensee and the licensor may also determine whether the costs of delivery are to be borne by the licensee or the licensor, as well as whether the licensee is entitled to reimbursement for the cost of the materials to be delivered.

Variations in Currency Values

Licensors should be aware that changes in the exchange rate can have an impact on the amount of royalties earned in U.S. dollars. Where exchange rates are volatile (as they are at the time of this writing), the time when royalties are computed and paid can be vital. Contractual negotiations should specify whether royalty conversions to U.S. dollars will be computed (1) at the time records are sold, (2) at the time of licensee's receipt of payment for records sold, (3) at the close of the royalty accounting period, or (4) at the close of the royalty accounting period when the licensee is contractually required to account to the licensor.

Currency fluctuations can work to the detriment of the licensee, who pays advances to the licensor in U.S. dollars at the time a license agreement is signed but then recoups those advances at later dates when the exchange rate may be less favorable.

Transmittal of Funds

Even the routine transfer of funds from a licensee to a licensor requires international bank transfers. If these transactions are by wire, additional charges may be involved. Some international licensees maintain U.S. dollar accounts for the convenience of all parties.

For the few areas in the world where governmental regulations impede the free flow of local funds to the United States for the payment of record royalties and guarantees, the licensing agreement may stipulate that the licensor has the option of directing the licensee to deposit the blocked funds to the credit of the licensor in a local depository designated by the licensor. The money then becomes available for local use by the licensor.

Jurisdiction over Disputes

Disputes may occur between the licensor and the licensee regarding the interpretation of the licensing agreement, royalty statements, or other matters in the agreement. The American licensor will seek to have U.S. courts or U.S. arbitration designated as the exclusive means of resolving such disputes. Naturally, the foreign licensee will resist this.

To determine whether the dispute will be adjudicated or arbitrated on American or foreign soil, negotiations are necessary. To avoid an impasse, some negotiators compromise by requiring the claimant to accept the jurisdiction of the responding party, thereby increasing the incentive to settle disputes. Given the cost and unpredictability of litigation, licensor-licensee agreements are increasingly specifying that alternative dispute resolution procedures, such as mediation and arbitration, be used. There may, however, be legal questions about the enforceability of adjudicated disputes if they do not conform to the due process requirements of the licensee's country, where enforcement is being sought. Legal counsel should be consulted in this area.

Default Clauses

It is advisable that the licensing agreement between the American licensor and the foreign licensee contain a complete, detailed clause setting forth the rights and obligations of the parties in the event of a default.

From the licensor's standpoint, the agreement should explicitly state that a default is deemed to be material if it is by reason of the licensee's failure to (1) pay guarantees and royalties when due, (2) render complete accountings when due, or (3) comply with contractual requirements as to minimum releases of the licensor's records. The licensor should also provide that the bankruptcy or insolvency of the licensee constitutes a material default (although this provision will be subject to the operation of local bankruptcy laws). The licensee will seek to include a provision under which it is entitled to a notice of default and a period in which to remedy it.

Ordinarily, where there is a material default, the American licensor has the right to cancel the agreement. When there is such a cancellation the licensee may not have the right, usually granted at the end of an agreement, to sell off any inventory of finished goods.

The default clause should reserve to the licensor all rights to seek damages, accountings, or other relief, in addition to canceling the agreement.

6

Labor Agreements

Two unions exist for performers in the record industry: the American Federation of Musicians (AFM) and the American Federation of Television and Radio Artists (AFTRA). Musicians, leaders, contractors, copyists, orchestrators, and arrangers of instrumental music are covered by the AFM; vocalists, actors, announcers, narrators, and sound effects artists are represented by AFTRA. Under the employers' agreements with both unions, employees must either be members of the union or become members by the 30th day of their employment.

Membership dues for the AFM consist of a one-time national fee of $65 plus local fees varying from a nominal $1 to $35; annual national dues of $46 and local dues of lesser amounts; and "work dues" of 1 to 5 percent of union-scale wages, of which 1 percent goes to the national union. The AFM has approximately 80,000 members. For detailed information about membership, benefits, payment schedules, etc., contact the AFM (see Appendix B, page 485; Web site: http://www.afm.org).

AFTRA has a uniform initiation fee of $1,000 covering both national and local membership, plus initial work dues of $442.50; additional work dues are billed annually on May 1 and November 1. These additional dues are based on the member's AFTRA earnings during previous year. During the year 2000, AFTRA implemented a uniform national schedule for local stages. AFTRA claims to have 110,000 professional musicians among its members, in the United States and Canada. For information regarding current dues, benefits, payment schedules, and membership rates, contact AFTRA (see Appendix B, page 485; Web site: http://www.aftra.org).

Key Labor Agreements

The main agreements between the two labor unions and the recording industry are the "AFTRA Code of Fair Practice for Phonograph Recordings" and the AFM "Phonograph Record Labor Agreement." Both agreements cover the essential negotiated points for members' services within the record industry, including minimum scale payments; residual payments; health and retirement provisions; vacation, overtime, and holiday pay provisions; union contractor requirements; and instrumental cartage for musicians. The recording industry also has certain obligations to the AFTRA Health and Retirement Funds and to the AFM's Special Payments Funds and the Phonograph Record Trust Fund.

Arbitration

Under the AFTRA Code of Fair Practice for Phonograph Recordings, any dispute between a record company and AFTRA, or between a record company and a member of AFTRA arising out of the AFTRA agreement or out of any contract made on or after April 1, 1987, must be submitted to arbitration.

If there is an exclusive recording agreement with an artist, and "the Company has reason to believe that the artist has recorded or contemplates recording in violation of the contract," the company may apply to any court having jurisdiction over the artist for an injunction and other relief arising out of the particular act.

As of this writing, AFM agreements do not provide for arbitration.

AFTRA and AFM Scale Payments

The AFTRA rates vary according to specific job classifications: soloists and duos; group singers; actors and comedians; narrators and announcers; and sound effects artists. There are also special rates for performers in original-cast albums and for vocalists "stepping out" of groups in recording sessions.

AFTRA scale payments for TV commercials vary according to on- or off-camera appearance, the duration of the commercial, and factors such as regional or national airing, cable use, Spanish-language versions, and "wild spots" (broadcast times designated at the discretion of the station at a discounted rate). Basic payments are supplemented as and when the on-air use occurs. AFTRA scale payments for radio commercials have complex formulas and involve factors such as single, duo, or larger groups; national or regional use; and, if regional, major cities included or excluded.

Under the AFTRA code, *nonroyalty* singers are entitled to additional union-scale payments, called *contingent scale payments,* depending on the number of records sold in the United States derived from recordings made on or after December 15, 1974. (A recording ceases to be considered a basis for additional payments 10 years after the date of its first release to the public as a single or as a part of an album.) Only sales in normal retail channels are counted. Record club, mail-order, and premium sales are excluded, but CD sales through the Internet are included, and sales from digital distribution are under discussion.

For albums other than cast albums, contingent scale payments (in addition to applicable minimum scale) are 50 percent of the applicable minimum scale, payable each time specified sales levels are reached. As of 2002, these levels were (a) 157,500, (b) 250,000, (c) 375,000, (d) 500,000, (e) 650,000, (f) 825,000, and (g) 1,000,000, (h) 1,500,000, (i) 2,000,000, (j) 2,500,000, (k) 3,000,000.

A recorded side that has been previously released in album form does not earn contingent-scale payments from further release in any other album. If released as a single, it does not accrue contingent-scale monies for release in any other single. If a single is incorporated into an album, it is then eligible for contingent-scale payments.

Contingent-scale payments to nonroyalty AFTRA artists may not ordinarily be recouped or charged against royalties or other payments due to AFTRA royalty artists. But the record company may, subject to the consent of the covered artist, credit overscale payments in excess of 2.5 times the minimum scale against contingent payments. All contingent-scale payments are subject to contributions to the AFTRA Health and Retirement Funds.

The AFM agreement makes provisions for minimum wages and other working conditions for instrumentalists, leaders, contractors, arrangers, orchestrators, and copyists. The provisions are detailed and extensive. The union should be consulted for specific terms.

As of February 1, 2001, a musician on nonclassical recordings became entitled to $313.45 as a basic session rate for a 3-hour session. There are also premium rates for recording sessions held on Saturdays after 1:00 p.m., as well as on Sundays, listed holidays, and during certain late night hours. Leaders and contractors receive not less than double the applicable sideman musician's scale. A musician who plays more than one instrument during a recording session (arbitrarily called "doubling") is paid an additional 20 percent of the base rate and the regular overtime payment. An additional 15 percent is paid for each subsequent instrument played during the session.

AFM Special Payments and Trust Funds

When employers sign the AFM Phonograph Record Labor Agreement, they also agree to contribute a percentage of their earnings to the AFM Phonograph Record Special Payments Fund, the Phonograph Record Trust Fund, and the Motion Picture Special Payments Fund agreements. Motion picture collections have substantially increased because sales to video, TV, and cable have raised both record sales and royalty collections. Compilation albums and licensing to clubs and film companies have also resulted in increased payments.

These funds are a major benefit of union membership. After deduction of expenses, the monies in the SPFs are disbursed as a continuing royalty to members of the AFM who have participated in the recordings on a nonroyalty basis. Payments are made yearly to those musicians who performed as union musicians at one or more sessions within the past 5 years. The amount of each recording musician's payment is determined by how many union recording sessions the musician has participated in. Participation is not limited to hit recordings or even to the actual commercial release of a recording once the session has been completed, and once qualified, the payments continue for 5 years.

In addition to the benefits paid by the Trust Fund to the participating non-royalty recording musicians, an equal amount is distributed, in a unique manner, in support of paying union member musicians at scale for live free concert performances:

> These musicians are not the same as the musicians who were involved in the recordings from which the earnings are paid. . . . They are selected by the promoters of the qualifying free concerts. Such free concerts are held throughout the United States and Canada at Veterans hospitals, community events, museums, prisons, parks, and nursing homes. They serve the function of using monies obtained from the recording industry to encourage the employment of live musicians for the public benefit. The funds so allocated since the commencement in 1950 have exceeded several hundreds of millions of dollars in aggregate and in many years have financed the presentation of over 25,000 such musical events.

Each agreement applies only to records containing music "which was performed or conducted by musicians covered by, or required to be paid pursuant to ... [the] Phonograph Record Labor Agreement." If the services of union members on a particular record consist solely of arrangements, orchestrations, or copying, then that record is not subject to either agreement.

The record companies' payments to the Phonograph Record SPF is based on record, tape, and CD sales. The schedule for payments is based on the manufacturer's suggested retail price, as follows: for records and tapes to $3.79, the rate is 0.54 percent; for records and tapes to $8.98, the rate is 0.52 percent; for compact discs to $10.98, the rate is 0.52 percent.

In computing payments, the record company must report 100 percent of net sales. There are certain allowances in connection with the computation of payments. First, there is a packaging deduction from the suggested retail list price in the country of manufacture or sale: 30 percent for tapes, cartridges, and compact discs. Second, there is an exemption for singles of the first 100,000 sold of each title. Third, excepting record clubs, there is an exemption of up to 25 percent of the total records, tapes, cartridges, and compact discs distributed, representing "free" records, tapes, cartridges, and compact discs actually distributed. And fourth, for record clubs there is an exemption for "free" and "bonus" records, tapes, cartridges, and compact discs actually distributed up to 50 percent of total distribution, with the record manufacturer paying the full rate on half of the excess of the free and bonus records, tapes, cartridges, and compact discs over the 50 percent, in addition to full-rate payments for all records actually sold by clubs.

Suggested retail list prices are computed exclusive of any sales or excise taxes. If a record company does not use the manufacturer's suggested retail price, it must negotiate a new equivalent basis for computing payments.

For each record subject to the Special Payments Fund Agreement, there is a 10-year limitation, from the year of release, on the sales for which payments must be made.

Record manufacturers pay lesser amounts for the Phonograph Record Trust Agreement. Payments are calculated on record sales at the rate of 0.23625 percent of the manufacturer's suggested retail list price. For compact discs, the maximum suggested retail price is $10.98. The allowances and exemptions are similar to those used to calculate payments to the Phonograph Record SPF, with some exceptions. There is an exemption for the first 25,000 units of a title for compact discs or other devices. There is a 5-year limitation for payments to the Phonograph Record Trust Agreement.

The Motion Picture Special Payments Fund is structured differently because revenues are generated differently in the motion picture industry. Payments are based on a musician's actual works in scoring a specific theatrical or television movie. Each union signatory producer contributes a percentage of the revenues for that specific project. Those payments are then divided among the musicians who performed the actual services. Musicians on that project receive SPF payments for that specific movie as long as the picture continues to be profitable for the union signatory company.

Finally, all sales, assignments, leases, licenses, or other transfers of master recordings are subject to the provisions in the Special Payments Fund Agreement and the Phonograph Record Trust Agreement. This applies to any person or company doing business in the United States, Canada, or Puerto Rico. Those who are licensed to do business outside the domestic area must agree to make the necessary payments to the licensor, who is responsible for remitting them to the appropriate funds.

AFTRA Health and Retirement Funds

The AFTRA Health and Retirement Funds provide medical coverage and retirement benefits for eligible AFTRA members. The record companies are required to pay to the funds an amount equal to 10 percent of the gross compensation paid to AFTRA members by the company. Included in the "gross compensation" are all forms of payment, including "salaries, earnings, royalties, fees, advances, guarantees, deferred compensation, proceeds, bonuses, profit-participation, shares of stock, bonds, options and property of any kind or nature whatsoever paid to the artist directly or indirectly." The 10 percent payment is limited to the first $100,000 of gross compensation paid in any calendar year.

Retirement and Death Benefits

Although the applicable rules of the AFM relating to death and retirement benefits are so complex that consultation with the administrator of the Retirement Fund is advised for important questions, there are several highlights worthy of note.

For each session an artist plays over his or her career, AFM sets aside a portion for retirement disbursement, which can arrive as early as age 55, or as late as age 70 and 6 months. Once an artist is vested—that is, has accumulated a specified number of months of service or attains retirement age while still a plan member—he or she is eligible for pension payments. If no application for benefits has been received by age 70 and 6 months, monthly payments begin automatically on the April after that age is reached.

Pension payments on retirement depend on age of retirement and on individual members' accrued benefits. For example, a member who retired at 65 with $25,000 vested benefits would receive a monthly pension for life of $1,115.

In the event of early death (before 100 months of retirement payments), there is a death benefit, to any qualifying heir, of the remaining balance between death and the "guaranteed" 100 monthly payments.

Royalty Performers

The AFM basic agreement makes a distinction between a musician who is a phonograph record "royalty artist" and one who is not. A royalty artist is one who "records pursuant to a phonograph record contract which provides for a royalty payable to such musician at a basic rate of at least 3 percent of the suggested retail list price of records sold (less deductions usual and customary in the trade) . . . or a substantially equivalent royalty," or "plays as a member of (and not as a sideman with) a recognized self-contained group." A recognized self-contained group consists of "two or more persons who perform together in fields other than phonograph records under a group name" and record under a phonograph record contract providing for a royalty "at a basic rate of at least 3 percent of the suggested retail list price of records sold (less deductions usual and customary in the trade) or a substantially equivalent royalty." Furthermore, all musicians in the group must be members of the AFM.

At the first session for a single record side a royalty artist receives only the basic session rate and related overtime rate regardless of whether he or she plays multiple parts, doubles, overdubs, or "sweetens" (e.g., adds strings, horns, or woodwinds to a previously recorded basic rhythm track).

The AFM agreement states that recording contracts must contain a covenant that the contract "shall become effective unless it is disapproved by the International Executive Board of the American Federation of Musicians of the United States and Canada, or a duly authorized agent thereof, within 30 working days after it is submitted to the International Executive Board. The parties acknowledge that this provision is not intended to provide a device for the parties hereto to avoid their obligations."

For recordings of the same side, the AFTRA code stipulates that a royalty artist shall receive minimum union scale, with a maximum payment of three times scale regardless of the length and number of sessions. The record company must state in the production memorandum that is filed after a recording session whether or not the performer is a royalty artist. The record company must also furnish the artist "at least semiannually and to AFTRA upon request, . . . so long as there shall be sales, a full and proper accounting in order to correctly ascertain the amount of royalty . . . due artist."

Contractors

Under the AFTRA code *contractors* are "those artists who perform any additional services, such as contacting singers, pre-rehearsing, coaching, or conducting singers, arranging for sessions or rehearsals, or any other similar or supervisory duties, including assisting and preparation of production memorandum." The contractor's duties include acting as liaison between the performers and producer, seeing that all AFTRA provisions are enforced, and completing and filing all appropriate forms with AFTRA within 48 hours. At each recording session, the contractor must fill out the pertinent information on the AFTRA Phonograph Record Sessions Report Form and deliver a copy of the form to the record company representatives. The record company initials the form, indicating that a recording session has been held, and the contractor files the report with AFTRA. This report is over and above Schedule A, a production memorandum, which the record company must furnish to AFTRA within 21 calendar days after the recording session. The production memorandum should provide sufficient information to permit a computation of the appropriate performing fee, as well as setting forth the gross fee paid.

A contractor is required for all engagements of nonroyalty group singers consisting of three or more persons. The contractor must be one of the singers unless the group is all-female or all-male. A contractor is also required for all original-cast albums employing a singing group of three or more; the contractor does not have to be a member of the singing group.

The contractor is to be present at all times during the recording session and receives, in addition to the regular union-scale payment for vocalists, an additional scale payment for services as a contractor. The AFTRA scale payment for contractors is the same as for additional vocalists.

The functions of a contractor are not generally defined in the AFM basic agreement. In practice, however, the contractor hires the necessary musicians for the recording session and often hires the AFTRA contractor, who in turn hires the required singers. An AFM contractor must be used if 12 or more sidemen are employed for any session. The contractor, who may or may not be one of the sidemen, must attend the entire session. The contractor is paid not less than double the applicable sideman's scale, with no extra payment for his or her services as sideman. It is the duty of the contractor to supply completed W-4 forms as well as B report forms to the record company for each recording session. The forms are due within 15 working days of the performance and are the basis for the payment of union scale by the record company.

Dubbing

Dubbing, also called *overdubbing,* is the addition of vocal or instrumental performances to music already recorded. The AFM basic agreement prohibits dubbing except as specifically permitted by other provisions of the agreement. Dubbing is allowed only if the record company gives prior notice to the union and pays union scale and fringe benefits for the new use. Both during and after a recording session, the record company may add live vocal and instrumental performances to a recording without additional compensation to the musicians who made the original recording.

Under the AFTRA agreement, dubbing also means converting or transferring a performance made in a medium other than phonograph records (e.g., radio, television, or motion pictures) for use as phonograph recordings. This is sanctioned by AFTRA provided that the record company meets certain conditions: providing a notice to AFTRA, paying AFTRA scale to the performers, obtaining the consent of the "star or featured or overscale artist," if any, and acquiring the consent of the artist who has performed the vocal soundtrack, if any, for the "star or featured or overscale artist." The provisions for payment are comparable to AFM reuse fees.

The AFTRA agreement does not prohibit overdubbing. It provides that if the "artist participates in multiple tracking (i.e., sings again to the original track at the same session), he shall be paid for the session as if each overtracking were an additional [record] side."

AFM and AFTRA Scales for New Media

In 1997, the AFM Electronic Media Services Division organized an Interactive/Multimedia Department, which put in place an experimental interactive/multimedia agreement that addresses requests for scales in all current existing interactive and new media areas. This agreement is renewed and updated every year. It outlines the new recording scales and guidelines for musicians' performances on CD-ROM, DVD, and dedicated console platform productions, for Web site and Web link menu music, and for live streaming performances on the Internet and World Wide Web. It also contains the scales for virtual reality rides and kiosks and the guidelines for new use of existing music on the Internet or as interactive product.

In 2002 the Industrial and New Technologies department of AFTRA drew up an Interactive Media Agreement which covers interactive programs such as games that appear on CD-ROM and the Internet, as well as other entertainment-oriented interactive programming.

Protections against Illicit Practices

Purchases or leases of master recordings by record companies are an accepted practice in the music business. There are established and well-financed independent producers who sell or lease master recordings made in accordance with union rules and regulations. There are also musicians who make master recordings on spec, inspired by faith in their own talents; lacking the capital to operate under union standards, these young entrepreneurs may record with nonunion musicians or with union musicians who are willing to accept less than scale.

AFTRA and the AFM are fully aware of the illicit practices in the field and recognize them as threats to the employment of union members and to the maintenance of minimum union pay rates. For this reason the unions have included certain provisions in their agreements that appear designed to make the record companies assist in policing the field.

Paragraph 17 of the AFM agreement prohibits a record company from acquiring recordings that were recorded in the domestic area or by a resident of the domestic area unless the musicians were paid wages and fringe benefits at least equal to the union scale in effect at the time the recorded music was produced. To satisfy its obligations if the seller or licensor was not a party to an AFM agreement when the recording was made, the record company may include certain stipulated clauses in its agreement to acquire the master recordings:

1. A representation and warranty by the seller or licensor that the recorded music does not come within the terms of Paragraph 17 or that the requirements of Paragraph 17 are satisfied
2. A statement that the representation and warranty were included for the benefit of the union and may be enforced by the union or by the person it may designate

AFTRA has equally protective provisions.

Attorneys are occasionally asked to advise a potential purchaser about future royalty obligations to the artists on the recordings. Unless the seller specifically agrees to continue paying royalties to the artist, a legal obligation is created between the artist and the purchaser even in the absence of a specific assumption. This is called a *lien,* which attaches to the property, which, in this situation, is the master. The union rights to the royalties are the same as those of the artist's.

The AFTRA Code of Fair Practice for Phonograph Recordings clearly attempts to solve this problem. It refers to any transfer of title to or rights in a master recording by "sale, assignment, pledge, hypothecation, or other transfer, or by attachment, levy, lien, garnishment, voluntary bankruptcy, involuntary bankruptcy, arrangement, reorganization, assignment for benefit of creditors, probate, or any other legal proceeding." Under the AFTRA code the transferee is responsible to the artist for royalties due under the artist contract for sales of phonograph records made by the transferee or its licensees. Such responsibility accrues after a default by the producer of the records in the payment of artist royalties and receipt by the transferee of written notice by the artist specifying the default, together with due proof of the artist's royalty arrangements. The transferee's responsibility is only in respect of sales after receipt of such notice.

The AFTRA agreement also requires that any transferee of title or rights to a master recording who is not a signatory to the AFTRA code shall sign an agreement with AFTRA assuming the obligations referred to in the previous paragraph. The transferer continues to have the same responsibility to the artist and to the AFTRA trust fund for all sales by the transferer's successor in interest, unless the successor is a Code signatory.

In agreements transferring an interest in a master recording, every record producer must include provisions incorporating the aforementioned royalty responsibility to the artist on the part of the transferee, as well as a covenant requiring the same undertaking in all subsequent transfers.

Domestic and Foreign Territory

The AFTRA agreement states that it applies to the making of phonograph recordings in the United States, its territories, and its possessions, which together are referred to as the "recording territory." No clause regulates recordings made outside the recording territory.

The AFM agreement is not so restricted. It covers recordings made in both Canada and the United States, or in a present territory or possession of either country, all of which is called the "domestic area." The agreement also encompasses any residents of the domestic area who are engaged to perform as instrumental musicians, leaders, contractors, copyists, orchestrators, or arrangers of instrumental music in the recording of phonograph records outside the domestic area.

According to AFM bylaws, its members are prohibited from rendering services outside the domestic area unless they have written authorization from the union to do so. Penalties for a violation include a fine not exceeding $10,000, or expulsion from the union, or both.

Other Income for Artists

Under the Rome Convention of 1961, broadcasters in signatory countries must pay a fee for the right to broadcast a recording to the public. The AFTRA agreement stipulates that if the fee is paid to the record company, within 30 days of a written request by either party, the record company and the union will bargain in good faith about the portion payable to the performers. If a separate payment is made to the performers, no negotiation is necessary.

In recent years the AFM, in conjunction with AFTRA and the Alliance of Artists and Recording Companies (AARC) (which represents 130 recording companies and 1,400 featured artists), has been successful in obtaining for American musicians a portion of Japanese record rental collections for U.S. sound recordings. AARC is also responsible for the distribution to its members of royalties paid to the U.S. Copyright Office by manufacturers of digital audio recorders and blank digital discs under the Audio Home Recording Act of 1992. Recent reports from AARC indicate that it has distributed over $2.3 million from these sources.

7

Copyright in Sound Recordings

Section 101 of the U.S. Copyright Act of 1976 clearly distinguishes phonorecords from sound recordings, as follows:

> "Phonorecords" are material objects in which sounds, other than those accompanying a motion picture or other audiovisual work, are fixed by any method now known or later developed, and from which the sounds can be perceived, reproduced, or otherwise communicated, either directly or with the aid of a machine or device. The term "phonorecords" includes the material object in which the sounds are first fixed. . . .

> "Sound recordings" are works that result from the fixation of a series of musical, spoken, or other sounds, but not including the sounds accompanying a motion picture or other audiovisual work, regardless of the nature of the material objects, such as disks, tapes, or other phonorecords, in which they are embodied.

Copyright Protection for Published and Unpublished Works

The 1976 Copyright Act defines *publication* as distribution "to the public by sale or other transfer of ownership, or by rental, lease or lending," as well as the offering to distribute "phonorecords to a group of persons for purposes of further distribution." A recording is considered published if it is sold to the public or offered to wholesalers or retailers for ultimate sale to the public.

Federal copyright protection went into effect for all sound recordings first fixed and published on or after February 15, 1972. However, unpublished sound recordings could not be registered for federal copyright until January 1, 1978. Once so qualifying for federal copyright, sound recordings have the advantage of duration of protection identical to that of songs. (This differs from foreign copyright provisions, many of which measure duration as 50 years from the initial release of a recording.) Sound recordings published before February 15,

1972, are not eligible for federal copyright protection, but they may be protected under common law or state antipiracy statutes. The Copyright Act limits this state law protection to 95 years; however; after February 15, 2067, sound recordings published on or before February 15, 1972, will fall into the public domain, notwithstanding any protection under state law.

Authorship

The Copyright Act states that the copyright of a sound recording rests initially with the "author" or "authors" of that recording. However, the act does not establish who the author is. At times this may be difficult to determine, inasmuch as the final recording reflects the contributions of various persons involved in the recording process. It is usual for the copyrightable elements in a sound recording to involve authorship both by the performers on the recording and by the record producer in charge of planning the recording session, recording and electronically processing the sounds, and assembling and editing them into the final sound recording. In some cases the record producer contributes very little and the performance is the only copyrightable element. In other cases, such as, for example, recordings of bird calls and airplane motors, the record producer's contribution is the sole copyrightable aspect.

Authorship, and ultimately ownership, of the recordings is a matter of bargaining between the parties involved. If there is no employment relationship or agreement by performers to assign the copyright to the record company, the copyright in the sound recording is owned by the performing artists and/or the producer. If the work is prepared by an employee in the course of his or her employment, it is a work for hire and the employer is the author. Virtually every recording agreement between a record company and an artist provides that the sound recordings are created for the company as works for hire. But just because it says so in the agreement does not necessarily make it so: this is a controversial issue that has yet to be determined on a case-by-case basis.

Rights of the Copyright Owner

The copyright gives the owner of a sound recording the exclusive rights to reproduce it, to distribute the records to the public, and to make derivative works based thereon. The copyright does not include cover or sound-alike records, i.e., sound recordings that imitate or simulate the original copyrighted sound recording; therefore the owner does not have the ability to prevent such recordings from being made and copyrighted by others.

There is no domestic provision for broadcast performance fees; the copyright owner is not entitled to license or receive royalties for the public performance and broadcasting of nondigital recordings. Since the United States is not a signatory to the Rome Convention, other signatories generally do not pay U.S. record companies, artists, or producers any share of that country's sound recording performance royalty pool. As a result, U.S. record companies, artists, and producers have lost an estimated $600 million or more of these royalties over the past several years. Limited performance fees are assessed for digital recordings. The practice of renting a lawfully purchased copy of a record was barred by a special act of Congress in 1984 and extended for the life of the copyright in 1993. This restriction does not apply to the lending of records for nonprofit purposes by public libraries or to the rental of motion picture soundtracks and videos, which are classified as audiovisual works.

Copyrightable Works

ALBUMS

Although an album consists of several separate recordings, notice of copyright (to the extent it is required; see discussion below) is not a complicated matter. Where there is only one copyright owner, one notice will suffice, and the album may be registered for copyright as a collective work in one application. In that event, only the overall title of the collective work will be indexed and cataloged in the records of the Copyright Office. For the separate indexing and cataloging of individual selections, the copyright owner may file a different application for registration together with a separate fee for each selection. If the album has been the subject of a registration, the application for registration of an individual title should indicate that the single is from the album.

DERIVATIVE WORKS

With respect to derivative works, sound recordings are treated like other works under the copyright law. If it is a new version of a public-domain work or a new version of a copyrighted work produced with the consent of the copyright proprietor, the new version is regarded as a "derivative work" and is copyrightable as such. Insofar as a sound recording contains recordings reissued with substantial new recorded material, or recordings republished with materially edited abridgments or revisions of the basic recording, the sound recording is considered a copyrightable derivative work. Many new recordings that use licensed samples of an earlier copyrighted recording fall within this derivative copyright status. If an original recording is rearranged, remixed, or otherwise altered in so substantially creative a manner as to constitute "authorship," it is worthy of derivative copyright. So is a remix of a 3-minute recording into a 5-minute version that emphasizes rhythm tracks and de-emphasizes vocals in a manner more suited to the demands of dance clubs. Of course, a remix and the use of instrumental loops in an authorized sample would eminently qualify for a new sound recording copyright in the resulting version.

The copyright in the derivative work applies only to the new material or to the changes or revisions in the underlying work. Where there are only minor additions to or variations from the original recording, it is not an original work of authorship able to be registered as a derivative work. The issuance of a tape of a sound recording previously released only in disc form would not qualify for a new registration.

If a notice of copyright is used for derivative works incorporating previously published material, the year of first publication of the derivative work suffices; there is no need to show the year of the earlier published material.

COMPILATIONS

Under the Copyright Act, a *compilation* is defined as "a work formed by the collection and assembling of pre-existing materials" or one that consists of "data that are selected, coordinated or arranged." The resulting work must be such that it "constitutes an original work of authorship" as a whole.

It is common for sound recordings to appear in compiled albums, which are very salable. "Greatest hits" series are released by many record companies. Each compilation is afforded statutory protection as such, without adding to or diminishing from the protection under the copyright law for individual selections. If the compilation contains selections that have had a substantial remixing or alteration or addition of sounds, these selections, in respect of the new matter or changes, are entitled to protection as new works.

If a notice of copyright is used for a compilation, it may contain only the year of the first publication of the compilation, not the earlier years of publication of the component selections or the names of the different owners of the individual selections. Unless there is an express transfer of the copyright, in whole or in part, the copyright owner of the compiled work is presumed to have acquired only the privilege of reproducing and distributing the separate editorial or other compiler's contribution.

AUDIOVISUAL RECORDINGS

As previously noted, sound recordings do not include sounds "accompanying a motion picture or other audiovisual work." But when a soundtrack album is released *before* the motion picture in which the soundtrack is contained, the recording is generally deemed eligible for a separate copyright notice and for copyright protection as a separate sound recording. The earlier release removes the recording from the category of "accompanying" the film.

Even if a soundtrack album comes out after the release of the motion picture, it is common for record companies to use the ℗ copyright notice and to file an application for copyright registration of the album as a sound recording. This is justified on the grounds that the soundtrack album usually contains edited, assembled, or rearranged versions of the basic motion picture soundtrack music or dialogue and may be construed as a compilation or derivative work.

Foreign Sound Recordings

Many sound recordings originate outside the United States. If they are unpublished they are subject to copyright protection in the United States without regard to the nationality or domicile of the authors. If they are published they may also be entitled to U.S. copyright protection, on condition that:

1. The author is a national or a resident of, or if the work is initially or simultaneously published in, a Berne Convention country.
2. The author is a national or a resident of, or if the work is initially or simultaneously published in, a foreign country with which the United States has copyright relations pursuant to a treaty.
3. The work is within the scope of a presidential proclamation extending protection to works of nationals or residents of a foreign nation that protects works of U.S. citizens or residents or works first published in the United States on substantially the same basis as the foreign country protects works of its own citizens or works first published there.

Often, in foreign countries, sound recordings are considered "a neighboring right" and are not afforded a full term of copyright protection. For example, in England a sound recording is entitled to only 50 years of protection; other copyrighted works, such as songs and books, receive protection for the life of the author plus 70 years.

Most commercially viable foreign recordings are now protected in the United States under provisions of the Berne Convention Implementation Act of 1988. This protects not only residents and citizens of Berne Convention countries but also recordings that were first or simultaneously published in any of the Berne countries as of the date of U.S. accession. As with sound recordings originating in the United States, there is broad coverage of foreign sound recordings published after February 15, 1972; foreign recordings made before February 15, 1972, are not protected by federal copyright law, but may be under state common law or antipiracy statutes.

Sampling

Sampling is the process of dubbing portions of previously recorded music into new recordings. These musical quotations are either duly licensed on a prior basis or they may be unauthorized copyright infringements waiting for claims to be presented.

There is no such thing as a "fair use" privilege for sampling music in a conventional commercial recording. In *Grand Upright Music v. Warner Bros. Records,* 780 F. Supp. 182 (S.D.N.Y. 1991), a U.S. district court held that rapper Biz Markie's use of the song "Alone Again Naturally" by Gilbert O'Sullivan was copyright infringement and imposed damages and attorney's fees. Moreover, the court referred the case to the U.S. Attorney General for possible prosecution as willful criminal infringement.

Samplings differ from conventional infringements in that they use not only the song's music and lyrics but the sound recording itself. Thus, there are two parties for any permissions, claims, or litigation: the song copyright proprietor (usually the music publisher) for a mechanical license and the sound recording copyright proprietor (usually the record company) for a master use license.

A sampling can be a musical insert within the body of an original song and recording, ranging from a few seconds to more extensive quotations. Or it can be the use of an earlier recorded segment in a recorded loop fashion, so that a short segment becomes an extended accompaniment, as in the accompaniment to a rap artist.

With the advent of digital technology, sampling has become quite prevalent. Among the issues yet to be addressed is whether a sampling that is otherwise substantial enough to be an infringement should be subject to injunctive relief or merely judicial awards of profits and/or damages.

Master Licensing

What may appear to be merely a nondubbing right of the sound recording copyright proprietor also covers the important role of master licensing for motion picture, television, or film and for sampling into other record derivative uses. Thus, a use of a post–February 15, 1972, master recording in a motion picture soundtrack for background or other purposes requires a license from the sound recording copyright owner. This derivative use of a sound recording in other media is subject to open negotiation and there is no compulsory license except in limited instances, such as "ephemeral uses" in broadcasting (see below).

There is full exemption for educational broadcasters in synchronization use of sound recordings. There is also inclusion of public broadcasting stations and networks within blanket compulsory performance licenses. However, in both instances, further negotiation is required before any such programming can be sold as a videotape or DVD to the public or for foreign or other uses outside of the specified permitted uses. Even commercial broadcasters can use protected sound recordings for what is known as "ephemeral" use—that is, where a copy is made for inclusion in a program for a single use and without repeated programming. For example, copying the sound recording into a TV show tape is permitted provided that it is limited to one showing.

Audio Home Recording Act

The 1992 Audio Home Recording Act (AHRA) was initially a great disappointment to the music industry, but since 1998 it has moved much closer to realizing two of its legislative intentions, those of easing the road for DAT equipment to enter the marketplace and collecting and distributing license fees on such equipment.

The AHRA protects hardware manufacturers, sellers of digital equipment, and blank-tape marketers from infringement liability on payment of a statutory blanket license fee: a 3 percent surcharge, collected as if it were a tax. One-third of the fee is split evenly between the music publishers and writers, and the remaining two-thirds is divided as follows: 60 percent to the record companies, 36 percent to the featured artist, and 4 percent to nonfeatured musicians and vocalists.

The complexities of appointing agents for this collection and distribution have brought traditional groups, such as RIAA, ASCAP, BMI, and Songwriters Guild of America, into action. A newly formed not-for-profit group called the Alliance of Artists and Recording Companies (AARC) has assumed responsibility for collections. AARC is operated by a board comprised of 15 featured artists and 15 record company representatives. By the end of 2001, a total of over $13 million had been collected, of which approximately $10 million had been collected domestically, and overhead costs had dropped considerably. The $3 million collected in foreign territories included $2 million for rental fees in Japan.

The Digital Performance Right in Sound Recordings Act of 1995

The Digital Performance Right in Sound Recordings Act (DPRSRA) of 1995 (Public Law 104-39) is similar to AHRA in that it attempts to fill the void in legislation for the protection of copyrighted works that are digitally transmitted over the Internet. The act deals with both the digital performance and the digital distribution of sound recordings.

DIGITAL PERFORMANCE RIGHTS

In the past, the United States, which is not a signatory to the Rome Convention, did not recognize any broadcast performance rights; only public performances of a musical composition were eligible for performance royalties. The Digital Performance Right in Sound Recordings Act changed that by creating a performance right in digital sound recordings.

Digital transmissions are classified according to whether they are nonsubscription, interactive, or subscription services. *Nonsubscription services* are free, noninteractive audio or video transmissions, often delivered via streaming. Like nondigital broadcast services (e.g., AM and FM radio), these services are not subject to a licensing fee under the act. *Interactive services* transmit digital sound recordings at the user's request. The service is free and often takes the form of a 45-second promotional music sample. *Subscription services* also transmit digital sound recordings at the user's request, but for a fee. Interactive transmissions are subject to a license that is voluntarily negotiated between the service and the record company, whereas subscription transmissions are subject to a statutory licensing fee.

The statutory licensing requirements mainly affect three subscription music services: Muzak's DishCD (part of Echostar's satellite-based Dish network); Digital Music Express (music subscription service owned by TCI Music); and Digital Cable Radio Associates, a jointly owned service of EMI, Sony, and Warner together with cable firms Cox, Time Warner, Continental, Comcast, and Adelphia. The statutory digital performance licensing fee that went into effect on June 1, 1998, is 6.5 percent of gross revenues from transmissions to residences by means other than conventional FCC-licensed broadcast, audiovisual cable, or television. (It is interesting to note that the RIAA originally sought a much higher rate, 41.5 percent, arguing that a music service ought to pay the same percentage for recorded music as cable firms have to pay for motion picture programming. The rate that was finally agreed upon, 6.5 percent, is more in line with the public performance rate.)

The receipts from statutory or voluntarily negotiated licenses under the DPRSRA and the Digital Millennium Copyright Act (see below) to make digital transmissions of sound recordings are administered on behalf of its members by SoundExchange (www.soundexchange.com), a nonprofit entity created by the RIAA, which collects and makes distributions to sound recording copyright holders; featured artists; the AFM (for nonfeatured musicians); and AFTRA (for nonfeatured vocalists). The payments are based on actual performance data furnished by subscription service providers, Webcasters, and other licensees.

Between 1996 and March 2000, SoundExchange licensed and collected payment for 80 million performances. The monies are divided among the companies themselves, the featured musicians and vocalists, and the nonfeatured musicians and vocalists, as follows: 50 percent goes to the record companies, 45 percent goes to the featured musicians or vocalists, and 5 percent is set aside in two equal escrow funds for distribution to nonfeatured musicians and vocalists. The escrow funds are managed jointly by the record companies and the unions. Recipients do not have to be union members.

When the collection of receipts is pursuant to a voluntary negotiated license, performers get paid in accordance with their individual contracts or collective bargaining agreements. In many instances, the artist contracts establish a percentage of net miscellaneous receipts and the collective bargaining agreements have their own provisions for miscellaneous revenues (or provisions for reuse or new media).

DIGITAL DISTRIBUTION RIGHTS

The DPRSRA also establishes a statutory digital mechanical license rate that differs from the conventional statutory rate for analog records (114(c)(3). When a digital record is transmitted for duplication over telephone lines, by cable, or by satellite, the act provides for a digital reproduction rate that is either voluntarily negotiated or statutory. This parallels the procedure used to set digital performance rates.

Section 115(c)(3) provides that artist-songwriters who have negotiated a controlled-composition rate in their record contract will be stuck with those rates, and will not get any additional benefit from the digital statutory mechanical license fees, only if one or both of the following applies:

1. The contract is dated on or before June 22, 1995 (a "grandfather clause" protection).
2. The contract, regardless of date, is entered into *after* the song has been recorded and the artist is then his or her own publisher.

Thus, many controlled-composition rates will not apply to digital phono-record delivery (DPD).

The Digital Millennium Copyright Act of 1998

In addition to implementing two 1996 World Intellectual Property Organization Treaties, the Digital Millennium Copyright Act (DMCA) of 1998 contains pro-visions designed to codify licensing for certain performances aired via digital media, including satellite radio and Internet radio. It renamed the subscription services covered in the DPRSRA as "pre-existing subscription services" and cre-ated three additional categories of service that could operate under a statutory license: pre-existing satellite digital audio radio services, new subscription serv-ices, and eligible nonsubscription services. The DMCA clarified the parameters of "ephemeral recordings"—copies made for the specific purpose of making licensed digital transmissions—and created a statutory license for multiple ephemeral recordings. The license fees for the statutory license retroactive to October 1998 were to be established by the U.S. Copyright Office, and the fees collected were to be split 50:50 between the artists and the copyright holders.

In early 2002, a three-person arbitration panel, the Copyright Arbitration Royalty Panel (CARP), was assigned by the government to set the terms of the license fees. (The Register of Copyrights chooses two members from a panel of more than 100 available experts in the field, and those two choose the third member, who serves as the chairperson. The CARP panel is only called into session if industry negotiators do not resolve an issue voluntarily.) In February, the panel recommended what was basically a per-performance fee schedule, including 0.07 cents per performance for simultaneous radio and Internet transmission, 0.14 cents per performance for Internet-only transmis-sion, and, for ephemeral rights, 9 percent of the performance revenue due. SoundExchange, supported by AFTRA and AFM, was to collect the fees once they were set.

None of the affected groups was totally happy with the CARP recommen-dations (many Internet Webcasters staged a day of silent protest on May 1, 2002), and in late May, the U.S. Librarian of Congress, who must approve the rates under the statute, rejected the proposed rates. Instead, the rates due to go into effect in October 2002 were a 7-cent performance fee per song per 1000 listeners for Internet Webcasters and commercial radio/Internet Web-casters and a 2-cent fee for noncommercial, non-CPB (Corporation for Public Broadcasting) stations, and an ephemeral license fee of 8.8 percent of per-formance revenue due.

As soon as the Copyright Office rejected the CARP rates, however, companies began to make separate deals with Webcasters. For example, Harry Fox Agency licensed the music of its clients to Streamwaves.com, to stream on-demand transmissions to consumers, for 10 percent of revenue. Small Web-based broadcasters claimed that even the 0.07 cent rate (retroactive to 1998, and with a $500 minimum fee) represented a potentially crippling expense.

In December of 2002, President Bush signed into law the Small Webcaster Settlement Act of 2002 (SWSA), the terms of which differed substantially from earlier recommendations: No specific royalty rates or fees were set, granting both sides the right to enter into a voluntary agreement and permitting Sound-Exchange, the receiving agent designated in the earlier legislation, to negotiate. It also suspended royalty payments due from noncommercial Webcasters until June 2003, so that noncommercial stations could reach voluntary agreements with the performance rights societies.

Bootlegging, Piracy, and Counterfeiting

In the record business, the bootlegger, the pirate, and the counterfeiter are all part of the same nefarious clan. They each misappropriate the services of the artist and the product owned and paid for by a legitimate manufacturer and benefit at the expense of record companies, performing artists, music publishers, and unions. Piracy may even threaten the sale of titles before they hit the marketplace, when bootleggers are able to obtain promotional copies ahead of release.

Labels have responded by curbing promotional release of records or, as in the case of 2002's *The Eminem Show,* moving the release date of the album forward before piracy can deplete initial sales. In some countries the illegal music market outnumbers the legal: according to the International Federation of the Phonographic Industry (IFPI), 61 percent of records sold in Mexico during 2001 (the equivalent of U.S.$400 million) were illegal.

Bootlegging is the unauthorized recording of a live or broadcast performance. *Piracy* is the unauthorized duplication of the actual sound recording. *Counterfeiting* is the duplication of the packaging, artwork, and label as well as the sound recording.

For example, a college student downloads an album from the Internet and e-mails it to a friend as a "gift"; this is bootlegging. The Brigand Record Company makes copies of a Decca recording of the Rolling Stones, slaps the Brigand label on the packaging, and sells the recording at a greatly reduced price; this is piracy. A guitarist on the roster of Universal Records records the theme for a television show that is a significant commercial success. The Brigand Record Company manufactures copies of the record, slaps on a duplicate of the Universal Records label, and markets them as the original product; this is counterfeiting.

The counterfeiter and the pirate can afford to charge substantially less than the legitimate manufacturer and still make a profit because their only costs are pressing and duplication charges, covers and labels, and distribution expenses. They only copy successful records, and therefore don't have to make up for the 85 percent of recordings released in the United States annually that, according to the RIAA, fail to make a profit. The record company incurs the recording costs, while the pirate and the counterfeiter steal the profits. The recordings are often of inferior quality, artists lose out on royalties, music publishers lose out on mechanical license fees, and union members lose payments to the trust funds.

According to information supplied by the RIAA, in 2001 the record industry worldwide lost about $4 billion due to piracy, including on-line piracy via peer-to-peer transfers or by other means. The United States alone was said to lose nearly $1 million a day. In 2001, over 122,000 counterfeit or pirated CDs, 152,000 illegally produced tapes, and 2.8 million counterfeit or pirated CD-Rs (compact discs, recordable) were confiscated. The number of cassette tapes confiscated dropped 12.8 percent from 1997, whereas the number of CDs confiscated increased 163 percent from 1997. These statistics reflect the considerable antipiracy efforts of the RIAA, as well as the respective rise and decline of consumer interest in particular formats. However, a drop in the number of confiscated goods reveals nothing about the extent of Internet piracy, which, despite the demise of Napster, shows no signs of abating.

Federal Legislation

Until 1962 it was not a federal crime to transport or sell phonorecords with counterfeit labels, and state laws were either nonexistent or ineffectual. In 1962, Congress passed a law making it illegal to counterfeit labels, but it was difficult to enforce, and penalties were modest. Federal copyright protection was finally granted to sound recordings published on and after February 15, 1972, and to all sound recordings, published or unpublished, after January 1, 1978. A violation of the exclusive rights of the copyright owner of a sound recording became a copyright infringement subject to civil action. The court could order an injunction, the impounding and destruction or other reasonable disposition of the infringing articles, and certain financial penalties: either (1) the copyright owner's actual damages and any additional profits of the infringer, or (2) statutory damages for any one work of $500 to $20,000, or (3) in the case of willful infringement, damages of $500 to $100,000, at the court's discretion. The court may also award court costs and reasonable attorney's fees to the prevailing party and order the destruction of all matrices, masters, tapes, film negatives, or other articles by which the records and tapes may be reproduced.

PIRACY AND COUNTERFEITING AMENDMENTS ACT OF 1982

Until 1982 a first-time charge of copyright infringement was merely a misdemeanor. However, with the passage of the Piracy and Counterfeiting Amendments Act in 1982, infringement of the copyright in a sound recording involving willful action for purposes of commercial advantage or private financial gain became punishable as a felony. Federal prosecutors are now more willing to pursue these crimes, and possible offenders are more effectively deterred.

Under the section "Trafficking in Counterfeit Labels for Phonorecords and Copies of Motion Pictures or Other Audiovisual Works" (18 U.S.C. 2318), any person who knowingly traffics in a counterfeit label affixed or designed to be affixed to a copyrighted phonorecord or a copy of a copyrighted motion picture or other audiovisual work may be fined up to $250,000 and/or imprisoned for up to 5 years. The prosecution no longer has to prove "fraudulent intent," merely that the offense of trafficking in counterfeit labels was knowingly committed. In addition, the penalty under this statute requires that all counterfeit labels be forfeited and destroyed or otherwise disposed of by the court.

Suppliers of equipment may also be liable under the section "Trafficking in Counterfeiting Goods or Services" (18 U.S.C. 2320). For example, in 1997 a supplier was found guilty of contributory infringement because he knew of the intended use of his duplicating equipment and proceeded to supply it nonetheless. Judgment of $7 million was granted the 26 record companies that acted in this infringement case. The computation was $1,000 for each of 56 recordings plus $7 million in trademark damages—three times the estimated profits of the defendant over a 2-year period.

URUGUAY ROUND AGREEMENTS ACT OF 1994

The Uruguay Round Agreements Act (URAA) of 1994 added a section to Chapter 11 of the U.S. Copyright Act, creating a new protection against international bootlegging by making it unlawful for anyone without permission "to fix, in copies or phonograms, sounds and/or images of a live musical performance or to reproduce copies or phonograms from such unauthorized fixations; to transmit or communicate to the public the sounds and/or images of a live musical performance; or to distribute, rent, sell, or traffic in copies of phonograms of live musical performances without consent of the performer."

Anyone who violates Chapter 11 of the Copyright Act is subject to the copyright infringement remedies set forth in the Act (injunctive relief, impounding, statutory or actual damages and profits, and costs and attorney's fees), and on conviction, courts are authorized to require the forfeiture and destruction of the illegal copies or phonograms, as well as, in the court's discretion, "any other equipment by means of which such copies or phonorecords may be reproduced, taking into account the nature, scope, and proportionality of the use of the equipment in the offense." The new law also provides that copies or phonorecords of live musical performances "fixed" outside the United States without authorization will be subject to seizure and forfeiture "in the same manner as property imported in violation of the customs laws."

The URAA also added a new section to the U.S. Code providing criminal penalties for the "unauthorized fixation of and trafficking in sound recordings and music videos of live musical performances" when done "knowingly and for purposes of commercial advantage or private financial gain" (18 U.S.C. 2319). Penalties include fines and/or imprisonment.

Prior to 1972, the record industry was forced to rely largely on lawsuits in state courts, under theories of unfair competition, to prohibit the piracy of recordings. This was not very effective. Apart from different interpretations of law in the 50 separate states, an injunction in one state did not bar a pirate from renewing his or her operations in another state. A pirate enjoined by one record company from duplicating its product could simply switch to copying records and tapes manufactured by another record company.

Under the 1976 Copyright Act, sound recordings that predate federal copyright protection will continue to be covered by state law until February 15, 2067, after which they will fall into public domain. Record companies can still seek redress against piracy in state court, but civil lawsuits have little deterrent effect on record pirates. As a result, the recording industry has been successful in convincing practically all the states in the United States to pass criminal legislation prohibiting the unauthorized reproduction and sale of recordings. These laws have proved very effective in limiting record piracy. For example, the antipiracy law of California provides for a graduated system of penalties of up to 5 years in prison and up to $250,000 in fines.

Compulsory License for Sound Recordings

At one time it was possible for pirates to obtain a compulsory license to mechanically reproduce songs contained in sound recordings, and they were thus shielded from possible lawsuits by or on behalf of the music publishers. Under the 1976 Copyright Act, they were no longer allowed to exercise compulsory licensing for illegal sound recordings. This represents a statutory enactment of the decisions of the federal courts interpreting the provisions of the prior Copyright Act. These decisions were the outcome of protracted litigation brought primarily by publishers affiliated with the Harry Fox Agency, the mechanical licensing agency for most U.S. publishers, which has been active in these lawsuits.

The pirating of recordings without the consent of the copyright owner constitutes a willful infringement of the music copyright. The pirate is subject to civil actions for such infringement under the 1976 Copyright Act; the remedies include injunctions, the impounding and destruction of infringing materials, and money awards for damages, the infringer's profits, court costs, and attorney's fees. For willful infringements of the music copyright there are also criminal penalties: a fine of up to $250,000, imprisonment of up to 2 years, or both. The maximum fine for organizations is $500,000.

Because many record companies are associated with music publishers who publish original music, music publishers are strongly motivated to pursue civil and criminal actions against pirates of the recordings issued by their affiliated record companies.

International Treaties Regarding Piracy

In 1971, representatives from approximately 50 nations, including the United States, met in Paris and drafted the Geneva Convention for the Protection of Producers of Phonograms against Unauthorized Duplication (Geneva Convention of 1971) to protect sound recordings against piracy. The United States ratified the treaty on March 10, 1974. Thus far, 67 countries have ratified the treaty, including such high-profile signatories as Japan, China, and the United Kingdom. Signatories agree to protect the nationals of other states against the making or importation of unauthorized duplications of sound recordings if the intent is to distribute them to the public. National legislatures are permitted to implement their treaty obligations by means of copyright law or other specific right or in other specifically enumerated manners.

The United States has long recognized the need for cooperation among foreign governments in order to achieve anticounterfeiting goals; local statutes must be passed and also enforced. Each year the U.S. Trade Representative publishes a Priority Watch List of countries deemed to be in violation of international trade laws controlling piracy and counterfeiting. This annual review examines the protection of U.S.-owned intellectual property in over 70 countries. The International Federation of the Phonographic Industry (IFPI) publishes an annual report which gives more specific data on offending countries. In 2001, the IFPI cited China, Russia, Brazil, Indonesia, Mexico, Italy, Spain, Taiwan, Poland, and Greece as the countries with the largest pirate markets in the world. The Chinese market for pirated product was estimated at U.S.$400 million (90 percent of all units sold). Worldwide sales of pirated CDs were 500 million, up from $475 million in 2000; sales of pirated CD-Rs were $450 million, up from $165 million in 2000.

Record Covers, Labels, and Liner Notes

Album packaging is one of the most effective advertising tools for records. An eye-catching illustration can attract consumers who may not be familiar with a new recording artist. Extensive liner notes, often featured on special reissues or boxed sets, may entice the devoted fan or music scholar to purchase recordings that they already own in order to learn more about their favorite artists or recordings.

The cost of packaging production, including design fees, photographer's fees, and preparation of artwork, can range from $3,500 to $10,000. Most record companies absorb these expenses as a cost of production but deduct 10 to 25 percent from the artist's royalty base for these packaging expenses. For example, a CD may sell for $17, but the packaging deduction of 25 percent will reduce the artist's royalty base to $12.75. The substantial $4.25 difference enables the record company to recover both creative and manufacturing costs for the album packaging.

Traditionally, album packaging includes the album title and attached labels, which may contain descriptive information, including the names of the songs, the artists, and the record company; illustrations; liner notes; and the names of the producer, the engineer, and the songwriter. Since 1958, the National Academy of Recording Arts and Sciences (NARAS) has given annual awards to art directors for Best Album Packaging. These awards are based on the illustrations (photographs and artwork) and the liner notes.

Album Titles

Albums feature various types of titles. Some albums are simply titled with the name of the performer; for example, *Ricky Martin* was the title of Latin star Ricky Martin's 1999 hit album. Other titles describe the album's musical content, for example, *Songs of the West, Love Songs,* or *Golden Hits of the Sixties.* Most titles, however, are creative titles chosen by the artists, such as Alanis Morissette's 1998 release, *Supposed Former Infatuation Junkie; I Am ... The Autobiography* by Nas; or *Amnesiac,* by Radiohead.

On Broadway cast albums, the name of the show is the title, and the phrase "original cast album" is featured. Motion picture soundtrack albums name the film in the title and prominently display the phrase "original soundtrack album" or, in the case of a re-recorded score, "original motion picture score."

Illustrations

Typically, illustrations—either photographs or artwork—grace the covers of many record albums. Photographers who supply pictures for album covers require their models to sign releases granting the right to use the photographs for commercial purposes. Without such releases, models may claim an invasion of their rights to privacy and publicity. They may further claim a violation of specific statutes that forbid the use of photographs for commercial endeavors unless the model consents in writing.

Under the Copyright Act, "pictorial, graphic, and sculptural works" are all eligible for copyright. These works are defined to include "fine, graphic, and applied art, photographs, prints, and art reproductions." The copyright in the artwork may be registered in the artist's name unless it was specifically created as a work for hire. For example, in the case of *Johannsen v. Brown*, 797 F. Supp. 835 (D. Ore. 1992), the court ruled that an artist who created an illustration on his own time and with his own tools and materials, who had absolute control over the project and was under no duty to furnish the illustration, was an independent contractor, and accordingly his illustration used for a cover design was not a work for hire.

After the effective date of the Berne Convention Implementation Act of 1998, a copyright notice is not needed in order to protect a work. However, the Copyright Act grants record companies the option of affixing a notice of copyright on each copy which is publicly distributed. The form of the notice should include the word "copyright," the abbreviation "copr.," or the symbol ©, accompanied by the name of the copyright proprietor, an abbreviation by which the name can be recognized, or a generally known alternative designation of the proprietor. For photographs, works of art, and reproductions of works of art, the Copyright Act does not require the year date in the optional notice. Record covers may be registered for copyright on Form VA for published or unpublished works of the visual arts.

In the case of soundtrack albums, the artwork is often the same as the artwork used to advertise the film and the copyright notice on the packaging should be consistent with the copyright notices employed by the motion picture company for the protection of the artwork and the photographs. Thus, if the name of the motion picture company and a particular year and date appear in its notice, caution prescribes that the same name and date be contained in the record packaging copyright notice placed in proximity to the artwork or photos. The copyright notice in the name of the motion picture company will also apply to the recording insofar as it is derived from the film soundtrack. If a record company elects to use a notice of copyright for a soundtrack recording, it is likely to employ a notice of copyright in its own name on the packaging in addition to that of the motion picture company.

Liner notes encompass the descriptive material on CD or cassette inserts or on the back of an album. This material may include the names of the songs on the recording, biographical information about the performers, comments on the contents of the album, the names of the producer, engineer, songwriters, and the like. Liner notes are protected by copyright under U.S. copyright law. However, as with artwork, copyright notice is optional. Liner notes of substantial length are registered for copyright on Form TX for published or unpublished nondramatic literary works.

Recording Identification

With the coming of compact discs, three-letter codes were developed to identify the nature of the original recording technology. These codes frequently appear on the back of the packaging. DDD indicates that a digital tape recorder was used for the recording session, the mixing and editing, and the mastering. ADD indicates that an analog tape recorder was used for the original recording session, but a digital recorder was employed for subsequent steps. AAD indicates that an analog tape recorder was used during the recording session and for subsequent mixing and editing, but a digital tape recorder was used for the mastering or transcription.

Many old monaural recordings are of interest to the present generation of record buyers. As a result, record companies have altered the monaural masters so that they can be played on stereophonic equipment. However, the Federal Trade Commission received complaints that the record companies were selling these altered recordings as if they were originally recorded for multichannel stereophonic reproduction, so it published a standard legend that must be printed prominently over the title of such recordings, as follows: "This Recording Altered To Simulate Stereophonic Reproduction."

Trademarks

Under the Lanham Act the words "Registered in U.S. Patent and Trademark Office," or "Reg. U.S. Pat. and TM Off.," or the symbol ® should be printed next to the trademark on album covers.

On occasion, a cover will include an unregistered trademark. Until a registration certificate is issued by the Patent Office, it is improper to use the notices referred to in the preceding paragraph. However, it is common to use the word "trademark" or the abbreviation "TM" in conjunction with an unregistered mark for the purpose of giving actual notice to the public of a claim to the mark.

Anticounterfeit Practices

Bar coding uses imprinted variant lines and numbers as an aid to inventory and sales control of records. The bar codes are usually printed on the jackets or on the back of inserts for CDs and cassettes, but they are also sometimes included in affixed stickers. Through computer readers, the retailer, wholesaler, and manufacturer can keep track of sales and inventory by categories such as record label, artist, title, and release number.

The latest technology in packaging was developed by Avery, a leading manufacturer of spine labels. The spine label, which is used to prevent tampering and theft, now includes both bar code and SoundScan digital data. The resulting technology combines shoplifting prevention and accurate sales reports in a convenient manner. In addition, the labels may now carry a record company's hologram in order to protect against counterfeiting.

In its 1994 annual report, the RIAA stated that its "legal arsenal against pirates includes state laws requiring recorded music to display the 'true name and address' of the manufacturer." In 28 states, the name and address of the record company must appear on each record distributed in the state. In California, failure to comply may result in fines of as much as $250,000 and jail sentences up to 5 years. Similar penalties exist in other states; some are more stringent, some more lenient. These initiatives have been especially effective because they empower state and local authorities to respond quickly to counterfeit activity without (literally) making a federal case out of it. In 1993 the "true name and address" statute in Washington state was upheld following a constitutional challenge by a convicted cassette counterfeiter.

In 1994 a federal antibootleg statute was created which, like the state statutes, made unauthorized manufacture and distribution of sound recordings illegal; it also provided for the seizure of bootleg recordings. (See Chapter 8, "Bootlegging, Piracy, and Counterfeiting.")

By virtue of the statutes, record companies or artists aggrieved by the misleading practices of other companies are better able to institute appropriate action to protect their rights by suits for injunction or damages or by complaints to federal, state, and local authorities.

Warning Stickers and Censorship Issues

In 1985 the Parents Music Resource Center (PMRC) initiated a movement to promote the labeling of albums that contained sexually explicit or perverse lyrics, or lyrics that promoted violence, rape, or the use of illegal drugs or alcohol. A number of states proposed legislation that would have required parental advisory warning labels on certain albums and held retailers liable for selling nonstickered records. In a hearing that same year before the Senate on Contents of Music and the Lyrics of Records, the late recording artist Frank Zappa, himself a father of four children, testified at length against the PMRC's proposals. (Among his many quotable remarks was this gem: "It is my understanding that, in law, First Amendment issues are decided with a preference for the least restrictive alternative. In this context, the PMRC's demands are the equivalent of treating a case of dandruff by decapitation.")

Encouraged by the retail and wholesale segments of the record industry, in 1990 the RIAA created a uniform label to be affixed to CD and cassette packaging in certain situations. The approved label, which reads "Explicit Lyrics—Parental Advisory," is now used by the 55 members of the association where the issuing company considers it appropriate. This voluntary practice was adopted as a practical means of heading off legislative action.

Opposition to the use of warning labels attracted alliances of diverse groups such as the American Civil Liberties Union, the Country Music Association, and the RIAA. They focused on the issue of free speech. Even a voluntary labeling supervised by the record industry trade association is perceived as a response to pressure from certain advocates imposing moral standards on the public at large. Making stickering a statutory requirement is a potentially complex and confusing procedure. Often vague and indefinite guidelines can jeopardize unsuspecting retailers, who have little time or inclination to act as censors.

The problem of stickering is to some extent part of the broader problem of attempting to define and restrict obscenity. Prosecutions for obscenity depend on an exception to the First Amendment constitutional right of free speech. In 1989, a U.S. district court judge in Florida held that the album *As Nasty As They Wanna Be,* by the rap group 2 Live Crew, was obscene, making it the first recording to be declared obscene by a federal court. A record store owner who continued to sell the album was arrested. Two members of the group were also arrested for performing one of the album's songs before an adult-only audience.

The ruling of obscenity by the U.S. district court was based on a three-part judicial standard set forth in a 1973 U.S. Supreme Court case:

1. Whether the average person applying contemporary community standards would find that the work, taken as a whole, appeals to the prurient interest
2. Whether the work depicts or describes, in a patently offensive way, sexual conduct specifically defined by the applicable state law
3. Whether the work, taken as a whole, lacks serious literary, artistic, political, or scientific value

All three standards must be satisfied to make a finding of obscenity.

On appeal, the district court was found to have failed to support the third essential test of obscenity in that the plaintiff/sheriff did not present evidence to contradict testimony that the work had artistic value. It was held that the judge could not, simply by listening to the recording, make a determination of "lacking serious artistic value" without independent testimony subject to cross-examination. Accordingly, the district court decision was reversed.

Obscenity cases represent a conflict between the First Amendment and the enforcement of community moral standards, including the need to protect children. According to one jurist, this necessarily presents a "penumbra," a shady region somewhere between black and white. There is no clear consensus as to what constitutes obscenity. In a 1964 opinion, Justice Stewart of the U.S.

Supreme Court famously stated that he could not define obscenity, but he knew it when he saw it. Many obscenity decisions are reached by divided courts with learned dissenting opinions, indicating the unknown and dangerous waters that may have to be traversed by record industry participants. Even community standards may vary from locality to locality.

It must be recognized that laws attempting to limit content raise grave questions, questions that reach back at least to 1799, when Constitutional founder James Madison said: "Truth of opinion ought not to be subject to imprisonment, to be inflicted by those of a different opinion. . . . There is a difference between the freedom and licentiousness of the press. . . . There is a property right in the ability to express opinions and the government which violates the property that individuals have in their opinions . . . is not a pattern for the United States."

Despite this, the possibility of criminal prosecution and fines for violations of state and local obscenity laws must be heeded by record industry participants, especially in connection with those albums that include overtly sexual or violent themes.

Part Three

Music Publisher and Writer Agreements and Practices

10

Copyright Law in the United States

Copyright literally means "the right to copy." The term, which refers to that body of exclusive rights granted by law to authors for the protection of their writings, includes the exclusive right to reproduce, publish, and sell copies of the copyrighted work, to make other versions of the work, and, with certain limitations, to make recordings of and perform the work in public.

Copyright is an intangible property right, best understood by distinguishing it from the physical property itself. In the words of the Copyright Act of 1976:

> Ownership of a copyright, or of any of the exclusive rights under
> a copyright, is distinct from ownership of any material object
> in which the work is embodied. Transfer of ownership of any
> material object, including the copy or phonorecord in which
> the work is first fixed, does not of itself convey any rights in the
> copyrighted work embodied in the object.

For example, someone who purchases a collection of letters written by a famous person owns the letters but not the right to publish copies of the letters; that right belongs to the person who owns the copyright. The right to copyright is based on authorship and exists separate and apart from its physical expression.

Copyright protects the expression of ideas, not the ideas themselves. The films *Star Wars* and *Star Trek* are both based on the idea of space travel. The films *Interview with a Vampire* and *Bram Stoker's Dracula* are both based on the idea of vampires. Similarly, the musical compositions "The Twist," "Twist and Shout," and "Let's Twist" all relate to the dance craze of the 1960s. None is a copyright infringement of another since each constitutes an original expression of the idea.

Copyright Revision, 1790 to 1976

Article 1 of the U.S. Constitution states that the purpose of copyright is "To promote the Progress of Science and useful Arts, by securing for limited Times to Authors and Inventors, the exclusive Right to their respective Writings and

Discoveries." These words are embodied in the Copyright Act of 1790, which provided protection against the copying of certain printed materials. Performance rights were granted statutory protection in 1889. The right of mechanical reproduction presently applicable to phonograph records was added in 1909, when piano rolls were prominent.

By the mid-1950s the Copyright Act of 1909 was completely antiquated. Supreme Court Justice Abe Fortas observed that administering the statute called "not for the judgment of Solomon but for the dexterity of Houdini." The act provided the courts with little guidance in coping with the vast technological changes that had taken place in the intervening years—innovations such as television, cable television, transcriptions, synchronization with film, offset printing, Xerox reprography, and long-playing records.

In 1955, the U.S. Copyright Office initiated a number of valuable studies in preparation for a general revision of the copyright act and circulated 34 reports on a multitude of problems to a panel of consultants and to the general public. It then prepared and circulated for review preliminary drafts of a new copyright statute and, in 1964, submitted a general revision of the 1909 copyright statute to Congress. A number of interested groups were opposed to particular provisions relating to cable television and jukebox performance fees and performers' rights in sound recordings, but finally, after 12 years of hearings and industry compromises, Congress passed the Copyright Act of 1976.

The Copyright Status of Sound Recordings

The 1976 Copyright Act defines *sound recordings* as "original works of authorship comprising an aggregate of musical, spoken, or other sounds that have been fixed in tangible form." *Phonorecords* are "physical objects in which sounds are fixed"—records, tapes, CDs, and so forth. Two factors affect the copyright status of a sound recording: when and whether it is published. *Publication* is "the distribution of copies of phonorecords of a work to the public by sale or other transfer of ownership, or by rental, lease or lending"; the offer "to distribute copies or phonorecords to a group of persons for purposes of further distribution, public performance, or public display, constitutes publication." (Public performance is not a publication.)

Sound recordings published on or after February 15, 1972, and all sound recordings published or unpublished on or after January 1, 1978 (the effective date of the Copyright Act of 1976), are covered by federal copyright. Sound recordings published prior to February 15, 1972, or unpublished prior to January 1, 1978, are covered by state common law until February 15, 2067, at which time they fall into the public domain.

Common Law Copyright

Works that are *not* fixed in sheet music, song folios, phonorecords, or other tangible medium of expression—for example, a musical composition improvised or developed from memory but not recorded or written down—do not qualify for statutory copyright. They are protected by a parallel system of *common law copyright,* which exists under individual state law. Common law copyright springs into being without any formality, registration, or notice. It offers an author, composer, or artist complete protection against the unauthorized commercialization of his or her work as long as it is not fixed in a tangible form sufficiently permanent or stable to permit it to be perceived, heard, or otherwise communicated for a period of more than transitory duration. Even a widely viewed "live" television or radio presentation of a song can be protected under common law if it is not recorded simultaneously with its transmission.

Until passage of the 1976 Copyright Act, common law copyright was perpetual and not limited to any number of years. At that time all common law works were brought under federal statutory provisions (called "pre-emption"), effective January 1, 1978, and measured in duration in the same manner as a new work created after that date. But where the author was already dead for the full period of the new statutory copyright, the former common law copyright was given a statutory minimum further duration. The minimum was until December 31, 2002, with a further extension, to December 31, 2047, if the work was put into published form before the original 2002 deadline.

Prior to January 1, 1978, common law protection covered works not "published," a term commonly used to refer to printed versions but, in the music industry, one subject to confusion and varied interpretation especially with regard to phonograph records. With the exception of sound recordings first fixed before February 15, 1972 (for which preemption is delayed until February 15, 2067), the 1976 Copyright Act as amended by the Copyright Term Extension Act has preempted any state common law or statutory protection for any of such works fixed in tangible form. It has legislated, with the exceptions noted below, the same duration of protection for previously existing common law works as is granted for new works created on or after January 1, 1978.

Statutory Copyright

Under the Copyright Act musical compositions may be copyrighted if they have been "fixed" in some visible or recorded form only under the federal copyright law, except for sound recordings first fixed before February 15, 1972. The federal statutory copyright applies to both unpublished and published works. The 1976 Copyright Act defines publication as "the distribution of copies of phonorecords of a work to the public by sale or other transfer of ownership, or by rental, lease or lending." It goes on to provide that the offer "to distribute copies or phonorecords to a group of persons for purposes of further distribution, public performance, or public display, constitutes publication." (Public performance is not a publication, regardless of the size of audience.)

In a 1995 decision involving the song "La Grange" recorded by the band ZZ Top, the 9th Circuit Court of Appeals ruled that a widely sold recording issued prior to 1978 was sufficient "publication" to have required a timely renewal of the song's copyright registration under the then-applicable law, thus forcing a song into public domain for failure to register and renew. The decision caused major concern throughout the music industry, which successfully petitioned Congress for a clarification of the 1976 Copyright Act. This resulted in a Congressional declaration in 1997 that a pre-1978 record release was not deemed a basis for forfeiture of a song copyright by reason of the absence of the then-required formality of copyright notice or of the renewal term of copyright of the song.

Copyright Registration

It is relatively simple to register a copyright claim with the Copyright Office. The copyright owner may register a work at any time during the copyright protection period. This basic registration secures the statutory benefits of registration to all authors and other owners of rights in the work. A qualifying "deposit" (in the form of a compact disc, cassette tape, printed copy, or unpublished manuscript) must be delivered to the Copyright Office at the time of registration. The U.S. Copyright Office reported registrations of works in the performing arts, including musical works, dramatic works, choreography, pantomimes, and motion pictures and filmstrips, for fiscal year 2000 as follows:

	Published Works	Unpublished Works	Total
Registrations, all performing arts	47,599	91,336	138,935
Registrations, sound recordings	13,665	20,625	34,290

For purposes of registration, the United States is considered the country of origin if:

- ▶ Publication occurred first in the United States.
- ▶ Publication occurred simultaneously in the United States and a non-Berne nation. ("Simultaneous publication" means within the first 30 days of publication.)
- ▶ Publication occurred simultaneously in the United States and another Berne nation that provides the same term of protection as, or a longer term of protection than, the United States.
- ▶ The work is unpublished, and all of the authors are U.S. nationals, domiciliaries, or habitual residents.
- ▶ The work is first published in a non-Berne nation and all of the authors are U.S. nationals, domiciliaries, or habitual residents.

It is prudent for a copyright owner to promptly register and deposit both published and unpublished works and thereby place the public on notice of his or her claims to copyright. In the case of a work of U.S. origin or a foreign work originating in a non-Berne nation, the copyright owner cannot commence an action for copyright infringement until copies of the work have been duly registered and deposited. Once this is done, legal action can proceed, even if registration is late and the infringement predates registration. For all works, regardless of origin, including Berne works not of U.S. origin, the possibility of recovering statutory damages and attorneys' fees is not available for infringements of unpublished, unregistered works unless the work is registered within 3 months after first publication.

The Copyright Act provides that in a judicial proceeding a registration certificate for a "registration made before or within five years after first publication of the work shall constitute prima facie evidence of the validity of the copyright and of the facts stated in the certificate." For subsequent registrations, the evidentiary weight of a registration certificate is within the court's discretion. Therefore, the statutory presumption is not available to late registrants who wait more than 5 years from the initial publication of their song. The 5-year registration deadline for the statutory presumption is not applicable to unpublished songs.

There is another benefit to registering a copyright: a claimant who wants to replace lost or mislaid certificates or deposits can apply for copies. Unpublished manuscripts or facsimile reproductions are kept for the entire period of copyright protection. Published manuscripts are retained for the longest period deemed practicable and desirable by the Register of Copyrights and the Library of Congress. Under their most recent determination, published copies delivered with the registration claim are not retained for more than 5 years from the date of such deposit except for visual arts works (pictorial, graphic, or sculptural works), which are kept for 10 or more years. However, the depositor or the copyright owner may request that the deposited material be retained for the full term of copyright protection, upon payment of an additional fee.

Some songwriters try to circumvent the need for registration of an unpublished song by sending a copy of their manuscript to themselves by registered mail and then leaving the sealed envelope unopened. They believe that the date on the envelope and the contents of the envelope, when shown in a court proceeding, conclusively demonstrates the priority of their authorship in suits against third parties for infringement. While there may be some merit to their position, copyright registration is likely to be immeasurably better than a self-addressed sealed envelope in proving that the work deposited with the registration was in existence on the date of the application and was not fraudulently concocted or modified just prior to the initiation of an infringement action in order to be similar to the defendant's song.

The Copyright Office has a liberal policy with regard to accepting applications for copyright registration. It has stated: "We will register material which we feel a court *might* reasonably hold to be copyrightable, even though personally we feel that it is not subject to copyright." For example, if a claimant unearthed an original version of Scott Joplin's "The Entertainer" in an attic and attempted to register it, the Copyright Office would reject the claim on the grounds that the composition is in the public domain. However, a brief melodic variation of a segment of the same work might be registered as an arrangement of a public domain work, even if there is some doubt as to the substantiality of the new material.

For many years, the United States was the only country that insisted on copyright formalities as a condition to the preservation or assertion of legal rights in copyrights. These formalities consist of:

▶ Copyright original and renewal registration
▶ Copyright notice
▶ Deposit of copyrighted works with the appropriate government agency

Other countries, notably signatories of the Berne Convention, refused to require these copyright formalities for protection under their appropriate copyright laws, while the United States refused to waive such formalities as to foreign works. However, desirous of joining the Berne Union, the United States made certain changes in its copyright law by enacting the Berne Convention Implementation Act of 1988. One modification was the abolition of the mandatory notice of copyright for works published for the first time on and after March 1, 1989, the effective date of the Berne Convention Implementation Act. Another change made non-U.S. Berne Convention works exempt from the requirement that the work be registered before a copyright infringement suit could be commenced. Another was the elimination of the requirement that a "transfer of copyright ownership" be registered in the Copyright Office before a transferee could institute a lawsuit in its name. Although these formalities often served valuable functions as a public record of ownership and transfers of ownership, it is now recognized that international copyright relations are more important.

Foreign copyrights originating with members of the Berne Convention have a unique ability to be revived from the public domain. Under the Berne Act, a foreign copyright which was in the public domain in the United States merely because of failure to comply with the formalities of copyright notice or renewal registration could be restored to full copyright status provided that the copyright would not otherwise have expired by reason of the passage of time.

Registration of Published and Unpublished Works

It is not necessary to register an unpublished work in order to re-register it when it is published. It is not necessary to reregister a previously registered unpublished work when it is published. However, if a published version of a previously registered published or unpublished work contains sufficient new matter to constitute a derivative work, a second registration of the derivative published work is necessary to protect the added material. (According to copyright law, "any work in which the editorial revisions, annotation, elaborations, or other modifications represent, as a whole, an original work of authorship" qualifies as a copyrightable derivative work. For example, a compilation of the greatest love songs of 2003 would be a copyrightable derivative work, the "original authorship" consisting of deciding which songs were the "greatest." Note that the creator of the derivative work must get permission from the holder(s) of the copyright(s) before publishing it.)

To register a copyright claim for a work, send the relevant application form, together with a copy of the work, to the U.S. Copyright Office, Library of Congress, 101 Independence Avenue S.E., Washington, DC 20559-6000. The kind of copy required depends on the work:

- *Unpublished works.* One complete copy or phonorecord of the work, whichever best represents it. (Retain a duplicate. Manuscripts and phonorecords are not returned.)
- *Works first published in the United States.* Two copies of the best edition of the work.
- *Works first published outside the United States.* One copy (as first published) of the work.
- *Works published only in phonorecords.* Two complete phonorecords of the best edition.
- *A contribution to a collective work.* One complete copy of the best edition of the collective work. (For a definition of "best edition," see page 92.)

A registration fee of $30 for first-time applications and $60 for renewals is payable by check, money order, or bank draft to the Register of Copyrights. Cash is sent at the remitter's risk.

The Copyright Office makes available, without charge, the following copyright application forms used in the music business:

- *Form PA* (for works in the performing arts). This form is used for published or unpublished musical works, including any accompanying works; dramatic works, including any accompanying music; pantomimes and choreographic works; and motion pictures and other audiovisual works. It is used for most applications for copyright registration of musical compositions prepared for the purpose of being "performed" directly before an audience or indirectly "by means of any device or process." Form PA does not cover sound recordings.
- *Form SR* (for sound recordings). This form is used for published or unpublished sound recordings. This is the only form that needs to be filed if the copyright claimant for both the musical or dramatic work and the sound recording is one and the same and if the claimant is seeking a single registration to cover both aspects of these works.

- ▶ *Form TX* (for nondramatic literary works). This form is used for all types of published and unpublished works written in words (or other verbal or numerical symbols) except for dramatic works, periodicals, and serials. The form includes lyric books as well as poems that may be used as lyrics.
- ▶ *Form VA* (for works of the visual arts). This form is used for published and unpublished "pictorial, graphic, or sculptural works," including two-dimensional and three-dimensional works of fine, graphic, and applied art; photographs, prints, and art reproductions; and maps, globes, charts, technical drawings, diagrams, and models. It covers pictorial or graphic labels and advertisements.
- ▶ *Form RE* (for renewal registrations). Note that in the rare instance of a published work that was not previously registered within its original 28-year term of copyright, it is now necessary to file a combined basic renewal registration and addendum (see copyright office circular 15 for further details). As of this writing the Copyright Office requires a fee of $30, in addition to the $60 fee for the Form RE, accompanied by a deposit of the printed copy.

In addition to these basic application forms, the following forms are used in the music business:

- ▶ *Form CA* (for supplementary registration). This is used to apply for a supplementary registration under Section 408(d) of the Copyright Act of 1976 in order to correct an error in a copyright registration or to amplify the information given in a registration.
- ▶ *Document cover sheet*. This form is required when U.S. citizens file assignments and transfers of copyright and other papers for official registration. It requires submission in duplicate, with a separate cover sheet for each document submitted. The required information includes the identification of the parties, the nature of the document, and the title of the work. If a photostat of an original signed document is submitted, it must be accompanied by a certification under oath that it is a true copy of the original document. This information should be sent to Document Unit LM-462, Catalog Division, Copyright Office, Library of Congress, Washington, DC 20559.

Each of the above forms contains simple instructions for its completion and filing. Copies of all of these forms can be downloaded from the U.S. Copyright Office Web site (http://www.loc.gov/copyright/forms). Once a work is registered, a copyright registration number is issued, preceded by the initials of the form used in the application: PA for performing arts, RE for renewal, VA for visual arts, and so on. Unpublished works are further identified by the letter U: for example, PAU for an unpublished work in the performing arts. All registrations prior to 1978 are recorded on index cards. Entries from January 1, 1978, to the present are recorded electronically. Entries are published in the *Catalog of*

Copyright Entries and available for inspection on microfiche in the Search Room of the Copyright Office and in the Library of Congress. Entries from January 1, 1978, to the present are also published on the Internet.

Because the duration of copyrights originating in and after 1978 is now generally measured from date of death of the author, except for works for hire, filers should provide the following information in compliance with Section 409 of the 1976 Copyright Act:

▸ The date of any author's birth and death
▸ A statement of whether the work was made for hire
▸ A statement of how the claimant obtained ownership of the copyright if the claimant is not the author
▸ Previous or alternative titles under which the work can be identified
▸ The year in which creation of the work was completed

If a compilation or derivative work is based on or incorporates a preexisting work, that work must be identified in the registration application, together with a description of the new material.

The Copyright Notice

As originally enacted, the 1976 Copyright Act required that all publicly distributed copies of published compositions bear a notice of copyright, but under the Berne Convention Implementation Act of 1988, this requirement no longer applies. Nonetheless, it is still highly recommended, especially for reprints of works first published with a notice before March 1, 1989. A copyright notice makes it easy to find the copyright holder who can provide the requisite permission or license.

Paragraph 401 of the Copyright Act states that the notice shall consist of either the word "copyright," the abbreviation, "copr.," or the symbol ©, accompanied by the name of the copyright owner, or an abbreviation by which the name can be recognized, or a generally known alternative designation of the owner. In the case of printed literary, musical, or dramatic works, the notice must also include the year of initial publication. A copyright notice usually looks like this: "© 2002 John Doe" or "Copyright 2002 by Jane Doe." The copyright notice for phonorecords uses a ℗ instead of the ©.

The 1909 copyright statute specified where the notice should appear for certain categories of work. This is still significant for works published before 1989 because an earlier failure to comply could be fatal to a copyright claim. For musical works, for instance, the notice had to be placed on either the title page or the first page of the music. Under the 1976 Copyright Act, the copyright notice is to be placed on "copies in such manner and location as to give reasonable notice of the claim of copyright." The Register of Copyrights may prescribe by regulation, as examples, specific notice positions to satisfy this requirement, although these specifications are not "exhaustive" of what may be otherwise "reasonable" notices.

The Universal Copyright Convention requires that each copy of a published work bear the symbol © accompanied by the name of the copyright proprietor and the year of first publication. The symbol should be placed in such manner and location as to give reasonable notice of claim of copyright. Other formalities, such as the registration and deposit of copies, are waived, but each country can require formalities pertaining to its own nationals and to works first published there.

The Deposit of Copyrighted Works

Under the Copyright Act, as amended by the Berne Convention Implementation Act of 1988, the copyright owner or the owner of the exclusive right of publication must deposit in the Copyright Office, for the use or disposition of the Library of Congress, two copies of the best edition of the work within 3 months of publication in the United States with or without notice of copyright. Deposit is mandatory, in contrast to registration (with accompanying copies), which is voluntary.

The following are deposit requirements for sound recordings:

1. For an unpublished sound recording, one phonorecord
2. For a published sound recording, two complete phonorecords of the best edition, plus accompanying text or visual matter (that is, the container or packaging, including any accompanying booklets)
3. For a sound recording first published outside the U.S., one complete phonorecord as so published

Best edition is defined as the one published in the United States before the date of deposit that the Library of Congress deems most suitable for its purpose. The Register of Copyrights may exempt such a deposit or require the deposit of only one copy. Literary, dramatic, and musical compositions published only in the form of phonorecords are exempt from deposit. ("Copyright Regulation 201: General Provisions" and "Copyright Regulation 202: Registration of Claims to Copyright" discuss deposits for the Library of Congress and for copyright registration. Regulations 201 and 202 and "Copyright Office Information Circular 7B: Best Edition" are available on the Copyright Office Web site.)

At any time after publication, the Register of Copyrights may demand the required deposit in writing. If the registrant fails to comply within 3 months, he or she will be liable to (1) a fine of not more than $250 for each work, (2) a payment to the Library of Congress of the total retail price of the copies or phonorecords demanded, and (3) an additional fine of $2,500 for willful or repeated failure or refusal to comply.

Deposit is required for registration but is not a condition of copyright protection. It serves two purposes: it identifies the work in connection with copyright registration and it provides copies for the use of the Library of Congress. The deposit of copies has been an integral part of the U.S. copyright system from its beginning in 1790. The administration of the registry system was placed in the Library of Congress in 1870; since that time, a single deposit has served both purposes.

A deposit as evidence of the copyrighted work must be viewed with some caution. While unpublished manuscripts or facsimile reproductions are kept on file for the life of the copyright, the Register of Copyrights and the Librarian of Congress may, at their discretion, dispose of published works after their retention for the longest period deemed practicable and desirable. This period for most works has been fixed at 5 years from the date of deposit. Under the Copyright Act of 1976 a request may be made for retention of deposited material for the full term of copyright upon payment of an additional fee (currently $425).

In 1939, music deposits received prior to 1928 and then retained were transferred to the Library of Congress's music division, where they are preserved and available for consultation. Additional musical compositions deemed appropriate for such preservation have been regularly transferred to the music division since that time.

Transfers of Copyright Ownership

Under the Copyright Act, there may be a "transfer of copyright ownership" in a copyright or in any of the exclusive rights included in a copyright. The transfer may be by means of a conveyance or by operation of law. The copyright or exclusive rights may also be transferred by will or by intestate succession. Transfer includes an assignment, mortgage, exclusive license, or any other conveyance, whether or not limited in time or place. It does not include a nonexclusive license.

The transfer, other than by operation of law, must be in writing and signed by the owner of the rights conveyed or an authorized agent. If the transfer is acknowledged before a notary public or other person authorized to administer oaths in the United States, the certificate or acknowledgment becomes prima facie evidence of the execution of the transfer.

The transfer of copyright ownership may be recorded in the Copyright Office. The recording fee is $80 for any document relating to a single title, plus an additional $20 for each group of up to 10 titles. When the ownership is recorded, the Register of Copyrights returns the documents together with a certificate of recordation.

Under the 1976 Copyright Act, following recordation, all persons are on constructive notice of the facts in the document recorded; in other words, all members of the general public are presumed to be fully aware of the facts of ownership. This is on condition that the work has been registered for copyright and that the document recorded specifically identifies the work involved so that a reasonable search under the title or registration number of the work reveals the document. Under the Copyright Act, the transferee could not begin an infringement action until the transfer had been recorded. This had the effect of encouraging the recordation of transfer of ownership. The Berne act eliminated this requirement. Recording a transfer is still encouraged by a provision of the Copyright Act, which states that in the event of conflicting transfers, the prior one prevails if it is recorded so as to give constructive notice (1) within 1 month after execution in the United States, or (2) within 2 months after execution abroad, or (3) at any time before recordation of the later transfer. Without such a recording, the later transfer prevails if recorded first in the manner required to give constructive notice, provided that the later transfer is made in good faith for a valuable consideration, or on the basis of an agreement to pay royalties, without notice of the prior transfer.

Nonexclusive licenses in writing, signed by the owner of the rights licensed or the owner's agent, whether recorded or not, are valid against later transfers. Such licenses also prevail against a prior unrecorded transfer if taken in good faith and without notice of the transfer. A transfer is always valid between the transferee and the transferor, with or without its recording, since both parties are on notice of their own acts.

Regardless of the transfer, the optional copyright notice may continue to contain the name of the prior owner. The new owner may substitute his or her name in the copyright notice. This change of name need not be preceded by recording the transfer in the Copyright Office.

Errors in the Copyright Notice

Under the Copyright Law of 1909, the omission of a copyright notice would generally invalidate the copyright. A distinction should be drawn, however, between the absence of notice on copies or phonorecords published or distributed *before* March 1, 1989, the effective date of the Berne act, and *on or after* March 1, 1989. On copies published or distributed on or after March 1, 1989, the absence of a copyright notice no longer divests a work of copyright protection. On copies published or distributed before March 1, 1989, the absence of a copyright notice is to be treated under the Copyright Act of 1976 (effective January 1, 1978) as it existed before the effective date of the Berne Act. Under the 1976 Copyright Act, omission of a copyright notice does not cause the automatic forfeiture of copyright protection or throw the work into the public domain. If notice is omitted from "no more than a relatively small number of copies" of phonorecords distributed publicly, the copyright is not invalidated. Even the omission from more than a relatively small number of copies does not affect the copyright's benefits where registration of the work has already been made or is made within 5 years after the publication without notice and where there are reasonable efforts to add the notice to copies of records publicly distributed in the United States after discovery of the omission. Similarly, there is continued copyright protection if the omission violated a written requirement by the copyright owner that authorized copies or records were to bear a prescribed notice.

Since the Berne Act is not retroactive insofar as works of U.S. origin are concerned, the copyright owner should take the necessary curative steps under the Copyright Act of 1976 to remedy any defect in order to avoid forfeiture of copyright.

Under some circumstances, innocence is a defense to an infringer. In that regard there is a difference between infringements before March 1, 1989, and infringements on or after that date. For copies of a work published on or after March 1, 1989, the absence of a copyright notice or error therein does not divest a work of copyright protection, but may result in the reduction of the actual or statutory damages awarded by a court to the copyright holder.

There are a number of results from omissions of, or defects in, copyright notices under the Copyright Act. If the infringer was misled, he or she would not be liable for maximum statutory damages prior to his or her receiving notice of a copyright registration. In that situation the court, in its discretion, might still allow claims for the infringer's profits, prohibit future infringement, or reduce the statutory award to not less than $200. This also applies in cases of an incorrect name in a copyright notice, where the infringer acted in good faith on the authority of the person in the notice and the Copyright Office records did not show the real owner in a copyright registration. Where there are relatively minor infringements by teachers, librarians, public broadcasters, and the like completed before actual notice of registration, a court may disallow statutory damages.

"Due diligence" in searching for official records of the Copyright Office for registered claims, assignments, etc., can be accomplished by paying the Copyright Office $80 per hour to conduct a search.

The Correction of Errors

The Register of Copyrights established procedures whereby an earlier copyright registration may be corrected or amplified, but not superseded, by a supplementary registration. Consequently, if a registration has been made with an incorrect name of the owner or an inaccurate date of publication, the error can be indicated in an application for a supplementary registration. This application identifies the earlier registration and is accompanied by a $30 registration fee, the same amount required for the prior registration. The Copyright Office has published Form CA for such supplementary registrations.

Titles of works are not subjects of copyright but merely a means of identifying a work. A change of title does not require a new copyright registration. It is the practice of the Copyright Office, when receiving a request in writing, to prepare without charge a cross-reference entry under the new title, to appear in the general indexes.

Fair Use

It is surprising how frequently songwriters and others in the music business think that copying four bars or fewer of someone's music is permissible despite copyright protection. This error may stem from a misinterpretation of the doctrine of *fair use,* which recognizes the right of the public to make a reasonable use of copyrighted material in special instances without the copyright owner's consent. For instance, book reviewers may quote lines from the book reviewed to illustrate their critical appraisal. Similarly, musicologists and other researchers may use reasonable extracts of copyrighted works in preparing a new scholarly text or commentary. These are clear examples of fair use.

Fair use has been applied for many years as a judicial exception to the exclusive rights of a copyright owner to print, publish, copy, and vend a copyrighted work. In the Copyright Act of 1976, the doctrine of fair use has been included in the statute itself. The provisions of the fair use section are generally consistent with what had been the treatment under case law prior to the statute.

It may be difficult to determine in advance what will be held to be a fair use, however, because the language of the statute is illustrative rather than absolute. It recognizes that the fair use of a copyrighted work may be used "for purposes such as criticism, comment, news reporting, teaching (including multiple copies for classroom use), scholarship, or research." The factors to be considered in determining fair use include:

1. The purpose and character of the use including whether such use is of a commercial nature or is for nonprofit educational purposes;
2. The nature of the copyrighted work;
3. The amount and substantiality of the portion used in relation to the copyrighted work as a whole; and
4. The effect of the use upon the potential market for or value of the copyrighted work.

The Music Publishers Association of the United States, the National Music Publishers' Association, the Music Teachers National Association, the Music Educators National Conference, the National Association of Schools of Music, and the Ad Hoc Committee on Copyright Law Revision have prepared a set of guidelines for the fair use of music for educational purposes. These guidelines set forth the extent of permissible copying of music for educational purposes, with a caveat that conditions may change in the future, so the guidelines may have to be restricted or enlarged. It is important to note that the guidelines are not intended to limit the types of copying permissible under fair use.

The guidelines permit emergency copying for a performance, making a single copy of a sound recording of copyrighted music for aural exercises or examinations, editing or simplification of printed copies, and making multiple copies (not more than one per pupil) of partial excerpts not comprising a performable unit, and not exceeding 10 percent of a whole work. There is a general prohibition, except as specifically exempted, against copying for performances, the copying of workbooks, exercises, and tests, and copying to substitute for the purchase of music.

The criteria for fair use codified earlier fair use standards reflected in case law. For example, in *Robert Stigwood Group Ltd. v. John T. O'Reilly et al.*, the court, faced with the defense of fair use by Catholic priests who had presented their revised version of *Jesus Christ Superstar,* ruled that the defendants' production could not qualify as "literary and religious criticism of the plaintiffs' work." The court stated that the defendants' presentation "(1) is obviously a substitute for plaintiffs' work; (2) copies almost all of the plaintiffs' lyrics, score, and sequence of songs; (3) undoubtedly has and will injure plaintiffs financially; (4) is definitely in competition with plaintiffs' performances; and (5) does not serve or advance the greater public interest in the development of news, art, science or industry."

In 1994, the U.S. Supreme Court ruled unanimously that a parody can qualify as a fair use exception to the copyright laws and that courts should decide on a case-by-case basis whether a particular work qualifies or infringes on a copyright. The case concerned a parody of the song "Oh, Pretty Woman" by the rap group 2 Live Crew. The court determined that a parody qualifies for exemption even if it is in relatively bad taste and that no royalties are required if the parody qualifies as fair use.

Litigation has not as yet settled the propriety of home audio recording of a broadcast or phonorecord for private use. However, in connection with the passage of the Sound Recording Amendment Act of 1971 creating a limited copyright in sound recordings, the House Judiciary Committee commented that "it is not the intention of the Committee to restrain the home recording, from broadcasts or from tapes or records, of recorded performances where the home recording is for private use and with no purpose of reproducing or otherwise capitalizing commercially on it."

In cases involving fair use, where there is doubt regarding its applicability, it is prudent to apply for a license from a copyright proprietor. The existence of the fair use exception tends to strengthen the bargaining position of the applicant for the license.

Copyright Protection of Song Titles

Copyright protection does not extend to the titles of songs or to other copyrighted materials insofar as they are titles. Indirectly, copyright may become involved if the words in the title are an important segment of the song lyric. However, while court decisions have tended to cloud the matter, titles that achieve a secondary meaning in the minds of the public by becoming associated with a particular work have traditionally been safeguarded by the doctrine of unfair competition. The courts invoke this doctrine to prevent the public from being deceived or defrauded as the result of a product being passed off as if it were the product of the plaintiff.

Record albums frequently use an individual song title as the featured title for the album itself. Use of the titles of popular songs helps to set the mood of the album, identifies the type of music contained, and attracts album buyers. No extra payment to the music publisher over usual mechanical royalties is customary. It is common for the publisher to insist on the full statutory mechanical rates when the title of its song is used in this manner, even though the songs in the remainder of the recording are licensed at lower rates customary for budget line albums.

Property rights in titles can be extremely valuable. Motion picture producers regularly pay large sums for the use of song titles such as "Ode to Billy Joe" or "Alexander's Ragtime Band." Not all titles are sufficiently unique for the assertion of legal rights against a motion picture use of the title, though. For example, when Disney released the movie *The Love Bug* without a license from the publisher of the musical composition, "The Love Bug Will Bite You (If You Don't Watch Out)," the court found that the "Love Bug" phrase was "oft used" and that the plaintiff had failed to establish the requisite secondary meaning and likelihood of confusion to support relief.

Compulsory Mechanical License for Recordings

Under section 115 of the Copyright Act, when the copyright owner authorizes a person or entity to distribute recordings of a musical composition, other than one originating in a dramatic show, to the public, any other person may also record and distribute recordings of the work after giving written notice consistent with the regulations of the Copyright Office and paying a statutory royalty rate on each record made and distributed. A record is considered to have been distributed if possession has been "voluntarily and permanently parted with." The written notice and the statutory rate together constitute a *compulsory license.* While author and music publishing groups have argued vehemently against the continuation of the compulsory mechanical license, record industry representatives have fought strongly and successfully for its retention.

A statutory rate of 2 cents was first established in the Copyright Act of 1909. The first review of statutory mechanical royalty rates occurred in 1987, and they are subject to periodic review. The 1997 rate was jointly proposed by the National Music Publishers' Association, the Songwriters Guild of America, and the Recording Industry Association of America and accepted by the Librarian of Congress at the recommendation of the Copyright Office. The rate as of January 1, 2002, is 8 cents per composition of up to 5 minutes' duration, or 1.55 cents per minute or fraction thereof, whichever is greater. These rates increase again on January 1, 2004, to 8.50 cents per composition or 1.65 cents per minute, whichever is greater, and again on January 1, 2006, to 9.10 cents or 1.75 cents per minute. The statutory rate will be reviewed again in 2007. The compulsory mechanical license fee is subject to review by the Copyright Arbitration Royalty Panel (CARP). (CARP is the successor to the Copyright Royalty Tribunal, which was created by the Copyright Act of 1976 as an appointive body charged with periodic review of the compulsory license rates. The Copyright Tribunal Reform Act of 1993 replaced the tribunal with the concept of a three-member arbitration panel that is called into action only if industry negotiators cannot resolve a licensing issue voluntarily. Two of the members are chosen by the Register of

Copyrights from a panel of more than 100 "experts in the field," and these two choose the third member, who serves as chair.)

The compulsory mechanical license for recordings allows the making of an "arrangement of the work to the extent necessary to conform it to the style or manner of interpretation of the performance." Even a "sound-alike" recording, with an arrangement similar to that of a prior recording, is permitted; however, a licensee must avoid changing the basic melody or fundamental character of the work. There can be no claim made to an arrangement as a derivative copyright unless consented to by the copyright owner.

The Copyright Act provides that "to be entitled to receive royalties under a compulsory license, the copyright owner must be identified in the registration or other public records of the Copyright Office." The copyright owner cannot require royalty payments for records made and distributed before being so identified, although the copyright owner can recover damages for records made and distributed after such identification. Accordingly, it is prudent for a copyright owner to register his or her copyright before records are made and distributed.

The copyright owner may negotiate the terms of a mechanical license instead of following the procedure for a compulsory license. A negotiated mechanical license ordinarily permits quarterly accountings and payments, instead of the monthly ones under oath required under a compulsory license by the 1976 statute, and usually dispenses with the requirement of cumulative annual statements made by a certified public accountant.

Record Rentals

Although there can be no legal objection to the well-established practice of selling and trading used CDs and cassettes, the rental of records has been a matter of major industry concern. After successful lobbying for statutory protection, a special restrictive amendment was passed in 1984. Under this Record Rental Act of 1984, regarding copies of sound recordings acquired on or after October 4, 1984, there can be no commercial rental, lease, or lending by the owners of the copies unless authorized by the copyright proprietors of the recordings and of the underlying musical works.

However, for rentals, leasing, and lending, a compulsory licensee is required to pay an additional royalty to the music copyright owner over and above that payable for the sale of records. The compulsory licensee must share its rental, lease, or lending revenues with the music copyright owner in the proportion that revenues from the sale of recordings are allocated between the copyright proprietors of the sound recording and the underlying music.

Jukebox Public Performance Fees

Jukeboxes reached their peak in the 1960s, with an estimated 300,000 in service. Usage declined from the late 1960s through the mid-1980s. Jukebox music now reaches an estimated 75 to 80 million Americans each week. About 85,000 boxes are currently licensed.

The 1976 statute defines a *jukebox* as "a coin-operated phonorecord player" that meets the following criteria:

- ▶ It performs nondramatic musical works and is activated by insertion of a coin.
- ▶ It is located in an establishment making no direct or indirect admission charge.
- ▶ It offers patrons a choice of works from a readily available list of titles.

Under the Copyright Act of 1909, owners of jukeboxes were generally exempted from paying public performance fees. After heated legislative hearings, the exemption was eliminated.

Under the Copyright Act of 1976, jukebox owners must obtain a compulsory public performance license for nondramatic works. The Berne Convention Implementation Act of 1988 amended the 1976 law to provide for negotiated public performance licenses between the jukebox operator and the copyright owner. The parties are encouraged to submit to arbitration if necessary to facilitate negotiated licenses. These licenses take precedence over the compulsory license, but compulsory licenses remain in effect if private agreements are not negotiated or if they are terminated.

The statutory fee was initially set at $8 per box, subject to later determinations first by CARP. The fee was increased to $25 in 1982 and $50 in 1984. Provision was made by the tribunal for later cost-of-living adjustments in the fee, as indicated by the consumer price index. As a result, the fee was set at $63 per jukebox in 1989.

In 1990, the Jukebox License Agreement, a 10-year licensing agreement, was negotiated between the Amusement and Music Operators Association (AMOA) and the three U.S. performing rights organizations, ASCAP, BMI, and SESAC. This agreement authorizes the jukebox performance of all the music handled by the three performing rights organizations. The agreement led to the formation of the Jukebox License Office, which administers the agreement. After administration costs, revenues are split by private agreement between the three participants. The license must be renewed yearly by March 15th. The 2003 annual rates were $364 for the first jukebox and $83 per box thereafter ($61 per box for AMOA members).

Licensing information can be obtained from the Jukebox License Office (Web site: www.jukeboxlicense.com).

Copyright and Cable Television Transmission

Television broadcasting is technically limited to the geographic area covered by the initial transmission, and unless there is a network extension of a broadcast area or syndicated use of videotaped programs, the audience of an originating television broadcast is necessarily confined. Nevertheless, signals from distant metropolitan stations are brought to more rural environs by means of sophisticated cable, CATV, and satellite facilities, thereby extending the audience beyond the area originally anticipated by copyright owners that licensed the broadcaster.

Cable television systems may be described as commercial subscription services that pick up television broadcasts of programs initiated by others and retransmit them to paying subscribers. In a typical system there is a central antenna for the receipt and amplification of television signals and a network of cables for transmitting signals to subscribers' receivers. In some cases, CATV systems initiate their own programming.

In a 1968 ruling concerning claims by copyright owners against CATV facilities, the U.S. Supreme Court held that cable television systems were not liable to copyright owners for the retransmission of copyrighted material. According to the Court, the cable systems were not active "performers" but merely retransmitters of already licensed material—extensions of the passive viewers whom they serviced.

The Copyright Act of 1976 changed preexisting law, requiring cable television systems to obtain a license from copyright owners for the retransmission of distant non-network programming. A cable television system can get a compulsory license on compliance with various formalities, including the recording of certain information by applying to the Copyright Office. Semiannual accounts must be submitted to the Register of Copyrights showing the number of channels used, the stations carried, the total number of subscribers, and the gross receipts from providing secondary transmission of primary broadcast transmitters. Section 111 of the 1976 statute sets royalty rates, to be paid semiannually by the cable systems and computed on the basis of specified percentages of the gross receipts. Receipts from subscribers for other services such as pay cable or installation charges are not included. Separate reduced-fee schedules are provided for smaller cable systems.

After deducting administrative costs, the Register of Copyright deposits the balance with the U.S. Treasury. After a further deduction for new administrative costs, CARP distributes the monies among the copyright owners or to their designated agents once a year. CARP also settles controversies among claimants and reviews cable television royalty rates periodically on the basis of standards and conditions set forth in the Copyright Act of 1976. CARP has the authority to revise the royalty rates every fifth calendar year. As of 1999 the aggregate sum distributed by the Library of Congress was over $113 million, but only a relatively small amount of this went to the music performance societies, with far greater portions going to owners of films and sports cable casts.

Licensing for Noncommercial Broadcasting

The Copyright Act grants noncommercial public broadcasting a compulsory license for the use of published nondramatic literary and musical works as well as published pictorial, graphic, and sculptural works. The license is subject to the payment of reasonable royalty fees, as established by CARP. With regard to music, public broadcasters are allowed to synchronize nondramatic musical works with their programs as well as to perform the programs. They are not allowed to broadcast an unauthorized dramatization of a nondramatic musical work or an unauthorized use of any portion of an audiovisual work.

The act encourages negotiated private agreements between copyright owners and public broadcasters. Voluntary agreements between such parties that are negotiated before, during, or after the determination of terms and rates by CARP supersede such terms and rates.

Satellite Carrier Compulsory License

Effective January 1, 1989, satellite carriers were authorized under section 119 of the Copyright Act of 1976 to retransmit the signals of television broadcast stations for the private home viewing of satellite dish owners. The compulsory license has been further extended at regular intervals.

A statutory rate was established at 17.5 cents per subscriber per month for each retransmitted independent broadcast station and 6 cents per subscriber per month for each retransmitted network-affiliated station or public broadcasting service. The distribution of these fees is subject to voluntary negotiations, which can now be referred to arbitration before a CARP panel appointed by the Copyright Office if unsuccessful. The Register of Copyrights receives the fees paid and, after deducting reasonable administrative costs, deposits the fees with the U.S. Treasury for later distribution by CARP to copyright owners who have filed claims. Although total collections for satellite carriers exceeded $80 million as of 1999, the music interests of the performance rights societies were relatively small compared to those of other claimants, for example, in the areas of sports and film.

11

The Duration of Copyright Protection

There are a number of major issues connected with the duration of copyright protection. One is determining when a work of orginal authorship becomes part of the public domain, "free as the air" so that anyone may use part or all of the work without becoming an infringer. Another is the issue of under what circumstances, and with what effect, the owner of copyright in a work can transfer that ownership to another person or persons.

Term of Copyright Protection

The first U.S. Copyright Act, in 1790, provided for a term of 14 years, renewable in the 14th year for a second 14-year period. Congress later extended the initial term to 28 years, renewable for 14 years. The Copyright Act of 1909 provided for a possible total copyright term of 56 years: an original copyright term of 28 years and a renewal term of another 28 years. In the early 1960s, Congress began extending the renewal term in increments—by 1 year each year. The Copyright Act of 1976 (which went into effect on January 1, 1978) set the renewal term for pre-1978 works at 47 years, giving them a total of 75 years of protection. It also eliminated the renewal requirement altogether for post-1977 works, giving them a term of life of author plus 50 years and a 75-year term for works made for hire. The Copyright Renewal Act of 1992 automatically extended the copyright term for works copyrighted between January 1, 1964, and December 31, 1977, to 67 years. The Copyright Term Extension Act (CTEA) of 1998—also known as the Sonny Bono Copyright Term Extension Act as a tribute to its sponsor, formerly of the well-known singing duo Sonny and Cher, who was a representative from California's 44th District from 1994 until his death in 1998—increased the total term of all works under valid copyright protection on January 1, 1999, by an additional 20 years.

In October 2002, in the case of *Eldred v. Ashcroft,* the Supreme Court heard arguments challenging the constitutionality of the CTEA. The petitioners argued that the 20-year extension violated the Constitutional requirement that copyright protection could be only for a "limited" time. They further argued that the extension violated the Constitutional rights of free speech to the extent that it unreasonably extended the time before which such materials entered the public domain.

The Supreme Court Decision on the Sonny Bono Copyright Term Extension Act

The Supreme Court rendered its decision in *Eldred v. Ashcroft* on January 15, 2003. In her majority opinion, Justice Ginsburg dealt with the two precedental issues presented: first, whether it is unconstitutional to grant 20 additional years of protection to works already under copyright protection (that is, a "retroactive" extension of protection); and second, whether such extension, by depriving parties who rely upon expectations of public domain status for works no longer subject to copyright, was a violation of free speech under the First Amendment.

The decision noted that a prime motivation of the 1976 Copyright Act, as amended by CTEA, was to align the United States copyright term with the prevailing international standard adopted in 1993 by the European Union. This "harmonization" was deemed essential to avoid the refusal of other countries to honor U.S. claims of foreign protection for a term longer than those in the United States. The decision approved the prior Court of Appeals statement that "harmonization . . . has obvious practical benefits" and is "a necessary and proper measure to meet contemporary circumstances rather than . . . a step on the way to make copyrights perpetual."

Justice Ginsburg also stated that "In addition to international concerns, Congress passed the CTEA in light of demographic, economic, and technological changes." In connection with this portion of the opinion, the Court footnoted Congressional testimony to the effect that increasing longevity, plus delayed childbearing, could be seen as justification for a longer term. The comments also noted "the failure of the U.S. copyright term to keep pace with the substantially increased commercial life of copyrighted works resulting from the rapid growth of communications media."

With regard to the issue of distinguishing new works from old works, the Court recognized an established history of each of the various extensions of the term of copyright, quoting a U.S. Representative named Huntington, who said in hearings on the 1831 act, "Justice, policy and equity alike forb[id]" that an "author who had sold his [work] a week ago, be placed in a worse situation than the author who should sell his work the day after the passing of [the] act." In this regard, the decision recognizes the maxim that "a page of history is equal to a volume of logic."

With regard to the free speech issue, future cases may very well consider this decision of great significance. In rejecting petitioner's contentions that the CTEA was a violation of free speech, the Court noted that copyright is actually an engine of freedom of speech in that it encourages publication and does not discourage comment or criticism. Fair use provisions safeguard comment and criticism, and, further, Congress has protected free speech by mandating specific compulsory licenses and exempting certain uses—for example, library uses and certain areas of public broadcasting—from those fees.

The Duration of Copyright

Copyright duration is best analyzed by considering the various periods of duration that now exist. In all cases the duration is determined by several factors, including the type of author (e.g., "natural person" or corporate author) and the date of creation or publication.

WORKS CREATED BY NATURAL PERSONS AFTER DECEMBER 31, 1977

The simplest category encompasses works created by a natural person—as distinct from a corporate author—in his or her lifetime any time after December 31, 1977. That measurement is life plus 70 years. If the work is a joint work as defined under copyright law (see Chapter 18 for a discussion of joint works), the 70-year term begins at the date of death of the last surviving author. If the work is known to have been created by a natural person, but is of anonymous or pseudonymous origin and the identity of the author, and hence the date of death, is unknown, the duration is the same as for a work for hire: 95 years from publication or 120 years from creation, whichever occurs first.

If the author of an anonymous or pseudonymous work is later officially identified in the records of the Copyright Office, the copyright endures for the life of the identified author plus 70 years.

WORKS FOR HIRE; ANONYMOUS OR PSEUDONYMOUS AUTHORS

The duration of copyright for works for hire where a corporate or other employer owns the copyright is 95 years from publication or 120 years from creation, whichever occurs first.

PRE-1978 WORKS

The duration of copyright for works originating before 1978 and after 1922 depends on the original date of copyright, and is 95 years from publication. However, if the work was published before 1964, formal notice of renewal had to be filed within the 28th year of copyright protection. As noted in Chapter 10 this formality was waived as of 1992. (Note that while the requirement to renew copyrights was not lifted for U.S. copyright owners until 1992, for Europeans and other Berne Convention nationals, renewal requirements were lifted in 1989, when the U.S. acceded to the Berne Convention. Thus, any copyrights belonging to Europeans that might have expired at any previous time because of failure to renew have been restored, even though the same is not true for copyrights belonging to Americans that expired during that period.)

Pre-1978 works published or copyrighted for the first time after 1978 are afforded the same protection provided new works: the life of the author plus 70 years. If the works are anonymous, pseudonymous, or works made for hire, the copyright now endures for 95 years from first publication or 120 years from creation, whichever occurs first. In all such pre-1978 works, the copyright endured until at least December 31, 2002. If the work was published before December 31, 2002, the copyright endures until at least December 31, 2047.

SOUND RECORDINGS

Federal copyright rules do not apply to sound recordings originating in the United States before February 15, 1972. For sound recordings originating in the United States between February 15, 1972, and December 31, 1977, the renewal requirements discussed above apply. For U.S. sound recordings originating on or after January 1, 1978, the duration of copyright is the same as the duration for songs. Note that the duration of foreign copyright for sound recordings originating in any country within the European Union is only 50 years from original publication.

WORKS IN THE PUBLIC DOMAIN

The statutory protection of works published in 1922 expired on January 1, 1998, and they became part of the public domain. Works published between 1923 and 1964 on which the copyright owner failed to renew his or her registration are in the public domain.

End-of-Calendar-Year Copyright Computation

Under the Copyright Act of 1909, an application for renewal had to be filed within 1 year of the expiration of the original term (day and month) of copyright. The Copyright Renewal Act of 1992 made renewal and extension automatic; inaction does not result in a lapse of copyright protection. Furthermore, the Copyright Act of 1976 extends copyright dates to the end of the calendar year in which they would otherwise terminate, which facilitates the computation of dates. This may result in a slight prolongation of a term that might otherwise expire earlier in a given year. For example, under the 1909 Copyright Act, the first 28-year term of a copyright obtained on July 1, 1972, would have ended on June 30, 2000; instead it ended on December 31, 2000. For a new work fixed on July 1, 1978, the term of copyright protection is the life of the author plus 70 years. If the author died on February 15, 1980, the 70-year period would expire on December 31, 2050, not on February 14, 2050.

The Duration of Copyright Protection for Joint Works

A *joint work* is defined in the Copyright Act as one "prepared by two or more authors with the intention that their contributions be merged into inseparable or interdependent parts of a unitary whole." A song can qualify as a joint work where authors write words and music together or where one or more authors write words and other authors separately write the music. For joint works fixed on or after January 1, 1978, the statutory term of protection is 70 years from the death of the last surviving author. This is beneficial to the heirs of the earlier-deceased coauthors because the heirs of the first author get the advantage of a longer term based on the later death date of the surviving collaborator.

The Determination of Date of Death

The computations of copyright term under the Copyright Act present practical problems with respect to determining the dates of death of obscure or unknown authors. The Register of Copyrights is obligated to maintain current records of author deaths. Any person having a copyright interest may record in the Copyright Office statements of the death or living status of an author, in compliance with the regulations of the Register of Copyrights.

After a period of 95 years from the publication of a work or 120 years from its creation, whichever expires first, any person may obtain a certification from the Copyright Office that its records disclose nothing to indicate that the author is living or has been dead for less than 70 years. In that case, the person may rely on a presumption that the author has been dead for more than 70 years. Such reliance in good faith is a complete defense to an infringement action.

Where the identity of the author remains unrevealed in anonymous or pseudonymous works or in the case of works made by an employee for hire, the duration of protection is 95 years from the year of first publication or 120 years from creation, whichever expires first. If the author of an anonymous or pseudonymous work is later officially identified in the records of the Copyright Office, the copyright endures for the life of the identified author plus 70 years.

Copyright Renewal

As noted previously, copyright renewal applies only to pre-1978 works in their original term of copyright as of January 1, 1978. The Copyright Renewal Act of 1992 eliminated the need to register renewal of copyrights in nearly all cases. Any copyright registered before January 1, 1964, had to be renewed within the 28th year of the initial term of copyright to maintain copyright protection for the full term. Because of the 1992 Act, any copyright created between January 1, 1964, and December 31, 1977, is protected for the full term without the need to register renewal. Automatic renewal benefits the original term publisher, who continues to collect on licenses issued before commencement of the renewal term. Thus, until December 31, 2005 (after which all new copyrights become subject to the 1976 Act, which eliminated the renewal term), it is still desirable (but not essential) for the author or, if deceased, the heirs to register renewals of songs. If the copyright is not affirmatively renewed, certain rights commonly known as the "Who's Sorry Now" benefits remain with the prior publisher *(Mills Music, Inc. v. Snyder* 469 U.S,153 [1985]). These rights, which include all continuing royalties that are based on a derivative copyright (including old copyrightable arrangements), will continue to flow to the prior publisher subject only to the original writer royalty agreement, even into the renewal term, unless a timely renewal claim is registered.

If there has been a valid assignment of renewal rights, the automatic renewal is for the benefit of the assignee if the assigning author survives into the renewal year. If there has been a death of the author or a failure of a surviving author to assign his or her rights of renewal, the automatic renewal benefits as to new uses accrue to the author or the statutory successors without further notification to the Copyright Office. In such a situation, notice should be sent to the performing rights society and mechanical or other licensing agents.

When considering renewal rights, in all applicable instances, if the renewal right was originally the author's, the appropriate renewal claimants are:

- ▶ *The author, if still living*
- ▶ *If the author is dead,* the widow, widower, or children of the author
- ▶ *If there is no surviving widow, widower, or child,* the executor named in the author's will
- ▶ *If there is no surviving widow, widower, or child,* and the author left no will, the next of kin of the deceased author

In the case of certain works (that were originally copyrighted by a proprietor), the right to renew rests with the original-term proprietor or assignee thereof. This includes posthumous works and periodical, encyclopedic, or other composite works, or works copyrighted by an employer or corporation that hired someone to create the work. Where there are collaborators on a song, the benefits of renewal accrue to each writer or his/her assignee if they survive into renewal or, if not, to their statutory beneficiaries as noted above. A renewal copyright is a new and independent right, and not merely a prolongation of the first term. While the courts uphold assignments of the renewal right, the fulfillment of the assignment depends on the survival of the author into the renewal year. In the event that the author does not survive, the assignee's rights are defeated by the beneficiaries designated in the Copyright Acts of 1909 and 1976, such as the widow, widower, children, executor, or next of kin.

In 1990 the U.S. Supreme Court considered a case involving Alfred Hitchcock's motion picture *Rear Window*, which is a derivative work based on a published story. The license to the film company purported to cover the original copyright term and the renewal term of the story. However, the author of the story died before the expiration of the original 28-year copyright period, and neither the renewal copyright owner nor its assignees had authorized the exploitation of the movie within the copyright renewal period. In a 6-to-3 decision, the Court ruled that without such authorization, the continued exhibition of the film or its exploitation in the form of videocassettes during the copyright renewal period constituted an infringement. This precedent would appear to apply also to derivative works based on music, where the author of the music dies before the copyright can be renewed. The *Rear Window* ruling is only applicable to renewal copyrights that are officially registered and does not occur if automatic renewal is relied on. This situation does not concern 39-year termination situations (19-year extension plus 20-year extension) where the 1976 and 1998 statutes specifically protect continued derivative uses.

The Copyright Act of 1976 stipulates that if the author of a work is dead, the renewal rights are owned by the author's widow or widower, children, or grandchildren. In 2002, a federal district court in Tennessee, in the case of *BMI v. Estate of Roger Miller,* ruled that Miller's widow and his seven children should be treated as equal members of a class, meaning that instead of being entitled to 50 percent of the rights, the widow was entitled only to one-eighth. This remarkable decision changes the arithmetic of participation for many old copyright renewal claims and is based upon the simple assertion by the Tennessee court that unless otherwise defined under statute, each class member is equal.

Prior to this decision the general practice in dealing with renewals of songs originating before 1978 was to apply the law of intestacy (death without a will) of the state where the decedent author resided. Thus, the shares to be allocated were always equal when there was only one child and one widow but if there were multiple surviving children, state law frequently allowed less than 50 percent—although rarely less than $33^1/_3$ percent to the widow. This trial court decision may be subject to appeal or review by courts in other states. Note that this case only deals with renewal rights and not termination rights (discussed below) where section 302 c(2)(A) specifies that a widow has a 50 percent interest.

It is important to recognize that U.S. renewal recapture rights do not normally affect the continuance of the grant of foreign rights. However, in a 1997 decision, a British court ruled that the copyright to the song "To Know Him Is to Love Him" reverted back to legendary producer-songwriter Phil Spector 28 years after publication because of a provision in the AGAC (presently Songwriters Guild) contract that provided for the reversion of world rights at the end of the original U.S. term of copyright.

Termination of Transfers

Before the Copyright Act of 1976, the total life of a copyright consisted of an initial term plus a renewal term. An important feature of renewal term rights was that even if an author had assigned all of his or her rights in a work to another party (a publisher or record company, for example) those rights reverted back to the author as the beginning of the renewal term. (Note that in the case of works for hire, the renewal copyright belonged either to the person who hired the author to create the work in the first place or to whomever the original owner had sold the right.) The legislative intent was to protect authors and their statutory beneficiaries from suffering permanent financial consequences as a result of entering into improvident agreements with publishing companies, record companies, and other parties. In addition to extending the duration of copyright for all copyrightable works, the Copyright Act of 1976 substituted the concept of *termination* for the concept of *renewal,* limiting renewals to those works created before January 1, 1978. The termination provisions apply to "transfer of copyright ownership," exclusive or nonexclusive licenses, and any other right within the copyright. Again, the intention of Congress was to continue to provide authors with a second chance to enjoy the fruits of their authorship, but now through a right of termination instead of the former renewal procedure.

An exception to the termination provisions applies to any "derivative work prepared under authority of the grant before its termination." For example, suppose the author of a book who has signed away his copyright to a publisher subsequently terminates the transfer of rights. A TV show based on that book that was created *before* termination can still exploit the rights to the show under the terms of the original agreement with the publisher.

PRE-1978 CONTRACTS (RENEWAL TERMINATION)

For a work the copyright protection of which is still valid, the creator of the work (or the statutory beneficiaries) can terminate the extended portion of renewal rights at any time during the 5 years beginning 56 years after the original copyright date. If the copyright was in its initial or renewal period at the time CTEA became effective (October 27, 1998), and the right to terminate the extended renewal period had not previously been exercised, a new right to terminate was provided, effective at any time designated within a 5-year window beginning 75 years after the original copyright date.

1978 AND POST-1978 CONTRACTS (TRANSFER TERMINATION)

The creator of the work (or the statutory beneficiaries) can terminate a transfer of rights during the 5 years beginning either at the end of 35 years from the date of publication of the work or the end of 40 years after the signing of the transfer agreement.

WHO CAN TERMINATE?

Notice of termination notice can always be sent by the creator. However, because the author may not survive to the date of intended termination, the statute requires designation as to who will be the statutory successor. The successor class consists of the widow, widower, children, or, if any of the children are no longer living, any children of the deceased children. The right to terminate an author's earlier grant has no provision for exercise of such rights by executors or next of kin. However, in the rare case in which an executor or next of kin was a signing party of a former renewal assignment, that person qualifies as a statutory successor.

For pre-1978 works in the extended renewal period where no actions have been taken under the 1976 Copyright Act's rights of termination, the CTEA stipulates that executors, administrators, personal representatives, and trustees may initiate termination, whereas the 1976 Copyright Act allowed only specified family members to initiate termination.

Complications arise when the original copyright is held by more than one person, for example, if there are two or three coauthors of a work, and the work originated in or after 1978 (renewal provisions apply to pre-1978 works). Termination in that situation requires a majority vote of the joint authors or their successors. Each coauthor has an equal voting status, regardless of how royalty benefits were originally allocated. If there are two joint authors, both must agree on the termination.

NOTICE OF TERMINATION

The creator or the creator's statutory beneficiaries must send a notice to the entity to whom the rights have been assigned (the assignee) not less than 2 or more than 10 years before the effective date of termination (which must be within the 5-year window). Of course, a well-advised terminating party will act at the earliest opportunity to send notice. It is important to note that a 2-year advance notice is *always* required before the effective date, so that the 5-year window is really only 3 years after the end of the 56th year (or 75th year if termination is sought under CTEA).

LEGISLATIVE IMPLICATIONS

A number of interesting legal cases concerning termination have been brought since the Copyright Act was enacted.

- ▶ *Mills Music, Inc. v. Snyder,* [469 U.S. 153 (1985)]. The authors of the musical composition "Who's Sorry Now" (composed in the 1920s) assigned their rights to a music publisher, Waterson et al., which subsequently, in bankruptcy proceedings, assigned the copyright to Mills Music. In 1940 the authors assigned all their renewal rights to Mills, including the exclusive right to act as publisher. In 1978, the widow and son of Ted Snyder, one of the original composers, terminated the grant to Mills and claimed exclusive right to all mechanical royalties. Ultimately, the Supreme Court, in a 5-to-4 decision that rested both on interpreting the phrase "term of the grant" and on deciding whether the derivative-work exception applied, determined that revenues from mechanical royalties on old records continue to flow to the old publisher subject to the old rate of royalties to the author's estate because they qualify as a "derivative work."
- ▶ *Woods v. Bourne Co.,* [60 F 3d 978 (2d Cir. 1995)]. The heirs of Harry Woods, the composer of "When the Red, Red Robin Comes Bob, Bob Bobbin' along," claimed that they should receive royalties from the song under the termination provisions of the Copyright Act. The music publisher, Bourne, argued that post-termination uses of the song were

derivative works prepared before termination and were therefore protected by the derivative-works exception. In this case, as in the Mills case, the courts ruled against the terminating parties. In effect, the "Who's Sorry Now" decision was extended to require ASCAP to credit performance royalties on the playing of old records and films to the old publisher.

▶ *Fred Ahlert Music Corporation v. Warner/Chappell Music, Inc.* 958 F. Supp 170 (S.D.N.Y. 1997). The copyright to "Bye, Bye Blackbird," written by Mort Dixon and Ray Henderson, was registered in 1926. The copyright was renewed in 1953, and each author subsequently assigned his interest in the copyright to Remick Music Corporation (later Warner/Chappell). In 1956 Warner granted A&M Records the right to record a Joe Cocker version (a derivative work) of "Bye, Bye Blackbird." In 1978, Dixon's heirs (Dixon died in 1956) transferred their termination interest in the original song to Ahlert's publishing company. In 1991, Ahlert issued a synchronization license to TriStar pictures giving them the right to use the song on the soundtrack of *Sleepless in Seattle.* The soundtrack, however, used a pretermination version of the 1969 Joe Cocker derivative. In 1993, a mechanical license to use the Cocker version on the soundtrack was issued to Sony (TriStar's affiliate) by the Harry Fox Agency on behalf of Ahlert. Warner-Chappell told Fox that it, not Ahlert, was entitled to all royalties from Cocker's version, and Fox subsequently canceled the license from Ahlert, granted one from Warner-Chappell, and gave royalties collected from Sony for the soundtrack album sales to Warner-Chappell. The courts eventually ruled (1) that the original grant from Dixon to Remick (later Warner-Chappell) covered the use of the Cocker derivative only on the A&M original Joe Cocker recording and not on the film soundtrack but (2) the right to authorize other new uses of "Bye, Bye Blackbird" to Sony was not within the terms of the grant by Warner to A&M and so reverted to Dixon's heirs, who had terminated the agreement with Remick (Warner-Chappell).

In the Mills case and the Woods case, the decisions mean that the protection of derivative versions under the terms of an earlier grant protects not only the derivative user but also the old publisher. The basic premise, however, is that an early investment in making a derivative version should not be jeopardized by disputes between authors and publishers, especially when major investments such as films are involved. Note that careful inspection of an earlier grant or license will sometimes disclose the existence of language broadly covering "any and all future formats in which the film can be presented, including new technology." Such "new technology" would include, for example, a new video or DVD of a classic theatrical film not previously licensed before termination, which would be analogous to a CD version of an LP licensed before termination. Only continuing uses under a prior grant made by the terminated party are still protected after termination.

Duration of Copyright and Protection
Outside of the United States

For the international protection of U.S. works under the law of a particular foreign country, U.S. publishers and authors can rely on the Berne Convention or on certain special laws and treaties discussed in Chapter 20, "International Copyright Protection." The United States joined the Berne Union on March 1, 1989, and it has been an adherent of the Universal Copyright Convention (UCC) since September 16, 1955. The Berne Convention and the UCC do not ordinarily protect the works of a U.S. author published in the United States before the date of adherence to the particular convention. However, compositions that were first or simultaneously published in Canada, England, or another Berne country qualify for Berne protection under the so-called back-door approach.

Under the Berne Convention, the United States and the 128 other Berne Union members have agreed to apply the minimum life-plus-50-years standard to works that qualify for Berne protection. Since Berne members agree to treat nationals of other member countries like their own nationals for purposes of copyright, U.S. authors often receive higher levels of protection than the guaranteed minimum. It should be noted that the Berne Convention does not cover minimum terms for sound recording copyrights.

12

The Uses of Public Domain

When the famed Hollywood composer Dimitri Tiomkin was called to the stage to receive one of his four Oscars for an outstanding motion picture score, he gave credit to his "collaborators," Bach, Beethoven, and Brahms. A number of years later composer Marvin Hamlisch, in accepting the Oscar for his contribution to *The Sting,* acknowledged his debt to the original composer of many of its tunes, Scott Joplin. In each of these cases, what was being acknowledged was music that was in the *public domain*—music unprotected by copyright. Reliance on music in the public domain may also be noted in the sheet music of such popular songs as "Our Love," "'Til the End of Time," and "Suddenly." Indeed, three of Elvis Presley's number one hits were based in part on music acknowledged to be in the public domain: "Love Me Tender" (based on "Aura Lee"), "It's Now or Never" (based on "O Sole Mio"), and "Surrender" (based on "Come Back to Sorrento"). In addition, experts can point out many thousands of songs based on undisclosed public domain sources.

Unsophisticated members of the music industry may think there is something unethical or shameful about reliance on music in the public domain, but certainly a great composer such as Dimitri Tiomkin was no less creative for his recognition of a cultural debt to the ages. As Goethe once correctly stated, "The most original modern authors are not so because they advance what is new, but simply because they know how to put what they have to say as if it had never been said before."

On the other hand, the frequent claim of full originality when a work in actuality is based partly on music in the public domain has been a source of confusion and even unfair business practices. The British *Performing Right Yearbook* once noted that one problem in the distribution of performance fees is the false claim of full originality for works that deserve only partial credit; in the same article, it went on to say that the majority of such false claims come from "overseas" (meaning the United States).

Music in the public domain is useful to a number of different people and groups.

- Music publishers use songs in the public domain in many folios and instructional series for reasons of budget economy and free adaptability.
- Record companies include varying numbers of songs in the public domain in albums, especially in budget albums, to avoid mechanical royalty payments.
- Artists who are composers obtain copyrights on arrangements of songs in the public domain presented in their repertoire.
- Television film scores and advertising jingles and announcements frequently use music in the public domain in order to avoid high synchronization fees and to have full freedom to adapt it in any form.

Works in the Public Domain

Public domain is the opposite of copyright: it lacks the element of private property granted to copyright; anyone can make full, unrestricted use of the material. It is literally "free as the air."

Copyright is granted for a limited time; once a work is published, it does not stay protected permanently. Find any sheet music published in the United States before 1923 and you can be certain that such version of the song is in the public domain. Most works in the public domain are so categorized because their term of copyright protection has expired or because they reached their 28th year of copyright protection and were not registered for U.S. renewal copyright. (Under the Copyright Renewal Act of 1992, renewal is now made automatically by the Copyright Office; failure to renew no longer places the work in the public domain.)

Other works fall into the public domain much earlier or may join the public domain from the time of their creation. Generally, anything written and published for the U.S. government is in the public domain from the outset. With limited exceptions, prior to January 1, 1978, the generally effective date of the Copyright Act of 1976, anything published without a copyright notice fell into the public domain regardless of later attempts to correct this situation. As famous a song as "The Caissons Go Rolling Along" became public domain material because of a defective copyright notice.

The omission of copyright notices for works first published between January 1, 1978, and March 1, 1989, the effective date of the Berne Convention Implementation Act of 1988, may invalidate a copyright under the Copyright Act of 1976, but there is greater flexibility and the omission may be forgiven. For works published for the first time on or after March 1, 1989, mandatory notice of copyright has been abolished, although voluntary use is encouraged by certain benefits that accrue from the use of notice.

The difficulty of determining public domain or copyright status in the international field is increased by the fact that most foreign countries respect copyright in a work for 50 or 70 years after the death of the author, whereas under U.S. copyright law, concerning works first fixed before January 1, 1978, protection is measured in terms of number of years from the original date of copyright or renewal of copyright. This results in a lack of uniformity when a specific work enters public domain status throughout the world. Accordingly, U.S. users who are relying on public domain status to compile a printed folio of songs, make a budget album, or synchronize the score of a film must investigate the foreign copyright status thoroughly before allowing the work to be exported. U.S. users should also be very cautious in determining whether the work is actually in the public domain.

The Uruguay Round Agreements Act (URAA), effective December 8, 1994, which implements the General Agreement on Tariffs and Trade (GATT) agreement on trade-related aspects of intellectual property rights (TRIPs), restores copyright protection to foreign works that were in the public domain in the U.S. but still under copyright protection in their source country, if that country was a member of the Berne Convention. To qualify for automatic restoration, the work must be in the public domain as a result of failure to comply with statutory formalities, lack of subject matter protection, or lack of national eligibility and must originate in a Berne Convention source country. Use of the restored work after constructive or actual notice of the intention to enforce restored copyright rights is an infringement, and full statutory remedies are available.

The Purposes of Public Domain

Songs registered or published prior to 1923 were not covered by the numerous interim extensions of copyright preceding the 1976 Copyright Act. Therefore, these songs did not qualify for the extension otherwise applicable to songs published in and after 1923. The U.S. Constitution authorizes copyright only "for limited times." Thus, the policy against perpetual private rights in writings is set forth in the highest law of the land. A study issued by the Copyright Office prior to the passage of the Copyright Act of 1976 stated the following reasons for this policy:

> It is generally believed to be to the benefit of the public that once the work has been created, and the author protected for a sufficient time to have produced the original incentive, the work should become available to be freely used by all. There is believed to be a greater probability of more varied editions of works of lasting value, and a wider opportunity to distribute existing works competitively, and use them as a basis for new creation, if they are freely available. It is basic to our economic system that profits in this area should be gained by more efficient manufacture, better distribution and the like, rather than by perpetual protection, once the purpose of the protection for a limited time has been achieved.
>
> In the words of Judge Learned Hand, one of the most respected federal appellate judges, "Congress has created the monopoly in exchange for a dedication, and when the monopoly expires the dedication must be complete."

The composer, naturally enough, may object to not being able to pass on property to grandchildren as easily as a neighbor who creates a shoe factory. However, consideration should be given to a policy that favors limited restraints on uses of what is thought to be the national cultural heritage. Imagine the block on cultural development if the heirs of Beethoven, Bach, or Brahms had to be located in order to grant a license for a sequenced jazz version or even a New York Philharmonic performance of the classics.

Prior to the enactment of the Copyright Act of 1976 and the Copyright Term Extension Act of 1998 (CTEA), arguments were advanced for a longer term of copyright and a more delayed entry into the public domain. A renowned German music industry leader, Dr. Erich Schulze, formerly the head of GEMA, the German performance and mechanical rights society, stated: "If the term were unlimited, arrangements would have to be made to ensure that the rights can be exercised even though a great number of heirs might be involved. If, at some later date, all of the heirs should have died, the copyright would have to pass to the state." Dr. Schulze pointed out that life expectancy in the United States had changed since the passage of the Copyright Act of 1909, which gave a maximum 56 years of copyright protection: "At the turn of the century, [life expectancy was] 48.23 years for newborn males and 51.01 for newborn females; in 1960, 67.4 for newborn males and 74.1 for newborn females." In 1987, life expectancy in the United States had increased to 71.5 years for males and 78.3 years for females. Since medical science had achieved the extension of life expectancy, Dr. Schulze contended, the term of copyright should be similarly extended to cover the lifetime of the author and his or her immediate family. This was the standard adopted by the Copyright Act of 1976—the life of the author plus 50 years and, for existing works, an extra 19 years equaling a total of 75 years. This standard had been adopted previously by a majority of the world's countries.

There has always been opposition from certain quarters to the CTEA of 1998, which provides for a further 20-year extension of copyright. Writing in the December 21, 1998, issue of *The Wall Street Journal,* Professor Richard A. Epstein of the University of Chicago stated: "Removing these works from the public domain works a huge uncompensated wealth transfer from ordinary citizens to . . . holders, corporate and individual, of preexisting copyrighted material. It also produces a net social loss by restricting overall level of use of this material." In a lead editorial dated February 21, 1998, *The New York Times* actively opposed a 20-year extension of copyright, arguing that "the tendency when thinking about copyright, is to vest the notion of creativity in the owners of copyright. But, artists . . . always emerge from the undifferentiated public, and the works in the public domain . . . are an essential part of every artist's sustenance." In *Eldred v. Ashcroft* (discussed at length in Chapter 11), the Supreme Court rejected these arguments.

The Court's decision in that case was based in part on the need for U.S. authors and other copyright parties to participate on an equal basis with their trading partners in the EU and with other Berne Convention countries that had already extended their copyrights to author's life plus 70 years. American corporations were afraid that other countries would fail to honor U.S. copyrights for the enlarged period if Americans did not have reciprocal extensions.

In some countries there exists what is known as a *public domain payant*. This is a state fund which collects royalties on public domain material for distribution not to heirs of the creator but to new and deserving artists and writers. This practice tends to reduce users' incentive to favor public domain at the expense of copyrighted works. It also encourages deserving new writers whose works may someday themselves be a part of a national cultural heritage.

Determining the Public Domain Status of Works

The public domain is like a vast national park with no guards to stop wanton looting, with no guides for lost travelers, with no clearly defined fences or borders to stop the innocent wayfarer from being sued for trespass. Much of the music material in the public domain is tainted by vague and indefinite claims of copyright in minimal or obscure "new versions." Even more of the musical public domain falls into oblivion because of the failure to maintain complete public archives. There are, however, various sources of information to help one determine whether copyright claims exist on a given work. These sources include the U.S. Copyright Office, the Library of Congress, editions of old songs, catalogs of performing rights societies, the Harry Fox Agency, and various reference materials.

U.S. COPYRIGHT OFFICE

The Copyright Office is exclusively concerned with works protected by copyright and has no jurisdiction over public domain. It keeps no separate record of works in the public domain. Because the Copyright Office does not list works in its *Catalog of Copyright Entries* that have not been registered for the renewal period of copyright, even though renewal registration is no longer required, it is the potential user of public domain material who must determine whether the renewal copyright is in effect. Moreover, if a faulty claim to copyright has been presented to the Copyright Office, there is no public notice of rejection by the Copyright Office.

However, the Copyright Office does perform some very valuable services in an investigation of copyright status. On request, its staff will search its records for a fee—at this writing, $65 for each hour or fraction of an hour. Based on the information furnished to it by the requesting party, the Copyright Office will provide an estimate of the total search fee. Anyone then requesting a search should include the Copyright Office's estimate in the letter. The office will then proceed with the search and provide a report either in writing or by telephone, at the option of the requesting party. The report will cover copyright registrations and claims. It will not certify the public domain status but it will give essential information as to whether there is another claimant to the copyright, whether the copyright has been renewed, and whether the initial claim for copyright is of such a date that public domain status, by reason of expiration of the period of protection or failure to renew, has occurred.

It is the basic policy under the Copyright Act that copyright deposits are to be kept as long as possible. However, the Register of Copyrights and the Librarian of Congress jointly have the power to dispose of them at their discretion when they no longer consider it practical or desirable to retain them. During the term of copyright, unpublished works may not be destroyed or otherwise disposed of unless a facsimile copy is made for Copyright Office records. For a fee of $365, the depositor of copies or the copyright owner of record may request that deposited material be retained for the full term of U.S. Copyright Office.

Once a copyright expires, the Copyright Office does *not* keep previously deposited manuscripts of unpublished or published music. Consequently, it is up to the potential user to locate a copy of the public domain manuscript unless, by chance, the Library of Congress chose in its discretion to keep a copy. Accordingly, a search for and inspection of copies of published or unpublished works registered for copyright should be made in *advance* of the expiration of copyright. The nature of copyright is such that the Copyright Office itself does not ordinarily make a copy of a published or unpublished work on deposit with it. Therefore, unless written permission of the owner is obtained to make a copy, in the absence of a certified need for litigation purposes, an on-the-spot inspection of a manuscript is required.

Other search services are available through the office of Thomson & Thomson Copyright Research Group (t-tlaw.com). Some film studios and other major users of material in the public domain, rather than risk a judgment involving substantial investment on the basis of only one such report, rely on two or more reports requested simultaneously.

LIBRARY OF CONGRESS

Not all copyrighted works are destroyed or lost when they are no longer within the copyright term of protection. The purpose of requiring a deposit of "two complete copies of the best edition" with the registration of claim to copyright is to offer the Library of Congress an opportunity, in its discretion, to keep a reference copy. Of course, even the more than 630 miles of shelves in the Library of Congress, holding over 88 million items, do not make it a universal archive of all previous publications. The Library of Congress has the right to transfer to its permanent and reserve collections one or both of the domestic editions registered for copyright and the one copy deposited for foreign works.

In practice, the Librarian of Congress determines which published deposits of the Copyright Office are to be transferred to the Library of Congress or other government libraries or used for exchanges or transfer to any other library. As for unpublished works, the Library of Congress may select any deposits for its collection or for transfer to the National Archives of the United States or to a federal records center.

EDITIONS OF OLD SONGS

If a copy of sheet music or other printed version bears a date earlier than 1923, the music and lyrics may be assumed to be in the public domain in the United States. Works created in 1923 and subsequent years up until January 1, 1978, have a full 95-year duration. Later works are measured by life of author plus 70 years.

The Lincoln Center Library of the Performing Arts in New York City maintains an extensive collection of old-time popular songs; an inspection of this collection is desirable for gathering available information from early editions. Sheet music and other published copies of old songs can often be obtained from private collections or dealers. It is important to have access to early editions so as to avoid copying a new version or new arrangement of a work that is otherwise in the public domain.

Some users of works in the public domain use a system of "most common denominator" as a means of determining true public domain. This is a method of gathering together many versions of a known public domain work as identified through the data banks of ASCAP and BMI and copying only those portions of words or music that appear in several different sources. The services of an expert musicologist are sometimes helpful here, especially in motion pictures, where great financial hardship might result if a valid claim were to be presented after initial use.

In cases where the melodic source for a popular composition is in the public domain, the new musical contributions made to the original source by a copyright claimant may be of a minor and limited nature. For example, a songwriter may write a song entitled "Darling, I Love You" based on a Bach sonata. Another songwriter would be entitled to write a new instrumental work on the same sonata or put new lyrics to it. In either case, the later songwriter also has a valid claim to copyright on the contributions in that new version, provided that the songwriter has not copied any of the earlier writer's additions to the underlying sonata. The later writer is well advised, however, to use a different title for the new version to avoid confusion in the collection of mechanical and performance fees.

CATALOGS OF PERFORMING RIGHTS SOCIETIES
AND THE HARRY FOX AGENCY

The ASCAP, BMI, and SESAC catalogs of songs as indexed on their Web sites are designed to provide convenient lists of copyright claimants. In some instances, they can be used to indicate the public domain status of the basic underlying work. For example, a listing of "arranger," with no claim by "composer," would appear to be a concession that only the new arrangement is original. If there are many listings of the same musical title under different publishers or performance right names, the underlying work is probably in the public domain. Rarely do the listings openly disclose public domain status. However, an ethical practice would be to give composer credit to the original-source composer even if the work is in the public domain.

The failure of ASCAP, BMI, or SESAC to list a work as public domain does not necessarily determine the issue, however. Some works filed as completely original may be based on a public domain composition, and the societies may not look behind the filing.

The Harry Fox Agency, which administers mechanical and synchronization rights on behalf of publishers in the United States, maintains voluminous files that contain significant information which also may be useful.

OTHER REFERENCE SOURCES

Finally, a number of print-based reference sources offer information regarding copyrighted material or public domain works. In 1993, a new subscription news-letter called the *Public Domain Report* was introduced. This publication offers reliable information on public domain status for U.S. purposes and includes an offer to deliver on request the original sheet music for a small charge. The newsletter is of particular interest to advertising agencies and film companies that may wish to have assured sources of such materials.

To date, *PDR* has reported nearly 13,500 public domain works to its reader-ship. Although originally available by mail order, *PDR* is now only available on-line to subscribers. This publisher also offers the *PDR Music Bible,* a two-volume series that includes more than 7,000 listings and reviews of public domain music. An extensive public domain sheet music library and custom copyright research services are available to all PDR clients. Their Web site is www.pubdomain.com.

BZ/Rights & Permissions (www.bzrights.com) also offers accurate public domain listings in their publication *The Mini-Encyclopedia of Public Domain Songs,* which lists the 800 best-known works in the public domain as well as information on composers to help determine copyright status of music throughout the world.

Record Research Inc. (www.recordresearch.com) has put out *Pop Memories, 1890–1954,* which presents in chronological order a detailed list of hit record-ings of each year and an artist-by-artist listing of over 12,000 songs.

A similar source based on song titles is found in a handy listing of a limited number of public domain songs in the ASCAP booklet *ASCAP Hit Songs.* The hit songs are listed by year, beginning in 1892. Among the well-known songs dated before 1923 are such classics as "Sidewalks of New York," "Sweet Rosie O'Grady," "Gypsy Love Song," "St. Louis Blues," "There's a Long, Long Trail," and "Alexander's Ragtime Band," as well as such recent additions as "Down by the O-Hi-O," "The Japanese Sandman," and "Avalon," George Gershwin's "Swanee," and Irving Berlin's "A Pretty Girl Is Like a Melody."

Copyright Registration of New Versions and Arrangements of Works

When filing for registration of a new version of copyright material, a copyright claimant must designate the new matter on which the claim is based; however, this designation rarely appears on printed copies of the music. For instance, a new arrangement of "The Star Spangled Banner" may show a copyright notice for the year 2003 in the same manner and form as would appear on a new and original composition. Therefore, it may be necessary to look up the application for registration in the Copyright Office to determine the new matter for which protection is claimed.

The Copyright Act dictates that applications for copyright registration of a compilation or derivative work include "an identification of any preexisting work or works that it is based on or incorporates, and a brief general statement of the additional material covered by the copyright claim being registered." The Committee on the Judiciary of the House of Representatives has stated Congress's intent that the "application covering a collection such as a songbook or hymnal would clearly reveal any works in the collection that are in the public domain, and the copyright status of all other previously published compositions. This information will be readily available in the Copyright Office."

As discussed in Chapter 10, application for copyright registration of works of the performing arts, including musical compositions, is made on Form PA. Item 5 of the form contains questions designed to determine whether an earlier registration has been made for the work and, if so, whether there is any basis for a new registration. Item 6 of the form calls for information on compilations or derivative works and requests the identification of any preexisting work that the current work is based on or incorporates: for example, "Compilation of 19th-Century Military Songs." It also asks that the applicant give a brief general statement of the additional new material covered by the copyright claim for which registration is sought.

The Copyright Office has stated previously that "new matter may consist of musical arrangement, compilation, editorial revision, and the like, as well as additional words and music." Thus, if a new folio of public domain works is published, a claim of copyright may be based on a "new compilation" if nothing else has been added to the public domain works. Another possible description of added material might be "new compilation, fingering, stress marks, and introductory material." Claims premised on new lyrics should show where the new lyrics occur, such as "new first and third verses." Most claims based on a new music arrangement merely designate in what lines the changed arrangement occurs, if limited to specified lines; if there is a new musical version arranged for soprano, alto, bass, etc., a statement to that effect may be made.

It is unfortunate for users that the designation of new material occurs only on official applications and is not available for inspection except in the files of the Copyright Office in Washington. However, it is only the deposited copy of the work that may not be copied; copies of applications may be ordered, with or without the consent of the claimant. A copy of the application can be obtained by supplying the details of the registration number from a search report and paying a fee in accordance with the form supplied by the Copyright Office.

13

Arrangements and Adaptations

The public does not hear songs or see them in written form until arrangements of the songs have been made. Songs usually require some development by arrangers, whose efforts may vary from mere transposition of keys and elaboration of chord structures to more creative work. Foreign-language songs are rarely presented to the American public with foreign lyrics; foreign lyrics must be substantially revised, and not just translated, in view of the necessary adaptation of rhyme and accents.

Jazz performers commonly make such substantial revisions to the basic song that it would take an expert musicologist to identify the source of the melodic material. Many rock and roll singers make their own impromptu arrangements of songs while performing, sometimes due to their inability to read music as well as to their desire for spontaneity.

The vital impact of rock music on the role of the arranger is well described in Milt Okun's *Great Songs of the Sixties:*

> What basically happened was that the rhythm section, consisting of
> bass, guitar, drums and piano, which formerly gave the underpinning
> to a band, stepped to the front and became the whole band . . . .
> Since most of the excitement comes from rhythmic development,
> plus improvisation, the trained arranger is not needed. Now there is
> arranging by group. One by-product of rock thus has been the unem-
> ployment of arrangers . . . . Music . . . has been stripped down to pure
> rhythm, or rhythms, categorized . . . with beat-specific names like hard
> house, techstep, jungle and speed garage . . . . On a hip-hop radio
> station . . . all that matters is the beat, the lyric and the grain of a voice.

Head Arrangements of Compositions

The traditional order of creative services goes from composer, to arranger, orchestrator, and copyist, to finished music fit for performance or recording.

However, with many forms of popular music—reggae, rap, hip-hop, dance, world, rhythm and blues, country, and others—there is more spontaneous development of music by "head arrangements" or layered recordings, and some of the traditional functions merge, and some may disappear entirely. When musicians do not read music, they develop alternative means to the end of arrangement and orchestration. Furthermore, when producers have a strong influence on a record session, they often perform the orchestrator and arranger role.

When tracks or "beats" are laid down before the addition of words and/or melody, the arrangement actually precedes the composing and there is confusion as to whether the underlying track is merely an arrangement of the resulting song or is a musical portion of the resulting song. This is even more confusing if the same track is used for successive competitive versions under different titles. When sampling of existing recorded music is used, the sample is sometimes the underlying track and thus is an arrangement in fully orchestrated form waiting for retroactive permission to be granted for inclusion.

The Copyrighting of Arrangements

Under the Copyright Act, arrangements may be copyrighted only if they are made by the copyright owner of the original work or with the owner's consent. Arrangements used on popular records rarely qualify for copyrighting under either of these conditions. The copyright owner, whether publisher or writer, ordinarily does not prepare the record arrangement and makes no claim for copyright in the arrangement. Moreover, the music publisher rarely gives consent to copyrighting the arrangement prepared for a recording of the song, and thus no copyright is taken by anyone in the arrangement used. The copyright owner issues a more or less standard mechanical license to record, which in practice is considered to indicate that no objection will be made to the arrangements required for purposes of recording. The license in this instance amounts to an agreement not to object rather than a consent or grant of rights. However, arrangements of works in the public domain may qualify for copyrighting without the consent of the former copyright owner.

There can be no question that in popular music the English-language version of a foreign song is truly a new version that requires creative effort over and above mechanical translation. English versions are nearly always undertaken on assignment from the music publisher controlling the basic copyright; unlike arrangements for purposes of record company sessions, the publisher will claim a further copyright in the new lyric version and the author of the new version will be given credit and royalties.

Arrangers and producer-arrangers rarely have any relationship with the music publisher and achieve no copyright status; they receive compensation solely from the record company or artists. Some arrangers do work directly for or with music publishers and printed music licensees, and the employer may obtain copyrights on their arrangements. These arrangers are the musically knowledgeable and trained persons who prepare songs for printing in sheet music, orchestration, or folio form. Frequently the songs have already been recorded. Separate arrangements may be required for single instruments and voice and for the diverse parts for different instruments in bands and orchestras. These arrangers are customarily employed on a weekly salary or assignment basis, with no right to royalties, and although their names may sometimes appear on the printed edition, as employees for hire they acquire no rights in the copyright or in renewal copyrights. The employer is considered the author of the work and the initial copyright owner. The arranger of a recorded work qualifies for American Federation of Musicians status as a union member with minimum payment standards plus other union benefits.

The Statutory Treatment of Arrangements

In the past there were disputes as to whether the person preparing musical arrangements was an employee acting within the scope of his or her employment or an independent contractor. The Copyright Act of 1976 clarifies the status of works prepared on special order or commission for use "as a supplementary work." Under the Act, if the parties expressly agree in writing that a supplementary work shall be considered to be "a work made for hire," the agreement is binding and the employer is regarded as the author and initial owner of the copyright. The act specifically defines "musical arrangements" as supplementary works for which such an agreement can be made.

The Copyright Act sets certain standards for permissible arrangements in sound recordings in connection with provisions for compulsory licenses. Under Section 115 of the Act there can be a compulsory license for making and distributing phonorecords of a work once they have been distributed to the public in the United States under authority of the copyright owner. A compulsory license permits the "making of a musical arrangement of the work to the extent necessary to conform it to the style or manner of interpretation of the performance." But the compulsory licensee cannot "change the basic melody or fundamental character of the work." The arrangement is not "subject to protection as a derivative work . . . except with the express consent of the copyright owner."

No Effect on Duration of Basic Work

The nature of musical arrangements or English-lyric versions assumes the prior existence of the basic work. A question arises as to whether the "derivative work," founded as it is on an earlier composition, has the effect of prolonging the term of copyright in the basic work. The Copyright Office has stated simply that the "protection for a copyrighted work cannot be lengthened by republishing the work with new matter." The Copyright Act of 1976 provides that the copyright in the derivative work "is independent of, and does not affect or enlarge the scope, duration, ownership, or subsistence of, any copyright protection in the pre-existing material."

In practical effect, however, copyrighted new versions created during the copyright term of the basic work may cause the public to accept the new version in place of the basic work, and the publisher may thereby obtain the benefit of the longer copyright term for the new version. Under the Copyright Act of 1976, the term of copyright runs until the 95th year following publication or the 100th year following creation, whichever is earlier, for new versions of a work created by an arranger who is an employee for hire.

Standards of Originality

Not all arrangements are capable of copyright protection, even if they are prepared with the consent of the copyright owner or if the basic work is in the public domain. An element of creative authorship must be involved, but how much is a matter of qualitative judgment that may eventually require judicial determination in case of conflict. The Copyright Office does not claim to compare the new arrangement with the basic work; it does require the copyright claimant to state what new material has been added. Its position is that "when only a few slight variations or minor additions of no substance have been made, or when the revisions or added material consist solely of uncopyrightable elements, registration is not possible."

There are no maximum boundaries on the extent of originality and creativity that can be contributed by arrangements. Béla Bartók once commented that it often takes more skill to make a qualified orchestral arrangement of a folk tune, while being loyal to its origins, than to write an entirely original work. The melodic basis of Brahms's "Academic Festival Overture" is found in the student songs of his day; similarly, Beethoven's "Country Dances" were developed from contemporary folk dances. Bach used already existing hymns in most of his chorales; for this reason he is considered one of the greatest arrangers in history. The great originality and creativity of each of these masterpieces lie in the development of the material.

The minimum requirements of originality and creativity for copyrightable arrangements are indefinite. Courts have made analogies to the rejection of patents for improvements "which a good mechanic could make." In 1850, in *Jollie v. Jaques* (13 Fed. Cas. 910), the Circuit Court for the Southern District of New York stated:

> The composition of a new air or melody is entitled to protection.... If the new air be substantially the same as the old, it is no doubt a piracy.... The musical composition contemplated by the statute must, doubtless, be substantially a new and original work, and not a copy of a piece already produced, with additions and variations, which a writer of music with experience and skill might readily make.

Applying these requirements, a later court rejected a claim of copyright infringement on an arrangement of public domain music even in the face of clear proof of copying. The new material in the arrangement, as copied by the defendant, involved adding an alto part and a few notes and rhythmical beats to smooth the transposition from Russian to English lyrics; the English words were not copied. Another court held that a student's piano collection of songs in the public domain could be protected as having "at least a modicum of creative work." This included editorial ingenuity in "fingering, dynamic marks, tempo indications, slurs and phrasing." The court also recognized some value in an original editorial grouping of a series of public domain works, together with original titles. [See *Lindsay Norden v. Oliver Ditson Co. Inc.,* 28 U.S. Pata. Q. 183 (D. Mass. 1936).]

The determination of a "modicum of creative work" may be difficult. In one case a Sicilian sailor was fortunate to have a bad memory and insufficient musical training, since his necessarily improvisational versions of folk songs were deemed to warrant a copyright. In another instance a respected teacher of music theory who was a choirmaster was found to have followed an original melody too faithfully to qualify for an arrangement copyright.

The decision by a leading California copyright jurist, the late Judge Leon R. Yankwich, sheds some light on the rationale for denying copyright to changes that could be developed by any experienced writer. Judge Yankwich said that too broad a basis of copyright in arrangements would lead to restricting the use of many works. It would result in permitting a Charles Laughton to forbid other actors from portraying Henry VIII in the same creative manner as that which he employed or in a Sir Laurence Olivier monopolizing the innovations in his portrayal of Hamlet. Judge Yankwich felt that a basic copyrighted work should not be subject to division into segments to the detriment of the original author or, in the case of works in the public domain, to the detriment of the public.

An important practical consideration in determining the extent of originality or creativity to be required by a court is the reluctance of members of the judiciary to qualify themselves as art or music experts. In *Bleistein v. Donaldson,* 188 U.S. 239, 250 (1903), Justice Oliver Wendell Holmes stated the prevalent judicial position, which is equally applicable to music and art:

> It would be a dangerous undertaking for persons trained only to the law to constitute themselves final judges of the worth of pictorial illustrations, outside of the narrowest and most obvious limits. At the one extreme some works of genius would be sure to miss appreciation. Their very novelty would make them repulsive until the public had learned the new language in which their author spoke. It may be more than doubted, for instance, whether the etchings of Goya or the paintings of Manet would have been sure of protection when seen for the first time. At the other end, copyright would be denied to pictures which appealed to a public less educated than the judge.

This refusal to become a critic of art and music is not just an expression of judicial modesty; it is essential for the orderly and efficient operation of the courts. The judge who passes on the minimum standards of originality or creativity of an arrangement (standards that are equally applicable to a completely new composition) does not have to put a stamp of cultural approval on the piece. In the words of the late Judge Sylvester Ryan of the U.S. District Court for the Southern District of New York, a judge must merely find sufficient "fingerprints of the composition" in the arrangement or succession of musical notes that can "establish its identity."

Derivative Works

The Copyright Act defines a *derivative work* as one that involves the recasting, transformation, or adaptation of a prior work. Among the examples given are musical arrangements and lyric versions of formerly instrumental works.

Musical arrangements are rarely categorized as derivative works because there are generally no major changes to the original. But an immediate practical effect of adding lyrics to instrumental works is the sharing of writer royalties and performing rights society credits. If the previous work is relatively dormant and can only achieve commercial value through the suggested change, the original composer is unlikely to object to the sharing of his or her income. But the composer of an established and popular work may resent the new writer who "horns in" on the original material, except where it is used in conjunction with the lyric, the new title of the lyric version, or other new arrangement.

The original writer and the publisher will be concerned with the selection of the new writer, the authorship credit, the publishing rights to be acquired from the writer, whether the writer will be credited with future earnings on the instrumental version as well as the new lyric version, and whether there will be a contractual limitation on obtaining still another lyric version.

Since the music publisher usually selects and engages the lyricist or arranger, the publisher may protect itself and the original writer contractually from some of the problems arising with derivative works. The Copyright Act makes special provisions for an arranger, by express agreement in writing, to be treated as an employee for hire, with all rights under copyright in the publisher as author. In the absence of such an agreement, the arranger or the new lyricist may still be an employee for hire acting in the course of his or her employment. Where there is an employee for hire, all rights under copyright for the new versions reside in the publisher, subject only to agreed-upon accounting and credit obligations. No right to terminate the grant of rights to the publisher at any time will vest in the new arranger or adaptor or his or her statutory heirs or successors. For the protection of the original writer, the agreement with the lyricist or arranger can provide that the first writer will continue to receive all writer royalties for the use of the earlier material in its original form.

As for works originating on or after January 1, 1978, the Copyright Act states that the owner of a lawful derivative work can continue to use and license prior uses of that work despite the exercise by an author of his or her right of termination. In the case of relatively simple musical arrangements of pre-existing works, questions arise as to whether the resultant works are the derivative works contemplated by the statute. It may be assumed that only arrangements with sufficient originality to be copyrightable will result in derivative works envisaged by the Act.

As an example, the legislative history refers to motion pictures, which may continue to be used despite termination by authors. Congress recognized that the continuing use of a multimillion-dollar investment in creating a motion picture version based on a prior published story or novel should not be jeopardized by the statutory heirs of the author of the prior literary work. Likewise, the continuing ownership of substantial new lyrics in an otherwise terminated song may well qualify the publisher-owner of such revised lyrics to continue to exercise rights in the entire song when such lyrics are used, notwithstanding termination of the earlier version.

Arranger credits were involved in the case of "When the Red, Red Robin Comes Bob, Bob Bobbin' Along" [*Woods v. Bourne Co.*, 60 F.3d 978 (2d Cir. 1995)]. This was a test action supported by the Songwriters Guild of America to contest the claim of the former publisher that, notwithstanding a valid termination of publishing grants, the old publisher continued to be entitled to receive ASCAP publisher credits when old records containing prior arrangements were performed.

After a full trial, the district court ruled that although musical arrangements are recognized as a possible derivative use to be protected against termination, the words should not be read in a vacuum. The court ruled that a mere cocktail piano arrangement or preparation of arrangement for sheet music or folio use does not qualify for a claim to all recorded renditions of the song involved. It is well known that most commercial recordings rely on the recording artist's own arrangement and not the standard sheet music form. In addition, the court recognized that it is likely that the arrangement as presented in the published sheet music might very well be substantially based on the original composer's demonstration version even though a simple lead sheet may have been the only registered version.

The court considered numerous versions of the one song and concluded that, except for a major choral version such as that by Fred Waring's Pennsylvanians, there was not sufficient showing that the publisher contributed copyrightable derivative material sufficient to stand on its own. The court required "unusual" new material rather than routine arrangement. In this respect, the *Bourne* court held that derivative works must have more than trivial variations for the former owner to qualify for continuing rights in the arranged version notwithstanding a termination, by the original creator's heirs, of the original grant of rights to the former owner.

Prior to the *Bourne case,* there was an important Supreme Court decision concerning the 1923 song "Who's Sorry Now" and the effects of termination by the statutory heirs. The original publisher, while acknowledging that termination had effectively taken place, relied upon the same specific exception of the statute allowing the former publisher to continue to collect royalties where a derivative work had been created prior to the termination. The publisher successfully asserted that a sound recording is a derivative work and that, although the recording artist is unlikely to have used standard sheet music arrangements prepared by that publisher, the statutory exception nevertheless accrues to the benefit of the original publisher. Thus, any flow of continuing mechanical royalties on such earlier recording under its original license from the former publisher would accrue to the original licensing publisher and not to the statutory heirs who attempted to terminate such status.

Sound Recording Sound-Alikes

Under the Copyright Act, the copyright owner of a sound recording cannot prevent the making or duplication of another sound recording that uses sounds (for example, an artist recording another version of a previously recorded song), even though the later recording imitates or simulates the earlier copyrighted recording. In effect, the copyright owner cannot prohibit cover records or sound-alike records that imitate the earlier recording. In this sense there is no protection of arrangements made for record company sessions.

The Arrangement of Works in the Public Domain

The contracts of many record companies state that the recording artist grants to the label a free mechanical right license for copyrighted arrangements of songs in the public domain that are recorded and controlled by the artist. This results in greater profits to the record company since there are no mechanical royalties to be paid. Where special provision is not made, normal mechanical license fees are charged for the use of copyrighted arrangements of public domain compositions.

ASCAP and BMI pay substantial performance monies to writers and publishers of copyrighted arrangements of works in the public domain. ASCAP has various categories calling for payment of 2 to 100 percent of the credit available for an original song:

- ► For nonreligious works copyrighted only in a printed folio: 2 percent
- ► For songs separately copyrighted and published or, lacking publication, for songs that are primarily instrumental works and available on a rental basis: 10 percent
- ► For new lyrics: 35 percent
- ► For new lyrics and a new title: 50 percent

- For changes in the music: 10 to 50 percent
- For transferring a primarily instrumental work from one medium to another: 35 percent

BMI pays performance monies for copyrighted arrangements of works in the public domain at a rate based on administrative valuation of the new material, up to 100 percent of the rate applicable to original songs.

Some folk artists and folk music publishers engage in unethical practices by changing song titles without modifying the lyrics or melody. They may claim full originality when they are really only "finders" of songs in the public domain. They register copyrights to such songs, claiming they are "original" works, and fail to set forth accurately the limited amount of any new material, thereby falsely and unfairly obtaining the benefit of the Copyright Act of 1976 provision that places the burden of proof of the invalidity of a certificate of copyright registration on an unauthorized user. This burden may be extremely difficult to sustain because the copyright claimant, as the true finder of songs in the public domain, may be the only witness who can describe the source of the particular song and may be unwilling to admit the public domain origin. The finder of such a song who wishes to legally protect his or her discovery may embellish it with new copyrightable material.

An additional category of new copyrightable versions of songs in the public domain is based on the compilation of parts of different compositions. While copyright cannot be obtained on a segment of a public domain work, the linking of various segments may require such an editorial creative endeavor, aside from original bridge music, that copyright will subsist in the collection as such. The "folk process" of developing folk songs by endless passage from person to person tends to add compilation material. The end product, a song in the hands of a finder, may still be a public domain work. However, the fashioning of a compilation composition by combining, say, a prison folk song with a riverboat work song and perhaps adding another bit or piece from other sources, may result in a copyrightable work.

Foreign Treatment of Arrangements and Adaptations

England, France, and some other major nations differ from the United States in their treatment of writers of arrangements, adaptations, translations, and other new versions. They do not require consent for the second copyright to arise. However, they insist on consent of *both* the original-version proprietor and the second-version owner before use. This results in a parallel set of protective rights that, without prejudice to the original owner, safeguards the creator of the second version.

In the past, the local performing rights societies in France and other European countries recognized the rights of arrangers of copyrighted published vocal works and generally allocated to them two-twelfths of the total performance royalties payable to writers and publishers. This was deductible from the total writer royalties, which for works of European origin usually equal eight-twelfths of the entire performance royalties payable to writers and publishers. If a sub-published work had both a local lyric writer and an arranger, the continental society would ordinarily allocate the two-twelfths between them. This practice was, in effect, an unfair "cut-in" of a local member, who would thus be paid at the expense of U.S. and British songwriters whose original songs were recorded by U.S. or British recording artists without any French or other foreign arrangements. The excuse for what appears to be an injustice was that it was too difficult to distinguish a Frank Sinatra recording of a song from a local recorded cover version. The same situation occurred with regard to lyric adopters of English-language songs into local-language versions. However, in 1991 CISAC, the umbrella organization for various national collection societies, adopted the so-called Amalfi resolution, whereby deductions from royalties due to the original writer are made only when the new version is actually performed. Unfortunately, many societies have not altered their databases with respect to the old catalogs and apply the Amalfi resolution only prospectively, from January 1, 1992.

Concerning noncopyrighted works, foreign continental societies normally have plans for grading arrangements in accordance with the amount of original work done by the arranger, and the arranger's share of performance royalties is determined by this grading.

14

Performing Rights Organizations

One of the greatest sources of revenue in the music industry comes from public performance payments collected and distributed by the major performing rights organizations. Yet the basis of operation of these organizations was nonexistent until 1897 because Congress had failed to include public performance rights within the copyright statute prior to that date. Even after its inclusion in the statute, there was no practical way to collect substantial monies, since only less important sources such as concerts, dance halls, and cabarets were available before the development of broadcasting, and the numerous copyright owners were not sufficiently organized to license and collect.

Today there are three performing rights organizations in the United States, and they perform valuable services for their members. All three have Web sites that provide information both to members and to nonmember users who want to learn more about the often complex world of performance rights societies. They collect substantial sums of money on behalf of their membership. As of December 31, 2000, ASCAP announced record revenues of over $635 million. It later made a retroactive distribution, in February 2001, of $60 million, collected from Viacom (owner of MTV), in settlement of disputed license fees. The best available comparative figure for BMI, for the fiscal year ending June 2001, was $540.8 million (exclusive of its own subsequent Viacom settlement) compared with $502.9 million for the prior fiscal year. SESAC, a privately held licensing organization, does not release its financial report. However, in a 1990 court proceeding concerning pay cable, it was determined that SESAC had 3 percent market share, compared to 43 percent for BMI and 54 percent for ASCAP. Here is the breakdown of major revenue sources for each of the three organizations.

	Television	Radio	Other Domestic	Foreign
ASCAP	33.84%	29.16%	14%	21%
BMI	33.45	30.89	13.94	21.72
SESAC	32	55	13	

Performance Monies and the World Economy

In its annual survey for the year 2000 (the most recent available), The National Music Publishers' Association reported that music publishing revenues worldwide amounted to nearly $8.1 billion, based on a flat currency exchange rate. There is little doubt that this figure dropped between 5 and 10 percent in both 2001 and 2002. Tables 14-1 and 14-2 show that performance revenues vary from country to country and catalog to catalog, but they are a significant part of the economy.

Table 14-1

Revenues from Music Performance and Reproduction-Based Income for Select Countries in 2000 ($ millions)

Country	Performance-Based Income*	Phonomechanical	Synchronization
United States	$811.90	$691.49	$156.72
Germany	316.03	258.67	67.76
Japan	283.17	311.32	80.51
United Kingdom	250.72	195.85	124.64
Worldwide	3,076.31	1,995.31	669.89

*Includes radio, television, cable, satellite, and live and recorded performances.

Source: NMPA International Survey.

Table 14-2

Breakdown for Publishers' Incomes, 1998

Publisher	Mechanical	Performance	Synchronization	Print*
EMI Music	54%	36%	10%	
Warner/Chappell	47%	33%	8%	12%
Peer Music	63%	25%	12%	

Warner/Chappell is a prominent independent printer; other publishers do not provide separate figures, but include print revenues in the total for mechanical license revenues.

Source: MBI, February 1999, p. ix.

Clearing Functions

Despite frequent grumbling by radio broadcasters at the necessity for paying sums akin to a gross receipts tax to performing rights organizations for the right to play music, it is generally conceded that without such organizations inordinate expense and chaos would result. There would be endless searches and bargaining for performing rights involving the owners of both established and obscure songs. Each station would require copyright clearance experts and would undergo programming delays while contacting the owners for each performance. The concept of a general clearance agency for a large group of music rights, undertaking a uniform system of collection and payment, is necessary for the orderly supply of music to radio stations. If it were not so, the government might close all performing rights organizations on the grounds of violation of antitrust laws.

A Solicitor General's brief, submitted to the U.S. Supreme Court in 1967, supported a lower court finding.

> A central licensing agency such as ASCAP is the only practical way that copyright proprietors may enjoy their rights under the federal copyright laws and that broadcasters and others may conveniently obtain licenses for the performance of copyrighted music. [The lower court] found that single copyright owners cannot deal individually with all users or individually police the use of their songs; and that a single radio station may broadcast as many as 60,000 performances of musical compositions involving as many as 6,000 separate compositions.

The staggering number of musical compositions currently available for broadcast—well into the millions—further demonstrates the necessity of central licensing. BMI, for example, now reports that each year it analyzes TV music totaling 6 million hours and radio airplay of approximately 400,000 hours. ASCAP does likewise for what it categorizes as "billions of performances licensed annually."

In general, all three organizations operate on a blanket license basis whereby their full catalogs are available to the licensed station or other user. There also exists a special per-program license applicable to programs such as news and sports where music is a minor component. The costs and delays involved in processing per-program licenses have resulted in the creation of service firms which report on specific music uses requiring per-program licenses, make provision for meeting monthly payment requirements, and monitor reporting requirements. Two such firms are Music Reports, Inc. (www.musicreports.com) and W. G. Slantz (www.wgslantz.com).

After many years of lobbying, the performing rights organizations and their author and publisher members and affiliates were able to engineer the repeal of the statutory exemption of jukeboxes in the Copyright Act, resulting in modest new sources of revenue. However, lobbying is a two-way street, as shown by the so-called Fairness in Music Licensing Act of 1998, under which small restaurant and café owners secured an exemption at the expense of the performing rights organizations as part of negotiations in Congress for passage of the Copyright Term Extension Act. Additional licensing sources established under the Copyright Act are retransmissions by cable broadcasters and by public and educational broadcasters.

The area of college concert dates is a continuing source of revenues for performing rights organizations. It was formerly assumed that college concerts were to be specially treated as low-budget nonprofit events largely in the field of serious music. However, popular artists regularly appear at college stadiums and halls before large audiences on a profitable tour basis having little or no relationship to the college's nonprofit educational purpose. Higher performing rights music fees have been required for college concerts in recent years.

American Society of Composers, Authors, and Publishers (ASCAP)

Founded in 1914, ASCAP is a membership organization. In early 2002, ASCAP had over 90,000 writers and 44,000 publishers, with new members being elected every month. ASCAP claims to have the oldest and largest repertoire in the United States, adding approximately 100,000 new titles annually. It gets its money by issuing a *blanket license* for its entire catalog to radio and television stations; the fee is based not on the extent of music use but on gross receipts of the station minus certain adjustments, such as agency commissions and wire charges. Its basic rate is just under 2 percent of the stations' adjusted gross receipts.

ASCAP pays an equal amount to publishers as a group and to writers as a group after an actual overhead deduction. In 2001, ASCAP's overhead expense was about 14 percent of total receipts, down from 16 percent in 1998 and 19 percent in 1994. ASCAP also deducts the cost of distributing royalties received from foreign societies, which has averaged between 3 and 4 percent of receipts in recent years.

Two of the most noteworthy services on the ASCAP Web site (www.ascap.com) are ASCAP's ACE on the Web and Internet licensing. The ACE on the Web feature is a song database that allows the user to search and identify songs in the ASCAP repertory. The service, which is updated weekly, identifies the credited authors/composers, the publisher, and the address of the administrator, as well as many of the artists who recorded the work. In 1998, ASCAP proudly announced that it was the first performance rights organization to make a distribution for licensed Internet performances. The amount was $100,000. In 2000, the Internet distribution was $2 million. On its New Media and Internet Licensing page, ASCAP offers downloadable license forms and a good-faith estimate of user costs through its RateCalc questionnaire. (See Chapter 42, page 408, for more information on RateCalc.)

ASCAP, primarily through the ASCAP Foundation (www.ascapfoundation.org), is a prominent benefactor of the musical arts, funding scholarships and competitive awards for songwriters, composers, musicians, and vocalists, and sponsoring workshops and artist-in-residence programs and community and secondary school outreach programs.

Broadcast Music Inc. (BMI)

BMI, a competitor of ASCAP, was established in 1940 in a move to increase competition and, according to BMI, to give an alternative to writers and publishers not represented by ASCAP. As of 2002, BMI represented about 300,000 songwriters and publishers. Its catalog consists of 4.5 million works. Like ASCAP, BMI operates primarily under blanket licenses and charges broadcasters a fee based on formulas applied to adjusted gross receipts. The BMI radio rate is less than ASCAP's—about 1.6 percent of adjusted gross receipts—and its television and general use licensing rates are also somewhat lower than ASCAP's. Although BMI is not technically a nonprofit organization, it has always operated on a break-even basis. BMI currently operates in three distinct administrative territories: Nashville, which covers the Southeast to Texas; Los Angeles, which handles everything west of the Rocky Mountains; and New York City, which handles the rest. It also has offices in London and Miami.

In 1976, BMI/Canada transferred its ownership and operations to a Canadian trust (PRO/Canada). In 1990, the two Canadian societies merged their operations to form the Society of Composers, Authors & Music Publishers of Canada (SOCAN).

The BMI Web site (www.bmi.com) offers a number of innovative services such as HyperRepertoire, the Songwriter's Toolbox, and the Licensing Toolbox. The HyperRepertoire service is an Internet song database that allows the user to search by song title, artist, publisher, or writer's name. The Songwriter's Toolbox is a unique educational service that provides information intended to assist songwriters to better understand what BMI does by providing an overview of performance rights, songwriting, music publishing, and copyright. Another part of BMI's educational services, the Licensing Toolbox, gives potential licensees a crash course on how to license music for public performance via radio, TV cable, and the Internet. BMI also has a feature that allows artists to review their catalogs and royalty statements online.

Like ASCAP, BMI is a significant supporter of the musical arts, sponsoring workshops and competitions around the country. In 2002, these included a number of BMI student composer awards and the BMI Foundation Peter Carpenter Fellowship for Aspiring Film Composers.

Society of European Stage Authors & Composers (SESAC)

SESAC, the smallest of the three performing rights organizations in the United States, is a private licensing company founded in 1930 and presently owned by Stephen Swid, Ira Smith, Freddie Gershon, and the investment banking firm of Allen and Company. The organization represents 8,000 publishers and writers and has a catalog of more than 200,000 compositions. It differs from BMI and ASCAP in that it allocates negotiated shares to its publisher and writer affiliates, after first deducting overhead expenses, with SESAC retaining the balance as its profits. SESAC substantially increased its status when Bob Dylan and Neil Diamond switched their writer and publisher catalogs to SESAC, reportedly for substantial financial inducements. SESAC is headquartered in Nashville and maintains offices in New York, London, and Los Angeles.

Fees charged by SESAC to licensees differ from those charged by ASCAP and BMI inasmuch as they are based on fixed determinants, such as market population served by the station and the station's standard advertising rates, rather than on a percent of gross receipts. SESAC uses a national rate card, applicable to all its broadcast licensees, which gives consideration to the factors of market classification (population) and spot rate. Fees for a full-time AM radio station range from $330 to $7,200 per year. A typical AM station, with an average market population of 300,000 and a maximum 1-minute advertising spot rate of $30, pays an annual fee of $1,020. Like ASCAP and BMI, SESAC licenses virtually the entire broadcasting industry. License fees for other users are also determined by relevant market factors. For instance, cable fees are based on subscriber audience numbers; college and university fees on student enrollment; and hotel fees on room rates, live or mechanical music use, and the number of rooms.

SESAC's Web site (www.sesac.com) offers services similar to those offered by BMI and ASCAP. SESAC's version of the on-line song database is called, simply, SESAC Repertory On-line. The database allows the user to perform a song title search, writer search, and publisher search. SESAC's Web site also offers the user information on licensing and the ability to download certain license forms and request others. The SESAC Web site also offers on-line song registration, as well as on-line password-protected access to members' catalogs and accounts. SESAC licensees can update and review their account balances on-line.

Title Registration

When new members join one of the organizations, they cannot sit back and expect works to be recognized for surveying and distribution purposes without registering the titles. Titles may be registered on paper forms, PC disks, or Macintosh disks. All three formats are available from ASCAP. As of 1995, ASCAP reported that 62 percent of its new titles were registered electronically. Bilingual Spanish-English registration is also possible.

ASCAP's Title Registration Information Center will, on request, supply computer-generated lists of all the member's registered works by title, along with a summary count of total titles.

When a song is administered by an ASCAP publisher, the writer does not need to register it. However, when a song has *not* been placed with an ASCAP publisher, it is essential that the writer register the work if it is expected to generate any broadcast, concert, or other ASCAP-logged performances. Furthermore, ASCAP does not independently record transfers, renewals, and terminations from the Copyright Office. When a song is transferred or subject to recapture by way of copyright renewal or termination, the writer should qualify as a publisher member and register the transferred composition. Failure to do this may result in payments being misdirected to the benefit of the former registrant. It is essential to trigger the new registration by complying with registration rules.

BMI uses the standard paper clearance form and the Automated Title System for registration of new works. When a work is assigned, even if recorded for assignment at the U.S. Copyright Office, BMI does not pick up the information unless specifically informed by the interested parties. BMI requires written documentation from both parties to change their records and further requests the effective date of the assignment.

SESAC uses both the newly created Common Works Registration electronic format and paper clearance.

Surveying Procedures

ASCAP and BMI both employ extensive systems of surveying and statistical sampling of actual broadcasts to determine monies to be paid to writers and publishers. Each television network performance is surveyed and credited for payment purposes by both organizations on the basis of an actual arithmetic count, without resorting to sampling. This is possible because the networks and the program producers supply program logs and music cue sheets to the performing rights organizations. ASCAP and BMI also make tapes of network television performances to verify the accuracy of the information furnished by the networks and program producers.

Tabulating performances on local radio stations necessarily involves statistical sampling; samples are multiplied by formulas established by leading statisticians who are selected separately by each organization. The formulas are used in order to have the sample represent most fairly total national performances without undertaking the inordinate expense of a universal count. Although BMI alleges that it samples more radio hours per annum than ASCAP, ASCAP asserts that its approach is sufficient to achieve fairness and equity.

The sampling methods used by ASCAP and BMI are also applied to local television performances other than syndicated programs, feature films, and movies of the week. ASCAP supplements its sampling techniques by reference to cue sheets and to *TV Guide* program listings (which include some 95 regional editions). In addition to references to cue sheets, since 1991 BMI has used television broadcast information compiled by a company called TV Data, which BMI claims offers more comprehensive coverage than *TV Guide*.

As of 2002, ASCAP expanded its "true count" survey, as distinct from sampling, as follows:

- ▸ All programs on network television, ABC, NBC, and CBS, and all Fox, Paramount, Warner Brothers, PAX, and Univision networks
- ▸ All PBS programs on stations paying more than $20,000 annually

- ▶ Major cable TV such as A&E, American Movie Classics, BET, Cartoon Network, Comedy Central, Country Music TV, Discovery, Disney, E!Entertainment, Encore, Lifetime, Family Channel, HBO, History, Showtime, and Turner Classic
- ▶ Local syndicated television programs, feature films, and movies of the week as well as all locally produced programs where ASCAP gets paid on a per-program basis
- ▶ Live concerts: All songs performed in the 200 top-grossing concert tours and other selected major live performance venues covering feature headliners and opening acts as well as live symphonic and recital concerts where the artist is paid over $1,500
- ▶ Background and foreground music services: FM satellite services of Muzak, The Environmental Channel, and the On-Premise and Star Tracks satellite services of AEI
- ▶ Other media: Ringling Bros. Circus, Disney on Ice, and Radio City Music Hall holiday shows

When relying upon samples instead of census counts, both ASCAP and BMI statistically weight the samples received in accordance with the size and importance of the surveyed station and the time of day of the program. ASCAP's method involves weighting their samples relative to the percentage of dollar receipts from the station involved. BMI also adjusts for the economic importance of the station-licensee by paying more for a Radio 1 network station performance than for a Radio 2 radio performance. Under BMI standards, a Radio 1 station is one that, in the year before the performance, paid a BMI license fee in the top 25 percent of all BMI radio station license fees. A Radio 2 station on a comparable basis paid a license fee in the bottom 75 percent of all BMI radio station license fees. The formula for BMI distribution to its affiliates is published on their Web page under Songwriter's Toolbox. Amounts payable are equal between writers and publishers of each applicable song except where there is an agreement to pay the publisher less than 50 percent, in which case the extra amount is automatically credited to the writer's account.

In 1993, SESAC formed a division called SESAC Latina, which was dedicated to representing Spanish-language music. SESAC Latina formed an alliance with Broadcast Data Systems (BDS) to employ its monitoring system to track performances and distribute royalties based on BDS data. Two years later, SESAC expanded its BDS usage to track affiliates' music across all major radio formats.

For radio formats not monitored by BDS, such as jazz and contemporary Christian, SESAC uses its chart payment system, which makes royalty payments based on chart positions in major trade publications, such as *Billboard, Radio and Records,* and *College Music Journal.* Although SESAC does not use a weighting system as such, it uses the peak position reached by a song in those publications' charts to determine the song's compensation. Distributions are made quarterly, with a goal of creating a 3-month gap between actual performance and payment.

SESAC uses TV data and cue sheets to track television and cable performances for its affiliates. In 1998, SESAC signed an agreement with Aris Technologies to use its MusiCode digital watermarking system for broadcast monitoring and royalty distribution. With MusiCode, segments of music as short as 3 seconds can be identified. SESAC reviews and analyzes all national network logs, pay-TV logs, and PBS/NPR cue sheets. It also spot-checks the programming of local radio and television stations and reviews regional editions of *TV Guide,* as well as *OnSat,* a guide to programming available by satellite. In addition, SESAC receives extensive information on syndicated television programming through cue sheets supplied by affiliates and producers and the *Nielsen Report on Syndicated Programming.*

Grievance Procedures

It is prudent for writers and publishers to recognize that the surveying and tabulation techniques of ASCAP and BMI are subject to interpretation, and that the reports by the organizations should be carefully reviewed. The late Billy Rose once observed that ASCAP's performance reports on certain of his songs showed in the column "Share" a lesser percentage for his participation vis-à-vis his collaborators than appeared on royalty statements rendered by his publishers. Where there were two other writers involved, he had been credited with one-third of the writer's share of performance fees. He pointed out in an informal ASCAP committee proceeding that he had written the words alone and that therefore his share was 50 percent and the other two collaborators should receive 25 percent apiece instead of one-third. Rose prevailed in his contentions, but ASCAP was careful to stress, in informing other members of the decision, that the writer has the burden of proving unusual divisions of performance fees.

Based on the ASCAP consent decree, the court appoints special distribution advisers to periodically examine the design and conduct of the ASCAP survey of performances, which establishes the basis of its distribution of revenues to members. They report to the court, to ASCAP, and to the U.S. government, making recommendations as to modifications of ASCAP's procedures and practices. Recognized functions of these special distribution advisers include making themselves available in person or by correspondence to ASCAP members who have questions concerning or problems with the ASCAP distribution system. Distribution adviser inquiries have been made into such matters as the credits for music performed at football games, the reduction of credits for qualifying works used as feature songs in films, and the basis for distribution of money received from unsurveyed background music licensees such as Muzak.

The relief that may be granted by the board of review in terms of monetary payment may not extend back beyond the time covered by the annual statement, unless the alleged injustice is such that the aggrieved party would not reasonably be put on notice of it by his or her annual statement; in that case, the relief given may reach back as far as, in the opinion of the board, is required to do justice. The board of review is obligated to set forth in detail the facts and grounds underlying its decision. There is a right to appeal any decision of the board of review before an impartial panel of the American Arbitration Association.

The BMI grievance procedure, as set out in its 1966 consent decree, requires that "all disputes of any kind, nature or description" between BMI and any writer, publisher, or music user be brought to arbitration in the City of New York under the prevailing rules of the American Arbitration Association.

SESAC is not subject to a court consent decree and has no established grievance procedure covering its relations with its affiliates.

Membership

Since 1960, ASCAP has operated under a court-administered consent decree with the U.S. Department of Justice with respect to the antitrust laws; the decree guides nearly every aspect of its operations. It requires ASCAP to accept for membership any applicant who is (1) a writer with at least one song regularly published or commercially recorded or (2) a music publisher actively engaged in the business with publications that have been "used or distributed on a commercial scale for at least one year." ASCAP actively solicits writers and publishers to join through its full-time staff members located in New York, California, Tennessee, England, and Puerto Rico, as well as through regularly placed trade paper advertisements. In fact, ASCAP acts promptly to accept publisher applications by active publishers, without any prerequisite period of operations. Under the consent decree, ASCAP must also permit members to resign and have procedures clearly in place; members may resign at the end of any calendar year by giving 3 months' advance notice in writing. The ASCAP consent decree is updated periodically.

Since 1966 BMI has also operated under a consent decree with the Justice Department. Under the decree, BMI must accept as an affiliate any writer who has had at least one composition commercially published or recorded and any publisher actively engaged in the business and whose compositions "have been commercially published or recorded and publicly promoted and distributed for at least one year." The decree prohibits contracts of more than 5 years' duration. In practice, the term of the publisher agreement is 5 years, and the term of the writer agreement is 2 years, with the following exception: BMI may continue to license compositions in existence at the date of termination until advances to the particular writer or publisher have been earned or repaid. In November 1994 the decree was revised to match ASCAP's. Throughout its history, BMI has been aggressive in soliciting and attracting new affiliates.

ASCAP collects an annual membership fee of $50 from publishers and $10 from writers. The dues, according to ASCAP, are used to aid elderly indigent members. BMI has a one-time $250 application fee for new corporate publisher affiliates and a $150 fee for an individual seeking status as a publisher, with no comparable fee for writers. There are no annual BMI charges for either publishers or writers.

SESAC is not bound by a consent decree in any of its operations. However, it actively solicits new publisher and writer members. The basic term of its publisher agreement is 5 years and the term of its writer agreement is 3 years. Such terms are automatically extended for similar periods unless canceled on 3 months' prior notice.

No writer or publisher can collect from more than one performing rights organization for the same songs at the same time, as dual membership or affiliation is not permitted. However, a writer or publisher can resign from an organization and still retain collection rights to songs that have been previously registered with, and continue to be licensed by, that organization.

Although ASCAP and BMI speak of release at the end of the license period of all rights to past songs of members or affiliates who resign, it rarely happens. The difficulty arises when a song is placed with a performing rights organization by both the writer and the publisher. This split origin of rights is rarely matched by joint resignations, and it has been judicially held that either the writer or the publisher can insist on maintaining the status quo with the first organization to which the performing right was jointly entrusted. There are, nevertheless, cases of split licensing. For example, BMI claims the right to license a former ASCAP writer's share while ASCAP continues to license the publisher's or co-writer's share. Or BMI recognizes the right of a BMI affiliate who resigns and joins ASCAP to take his or her share of the rights with him while BMI continues to license the rights of the publisher or co-writer who continues as a BMI affiliate.

Where an ASCAP writer collaborates with a BMI writer and the song is licensed by both societies, both will pay only their own publishers and writers. In the case of a collaboration between an ASCAP writer and a writer not affiliated with a performing rights organization, ASCAP will pay both writers if the unaffiliated writer's contribution is published by an ASCAP publisher and the unaffiliated writer does not give licensing rights to another performing rights organization. When a BMI writer collaborates with a writer not affiliated with a performing rights organization, BMI will not pay the unaffiliated writer.

The Fairness in Music Licensing Act of 1998

Under the Fairness in Music Licensing Act of 1998, bars and restaurants of less than 3,700 square feet and retail stores of less than 2,000 square feet that play music via radio or television sets are exempt from paying performance royalty fees. A protest against the Fairness in Music Licensing Act was filed by music publishers and songwriters residing in European Union countries signatory to the Berne Convention, led by the Irish Music Rights Organization. The protestors claimed that the exemption violated World Trade Organization (WTO) intellectual property rules. The claim was referred to the WTO dispute resolution panel, which decided in July 2001 that the claim was justified and gave the United States until the end of 2001 to repeal the offending legislation or face damages of $1.1 million per year retroactive to 1998. In 2002, the United States submitted a status report on what it assured the WTO were productive discussions directed toward arriving at a compensatory series of subsidies for the benefit of EU music creators. As of this writing, a final settlement had not been reached.

The ASCAP Payment System

For over 25 years, all new ASCAP writer members elected to be paid in the same way as the publishers: on the *current performance plan*. This is a relatively simple calculation based on the number of performance credits recorded by the ASCAP logging system during the most recent available fiscal survey annual year multiplied by the monetary value of a credit for that period. This monetary value is arithmetically determined by the simple division of total credits into total available net earnings to be split among the total group of writers in the plan. For example, the credit value as of January 2003 was $5.67. In 1989 there were substantially fewer available dollars and thus less credit value—somewhere between $2.62 and $2.98 for the applicable total annual collections.

Effective July 1999, ASCAP writers have the choice of one of two methods of payment: the current performance plan or the *averaged performance plan*. All publishers are enrolled in the current performance plan. New writers are automatically enrolled in the current performance plan, but writers can switch from one plan to the other at the end of any 12-month period. Under either plan, payments are calculated using a formula based on the dollar value of an ASCAP *credit*. The number of credits allocated for each performance of a work depends on a number of factors, including:

- ▶ Type of performance
- ▶ "Hookup" factor—e.g., with network television, the number of stations carrying a broadcast
- ▶ "Follow the dollar" factor—the money that ASCAP receives from any medium is paid to writers and publishers for performances in that medium
- ▶ Time of day—e.g., prime-time performance of a work is worth more than early morning performance of the same work

In addition, "premium" credits are allocated to songs that earn a predetermined number of radio feature credits during a particular quarter.

The quarterly royalties for writers who choose the current performance plan are calculated by multiplying the number of credits earned during that quarter by the current dollar value of a credit. For example, a writer with 475 credits in the fourth quarter of 1998 would have been owed royalties of $2351.25.

The averaged performance plan replaces an unwieldy system, the four-fund plan, which calculated payments using a system of "redeemable credits" rather than dollars earned and taking into account such factors as length of ASCAP membership and whether a song was a "recognized" work. Like the current performance plan, the averaged performance plan pays quarterly royalties on the basis of the monetary values of members' credits. However, 20 percent of each distribution is based on current performance dollars, 60 percent on a 5-year average, and 20 percent on a 10-year average, providing a steadier stream of income.

The dollar value of a credit will fluctuate with the amount of ASCAP receipts and the total number of ASCAP performance credits. In the follow-the-dollar policy of valuation of surveyed performances, ASCAP recognizes that a network TV sponsor pays more on weekends and during prime hours. Performances on Monday through Friday receive 50 percent, 75 percent, and 100 percent of full credits, depending on the time of day, whether morning, midday, or after 7 P.M. For weekends, the midday credits are eliminated in place of a full-payment prime time commencing at 1 P.M. Similar follow-the-dollar formulas are applicable to revenues from radio stations and networks.

One of the most novel concepts in the ASCAP system of credits is the "qualified work" designation. Under this part of the system, a song with a history of 20,000 feature performances, of which the most recent 5 years contributed a total of at least 5,000 feature performances a year, is given higher credits when used in nonfeature roles such as background, cue, bridge, or theme; not more than 1,500 feature performances are to be counted in any one of the 5 years to meet the 5,000 requirement. For purposes of jingle payments, there is also a form of qualified work dealing with works that show 150 feature performances logged by ASCAP in its radio and television surveys within the 5 prior years.

The justification for higher credits is that when a background strain or a theme is based on a well-known old standard, such as "Raindrops Keep Fallin' on My Head," the user is getting more value from the use and accordingly recognizes that ASCAP's bargaining power for general license fees is greater than if the tune were a new song previously unknown to the public and commissioned by the user especially for that purpose. It is also considered that background uses of well-known songs may advance the plot, without explicit exposition, because the public will associate such songs with special moods or images.

This simplified explanation leaves aside the more difficult issue of describing or justifying the different rates of payment. A qualified work used as a theme is accorded half a feature credit, while an unqualified work in the same form receives one-quarter of a feature credit. A background use of even 5 seconds of a qualified work gets half a feature credit, but an unqualified work requires a 3-minute total use for 42 percent of a feature credit, with a proportionate reduction for lesser use, measured by each second of timing, with a minimum payment of 1 percent per use. Except for emergencies, ASCAP does not give advances.

The BMI Payment System

The BMI standard forms of writer contract and publisher contracts do not mention payment rates. Each states in effect that payments will be made in accordance with the current practices and rates of BMI. The regular rates of payment for writers and publishers are the same. Actual payments to writers or publishe distinguish between radio and television performances and between network and local performances. In the case of a network performance, the rate allotted is multiplied by the number of interconnected stations carrying the broadcast. The rate allocated to a local station performance is multiplied by a statistical multiplier based on the ratio of stations logged to stations licensed in each station classification.

BMI's performance payment schedule, which is distributed to all its affiliates and is available on its Web site, specifies BMI's minimum rates. The actual payments made—all monies other than those needed for overhead and reserve—may be and have been higher than the minimum rates. Each payment rate under the schedule covers combined writer and publisher compensation and should ordinarily be divided in half to arrive at the separate payments to a writer and a publisher. In the absence of a publisher, the rate stipulated in the payment schedule is payable entirely to the writer, and if copublishing status is agreed upon, the designated share can be added to writer payments.

Under this system, a writer does not need to form a publishing firm in order to collect more than 50 percent of the total performance fees paid, and the number of prospective BMI music publishing firms is reduced. BMI states that its system is "similar to that of other performing rights organizations throughout the world."

On the assumption that there is a publisher and that the writer and publisher share equally in the payment rate, their respective shares under the BMI payment schedule are as follows: There is a payment of 12 cents for a feature radio performance of a popular song on each radio network station and on each Radio 1 station (a station whose BMI license fee is in the top 25 percent of all BMI radio station license fees in the year prior to the performance). There is a payment of 6 cents for a feature radio performance on each Radio 2 station (a station whose BMI license fees are in the bottom 75 percent of all BMI radio station license fees in the year before the performance). A local television feature performance is allocated a rate of $1.50 for hours between 11 a.m. and 4:00 p.m. the next day and double that amount for prime time, between 4:00 and 11 p.m. Network television feature performances in prime time, between 6 and 11:00 p.m., earn $11.50 per station, and in other than prime time, $5, $6, and $9 depending on the hour of performance. When a performance is shorter than 45 seconds, the rate is pro rated by actual time. There is no distinction made between AM and FM feature performances on radio. Concert works on radio receive substantially higher payments than performances of a popular song.

Under this system, an individual song receives the base rate in the BMI payment schedule discussed above until a certain plateau of U.S. feature broadcast performances of the song is reached. At this plateau, a higher payment rate ensues under what is called a "bonus level." Works receive bonus station credit on the basis of all feature broadcast performances from January 1, 1960, on.

An *entry-level* bonus payment at 1.5 times the base rate is made for those songs with a cumulative history of at least 25,000 U.S. feature broadcast performances. For those songs with the next higher cumulative history whose current quarter's performances constitute 25 percent of the current quarter's radio and television performances of all BMI songs, there is a *midlevel* bonus payment of 2 times the base rate. An *upper-level* bonus payment of 2.5 times the base rate applies to those songs with the next higher cumulative history whose current quarter's performances constitute 15 percent of the current quarter's radio and television performances of all songs. A *super-bonus* payment of 4 times the base rate is given to those songs with the highest cumulative history whose current quarter's performances make up 10 percent of the current quarter's radio and television performances of all BMI songs. Bonus payments are instead of, and not in addition to, the base rate.

Some of the songs in this super-bonus category are "Amapola," "Bye Bye Love," "Don't Be Cruel," "Killing Me Softly with His Song," "Never on Sunday," "Sounds of Silence," "Sunrise, Sunset," and "Up, Up and Away."

Regardless of its prior cumulative history, any song that has 100,000 or more U.S. radio performances in one quarter will be awarded, for all such performances in that quarter, the next higher level of bonus payment than it would ordinarily be entitled to receive.

BMI provides for immediate entry to a super-bonus level for songs identified originally as "show music." These songs originate in (1) a first-class Broadway show or (2) an off-Broadway show that opened after October 1, 1966, and was released as an original-cast album.

Special credit is also stipulated for a "movie work." This is described as a complete musical work originating in and performed for not less than 40 consecutive seconds as a feature work or theme in a full-length theatrical or television motion picture lasting 90 minutes or more that has been released in the United States after October 1, 1966. Such a work is awarded not less than the midlevel bonus payment.

While U.S. network television and public broadcasting station feature performances are counted in computing the cumulative history of a song for bonus purposes, such performances themselves are not eligible for bonus payments. BMI, like ASCAP, does not give advances except in emergency situations.

Loan Assistance

With the cessation of ordinary advances by ASCAP and BMI there has arisen a greater need on the part of some writers and publishers for bank loans or loans from other third parties.

BMI currently has excellent relations with Bank of America, which is headquartered in Nashville, Tennessee. When the bank makes a BMI member writer a loan of 70 percent of average 3-year earnings, BMI transfers 100 percent of the writer's or publisher's account, foreign and domestic. The member writer's royalties are assigned directly to the bank. The bank offers a preferred interest rate, historically as low as 1 point above prime. The bank runs a normal credit check on the applicant and is provided with information from

BMI about the affiliate's royalty income stream. Mere affiliation with BMI alone is not sufficient to secure such a low-interest loan; such loans are only possible if the writer can show a reliable past and continuing flow of performance royalties. Because of the process of funneling funds directly to the bank, in some cases where the writer or publisher has a particularly strong catalog, BMI has been able to influence the acceptance of its affiliates. BMI may continue to license compositions in existence at the date of termination until outstanding loans or emergency advances to the particular writer or publisher have been repaid or earned.

The Bank of America has a similar arrangement with ASCAP for member loans. ASCAP and BMI use the same procedure with any bank nominated by its affiliate or member, but many banks are unfamiliar with the system and Bank of America thus has a preferred status.

ASCAP maintains two separate and distinct loan services to its members. While offering bank services similar to BMI, ASCAP also offers its members a credit union membership through USAlliance Federal Credit Union. USAlliance offers ASCAP members a variety of services, including low-interest loans, 24-hour customer service, 24-hour worldwide ATM service, and retirement plans. USAlliance also offers services exclusively to ASCAP members such as direct deposit of performance royalties, loans based upon the value of the member's catalog, interest-only payments for royalty-secured loans, and a member services staff specifically trained to deal with the unique needs of ASCAP members.

Insurance Plans

ASCAP and BMI both offer insurance coverage for health and musical instruments. ASCAP endorses MusicPro Insurance Agency LLC (musicproinsurance.com), which has been specifically created to provide one-stop insurance at a reasonable cost to meet the needs of working musicians and composers. It offers insurance coverage against theft, loss, and other insurable damage to instruments, equipment, computers, and software, as well as studio liability, tour liability, travel and accident, long-term care, major medical, term life, and even dental insurance.

BMI arranges medical, dental, life, and musical instrument insurance to its members through 10 distinct coverage options. The musical instrument insurance, administered by J&H Marsh & McLennan, covers loss for any type of musical instrument or electronic equipment; it also covers sheet music from theft, fire, vandalism, and natural disasters all over the globe.

SESAC has insurance coverage available to its affiliates around the country through Near North Insurance Brokerage of New York. Group medical insurance, excess major medical insurance, Medicare supplemental insurance, accidental death and dismemberment insurance, group term life insurance, and equipment insurance are all available.

Writer Awards

The ASCAPlus$ program is a system of "awards to writers whose works have a unique prestige value for which adequate compensation would not otherwise be received by such writers, and to writers whose works are performed substantially in media not surveyed by the society." There is a two-part special awards panel composed of people of standing who are not ASCAP members: the Popular Production Panel makes special monetary awards to popular music composers, and the Standard Awards Panel allocates such awards to composers of symphonic and concert music. In 1998 a total of $1.8 million was awarded. In 2001, a total of $2.2 million was awarded. Currently, $15,000 is the top award for the Popular field and $20,000 for the Standard field.

For more than 40 years, BMI has presented annual cash awards to student composers of serious music. Six of the recipients of these awards have subsequently received Pulitzer Prizes. The awards, aggregating $15,000 annually, are available to students under the age of 27 who reside in the Western Hemisphere. Awards recipients are selected by a panel of distinguished composers, musicians, and publishers.

SESAC honors its top songs and songwriters throughout the year with various awards ceremonies. Awards are based on cumulative broadcast performances for a 12-month period.

Foreign Collections

Both ASCAP and BMI play a valuable international role for publishers, writers, and users of music. They collect from abroad for their members or affiliates and collect from users in the United States on behalf of foreign societies. Foreign collections are made through affiliated societies in each country and remitted through the domestic organization. It would be an extremely difficult task for each writer or publisher to supervise the licensing of rights in every country of the world where American music is used. ASCAP has more than 40 foreign affiliates, and BMI has substantially the same; most often the same foreign society represents both organizations, for the United States is unusual in having more than one performing rights organization.

BMI charges 3.6 percent of foreign collections as a service fee, which is deducted from remittances to its affiliated writers and publishers. Revenues received by ASCAP from foreign sources are distributed to writer and publisher members on a current-performance basis. ASCAP makes an overhead charge of about 3.5 percent for its foreign collection services. ASCAP distributes foreign revenues to members on the basis of performances reported by the foreign society if the revenue from the society exceeds $200,000 a year. The reports furnished to ASCAP allocate credit in reasonably identifiable form separately by compositions performed and indicate the members in interest.

ASCAP distributes foreign income to its members based on reports received from local societies, even when the fees remitted are under $200,000, as long as the reports identify the works performed and the ASCAP members in interest. ASCAP receives more than $200,000 per year from Australia, Austria, Belgium, Canada, Denmark, England, France, Germany, Holland, Italy, Japan, Spain, Sweden, and Switzerland. With the exception of Canada, a member's credits in these countries are used as the basis of proportional distribution of all other foreign income that is not received in accordance with surveying reports. A similar procedure is used for the distribution of foreign film and television income when it is also not distributed in accordance with surveying reports.

A great majority of American music publishers, despite the convenience of collecting through ASCAP or BMI, have their share of foreign collections in important countries paid to foreign subpublishers or agents. They explain that a local subpublisher will expedite collections and will be more vigilant in claiming rights; some publishers desire to have foreign revenue collected abroad and retained there for capital acquisitions or other local expenditures. Another purpose is to maximize the advances to be paid to the American publisher.

ASCAP and BMI have both made progress in expediting payments from foreign performing rights organizations, which have in the past arrived only after long delays. This benefits their writer members and those publisher members who elect to have their foreign performance earnings collected other than through subpublishers. Examples of expedited payments were shown in the ASCAP February 1999 distribution, which covered Sweden, Switzerland, Japan, and Germany through December 1997 and an even more expedited distribution from France and Britain through June 1998.

A major cause of concern for American publishers and writers is the large sum of foreign performance collections not paid to U.S. copyright holders because of claimed difficulties in identifying American songs under translated or new local titles. Such so-called "unclaimed" monies go into general funds which, after a period of time, are distributed by the foreign performing rights societies among their memberships, without participation by American writers or publishers. The problem of this so-called *black box* distribution can be alleviated if U.S. publishers appoint a local representative to identify and claim a song in all its varied forms so that performance income can be properly allocated.

Often a subpublication agreement allows the subpublisher to designate a local translator or adapter of the song lyric, who is entitled, among other things, to 25 percent of the total writer's share of performance royalties in the territory. Formerly, in a number of countries, the translator or adapter was paid 25 percent of the monies that would normally belong to the original writers, regardless of whether the performance was of the original lyric or of the translated or adapted lyric. This was true even when the two versions had different titles and there was no problem identifying which version was performed. This is no longer done, as least with regard to new works. However, to protect their writers, American publishers may prohibit translations or adaptations without their consent, especially where the original lyric version is likely to be used widely.

Dramatic Performance Rights

Dramatic performance rights, frequently called "grand rights," are to be distinguished from nondramatic performance rights, or "small rights," by the type of use involved and in the practical manner of who administers the rights.

The Copyright Act grants the exclusive right to perform or represent a copyrighted work publicly if it is a dramatic work. A dramatic work includes material dramatic in character such as plays, dramatic scripts designed for radio or television broadcast, pantomimes, ballets, musical comedies, and operas. In contrast to a nondramatic work such as a musical composition, compulsory licenses under the Copyright Act for phonograph recordings, jukebox performances, and performances on public broadcasting systems do not apply to dramatic works. Consequently, the copyright owner of a dramatic work, for example, the musical *The Lion King*, has the absolute exclusive right to authorize or to withhold authorization of the recording or performance in public of the work.

A dramatic performance does not make the material a dramatic work. An example of a dramatic performance might be the portrayal of the story line of the song "Tie a Yellow Ribbon Round the Ol' Oak Tree" in a dramatic fashion, such as for a television show using background scenery, props, and character action to depict the plot of the composition.

The ASCAP television license represents the music industry and broadcasting industry representatives' best effort to reach a definition of dramatic performance rights. The effort is necessary because ASCAP obtains from members only nondramatic public performance rights, not dramatic performance rights. Concerning the dramatization on television of a single musical composition that does not necessarily stem from a musical play or other dramatic production, the latest television license states:

> Any performance of a separate musical composition which is not a dramatic performance, as defined herein, shall be deemed to be a nondramatic performance. For the purposes of this agreement, a dramatic performance shall mean a performance of a musical composition on a television program in which there is a definite plot depicted by action and where the performance of the musical composition is woven into and carries forward the plot and its accompanying action. The use of dialogue to establish a mere program format or the use of any nondramatic device merely to introduce a performance of a composition shall not be deemed to make such performance dramatic.

The television license defines the dramatic performance of dramatic musical works such as musical plays as follows:

This license does not extend to or include the public performance by television broadcasting or otherwise of any rendition or performance of (a) any opera, operetta, musical comedy, play or like production, as such, in whole or in part, or (b) any composition from any opera, operetta, musical comedy, play or like production (whether or not such opera, operetta, musical comedy, play or like production was presented on the stage or in motion picture form) in a manner which recreates the performance of such composition with substantially such distinctive scenery or costumes as was used in a presentation of such opera, operetta, musical comedy, play or like production (whether or not such opera, operetta, musical comedy, play or like production was presented on the stage or in motion picture form).

The standard BMI contract with affiliated writers and publishers gives BMI the right to license dramatic performances, but these rights are restricted. As a result, BMI is not authorized to license the performances of more than one song or aria from an opera, operetta, or musical comedy, or more than 5 minutes from a ballet if the performance is accompanied by the dramatic action, costumes, or scenery of that opera, operetta, musical comedy, or ballet. The writers and publishers of a work may jointly, by written notice to BMI, exclude from the grant of rights to BMI any performances of more than 30 minutes' duration of a work that is an opera, operetta, or musical comedy; exceptions are (1) the score of a theatrical film when performed with the film and (2) the score written for a radio or television program when performed with the program.

The standard SESAC license excludes grand rights, which it states includes "the right to perform in whole or in part dramatico-musical and dramatic works in a dramatic setting." These rights are licensed separately by SESAC.

Where a performance is found to be dramatic, the presentation of the whole or part of a musical play will usually be administered by the writers, based on rights reserved to them by Dramatists Guild contracts. In the case of most music publishers who publish show music, copyright is maintained in the name of the writer, and, accordingly, publishers do not acquire dramatic rights. In many instances, shows previously produced on the Broadway stage are licensed by writers' agents such as Tams-Witmark Music Library and Rodgers & Hammerstein Repertory to amateur and stock groups and to television for dramatic performances.

For music not originating in plays, operas, and the like, the copyright is normally held by the music publisher, who obtains the dramatization rights, although some writer contracts, such as those of the Songwriters Guild, require consent of the writer for the dramatization of a composition. There are also some contracts, especially older ones, where the writer specifically reserved all dramatic rights.

15

Mechanical Rights

The copyright owner owns the exclusive right to reproduce and distribute to the public copyrighted musical compositions on phonorecords, which include compact discs, tapes, and any other material object in which sounds other than those accompanying motion pictures and other audiovisual works are fixed. This right is commonly called a *mechanical right* and the authority to exercise this right is called a *mechanical license*. These terms date from the days when records were reproduced mechanically, rather than electronically. Mechanical rights are an important and lucrative aspect of copyright, different from other rights protected under copyright, such as synchronization rights used in motion pictures, video, and television; print rights; and public performance rights.

Under the Copyright Act of 1909, Congress recognized for the first time the copyright owner's exclusive ownership of recording and mechanical reproduction rights in musical works. Congress's reason for doing so was twofold. Not only did it want to protect the composer's rights of mechanical reproduction, it also sought to prevent the creation of a monopoly in this area. At the time, millions of piano rolls (the ancestor of records) were being sold every year. The Aeolian Company, a leading manufacturer of piano rolls, had made exclusive contracts with most of the major music publishers to reproduce all the compositions that they owned or controlled. Section 1 (e) of the 1909 Copyright Act changed that. It provided that if the copyright owner used or permitted the use of a copyrighted composition for mechanical reproduction, then anyone else might also mechanically reproduce the composition on payment to the copyright proprietor of a royalty originally set at 2 cents "on each such part manufactured." This is usually referred to as a *compulsory license* and the license rate is referred to as the *statutory rate*. Although the compulsory license provision called for the payment of the statutory rate "on each such part manufactured," the music industry has interpreted this provision to mean that payment is required for each composition on a record, that is, for each song.

Under the Copyright Act of 1976, the concept of a compulsory mechanical license was continued and clarified. If phonorecords of a nondramatic composition have been distributed to the public with the authorization of the copyright owner, any other person may record and distribute phonorecords of the work by giving a specified notice and paying a statutory royalty. A record is considered distributed if possession has been "voluntarily and permanently parted with."

The National Music Publishers Association, the Songwriters Guild of America, and the Recording Industry Association of America jointly negotiate, for industrywide purposes, 10-year maximum mechanical royalty rates with recourse for final determination, if necessary (that is, if the industry cannot reach an agreement), to a Copyright Arbitration Royalty Panel (CARP) (see Chapter 7, page 67). The mechanical royalty rate until December 31, 2003, is 8 cents per song per record distributed for songs up to 5 minutes in length or 1.55 cents per minute or fraction thereof for songs over 5 minutes. The approved escalations come in two-year units, so that for the period 2004–2005 the rate goes up 0.5 cent for songs up to 5 minutes, to 8.5 cents, and up 0.1 cent a minute, to 1.65 cents, for songs over 5 minutes. In 2006 those rates will be, respectively, 9.10 cents and 1.75 cents.

The compulsory license provisions of the Copyright Act expressly permit the making of an "arrangement of the work to the extent necessary to conform it to the style or manner of interpretation of the performance." Even a sound-alike recording, with an arrangement similar to that of a prior recording, is permitted. However, a compulsory licensee must avoid changing the basic melody or fundamental character of the work. The author of an arrangement cannot claim a derivative copyright in the arrangement without the consent of the copyright owner. Such consents are rarely given.

Compulsory mechanical licenses under the Copyright Act apply solely to audio recordings primarily intended for distribution to the public for private use. They are not available for purposes of background music services, broadcast transcriptions, television films or episodes, or any motion picture synchronization. A compulsory license applies only to the use of musical compositions in new recordings. There can be no compulsory license for compositions used in the duplication ("dubbing") of a prior sound recording, unless consent has been obtained from the owner of the prior recording, which itself was fixed lawfully. This acts as a significant restriction on the pirating of recordings.

Parting with Possession; Returns

Under the Copyright Act a record is not considered distributed (and no statutory mechanical royalty is due) unless its possession has been "voluntarily and permanently parted with." In 1976, the House Committee on the Judiciary stated:

> The concept of "distribution" comprises any act by which the
> person exercising the compulsory license voluntarily relinquishes
> possession of a phonorecord (considered as a fungible unit),
> regardless of whether the distribution is to the public, passes title,

constitutes a gift, or is sold, rented, leased, or loaned, unless it is actually returned and the transaction canceled. (H.R. Rep. No. 1476, 94th Cong., 2d Sess. 106)

In the legislative history preceding the Copyright Act, there is recognition of a record industry practice of distributing records with return privileges.

Phonorecords are distributed to wholesalers and retailers with the privilege of returning unsold copies for credit or exchange. As a result, the number of recordings that have been "permanently" distributed will not usually be known until some time—six or seven months on the average—after the initial distribution. In recognition of this problem, it has become a well-established industry practice, under negotiated licenses, for record companies to maintain reasonable reserves of the mechanical royalties due the copyright owners, against which royalties on the returns can be offset. The Committee recognizes that this practice may be consistent with the statutory requirements for monthly compulsory license accounting reports, but recognizes the possibility that, without proper safeguards, the maintenance of such reserves could be manipulated to avoid making payments of the full amounts owing to copyright owners.

The committee recommended that the regulations to be published by the Register of Copyrights should

Contain detailed provisions ensuring that the ultimate disposition of every phonorecord made under a compulsory license is accounted for, and that payment is made for every phonorecord "voluntarily and permanently" distributed. In particular the Register should prescribe a point in time when. . . . a phonorecord will be considered "permanently distributed," and should prescribe the situation in which a compulsory licensee is barred from maintaining reserves (e.g., situations in which the compulsory licensee has frequently failed to make payments in the past).

The Register of Copyrights has promulgated regulations that, in effect, give a compulsory licensee 9 months at the most, from the month in which the records are relinquished from possession, to hold mechanical royalties in a reserve fund. However, the regulations deny the privilege of holding reserve to a habitual nonpayer of mechanical royalties. Such a licensee is one who, within 3 years from when a phonorecord was parted from possession, has had final judgment rendered against it for failing to pay mechanical royalties on phonorecords, or within such period has been found in any proceeding involving bankruptcy, insolvency, receivership, assignment for the benefit of creditors, or similar action to have failed to pay such royalties.

The Register of Copyrights did not establish any specific criteria for what a reasonable reserve would be. In their absence, this is governed by customary music industry practice.

Notice of Intention

Anyone who proposes to invoke the benefit of compulsory licensing provisions under the Copyright Act must serve a "notice of intention" in a form and manner prescribed by the Register of Copyrights. Pursuant to Section 115 of the Copyright Act, the notice must be sent to the copyright owner either before any records are distributed or within 30 days after distribution. If the records of the Copyright Office fail to identify the copyright owner and his or her address, then the notice requirements can be met by sending the notice to the Copyright Office along with a $12 fee.

Failure to timely serve a compulsory license notice "forecloses the possibility of a compulsory license." In other words, the making and distribution of phonorecords is copyright infringement and the copyright owner has various remedies available.

Compulsory License Accountings

A compulsory licensee must make monthly royalty payments on or before the 20th of each month for records made and distributed during the preceding month. Accompanying each payment must be a detailed accounting statement made under oath. The copyright owner is also entitled to cumulative annual statements certified by a certified public accountant.

Under the Copyright Act there is an automatic termination of a compulsory license for failure to render monthly payments and the appropriate accountings when due if the default is not cured within 30 days after written notice by the copyright owner. If a default continues beyond this period, there is an automatic termination of the compulsory license. In addition, once a license has been terminated, parties can be sued for copyright infringement if they continue to make and distribute phonorecords for which royalties are unpaid.

Copyright Owner Identification

There is no obligation under the Copyright Act of 1976 to pay compulsory license royalties to a copyright owner unless the owner is identified in the registration or other records of the Copyright Office. A copyright owner is entitled to receive compulsory license royalties for phonorecords made and distributed after this identification is made, but the owner cannot collect royalties for phonorecords made and distributed before the identification. This provides a strong incentive for early copyright registration by an owner.

Negotiated Licenses

The procedure for monthly accountings and payments is a strong deterrent to resorting to compulsory licenses. In the music industry it is standard practice for a record manufacturer to account for and pay mechanical royalties quarterly, not monthly, and statements are not usually made under oath. In addition, it is unnecessary to serve a notice of intention to obtain a compulsory license if the publisher issues a negotiated license.

A compulsory license is inapplicable to the first recording of a copyrighted composition. The copyright owner has complete control over his or her decision to make the first recording as well as over the terms and conditions with respect to that recording of the composition. Thus, the copyright owner could, in theory, insist that higher mechanical royalties be paid, or that the record couple two compositions controlled by the copyright owner, or that the next recording by the same artist include a copyrighted composition from the catalog of the copyright proprietor, but this rarely, if ever, occurs. Finally, and most importantly, the possibility of obtaining a mechanical royalty rate of less than the statutory rate militates in favor of a negotiated license. By reason of the compulsory license provisions, the statutory rate has the effect of serving as a ceiling on negotiated mechanical license rates for records distributed in the United States. In practice, however, publishers usually grant initial licenses at the prevailing statutory rate and without additional restriction. It is rare that the maximum statutory rate is exceeded. Indeed, record companies, by the use of "controlled composition" clauses, usually provide for mechanical licenses to be issued at 75 percent of the basic per-song statutory rate, regardless of the song's duration.

The Harry Fox Agency

The National Music Publishers Association (NMPA), which was founded in 1917, is a trade association of music publishers. It represents the interests of more than 750 of the leading U.S. music publishers in all pertinent national and international copyright issues, including legislation and U.S. intellectual trade policy. NMPA's far-ranging activities are supported in large part by commissions earned by its wholly owned subsidiary, the Harry Fox Agency (www.nmpa.org/hfa.html).

The Harry Fox Agency was established in 1917 to administer mechanical rights in the U.S. for publishers who wished to use its services on a commission basis. Effective June 30, 2002, it discontinued its synchronization licensing division, since by then most publishers were handling synchronization licensing directly, but in early 2003 announced that it would issue a joint mechanical and synchronization license for DVD audio allowing visual elements such as lyric reproduction. The agency represents more than 27,000 music publishers, many of whom are unaffiliated with NMPA, who in turn represent the interests of over 160,000 songwriters. In 2001, the agency's annual gross collections were $441.8

million, a significant decrease from the previous year, reflecting the general contraction of the music industry.

The agency's services include the issuance of mechanical licenses and the supervision of collections from record companies. It employs auditing firms to regularly check the books of record companies and other licensees in order to ensure proper accountings of mechanical license fees. On behalf of publishers that it represents, the Harry Fox Agency has instituted litigation to pursue delinquent record firms and record pirates, as well as to settle disputes stemming from diffent interpretations of the Copyright Act. For its mechanical license services, the agency presently charges a commission of 5.75 percent on royalties distributed.

Under the basic mechanical license issued by the Harry Fox Agency on behalf of the publishers it represents, the record company must account and pay for all records manufactured and distributed. The license calls for quarterly accountings and payments and provides that failure to make accountings and payments constitutes grounds for the revocation of the license. It also states that service of a notice of intention to obtain a compulsory license is waived.

The license further states that the record company has requested a license under the compulsory license provision of the Copyright Act. It provides that the licensees have all the rights granted to and all the obligations imposed on users of copyrighted works under the compulsory license provision, with certain exceptions relating to quarterly instead of monthly or annual sworn accountings and a waiver of the notice requirements.

The courts have held that the Harry Fox license form is a modification of the compulsory license provisions of the Copyright Act and is not a separate, private contract. This preserves the statutory remedies afforded by the Copyright Act as well as federal jurisdiction. The Harry Fox license is generally nonassignable, and a separate license is required for each type of phonorecord configuration the licensee desires to manufacture or distribute, (i.e., CDs, cassettes, and singles).

In 1987, in the case of *T. B. Harms Co. v. Jem Records* (655 F. Supp. 1575), a federal district court in New Jersey ruled that according to the U.S. Copyright Act, the importation of phonorecords into the United States (regardless of whether such records were legally manufactured abroad and were subject to royalties at the place of manufacture) still requires a license from the owner of the U.S. copyright in the songs contained in the imported record. Although this case was never appealed to the Third Circuit Court of Appeals and is not technically binding in other judicial circuits, since that time the Harry Fox Agency has required that import licenses be obtained by record importers for the mechanical use of copyrighted music. Under this type of mechanical license, royalties are payable on all goods imported, whether or not they are ultimately sold.

Other U.S. Mechanical Rights Organizations

A number of other agencies handle the licensing of mechanical rights in the United States, although their annual receipts are very small in comparison with those of the Harry Fox Agency. The largest of these is probably the American Mechanical Rights Agency (AMRA; e-mail: amracalif@aol.com). Organized in 1961, AMRA licenses mechanical and synchronization rights for music publishers and writers, charging a fee of 5 percent of the gross collections, and represents a number of foreign mechanical rights societies.

The Canadian Mechanical Rights Organizations

The Canadian Musical Reproduction Rights Agency Limited (CMRRA; www.cmrra.ca) performs the same functions in Canada as the Harry Fox Agency does in the United states. Another Canadian mechanical and synchronization licensing agent dealing with French-language recordings in Quebec is Société du Droit de Reproduction des Auteurs (SODRAC; www.sodrac.com).

International Mechanical Rights Societies

The Harry Fox Agency has affiliations with various territorial mechanical rights societies and can make arrangements for them to act as agents to collect local mechanical license fees on behalf of U.S. publishers in more than 60 countries other than Canada. The collection fees charged by the local societies tend to average under 10 percent, to which is added the applicable percent Harry Fox Agency commission. Following is a list of the principal foreign mechanical rights organizations that make collections for the Harry Fox Agency.

- ► Argentina: SADAIC
- ► Australia and New Zealand: AMCOS
- ► Bolivia, Colombia, and Peru: FONOPERU
- ► Former Soviet Union countries: RAO
- ► France, the former French colonies, Belgium, and Luxembourg: Société pour l'Administration du Droit de Reproduction Mécanique (SDRM)
- ► Germany, Austria, Bulgaria, Rumania, Hungary, Czechoslovakia, Poland, South Korea, Taiwan, Yugoslavia, Turkey, and the Philippines: GEMA
- ► Great Britain, Scotland, and Northern Ireland: Mechanical Copyright Protection Society (MCPS)
- ► Israel: ACUM
- ► Italy: SIAE
- ► Japan: JASRAC
- ► Netherlands: STEMRA
- ► Portugal: SPA
- ► Scandinavia (Denmark, Estonia, Finland, Iceland, Lithuania, Norway, Sweden): Nordisk Copyright Bureau (NCB)
- ► Spain: SGAE
- ► Switzerland: SUISA
- ► Trinidad and Tobago: COTT

Some of the societies handle performing rights licensing and collections as well as mechanical rights licensing and collections. American publishers can make direct arrangements for the collection of mechanical right fees in some foreign territories; among these are MCPS, SDRM, GEMA, and NCB. JASRAC and SIAE do not permit such arrangements. Through direct dealings with mechanical rights societies, American publishers can eliminate the Harry Fox Agency charge, but they forgo the convenience of having different territories serviced through the one agency.

Each society operates under the customs and laws of its applicable home base. However, in the European Union, consolidated negotiations have resulted in a mechanical rate of 9.01 percent of published price to dealer (PPD) for the Continent and 8.5 thereof for the United Kingdom and Ireland.

The Writer's Share of Mechanical Fees

In contracts between publishers and songwriters it is standard for the writer to receive 50 percent of the mechanical license fees collected by the contracting ("original") publisher. Where foreign subpublishers are entitled to retain 50 percent of the mechanical fees collected by them and they remit the balance to the original publisher, the writer in effect receives one-quarter of the amount collected at the source by the foreign subpublisher. In computing royalties due to the original publisher (and which the original publisher shares with the writer), it is common to disregard charges made by the local mechanical rights society that collected mechanical license fees from local record companies in the first instance, since the royalty to the original writer is customarily computed only on the balance remitted by the subpublisher to the original publisher (after the subpublisher has deducted its charges).

It should be noted that the writer share of public performance income is more favorable to the writer because it is computed at the source in each country and remitted through affiliated societies, whereas the writer share of mechanical income is filtered through the publisher and subpublisher.

Record Clubs

Historically, record clubs did not obtain their own mechanical licenses when they reissued products under club imprint. The record clubs aimed to be an extension of the original record manufacturer, and in most instances they relied on industry custom in paying 75 percent of either the compulsory license rate or the negotiated or controlled-composition rate for a composition re-released through a club.

The Harry Fox Agency has taken the position that clubs should no longer rely on industry custom and usage but should have specific mechanical licenses for each record club release, which sets forth the manner of computation of royalties and the basis on which an audit can be conducted. The agency noted that previous difficulties have become even greater now that many royalty statements are rendered electronically. The reason for this is the absence of an electronic database with separate licenses against which automatic tracking and verification could otherwise be done. The agency also noted that the court in the *Sleepless in Seattle* decision (see page 112) ruled that when old recordings are issued by a new licensee, new licensing rates must be negotiated for club release (on which a 75 percent rate is customary, as noted above). It is obviously in the best interest of publishers to try to update the mechanical royalty rates as the statutory (compulsory) rates increase.

Title Use Restrictions

According to instructions from certain publishers, a Harry Fox Agency license may contain a restriction against the use of a licensed song as the title of a record album. Such uses may be the special concern of publishers affiliated with motion picture companies or with record companies that release soundtrack albums or original cast albums. Where the title song of a film is named after the film—for example, "Never on Sunday"—an album with the same title as the song may be confused by the public with the soundtrack album from the motion picture. The same would apply to a song from a show that has a title identical to that of the show, for example, "Oklahoma." The publishers that impose the restriction seek to avoid this confusion and regulate this type of usage.

Record Rentals

The Record Rental Act of 1984 provides that no copies of sound recordings acquired on or after October 4, 1984, may be commercially rented, leased, or lent by the owner of the copies unless authorized by the copyright proprietors of the recordings and of the underlying musical works. This legislation represents a modification of the so-called *first-sale concept* of copyright law, according to which a purchaser of a phonorecord or an audiovisual recording, whether disc, tape, compact disc, or other configuration, had been permitted to rent, lease, or lend it without the consent of such copyright proprietors. An unauthorized commercial rental, lease, or lending constitutes a copyright infringement subject to civil but not criminal infringement penalties under existing copyright laws.

The Record Rental Act was passed in recognition that there was a potential threat of a substantial loss in sales for manufacturers, distributors, and retail record stores. Public libraries were exempted. In 1994, its provisions were made permanent. Accordingly, the commercial rental of recordings now requires the consent of both the music publisher and the record company.

16

Songwriter Contracts and Royalty Statements

An article in *Billboard* once remarked that the music business was similar to the meat-packing business in that it used everything on the animal but the squeal. (Some music critics might even include the squeal.) Yet there are songwriters who sign agreements that make specific provisions for their participation in print music receipts and receipts from the sale of phonograph records and film synchronization licenses but fail to provide for their participation in many other commercial uses, such as advertising jingles and new technologies. Many writers have found a solution to this problem by providing that they must share equally in all receipts from unspecified sources. Other writers, especially writers for theater, put the burden on the music publisher to specify sources of income in which the publisher shall have any participation.

Unfortunately, many novice songwriters sign whatever is placed before them fearing that otherwise they may jeopardize the music publisher's willingness to enter into an agreement. Unlike the typical book publishing or theatrical contract, all rights under copyright are customarily assigned to the publisher of popular music. Thus, if writers are not protected by a well-constructed contract, which includes language covering approval of new lyrics and recapture of rights (discussed below), there is little likelihood that their rights will be safeguarded.

Duration of Copyright Assignment

It is essential that both parties to a songwriter contract be fully aware that the relationship is likely to last a long time. How long a music publisher may continue to exploit and administer rights is determined both by the songwriter contract and by statute. As noted below, some contracts, such as the 1948 and 1969 Songwriters Guild contract forms, expressly limit the publisher's worldwide rights to 28 years, subject to certain notices applicable to foreign rights.

Where the duration of the contract is expressed as the duration of copyright, this would mean the 28-year initial term of copyright and a 28-year renewal period; generally speaking, U.S. rights reverted to the author or the author's successors at the end of the initial term of copyright unless the author also expressly granted rights for the renewal term to the publisher. However, even if the U.S. renewal-term rights reverted, rights would remain with the publisher in foreign territories for the full duration of copyright protection there.

The Copyright Act of 1976 added a 19-year extension to the renewal term, subject to a right of termination of the additional 19 years in favor of the author or the specified statutory heirs. It also created a right of termination of grants or licenses of U.S. rights made by the author for compositions first fixed on or after January 1, 1978. The termination becomes effective within a period of 5 years from the end of the 35th year following the date of the grant or license, provided that timely notice is given by the terminating writer or designated successors. If the grant or license covers publication, the 5-year period begins at the end of 35 years from the date of publication or 40 years from the execution of the grant, whichever is earlier. This right of termination takes precedence over contrary contractual provisions. However, the parties are free to contract for a term of rights that is less than 35 years.

The subject of duration of copyright, including renewal term and termination, is more extensively covered in Chapter 11. The significant point here is that whatever the duration is—28 years, 35 years, or longer—the extensive length of the relationship between a songwriter and a publisher means that a carefully written publishing agreement is a necessity.

Songwriters Guild Contracts

The Songwriters Guild of America (SGA), originally founded in 1931 as the Songwriters Protective Association, is an organization of songwriters with a present membership of over 3,500 writers. It is presently headquartered at 1500 Harbour Blvd., Weehawken, NJ 07087 and maintains branch offices in New York, Nashville, and Los Angeles. The organization recommends to its members that they use a standard songwriter contract form published by the SGA. The contract was originally issued in 1948, revised slightly in 1969, and amended substantially in 1978 in light of the Copyright Act of 1976.

Under the 1948 contract and the revised 1969 contract, the grant of worldwide rights to the publisher was for the original period of U.S. copyright, 28 years, or for 28 years from publication, whichever was shorter. However, writers would forfeit the right to recapture foreign copyrights, other than in Canada, if they did not give the original publisher at least 6 months' written notice of their intention to sell or assign to a third party their rights in U.S. renewal copyright or any of their rights in the United States or elsewhere for the period beyond the original grant.

The 1978 SGA contract form increased the 28-year period to a worldwide maximum of 40 years from the date of the agreement or 35 years from the first release of a commercial sound recording of a composition, whichever is earlier; however, the parties can specify a lesser period. At the expiration of this period, worldwide rights revert to the writer even though the term of copyright extends until 70 years from the death of the last surviving collaborator on a song in most major countries. Because of the contractual limitation on duration, there is no need for designated statutory notices to effectuate the right of termination under the Copyright Act of 1976. Termination is automatic and applies to worldwide rights, whereas the statutory right of termination covers only U.S. rights.

Many music publishers argue that a recapture right on the part of the writer is wrong in principle because it fails to recognize the importance of the publisher's efforts and expenditures in establishing the popular acceptance of compositions. These music publishers attempt to obtain an assignment of copyright including full administration and publishing rights for the maximum possible period for any and all countries of the world. In negotiations between publishers and songwriters, a full understanding of the applicable statutory provisions concerning the duration of the agreeement and the right of termination is essential.

While recognizing the merit of certain provisions in the SGA contract form, such as the right granted to the writer to participate in all possible revenue from a song, publishers contend that some clauses are outdated and tend to impede the proper administration of a publisher's functions. They assert, for instance, that a writer's consent should not be required for issuance of television or motion picture synchronization licenses.

Copyright Divisibility

Except in rare instances, the music industry customarily treats all aspects of music copyright as a single bundle of rights exclusively owned and administered by the music publisher. As owner and administrator, the music publisher handles the separate rights of mechanical reproduction, preparation of derivative works, reproduction in printed editions, and publication.

Before passage of the Copyright Act of 1976, copyright was generally considered indivisible. There could be only an inseparable ownership of the rights under copyright, although such rights might be the subject of exclusive or nonexclusive licenses. The 1976 Copyright Act expressly recognizes, for the first time, that copyright is divisible. There can therefore be a separate transfer and ownership of any of the exclusive rights that collectively comprise a copyright.

Thus, it is possible under the statute for a writer to assign to a publisher the ownership of certain rights under copyright while reserving the ownership of one or more other such rights. Conceivably, a writer could assign the ownership of some rights to one publisher and ownership of other rights to another publisher. In practice, however, a single publisher generally owns and administers all rights, except in the case of "split copyrights."

Royalty Statements

Obtaining a satisfactory contract is only part of a songwriter's job. A writer must also know how to read the publisher's royalty statements. In the past songwriters would sometimes boast of their ignorance in this respect by saying that they filed royalty checks in the bank and royalty statements in the wastepaper basket. In an era of computerized royalty statements with code letters or numerals instead of clearly understandable designations, songwriters may be even more tempted to ignore such matters. However, machine-prepared royalty statements can contain mistakes because somewhere in the data chain there is a human operator and each operator works from a source document. Reading the royalty statement not only informs writers as to the source of their livelihood but also keeps them alert to possible areas of exploitation that may not have been tracked.

An alert writer should have in mind specific questions when reading royalty statements:

- Is a certain song's advance being charged against the writer's other songs handled by the same publisher?
- Is the 50 percent division of mechanical royalties being properly allocated among collaborators, as in the case of a song with two lyricists and only one composer, where contractual provision is made that the sole composer is entitled to half of the writer royalties?
- Is payment being made immediately in respect of a foreign advance obtained by the publisher? Or is it being withheld pending the publisher's receipt of foreign royalty statements showing actual earnings against that advance—usually a long time later?
- Is the Harry Fox Agency commission being deducted in full by the publisher from mechanical receipts?
- Are the public performance license fees collected from a motion picture producer for U.S. theater performances being distributed at the same time as the synchronization license fees?

These and other questions can be raised only if the contract contains appropriate provisions.

Recapture of Rights

Writers must try to ensure that a composition does not lie unnoticed on a publisher's shelf for an extended period of time. Under the 1978 SGA contract form, the writer is entitled to recapture rights from the publisher after 1 year from the date of the agreement, or such shorter period as may be specified, if the publisher has not licensed a recording or other use. However, if prior to the end of this period the publisher pays the writer a nonrecoupable bonus of $250 (or any larger amount that has been mutually agreed on), the period to obtain the release of a commercial recording is extended for up to 6 months (or such lesser period as may be specified by the parties).

Some non-SGA publishing agreements make no provision for the recapture of rights by the writer for a publisher's failure to exploit a song. Other agreements may forestall recapture by one or more of the following acts on the part of the publisher: (1) printing sheet music copies, (2) obtaining a commercial recording of the composition, (3) licensing the music composition for inclusion in a television, motion picture, video, or dramatic production, or (4) paying a certain amount of money. The publisher may protect itself by a clause that requires the writer to give a 30-day (or longer) notice of intention to recapture, during which period the publisher may cure any default.

Printed Editions

A customary provision in a songwriter's contract is for the payment to the writer of 8 to 12 cents per copy of sheet music sold in the United States and Canada, plus 50 percent of the sheet music royalties received by the publisher for sales in other countries. (The publisher usually contracts to be paid 10 to 12.5 percent of the retail selling price of sheet music sold outside the United States and Canada.) In common practice, most printing is done under license, and 50 percent of net receipts is the basis of print music royalties, just as it is with mechanicals.

For compositions included in printed song folios, the SGA contract provides for the writer to be paid a royalty of 10 percent of the wholesale selling price (less trade discounts, if any) prorated downward by the ratio between the number of compositions written by the writer and the number of other copyrighted compositions in the folio. If the publication contains more than 25 compositions, the 10 percent royalty rate is increased by an additional 0.5 percent for each additional composition. It is not uncommon for publishers to issue deluxe higher-priced folios containing as many as 45 to 50 songs, and usually writers gladly consent to such editions and waive extra royalties.

With respect to folios, many songwriter contracts provide for the payment of a one-time fixed sum to a writer, ranging anywhere from $1 up to about $25, irrespective of the number sold. If the lump-sum payment is reasonable no substantial harm results, since the sales of folios are often limited. There have been exceptional folios that sold in excess of 100,000 copies, such as those comprising the songs of Paul Simon, Andrew Lloyd Webber, Michael Jackson, or Lennon-McCartney. That having been said, it is generally advisable to avoid fixed-fee buyouts.

In the exploitation of music, the publisher is called on to distribute promotional or professional copies of printed editions. These copies may be given to the A&R personnel of record companies whose function it is to acquire material that has the potential to be recorded by artists under contract to their companies. Other copies may be delivered to orchestras or vocalists in order to encourage their performance of the composition. Additional copies may be sent to managers, agents, and producers. The SGA contract and most songwriter agreements provide that the publisher is not obligated to pay royalties for promotional or professional copies.

Sheet Music Sales

Over the past few decades sales of single copies of sheet music of most individual popular songs have slowed to a mere trickle in the United States, at least sales in bricks-and-mortar wholesalers and retailers, although some hit songs can still sell in large quantities. (The sale of folio and other collections is still big business—in 2000, a total of $316 million in the United States and $728 million worldwide.) Further, even the major retailers carry at most 10,000 selections, and even if a selection *is* in stock, it is likely to be available only for the piano and/or guitar instrumentation. On-line distribution, a relatively recent phenomenon, has changed all that, and numerous Web sites offer downloadable sheet music for sale. One of the largest, sheetmusicplus.com, claims to have over 366,000 titles. For more information on sheet music offerings on the Web, see Chapter 29.

Mechanical Rights

As discussed in Chapter 15, the holder of the copyright to a musical composition has the sole right to reproduce that composition by mechanical means, including CDs, whether distributed as finished product or digitally. The songwriter grants that right to the music publisher, which then gives a mechanical license to a record company, under which a royalty based on the statutory rate is payable. As of January 1, 2002, the statutory rate was 8 cents per composition for each phonorecord made and distributed up to 5 minutes' duration or 1.55 cents per minute or fraction thereof, whichever is greater.

In some instances the mechanical royalty for a composition included in an album will be less than for a single because of the number of compositions on the album. This is often the case where the artist or producer is the writer and the recording agreement has a controlled-composition clause with a cap on the number of compositions. (Recall that a controlled composition is any composition written, owned, or controlled, in whole or in part, by the artist or producer.)

A great majority of the active publishers in the United States use the services of the Harry Fox Agency for mechanical licensing. In the agreement between a songwriter and a publisher, provision is made for the writer to share in mechanical license fees received by the publisher. The customary share is 50 percent of the publisher's receipts in the United States. This means 50 percent of 100 percent of license fee payments from U.S. record companies, after deducting the Harry Fox Agency collection charge of 5.75 percent on mechanicals. For mechanical license earnings outside the United States, the writer is usually entitled to 50 percent of the net sums received domestically by the U.S. publisher.

A similar division applies to a publisher's receipts from licensing the synchronization or reproduction of music on television, video, motion picture soundtracks, video games, and even bell tones for cellular telephones. Such licenses are referred to as *synchronization licenses*. Harry Fox no longer administers synchronization rights for publishers.

In promoting a new recording, a publisher may spend money in trade paper advertising and in the purchase and distribution of promotional records. These expenses are not normally chargeable either in whole or in part to the writer. Some publishers charge the writer's royalty account for one-half of these expenses by authorizing the record company to undertake the entire expense of the advertisements or promotional records and then deduct the portion of that expense that the publisher would usually bear from mechanical record royalties otherwise payable to the publisher. The publisher is obligated to pay the writer one-half of the receipts, but by allowing the record company to deduct the cost of advertising and promotion off the top—that is, from the mechanical royalties that it sends to the publisher—the publisher receives, and shares with the writer, reduced remittances. This practice is a violation of some songwriter agreements, including the SGA standard songwriter agreement. However, it is difficult to determine the extent of the practice without a detailed audit. The SGA recommends that all songwriter agreements include an audit provision with no time restriction.

Accountings and Audits

The SGA agreement stipulates that the publisher will account to writers either quarterly or semiannually, depending on what period is customary for the publisher, within 45 days after the end of the applicable period. Other agreements usually provide for semiannual accountings. Quarterly accountings are obviously more desirable for a writer than semiannual accountings. Naturally, a publisher seeks fewer accountings, which lessens administrative costs and overhead.

Songwriters should be alert to provisions by which they waive any objections to royalty accountings unless such objections are lodged within a given period, such as one year. These provisions are generally enforceable. Of course, a publisher is entitled to some protection against complaints received long after events transpire.

Frequently, a basis for complaint regarding an accounting can be found only on an audit of the books of the publisher. Many reputable publishers will cooperate with a request for an audit even in the absence of a contractual provision permitting the songwriter to audit. Other publishers require such contractual provisions before they are willing to allow an audit. A contractual provision has the advantage of fixing rights and obligations without requiring a court order, although such orders are generally granted, even in the absence of contractual provisions.

Under the SGA contract, any writer may demand a detailed breakdown of royalties on 60 days' written notice, showing the receipts attributable to each record label for each song as well as the details of other uses and the number of copies sold in each royalty category. The writer must pay the cost of the examination; but if the audit reveals that the writer is owed 5 percent or more of the amount shown on royalty statements the publisher must pay for the cost of the examination, up to 50 percent of the amount found to be due to the writer. When a record company and a publishing company are under common ownership and the publishing company does its own licensing of sound recordings, the writer may examine the books of the record company if royalty payments are questioned.

The SGA Collection Plan is a compulsory system of collection and auditing required of all members of SGA. It is designed to avoid the expense and delay involved for a songwriter in the auditing of publisher's books. The charge is 5.75 percent of the writer royalties collected from publishers, with a maximum charge of $2,170 a year. Under the system the writer directs publishers to send his or her checks and statements to the SGA office. Not all publisher accounts are audited, since the time and expense would be inordinate. SGA accountants make a random selection of publishers for the purpose of auditing the accounts for several years at the same time. Many responsible publishers welcome the opportunity to be audited in order to reassure their writers of their accounting integrity. Furthermore, by dealing with an accountant who represents many writers, the publisher avoids the loss of time required to make individual explanations to writers.

Many songwriters have requested that SGA charge only for collections and audits to particular publishers designated by the writers, rather than to all publishers audited by the SGA. This is not permitted on the grounds that the 5.75 percent fee, in respect of publishers who pay regularly and honestly, is required to subsidize the expense of auditing and collecting with regard to the less scrupulous publishers. However, if a publisher is owned in whole or in part to the extent of at least 25 percent by an SGA writer, the songwriter can exclude the royalties from that publisher in the collection plan and still use the collection service for other publishers.

Default

Occasionally a songwriter complains that royalties are not paid when due and that statements are insufficient in detail. In the face of continued refusals to account, a claim can be made of a breach in the contract between the writer and the publisher. The writer can sue in the courts for an accounting, and under usual court procedure the writer will be able to examine the books and records of the publisher in support of the writer's action.

The writer may also take the position that the breach justifies termination of the contract and that on such a termination all rights in the copyright revert to the writer. It may be expected that the publisher will strongly oppose this position. A court has to decide whether the breach is material or immaterial— that is, whether or not it goes to the essence of the agreement and therefore permits the aggrieved party to cancel it. A refusal to account for one period may well be deemed immaterial, whereas failure to account for several periods, during which repeated requests for accountings were made by the writer, may be judged material.

The prospect of court litigation discourages many songwriters from moving to obtain accountings or to nullify their agreements with publishers. There are at least two practical approaches for a writer to avoid having to pay for litigation. Under one approach, the writer may assign all publication rights to another publisher, and the writer and publisher may join in notifying the performing rights organization that the original publisher's rights have been canceled and that the publication rights have been vested in a new publisher. On such notice BMI may hold up payments of the publisher's share of performance royalties to the original publisher with a doubtful credit standing. ASCAP will hold back payments of the publisher's share of performance monies but will resume payments within 6 months if a suit is not filed or within 1 year if a filed suit is not adjudicated, provided the original publisher files an agreement to indemnify ASCAP against claims by the other publisher and, in addition, in disputes over renewal rights, files documentary support of its position. The performing rights organization's action may by itself be sufficient to make the original publisher willing to negotiate an agreeable settlement of the controversy.

Using the second approach, the writer, as a condition of the assignment to the new publisher, may require it to finance all litigation to establish the new publisher's rights to the material.

Obviously, it is to the writer's advantage to insert a clear and appropriate default clause in the songwriter's agreement. It should be provided that certain specified events constitute grounds for requesting arbitration or for the termination of the agreement. Among these events would be the failure to supply royalty statements and remittances, and the publisher's refusal to allow an inspection of its books and records.

The publisher may strongly oppose the default clause and claim, arguing that the writer is protected by law in case of a material breach. While this may be true, it entails the potential expense of litigation to establish the materiality of a breach and does not meet the objective of the writer to avoid litigation. The writer can counter with an offer to give adequate notice to the publisher of a default and a sufficient opportunity to cure it. Another counteroffer may be one calling for alternate dispute resolution by mediation or arbitration in the event of a dispute.

Performance Fees

As discussed in Chapter 14, performance fees are collected by performing rights organizations—ASCAP, BMI, and SESAC in the United States—from radio and television stations and from other commercial users of music, such as nightclubs and hotels, for the right to publicly perform copyrighted music.

Under the Copyright Act of 1909, the performance would ordinarily have to be for profit. The Copyright Act of 1976 deletes this requirement, but it substitutes certain specific and limited exemptions set forth in Section 110, such as non-commercial performances during religious services in places of worship or in face-to-face classroom instruction. The performing rights organizations make distributions separately to the writers and publishers of musical compositions. They will not pay the writer's share to the publisher. As a consequence, song-writer agreements with publishers do not provide for the payment of perform-ance fees by the publisher to the writer. To clarify the matter, agreements often state that the publisher is not obligated to pay any public performance fees to the writer.

The SGA contract specifically denies the right of the writer or publisher to share in the revenues distributed to the other by the performing rights organi-zation with which both are affiliated.

Assignments

Many songwriter agreements permit a publisher to assign its rights. Consequently, a songwriter who enters into an agreement relying on the personnel and integrity of a particular publisher may find that by virtue of an assignment the writer is dealing with a different entity. The SGA contract meets this problem by requiring the writer's consent to an assignment by the publisher, except if the song is included in a bona fide sale of the publisher's business or entire catalog, or in a merger, or as part of an assignment to a subsidiary or affiliate. However, in all cases a written assumption of obligations must be delivered to the author by the new assignee-publisher.

It is clear that over the long life of a copyright many situations may arise that can be handled more flexibly and expeditiously if a publisher can assign his or her rights. The principals of independent publishers die and estates may be forced to sell interests in a copyright, or they may retire and desire to dispose of their music publishing interests. There can be little cause for concern when the assignment is made to a large, established, reputable publisher, as is the ten-dency, since this type of purchaser is generally able to make higher offers.

Lyrics versus Music

A song may be written for instruments alone, without lyrics, but more fre-quently it consists of both music and lyrics. While there are writers who write both music and lyrics, it is more common for an artist to be either a composer or a lyricist. The wedding of lyrics and music is an integral part of the business of a music publisher. A good publisher must know the commercial potential of various types of lyrics as well as qualified lyricists who can write them.

Through the grant of all rights under copyright, the publisher obtains the right to set words to the music and to modify and adapt the music. These powers are usually necessary for the proper exploitation of a composition. A publisher must be careful to determine whether the writer has the right to approve changes in the music, including any new lyrics, as well as whether the writer has agreed to share royalties with the lyricist or other writer engaged by the publisher. Where the SGA contract has been used, it is prudent to draw a new agreement that includes all of the writers of the final version of the song and thus avoid any later problem of consent or sharing of royalties. Under the SGA agreement, unless specifically agreed otherwise, the royalties are shared equally among all the writers, regardless of the total number. Consequently, if there is only one lyric writer and there are three melody collaborators, each receives 25 percent. An agreement among the writers changing their participation may be required to avoid an injustice.

Earlier sections of this chapter deal with royalties payable to writers for printed editions and mechanical licenses. Normally, these royalties cover the writers as a collective unit rather than composer and lyricist separately. The total writer royalties are ordinarily shared equally between the composer and lyricist. Specifically, a royalty of 6 cents per copy of sheet music sold is remitted as follows: 3 cents to the composer and 3 cents to the lyricist. Similarly, mechanical license royalties, which are usually 50 percent of the publisher's collections, are paid half to the composer and the other half to the lyricist. If there are three or more collaborators on a song, they usually determine among themselves their respective shares of the total writer royalties.

It should be recognized that some songs never reach the public eye and the writers may wish to attempt to salvage their individual contributions of title, words, or music for future use.

Royalties Held in Trust Funds

A potent weapon to ensure that songwriters receive the monies they are due is to provide that these monies collected by the publisher are held in trust by the publisher. A fiduciary relationship between the publisher and the writer is thus created in place of a debtor-creditor relationship. Under the debtor-creditor status, the failure to account to the writer might entail only a simple claim against the publisher. This claim has the same standing as that for any other debt owed by the publisher. The bankruptcy of the publisher erases the debt to the writer in the same way that other debts are canceled.

However, under the trust concept the writer becomes the legal owner of the funds, and the publisher is the custodian on behalf of the writer. The claim of the writer is not then dischargeable in the bankruptcy of the publisher, and the writer achieves a preferred status in relation to other creditors. Furthermore, there is a basis for criminal prosecution if the publisher becomes insolvent and does not pay writer royalties, since there will have been a misappropriation of funds that belong to another, namely, the writer. A similar charge may be brought in case the publisher refuses to pay.

The trust concept is clearly established under the SGA contract. Publishers using other songwriter forms will oppose the insertion of trust clauses because of the drastic consequences that may ensue. They point out, and with merit, that they may be unjustly prosecuted criminally if an honest dispute develops, for example, concerning whether monies are actually owed to the writer. Publishers also contend that innocent officers in a publishing enterprise may become tarred with a criminal brush because of acts or defaults of other officers. They argue that, for full protection of personnel, there has to be established separate and burdensome trust accounts and other administrative procedures that the average publisher cannot afford in terms of either time or expense.

Arbitration

As may be expected, disputes arise between publishers and writers concerning their respective rights and obligations under their agreements. If they cannot compromise, the SGA contract relegates both parties to arbitration, before a sole arbitrator, under the prevailing rules of the American Arbitration Association. A decision by the arbitrator is enforceable by the courts. Some songwriter agreements follow the example of the SGA contract in providing for arbitration. Many do not.

From the writer's point of view, arbitration is desirable since it affords a relatively inexpensive and expeditious method for resolving conflicts. Many music publishers favor arbitration for the same reason. Due to the technical aspects of copyright law and the tendency of arbitrators to compromise differences rather than decide disputes on principle, other publishers prefer the courts. Moreover, publishers can often bear the expense of litigation more readily than writers, and the expense may well force writers to settle for less than they might be entitled to under a court decision.

Exclusive Writer Agreements

Publishers interested in a continuous supply of good material may attempt to negotiate an exclusive agreement with a desirable composer or lyricist. Most major exclusive writer deals with large advance payments concern writers who are also producers or featured artists with recording commitments and therefore the possibility of significant publishing revenues. Under an exclusive-writer agreement the writer assigns all compositions written during its term solely to the publisher, which becomes the owner of all copyrights. Royalties payable to the writer under an exclusive writer agreement are usually the same as those paid in the absence of an exclusive writer's agreement.

A songwriter is not likely to sign an exclusive contract unless he or she is to be paid a cash consideration in the form of a lump sum or weekly payments. Frequently, a payment beyond an initial advance is conditioned on the commercial U.S. release of an agreed number of recordings on a major label. All the payments are deemed to be advances against, and recoupable from, royalties that otherwise become payable to the writer.

It is a customary provision in exclusive writer agreements that the publisher has one or more options to extend the term of the agreement, either on the same or modified terms. When the songwriter is not also a producer or featured artist, it may be that the publisher cannot exercise the option unless the publisher has passed certain performance tests indicating that it is actually working in the interest of the writer. One test may be that a certain number of the writer's compositions have been recorded commercially. Most agreements (especially those where there is a producer or featured major-label artist involved) provide for an escalation in the cash consideration to be paid in option periods. Some writers may be able to negotiate their right to copublish all works written in any option periods.

In recent years publishing affiliates of major label record companies offer to copublish, or to be the full publisher of, music of songwriter-artists on affiliated labels by offering special inducements. A major inducement is to have the record label waive its normal controlled-composition 75 percent of statutory rate request and to allow the full statutory rate to be applied. However, if there is a copublishing relationship, the net to the writer-copublisher is usually somewhat less than 75 percent of the statutory rate after the deduction of a copublisher share and an administrative charge. A simple explanation will demonstrate this. The publisher usually takes 10 percent off the top as administrative charges; 50 percent goes to the writer, leaving 40 percent of the statutory rate. The remaining balance of 40 percent is divided equally between the writer (copublisher) and publisher. The final outcome is that the writer receives 70 percent (50 percent plus 20 percent), which is less than the normal 75 percent statutory rate applicable if no copublishing deal had been made.

A more conventional inducement is the payment of a substantial advance on signing plus additional advances during successive option periods, which usually run parallel to the record company option periods, extending for as many as seven albums. Such advances can be significant sums but are usually based on the assumption that all or substantially all of the compositions recorded by the songwriter-artist are subject to the agreement. If a lesser number are delivered, there is a proportionate reduction in the advance.

Further negotiations sometimes provide not only that the stated minimum advances be escalated as each successive album is delivered but also that such amount be a minimum, with a higher amount applicable if 66.67 percent of earnings on the preceding album justify this amount, provided that even with a blockbuster sale the formula payment can never exceed 200 percent of the negotiated minimum payment. A pro-rated schedule of minimum and maximum amounts per album is usually set out, together with the formula of a 6- to 9-month period after release of the prior record. For formula purposes, customary reserves are usually disregarded.

If a writer is signed to an exclusive contract, the status of the works becomes a matter of debate: Are they to be considered works for hire or independent contractor works under the Copyright Act? This is a complex subject that will be discussed in Chapter 17. The decision affects the initial ownership of copyright, the duration of copyright, the owner's copyright renewal rights, and the copyright termination rights.

If minors who are songwriters are asked to sign exclusive writer contracts, questions arise as to whether the minors can be legally bound and, if so, in what manner. These issues are considered in Chapter 3.

17

Works for Hire

Section 101 of the Copyright Act provides two legal categories of a work made for hire:

1. A work prepared by an employee within "the scope of his or her employment," for example, work created by a conventional salaried employee
2. A work specially ordered or commissioned for use as a contribution to a collective work, as a part of a motion picture or other audiovisual work, as a translation, as a supplementary work, as a compilation, as an instructional text, as a test, as answer material for a test, or as an atlas, provided that the parties expressly agree in writing that the work shall be considered a work for hire. Notice that nine types of work are specified in the second category. A work of one of these types is generally created by an independent contractor who has agreed in writing to such treatment. Subsequent cases have determined that the written agreement must be entered into *before* the work is created.

Whether or not a composition or a recording is a work for hire can have profound significance. It affects the initial ownership of copyright, the duration of copyright, copyright renewal rights (if created before 1978), and copyright termination rights.

The Copyright Act provides that "copyright in a work protected under this title vests initially in the author or authors of the work." But if a work is "for hire," the Act considers the hiring party (the employer or qualifying commissioning party) to be the author of the work and (absent any written agreement to the contrary) the owner of copyright in the work.

Copyright in works for hire written in 1978 or later last for 95 years from the year of first publication, or 100 years from creation, whichever is shorter. If the work is not a work for hire, copyright remains in effect for the author's life plus 70 years. An independent contractor who has not created a work for hire can usually terminate his or her grant of rights after 35 years, subject, however, to the right of the owner to continue to use derivative works prepared before the termination. There can be no such termination by the actual creator of the work in the case of a work for hire.

Most recording agreements state that the recordings made under the agreement are deemed to be "works made for hire." However, given the absence of regular work hours, withholding of taxes and social security, and other indications of a conventional employer-employee working relationship, the recording artist is likely to be considered an independent contractor. Of course, recordings made by an independent contractor may still be deemed works for hire if they fit within one of the nine categories specified in the 1976 Copyright Act. Whether or not they do is an issue that remains to be resolved (see discussion below).

Factors Determining a Work-for-Hire Relationship

A written statement in a contract as to whether a work was prepared by an employee in the scope of his or her employment is not by itself decisive of this issue. In *Community for Creative Non-Violence et al. v. Reid*, 109 Sup. Ct. 2166 (1989), the Supreme Court stated that the standard for determining the existence of an employment relationship is the common law of agency. The Court rejected a test based simply on whether the hiring party controlled or had the right to control the production of the work and instead set forth various factors to be considered in deciding whether an employment-for-hire relationship exists. The Court further stated that each factor is one among other factors, with no one factor being determinative.

These are some of the factors identified by the Supreme Court as they apply to recording artists and songwriters.

▶ *The skill required.* This factor might weigh in favor of finding that a recording artist and an exclusive writer are independent contractors, not employees, since it requires great skill on the part of the artist and songwriter to create these works.

▶ *The source of the instrumentalities and tools.* This factor favors both artists and writers because rarely do artists record at studios owned by the record company, and typically the company provides the artist with a recording fund, which the artist uses to create and deliver master recordings.

▶ *The location of the work.* This factor also favors both artists and writers because, as referred to above, rarely do artists and writers record or write on the premises of the company or publisher.

▶ *The duration of the relationship.* Since artist and writer exclusive agreements are usually for a period of years, this factor may favor the hiring party being defined as the "employer."

▶ *The hiring party's option to assign additional projects.* Many recording contracts call for additional recordings at the option of the record company. Exclusive writer agreements may not contain similar provisions.

- ▶ *The extent of the hiring party's discretion over when and how to work.* A record company's control is usually limited to choosing (or approving) producers, material to be recorded, and recording budgets. Publishers do not control the manner in which writers write music.
- ▶ *The method of payment.* While writer agreements often provide for periodic advances, the recording artist is more likely to receive advances only in conjunction with specific recording projects. Both writers and artists receive compensation in the form of royalties which are contingent upon success. Additionally, neither publishers nor record companies customarily deduct withholding taxes or contribute to social security, as regular employers are required to do.
- ▶ *The hired party's role in hiring and paying assistants.* This is not usually a factor in exclusive writer agreements, but it would ordinarily relate to hiring and paying musician sidemen for recording sessions.
- ▶ *Whether the hiring party is in business.* Both the record company and the music publisher are obviously in business.
- ▶ *Whether the work is part of the regular business of the hiring party.* This factor favors the record company and the music publisher.

Subsequent cases have attached greater weight to some of these factors than to others. However, on balance it appears that recording artists and songwriters are not employees of either the record company or the music publisher. In the case of *Forward v. Thorogood,* 758 F.Supp 782 (D.MA 1991) aff'd 985 F.2d 604 (1st Cir. 1993), Forward had arranged and paid for two 1976 recording sessions for Thorogood's band. The band let Forward keep the tapes. In 1988 Forward sought to sell the tapes to a record company for commercial release, claiming ownership under the work-for-hire doctrine. The court rejected Forward's claim, holding that there was no evidence that he employed or commissioned the band members.

Commissioned Works

Since recording artists and songwriters are not likely to be considered conventional employees of a record company or music publisher, the second definition of a work made for hire is the one most likely to be brought into play.

Works which are specifically created for a motion picture or other audiovisual work make up one subcategory of commissioned works. This subcategory clearly covers music specifically created for use in motion pictures, television, films, and videos, as well as for the soundtrack recordings, but not pre-existing music used in such works. However, most popular music recordings do not fit into this category.

Another category of commissioned works with possible relevance to the music industry is a compilation. A *compilation* is defined in the Copyright Act as "a work formed by the collection and assembling of preexisting materials or of data that are selected, coordinated, or arranged in such a way that the resulting work as a whole constitutes an original work of authorship." The determination of whether an album is in fact a compilation and whether recordings are specially commissioned as part of the album is not easily made. In order to be separately copyrightable as a compilation, sufficient original authorship must be involved in the selection and arrangement of the works. If an artist delivers 12 songs, all of which are included in an album, there has been no selectivity. If the record company omits certain individual recordings delivered by the artist and otherwise changes the order in which the artist has delivered the album, one might argue there has been original authorship. In the case of "greatest hits" albums, which are clearly compilations, one cannot argue that the component songs (presumably pre-existing) were specially commissioned to be included in the compilation.

A third category of commissioned works which might relate to the music industry is supplementary work. A *supplementary work* is defined in the Copyright Act as one "prepared for publication as a secondary adjunct to a work by another author for the purpose of introducing, concluding, illustrating, explaining, revising, commenting upon, or assisting in the use of the other work, such as forewords, afterwords, pictorial illustrations, maps, charts, tables, editorial notes, *musical arrangements,* answer material for tests, bibliographies, appendixes, and indexes" (emphasis added). This category seems applicable to those portions of printed editions of musical compositions which are forewords, illustrations, and special musical arrangements, but not to the musical compositions themselves.

In 1999, Congress passed a so-called "technical" correction to the second part of employment for hire definitions of the Copyright Act of 1976. In doing so, it added the words "sound recordings" to the Copyright Act's list of specific categories of works for which an independent contractor can be deemed an employee if the contract so provides. This provision, which was passed without public notice or hearings, and as part of a bill that had no clear relation to recordings or works for hire, was immediately controversial. Recording artists claimed that the provision deprived them of their rights as independent contractors to terminate record companies' rights in recordings made after the effective date of the Copyright Act of 1976, beginning in 2013. Record companies, represented by the Recording Industry Association of America (RIAA), claimed that the disputed inserted language was merely a "clarification" of existing practices.

Congress resolved the dispute by the Copyright Corrections Act of 2000, which removed the "sound recording" category that had been added, but also stated that no legal significance should be given either to the technical insert or the removal thereof. This result clearly showed a Congressional intention to avoid a final determination of whether recording artists are or are not to be treated as employees and to leave the issue for the courts to decide. This was in deference to the RIAA, which feared that an outright repeal of the 1999 correction would be interpreted as an indication that Congress in fact intended sound recordings *not* to be eligible to be considered works for hire. Informed commentators generally feel that continuing record company ownership of a sound recording is unlikely to survive an appropriate notice of termination by the artist, except in the case of sound recordings made as part of a video and thus falling within the protected "audiovisual" format.

Assignments of Copyright

In agreements that state that a work is deemed to be a work for hire, there is often a further provision assigning the copyright, including any renewal and extension rights, to the hiring party. This should not technically be necessary because (as recognized in the first section of the definition of works made for hire) a true employment relationship leads to the employer owning the products of the employee made within the scope of the employment. Some contracts simply state that the parties intend that the results and proceeds of the services involved belong to the hiring party. In the absence of direct language of assignment to the hiring party, a court may decide that the contractual characterization of the work as one for hire indicates an intention to make an assignment to the hiring party. As a result, even though a court may declare the work not to be a work for hire, the court might also find that the hiring party (that is, the record company or music publisher) owns the copyright by assignment.

Works commissioned and created prior to January 1, 1978, the effective date of the Copyright Act of 1976, were generally presumed to be owned by the commissioning party. As discussed above, the 1976 Copyright Act changed this presumption by providing that only certain categories of commissioned works, created under an agreement in writing signed by the parties, would be eligible for work-for-hire status. For pre-1978 compositions, the right to renew for the 28-year renewal period and the right to continue for the full copyright extension period runs in favor of the independent contractor or his or her successors under certain circumstances, as previously indicated. For compositions created on or after 1978 that are not works for hire, the assignment to the hiring party can usually be terminated after 35 years. Since the first notices of termination can be sent as early as 2003 (10 years before the expiration of 35 years from the effective date of the 1976 Copyright Act), this issue will soon be tested in the courts.

Notwithstanding the status of a writer of words or music for ownership of copyright purposes, both ASCAP and BMI will continue to pay the writers their writer share of performance income. Thus, film music, which is customarily written under an employment contract, will still generate performance earnings, even in the rare situation where mechanical royalties might be forfeited.

Joint Work Status

In *Community for Creative Non-Violence et al. v. Reid,* the district court had to decide whether the product created was a joint work, with the hiring party and the independent contractor as joint authors. According to the Supreme Court, this depends on a determination that the parties prepared the work with the "intention that their contributions be merged into inseparable or interdependent parts of a unitary whole." The language quoted from the Court opinion is itself contained in the definition of a joint work in the Copyright Act.

Whether or not a joint work was created as such is an issue of fact. The intention at the time of creation is the touchstone. To qualify as a joint author, the commissioning party must materially contribute to the creation of the work. Each contribution must be more than minimal. It is not sufficient that the commissioning party merely furnish the financing for the work. It may be expected that the written expression of the parties' intention—that the work is one for hire—may influence whether a joint work is determined to exist.

What might the contributions of a record company or a music publisher be to the creation of a joint work? The record company's A&R personnel may suggest the compositions to be recorded, the appropriate commercial music arrangements, the special effects from synthesizers or other recordings, the proper makeup of the orchestra, and so on. The record producer may supervise in great detail the entire recording session and may have significant input into the editing of the recording sessions after their completion. In *Forward v. Thorogood* (cited above, page 178), the court found no evidence that the producer had made any musical or artistic contribution which was sufficient to reach the level of joint ownership. In another situation, however, the result might be different.

The professional personnel of the music publisher may suggest the subject and titles of compositions to be written and may participate in changing the words and music or the arrangements in order to make the product more attractive. They may also supervise the production of demonstration records and initiate arrangements and make editing decisions that enhance the appeal of otherwise raw compositions. A court may consider such participation in deciding whether the music publisher should be considered a joint author.

If a work is determined to be a joint work, the commissioning party is assured of sharing in the work for the full duration of copyright. Although the independent contractor or his or her heirs is thus entitled to participate in ownership of the work, there is a joint sharing with the commissioning party, as in the case of multiple authors of other joint works.

18

Co-Ownership and Joint Administration of Copyrights

Even a cursory review of recent chart hits reveals that the practice of two or more publishers sharing the ownership of popular songs is common. *Co-ownership* exists where there are two or more writers of a joint work, with each being a co-owner of the entire copyright and entitled to assign his or her interest to a separate publisher.

Sharing of copyright often occurs when the recording artist and a producer each contributes to the writing of a song and each has his or her own publishing firm. It may also occur when a record company's publishing affiliate has been granted a stake in the copyright in order to induce the record company to sign an artist-writer, or when an established song is in the renewal term of copyright and each of the two writers has granted his or her renewal rights to a different music publisher.

Joint ownership, or co-ownership, of copyright is sometimes called a "split copyright." In theory, this phrase is a misnomer because prior to the Copyright Act of 1976, the courts regarded a copyright as "indivisible." In practice, however, while there could be only one legal owner of a copyright, this was not regarded as barring joint ownership of undivided interests in the bundle of rights that constitute a copyright. Under the Copyright Act of 1976, there was a statutory recognition of the divisibility of copyright. Now, any of the exclusive rights under copyright, and any subdivision of them, can be transferred and owned separately. Most agreements between joint owners relate to the entire copyright and its undivided interests or shares, although under the Copyright Act of 1976 there is no bar to joint ownership of a particular exclusive right, such as the right to reproduce printed copies of a musical work.

Registration and Notice

The Copyright Office recognizes joint ownership of copyright as an appropriate matter to be registered. When there is joint ownership of copyright, the notice of copyright on copies should contain the names of all co-owners, and such names should be the same as the names of the copyright owners on the copyright registration form.

The General Rights of Co-Owners

A joint owner of a copyright is free to use or license the use of the work without the knowledge or consent of the other co-owners, provided that the use does not amount to a destruction of the work. Judges use the analogy to joint ownership of real estate. If two or more persons own a cabin on a wooded plot of land, any of the owners can make use of the property or may authorize third parties to use it. However, no joint owner may chop down the trees or authorize third parties to destroy the joint property without the consent of the other owners.

The courts have uniformly held that when any one of the co-owners of a copyright licenses the use of the work, he or she must account to the other co-owners for their share of the profits. Although there is a split of opinion among music publishers regarding the need to account to co-owners for profits from a music publisher's own printed editions as distinguished from usages licensed for exploitation by third parties, current industry practice favors a requirement to account.

Even the field of printing and distribution of printed sheet music and folios is adapted to co-ownership. Firms such as Warner Bros. Music and Hal Leonard Publishing Corporation serve as licensees to handle printing and distribution and to remit to the joint owners their respective shares of the net receipts.

The Problems of Co-Ownership

Limited problems do exist in the administration of a jointly owned copyright for purposes of licensing and collection. ASCAP, BMI, and SESAC have no difficulty in administering jointly owned performing rights, provided that all co-owners are affiliates or members of the same performing rights organization. Even where the performing rights are divided among several performing rights organizations, they will generally honor directions to divide publisher and writer credits as directed by the co-owners. Some dissatisfied publishers claim that they are forced to share copyrights with recording stars and record company publishing affiliates, and that this is akin to payola; however, the practice appears uncoerced from a legal point of view.

At times the co-owners may have a conflict of interests. For instance, a record company co-owner may wish to grant itself a favorable reduced mechanical licensing rate, despite the decrease in publisher receipts that will result. Record company and artist co-owners may want to discourage obtaining and exploiting cover records of the same song by other artists and record companies.

In making a deal with a record company to share in the copyright, the publisher or artist-writer should contractually provide for the minimum mechanical license rate that the record company must pay. Otherwise the label may be in a position to grant itself a favorable rate, despite the objections of the co-owner, subject to a possible claim for breach of trust.

With regard to cover records, neither joint owner can bar the other, except contractually, from seeking and exploiting those records. On the other hand, no joint owner can insist, in the absence of a contractual provision, on joint expenditures for advertising and exploitation of any nature, whether they be for a cover record or otherwise.

Synchronization Rights

Although it would be simple to instruct that synchronization fees be divided in the same manner as mechanical license royalties received from record companies, synchronization rights may require different treatment. Since synchronization rights apply worldwide, the joint administration agreement must provide for an allocation of the synchronization fee between the United States and elsewhere when the co-ownership involves only U.S. rights, as may occur in the case of joint ownership during the renewal term of the U.S. copyright of pre-1978 works.

Many publishers agree that 50 percent of the synchronization fee should be attributable to the United States and the balance to the rest of the world. Some knowledgeable industry accountants, however, state that the percentages should be 45 percent for the United States and 5 percent for Canada, with 50 percent for the remainder of the world.

In the case of motion pictures, synchronization license fees must be distinguished from fees for the license of U.S. performing rights. A motion picture producer or other user of music who seeks a synchronization license must also acquire a U.S. public performance license. In the United States, ASCAP is barred by a court decree based on anti-monopoly laws from licensing theaters to perform music contained in films. Because of this, specific licenses for the U.S. performance of the music in motion pictures is customarily issued to the producer by the publisher at the same time as the worldwide synchronization license. If the co-owner has only a U.S. interest (such as under a renewal copyright ownership), the total combined license fees must be divided to reflect the respective interests of the co-owners.

Foreign Rights

Agreements for the co-ownership of songs should provide for one or the other of the owners to have sole control of foreign rights or should set forth the basic terms for acceptable foreign licensing contracts. This provision is essential because in a number of foreign countries, including England, either joint owner may arbitrarily veto a license negotiated by the other. This is in contrast to the freedom to license accorded to each co-owner under U.S. law.

Where joint ownership pertains to pre-1978 songs for their U.S. renewal period, it may also involve foreign administration of the songs if the foreign rights were reacquired by the writers beginning with the renewal term of the U.S. copyright. This reacquisition is provided for in the Songwriters Guild of America standard agreement between publishers and writers relating to pre-1978 songs. Prior to the 1948 and 1969 forms of the American Guild of Authors and Composers (the SGA's predecessor organization), most agreements with writers did not limit the term of foreign rights.

Consent by Silence

Many joint ownership agreements provide for consultation and reasonable consent before either owner grants a license to a recording company at rates less than the compulsory license rate per composition. Where the co-owner may be unavailable for consultation and consent, it is advisable to provide that, a reasonable amount of time after notification by registered or certified mail, consent shall be assumed in the absence of written objection.

Restrictions on Assignment

As in any partnership or joint venture, there may be a strong element of reliance on a specific individual or company in selecting the co-owner. If the joint owner is a top recording star or a respected publisher, it may be appropriate to have different provisions relating to assignment than would be the case if the co-owner had only a financial interest. Where the joint administration agreement is based on such factors, it may be desirable to provide that neither co-owner may assign his or her interest without the approval of, or rights of first refusal in, the other co-owner.

The Writer's Interest in Co-Ownership

Especially with regard to renewal copyrights of pre-1978 compositions, writers are often cautioned against allowing joint ownership of copyrights. In actuality, there is little practical effect on the writer's royalty computations, although there may be a more significant effect on the exploitation of the song involved. Critics of the practice of "splitting copyrights" point out that the incentive to promote a song may decrease when a publisher's share is decreased.

If there are two writers on a musical work and each grants publishing rights to a different publisher, the writers will normally look solely to their own publisher for their share of royalties unless both publishers agree that one of them will assume full writer royalty obligations with respect to the entire composition. Where two publishers share equally in the mechanical license fees payable for a song, each publisher pays its own contributing writer as if there were no collaborator on the song. Each publisher will pay its writer one-half of its mechanical license receipts (which is the usual total writer's rate), and since each publisher receives 50 percent of the total mechanical license fees, each writer in effect receives 25 percent of the combined publishers' receipts. This is the same rate and amount that would be payable to each writer if there were only one publisher and two writers.

For sheet music and other printed uses, there is no difference to the writers whether the publishers agree to account to each other and to the writers for their separate publications or they use the same printer, such as Warner Bros. Publications, which is directed to render separate accountings to each publisher. Without such arrangements, writers obtain print royalties only from their own publisher and receive no accountings from the other publisher. This may prove inequitable if the other publisher is more energetic and capable and achieves greater sales of printed editions. This situation occurs rarely, however, and in view of the limited sales of printed editions, the harm to a writer is not likely to be serious.

It has been observed that publishers with less than a 100 percent interest in a song have sometimes used the split copyright as a loss leader in the form of reduced mechanical license fees in order to induce a record company to take other songs from the publisher's catalog at a higher rate. Obviously, in such cases the writer and the other publisher both lose. Flagrant abuses of this sort can lead to a claim by the writer of a breach of the obligation of the publisher to exploit the composition equitably and fairly, and may result in an enforced accounting by the publisher for additional royalties. Similarly, the other co-owner may contend that any discount must apply to all the licensed compositions rather than to the one composition alone. On the other hand, the participation of another publisher in the song proceeds may add an extra measure of exploitation, to the ultimate benefit of the song.

The "Cut-In"

As an alternative to the joint ownership of copyrights, some songwriters and publishers recommend that, wherever feasible, the record artist or the record company should receive a "cut-in," an authorized participation in publishing income instead of an interest in the copyright itself. In this instance the financial reward does not need to include management rights in the copyright. This leaves in the hands of the publisher the control of license rates, foreign deals, collection vigilance, and exploitation, subject only to money payments out of receipts to the person or firm that helps to launch, or "break," the song. In some instances the cut-in is limited to a share of the publisher's earnings derived from the particular recording.

It is important to make sure that the cut-in is nullified if the record is not released. The mere making of a recording is no guarantee that it will be released. Accordingly, many publishers insist that the actual general release of a single record on a specified label by a designated artist must occur before the cut-in takes effect. Others permit the agreement to become effective but provide for a right of recapture in the event that the specified recording is not released within a given period of time.

The cut-in is a practice that is often condemned. When given to record company personnel without the knowledge of the employer, it may constitute commercial bribery under state laws. It can be argued that when properly and openly made, a cut-in is acceptable as a reputable business device that preserves the integrity of management of a copyright and is an appropriate way to provide benefits that are not automatically provided by copyright law, to the artist who establishes the popularity of the song or to the record company whose arrangers are responsible for the song's successful commercial presentation. Asking for a cut-in is not the same as demanding to be named a co-writer of the composition in order to obtain a share of the writer credits and payments from ASCAP or BMI. The latter practice may constitute a fraudulent registration in the Copyright Office.

When a songwriter regrets or renounces a cut-in deal, it is important that he or she take action expeditiously. In a 1999 case concerning writer credits for the 1959 song "The Sea of Love," the writer threatened legal action unless he got 100 percent of writer royalties. The court ruled that any such action had to be taken within 3 years of discovery. In this case, 40 years had passed, the statute of limitations had been exceeded, and the case was rejected. However, when a pre-1978 song is the subject of potential renewal in its 28th year, a timely action can still be taken to contest the claimed authorship of the cut-in "writer." This is especially desirable if the cut-in was not listed on the original copyright registration.

19

Copyright Infringement

Copyright infringement lawsuits are common in the music industry, and no song or artist is immune. Cases of infringement have involved such important figures as Andrew Lloyd Webber, Michael Jackson, Michael Bolton, and The Rolling Stones. There are two basic types of copyright infringers: (1) those who use copyrighted material without obtaining the requisite permission, in the form of a license, and (2) those who claim to originate a work but, consciously or unconsciously, copy another's original work.

Not all infringements are intentional. For example, the great composer Jerome Kern was found to have infringed an earlier work, "Dardanella," in one of his compositions; a recognizable copy of the "Dardanella" bass line had somehow crept into Kern's subconscious and emerged in his allegedly original work, "Kalua." Even though it was unconscious, it was nonetheless a copyright infringement. George Harrison, the former Beatle, was found guilty of copyright infringement; the court found that Harrison's 1970 hit "My Sweet Lord" was plagiarized from the 1962 tune "He's So Fine."

Proof of Access to a Copyrighted Work

Whether conscious or subconscious infringement is involved, an indispensable prerequisite to a finding of infringement is the *access* of the second writer to the work of the first. No infringement occurs merely because the identical melody or lyric is reproduced in the second writer's song. The copyright owned by the first writer is protection against being copied, but it does not provide a basis for a claim against a second person who independently creates the same result. An obvious example would be a copyrighted photograph of New York City's George Washington Bridge at sunset taken from a position that permitted the inclusion of the nearby little red lighthouse in the same picture. A second photographer might independently take the same picture at the same time of day and from the same vantage point without having had access to the first photograph and thus without infringement of copyright. Similarly, a simple melodic line from one popular song might be duplicated in another popular song by sheer coincidence.

Consequently, it is important for an infringement claimant to establish access to the copyrighted—and allegedly copied—work by showing that the song was publicly disseminated through the release of sheet music or recording and public performance, or by proving that the defendant had actual personal contact with the copyrighted song. Clearly, a willful wrongdoer will deny having had any contact with the song, whether receipt of a demo in the mail or otherwise, and this makes proving access difficult. However, the courts will recognize circumstantial evidence as establishing proof of access. The access of a linking third party, such as a record producer, can suffice to show the required access to the copyrighted material. Similar complexities in the original work and the copies are considered to demonstrate the presence of access. Extended duplication in more than isolated bars of music has been defined by one court as "a striking similarity which passes the bounds of mere accident."

Even when access can be shown, there is no copyright remedy for minimal similarities. There must be substantial copying; this refers to quality and not necessarily quantity: There is no "four-bar exception." In a 1994 infringement action, in which the Isley Brothers charged that the song "Love Is a Wonderful Thing" by Michael Bolton and Andrew Goldmark was an infringing use of their song of the same name, access was shown simply by the fact that the song had played on radio stations in the areas in which the infringing authors had been raised and that Michael Bolton was an avid Isley Brothers fan. In 1998, two rap musicians brought suit against M.C. Hammer, claiming that the song "Here Comes The Hammer" was a copy of the "hook" in the plaintiff's song. The hook involved the syncopated, quadruple repetition of the slang term "uh-oh." The court stated that "the repetition of the non-protectible word 'uh-oh' in a distinctive rhythm comprises a sufficiently original composition to render it protectible by the copyright laws."

Another court held that common errors in a plaintiff's version of music in public domain and in the defendant's use of this music, such as the misspelling of an author's name and the failure to carry over a musical "slur" mark at the same exact place in the composition, although technically and musically required, "are unmistakable signs of copying."

The Use of Music in the Public Domain

A common defense against a charge of having infringed a copyrighted song is that the musical work is in the public domain. This can result from the forfeiture of copyright by the plaintiff through failure to use proper notices of copyright in printed copies before 1978 when such notices were required by law, or failure to renew the copyright when such renewals were required prior to 1992. It can also result from the defendant's proving that the duplicated melody line or lyric originated from sources other than the plaintiff. In an infringement action against the producers of the children's TV show *Sesame Street*, the court found the original source to be an old Russian folktale and held that "the most that could be said is that [the defendant] read the plaintiff's work and retold the story in [his] own words. Such a finding will not, given the derivative nature of plaintiff's work, support a course of action for copyright infringement."

Copyright is not jeopardized by the acknowledgment that a composition in the public domain is the basis of the writer's song. In such a case, however, the copyright obtained is not on the work in the public domain but on the arrangement, revision, or other new material added. Consequently, a user could record the original Chopin *Polonaise* melody, which is in the public domain, but not the arrangement or adaptation of the melody contained in the song "'Til the End of Time."

Vicarious Liability

When a song or recording is determined to be an infringement of copyright, retail stores or other intermediaries between the customer and the original infringer cannot hide behind their own ignorance. The H. L. Green chain store was held liable for infringement in connection with the sale of bootleg records by a concessionaire that operated its music department. Similarly, the advertising agency Batten, Barton, Durstine & Osborn was held liable for a commercial jingle supplied by an infringer. The various infringers are not only jointly liable, but also individually liable if the other parties are unable to bear the cost of the settlement. For this reason, suits may be aimed at the more financially responsible member or members of the infringing group—a pressing plant, a distributor, a record or music store, as well as the composer of the infringing work.

The Copyright Act of 1976 took a more liberal approach than previous copyright legislation toward authors who had failed to register their copyright in a timely or correct manner. At the same time, the act tried to provide some protection to copyright infringers who had been misled by the absence of a copyright notice: The innocent infringer was granted a complete defense in cases of an incorrect name in a copyright notice as long as the infringer acted in good faith under the authority of the person in the notice and the Copyright Office records did not show the real owner in a copyright registration or in a document executed by the person named in the notice. The infringer was not liable for actual or statutory damages prior to receiving notice of a copyright registration. In that situation the court might (1) allow claims for the infringer's profits, (2) enjoin future infringement, or (3) require the infringer to pay the copyright owner a reasonable license fee fixed by the court in order to continue the venture.

Works published on or after March 1, 1989, the effective date of the Berne Convention Implementation Act of 1988, no longer require a copyright notice to receive copyright protection. The presence of a proper copyright notice defeats a defense of innocent infringement. If a defense of innocent infringement *is* sustained, the actual or statutory damages awarded the copyright holder may be limited. In allowing or disallowing injunctive relief, the court's discretion is involved. The innocent intent of an infringer can be a factor in the exercise of a court's discretion.

Who May Sue for Infringement

Prior to the Copyright Act of 1976, generally only the holder of the copyright was considered to be entitled to bring an action for infringement. Exclusive licensees might sue for infringement on the condition that the copyright holder was joined as a party to the suit. This policy was aimed at avoiding a multiplicity of suits. A copyright was usually regarded as an indivisible bundle of rights as far as infringement actions were concerned.

The 1976 Copyright Act effected a major change in copyright law. All rights under copyright, including performance rights, printing rights, and mechanical reproduction rights, are now clearly divisible. As a result, the owner of an exclusive right can bring an action in his or her own name for infringement of the owner's right. For example, if a firm such as Hal Leonard Publishing Corporation is the exclusive licensee of the right to print a particular song, it can sue infringers of that right without the participation of the licensor.

The beneficial owner of an exclusive right, as distinct from the legal owner, is also entitled to sue for infringement. An example of a beneficial owner is an author who has assigned his or her legal title to a copyright in return for the right to receive percentage royalties computed on the basis of sales fees or license fees.

In recognition of the fact that an action for infringement can affect the rights of others who have an interest in the copyright, a court can require that the plaintiff provide written notice of the action to any interested parties. The court may also require or permit any persons whose rights may be affected to join in the action. A copyright action may be brought only by the legal or beneficial owner, and the ability to join in the suit is limited to those who have an interest in the copyright. Licensing agents such as Harry Fox have neither ownership nor beneficial interest in the copyright; consequently, litigation is invariably commenced in the name of the publisher.

Civil Remedies for Infringement

There are various remedies available to a plaintiff who claims the infringement of a copyright. The plaintiff may seek a court-ordered injunction. The plaintiff may request that the infringing copies, as well as the plates, molds, matrices, tapes, and other means of reproduction, be impounded or destroyed. More commonly, the plaintiff will sue for his or her actual damages and any additional profits made by the infringer from the infringement that are not taken into account in computing those damages.

In suits for an infringer's profits, the burden of proof tends to be on the defendant. The Copyright Act states that the copyright proprietor need prove only "the infringer's gross revenue, and the infringer is required to prove his or her deductible expenses and the elements of profits attributable to factors other than the copyrighted work." In the past, determining an infringer's gross revenue has been a difficult task for plaintiffs attempting to calculate damages. However, in current practice, judges can rely upon the sales figures compiled by SoundScan to determine the amount of damages to be paid. (For over a decade, SoundScan has been tracking sales of music by combining point-of-sale entries from thousands of record outlets using bar-code scans with data from online and mail-order retailers.)

At any time before final judgment during a legal action, a plaintiff under the 1976 statute can elect to recover statutory damages in lieu of actual damages and the additional profits of the infringer. For such damages the court must generally award between $750 and $30,000 for nonwillful infringements of works registered prior to the act of infringement. However, where there is a willful infringement, as in the case of a defendant who infringes a copyright after written notice, the court may award up to $150,000 for statutory damages. A reduction to a minimum of $200 can apply if the court finds that the defendant "was not aware and had no reason to believe" that the act was an infringement. The court may also omit any award against instructors, librarians, and archivists in nonprofit institutions who honestly but mistakenly relied on fair use where there were reasonable grounds for the belief that fair use was applicable to their reproductions.

A 1998 Supreme Court decision regarding a television station's copyright infringement in syndicated programs after the expiration of a negotiated license also applies to the music industry. The decision held that though the Copyright Act does not specify or provide for a jury trial to determine damages, there is a constitutional right to a jury trial in such situations.

An example of the computation of statutory damages under the Copyright Act of 1909 is offered in a court decision in an action regarding the copyright infringement of songs from the musical play *Jesus Christ Superstar*. A series of 48 live performances in the United States resulted in a judgment for $48,000. The computation was based on the then applicable minimum statutory damage amount of $250 per each of the four infringed copyrights, multiplied by the number of performances.

In the 1994 infringement case involving the Isley Brothers (see page 189), it was ruled that Bolton and Goldmark's song infringed upon 66 percent of the Isley Brothers' song and contributed to 28 percent of the profits from Bolton's multiplatinum album (10 million copies sold) *Time, Love and Tenderness*. The disputed song was only one of the many songs on the album. As a result, the Isley Brothers are entitled to 18 percent of the revenues earned by the album as well as 66 percent of the entire income of the song from music publishing.

In addition to infringements by unauthorized performances, statutory damages are also applicable to other infringements, such as by printed copies, film synchronization, mechanical reproduction other than under a compulsory license, transcriptions, or unauthorized Internet activities.

The reason for statutory minimum damages is that frequently proof of actual damages or profits is difficult or impossible to achieve, even though other elements of infringement, such as access to the plaintiff's original work and a substantial similarity, are shown. The availability of minimum damages to a successful plaintiff is an important deterrent against infringements. In fact, such a remedy is considered valuable, if not essential, to performing rights societies such as ASCAP, BMI, and SESAC, especially in dealing with smaller broadcasting stations that might otherwise be tempted to risk infringement on the chance of nondiscovery or the inability of a plaintiff to prove damages or the defendant's profits.

Court Costs and Attorney Fees

In 1990 Ray Repp, a relatively unknown composer, brought an infringement case against composer Andrew Lloyd Webber. Repp claimed that the central theme of *Phantom of the Opera* was taken from "Till You," a little-known song that Repp wrote in 1978. Although Repp's composition earned less than $100, he claimed that Webber had had access to the song. Ultimately, the jury found for Webber, but what was noteworthy about the case was the over $1 million in legal fees reportedly incurred by Webber in his successful defense.

When sued for copyright infringement, a defendant may request a summary judgment (i.e., a finding that the plaintiff's case has no merit and should be dismissed out of hand). If this request is denied, the defendant may seek a finding that there is a "likelihood" of the defendant's success at trial. This is a way of putting financial pressure on a plaintiff, because such a finding may lead the court to require that the plaintiff post a bond for "costs" in the event of the defendant's success. In copyright actions, costs can include sizable attorney's fees. However, in the case of *Selletti v. Mariah Carey,* 173 F.3d 104 (2d Cir. 1999), a court said that "the imposition of a security requirement may not be used as a means to dismiss suits of questionable merit filed by plaintiffs with few resources."

Many copyright actions involve long, expensive, and burdensome trials with verdicts of fairly small awards based on actual or statutory damages. In such instances, the plaintiff is faced with empty justice if he or she has to foot the bills for court costs and legal expenses. The court may award reasonable attorney's fees and court costs to the successful party in a copyright suit. This is a double-edged sword, however, since the successful defendant can also obtain such relief.

In the 1994 *Fogerty v. Fantasy Inc.* decision, the U.S. Supreme Court leveled the playing field for plaintiffs and defendants on the subject of lawyers' fees. The Court overturned a ruling that required successful copyright defendants to prove that the suit was frivolous or brought in bad faith in order to recoup their lawyers' fees. The case dealt with lawyers' fees of $1.35 million. Fantasy appealed the $1.35 million award, claiming that it had brought its action in "good faith" and was thus "blameless." The appellate court stated that "a court's discretion may be influenced by the plaintiff's culpability in bringing or pursuing the action, but blameworthiness is not a prerequisite to awarding fees to a prevailing defendant." The court also allowed John Fogerty to collect additional attorney's fees in his defense of Fantasy's unsuccessful appeal of the attorney's fees issue. This ruling will obviously make prospective infringement claimants give more thought to settling out of court or dropping their suits altogether.

Some copyright cases have proved to be so complex that attorneys' fees, based on the amount of work involved, the skill shown, the results obtained, and the responsibility indicated by the decision, have been awarded by the courts in amounts up to $10,000, even in cases where the awards for infringement were less. However, attorneys' fees awarded by courts are often not for the full amount of the fees incurred. Under federal as well as local court rules, there are procedures to order sanctions against the attorneys as well as the party who failed to make a reasonable investigation before bringing copyright actions.

As a result of these rules, the claimant as well as the attorney should compile and review all information for accuracy and investigate any discrepancies found, review any and all information publicly available concerning the factual issues, and interview any person with knowledge of any relevant information. These same sanction rules also apply to wrongfully continuing an action that might initially have been justified but subsequently was shown to lack a justifiable factual issue. Engaging a qualified musicologist before beginning the action and not merely shooting from the hip is an essential first step. Similarly, a defendant faced with what appears to be a meritorious claim should get expert guidance as to melodic comparisons.

Criminal Remedies for Infringement

In a recent sampling case involving rap music, a judge who was sitting in a civil case found that the infringement was so blatant that he referred the case to the U.S. Attorney for possible criminal action. "Thou shalt not steal" stated the judge, quoting the ancient prescript as the criminal basis of copyright law. The Copyright Act provides that a willful infringement for commercial advantage or private financial gain by an individual can result in a fine of not more than $250,000, or imprisonment for not more than 5 years, or both. The maximum criminal fine for an organization is $500,000. The No Electronic Theft Act (NET Act) changes the standard of financial and commercial gain to include anything of value, including the receipt of other copyrighted works. The act is aimed at hackers on the Internet who do not have the profit incentive of conventional counterfeiters and bootleggers.

Mechanical Right Infringement

The Copyright Act provides a special limitation on the exclusive right to record musical compositions. If the copyright owner has authorized a recording that has been distributed to the public in the United States, the compulsory mechanical license provisions of the act are applicable. Without the proper notice of intention to rely on those compulsory license provisions, these provisions do not pertain, and the making and distribution of records become actionable acts of infringement for which full civil and criminal remedies are available. In *Harris v. Emus Records,* 1984, a California court held that once a record has been distributed, it is too late to rely on this compulsory license provision. In that case, Emmylou Harris succeeded in having the court rule that the owner of an unlicensed master who had already issued the record without a license could thereafter "listen to the master in his own living room" but make no other use of it.

Under the compulsory license provisions, the copyright owner is entitled to receive monthly payments and statements of mechanical royalties as well as cumulative annual statements certified by a public accountant. If the monthly payments and the monthly and annual statements are not received when they are due and the default is not remedied within 30 days after written notice by the copyright owner, the compulsory license is automatically terminated. At this point, the making or distributing of all records for which royalties had not been paid become acts of infringement for which civil and criminal remedies apply.

Infringement by Importation

One of the rights of a copyright owner is to prevent the importation of copies or phonorecords of a work. Importation is an infringement of the owner's exclusive right to distribute copies or records; civil and criminal remedies for an infringement apply.

As provided by the 1976 Copyright Act, however, individuals arriving from abroad can include a single copy or record as a part of their personal baggage. In addition, a nonprofit organization that operates for scholarly, educational, or religious purposes may import not more than one copy of an audiovisual work, such as a motion picture, for its archives and not more than five copies or records of any other work for its archives or for library lending.

The Copyright Act bars the importation of pirated copies or phonorecords, namely, those whose manufacture would be a copyright infringement if the Copyright Act had been applicable. While the manufacture may be lawful in the country where it was made because, perhaps, that country has no copyright relations with the United States, importation nevertheless is prohibited if the making would be illegal under the U.S. Copyright Act. In the 1991 case *BMG Music v. Perez* the court determined that the first-sale doctrine is not a valid defense where records lawfully made in the country of manufacture and first sale are thereafter imported in bulk into the United States without the copyright license from the U.S. owners. Further, the payment of copyright fees abroad is not enough in itself, said the Circuit Court for the Ninth District, thereby endorsing a prior 1987 New Jersey decision of Jem Records importers. The U.S. Customs Service is authorized to prevent the importation of unlawful copies or records.

Whether the making is lawful or unlawful, the Secretary of the Treasury may publish procedures whereby an individual claiming an interest in a copyrighted work can, for a fee, become entitled to notice from the U.S. Customs Service of the importation of copies or phonorecords.

When finished goods have been manufactured in the United States and shipped abroad for a bounce-back into U.S. markets, the first-sale doctrine has been considered a sufficient defense. The *first-sale doctrine* refers to a rule of law that any right of distribution stops after the first authorized sale of a copyrighted item, and that a subsequent holder in due course can sell again, ad infinitum, provided that authorized first sale was by or authorized by the U.S. copyright proprietor. However, when the overseas source is the place of manufacture, the import into the United States of any such finished record of other goods is not granted this defense because the Supreme Court has determined that the first-sale doctrine applies only to goods manufactured under license within the United States and not abroad.

The recent success of on-line book and CD distributors has complicated this issue. These on-line distributors have caused the long-standing concepts of territorial publishing rights to vanish. In 1999, amazon.com began selling copies of *Harry Potter and the Prisoner of Azkaban,* an immensely successful British children's book that had not yet been published in the United States, much to the dismay of the U.S. publisher who paid for the rights to release the book in the United States. Current laws do not address the issue of individual copy importation such as by mail order or Internet. As a result, the Association of American Publishers (AAP) is considering lobbying for legislative change.

Copyright Registration

The 1976 Copyright Act, as modified by the Berne Convention Implementation Act of 1988, encourages copyright registration by making it a prerequisite to the start of an infringement action involving works of U.S. origin and foreign works not originating in a Berne nation. By virtue of the Berne Act, there is no requirement of registration for copyright of a Berne work of non-U.S. origin as a prerequisite to initiation of an infringement action with respect to such work.

The failure to register where required constitutes grounds for dismissal, but after registration the suit can proceed with regard to both past and future infringements. There is, however, a penalty imposed for failure to register those works where registration is a prerequisite to an infringement suit. Despite registration, the remedies of statutory damages and attorneys' fees are not available to acts of infringements commenced prior to registration unless the registration was made within 3 months after initial publication.

The Recordation of Copyright Transfer

Under the law in effect before March 1, 1989, the owner of an allegedly infringed copyright or exclusive right who had obtained the rights by a transfer of copyright could not institute an infringement action until he or she had recorded the instrument of transfer in the Copyright Office. After recordation the owner could sue on past infringements. The above requirement was eliminated by the Berne Act.

Time Frame for Legal Actions

The Copyright Act provides for a 3-year statute of limitations for the start of a court action or criminal proceedings for copyright infringement. This means that a lawsuit must begin within 3 years after the claim arises and a criminal proceeding must be instituted within 3 years after the cause of action occurs.

Infringements concerning phonograph records or printed editions may continue for longer than 3 years. Only those infringements that occurred before the latest 3-year period are barred by the statute of limitations.

For injunctive relief, as distinguished from claims for monetary damages or profits, a suit must be brought within a reasonably prompt period after the discovery of the infringement. The failure to institute the action within such a period, which is likely to be less than 3 years, may cause a court to deny the injunction on the ground of the plaintiff's "laches," or undue delay in seeking legal redress.

Sampling and Copyright Infringement

An entire industry—sampling—has been created based on copyright infringement. Sampling is a double infringement—of sound as well as song. A segment of an earlier recording is incorporated into a new recording, either alone or together with other segments. A brief musical accompaniment may be created by "looping" a short segment of sound recording from a prior record and repeating it for extended periods as an accompaniment, often to rap lyrics. When it is without license, it is an infringement.

The customary practice in regard to sampling is to appropriate a brief segment of the original source and to loop it for continuous usage within the new recording, often of a duration much longer than the original segment itself. Thus, a segment of only 6 seconds can be used for as much as 90 seconds within, and often as background to, the new recording. Plus, the original brief segment can be digitally altered. In the case of *Jarvis v. A&M Records* 827 F. Supp. 282 (D.N.J. 1993), the court categorized the process as "the conversion of analog sound waves into a digital code [which] can then be reused, manipulated or combined with other digitized or recorded sounds using a machine with digital data processing capabilities, such as a computerized synthesizer."

Record companies have learned to discipline artists and producers by making them bear the full responsibility of unlicensed sampling. They have learned that to search out the two owners (record company for sound and publisher for song) is not only expensive in itself; it is a mere preliminary to the expense of a retroactive license after the record is already issued. Numerous research and negotiating service houses have arisen for handling these claims. When it is possible to clear in advance, the price is obviously cheaper, since there is the possibility of switching tracks to a more cooperative source if there is resistance from the first selection. When a retroactive license has proved impossible, records have been withdrawn from the market at great expense; this is in addition to payment of considerable damage claims for past sales. A frequent negotiation that avoids such consequence is to transfer all or part of the copyright in the new version to the owner of the sampled song.

In the 1999 case *Emergency Music v. Isbell,* involving the use of a sample of the song "I'm Ready" in the hit song "Whoomp! There It Is!" by the one-hit wonder Tag Team, a district court ordered the defendants to pay $707,766.47 in damages even though the defendants had obtained a license for the sample. Because the defendants had failed to pay at the appropriate payment periods, even after receiving written notice by the plaintiff, the court ruled that the license was terminated. This made use of the sample a copyright infringement.

Negotiations for the clearance of sampled material necessarily involve knowing the nature of the use. An analysis of the use should cover the following:

- ▶ Length of basic material sampled
- ▶ Whether the sampled material is extended in its actual intended use through looping or other repetitive devices
- ▶ Whether the sampled material is the primary focus of audience attention or just in the background
- ▶ Whether the other interested party—the record company or the music publisher—has already cleared the sample use as well as price or other form
- ▶ Whether this is the only instance of sampling in the resulting song or one of several, and if so, what deals were offered to the other parties
- ▶ The past sales history of the artist who did the sampling as an indication of likely volume of sales on the current recording
- ▶ The name of the publisher of the sampled song and the owner of the sampled sound recording

With this information in hand, it can be determined whether an outright fixed price for permission to sample is appropriate or whether a demand should be made for a share (or all) of the copyright in the resulting song. Since the law does not permit an unauthorized adaptation, it is possible to insist on a delivery of 100 percent of the copyright in the resulting song. Whether it is part or all of the song, the next question pertains to the mechanical royalty rate: Will it be a reduced rate consistent with any controlled-composition requirements of the artist's contract with the record label, or will the full statutory rate apply? Finally, should an advance be paid against the resulting royalties, thereby guaranteeing a certain sum that would normally be substantially less than if an outright sale were made?

Record company negotiations for clearances of sound recordings usually operate on a fixed sum, while the negotiations of music publishers more often involve a continuing royalty claim. Some observers note that a record company may be more leniently disposed toward clearing samples of a fellow record company in recognition that the next time around the negotiating sides will be reversed and a courtesy given may be reciprocated. Music publishers rarely feel that way.

Successful records are rarely limited to the United States. Consequently, a sample clearance should be worldwide. Nonetheless, some U.S. music publishers who have granted foreign rights to subpublishers prefer to get a larger up-front payment and, in that event, have a confidentiality clause that gives limited protection to the infringing companies. The same applies if a co-publisher pursues a sampling claim without confiding in the other partner or intending to share the results. This is not only unethical, but it is also illegal, as copublishers have a duty to account for profits to their partners.

Sampling clearances that do not get settled on outright sums usually refer to 100 percent or lesser shares of statutory compulsory mechanical royalty rates. However, a hard-hitting negotiator dealing with a sampled recording that has already been released has a hidden weapon for asking for even higher rates, since compulsory rates do not apply once a recording has been distributed without a license.

A note of caution: With the assignment of the offending copyright can come possible claims from other affronted sampled parties who might not have been disclosed by the assignor.

Is there a defense available to the sampler? The defense of fair use is not available because the use is invariably commercial and not done for the purpose of socially constructive criticism, parody, or reference, and although the sampling may not diminish sales or licenses of the original, it is a "taking without compensation," with the intention of saving recording costs. Frank Zappa sampled his own material, which was perfectly legal because he owned both the music and the sampled version. Other strategies are for the interested record company to invite licensed uses of its own recorded library. Many artists of earlier recordings would welcome recognition and payment resulting from an authorized sample.

The major defense in sampling is that the use is not "substantial." If the resulting sound is unrecognizable by the ordinary audience, it may escape the onus of copyright infringement even though it is an unlicensed and unfair appropriation of the work product of the original recording artist and production company. However, if it escapes detection and is as a result not "substantially similar," it also escapes the normal goal of sampling, which is often seen as a game of hide-and-seek and an appeal to subliminal or actual nostalgia for the sounds of yesteryear. There is no need to settle a case of noninfringing use, so the question arises: Why was it taken in the first instance if the purpose was to tease the listener with recognizable snatches of older recordings?

Record companies defending or negotiating sample clearances are usually fully aware that they can charge 100 percent of the costs against the artist's account. They also have the right to charge the producer's account under the usual warranty. Yet producers are not customarily charged unless the artist or artist's manager insists.

When a music publisher settles a sampling claim, it has a legal right to look to the sampling songwriter to indemnify against costs. A flat-sum settlement is easily charged against a songwriter's royalties, but whether a reduction or abandonment of publisher shares can result in such a charge against the songwriter raises major questions of publisher-writer relations and is usually avoided by taking the reduction "off the top," to be shared between publisher and songwriter.

Because of the complexities of obtaining the appropriate sampling licenses, record companies often turn to sample clearinghouses. Duties performed by the clearinghouses include searching out the potential licensors and negotiating the terms and conditions of the licenses. The clearinghouses are usually compensated for their services on a fixed-fee basis, the rates for which are currently around $200 for finding the owner of the sound recording and $200 for finding the owner of the underlying musical composition. These fees normally include the clearinghouse's negotiating services, but if there are extended negotiations, additional charges may apply.

20

International Copyright Protection

Although the U.S. balance of trade since the mid-1980s has been characterized by substantial deficits, the nation's copyright industries have consistently continued to produce a trade surplus. In recognition of the importance to the U.S. economy of safeguarding this area of trade, Congress voted in 1988 to ratify the international Berne Copyright Convention, the world's oldest, most comprehensive, and most protective reciprocal copyright treaty, as part of an effort to maximize copyright protection for American works in foreign countries.

The Berne Convention

The Berne Convention for the Protection of Literary and Artistic Works is a century-old copyright treaty that has undergone several revisions, the most recent known as the Paris Act of July 24, 1971. Berne stipulates specific minimum levels of copyright protection that must be enacted by member nations for the benefit of eligible copyrighted works (except phonorecords), including a minimum term of protection for copyrighted works of the life of the author plus 50 years in most cases; protection of foreign copyrights without the requirements of notice, deposit, registration, and other formalities; and limited moral rights for authors.

Advocates of U.S. adherence to the Berne Convention argued long and hard in the intervening years between 1955—when the United States first joined the less stringent but popular international copyright treaty, the Universal Copyright Convention (UCC)—and 1988 that UCC membership alone was inadequate to protect U.S. copyrights abroad. Their argument centered on the fact that the United States, as the world's leading copyright nation, greatly diminished its influence in the international copyright community and invited retaliatory and discriminatory treatment of American works in foreign countries by continuing to rely on a "free ride" for U.S. works on Berne. By illustration, American works were often accorded Berne-level protection through the back door because many UCC countries were also Berne members whose national copyright laws had been made compatible to Berne. U.S. works benefited on a nonreciprocal basis, even as the United States steadfastly refused to join the Berne Union.

With the enactment of the revised 1976 U.S. Copyright Act, which raised the term of U.S. copyright protection to the minimum Berne level of author's life plus 50 years (which has now been extended to life plus 70), adherence became more of a possibility. It took 12 more years, however, for Congress to pass the U.S. Berne Convention Implementation Act, finally bringing the United States into Berne compliance. The official entrance into the Berne Union of the United States came in March 1989.

The Effects of Berne Adherence

Works of American authors are now protected automatically in all countries of the Berne Union. There is a minimum level of copyright protection agreed to by members of the Union, and each Berne country provides at least that guaranteed level to American authors. Since members of the Berne Union agree to treat nationals of other member countries like their own nationals for purposes of copyright, American authors frequently receive greater levels of protection than the guaranteed minimum.

Works of foreign authors who are nationals of a Berne Union country and works first or simultaneously published in a Berne country are automatically protected in the United States. This is especially important for certain material formerly in the public domain. As was discussed in Chapter 12, a significant revision of U.S. copyright policy now allows retroactive copyright protection for certain foreign works that were in the public domain only by virtue of the fact that U.S. copyright formalities had not been followed.

The Berne Convention Implementation Act of 1988 amended the Copyright Act of 1976 in several significant ways: copyright notice was eliminated as a prerequisite for U.S. copyright protection; the necessity for recordation of copyright assignments and documents of transfer as a prerequisite to suit was abolished; and the necessity for copyright registration of foreign works originating in other Berne member countries as a prerequisite to suit was also eliminated.

However, various incentives were included in the Copyright Act amendments to encourage copyright owners to continue to register and deposit copyrighted works with the U.S. Copyright Office, to include copyright notices on all copies, and to register works prior to suit. For instance, statutory damages and attorneys' fees are available only for registered works, and a certificate of registration acts as prima facie evidence of the validity and ownership of a copyright. In addition, if an infringement suit is instituted and there has been a copyright notice, the defendant cannot successfully mitigate actual or statutory damages by the defense of innocent infringement.

Under the Berne Act, Congress has made clear its view that existing statutory and common law in the United States satisfies the Berne moral rights standard without the need to amend U.S. law. The Berne standard provides that an author "shall have the right to claim authorship of [his or her] work and to object to any distortion, mutilation, or other modification of, or other derogatory action in relation to [his or her] work, which would be prejudicial to his honor or reputation."

An immediate effect of the entry of the United States into the Berne Union was the establishment of copyright relations for the reciprocal protection of copyrighted works in at least 24 non-UCC nations with whom the United States had no prior copyright treaties, including Egypt, Turkey, and Romania.

As Senator Patrick Leahy stated in introducing his Berne adherence bill in the U.S. Senate, "Vital American interests can be fully represented in the international copyright system only if we get off the sidelines and onto the playing field, by joining the Berne Convention." Illustrative of Senator Leahy's point, revision of the Berne Convention requires a unanimous vote of Berne members. By joining the Berne Union, the United States immediately acquired the right to veto amendments to Berne that could injure U.S. interests. In addition, in this age of rapid technological developments and increasing worldwide popularity and use of U.S. music, the United States gained a voice in the administration and management of the most important international copyright treaty.

Trade Negotiations and GATT

The United States has recognized that its copyright industry of film, records, music, and books are major contributors to its strength as an exporting nation. This "invisible export," linked as it is to copyrights in software, is, in fact, second in importance only to the aeronautics industry. Berne membership has also strengthened the ability of the U.S. Trade Representative to lobby for tougher copyright protection and more active enforcement of existing laws in foreign countries. This is especially true in regard to "pirate-haven" nations, which often used the U.S. failure to join Berne as an excuse not to heed U.S. demands for more active protection of U.S. works.

By joining Berne, the United States increased its ability to influence the initiative of the international General Agreement on Tariffs and Trade (GATT) (now the World Trade Organization [WTO]) to develop a new international code of minimum copyright protection and enforcement. In its 2002 Music Report, the International Federation of the Phonographic Industry (IFPI) estimated that piracy (including both physical product and downloading from the Internet) represents about U.S.$4.3 billion annually and that in China as much as 80 to 90 percent of available product is pirated. In his January 2003 MIDEM keynote address, Jay Berman, Chairman and CEO of IFPI, reported that action on the piracy front may be more successful in the future, as EU member nations implement antipiracy measures in the EU Copyright Directive, which derives from the WIPO treaties (see below). No longer ostracized for its failure to join Berne, the United States is in a better position to be a leader among the approximately 100 World Trade Organization nations in striving for maximum international protection of intellectual property rights.

U.S. Trade Representative

The office of the U.S. Trade Representative (USTR) has an important function in motivating foreign nations to protect U.S. copyrights. Under the strengthened Section 301 provisions of a recent omnibus trade act, the USTR may place those foreign nations engaging in unfair or lackadaisical treatment of U.S. intellectual property rights on its Priority Watch List. Once added to the list, those nations have 6 months to demonstrate "a full commitment toward the resolution" of intellectual property protection problems or face the possibility of trade sanctions. In the year 2001 the Watch List included China, Russia, Brazil, Indonesia, Mexico, Italy, Spain, Taiwan, Poland, and Greece.

The USTR may also recommend that countries receiving trade preferences from the United States be denied such privileges for failure to protect U.S. intellectual property within their national borders.

The International Intellectual Property Alliance, a group of seven major U.S. copyright industry associations, is dedicated to assisting the USTR in evaluating the treatment of U.S. works abroad and advising the USTR as to which nations the U.S. private sector believes should be targeted for inclusion on the Super 301 priority watch list.

Geneva Phonogram Convention

The Geneva Convention of October 29, 1971, for the Protection of Producers of Phonograms against Unauthorized Duplication (Geneva Convention of 1971) is an international treaty to protect sound recordings against piracy. Under the treaty, ratified by the United States on March 10, 1974, the participating countries agree to protect the nationals of other states against the production or importation of unauthorized duplicate recordings if the purpose is to distribute them to the public. The method used to accomplish this result is determined by the domestic law of each participating country and includes one or more of the following:

- ► Protection by means of the grant of copyright or other specific right
- ► Protection by means of the law relating to unfair competition
- ► Protection by means of penal sanctions

The United States, which became a member on March 10, 1974, implements the treaty through the federal copyright in sound recordings. However, the Geneva Convention is considered an inadequate alternative to the Rome Convention of 1961, which the United States has never signed.

WIPO Treaties

In December 1996, the World Intellectual Property Organization (WIPO), an intergovernmental organization based in Geneva that has been in existence since

1967, concluded two important treaties designed to establish minimum standards of copyright protection within the digital environment: the WIPO Copyright Treaty and the WIPO Phonograms and Performances Treaty. According to WIPO:

> These treaties contain a general update of the legal principles underpinning international protection of copyright and the rights of performers and phonogram producers in cyberspace. They also clarify that national law must prevent unauthorized access to and use of creative works which, given the global reach of the Internet, may be distributed, accessed, and reproduced anywhere in the world at the push of a button.

The United States is one of 34 countries that have ratified the Performances and Phonograms Treaty and one of 35 that have ratified the Copyright Treaty. A minimum of 30 countries had to become signatories before either of the treaties could become effective. The WIPO Copyright Treaty became effective on March 6, 2002, and the Performances and Phonograms Treaty on May 20 that year.

With the signing of the Digital Millennium Copyright Act (DMCA) in the fall of 1998, the United States was in compliance with both treaties. The main provisions of the treaties:

- ▶ Confirm protection of traditional copyrighted materials and distribution mechanisms
- ▶ Clarify how copyright and related rights apply in the digital environment
- ▶ Protect the use of technological measures designed to control unauthorized copying, transmission, and use of copyrighted products and at the same time make it illegal to circumvent these measures

The WIPO treaties were initially characterized by some groups in the United States, including the Consumer's Union and various library associations, as an anticircumvention meat axe broadly swinging at all electronic technology designed for a digital environment. Libraries and consumers also worried that the treaties would make fair use of copyrighted material—in, for example, private homes, libraries, and educational research centers—impossible in the digital environment. Finally, there were fears that the technology used to prevent Internet piracy might, if not implemented with precision, simply add a digital virus to consumers' home machines, even if they were not themselves engaged in illegal activities. Although various provisions of the DMCA are still being tested in the courts, the DMCA does not undermine the principles of fair use as they have traditionally been applied.

Chapter 42, "Technology and Music," in the section on Copyright Legislation, discusses some of the ramifications of the DMCA for providers of music on the Internet.

21

Foreign Publishing

In the past, American music publishers derived most of their income on a composition from its exploitation in the United States and Canada. Only a rare song, such as one from a motion picture or musical play, could pierce the barriers of foreign languages and different tastes abroad. Consequently, American publishers often negotiated foreign subpublishing deals that emphasized obtaining a locally originated foreign recording (in trade parlance, a "cover record") or an immediate advance of monies. There was a minimum of bargaining as to the amount of royalty, the extent of the territory licensed, the duration of the license, and the minimum exploitation to be guaranteed by the subpublisher.

Today the international aspects of the music industry are firmly established and foreign earnings have become a major factor in the profit-and-loss figures of American publishers. It is now possible for sales of an American recording in Europe to equal or even surpass sales in the United States. Language barriers are disappearing. Young people throughout the world have learned at least some English, often from listening to popular music. Despite the efforts of some countries, such as France, to preserve national culture by requiring that broadcasts contain a minimum content of local music, English is still the most important language for lyrics on a worldwide basis.

A number of factors contribute to the internationalization of popular music: airings on local stations, the influence of Armed Forces radio stations, international tours of recording and concert stars, promotional videos disseminated via the Internet, cheaper air freight charges for finished records, worldwide marketing of motion pictures and syndicated television shows, reduced trade barriers, and the increase in disposable income in many countries.

In the past, American jazz, film, and show music were particularly strong in the international market. More recently, American rhythm and blues, rock, and even country music have gained international acceptance. As a result, competition to acquire foreign rights to successful American songs is intense.

The World Market for Music

Based on statistics compiled by the International Federation of the Phonographic Industry (IFPI), worldwide sales of sound recordings in the first half of 2002 were down 9.2 percent in value and 11.2 percent in units. Sales in the United States and Japan, which together account for over 50 percent of the world market, were down 6.8 percent and 14.2 percent, respectively, from the same period in 2001. France saw an overall rise of 5.2 percent, mainly due to sales of domestic artists.

According to the National Music Publishers Association (NMPA), total 2000 worldwide music publishing income from all sources was $8.1 billion. This represents an increase of 6.7 percent from 1999 figures. This included income from performance (radio, cable and satellite TV, and live performance), reproductions (phonomechanical, synchronization and transcription, and private copy), distribution (sale of printed music and rental and public lending), and miscellaneous sources (including interest and investment income).

Table 21-1 gives a breakdown of regional shares of worldwide publisher income from sound recordings. Table 21-2 gives dollar figures for publisher income in the year 2000 for the United States, Japan, and the major European markets.

Table 21-1

Regional Share of Publishing Income in 2000 from Sound Recordings

North America	36.56%
Europe	42.06
Japan	15.6
Latin America	2.80
Rest of the world	2.80

NMPA International Survey.

Table 21-2

Worldwide Music Publishing Income in 2002 from All Sources ($ millions)

United States	$2006.53
Germany	834.01
Japan	820.70
United Kingdom	666.58
France	601.22
Italy	358.37
Spain	207.16

NMPA International Survey.

Representation by Subpublishers

Foreign publishers who represent American music are called subpublishers, while the American publishers that own the music in the first instance are called original publishers. Agreements with subpublishers are commonly referred to as subpublication agreements. Apart from differences in geographical scope, subpublication agreements may be limited to one or more compositions or may encompass all compositions owned or controlled by the original publisher. The latter agreement is called a catalog subpublication contract.

American music publishers have various options for achieving proper representation abroad. If the original publisher chooses to deal with a large international publisher such as Warner/Chappell or EMI Music Publishing, it enjoys the convenience of a single point of contact. The original publisher may also obtain a larger advance from a single entity than it can from making separate territorial deals, since the advance will be cross-collateralized out of earnings from multiple territories. On the other hand, through the wise selection of separate subpublishers in various foreign territories, a U.S. publisher may achieve better overall representation, including more aggressive promotion in each territory. The territory-by-territory approach necessarily assumes a much greater investment in time and effort on the part of the original publisher to investigate and become familiar with the music business and publishers in each territory and to correspond and enter into contractual relations with them.

Whether the subpublication agreement includes a single composition or an entire catalog, there are various provisions to be negotiated. Most important among these is the division of royalties between the original publisher and the subpublisher and whether the division of royalties is to be calculated "at the source" when more than one territory is involved. Also to be negotiated are the subpublisher's ability to retain rights beyond the expiration of the term if a local recording or some other substantial level of exploitation is attained as a result of the subpublisher's efforts, and whether the royalty division changes in favor of the subpublisher if this occurs.

Foreign Performing Rights Societies

Performing rights societies exist in most countries of the world to license performing rights and collect fees for such licenses. In some instances the same society also licenses mechanical rights. In terms of collections, the largest societies outside the United States and Canada are GEMA in Germany, JASRAC in Japan, the PRS/MCPS alliance in the United Kingdom, and SACEM/SDRM in France.

There are two important aspects of foreign publishing contracts that need to be recognized. First, an original publisher may (but usually does not) require that its share of public performance income be routed back to its own performing rights society, in accordance with multilateral agreements between the various societies, rather than being collected by the subpublisher. Second, the writers' share of public performance income may in some instances be automatically reduced by the share payable to foreign translators and arrangers under the rules of the local performing rights society.

Foreign Mechanical Licensing

Many American publishers use the services of the Harry Fox Agency to license and collect mechanical royalties. Although the agency has traditionally asserted jurisdiction only over phonorecords distributed within the United States and permitted records made domestically to be exported without payment of American mechanical royalties where it had reasonable assurance that mechanical royalties would be paid in the country of sale, it has taken the position that U.S. mechanical royalties must be paid even on exports, owing to alleged difficulties in obtaining verification of foreign mechanical royalty payments. This position has irritated foreign mechanical societies and created some new problems in the negotiation of foreign subpublication agreements.

Outside the United States, and particularly in Europe, the usual method of collection of mechanical royalties is through national mechanical rights societies. With the exception of the United Kingdom, the national societies in Europe negotiate industrywide licenses for phonorecord reproduction rights through a confederation known as BIEM (Bureau International des Sociétés Gérants des Droits d'Enregistrement et de Reproduction Mécanique), which negotiates with IFPI, the record industry trade association. These negotiations are on two levels. On an international basis BIEM and IFPI negotiate the general licensing system and the standard rate. Then the national societies settle such things as the amount of deductions from the standard rate and the minimum royalty.

The structure of BIEM licensing is conceptually different than in the United States. In the United States the reproduction of each musical composition on each phonorecord is individually licensed, whereas the BIEM-IFPI agreement grants phonograph record manufacturers a blanket license, similar to the music licenses that performing rights organizations grant to broadcasters. In the United States the current statutory rate is 8.0 cents per song per phonorecord sold, whereas the net BIEM rate (after deductions for discounts and packaging) is 9.009 percent of the published price to dealers (PPD) on full-price product under the BIEM-IFPI agreement. This agreement technically expired on June 30, 2000, but continues while being renegotiated. One of the principal bones of contention is the IFPI's demand that the new rate be based on actual (or average) realized price to dealers (ARP). Depending on the rate of exchange and relative prices, the BIEM rate generally works out to a higher amount (in dollars and cents) than the mechanical royalty rate in the United States.

The European scene has undergone substantial changes. Since the formation of the European Union, any member-country society can license reproduction rights, regardless of the place of ultimate sale. This initially led to intense competition between the various national mechanical rights societies to make "central licensing" deals with international record companies. PolyGram initially made a deal with STEMRA in the Netherlands and subsequently with MCPS in the United Kingdom; BMG and Warner dealt with GEMA in Germany; and Sony dealt with SDRM in France.

In order to deal with the issues such as the "social and cultural" deductions levied by various national societies (especially GEMA in Germany and SACEM in France), as well as high administration costs, the principal publishers and the European societies struck an agreement in Cannes in January 1997. Under this so-called Cannes Accord, the societies pledged to reduce their average administration charges from more than 8 percent to 7.1 percent as of December 1998, 6.27 percent as of June 2000, and 6 percent as of June 2001. The Cannes Accord also established an ultimate goal of distributions within 90 days of each calendar quarter.

Piracy—unauthorized reproduction of music—is a worldwide problem, and is particularly rampant in Brazil, Indonesia, China, Mexico, Panama, and Russia according to IFPI reports. This problem threatens to become even more serious as digital recording devices such as CD-Rs proliferate.

The Harry Fox Agency represents the mechanical rights controlled by most of the foreign mechanical rights societies (and through them their publisher affiliates) in the United States. Many of these foreign societies accept direct membership by U.S. publishers without the intercession of a local publisher. Through its relationship with foreign societies, the Harry Fox Agency can act as agent for those American publishers that have not directly affiliated with the foreign societies and have not authorized a local foreign publisher to subpublish their copyrights.

As noted previously, mechanical license fees relate to a license to use copyrighted compositions on records. Mechanical license fees are customarily based on the number of copies of a record that are sold and are divided proportionately among the copyright owners of the music used on the record.

When subpublishers are granted subpublication rights in a composition, they customarily receive the power to collect mechanical license fees and the publisher's share of performance fees. (Only the remaining "publisher share" is remitted to the subpublisher when it has the right to collect performance fees; the U.S. writer's share of performance fees—usually 50 percent of total performance fees—is reserved for the writers by the local performing rights society and remitted directly to the writer's society.) The historical division of collections between the original (U.S.) publisher and the local subpublisher is 50-50. However, competitive forces have tended to increase the percentage paid to the U.S. publisher to 75 percent (and sometimes more) of the amounts collected by the subpublisher.

If a composition has been released on a commercial record in the United States and the same recording has been or is likely to be released in the foreign territory, the original publisher in the United States may insist on receiving more than the usual share of performance fees and mechanical fees. The argument for this is that the subpublisher is only a collecting agent, and therefore only a collection charge, from 10 to 15 percent, should be retained by the local subpublisher. Some subpublishers accede to such arguments.

Other subpublishers oppose any reduction in their fee. They contend that they may be the moving force in causing the local release of the original U.S. recording. They must spend time and money promoting the U.S. recording to make it successful. They also point out that performance fees are earned by live as well as record performances and that a reduced fee would unfairly compensate them for their efforts in printing, arranging, and distributing the composition so that it will be performed by orchestras and vocalists. Their position is reinforced if they obtain local cover recordings. They also argue that the performing rights societies' records do not adequately separate performances of the original U.S. recordings from other performances.

In the area of motion picture and television film performance fees, the subpublisher will generally agree to a fee of 10 to 15 percent because only a collection arrangement is involved. Music cue sheets that list the music in American films are received from the United States and are filed with the performing rights society. The society makes clear and separate accountings for each film, and the subpublisher can do little to affect the amounts collected. In Europe, motion picture performance fees for theatrical films are collected from theaters as a small percentage of box office receipts. Television film performance fees are received from the television stations.

Under some contractual arrangements a subpublisher retains from 10 to 25 percent of receipts in its territory on compositions for which there is no locally originated recording and a higher percentage after a local recording is obtained. The increased rate may be 30 to 50 percent of all receipts from the composition; or the higher rate may be limited to mechanical and synchronization income from the local version only. If the local version has a different title than the original song, it is possible to distinguish the performance earnings of the original and local versions and to accurately allocate to the subpublisher a lower percentage of income from nonlocal recordings and a higher percentage of income from the local version.

Synchronization Fees

A synchronization license fee is payable for a publisher's consent to the recording of a composition as a part of the soundtrack of a motion picture or television film. When a composition is subpublished, it is standard for the subpublisher to acquire the right to grant worldwide nonexclusive synchronization licenses for motion picture or television films originating in the local territory. Fifty percent or more of the synchronization fees are payable to the U.S. publisher. For films originating outside the subpublisher's territory, the U.S. publisher usually reserves the right to issue worldwide synchronization licenses for fees in which the local subpublisher does not share, even though the film may be shown in the local territory. However, the subpublisher participates in local performance income from the music in the film.

The producers of audiovisual devices such as videocassettes or videodiscs customarily request worldwide licenses for synchronization and marketing rights. To facilitate such licenses, original publishers may deny subpublishers the right to license and collect fees on audiovisual recordings that originate outside the subpublisher's territory, even though the devices containing such recordings are distributed in the subpublisher's territory.

Printed Editions

The royalty customarily payable by the local subpublisher to the original publisher in the United States for printed editions is 10 to 12.5 percent of the suggested retail price of such editions. If folios or albums are printed, and the U.S. publisher's composition is included with other compositions, the American publisher receives a prorated share of 10 to 12.5 percent computed in the ratio that the composition bears to the total number of compositions in the edition. Many agreements provide that public domain compositions in the editions be excluded in calculating the publisher's prorated share.

Provision should be made for sample copies of printed editions to be supplied gratis to the original publisher. A reasonable number of copies—four, for example—may be required.

Local Lyrics and Versions

A subpublisher usually acquires the right to make translations, adaptations, and arrangements of a composition so that it may be exploited commercially in the local territory. This includes the right to provide new lyrics and a new title. For compositions other than instrumentals, the subpublisher will have difficulties marketing the composition if it cannot be adapted for use in the subpublisher's territory by the addition of lyrics in the local language, a new title, and appropriate musical arrangements. For instance, the popular song "Never on Sunday" is called "Enfants du Piree" (Children of Piraeus) in France and "Ein Schiff Wird Kommen" (A Ship Will Come) in Germany, and there are different lyrics in each language. The song would not have achieved its worldwide popularity without these local versions. In fact, one criterion in selecting a subpublisher is its ability to arrange for appropriate adaptations of a composition to be made and recorded by popular local artists.

Local Writer Royalties

Royalties payable to a sublyricist—the person who writes lyrics for the local version—are frequently 12.5 percent of the subpublisher's gross receipts for mechanical and synchronization uses, 25 percent of the total writer's share payable in the territory in respect of public performance income, and 50 percent of the usual lyric writer royalties for territorial printed edition sales. It is customary for the subpublisher to bear, out of its share, the royalty payable to the local lyric writer for mechanical and synchronization uses and for the sale of printed editions. The subpublisher can more easily afford this when provision is made for its royalties to increase when there are local cover records. The share of public performance fees due the local lyric writer is usually deducted by the local public performance society from the share of the original writer. If the music and lyrics of the original song were written jointly by two separate writers, the public performance fees payable to the local writer are deducted equally from the shares of the original writers.

Some public performance societies provide for local arrangers to receive a portion of the original music writer's share of public performance fees. For many years, local lyric adapters of successful English-language songs participated even when the original version was played or sold. The arguments were (1) that the local version helped to popularize the original version in the local territory and (2) that it was more efficient to have a uniform royalty division for all versions of the song. The result was grossly unfair to original writers, and much money was diverted to local writers who had nothing to do with the work actually performed. Under more recent rules adopted by CISAC (the international association of performing rights societies), sublyricists participate only when their local version is actually used, at least on a prospective basis, but this does not affect some pre-existing situations where the local adapter had nothing to with the original recording yet continues to receive a portion of the original writer's share.

Copyright and Term of Rights

Subpublishers once sought to have rights conveyed to them for the entire term of copyright in their territory rather than for a limited number of years. It is in the interest of the U.S. publisher to limit the duration of the grant of rights, but not to the point of discouraging activity by the subpublisher. In recent years the trend has been to grant rights for shorter periods, usually not less than 3 years, with the possibility of an extension where cover records are made or synchronization rights for use in a motion picture are obtained. Some foreign societies, such as GEMA in Germany, may not recognize a subpublication agreement unless it has a minimum duration, ordinarily 3 years, although they may accept a reversionary clause that is activated sooner by the subpublisher's failure to achieve certain performance tests.

Under the Copyright Act of 1976 as amended in 1998 by the Copyright Term Extension Act, copyrights now last for the author's life plus 70 years, the same as the term of copyright in most European countries. Although the author may have the right to terminate grants after 35 years, the exercise of this termination right will not affect foreign subpublication rights.

While all rights under copyright may be granted to a subpublisher, the original publisher normally reserves the ownership of the copyright. This is a necessity if the agreement with the writer is a Songwriters Guild of America contract. The subpublisher should agree that each copy of the composition published by the subpublisher will bear a notice of copyright in the name of the original publisher.

A problem may arise, however, regarding local arrangements, translations, and adaptations, as well as local lyrics and titles. The subpublisher may attempt to retain the copyright for these local modifications and versions insofar as they contain new material. An experienced U.S. publisher will oppose this because, unless that publisher acquires the copyright in new material, it may be unable to exploit the composition fully in the local territory after the subpublisher's rights expire. In addition, the subpublisher who owns the copyright in new material would have to be asked to consent to its use by another subpublisher in a different territory and would presumably require a royalty payment as the price for such consent. The U.S. publisher should insist upon acquiring all rights in new material.

In catalog deals it is common to provide that compositions revert to the original publisher at the end of the term. Exceptions are sometimes made for compositions that have been printed locally, or released on a locally originated record, or both printed and released on records. The subpublisher may contend that the local release of the original U.S. recording should justify continuing rights in a composition, since the subpublisher may cause such release. The duration of the continuing rights is a matter of negotiation between the original publisher and the subpublisher. Provision is sometimes made for some extension of rights in compositions that are made available to the subpublisher only toward the end of the catalog deal and for which there has been printing or release on a local record, or both, before the close of the term; otherwise, the subpublisher would have little or no incentive to promote such songs.

Fees from All Usage, Accounting, and Audits

Subpublication contracts specify the royalties payable to the original publisher for various uses of a composition. In order to avoid being penalized for failing to set forth all conceivable uses, the U.S. publisher must be careful to provide that it is entitled to a stipulated percentage of all monies collected by the subpublisher for any use other than those specified in the agreement, whether or not such use is presently known or subsequently invented. There should be no objection by the subpublisher to the inclusion of this provision.

Problems may develop regarding accountings and royalty payments due to the U.S. publisher. The subpublication contract should clearly define the subpublisher's obligation to account for and make payment. A common provision requires the subpublisher to send the original publisher an itemized and detailed royalty statement every 6 months within 90 days of the end of each calendar half-year, and at the same time to remit all royalties shown to be due. It is advisable to specify the items to be included in the statement so that disputes about the completeness of the accounting may be avoided. For mechanical income these items may consist of a list of the individual records released in the territory, the names of the artists and record companies on the records, the number of records sold, and the total fees received. Accountings for printed editions should itemize separately the different editions, the retail price, and the number of copies sold.

Most countries have reciprocal tax treaties with the United States under which copyright royalties are exempt from withholding taxes or subject to reduced withholding taxes. Japan is an example of the latter. Where there are foreign withholding taxes on remittances to the original publisher, the latter should be furnished with an appropriate certificate to enable the original publisher to obtain a U.S. tax credit for foreign taxes paid.

In order to verify and facilitate the collection of royalties due, U.S. publishers may wish to have royalties paid directly to their own performing rights society and mechanical rights collection agency. In these cases, the subpublisher may be required to instruct its local performing rights society to pay the original publisher's share to that publisher's own performing rights society. If the U.S. publisher has entered into an affiliation agreement with a local mechanical rights society, that society may be instructed to pay the appropriate share of mechanical rights collections directly to the U.S. publisher. Alternatively, the Harry Fox Agency may serve as the U.S. publisher's representative abroad and receive the U.S. publisher's share of mechanical rights collections on the U.S. publisher's behalf. The Cannes Accord, discussed above, is one attempt to reduce delays in remittances from abroad as well as administrative charges by the foreign societies.

There are also risks of loss caused by commingling the accounts of many publishers or by the failure to identify foreign version song titles. These risks may be worthwhile if the appointment of a subpublisher results in the receipt of greater overall royalties, some of which might otherwise fail to be accounted for. A prudent U.S. publisher will obtain the right to inspect and audit the account books of the subpublisher. If it is not practical for the U.S. publisher to exercise the right through its own employees or regular accountants because of the expense involved, the publisher may choose to have its audit rights exercised by a local accountant at a lower cost.

Subpublication for Diverse Territories

A U.S. publisher may contract with a subpublisher for several countries under one agreement. However, within the 15 member states of the European Union, where free trade is mandated by EU directive, the traditional country breakdowns seem increasingly irrelevant. To the extent that the original U.S. publisher considers it desirable to enter separate subpublishing agreements for various territories, the following are the traditional groupings (italicized names represent countries that may also be licensed alone):

- European Union, excluding the United Kingdom and Ireland
- *Germany*, Austria, and Switzerland
- Scandinavia, including Sweden, Norway, Denmark, Finland, and Iceland
- *Spain* and Portugal
- *United Kingdom and Northern Ireland*
- *France* and territories under the jurisdiction of SACEM
- *Japan*
- Far East, excluding Japan but including China, Singapore, Malaysia, Taiwan, and Thailand
- *Belgium, the Netherlands,* and Luxembourg, often collectively referred to as Benelux. (Belgium is sometimes included with France, and Luxembourg is split between Germany and France on a language basis.)
- *Italy*, Vatican City, and San Marino
- *Australia* and New Zealand
- *South Africa*
- *Mexico*, Central America, Venezuela, Colombia, Ecuador, and Peru
- *Argentina*, Uruguay, Chile, Paraguay, and Bolivia
- *Brazil*
- *Greece*
- Russia, Poland, the Czech Republic, Slovak Republic, Romania, Hungary, and former nations of the Soviet Union.

As indicated above, the original U.S. publisher receives royalties equivalent to negotiated percentages of various types of income collected by the subpublisher. Where the subpublisher's territory includes more than one country and the subpublisher uses the services of one or more secondary subpublishers in other countries, the latter will deduct a fee before remitting collections to the former, which can reduce the royalties paid to the original publisher. For example, if the secondary subpublisher's fee is 50 percent, the primary subpublisher will be paid only 50 percent of the funds earned "at the source." If the primary subpublication contract requires 50 percent of collections to be remitted to the U.S. publisher, the U.S. publisher would then be entitled to be paid only 25 percent of the earnings "at the source." As a result, nearly all subpublishing calculations are required to be made "at the source," thus requiring the primary subpublisher to absorb the cost of collection commissions deducted by the secondary subpublishers. Moreover, as the original U.S. publisher must usually pay 50 percent of its own receipts to the writer, the writer is also vitally interested in not allowing the diminution of monies as they pass from one country to another.

It should be noted that 50 percent of performing rights society monies are invariably collected and paid at the source to the account of the writer's originating society so that only the publisher's share of performing rights monies are involved in the subpublishing collection and payments. The writer does not get paid again out of the publisher's share of performing rights income remitted to the original publisher.

The European Union

At present there are 15 member states in the European Union: Austria, Belgium, Denmark, England, Finland, France, Germany, Greece, Ireland, Italy, Luxembourg, the Netherlands, Portugal, Spain, and Sweden. Relations among members are governed by the Treaty of Rome, which provides for the abolition of tariff barriers and the free and unrestricted movement of goods across state borders. Territorial sales restrictions in license agreements among the EU countries are generally invalid. Similar restrictions apply to the four nations in the European Free Trade Association: Iceland, Liechtenstein, Norway, and Switzerland.

Questions arise as to the enforceability of exclusive subpublishing agreements with publishers in different EU states. For example, there may be one agreement with a subpublisher in England covering exclusive rights there and another with a subpublisher in France providing for exclusive rights in that country. Must each of these subpublishers respect and recognize the exclusive rights of the other? In practice, if a subpublishing agreement is for a limited term, the prospect of nonrenewal by the original U.S. publisher may tend to keep each subpublisher within the bounds of its own territory. But third parties, such as companies that buy phonograph records lawfully licensed for manufacture in France are free, under the Treaty of Rome, to export the records into England and other EU countries. The same also applies to printed editions manufactured in one EU state and bought for export to another.

The Treaty of Rome has been said not to affect the exclusive rights of copyright proprietors with respect to such matters as rented sheet music or the licensing of the public performance of copyrighted works. To what extent the Treaty of Rome restricts exclusivity and territorial restraints in subpublishing agreements is not entirely clear, and consequently the advice of local counsel should be obtained. Infringements of the treaty may involve not only the negation of business deals but also, in certain cases, prosecution and fines by the European Commission, which is one of the five governing institutions within the European Union.

Default Clauses

It is difficult and often impossible to anticipate the legal effect, especially in a distant territory, of a default by a subpublisher in the performance of an obligation without a clear statement in the agreement of the effect intended by the parties. For example, if an accounting statement or a royalty payment is delayed, can this be grounds for canceling the agreement?

It is therefore advisable to include in the subpublication agreement a clause that defines the rights and obligations of the parties in case of default. From the U.S. publisher's point of view, it can be provided that there will be a material default if the subpublisher fails to (1) make periodic accountings, (2) pay royalties when due, or (3) release local cover records if that has been promised. Such a failure may give the U.S. publisher grounds to terminate the agreement and cause a reversion of all rights in the composition. The subpublisher can in turn guard against cancellation by a clause under which the subpublisher must receive written notice of any default and an opportunity for a certain period, perhaps 30 days, to cure the default.

The default clause may further state that the U.S. publisher can cancel the subpublication agreement in the event an insolvency or bankruptcy proceeding is begun by or against the subpublisher and is not dismissed within a given period, such as 30 to 60 days.

Jurisdiction over Disputes

Despite careful draftsmanship, subpublication contracts may still result in disputes regarding their interpretation. Because of this, and because of the expense involved in litigating a matter in a foreign country, U.S. publishers strive to provide in subpublication agreements that the exclusive forum for the determination of controversies will be U.S. courts or a U.S. arbitration tribunal in a specified location (customarily where the original publisher's main office is located) and that the subpublisher consents to that jurisdiction. Even when such a clause exists in a subpublication agreement, there may be problems enforcing an award in a foreign jurisdiction if the due process standards of that jurisdiction are not complied with.

Catalog Agreements

It has been previously stated that if all the compositions of a U.S. publisher are the subject of a publication agreement, the agreement may be considered as a catalog subpublication contract under which all compositions are subpublished by the subpublisher for the term of the agreement. A catalog subpublication agreement has the advantage of relieving the U.S. publisher of the burden of negotiating separately for representation in the territory of each composition in the catalog. However, it also means that the U.S. publisher cannot shop for the largest cash advance among the various foreign subpublishers that may be interested in a musical work.

On the other hand, a U.S. publisher can require an overall cash advance for its catalog as the price for committing its entire catalog to a single subpublisher. It is possible that the overall advance will exceed the separate advances that might be negotiated for individual compositions. In negotiating a catalog deal, a U.S. publisher may be able to obtain other concessions, such as increased royalty rates and a shorter term for the subpublisher's interest in copyrights, which would not be granted if single compositions were involved.

Local Firms

Larger U.S.-based publishers may eventually try to establish their own firms in a local territory. However, if the catalog is not suitable for and potentially strong in the territory, the investment required—for office space, personnel, and over-head—may be financially unsound.

Some foreign performing rights societies tend to discourage foreign-controlled publishing firms. As a condition of membership, a society may insist that a new firm control a stipulated amount of locally originated material. Generally, lower-rung memberships in societies may be permitted, which gives the right to be represented by the society and to receive publisher distributions. Becoming a full member with additional voting and other rights can be more difficult. For example, PRS, the British performing rights society, requires an associate member to earn a minimum of about £17,000 a year in at least 2 of 3 recent years before qualifying for full membership.

At times the problem of attaining full membership can be solved by the purchase of local publishing firms that have already qualified for such memberships. On the other hand, a U.S. publisher may be satisfied with a lower-rung membership provided that, as is commonly observed by societies, the lesser members receive distributions on an equal basis with full members. The practices of each society should be investigated prior to the establishment of a local firm by a U.S. publisher.

Joint Firms

Recognizing the perils and problems represented by a firm that is wholly owned locally, many U.S. publishers have in the past embarked on joint publishing ventures with an established local publisher. Together the parties create a jointly owned firm. In this way the U.S. publisher acquires local management and know-how at minimum expense. Advantageous arrangements can be made whereby the local partner manages the joint company and supplies the necessary office and other facilities for a fee, which is commonly a percentage of gross revenues of the joint company. The fee may be roughly 10 to 15 percent and is generally exclusive of direct expenses billed to the joint company for costs of demonstration records, advertising in trade publications, salaries of personnel who work solely for the joint company, and special legal and accounting services. In some instances the local partner will absorb all expenses in return for a negotiated fee.

Where a new joint firm is organized, the local partner arranges for its formation through territorial counsel. The local partner may advance the organizational expenses as a charge against future net income of the joint company. Because it is prudent for the U.S. publisher to be fully aware of the impact of territorial laws and practices, it should give serious consideration to being represented by its own local counsel who is completely familiar with the music business in the area, including the practices of the performing rights society.

If the local performing rights society will not qualify a new firm for membership unless it controls locally originated material, arrangements must be made with the territorial partner to supply this material so that membership can be obtained. Otherwise the joint firm will continue to be dependent on firms with membership for relations with the society.

A problem in the operation of joint firms is that they may be administered by the local partner as if they were catalog deals. In other words, only the material from the U.S. publisher goes into the joint firm, and nothing is done by the local partner to develop the firm's status as a local publisher that vigorously seeks to acquire and exploit territorial copyrights. This makes good business sense for the local partner, since it has merely a 50 percent interest in the joint firm. In effect, the local partner tends to treat a joint firm as a catalog deal in which the U.S. partner's 50 percent interest is equivalent to an increased royalty; in return for the increased royalty the territorial partner is assured of a flow of desirable product for a number of years.

Overcoming the inertia of the territorial partner is not easy. One approach may be to employ a professional manager who works solely for the joint firm. This can result in a large financial burden for the firm, which the U.S. partner and the territorial partner may be unwilling to risk. The local partner is ordinarily the one who chooses the professional manager and may therefore be able to influence the manager to permit choice copyrights to remain with the local partner's publishing firm. Or the territorial partner may consciously choose an ineffective professional manager so that the joint firm is not built up as a strong competitor in local publishing.

Joint firms do, however, have a number of advantages over catalog arrangements. For example, if the joint firm is a member of the local performing rights and mechanical rights societies, the accountings for copyrights controlled by the firm will be completely segregated, and losses due to improper accountings by the local partner will be avoided. Where the subpublisher's honesty and dependability are above reproach, this advantage may be of little importance. The U.S. publisher may anticipate a greater overall return from a joint company than would otherwise be derived from a catalog deal, but if the publisher fails to assess all the factors adequately, there may ultimately be a negative effect on the company's earnings.

It can be argued that a U.S. publisher with a joint firm is better able to acquire from other U.S. publishers foreign territorial rights in U.S. copyrights. A joint firm, which is doing business in the territory as a separate entity from the U.S. firm, may be able to actively engage in pursuing territorial rights in attractive U.S. copyrights. It may have the authority to execute subpublication agreements with and make cash advances to U.S. publishers on behalf of the joint firm.

Finally, it must be recognized that while a catalog deal is designed to exploit a catalog and result in a profit to the U.S. publisher, the joint firm not only accomplishes the same purpose but can also act as a necessary first step in setting up a wholly locally owned publishing enterprise.

The Termination of Joint Ownership

Inherent in the formation of a joint company is the agreement on the part of the U.S. partner to make a catalog deal with the company for a period of years. The number of years is subject to negotiations: 3 to 5 years is common.

It is usual to provide for the manner in which the joint firm will continue after the period of years expires. The U.S. partner will wish to have an option to buy out the local partner so that it has a wholly owned firm in the territory. This option may be exercised in many ways. An agreement may be struck that the purchase price for the half-interest of the local partner will be computed as a certain number of times local partner's average net income or the previous year's net income. Assuming it is reasonable to value a publishing company's net income in a range of 6 times such income, the parties might then fix the purchase price for a half-interest at 3 times the net income. For instance, if the company's net income is $10,000, the purchase price for the half-interest may be stipulated as $30,000 plus half the costs of organizing the company, which are usually low and may come to only a few hundred dollars.

A second method of obtaining an option to buy out a local partner is to provide for negotiations on the price and, if the parties are unable to agree, to have the price settled by designated arbitrators. A third method is to have a local partner divide the copyrights into two lists of equal quality and give the U.S. partner the right to elect to take either list plus the stock interest of the territorial partner. Again, the U.S. partner may agree to reimburse half of the costs of organizing the company to the local partner.

The parties may also agree on a buy or sell clause whereby either party has the option of making an initial bid to buy the other's interest, but with the understanding that the other party may instead buy out the bidder for the same price. Here once more, the local partner may be the final buyer and thus frustrate the purpose of the U.S. partner.

To avoid the necessity for a complicated procedure for either party to acquire the other's interest, the U.S. publisher may trade a long-term catalog deal—say, 10 years with the joint company—in return for an assignment to it gratis of the local partner's interest at the end of that period. An alternative approach, with practically the same economic results to the local partner, might be for the U.S. partner to retain 100 percent ownership at all times but have the firm managed by the local publisher on a basis that would give the same net return to the local publisher that it would receive if it were a partner; this scenario may not be practical where the joint firm must have some local ownership in order to qualify for membership in local societies.

22

The Writer as Publisher

Thousands of music publishers participate in the U.S. music industry. Some, such as Warner/Chappell and the EMI group of publishers, have extensive administrative and promotional offices. Some rarely have cash reserves equal to the next month's rent. Many are private firms owned and operated by the writer with the assistance of the writer's own attorney and accountant, and these firms usually handle shares of songs written by the writer that have not been placed with conventional publishers or with such interests recaptured due to statutory provisions.

No license is required to become a music publisher. The Constitution of the United States provides for freedom of the press, which is not limited to newspaper, magazine, and book publications. Anyone can publish printed products. However, in the music industry a publisher is more likely to be interested in other, more profitable aspects of music publishing, such as collecting broadcast and other performance fees through ASCAP, BMI, SESAC, and foreign performing rights societies and granting mechanical rights licenses for phonograph records.

Both ASCAP and BMI operate under consent decrees that tend to encourage people to qualify as publishers. ASCAP is required to advertise in music trade journals that anyone can become a publisher member with proof of being actively engaged in the music publishing business, and with musical compositions that have been used or distributed for at least one year. The BMI consent decree requires the acceptance of any publisher engaged in the music publishing business whose musical publications have been commercially published or recorded and publicly promoted or distributed for at least one year. In fact, ASCAP and BMI move promptly to grant publisher membership to persons active as publishers without insisting on any set prerequisite time period of operations. Writer membership in ASCAP or BMI is available to any composer or lyricist who has had at least one work published or recorded.

Publisher membership in ASCAP involves a $50 annual fee. BMI publisher status does not call for a fee—only a one-time $150 application charge. SESAC, a for-profit corporation, does not charge an application or annual fee; however, affiliation is not available to all applicants, as SESAC grants membership only to those applicants they approve.

Writer-Publisher Joint Firms

For many years, successful writers such as Stevie Wonder, Henry Mancini, Richard Rodgers and Oscar Hammerstein, the Gershwins, and Irving Berlin have founded publishing firms for their compositions in conjunction with and administered by established publishers. This type of writer-founded firm frequently involves common stock participation by the writer and the administering publisher in proportions commensurate with the bargaining power of the writer.

The supervising publisher usually requests an administration fee—a fixed percentage fee ranging from 7.5 to 25 percent of gross receipts—in lieu of charges for rent, local telephone services, management salaries, and other general overhead. In some instances, again dependent on the bargaining power of the composer or lyricist, the administration fee will be waived. In effect, the firm jointly owned by a writer and a publisher is a device for increasing the earnings of the writer as well as providing more control over his or her copyrights.

Self-Publishing

Increasingly, successful writers are acting as their own publishers, with limited administrative assistance performed or supervised by their accountants and attorneys.

Less successful writers may decide to act as their own publisher because no other publishing company is interested in their compositions. These writers have to make demonstration records and attempt to place their compositions with record companies and artists. Some composers are by nature very active in promoting the recording of their compositions and their performance on the air, and they can easily claim that they are performing as a publisher. Until such time as they find an alert publisher that will match or exceed their efforts, they see no reason to share publishing income with another entity. They keep 100 percent of the publishing income by forming one of the thousands of music companies in existence and by qualifying the firm for membership in ASCAP or affiliation with BMI, depending on their own writer status. However, they also have to assume all the advertising, promotion, accounting, and other expenses, which may sometimes prove to be high.

Songwriters who are their own publisher rarely print their songs; if they want printed copies, they can deal with independent sheet music printer-distributors. They may arrange for the Harry Fox Agency to license and collect mechanical license fees for recordings of their compositions. The Harry Fox Agency will act on their behalf in the same manner as it does for larger publishers.

Among the numerous companies that offer administrative services to writers are Bug Music, with offices in the United States, Germany, and the United Kingdom (www.bugmusic.com); Copyright Management International or Blue Mountain Music in Nashville; and Reach International and Spirit Music in New York. Charges for administrative services range from 10 to 15 percent of gross receipts, and 25 percent on cover recordings secured by the administrator.

The Songwriters Guild of America in New Jersey has recognized that more and more of its songwriter members own the publishing rights as well, either through initial retention of rights or their recapture of rights in renewal periods. The SGA offers a limited catalog administration plan for the administration of the publishing rights of its members. The fee is 9 percent of the gross receipts, with a lesser charge of 3 percent of publisher small performance (ASCAP, BMI, or SESAC) income. There is a one-time setup charge of $2 per song. A writer-publisher in the SGA is not required to pay the service fee of 5.75 percent otherwise payable under the SGA's collection plan; this is a compulsory system of collection and auditing applicable to all members and relates only to writer royalties collected from third-party publishers subject to a maximum per year of $1750.00 for any individual writer or estate thereof. The services offered by the SGA do not include the negotiation of contracts for printed publications or foreign subpublishing. Grand rights, or dramatic rights, are not administered under SGA or other customary administrative plans. However, firms such as Tams-Witmark Music Library, Music Theater International, Rodgers & Hammerstein Repertory, and Samuel French are available for such services.

Under the Copyright Act of 1976, the period of copyright of pre-1978 songs was initially extended by 19 years and under the Copyright Term Extension Act extended for a total of 95 years. A writer who has terminated a grant of rights may want assistance in evaluating the monetary value of the additional period and determining whether to keep the ownership of the publishing rights or reassign the composition to a publisher. The SGA, through its catalog evaluation plan, offers to provide the valuation for an hourly fee, which is lower for members than for nonmembers.

In certain instances, a writer will make a joint copyright ownership arrangement with a publisher and retain a portion of the customary publisher's share, which is 50 percent of gross income. If the writer is able to retain a part interest in the copyright of a composition, he or she can organize a publishing firm and register as an ASCAP or BMI publisher member. This procedure is often chosen by recording artists who write their own material. In fact, many record companies will negotiate with recording artists for a joint copyright ownership by the company's affiliated publishing firm and the artist of all original songs written or controlled by the artist and recorded during the term of the recording contract. Negotiations will determine who administers the copyrights and the extent of any administration fee.

der the current BMI payment schedule, if there is no publisher, writers title to receive the performance fees ordinarily payable to both the publisher and the writer. It is possible for the writer's share of performance fees to exceed 50 percent of the combined writer-publisher total, although the publisher's share cannot exceed one-half. This practice eliminates the need for a writer to form a publishing firm for the purpose of collecting more than the usual BMI writer's share of performance fees.

Sources of Copyrights for the Self-Publisher

Self-publishing starts with ownership of all or part of the musical copyright. This obviously includes the many songs which are written and recorded prior to placement with a conventional music publisher. Garage bands and and Internet-reliant artist/composers alike retain publishing rights when no deal has been made to assign them to a third party. Similarly an author, if still living at the vital 28th year of a copyright first published before 1978, or the author's statutory heirs, become full owners of any previously assigned publishing rights unless a specific sale of "renewal" rights has been made by the qualifying renewal claimant. This, of course, is an ever-diminishing library of songs: the retention of copyright for songs published on or after January 1, 1978, is governed not by automatic reversion upon the 28th year after publication but by the termination provisions of the Copyright Act, which are covered in detail in Chapter 17.

23

Music for Motion Pictures

Music is very important to the motion picture industry and, reciprocally, motion pictures are of prime importance to the music industry. A considerable amount of music appears in the average film. Films usually get broad exposure to the public, and there is commensurate exposure of the music in the picture.

Motion pictures are a prime source of music evergreens, which, in turn, helps the box office appeal of motion pictures. For example, the music in the films *Moulin Rouge, The Crow,* and *The Pink Panther* have contributed significantly to the success of the films themselves. Historically, songs launched within film scores generated a large number of cover records, for example, "Moon River" (55 covers), "More" (54 charted covers), and the venerable "White Christmas" (74 charted covers). The song "Unchained Melody" was first issued as the theme song of the film *Unchained* and some 30 years later was featured in *Ghost;* the result was two records on the *Billboard* chart at the same time.

The distribution and promotion of these films and many others have aided materially in popularizing the music on their soundtracks. Similarly, film soundtracks can turn into best-selling albums, which serve to promote the films at the box office: for example, *Saturday Night Fever* and *Flashdance* in the 1970s; *Dirty Dancing* in the 1980s; *Titanic* in the 1990s; and *Coyote Ugly* and *O Brother, Where Art Thou?* in the early 2000s.

Billboard's Top-Selling Album Chart published June 29, 2002, shows 13 soundtrack albums reaching the pop charts, with notable successes for *O Brother, Where Art Thou?* (listed for 77 weeks), *Shrek* (57 weeks), and *Moulin Rouge* (52 weeks). Soundtracks have garnered such notable success in recent years that companies have occasionally released follow-ups to original soundtrack album hits, two notable examples being *Back to Titanic* and *More Music from Save the Last Dance.* In fact, motion picture soundtracks have been so successful that television studios have begun promoting their shows through album releases such as *Touched by an Angel: The Album,* which reached number 11 on the charts, *The Osbourne Family Album,* which peaked at number 13, and *The Sopranos: Music from the HBO Series.* The *Sopranos* album, like the soundtrack albums for *O Brother, Where Art Thou?* and *Sleepless in Seattle*, does not consist of music specifically composed for the show played by studio orchestras with featured artists but of licensed songs performed by the original artists.

Rights Required for Films

In order to use music in a motion picture, the producer must acquire several fundamental rights. These include the *synchronization right*, the right to record the music in synchronized or timed relation to the pictures in a film, video, or laserdisc; *the performance right*, the right to perform publicly the music that is recorded under the synchronization right; and the right to make copies of the film, video, or laserdisc and to distribute them to the public by sales or rental. Ordinarily the right to make copies and distribute them, for the purpose of negotiations, is encompassed under the synchronization and performance rights.

In the discussion that follows, it may be assumed that when a producer applies for a synchronization and performance license for a film, the producer is seeking the fundamental rights required to make and exploit the film. A typical industry checklist for film licensing now specifies fee quotations for world synchronization, U.S. theatrical performance rights, and videogram rights, as well as new media to cover DVD and other new technology. Also included in the rights package are so-called free broadcast television—whether network, syndicated, or local and whether commercial or public television—as well as cable in various formats—basic, subscription, pay-per-view, closed-circuit hotel television, and satellite.

Employee-for-Hire Agreements

If the producer wishes to have original music created for a motion picture, the producer customarily makes an employee-for-hire agreement with a composer, according to which fundamental rights are acquired from the composer. Under the contract the composer will create the music and in addition will usually arrange the music and select and conduct the orchestra. All rights under copyright in the music will reside with the producer as the so-called author under copyright law, including all rights of recording, performance, and music publishing. Motion pictures are, of course, audiovisual works and consequently fit into the 1976 Copyright Act definition of a work for hire: a work that is not only prepared by an employee in the scope of his or her employment but also specially ordered or commissioned, if the parties expressly agree in writing that the work shall be considered one made for hire.

The great body of motion picture music has always been written on a work-for-hire basis, which vests copyrights in the film producer or other employer. In the rare instance where a song or score used in a film does not fit within the work-for-hire category, problems can arise, particularly when the work originated before 1978, with regard to the appropriate licensor and the duration of the license. One solution has been to have family members of the creators of such works agree to be bound by a renewal grant. When dealing with film music created on or after January 1, 1978, there is no right of termination to be considered because the termination statute itself clearly specifies that derivative works previously authorized are not affected by exercise of termination by composers or the composer's statutory heirs.

Synchronization and Performance Licenses

A producer's alternative to contracting with a composer to create original music for a film is to use music not specifically composed for the picture. In that event, the producer will seek a synchronization and performance license from the copyright proprietor, who is likely to be a music publisher. This is commonly referred to as "interpolation."

In negotiating a synchronization and performance license, the producer and publisher must come to terms on the nature of the license that the publisher is willing to grant. A producer will seek a broad license that permits the exploitation of the film in all conceivable media throughout the world. The publisher, on the other hand, will seek to limit the license to theatrical exhibition in theaters and to reserve the right to collect further fees for other uses, such as exhibition over free television or pay-TV or distribution of the film on videocassettes or DVDs for sale or rental to the public. Prolonged negotiations may be necessary before mutually agreeable license fees are arrived at.

In the 1948 case of *Alden-Rochelle v. ASCAP*, the courts held that under antimonopoly laws, performance licenses for ASCAP music in theatrical films cannot be required of theaters. However, in foreign countries, theaters are granted blanket licenses by the local performing rights society for the performance of music in conjunction with films; theaters usually pay a small percentage of their net box office receipts after taxes as consideration for the license. The local performing rights societies outside the United States operate under agreements with ASCAP and BMI, according to which the foreign societies are authorized to grant licenses for the performance of music controlled by ASCAP- or BMI-affiliated societies. BMI and SESAC honor the Alden-Rochelle rule with regard to their own repertoires.

Prices charged by publishers for synchronization and performance licenses vary with the proposed use of the music in the film. For background instrumental use, the price is less than for a background vocal use, and visual performances command higher fees than background performances. The fee is usually structured on a one-time flat-fee basis that includes both types of licenses (U.S. performance plus world synchronization). The performance license is usually determined by simply taking half the U.S. portion of the worldwide synchronization fee. The U.S. portion is sometimes one-half of the world total and sometimes somewhat less; the Canadian share may be up to one-tenth of the North American share, but is subject to negotiation, especially where a different publisher controls Canadian rights.

Although limited to licensing performance rights in film music to television and not theaters, BMI recognizes the special value of film music in its repertoire by two special treatments. It pays two times a conventional performance royalty for feature performances on television or radio of music originating in films. It also sponsors a tuition-free workshop annually—the BMI Film Conducting Workshop.

Licensing Agents and Research Firms

In June of 2002, the Harry Fox Agency discontinued the service of licensing synchronization rights for motion pictures. Negotiating a synchronization license for a motion picture or TV film or for a commercial jingle must now be done directly with the publisher or appointed agent of the author. The Harry Fox Agency will, however, provide information regarding who controls the music rights. Other sources of information are ASCAP, BMI, and the Copyright Office.

As to musical works originating before 1978, producers should exercise caution concerning the owner or potential owner of renewal rights. Under a 1990 Supreme Court decision concerning the film *Rear Window,* it was determined that agreements made in the initial 28-year term of copyright for a pre-1978 work do not necessarily extend to the renewal period. In this case, the author of the short story on which the film *Rear Window* was based sold the movie rights to a production company which in turn assigned them to the makers of the film. The author died before the start of the renewal term for the story, but his statutory heirs filed for renewal in 1970 and then sold the renewal rights in the story to the plaintiff. Later the film company authorized its distribution first by broadcast on national television and later for release in theaters, on cable TV, and for use on videocassettes. The plaintiff sued for infringement of his renewal-term copyrights, and the Supreme Court ruled in his favor, holding that the film was, under the circumstances presented, a "derivative work" of the original short story. In practical terms, the case means that a song originating in 1975 might have a valid synchronization license issued in 2003 that could lose its validity in the United States as of 2004, requiring further negotiations at such time, if the potential renewal claimant had not endorsed the original license at or before the time of issuance. No such problem exists for compositions originating in and after 1978.

It is quite common for a producer to refer such a matter to a copyright search firm that specializes in rendering copyright reports. It frequently happens that the particular matter has been researched previously and a quick reply can be forwarded to the producer. Among copyright search organizations are Thomson & Thomson Copyright Research Group, a firm with offices in Boston and Washington, D.C., and Government Liaison Services of Washington, D.C. Of course, the Research Division of the Copyright Office can make a report at their rate of $65 per hour. If an interpretation of law is required to clarify a search, the producer has to refer the report to specialist copyright attorneys for an opinion.

Videos and DVDs

In the United States, video and DVD rental and sales have the potential to earn more revenue than the theater release of a feature film. In the past, the release date of a video was almost always delayed until the end of the original theatrical run, and further delayed during pay-cable showings, but this practice is no longer routinely followed. Revenues from video marketing are an essential part of any film's financial projections. For purposes of large-volume sales, a lower price, between $15 and $25, is applicable in what is called "sell-thru" marketing to the consumer, as distinguished from the original higher price, which is usually over $70.

In 2002, International Recording Media Association (IRMA) statistics revealed that 90 percent of American homes had VCRs, up from 85 percent in 1998 and that 30 percent of American homes had acquired a DVD player since the introduction of that format. In North America in 2001, according to IRMA, 920 million VHS cassettes and 435 million DVD discs were produced. Most observers believe that DVDs will replace videocassettes at a much faster rate than CDs replaced tapes and records.

Producers of feature films generally insist on music licenses from publishers that permit the use of their product in the form of videos. Publishers, and through them the songwriters they represent, seek to share in the substantial revenues to be generated by videos. Negotiations between producers and publishers are initiated by a producer application for a synchronization license.

Where the use of music is limited, a music publisher may agree to a customary type of synchronization fee, with an extra payment added for video rights. Or the producer may be granted an option to secure video rights, for a fixed sum within a given period. As of this writing, there has been a nearly uniform approach of the licensee to seek a flat-fee buyout of video rights. Publishers often seek to negotiate a "rolling advance" based on a figure roughly double the applicable royalty statutory rate (until December 31, 2003, 8 cents) and payable in advance of each set of 30,000 to 50,000 units. However, in the overwhelming majority of negotiations for such uses, the film producers have succeeded in worldwide buy-outs at prices ranging from $5,000 to $15,000, depending on the expected video sales and importance of the song to the film score. Negotiations for this type of use recognize that the normal expected collections from ASCAP or BMI of television and foreign theatrical payments are reduced by the growing popularity of home video rental or purchase and that the negotiated fixed flat or royalty payment is the only benefit to be obtained for video use.

Where preexisting recordings are licensed for inclusion in a film, producers have to clear the right to incorporate the recordings into videos. The bargaining with record companies is analogous to negotiations with music publishers. A special obstacle may be the need to obtain the approval of the recording artists. This subject is discussed in Chapter 24, "Licensing Recordings for Motion Pictures."

Music Publishing Rights

Music publishing rights for original film score music are ordinarily covered by employee-for-hire language, by which all rights of every nature and description reside with the producer. The royalties paid to the composer fall into several categories, similar to those in agreements with composers who are submitting pop tunes to a publisher. For printed editions, the composer will be paid a specified amount, perhaps 8 to 12 cents, for piano copies sold in the United States and Canada, and 10 percent of the wholesale price (after trade discounts, if any) of other printed editions sold and paid for in those countries. For foreign printed editions, the standard royalty is 50 percent of the royalties received by the original publisher. The composer is usually paid 50 percent of the mechanical license receipts of the original publisher. Composer royalties are split evenly with the lyricists, if any.

Recording Artist Royalties

Motion picture producers are reluctant to provide contractually for a royalty to be paid to the composer-conductor on sales of soundtrack recordings. The reason for this is that such a payment, which is in the nature of a recording artist royalty, is ordinarily deducted from royalties otherwise payable to the producer. However, in the case of more prominent motion picture composers, some of whom are recording artists in their own right, the agreement provides for a special royalty to be paid on the sale of commercial phonograph records manufactured from any part of the soundtrack recorded by the orchestra conducted by the composer. This royalty may be 6 percent of the retail list price of records sold in the United States (less taxes and price of the album cover), frequently with the provision for lower royalties for foreign and record club sales.

In the case of composer-conductors who are recording artists in their own right, the royalties may exceed 6 percent. If the composer-conductor undertakes the obligation to prepare an edited soundtrack recording tape as a basis for the manufacture of phonograph records, the royalty otherwise payable is likely to increase by about 2 percent for such services. The royalties are generally subject to reduction to the extent that royalties are payable to other artists and are likely to be payable only after recoupment of all or a portion of union reuse fees that must be paid if records are manufactured from a soundtrack. (Under agreements that producers enter into with the American Federation of Musicians covering the studio orchestra, arrangers, and copyists used to make a film score, the union must consent to the use of a soundtrack for the manufacture of records. Consent is usually given on the condition that the musicians, arrangers, and copyists involved in the original recording are paid full scale for the music that appears on the record. It is not unusual for union reuse fees to reach $12,000 or more for a soundtrack album. For expensive films with large orchestras, the reuse fees can easily exceed $100,000.)

Soundtrack Album Contracts with Record Companies

From time to time, the larger record companies have complained that soundtrack albums are preempted by the record companies affiliated with the motion picture companies. For example, films released by the Disney affiliates Miramax Films and Touchstone Pictures sometimes issue the soundtrack records through Disney's own affiliated record companies, Hollywood Records or Walt Disney Records. This was the case, for example, with the soundtrack albums for *The Crow, Mission Impossible: 2, Il Postino,* and *Monsters, Inc.* However, MGM-UA, Paramount Pictures, and 20th Century Fox no longer have active record company firms, and even when a motion picture company has an affiliated record firm, it may choose to assign the soundtrack album rights to an unaffiliated record label. In the case of the film version of *West Side Story,* CBS Records (now Sony) issued the soundtrack album because it had reserved the right to the soundtrack when it contracted for album rights to the Broadway show. Soundtrack album rights may also be acquired by an unaffiliated record company for foreign motion pictures that are not committed to the record company subsidiaries of the film's distributors.

In cases where soundtrack album rights are acquired by unaffiliated record companies, the agreement between the record company and the producer may represent the result of intensive bargaining on such matters as the royalty percentage; advances against royalties; promises of singles records by outstanding artists; and the use, exclusive or otherwise, of the art, logo, and stills from the picture. If the soundtrack was recorded by members of the American Federation of Musicians, the problem of reuse fees would have to be covered; usually there is a provision that the record company will pay such fees as an advance against royalties.

The prospect of synergy in the music promoting the film and the film promoting the music comes to the forefront in the case of sales of soundtrack albums. There are film buffs and souvenir purchasers who will buy a soundtrack of a film for its own sake. Recent trends in the R&B and hip-hop market have seen soundtrack sales as independent from the success of the film. *How High, The Fast and The Furious,* and *Save the Last Dance* all reached the *Billboard* charts with a compilation of popular rap and R&B artists. However, the multi-platinum pot at the end of the rainbow looms large when a major film is accompanied by a significant score. For example, the soundtrack to the hit 1997 movie *Titanic* has sold over 9 million copies to date.

Television is also quickly becoming a lucrative market for popular music. The soundtrack to the Fox series *Ally McBeal,* featuring vocalist Vonda Shepard, sold over 1 million copies. Sometimes, as part of negotiation for the basic synchronization, U.S. performance, and video buyout terms, the astute music publisher will insist on a guaranteed inclusion within the possible soundtrack album.

Component Parts of Films

Under the Berne Convention, the use of a copyright notice to protect films and music is optional. In the past, music publishers associated with film companies wanted to be named as the copyright owners in notices of copyright for the new music in films. This has been traditional and prestigious and has facilitated the administration and exploitation of the music.

For some years the Copyright Office, for purposes of deposit and registration, considered a copyrightable component part of a motion picture, such as the new music, an integral part of the film. If the film had been released prior to the publication or registration of a copyrightable component part, the Copyright Office refused separate registration for the component part unless a separate copyright notice for that part had been placed on the film: for example, an individual notice naming the music publisher as the copyright owner of the music. Based on the Copyright Act of 1976, which requires a copyright notice only on publicly distributed copies of works that could be "visually perceived," the position of the Copyright Office changed. Music in films is not visually perceptible, and the conclusion followed that a separate copyright notice was unnecessary. The Berne Act further removed formalities such as notice of copyright as essential to copyright claim or registration.

The Copyright Office now accepts the simultaneous registration of separate copyright claims for a film and for the new music in the motion picture. The multiple registrations can be made by different copyright claimants, with the deposit of only one "copy" of the film, which can be a videocassette or DVD. There is no need to make separate deposits of "lead sheets" or other copies of the music.

While a soundtrack recording is an integral part of a motion picture, record companies have not had the same problem with the Copyright Office as the music publishers. By editing, mixing, assembling, and altering the movie soundtrack for a soundtrack album, a record company becomes entitled to treat an album as a derivative work for which the notice of copyright can be in the name of the record company.

Performances in Europe

There can be substantial earnings based on performances of the music contained in films exhibited in Europe. Under the system prevalent in Europe, performing rights societies license theaters on the condition that the theaters pay to the societies a percentage of the box office receipts. These payments, which are based on music cue sheets, are then divided between the publishers and writers of the film scores. Payments are related to the success of a film, and it is not unusual for a successful film to earn thousands of dollars. The percentages collected generally range between 1 percent and slightly over 2 percent of the net box office receipts after taxes; England, France, and Italy generate the greatest film performance earnings. Although ASCAP and BMI are barred from similar collections in the United States, U.S. publishers and composers can expect performance compensation when the films are shown on television in the United States and elsewhere.

24

Licensing Recordings for Motion Pictures

Frequently, record companies with sizable catalogs or current hits receive requests for permission to use their recordings in various media. There are three main categories of media to which requests relate.

1. Full-length theatrical films. *Saturday Night Fever,* which featured hits by the Bee Gees, is one of the earliest examples of the successful use of preexisting recordings, but the practice is extremely common today.
2. Nonprofit, educational, or religious films, such as a film on race relations, which might contain recorded recitals of gospel music.
3. Television features or series that use actual source recordings for portions of their score.

Film producers favor certain recordings because they present in tangible form the exact flavor desired for particular scenes. A rendition of Aretha Franklin issued by Atlantic Records or a performance by Herb Alpert on an A&M release may present a background that a studio orchestra would be hard-pressed to duplicate. The actual recordings dispel the need to guess at how a future rendition, made especially for the film, will sound.

The Protection of Recordings

Before using existing songs and recordings in films, film producers must obtain the requisite licenses and approvals from record companies, music publishers, recording artists, and the affected unions.

The legal bases for the protection of property interests in recordings are multiple and complicated. The rights of the copyright proprietors in sound recordings that were fixed and published on or after February 15, 1972, and before January 1, 1978, are protected under the Copyright Act of 1909, as amended. Effective January 1, 1978, sound recordings fixed on or after that date, regardless of whether they are published or unpublished, are given copyright protection under the 1976 Copyright Act. The rights of the owners of the underlying compositions are protected under copyright statutes regardless of the date the recordings are made or released.

Pre-February 15, 1972, recordings are safeguarded state by state under state common law and under statutes against record piracy. Pursuant to the 1976 Copyright Act, all common law rights will end on February 15, 2067.

In some instances, plaintiffs have asserted claims derived from the performer's right of publicity in regard to the use of the artist's name and likeness.

The Consent of the Music Publisher

Chapter 23, "Music for Motion Pictures," discusses the film synchronization and performance licenses that should be sought from music publishers. These ordinarily relate to existing music that is proposed to be recorded in the soundtrack of a film. The same types of licenses must be acquired for music embodied in existing recordings proposed to be integrated in a film.

One publisher, Warner/Chappell Music, Inc., has made licensing music easier for film producers by establishing Onestoptrax.com, where producers can choose from a catalog of songs plus master recordings that have been precleared to license, at set fees. For example, the fee to license any of the listed songs for use and rendition thereof in the main title sequence in a worldwide cinema release is as low as $10,000.

Union Reuse Fees

Under union agreements with the American Federation of Musicians and the American Federation of Television and Radio Artists, the record company must pay reuse fees if domestic phonograph recordings are used in different media, such as theatrical films, television films, or film commercials. The record company is liable to the vocalists, musicians, conductors, arrangers, orchestrators, and copyists for reuse fees in an amount equal to applicable union scale for that medium for the services previously performed. The reuse fees may be substantial, depending upon the number of union members involved in the original recording and the extent of their services. In 1968, at a time when union-scale payments were much lower than today, the chief counsel for Capitol Records observed: "When a record company says 'yes,' the record company would be obligated to pay all the musicians, all the AFTRA performers, the arranger, the copyist, everybody, a new additional scale payment. If you want to do that for a symphony, the cost to the record company may well be $50,000." Standard licensing agreements provide that the cost of union reuse fees are assumed by the licensee.

In certain instances, the unions on application may grant waivers of reuse fees if the film is of a nonprofit public service nature. Since the record company may be charging little or nothing for its consent, it may require the film producer to apply for the waiver. Otherwise, unremunerative staff time may have be devoted to the application.

Artist Contract Restrictions

If the film producer is not discouraged by reuse fees and by the need for music publisher licenses, the record company must still examine its own files to determine whether permission may be granted and on what terms. The record company will turn first to the recording contract under which the recording was originally made. In many cases, the contract will not limit the type of usage of a recording. This is especially true for recordings by newer artists. For established artists, another situation may prevail; the artist may have negotiated a restriction on the sale or use of the recording to home phonograph records or tapes, or the contract may require the artist's consent for the synchronization of the recording in films.

In such situations, where there are restrictions or a consent is required, the record company must furnish the details to the film producer if it elects to require the film producer to obtain the necessary waivers. Then, the producer must proceed to obtain the appropriate consent of the artist. If a license fee is to be paid to the record company, the artist may request a portion of the fee as the price for consent.

Soundtrack Albums

Additional problems may arise when the film producer plans to release a soundtrack album that includes recordings in the film. For instance, if the record company has granted exclusive foreign phonograph record rights in the recording to foreign record companies, the film company cannot obtain worldwide record rights without the consent of those companies. Assuming this and other problems have been solved, the record company may request a royalty based on sales of the proposed soundtrack album. This may be necessary in order to meet commitments to the artist, who is entitled to a royalty on all sales of the recording. Depending on what the traffic will bear, the royalty will vary. For example, if the artist must be paid a royalty of 7 percent of sales, prorated in relation to the number of selections in the album, the record company will seek a higher royalty to provide the company with a profit after the deduction of the artist royalty.

In licensing the music publishing rights to a song originally issued for a former commercially released recording, the parties should bear in mind a case concerning singer Joe Cocker's recording of "Bye, Bye Blackbird" in the film *Sleepless in Seattle*. The soundtrack album was issued on a new label and thus required a new license from the new publisher. The continuing sales of the original Joe Cocker version by its original record company required license payments to the former publisher. This complex situation, which concerns the right to terminate grants and licenses as of the 57th year of copyright, is discussed in detail in Chapter 11, page 112.

25

Music for the Theater

It is a rare popular songwriter who doesn't aspire to write show music for the theater. Yet it is a rare show music writer who writes popular music outside the framework of a show. For example, Ira Gershwin's "Fascinatin' Rhythm," "Embraceable You," and "It Ain't Necessarily So" are all strong contenders in any popular music category, yet each of these was written for a specific Broadway show; so were "Don't Cry for Me, Argentina," which Tim Rice and Andrew Lloyd Webber originally wrote for *Evita*, and "Send in the Clowns," which Stephen Sondheim wrote for *A Little Night Music*. Yet ask most show writers for a hit song they have written independently of a show, and they will have difficulty pointing to one.

The reverse is not the case. Cy Coleman, who wrote the popular tunes "Witchcraft" and "The Best Is Yet to Come," later came to Broadway and enjoyed considerable success with such shows as *City of Angels, The Life,* and *Ziegfeld Follies,* for which he was awarded two of his six Tony Awards. On the other hand, Paul Simon, one of the world's most acclaimed popular songwriters, whose credits include "Mrs. Robinson," "Bridge over Troubled Water," "Slip Slidin' Away," and "Cecelia," flopped on Broadway in 1998 with *Capeman.* Simon described what happened to the lavish production, which ran for only 20 performances after extended previews and major rewrites, as "one of the biggest beatings that I have ever taken. It hurt, it really hurt."

Sometimes there is a successful crossover from film composing to show music. *A Chorus Line* represented the first Broadway credits for composer Marvin Hamlisch and lyricist Edward Kleban. The composer had won an Oscar for his earlier adaptation of Joplin's music for *The Sting* and awards for the score and song for the film *The Way We Were.* Kleban previously had written only for television and was known as a composer rather than a lyricist.

The Rights of Producers and Writers

The Dramatists Guild is not a union. It is a voluntary association that is responsible in large part for the contractual strength of composers and lyric writers.

Composers, lyric writers, and playwrights are accepted as full members of the Guild. The Approved Production Contract (APC) of the Dramatists Guild indicates acceptable terms regarding the rights of composers and lyricists in show music. The basic concept expressed throughout the contract is that legal title to the book, music, and lyrics is at all times reserved by the writers, subject only to limited rights licensed to the producer and to a limited financial participation accorded to the producer in certain "subsidiary rights." The latter include motion picture, television, and radio rights to the play; touring company rights (other than a first-class company); stock rights; amateur rights; concert tour rights; and grand opera versions. The producer is granted no interest in music publishing rights, which would include payments of mechanical license fees by record companies for cast albums sold, all ASCAP or BMI performance payments for the songs, and all other royalties or income from printed editions or from licensing to record companies, Muzak, commercial jingles, or other music uses.

The producer's rights are confined to uses on the stage in the United States and Canada, and even these rights are dependent on the show reaching the stage in a specified reasonable time. These rights can be extended to the United Kingdom, Ireland, Australia, and New Zealand within 6 months from the closing of the play in New York City and can be further extended by payments of specified amounts. Even with regard to stage rights, the writers reserve the right to protect the integrity of their work. A song cannot be added without their approval, nor can deletions occur without their consent. Any deleted material belongs to the writers completely, and any corrections, additions, or changes made with or without their consent are nevertheless the property of the writers subject only to the limited rights licensed to the producer; consents are determined by the majority vote of the composer, lyricist, and author of the play. The writers have the right to approve the cast, director, conductor, and choreographer.

Under many of the older contracts, all writers receive fixed-option payments for the preproduction period of the show, and thereafter they are normally paid a royalty of 4.5 percent (going to 6 percent after recoupment of production costs) of the gross weekly box office receipts, shared among the book writer, lyricist, and composer. In a typical case, the book writer receives one-third, and the remaining two-thirds is shared equally among composers and lyricists. During the weeks when the show is not operating at a profit, the book writer, lyricist, and composer forgo percentage royalties and each is paid a minimum weekly amount of $1,000.

An alternative to this, which has been adopted for almost all current musicals, is the profit pool. Under the profit pool concept, royalty recipients share in operating profits, not gross receipts, with a minimum weekly guarantee. In almost all cases these recipients get less royalty money per week than they would under the gross percentage plan, with the result that more money is available to the investors. Running (operating) expenses for this purpose include theater rental, cast, stagehands, insurance, legal and accounting, general and company managers, as well as any minimum weekly guarantees that are not covered by the pool. The accompanying chart shows the flow of monies under a profit pool plan where 40 percent of net box office goes to the creators' royalty pool and the remaining 60 percent is applied first to recoup investment and then split equally between producers and investors. Note that the 40 percent–60 percent division is negotiable, and depends on whether the production is intended for Broadway or Off Broadway. The goal of the profit pool is to give the investors a better chance to recoup the costs of producing the show and to have a greater investor share in profits. The incentive to royalty participants is a guaranteed weekly payment within the 40 percent share, and given the practical realities of the industry—in most cases, investors and producers insist on a pool—they really have no choice.

Another innovation that is gaining acceptance is what is known as an "amortization factor," where the operating profit royalty pool is subject to a priority

ROYALTY PROFIT POOL

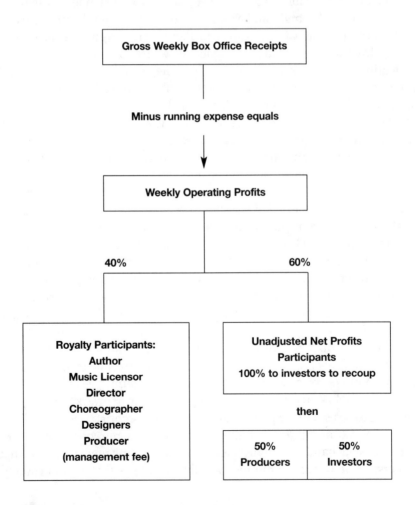

deduction—2 percent of the production budget—which is distributed to investors. For a show that generates substantial profits in a short period of time, investors may see a return on capital within a year. The royalty pool during the period before investors have recouped their capital is reduced, and so creative-team royalty recipients try to get some compensation, usually by an increase in the weekly guarantee and sometimes a share in the partnership profits. This deduction, like the profit pool, is driven by practical realities. Authors must face the fact that given the enormous costs of mounting a musical today, it would be difficult to attract investors without such incentives.

Original-Cast Albums

By their very nature, original-cast albums require performances by the members of the cast as well as the use of the musical and literary material. Because of the cast participation and by custom, the producer preserves a strong role in bargaining for the cast album placement. Frequently the producer and the writers' representatives collaborate in the bargaining. In all instances the approval of the writers is required.

The royalty for the cast album is customarily 12 to 15 percent of retail; the writers ordinarily receive 60 percent of the total royalty and the producer is paid the balance. Royalties are commonly subject to the recoupment of the cost of production of the cast album. Depending on the agreement between the collaborators, the royalties payable to the writers are ordinarily divided two-thirds between the composer and lyricist and one-third to the book writer. The writers' music publisher, who is selected by the composer and lyricist without any voice, other than advisory, by the producer, is also paid mechanical license fees by the record company.

Compared to the sales of such older popular musicals as *My Fair Lady, South Pacific,* and *Sound of Music,* sales of recent cast albums have greatly diminished. With the notable exception of the original Broadway cast album for *The Lion King,* which was certified Gold in 2001, average original cast album sales for recent Broadway shows have been between 20,000 and 25,000 units—hardly an attractive number considering the high recording costs.

Subsidiary Rights

Investors are increasingly aware that when a show is highly successful, the benefits in residual income such as performance and mechanical royalties of the composer and lyricist often are more attractive than those obtained by the investor. The producer and the investors receive from the writers the right to share in certain subsidiary rights; this is dependent on the producer's rights being vested in the territory on the basis of the play having been presented there for a specified number and type of performances. For a producer to be vested, the play has to have been presented in a territory for a specified number and type of performances. The share and the period of participation of the producer vary, depending on which of the alternatives in the APC the producer has chosen. Under all alternatives the producer shares perpetually in the proceeds from audiovisual productions, which include motion pictures, television productions, videocassettes, and soundtrack albums. Depending on the alternative chosen, the participation of the producer ranges from 30 to 50 percent.

As for stock and ancillary performances, the periods of participation under the different alternatives may be 10 years, 36 years, or 40 years, and the participation may be from 20 to 50 percent. In all these instances the writers have the sole bargaining power concerning subsidiary rights, except with respect to original-cast albums and the sale or lease of motion picture rights. Film rights are within the purview of the negotiator of the Dramatists Guild under special provisions.

The widespread use of musicals in stock and amateur productions is an all-important revenue source after a successful—or even not so successful—Broadway run. Even 50 years after its opening, *Oklahoma,* revived on Broadway in 2002, was grossing nearly $1 million per performance. It has been licensed to as many as 900 theaters a year in North America. *Variety* magazine reports that in the 2001–2002 season Broadway box office receipts were over $642.5 million and road box office receipts over $630 million. Amateur groups may pay between $75 and $125 a performance on average for the rights to an entire musical, while professional groups pay minimum weekly guarantees up to 10 percent of box office receipts. Both types of groups must also pay rental fees for the conductor's score and choral parts.

Licensing agents in the field include Tams-Witmark Music Library, Music Theater International, Rodgers & Hammerstein Repertory, and Samuel French, Inc. The in-house Rodgers & Hammerstein licensing company takes in more than $10 million in licensing revenues a year for such uses, which often include foreign productions as far away as Japan and Denmark as well as regular uses in Britain and Australia. Usually only successful plays are handled by the licensing agents.

American Productions Abroad

If a producer whose domestic production qualifies him or her under the APC provisions produces or, with the consent of the writers, arranges for the production of a show in the United Kingdom, Ireland, Australia, or New Zealand, royalties are payable to the writers based on gross weekly box office receipts. For shows in the United Kingdom and Ireland, the royalties are 4.5 percent of such receipts, rising to 6 percent after the recoupment of production costs; royalties with respect to performances in Australia or New Zealand are 6 percent of such receipts. If the producer fails to produce or arrange for the production of the show, the producer and the investors participate in 25 percent of the net proceeds received by the writers on contracts for such production in the United Kingdom and Ireland executed within 7 years from the date when the producer's rights vest in that territory. In Australia or New Zealand, the percentage is 35 percent on contracts executed within 7 years from the vesting of the producer's rights in the particular territory. In foreign areas other than the United Kingdom, Ireland, Australia, and New Zealand, the writers control the production of the show, and they pay the producer and the investors 25 percent of the writers' net proceeds received by virtue of contracts made within 7 years from the New York opening.

Writing a Show

On the practical side, the job of writing a show score is sometimes assigned by a producer who owns rights granted by the author of the book; usually the author assigns rights on options only, for a limited time. The 2002 Broadway production of *Hairspray,* based on a John Waters film, is an example of the long-term dedication that producing a Broadway show requires. Despite the fact that *Hairspray* was originally a musically scored film, the show was in development for almost three years before reaching Broadway. Creative teams for Broadway shows such as *Grease, Jelly's Last Jam,* and *Cats* also had to search for a producer after completing the initial stages. Such a collaboration may begin prior to the solicitation of a producer.

If underlying rights to a film, a play, or a book are involved, they might negotiate for an option period that may expire unless a producer is obtained within the stated term, such as a year. The producer in turn acquires a secondary option from the author for a given period, which under the APC is 1 year from the contract date or 1 year from delivery of the unfinished play, whichever is later, within which the show must be produced.

Music in Dramatic Shows

Some shows use music only as background to dramatic action. In such instances, the composer usually is not covered by the Dramatists Guild contract, and his or her compensation and rights will be different from those of the author of the play. A common arrangement is for the composer to receive a single stipulated payment plus specified amounts for each week of the run, as distinguished from a royalty based on box office receipts. There is no fixed rule as to the amount or nature of payment; a top-rated composer may be able to obtain an initial fixed payment plus a percentage of gross weekly box office receipts, such as 0.5 percent. The agreement with the composer ordinarily covers the use of the music for stock and amateur rights or for a television production, with appropriate payment to the composer for such use.

Incidental music is often used in a "straight" drama. For example, the 1998 production of *Blue Room* starring Nicole Kidman used Elvis Presley's recording of "Love Me Tender." A dramatic script may call for one of the characters to play a specific record, for which the producer frequently pays a fee of $100 per week to the music publisher. Sometimes an authorized title song is written for a Broadway hit, although this is more common with motion pictures. Such a tie-in helps promote the musical or film through air play and may at the same time provide a promotional head start for the song based on public interest in the play.

Investment in Musical Theater

Until the 2001–2002 season, musical theater in the United States enjoyed 10 straight box office record-breaking seasons. In the 2001–2002 season combined Broadway and road box office receipts were about $1.3 billion—down from the previous season, but by less than 1 percent. On Broadway, box office attendance was down by 8.2 percent, but gross receipts ($642.5 million, almost three-quarters of which was generated by musicals) were down only 3.4 percent. However, the sad story is that despite the phenomenal success of Mel Brooks's *The Producers,* which won a record 12 Tony awards and sold $2.8 million in tickets in its first day, a box office record, only 3 of the 10 musicals that opened in 2001–2002 were able to repay investors during the same season.

A popular song can be launched with only a few hundred dollars, a demonstration record or master, and a lot of effort. However, Broadway musicals historically involve rapidly escalating costs that may reach many millions of dollars. The Canadian-based company Livent went bankrupt in 1999 after investing some $40 million in *Ragtime, Fosse,* and *Showboat*—three seemingly successful shows with long runs that continued even past the date of bankruptcy. Apparently, the high costs of these productions, coupled with the costs of launching second companies running simultaneously, exceeded the available bank accounts. Even the most impressive team of collaborators won't guarantee success. *The Sweet Smell of Success,* produced by Miramax's Weinstein brothers and Clear Channel Entertainment, and with a musical score by *Chorus Line* composer Marvin Hamlisch, closed in 2002 after only 108 performances, with a $10 million loss. This was despite a $4 million advance ticket sale. A revival of *The Music Man* also closed after a year's run, failing to recoup its $8.5 million investment. The lesson here is that musicals rarely get to Broadway without multimillion-dollar investments, and without extended runs and a steady stream of people willing to pay top dollar for tickets (it is estimated that the blockbuster shows require a ticket gross of six figures per performance to survive), those investments cannot be recouped. Legendary hits like *Cats,* which closed in 2002 after 7,485 performances; *Les Miserables,* which opened in 1986 and has since logged over 6,000 performances; *Beauty and the Beast;* and Disney's *Lion King,* which by mid-2002 had sold all available tickets, are exceptions. Even when a show garners rave reviews and/or a slew of Tony Awards, it requires additional funds to let potential audiences *know* of such success, and while full potential box office sales build up, high day-to-day expenses must still be paid. *Lion King,* for example, despite pulling in approximately $1 million weekly, took four years to recoup its investment.

Some musicals which do not do well on Broadway are able to recoup their investment on tour. *Ain't Nothin' but the Blues* was initially capitalized at a modest $900,000. It required an additional $700,000 for its first move to Lincoln Center's Vivian Beaumont Theater, where it lasted for 19 weeks, and an additional $300,000 for its move to the Ambassador Theater on Broadway, where it lasted another 18 weeks. By the time the show closed, in January 2000, it was running at an average weekly loss of $10,000. However, the show, which was nominated for four Tony awards and received favorable Broadway reviews, did well on tour.

Stage musicals that are never meant for Broadway, although still relatively expensive to produce, generally do not require Broadway-level backing and are therefore not such high-risk investments. One example is the stage version of the classic film *Some Like It Hot*, a $4 million production which opened in June, 2002, at Houston's Hobby Center and proceeded to tour to other cities, including a stop at Las Vegas' Aladdin Hotel. Another is the Rodgers and Hammerstein children's show *Cinderella*, which never played on Broadway but which began touring in 1997 with a $2.2 million capitalization, cashing in on a family audience, some of whom were a guaranteed subscription audience ticket base. In 2001, Ann-Margret starred in a $2.5 million touring revival of *The Best Little Whorehouse in Texas*, and her contract stipulated that she would not be scheduled for Broadway.

Some highly successful musicals, such as *Rent* and *Annie*, did not open on Broadway, but had regional, low-budget, or workshop initial stagings. A revival of Lerner and Loewe's *Paint Your Wagon* was mounted for under $150,000 from private backers; this was possible because it first opened at the Goodspeed Opera House in East Haddam, Connecticut, with the help of state and other subsidies. Goodspeed Musicals, Inc., originated *Annie, Shenandoah,* and *Man of La Mancha*. Since 1984, Goodspeed has operated, in addition to the Goodspeed Opera House, the Norma Terris Theater in Chester, Connecticut, which mounts three new musicals each year, some of which have gone on to regional success. For the 2002–2003 Broadway season, *Harlem Song* got a head start by premiering at the Apollo Theater in Harlem several months before its Broadway opening. The National Alliance for Musical Theater's Festival of New Musicals, created in 1989, has introduced 125 musicals, including *Thoroughly Modern Millie,* which went on to success on Broadway in 2001, and *Summer of '42,* which was a regional success. Music Theater International (www.mitshows.com) licenses an average of 30,000 performances of 6,000 different productions every year to universities, high schools, and small theaters across the United States.

Many of the works that emerge from these forums are developed in a non-profit environment at ASCAP's Musical Theater Workshop or BMI's Lehman Engel Musical Theater Workshop. In ASCAP's program, which is run semiannually, four or five musicals are selected and workshopped over the course of a few weeks and then are presented to industry panels comprised of such major talents as songwriter-composer Steven Schwartz, who offer critiques. The revised works are presented to the public at a cabaret night. In 2002, several of the works developed in ASCAP workshops were presented at the Kennedy

Center for the Performing Arts in Washington, D.C., in performances funded by Disney's Buena Vista Theatrical Group, among others.

Sources of Investment

Investors frequently include the Schubert Organization, Nederlander Organization, and Jujamcyn Theatres, a phenomenon of the past two decades. Previously, such theater owners would have merely leased the theater and personnel for about 30 percent of the box office receipts, without investing as a partner. The practice today is more complicated, with the producer's out-of-pocket costs such as box office personnel, stage crew, and utilities being covered first, then show costs, with 5 to 10 percent of gross weekly box office receipts being paid as rent.

Long recognized as a most vital part of the world of musical theatricals is the Schubert Foundation. Founded by the Schubert brothers and part of theater history, this organization owns 16 Broadway theaters and a half-interest in another, as well as theaters in Boston and Philadelphia. The Schubert Organization, a subsidiary of the foundation, manages the National Theater in Washington, D.C., and, through lease arrangements, a major Los Angeles theater. It is considered to be worth well over $100 million, and it generates enough profits to have paid out grants of $8.283 million in 1998. In one outstanding example, the Schubert Foundation bestowed money on Playwrights Horizons, a nonprofit Manhattan theater company. Its production of *Sunday in the Park with George,* by Stephen Sondheim and James Lapine, went on to play at the Schubert Theater in 1984.

In recent years record companies have generally had little interest in or incentive to finance musical plays in order to obtain cast album rights. The present tendency is for a record company to await the opening of a play in out-of-town tryouts or on Broadway before determining whether to invest in the play or in the large recording costs of a cast album, which often amount to over $100,000.

The lack of major-label interest in original-cast albums created a vacuum that is being filled to some extent by smaller record labels. DRG Records, for example, released a cast album for the 1999 revival of *Kiss Me Kate* which sold 68,000 copies.

AFM Union Scale

The pit orchestra members and conductor are subject to AFM-scale minimum rates. These minimum rates require that each musician be paid for eight weekly performances at a base rate of $1,231 per week, to which vacation and pension pay is added. Additional pay is required for doubling on more than one instrument, for instrument maintenance, for extra rehearsal calls; further sums are also paid if the musicians are required to appear on stage or in costume. The conductor's base pay starts at $2154.34 a week, with extras amounting to a gross weekly pay of about $2,500. Associate union scale for conductor and musicians appearing for a cast album amounts to additional pay equal to 1 week of regular performances.

26

Commercial Jingles

The early success of "Pepsi-Cola Hits the Spot" heralded an ever-growing reliance by the advertising industry upon commercial jingles. The production of jingles has developed into a specialized segment of the music industry, employing not only composers and arrangers but also many successful recording stars, such as the Spice Girls, Ray Charles, and Brandy.

Some of the standards of commercial jingles have been Coca-Cola's "I'd Like to Teach the World to Sing" and "It's the Real Thing," as well as Lowenbrau's "Here's to Good Friends." In addition, there have been such long-running successes as Ford Mercury Cougar's use of Steppenwolf's rendition of the song "Born to Be Wild" as part of a campaign aimed at a younger market, Nike's use of the Beatles song "Revolution," and Fruit of the Loom calling on Graham Nash of Crosby, Stills and Nash for his song "Teach Your Children." The practice of using songs as commercial jingles is becoming more and more popular. In 1999 Burger King used such classic soul tunes as Minnie Ripperton's "Loving You" and Chick's "Le Freak" to sell flame-broiled hamburgers, while Gap commercials featured Bill Wither's "Lovely Day" and "Dress You Up in My Love" by Madonna.

Uses of Music in Commercial Jingles

Music can be used in two ways in commercial jingles. Established songs can be used in either derivative or integral ways. A derivative use is a new version of a previously established song, such as R. Kelly's "I Believe I Can Fly," used in a McDonald's advertisement with revised lyrics. An integral use is when the original version of an established song is used, such as the use of Bob Seger's "Like a Rock" in the Chevrolet truck commercials.

Music for jingles can also be newly created for a specific purpose. Considered works for hire under copyright law, these songs are owned by the advertising agency that commissioned the work. Some of the more notable examples include the Folger's coffee jingle "The Best Part of Waking Up" and Coca-Cola's "Always Coca-Cola."

New technology has also created new uses for commercial jingles. Negotiations for jingle use are now likely to cover in-store video monitors, 800 phone order lines, and outdoor video screens, in addition to network and cable television and/or radio. The territories that may be covered have also been expanded from the traditional ones—the United States and Canada—and licensing agreements for jingles about products with international appeal sometimes include the U.K., France, Germany, and Japan. In 2002, for example, Gap Clothing licensed the song "Bend Me, Shape Me," a 1968 Top 10 hit, for use not only for television commercials, but also for in-store monitors and an 800 order line, as well as outdoor screens in the U.K. and Japan.

Payments for Music Used in Commercials

In payment formulas for the use of music in commercials, ASCAP distinguishes between well-established songs, called *qualifying works;* and songs written specifically for advertising purposes or lesser-known songs adopted for advertising purposes. The measurement of what is "qualified" requires a statistical review of prior ASCAP credits for radio or television feature performances. A qualifying work is one that has accumulated 20,000 such credits since October 1959 or 5,000 feature credits within the last 5 years, of which not more than 1,500 can be counted in any one year. Such qualifying works get 12 percent of what a regular featured performance would earn, whereas a nonqualifying work receives a mere 3 percent. The reason given for such a substantial difference is that a qualifying work offers the advertiser a well-established audience identification, which is a bargaining tool in the ASCAP licensing negotiations with broadcasters. Newly created works, the use of which is tailor-made for the advertisement, may make up for this difference, to some extent, through a higher creative fee.

As ASCAP defines it, a commercial jingle is "an advertising, promotional or public service announcement containing musical material (with or without lyrics)" in which:

> (a) the musical material was originally written for advertising,
> promotional or public service announcement purposes, or (b)
> the performance is of a musical work, originally written for other
> purposes, with the lyrics changed for advertising, promotional or
> public service announcement purposes with the permission of the
> ASCAP member or members in interest, or (c) the performance
> is of a musical work, originally written for other purposes, which
> does not have at least one hundred and fifty feature performance
> credits recorded in the Society's radio and television surveys
> during the five preceding fiscal survey years.

Commercial music can also be used as background for a spoken message, such as a strain from "Rhapsody in Blue" for an international ad campaign of United Airlines. This category is defined by ASCAP as "a musical work (other than a jingle) used in conjunction with an advertising, promotional, or public service announcement." For such a use, ASCAP generally accords the credit as

> the greater of (i) the credit for use of the work in a single program computed on a durational basis . . . or (ii) 50% of a use credit for the first such performance on a single program, and only 5% of a use credit for each subsequent such performance on such program, provided, however, that in the event credit is computed as set forth in (ii) of this subparagraph . . . no work shall receive more than one use credit for a single program.

ASCAP will not pay performance fees to a jingle composer who writes the music for an advertiser as a work for hire or under an agreement that prevents it from licensing the performing rights. ASCAP monitors the usage of music used in commercials by "media buy" schedules provided by advertising agencies, International Standard Commercial Identifier (ISCI) codes (the ISCI number, which consists of four letters and four numbers, is an identifying code used by the advertising industry and broadcast media for airing and billing purposes), and by the opening lines of the commercial's copy.

Since July 1981 BMI has been making payments for the use of music as jingles. These payments do not, however, include uses for "network or station promotional or public service announcements." This is because no revenue is earned by the station for such uses.

To qualify for payment, the music must be the sole focus of audience attention for at least 15 seconds during the commercial. There is also a payment schedule for background and underscore music for ABC, CBS, and NBC only, with a minimum of 7 seconds of original music. In addition, there is payment for feature performances on the ABC, CBS, and NBC network TV with a minimum of 15 seconds of sole focus of original music. There is even a bonus for works that have received a minimum of 25,000 feature performances on American radio and local television (ABC, CBS, and NBC only) as measured by BMI.

In addition to sending the required notice of the commercial to the BMI Jingle Department on forms supplied and processed by that department, an audiotape of the commercial as broadcast must be submitted. In the case of a television commercial, the sender can supply a videotape if he or she desires. Another item that must be submitted is a list of the broadcast time bought on behalf of the sponsor. The music will not qualify if written for the advertiser as a work for hire or written according to any agreement whereby BMI is unable to license the performing rights.

Recent rates paid by BMI, to both the writer and the publisher, are 1 cent for a local radio performance, 37.5 cents for a local television performance, and $30 for a television network performance on ABC, CBS, or NBC. The rates are subject to change by BMI.

In the world of the commercial jingle, BMI and ASCAP recognize that invariably their members receive significant license payments for the right to synchronize songs for advertising purposes. However, they remind members that synch licenses do not necessarily include the right of public performances. Customarily, ad agencies permit language in the agreement reserving the right of the applicable performing rights society to license nondramatic public performance.

Both BMI and ASCAP identify performances for radio, local television, and most cable television surveys by the product and the first line spoken or sung and request that their members provide them with this information. They also request the television commercial reports, which can be obtained from the advertising agency. On each report, ASCAP and BMI ask for the name of the network, the name of the program, the date of the performance, and the ISCI code. For existing works used in a commercial, ASCAP and BMI request that the member indicate whether the work is being used as instrumental, with original lyrics, or with lyrics which the owner has authorized to be changed for the commercial.

Negotiations for Licensing Fees

Much money can be made from the licensing of well-known songs for jingles or from commissioning the creation of original jingle music and lyrics. Jingle rights to well-recognized songs for use in commercial jingles have been known to command impressive fees, reaching above $500,000 in some instances. Such songs include "You'd Be So Nice to Come Home To," used by Chanel perfumes, "Stand by Me," used by Citibank, "It's Impossible," used by Polaroid, and "Bye Bye Blackbird," used by Pontiac. In 2001, Microsoft licensed the Madonna song "Ray of Light" for the launch of Windows XP, reportedly for around the same $12 million it paid the Rolling Stones to license "Start Me Up" to launch its Windows 95 product. Although payments in excess of $150,000 are relatively rare for U.S. rights, fees approximating $75,000 are often negotiated. For regional ads, where full U.S. rights are not required, payment is proportionately reduced based on the share of the population that the region represents. Regions can be as large as a group of states or as small as a specific city. These fees are significant when compared to annual earnings from conventional music sources, but the amounts are small in relation to the large amounts— even millions of dollars—that may be spent in the advertising campaign built on a jingle.

To put licensing fees in the context of an advertising agency budget, keep in mind that a single 30-second commercial on a popular network show such as *E.R.* costs $600,000 in air time alone and that even moderately successful network shows charge an average price of almost $200,000 for each similar 30-second spot. In contrast, music license fees are for an unlimited number of spots within the negotiated time period. An agency may not wish to jeopardize a costly campaign by negotiating a nonexclusive license that might permit another competing advertiser to use the same tune. Advertisers usually request category exclusivity, such as "soft drinks," "automotive supplies," or "air transportation," thus permitting the same song to be used to advertise a noncompeting product. In practice, the simultaneous use of one song to advertise different products is infrequent. It does, however, sometimes happen, as in the case of "The Pink Panther Theme," which was used in commercials advertising an insurer and a supplier of building products.

Negotiations for the appropriate license were formerly initiated by the advertiser through the Harry Fox Agency, but they are now directly negotiated by the advertising agency and the music publisher. It is not uncommon for an advertising agency to shop around for alternative tunes to test-market, and then, when they have settled on two or three choices, get bids for airing the various choices. Publishers have learned that in such a high-stakes competition it is best to agree to test-marketing for a portion of the licensing fees (usually 10 percent), with the balance of the fee to be paid if the test is successful.

Among items of negotiation in the licensing of songs for commercials are exclusivity, the extent of the licensed territory, the duration of the license (including options to extend the term, usually at escalated fees), and the scope of the license (for example, does it cover cable TV usage as well as standard, that is, free, radio and television?). Many sponsors seek an extension of rights to cover trade shows and sales meetings. The most important factor is whether the song is widely known. If it is a current or recent hit, the advertiser will want the commercial to be released while the tune is fresh in the listener's memory. The publisher and writer usually prefer to wait until the song is declining on hit charts, so as not to detract from record sales and regular air play.

Some composers object to *any* commercial use of their music as an affront to artistic integrity, as potentially damaging to their reputation, or as detracting from normal use of the song. For decades composer Bob Dylan refused to allow his songs to be used in jingles, but he finally relented. He allowed the international accounting firm of Coopers and Lybrand to use "The Times They Are A-Changin'" provided that they not identify it further by direct or indirect use of his name or likeness. Graham Nash, of Crosby, Stills and Nash, was less demanding. He allowed not only his song "Teach Your Children" to be used for Fruit of the Loom underwear ads, but his voice as well, noting modestly, "We're not talking Mozart, here."

Warranties and Indemnities

A further item for negotiation in the licensing of songs for jingles is the matter of warranties and indemnities sought by advertisers from the licensors of the music. Advertisers who plan to invest substantial sums in the production and use of a jingle are naturally concerned about obtaining clear and unimpeded rights to the music. They fear infringement claims that might result in an obligation to pay damages or a share of profits greatly in excess of the license fees or other costs paid to the supplier of the music. The potential liability, as well as the possibility of high attorney's fees involved in such litigation, impels advertisers to require appropriate warranties and indemnifications, even if they carry their own "errors and omissions" insurance.

The standard license form or other form submitted by or on behalf of the advertiser contains unlimited warranties and indemnities. At the same time, publishers, composers, and producers seek to limit their exposure, ordinarily to the amounts paid or payable for the rights to the jingle. The advertiser and its agency are commonly protected by any errors and omissions insurance policy, whereas such insurance may be unusual for the music licensors. The latter, for their protection, can attempt to negotiate being named as additional insured parties in the advertiser or agency's insurance policy.

Uses of music "in conjunction with" advertising messages, such as in background instrumental form, fall within the general ASCAP license and do not usually require a special performance license for the arrangement or adaptation. However, advertising campaigns are not founded on a live use of background music, and accordingly, a license is necessary for synchronizing the music with the taped television film or for mechanical reproduction on a transcribed announcement.

The Packaging of Jingles

Writers commissioned to create tailor-made jingles sometimes prepare the entire package of the musical composition, lyric, performance, and recording, thereby reaping a financial benefit in addition to the flat fee for composing and writing the jingle. Even when the advertiser receives rights free of writer royalty obligations, the writer may attempt to retain the right to collect any performance fees payable by a performing rights organization. It is not uncommon, however, for writers to retain no rights whatsoever.

Many commercial jingles are purchased in package deals from producers specializing in music for commercials. They frequently have their own staff of writers and composers who receive guaranteed earnings either as salary or as advances. A study conducted by the American Association of Advertising Agencies (AAAA) in 1993 determined that such packagers charged a markup of about 28 percent over actual production costs, representing profits and overhead. Nonetheless, having the creative services of multiple professionals beyond the jingle composer, including director, editor, engineer, musicians, actors, and voice-over narrators as a team, can result in budget savings and competitive bidding advantages as well as economies of time on tightly scheduled assignments.

Participation in the creation and production of a jingle can carry with it the advantage of becoming one of the singers and musicians in the production sessions or choosing the personnel for the session. These performers receive union residual payments that often are substantially greater than the fixed fees paid to the creator or producer. Creators and producers sometimes successfully bargain that if they are not engaged for a follow-up to the initial campaign, they will receive the union rate payable to a singer on future versions of their original jingle.

Payments to Singers and Instrumentalists

Minimum payment rates to singers who perform in commercial jingles are governed by the applicable American Federation of Television and Radio Artists (AFTRA) or Screen Actors Guild (SAG) rate schedules. In general, jingles for radio are subject to AFTRA jurisdiction, and those for television are subject to SAG jurisdiction, although in a field such as video, where tape is employed instead of film, the user can opt for either AFTRA or SAG jurisdiction. Union scale under either jurisdiction is similar.

AFM rate schedules cover minimum rates of payment to instrumentalists, orchestrators, arrangers, and copyists. Payments under union agreements are usually geared to particular periods or cycles of use, and additional payments are commonly required for continued use beyond the original period. For example, a 1-hour-minimum call session fee is $98.50 per musician. Use, reuse, dubbing fees, and so forth are also applicable. The pension contribution for both radio and television commercials is 10 percent, based upon their respective union scales.

Singers can earn substantial monies by participating in commercial jingles for radio and television. The combined SAG/AFTRA rate for on-camera solo or duo performance starts at $500; for off-camera performance, at $375. A TV demo rate is $189. To this is added a pension and health contribution of 13.3 percent. More information and details can be found at the respective AFM and AFTRA Web sites.

The Simulation of an Artist's Style in Jingles

It is obviously more economical for an advertiser to use studio musicians and singers for commercials than to hire famous stars. When a synchronization license for a commercial jingle is obtained from a music publisher for a song made famous by a top star, it is quite tempting for the advertiser to simulate the star's arrangement and style in the jingle. Nancy Sinatra's rendition of "These Boots Were Made for Walking" was imitated for a Goodyear Tire and Rubber Company commercial, and the Fifth Dimension's style was used for TWA's "Up, Up, and Away" advertising campaign. In separate suits brought for each of these two cases, the courts held that the artists had no property rights in their style of rendition or arrangement and that there was no unfair competition.

However, in a 1988 case involving the imitation of Bette Midler's voice in a Ford Motor commercial, the U.S. Circuit Court for the Ninth District held that the deliberate imitation of the plaintiff's distinctive voice gave rise to a cause of action under California common law. One commentator noted:

> The Midler case signals a possible end to judicial resistance to the concept that a performer may be as readily identifiable by voice as by mere facial appearance. . . . As commercial exploitation of a persona expands to encompass name, likeness, voice, and style,

judicial and legislative protection must expand as well. The common thread of this fascinating body of law is preventing one who has not expended the "sweat equity" in achieving distinction from reaping the commercial benefits that come with public recognition and success.

In 1992, the U.S. Circuit Court for the Ninth District, building on the Midler decision, affirmed a $2.4 million award to artist Tom Waits against Frito-Lay for running an ad using a sound-alike singer to sing Waits's song "Step Right Up" and to imitate Waits's distinctive, raspy, gravelly singing voice. The court described the sound-alike as "near perfection" and ruled "when a distinctive voice of a professional singer is widely known and is deliberately imitated in order to sell a product, the sellers have appropriated what is not theirs and have committed a tort in California." The court went on to rule that "a voice is a sufficient indicia of a celebrity's identity and the right of publicity protects against its imitation for commercial purposes without the celebrity's consent."

In New York, in 1994, U.S. District Court Judge Charles S. Haight, Jr., ruled that the distinctive sound of the group the Fat Boys was available for protection and denied summary judgment to Miller Brewing Company which the Fat Boys sued after a Miller Lite commercial aired featuring three Fat Boys look-alikes performing in the group's distinctive style.

It would appear that the risks of a successful lawsuit against them are likely to dampen any continued interest by advertisers and their agencies in simulating a star's arrangement and style for a proposed commercial jingle.

27

Buying and Selling Music Publishing Companies and Record Companies

The ever-active transactions involving the buying and selling of assets within the music industry can be broken down into two principal areas: (1) the buying and selling of record companies which own and exploit sound recordings and (2) the buying and selling of publishing companies which own and exploit musical compositions. Both sound recordings and musical compositions are protected by copyright law.

Most record companies have publishing affiliates, although this is not always true of publishing companies. A record company with one or more publishing affiliates will generally sell the record company branch of the business and the publishing company or companies in separate transactions, to obtain a better overall price. A record company may also sell either its publishing operation or record operation, retaining the other. An example of the former is Universal's acquisition of A&M Records and its subsequent acquisition of A&M's publishing affiliate Rondor Music. BMG initially acquired merely an interest in Jive Records, but in a subsequent deal, BMG acquired Jive's publishing affiliate Zomba Music as part of the $2.74 billion transaction in which it acquired the balance of the Jive record group. Other examples are the sale of Roulette Records to Universal Records and the separate sale of its affiliate Planetary Music to FujiPacific and the acquisition of Columbia Records by Sony while Columbia's publishing affiliates, April Music and Blackwood Music, ended up in the hands of EMI.

THE BUYING AND SELLING OF CATALOGS

Songs are not interchangeable commodities like ears of corn or tons of steel. A hit song obviously generates substantially more income than an unrecorded song in manuscript or demo form. Consequently, sophisticated participants in the music publishing field look to earnings history, among other factors, for the valuation of a catalog.

Large Catalogs

In recent years, there has been substantial competition in buying and selling large music catalogs.

- *Universal Music Group.* In 1999, Universal Music Group added the music publishing interests of PolyGram Music to its MCA holdings and in 2001 acquired the Almo-Irving catalogs. Universal Music Publishing now controls more than 700,000 copyrights and over 26 percent of the market share.
- *BMG.* The 2002 acquisition by BMG Music of the Jive-Zomba operations added substantially to its prior catalog of over 250,000 titles.
- *Sony/ATV.* In 2002, Sony/ATV Music Publishing purchased the important Acuff-Rose country music catalog, featuring such standards as "Your Cheatin' Heart" and "Pretty Woman," a deal which followed Sony's previous acquisition of the administrative rights to the Tree Music catalog and the Word Catalog. Sony/ATV was born in 1995 when Sony acquired the administrative rights to the ATV catalog, which Michael Jackson had purchased from its original owners for $47 million in 1985. (For a number of years, EMI administered the rights to that catalog under a form of lease that did not include full transfer of title.) Sony and Jackson announced that they had formed a new worldwide joint venture that would encompass all the present and future music publishing interests of both parties (except for Jackson's own compositions in his MIJAC catalog, which continue to be administered by Warner/Chappell). The ATV catalog, which included the 251 Beatles titles as well as such other hits as "He's So Shy," "Lucille," "Long Tall Sally," "Ramblin' Rose," and "Girl's Night Out," was a significant addition to Sony's existing catalog of songs recorded by Willie Nelson, Little Richard, Elvis Presley, Lloyd Price, the Pointer Sisters, Babyface, and Cyndi Lauper. At the time of writing, both Sony and Mr. Jackson were trying to purchase the other's share to end the partnership.
- *Warner/Chappell.* The Warner group acquired the Chappell catalog, with its wealth of standards, for twice as much as was paid in 1985 when PolyGram, the former owner of the catalog, sold it for about $140 million to a consortium of various private banking and other investors organized and administered by Bienstock Enterprises, the owner of Carlin Music Ltd. of England as well as important U.S. catalogs. Prior to this, the Bienstock organization had acquired the E. B. Marks Music Company in association with the estates of Richard Rodgers and Oscar Hammerstein. The Rodgers and Hammerstein catalogs were administered, though not owned, by Chappell; therefore, they were not a part of the Warner purchase.
- *EMI.* In 1990, EMI acquired another major group of old-line music firms in Robbins Music, Feist Music, Miller Music, and later Mills

Music. These firms had been assembled through the years by various transfers to and among United Artists, CBS Songs, Belwin Music, and Filmtrax. Just two years prior to the eventual EMI acquisition, a portion consisting only of Robbins, Feist, Miller, and CBS Songs was sold to SBK (eventually part of EMI) for $170 million and thereafter repackaged with the Filmtrax-Belwin-Mills copyrights for a considerably higher total sales price. In 1999, the Windswept Pacific catalog of approximately 40,000 songs was sold by its owner, Fujisankei Communications of Japan, to EMI for a reported $200 million.

Factors to Consider

The number of songs in a catalog is not as important as their earning power. However, the historic earnings of a former hit are not sufficient assurance of value. While it is desirable to have songs that will likely continue to be popular, it is also desirable to avoid putting all of one's eggs in one basket, with only a few major earners instead of the more desirable broad-based catalog with the same earnings being generated by a larger number of songs, each with its own following, history of past hit records, and likely recurrence of earnings in the future. How far into the future is important as well, and the formula for valuation must always include the duration of copyright and contractual rights owned or controlled by the seller.

Foreign earnings and the status of subpublisher commitments are also factors to be considered. An important U.S. catalog with long-term 50-50 deals throughout the world is obviously less desirable than a catalog available for worldwide exploitation and administration without extended prior commitments. On the other hand, when BMG acquired Italy's largest firm, G. Ricordi, it acquired the right to administer numerous songs that would otherwise have been in its competitors' catalogs, because Ricordi had previously made long-term deals on many important songs copyrighted in the United States. Another consideration is the ability to acquire or consolidate foreign operations, as shown by the PolyGram acquisition, which enabled MCA to take over PolyGram's existing offices in Latin America and Southeast Asia without incurring the expense and effort of setting up its own operations in these territories.

In the past, purchasers might have a windfall benefit from increased mechanical royalty collections due to rising sales. This is no longer a source of increased income. Another past windfall was the surge in earnings brought about by the re-release of many records in CD format, which is likely to be replicated only to a modest extent with the advent of the DVD format. At this time, industry observers are concerned about rampant unlicensed duplication made possible by new technological developments. Whether such uses can be prevented by antipiracy measures remains to be seen.

New financial growth may also result from increased commercial radio and television in foreign territories previously dominated by state-owned and low-royalty-paying public bodies, as well as Internet-generated revenues. The 1994 adoption of GATT, with its emphasis on intellectual property rights, has resulted in legal and economic recognition of copyrights in some countries, mainly in Southeast Asia, that had been major sources of international piracy. All these factors help sustain the historical rise in publishing earnings.

Smaller Catalogs

It is beyond dispute that the music publishing industry is becoming more centralized and that true independents, although numbering in the thousands, are capturing less of the total cash flow of the industry. In 2002, the three most important independent music publishers were Peer, Music Sales, and Carlin Music.

Certain smaller independent publishers and even some individuals have, like the majors, engaged in a deliberate course of investment in copyrights and interests in copyrights. This demonstrates that sophisticated professionals are convinced that copyrights represent excellent investments. Their principal interest, of course, lies in established musical compositions rather than untried, unproven ones. Some publishers have prospered by buying half-interests, and even quarter-interests, in music copyrights.

There are various incentives for selling music publishing catalogs: for example, the death of a principal owner (and the possible need to raise cash to pay estate taxes); the retirement of a principal owner; a disagreement among joint owners; and the fear of decreasing value as the catalogs mature without new promotion. In addition, tax benefits can be a powerful incentive in a stock-for-stock transaction where the catalog is transferred to a publicly traded entity. If the seller is not the original composer, author, or donee of the compositions, capital gains treatment may be applicable at a lower tax rate than the otherwise applicable income tax rate.

Public corporations may regard the acquisition of a broad-based, well-managed music publishing catalog as a sound way to enter or expand their presence in the "content" side of the entertainment market. It may also be seen as a way to enhance the earnings on their common stock, especially when the price paid for the acquisition compares favorably with the price of the purchaser's stock and its past earnings. For example, purchasing a music catalog at 10 times the amount of average expected annual net earnings would be particularly advantageous if the stock of the purchasing company were being valued at 20 times its average net earnings.

Sources of Individual Copyrights

The sources of individual copyrights are largely smaller publishers (including artists and writers who may have retained all or part of their ownership in works) and composers who have obtained control of their copyrights during the renewal term of copyrights, that is, after the initial 28-year period. Under the Songwriters Guild of America contract developed in 1948 and used before the 1978 effective date of the Copyright Act of 1976, worldwide ownership of copyrights in the renewal period can vest in the writer.

Knowledgeable publishers interested in renewal copyrights study the Register of Copyright publications and ferret out the better copyrights that will shortly be up for renewal. They then initiate negotiations with the writers or their estates for the right to publish the copyrighted material in the renewal period. Until the year 2005, such renewal opportunities still exist for songs originating prior to 1978. This is obviously a diminishing pool of available acquisitions. Subsequent compositions are governed by the Copyright Act of 1976 and are subject to return of U.S. rights either at the 35-year mark from date of publication in print or record form or 40 years from date of execution of grant, whichever is earlier. Most songs are in the 35-year termination situation. The prospective buyer must make a full and thorough examination of the contracts entered into by the writers and the prior publishers in order to determine what rights and territories have not previously been assigned to third parties.

Purchasers of older copyrights must recognize that historical business patterns may have resulted in widely varying foreign publishing relationships, which require detailed analysis. A single composition may have been subpublished by many different subpublishers in various territories under separate agreements, each with its own terms. In certain areas, the composition's subpublishing rights may have been assigned for 10 years, in others, for the original period of the U.S. copyright, and in the balance, for the entire term of copyright in the particular territory. In the major music territories, the term of copyright is often the life of the writer plus 70 years. Buyers must ascertain whether they are purchasing the full publishing rights for each country or only the right to receive royalties from a subpublisher already in place, and if the latter, for how long.

Renewal and Reversion Rights

In the case of purchases of compositions first fixed before 1978 that are in the original 28-year period of the U.S. copyright, the status of the right to renew the U.S. copyright is important, even though the formality of actual renewal registration is not required after the Copyright Renewal Act of 1992. (Of course, this does not include songs that are works for hire.)

The buyer who purchases a pre-1978 copyrighted composition from a publisher who does not control the renewal right must understand that the acquired rights for the U.S. market will cease at the end of the 28th year from the inception of the copyright. If the publisher is also selling the renewal right, the buyer must recognize that the seller can convey only a contingent interest in the renewal period and that the contingent interest will vest only if the writer who granted the renewal rights is alive in the 28th year. The same contingency is present if the seller is also the writer. Should the writer not live to the 28th year, the renewal right belongs to the surviving spouse and children; if there is no such immediate family and the writer left a will, the right goes to the executor of the writer's estate; if there is no will, the renewal right vests in the writer's next of kin. It should be noted that for compositions written on a work-for-hire basis there is no reversion in the event of the writer's death before the 28th year.

For compositions written in and after 1978 (again, with the exception of works for hire) there is a right of termination between the 35th and 40th year from the date of the grant of copyright. This right cannot be waived any earlier than 10 years before the effective date of any such termination. Nevertheless, as the risk of termination is not automatic in the absence of affirmative action by the terminating party, some value may be attributed to the possibility of inertia when purchasing compositions otherwise subject to termination.

Locating the wife or husband and children may be a long and expensive task, sometimes further complicated by the status of children born out of wedlock, who are, under the Copyright Act of 1976, recognized as "children."

In the case of compositions already in the renewal term, consideration must be given to the author's right under the Copyright Act of 1976 to terminate after the 56th year. For compositions first fixed after 1977, the author's right, under the same statute, to terminate after the 35th year must be taken into account.

There may be a special problem in the case of copyrights created before 1957 in the U.K., Canada, Australia, and other nations or territories that were in the British Commonwealth at that time. Under the applicable law concerning such compositions, the copyright will revert to the estate 25 years after the writer's death for the balance of the period of the copyright protection. Any prospective buyer of older copyrights must reckon with this right of "reversion" of copyright.

As for works originating in or before 1934, purchasers of such works should be aware of possible similar problems with regard to German rights. The issue concerns whether a publisher/assignee or the heirs of a composer benefit from a statutory extension of the life of a copyright. On December 13, 1934, the period was extended from 30 years to 50 years after the death of the composer. The duration for Germany was subsequently further extended to 70 years after death.

The Purchase of Assets or Stock

Where the entire catalog of a publisher is for sale, the buyer usually prefers to acquire the copyrights rather than the corporate stock of the publisher, in order to obtain the right to depreciate the cost of the acquisition for tax purposes. One advantage of purchasing assets instead of stock is the opportunity to amortize the assets over several years for tax purposes of sale, thereby establishing a new valuation basis as well as preserving a corporate shield against the corporate seller's possible prior underpayment of taxes. However, in some instances, it is possible that the corporate entity of the publisher may offer some tax-loss benefits, or that purchasing the corporate entity may have some advantage, for example, the avoidance of restrictions against the assignment of copyrights or writer contracts.

In some instances, the seller insists on the sale of the corporate stock. Acquiring the corporate entity may create complicated legal and accounting problems, since the buyer then inherits the corporate liabilities, including possible claims for back taxes, writer suits for royalties, etc. If the individuals who are the owners of the corporation are financially responsible, it is possible for the buyer to achieve some measure of protection in buying the corporate stock by obtaining guarantees and indemnifications from those individuals. Additional protection may be provided if the consideration for the sale is payable over a period of years, so that any adverse claims will likely appear while a significant portion of the consideration is still unpaid. It may also be specifically provided that a portion of the price will be held in escrow for a certain period, to satisfy tax and other claims. To ensure that tax claims are made promptly, the buyer may request a government tax audit of the returns for past years.

Whether the underlying copyrights or stock is purchased, it is wise for the buyer to insist on warranties and indemnities relating to the absence of litigation or threats of litigation and to the fact that the copyrights are original, do not infringe the rights of any third party, and are not subject to any liens or other encumbrances.

The Price of Purchasing a Copyright

In arriving at a price to be paid for a copyright, the buyer requires information about the past earnings of that copyright. These earnings generally fall into four categories: performance fees, mechanical and synchronization fees, earnings from printed editions, and earnings from foreign sources. The buyer requests that the owner of a copyright submit financial data for a period of years, including copies of statements rendered by ASCAP or BMI as well as by the Harry Fox Agency, if it represented the owner in the collection of mechanical and synchronization fees. If the printed editions were handled by independent organizations, the buyer should have access to the statements rendered by those organizations.

In the distant past, a common rule of thumb in the music publishing industry was that the buyer would pay the seller a price equal to from 5 to 8 times the average yearly performance earnings paid by ASCAP or BMI for a musical composition over a representative period such as 5 years. This figure was without reference to mechanical and synchronization fees or foreign earnings of any kind.

The current tendency is to increase the weight given to mechanical and synchronization fees and to foreign earnings, although banks which lend money to finance a purchase continue to rely on ASCAP or BMI earnings history. A further reason is the possibility of periodic raises in the compulsory mechanical license rate. In January 2002, the mechanical rate was raised to 8 cents per song, or 1.55 cents per minute (previously, the rates were 7.55 cents per song or 1.45 cents per minute). In January 2004 the basic rate will go up to 8.5 cents per song or 1.65 per minute, and in January 2006 it will go up again, to 9.10 cents per song or 1.75 cents per minute.

In recent years cable TV, home video, CD releases, and commercial jingles have been making greater use of classic films and film clips. A good example of this is the authorized, royalty-producing use of a computer-aided sequence on a vacuum cleaner commercial showing Fred Astaire dancing with the advertiser's product. As digital techniques become ever more sophisticated, new sources of music publishing revenues may emerge.

The expansion of satellite broadcasting stations, as well as the replacement in Europe of state-supported stations by private commercial stations, may also generate new sources of income in the near future. Paralleling this is growth of commercial television programming in the American pattern; for example, in England, annual program output is expected to increase more than 300 percent in the next decade, with music in its customary participating role, thereby generating performing rights and synchronization payments.

Other new or enlarged music income sources are coming from developing countries. These substantially improved music earnings are the result of GATT negotiations and the American endorsement of the Berne Convention.

As a consequence, the old rule of thumb of 5 to 8 times the average yearly performance earnings is now obsolete. A more likely figure is as high as 12 to 13 times—or more—of the total of (1) the average performance earnings, (2) the average over the same period of the publisher's share of mechanical earnings, that is, the gross mechanical earnings less the writer's mechanical royalties, and (3) the average of the publisher's share of foreign performance income and foreign mechanical earnings remitted to the United States.

Under Internal Revenue Service tax law, a seller who receives all or part of the sale price after the year of sale can treat the transaction as an installment sale provided the sale is at a gain. The seller is thus entitled to file a return for each year showing only the payments received in that year. A portion of each payment will represent a part of the gain, with the profit percentage or ratio applied to each payment being computed by dividing the gross profit by the gross selling price. If the contract fails to charge interest at a minimum rate, the IRS will impute interest at that rate. Under this approach, a portion of each installment payment is considered to be a payment of interest rather than a capital gain. Like depreciation costs, interest payments are tax-deductible. Accountants or attorneys should be consulted as to the rules and regulations covering the computation of the minimum rate.

Users of Copyrights

Some purchasers of copyrights are in a special position because they are users of copyrights in addition to being music publishers. The five major label record companies are obviously users of copyrights. In addition, three of them (Universal Music Group, Warner/Chappell, and Sony/ATV) are affiliates of motion picture companies. They are therefore capable of enhancing the value of a composition by planned exploitation, which results in increased earnings from mechanical fees and performance fees, as well as more frequent opportunities to earn synchronization fees.

The increased earnings from mechanical fees result from recordings by the record company, while the earnings from performance fees increase from performances of the records and of the television shows or films and motion pictures in which the composition appears. Synchronization fees are payable for use in television and motion pictures. It is obvious that the user-purchaser is frequently able to justify a higher purchase price for a composition than a purchaser who is not a user. With the judicious, planned use of a composition, user-purchasers may recoup their investment more quickly than other purchasers.

Capital Gains

A problem that confronts a seller of copyrights is whether to report the sum received as the proceeds from the sale of capital assets, which are taxable at capital gain rates, or whether to consider the income as royalties. Under the Internal Revenue Code, the term capital asset does not include musical copyrights held by the writer or the writer's donee, and therefore if such individuals are the seller, they must report the amount received, or the value of property acquired in exchange, as ordinary income, not as capital gain.

In contrast, other sellers, including the heirs of a writer, have the benefit of capital gains treatment. For this purpose, heirs include "statutory heirs" for U.S. renewal and termination rights, whereas British reversions are for the benefit of "heirs under will." With regard to assets obtained from a legatee under a will, a "stepped-up" tax basis valuation applies, and the heirs are not considered donees of the composer. For U.S. renewal and termination assignments, the statutory heirs use a capital gains basis of valuation at the effective date of acquisition of the copyright interest. Other sellers, including, as noted above, the heirs of a writer, have the benefit of capital gains treatment.

Due Diligence

A "due diligence" investigation is a detailed review of the chain of title and other aspects of what is being sold and the value of the catalog being purchased. It is usually conducted by qualified expert attorneys or accountants and is essential in any purchase transaction. This is especially true if the purchase price is financed in whole or in part by a bank or third-party loan, since the purchaser must usually warrant and represent to the lender that all third-party obligations, including all licenses, agency agreements, foreign subpublishing deals, outstanding advances, collaborator status, and related essential status reports have been fully disclosed. The following is a due diligence checklist that might be used in a typical purchase:

- Name, address, tax identification number, and legal status of owner of songs (i.e., the owner as shown in the Copyright Office registrations and performing rights society affiliations).
- Song-by-song list of those songs that together constitute 80 percent of the net publisher share (NPS) of the entire catalog, showing author and publisher splits, copyright registration data (date of filing and registration number), NPS, and recording information.
- List of songwriters currently under contract, including contract date, current period and options, ongoing advance obligations, as well as copies of the songwriter agreements.
- List of unrecouped advance balances to songwriters,
- List of subpublishing licenses, including date of license, territory, term, retention and collection period, advances and unrecouped balances, along with copies of the licenses.
- List of any other advances recoupable from earnings of the assets (e.g., BMI or ASCAP advances, to be cross-checked with the societies).
- List of print contracts, including term, advances, and unrecouped balances; sell-off rights; and copies of the contracts.
- Copies of recording agreements, including controlled-composition provisions.
- Copies of all other pertinent contracts, other than Harry Fox Agency standard form mechanical licenses and other nonexclusive licenses.
- Copies of copyright documents, including registrations, assignments, etc.
- List of the names, addresses, and ages of all the songwriters and their spouses and children (natural or adopted), if any of the major compositions are pre-1978 and are not works for hire.
- Addresses for the last 5 years of each owner (as reflected in the Copyright Office records).
- If the seller is a corporation, a recently certified good-standing certificate and tax good-standing certificate; at closing, minutes of directors meeting approving the transaction certified by the secretary of the corporation. If the seller is "doing business as" (dba), a recently certified copy of the fictitious name filing.
- Copies of all source royalty statements received by company from record companies, the Harry Fox Agency, performance societies, subpublishers, etc. (5 years).
- Copies of all royalty statements issued to songwriters, co-publishers, etc. (5 years).
- Cash receipts book (5 years).
- Cash disbursements book (5 years).
- Bank statements (5 years).

- All available financial summaries relating to the compositions.
- Seller's federal tax returns (5 years).
- Authorization executed by seller authorizing BMI, ASCAP, and the other societies to turn over complete song lists, statements, and account status.
- Documentation on any pending claims or litigations relating to the catalog, including audit claims.
- Documentation relating to any liens, pledges, or security agreements relating to the catalog.
- Copy of publisher's current society affiliation agreements.
- Copy of publisher's current Harry Fox Agency agreement.
- List of all mechanical licenses, including song title, artist, label, selection number, and release date.

BUYING AND SELLING RECORD COMPANIES AND MASTERS

Consolidation

Consolidation is the word which best describes the recent changes of ownership of record companies and significant catalogs of master recordings. With the absorption of PolyGram and MCA and their subsidiary and previously acquired masters into Universal, there are now only five significant major labels, Universal, Warner, Sony, EMI, and BMG. Table 27-1, on page 270, lists the labels owned or distributed by these companies. A December 2002 SoundScan report reported the following U.S. market shares for the big five: Universal Music Group, nearly 29 percent; Warner Group, 17 percent; BMG, nearly 15 percent; Sony, over 16 percent; and EMI, slightly over 9 percent. The independent companies as a group have slightly over 13 percent. The largest of the indies, Madacy, approached 1.5 percent, and three of the others, Fonovisa, TVT, and Laserlight, each had less than 0.5 percent.

A SoundScan analysis of major label sales in Germany is representative of the other European markets: the Warner Group of labels (including Warner, Elektra, and Atlantic) had 12 percent of that market, the Universal Group had 38.9 percent, Sony had 17.1 percent, BMG had 15.5 percent, EMI had 6.7, and the indies had 9 percent.

Despite their relatively small market share, independent labels continue to spring up in all parts of the world, and there are currently over 500 members of the National Association of Independent Record Producers. These companies are spearheaded by people who are willing to invest time, money, and creative energy for possible sales only in the low five figures, between 10,000 and 50,000, and who often actively nurture new talent. Sometimes the result is gold, as with George Thorogood (originally launched by Rounder, before becoming a star with EMI), Little Richard (launched by Specialty), and—the most famous case—Elvis Presley (launched by the Memphis-based Sun Records). In contrast, only artists with a reasonable expectation of hundreds of thousands of sales are generally considered appropriate for inclusion in the priority catalogs of the majors and backed by expensive promotional campaigns.

As the above statistics make clear, the industry is overwhelmingly dominated by the majors. With their deep pockets and distribution and promotional clout, the majors seem to regard some of the indies the way major league baseball teams regard their farm teams, as a training ground for potential stars. Minor labels may even be financed in part by the majors, and many so-called independent labels hitch up with the majors for distribution. Furthermore, once an indie has proved its credibility in the marketplace, it is ripe for acquisition by one of the majors. The 2002 acquisition by BMG of the Zomba/Jive group is a revealing case study.

As reported by *Billboard,* the story started in 1971 when a former correspondent for *Billboard* from South Africa, Clive Calder, teamed up with Ralph Simon to form a South African firm. Calder moved in 1974 to London and proceeded in 1978 to open a New York branch.

In 1981 "Back to the Sixties," distributed in the United States by Arista Records, was Jive's first charted single and in 1982 Jive reached #1 on the British charts for "The Lion Sleeps Tonight." By 1984 Jive's artist Billy Ocean reached #1 in the United States for "Caribbean Queen (No More Love On The Run)," and U.S. producer Barry Eastmond was engaged for trans-Atlantic flights for further Billy Ocean production. Jive reached #1 on the U.S. album charts in 1995 with an R. Kelly album. In 1999–2000 Jive had its first #1 album in the U.K., *Spectacular,* and six Jive albums sold a total of 40 million copies in the United States.

In 1987 the label switched from Arista to BMG for international distribution.

In 1990, Calder and Simon split, and Calder started what turned out to be aborted negotiations with EMI for the sale of a minority interest. However, by 1991 BMG had acquired a 25 percent interest in Jive's publishing arm, and in 1996 BMG bought a 20 percent interest in the record arm, for an estimated $50 million, which enabled Jive to acquire, for $25 million, a 75 percent interest in the U.K. publishing firm Pinnacle.

In 2002, Calder's careful grooming of hits, his sound management policies, and the emergence of Britney Spears and 'N Sync as major stars, had made Jive such a desirable property that BMG came through with nearly $3 billion for full acquisition of Jive's recording and publishing arms.

Other examples of consolidation are Sony's acquisition of three CBS (Columbia) labels in 1988 for $2 billion, as well as the sale of Motown Records for $61 million in 1989 to a joint venture of which MCA (thereafter acquired by Universal) was the leading member. After litigation among partners, Motown was again sold but this time for $301 million to PolyGram (since acquired by Universal). Other historic sales were Virgin Records to EMI for $872 million and Geffen Records to MCA in 1990 for $550 million in stock.

The questions remain, Does consolidation of corporate ownership of record labels inevitably lead to stagnation? Are corporate major label A&R personnel as inspired as the people running the independent labels in this country? Some of the majors have answered by developing alternative strategies, furnishing major "parental" financial support while preserving independent creative freedom. Activity of this sort, as well as the development of the in-house independent labels referred to above, has stepped up considerably since the success of Nirvana, the punk-metal group that went from relative obscurity with the Seattle-based indie Sub Pop to the top of the album charts with their second album, *Nevermind,* which was released by Geffen and has sold over 5 million copies in the United States.

The last word on this subject comes from Jerry Wexler, one of the partners who sold Atlantic to Warner. In his autobiography, he offered the following thoughts on the concept of subsidiary label deals:

> I always pushed the idea of a subsidiary label. It didn't cost a lot and was an easy way to pacify an artist or a heavyweight manager. CBS's credo may have been "it's gotta come out on our label and we won't pay more than five percent," but our credo is" we'll put your record out on any damn label you choose and we'll pay ten percent." As a result we had a slew of successful sub-labels: Dial, Fame, Dade, Alston, Stax, Volt, Capricorn, Rolling Stone, and so forth. While the majors were sleeping on this issue, we mopped up. Today . . . the practice is so standard it is practically meaning-less. It always was.

Factors to Consider

One informed industry veteran has the following general advice when consid-ering the purchase of a record company: "When buying a music-publishing firm, treat it like the purchase of an insurance company annuity with some side benefits available . . . . When buying a record company, treat it like the purchase of an expensive jet liner already flying high in the air and make sure that you have a qualified pilot and enough gas."

There is a vast difference between acquiring one or more masters as indi-vidual items to augment a catalog and the acquisition of an existing operational label. The latter involves ongoing exclusive artist recording contracts as well as administrative, A&R and promotion staffs, trademarks and logos, and good will of the label. Many newly acquired record companies share marketing, sales, advertising, and publicity offices with the new parent, but they usually retain at least their original A&R employees with their standing industry relationships. In determining purchase price, value-added factors can result in a negotiated price as high as 20 times current net earnings.

In contrast, when acquiring a master recording that has been previously released, its historical earnings are not necessarily reflective of future sales inas-much as it is unlikely that the number of future purchasers will be the same number as past purchasers. For example, a regional hit acquired by a major label can have substantially increased sales due to the major's national and international distribution clout and ability to finance more pressings and promotion. Thus, the multiple for acquisition of an existing master that has been released in the past may be quite low, even as little as 3 to 5 times average annual net earnings.

LEADERSHIP OF THE NEWLY ACQUIRED LABEL

When Sony acquired CBS Records, the $2 billion price was agreed upon only in conjunction with additional payments to top management. This was not merely part of an inducement for company leaders to back the basic deal, but rather an essential insurance policy designed to make sure that key personnel would not abandon ship, link up with competitors, and lead current recording stars to switch companies when their contracts ran out.

Indeed, presuming that the reason for agreeing to a high multiple-of-earnings purchase price is that the venture being acquired is a highly successful ongoing venture, it is important to retain existing key personnel through such measures as bonuses, stock options, and assured salary payments.

Due Diligence

Two items on the due diligence checklist, a review of key personnel agreements and a review of liabilities, deserve special attention.

The acquiring company must be sure to review top artists' agreements for the existence of "key man " provisions that would allow them to desert the label if a designated key officer is no longer employed. If such provisions exist, the best course of action may be to lock in the employment of the key officer. Clive Davis of Arista has been named as such a key man in numerous important artist deals, thereby giving him considerable leverage in dealing with top-level BMG management.

An investigation of the current status of all artist accounts (and of publisher mechanical royalties) is another essential part of the due diligence investigation. Many acquiring firms have a "one-way street" mentality, hoping to claim all unrecouped recording cost credits while disregarding unpaid artist royalties of fully recouped accounts. In 1992, in connection with the acquisition of the Springboard catalog by Gusto Records of Nashville, a Federal Court of Appeals ruled that the acquiring company acquired not only master rights but liabilities as well. It is general law that one cannot acquire a bulk sale of a company's assets without clearing or assuming all liabilities of the seller. However, unpaid artist royalties, even those of a former bankrupt owner, were declared the liability of the acquiring label, with no reference to a time limit under the statute of limitations.

Following is a partial list of what should be reviewed before purchasing a record company.

- ▶ A Copyright Office report by at least one source and possibly two reference services as to all sound recording copyright registrations, to assure no conflicting claims to copyright.
- ▶ Reports on trademarks or service marks involving record labels used or artist names controlled .
- ▶ A Dun and Bradstreet credit report on the credit status of the acquired label and recent history of payment of bills. It is desirable to get a solvency opinion if any credit is to be extended based on delivered assets. This is to avoid risk under the Uniform Fraudulent Conveyance Act, Bankruptcy Code, and certain state common law provisions. Optimally, someone other than the seller's Certified Public Accountant would vouch that:
    - ▶ The present fair market value of the assets exceeds the liabilities of the borrower, including royalties due and other contingent liabilities.
    - ▶ The borrowing entity will be in a position to meet its intended obligations, including royalties and other contingent liabilities.
    - ▶ The entity will not be left with an unreasonably small capital balance so as to jeopardize continued normal operations of its business.
    - ▶ Certified financial statements for a specified period and unaudited statements for the current period signed by the officially designated Certified Public Accountant of seller.
- ▶ A report of amounts and collectability of receivables (aging schedule), which should include a statement of adequacy of allowance for possible returns and whether there are any agreements with purchasers of inventory as to return privileges, title or consignment, and so on.
- ▶ A report of audit claims (i.e., music publisher claims for mechanical royalties and artist royalty review), and a report of litigation in process, including unsettled claims.
- ▶ A warehouse inventory, listing in detail all available product and configurations of each catalog item, including titles and catalog numbers, and designation of location and amounts of any items sold on a consignment basis; a catalog of masters owned, whether or not in current release.
- ▶ A list of pressing plants utilized within the past several years and a report of pressing activity, as well as a list of all masters in the possession of each plant.
- ▶ A list of foreign distributors and a designation of duration of each deal.
- ▶ A list of union contracts and books and records as to compliance with pension, welfare, and other payment requirements.
- ▶ A list of banks and insurance accounts currently in force.
- ▶ A list of real estate owned or leases in force, including equipment and furniture valuations.
- ▶ Representation that mechanical licenses have been obtained for all recorded materials and indication of which of such licenses are at higher than 75 percent of statutory rates.

- A list of any retained music publishing rights on songs recorded.
- A list of any outstanding licensing arrangements (record club, premium licenses, K-Tel-style licenses, etc.); a list of domestic special marketing, promotion, or merchandising rights and obligations.
- A designation of all continuing artist agreements and terms of options thereof.
- A designation of unrecouped deferred recording costs and advances to be charged against artist and/or producer (or other) royalty accounts.
- A list of all producer agreements with continuing royalty obligations.
- Key personnel agreements, including pension plans and fringe benefits and reference to key personnel in any outstanding artist agreements.
- Distribution agreements and return privileges outstanding, together with a history of returns.

Table 27-1

Distribution Groups

BMG	EMI	Sony	Universal	Warner
Arista	Angel/Bluenote	550 Music	A&M	ATCO
Bad Boy	Capitol Records	Columbia	CURB	Atlantic
BMG US Latin	Capitol Nashville	Epic	Def Jam/Def Soul	Assylum
BNA Entertainment	Christian Music Group	Independent	Deutsch Grammophone	Blackbird
Buddha	EMI Latin	Legacy Records	Disney/Buena Vista	Classics
J Records	EMI Manhattan	Lucky Dog Records	Fonovisa	Elektra
Jive	EMI Metro Blue	Loud	Geffen Records	East West
Kinetic Rec	EMI Philadelphia Int'l	Ovum Records	Hip-O-Records	Erato
Razor & Tie	EMI Sparrow Label Group	Portrait	Hollywood Records	Lava Records
RCA	Priority	Red Ink	Interscope	Maverick Recording Co.
RCA Victor	Right Stuff/Special	RPM Music Prod.	Island Def Jam	Nonesuch
Robbins Ent.		Sony Classical	MCA Records	Reprise
Santuary/CMC		Sony Discos	Mercury	Rhino Entertainment Co.
Silvertone			Refuge	
V2			Rounder	Tommy Boy
Verity			Ruff Ryder Entertainment	WEA Latin
Volcano			Thump	Word/Curb
Windham Hill			Trinity Records	
Wind-up Entertainment			Universal Music Latin	
Zomba			Verve	
			Virgin	

28

Loans to Music Publishers

There are many sound business reasons why a music publisher might require a loan: catalog acquisitions, writer royalty advances, new physical studio or equipment costs, costs of preparing new demonstration records, costs of preparing or financing others to make master recordings, and selective advertising and promotion of songs or recordings. Until relatively recently, however, it was difficult to conceive of any group less likely to be regarded favorably by conservative bankers than the thousands of smaller music publishers in New York's Tin Pan Alley, in Nashville, and in Hollywood. Assets literally worth no more than a song and administered through a highly subjective system that emphasizes promotion, contacts, and ever-changing market conditions would hardly seem reassuring to a potential lender.

But today banking relationships are no longer exceptional in the music industry. Knowledgeable lenders have noted that ASCAP, BMI, and SESAC pay out millions of dollars a year to music publishers. Many loans are made on the basis of certified ASCAP and BMI reports of past performance fee earnings. Low-cost collection agencies, such as the Harry Fox Agency, which collects mechanical license fees from record companies for a fee of 5.75 percent of gross receipts, help materially to bolster the credit rating of the music business.

Some lenders, recognizing that music copyrights are a good form of collateral, have made something of a specialty of music industry loans. One informed banker commented that any major loan requires two areas of security: first, the asset and cash flow of the entity being acquired, and second, the backup assurance of the borrower's basic business. In recent years, many of the major acquisitions have been financed by private investment bankers, such as Boston Ventures, rather than commercial banks.

As the banking world has acquired a basic understanding of the peculiar needs and resources of the music industry, they have increased loans to industry members. A method of securing loans initially established in the film industry— a lien against future earnings—has become common in the music business. The first entity to successfully launch this concept in the music business was the Pullman Structured Asset Sales Group,[1] which successfully organized a $50 million loan secured by David Bowie's future artist and songwriter royalties. Pullman followed this with a loan secured by the Holland-Dozier-Holland producer and artist royalty streams and then one secured by the Ashford and Simpson artist and songwriter royalty streams. Others followed Pullman's lead. Owing to the expense of organizing, evaluating, and selling securities, however, only large loans can be "securitized" in this way. Pullman-type bonds have an average life of 10 years but can go up to 15 years. Their attraction is that monies are not taxable when initially received but only as and when the loan is liquidated.

The Special Risks in Loans to Music Publishers

Annually, more than 120,000 new songs compete fiercely for the few spots on the record charts. The fact is, most new songs make no impact whatsoever in the music marketplace. As a result, in evaluating a proposed loan, lenders generally focus only on income from established songs with a proven financial record. In considering the business expenses of a music publisher, lenders focus on writer royalties, which is a publisher's most important cost of doing business. On mechanical license income, the writer's royalty is usually 50 percent of the receipts; rent, salaries, independent promotion, and travel and telephone costs are the other principal items of expense.

Lenders must be aware of the special risks involved in loans to music publishers. An unscrupulous borrower may apply for a bank loan after having exhausted all other methods of obtaining money by way of cash advances against future earnings. Such advances may have been obtained from copublishing deals, print licensees, or foreign subpublishers. Lenders who rely on earnings from such sources may later find that the advances must be recouped before the earnings are available to repay the loan.

Another special risk involved in loans to music publishers is the duration of the borrower's rights. On copyrights originating before 1978, the borrower may not possess rights beyond the original 28-year term of copyright because he or she has failed to obtain renewal rights from the author or a deceased author's statutory successors. As with all copyrights, consideration should be given to statutory rights of termination granted under the Copyright Act of 1976. If the copyright is of foreign origin, the borrower may have acquired U.S. publishing rights for only a limited term (for example, 10 years from the original foreign publisher). It should be remembered that all copyrights go into the public domain after the expiration of the applicable statutory periods of copyright.

Another copyright-related risk involves the possibility that through negligent administration, rights have been forfeited. This is now much less likely than it used to be because the current statute—the Copyright Act as amended under the

---

[1] Contact at info@pullmanbonds.com or www.pullmanbonds.com

Berne Implementation Act, effective in 1989—is much more liberal with regard to omissions or imperfections in notice and registration. The Copyright Renewal Act of 1992 provides further protection against forfeiture for failure to renew older copyrights in their 28th year. Nevertheless, there are still circumstances in which failure to comply with formalities, such as failure to register renewals for works originating before 1964 or to affix correct notice on works published before 1998, results in forfeiture of benefits, for example, recovery of statutory damages and attorney's fees.

The Copyright Act provides that a copyright owner cannot collect mechanical royalties under a compulsory license for records made and distributed before the owner is identified as such in the records of the Copyright Office, although recovery can be made for records made and distributed after such identification. A lender might therefore wish to check the status of current registrations of copyrights.

A more basic threat to music copyrights is the failure to defend adequately against litigation that attacks the validity of the copyright. This can result from the frequent defense of nonoriginality in lawsuits brought by the borrower.

A lender should also have the right to approve any litigation involving copyrights which the borrower proposes to commence, given the fact that the defendant will invariably attack the validity of the copyright. The lender will not wish to jeopardize the validity of a weak copyright in such litigation.

The Amount of a Loan

A simple protection available to lenders in the music field is to limit the amount of a loan to the anticipated receipts of the borrower from sources akin to "accounts receivable" in other fields, that is, monies which, although they may not be currently held assets, will come through the "pipeline." This alleviates the necessity for a full investigation of copyright ownership and duration. It does, however, require access to information concerning (1) recent uses of compositions in the borrower's catalog and (2) advances against earnings previously obtained by the borrower.

A typical anticipated payment is the quarterly accounting by ASCAP or BMI based on public performances logged from 6 to 9 months prior to the accounting. Similar in regularity are the Harry Fox Agency quarterly distributions of mechanical royalties collected on a quarterly or semiannual basis from record companies. More delayed payments, often as much as one or two years behind domestic payments, may come from foreign agents or licensees, who ordinarily remit 50 percent or more of their territorial earnings from all sources except print uses, which are usually accounted for at a minimum rate of 10 to 12.5 percent of the retail selling price. These anticipated receipts, subject to outstanding advances, can be considered an appropriate basis for a short-term loan. A lender usually requires the added protection of a notification to the appropriate society or collecting agency to make payment directly to the lender.

An estimate of uncollected mechanical royalties can sometimes be made on the basis of public announcements of verified sales of hit records. The song of a proposed borrower may be contained in an album or single certified by the Recording Industry Association of America (RIAA) as a gold record or a platinum record. (The former relates to a certified shipment by the manufacturer of 500,000 units, and the latter to 1 million units.) Caution, however, must be exercised before anticipating royalty receipts computed on the basis of RIAA certification. Actual royalties are generally less than a simple units-shipped calculation would indicate because of possible returns, reserves, and nonroyalty sales. Alternatively (or additionally), a lender may look to sales reported by SoundScan. Based on actual net sales of 1 million units, a composition licensed by the publisher at 8 cents would result in the publisher's collecting $80,000, of which $40,000 would remain for the publisher after the usual 50 percent writer royalties. This computation makes no deduction for the Harry Fox Agency commissions, which would reduce the amount collected by 6 percent.

Both ASCAP and BMI promptly respond to written requests from a member for a statement of outstanding advances and of the amounts of the most recent distributions. Both ASCAP and BMI permit instructions for a general assignment to be irrevocable, providing the lender with further assurance that the instructions will not be revoked at a later date. (Note: When an "irrevocable" assignment is made, it is up to the *borrower* to make provision for the lender to reassign all such rights once the loan has been fully repaid.)

The Harry Fox Agency will accept an irrevocable direction, signed by the publisher and the bank, for payment to the bank of monies otherwise due to the publisher for mechanical license fees.

Copyright Search Report

One advantage of the federal copyright system is the maintenance of a public registration procedure that makes available essential title information, including the history of recorded assignments. The original copyright registrations of published and unpublished musical works are listed in the *Catalog of Copyright Entries* issued by the Copyright Office and available at many libraries throughout the country as well as over the Internet. The Internet data bank (www.loc.gov/copyright) starts with 1978 registrations.

However, the prospective lender should not rely on this listing alone because no reference is made to assignments or other recorded documents relating to the work. Complete reports are obtainable only by actual inspection of the copyright records maintained by the Copyright Office in Washington, D.C. The Thomson & Thomson Copyright Research Group makes private reports based upon actual inspection of Copyright Office records. The Copyright Office itself also offers search reports. Some lenders may prefer to use two or more of these services to cross-check for accuracy before making a substantial loan. All search reports should be examined closely to discern the effective date of the information contained as well as to determine whether the report includes the inspection of pending files. Because of the tremendous volume of recordations and the intricacies of Copyright Office filings, there is some delay between the date of receipt of assignments or related documents and their actual recordation.

It is also important to be aware of the hiatus permitted under the Copyright Act whereby a prior assignee or mortgagee can delay recordation of a document for up to 1 month from execution in the United States and up to 2 months from execution abroad without losing his or her right to priority over a subsequent purchaser or mortgagee.

The Recordation of Loans in the Copyright Office

In music copyright matters the preferred form of security for a loan is referred to in the Copyright Act of 1909 as a "mortgage," although the Copyright Act of 1976 lumps mortgages together with other assignments of copyright interests under the phrase "transfer of copyright ownership." As a matter of standard practice, lenders should record their mortgages in the Copyright Office. For a single fee and by a single act of filing with the Copyright Office in Washington, D.C., the lender can obtain a nationwide protection against conflicting mortgages or assignments.

The procedure for recordation of a mortgage is the same as the recordation of a regular assignment of copyright. Recordation of a transfer of copyright ownership is provided for in Section 205 of the Copyright Act. No specific form of mortgage is indicated in the Copyright Acts of 1909 or 1976. Section 204 of the 1976 Copyright Act simply provides that there may be a transfer of copyright ownership (which includes a mortgage) by an instrument in writing signed by the owner of the rights conveyed or by his or her authorized agent.

As stated above, the period within which a mortgage must be recorded for protection against subsequent assignees or mortgagees who obtained their interest for value without notice is set by the Copyright Act as 1 month from execution in the United States and 2 months from execution abroad. This permissible delay represents a convenience to a mortgagee. However, it creates a period of hiatus during which a lender cannot be certain that it is not a subsequent mortgagee lender being defrauded by the borrower. The only assurance possible is to make the mortgage commitment for payment effective 2 months after execution, provided there is a clear title report; of course, it will be a rare borrower who is willing to wait that long. The study made by the Copyright Office, in preparation for copyright act revision, is somewhat reassuring to the prospective bona fide lender in indicating that a significant majority of recordations of assignments or mortgages are made within 1 month of execution.

The procedure for recordation is to send the original mortgage document to the Copyright Office, preferably by registered or certified mail, along with the recordation fee of $80. For additional titles, the fee is $20 for each group of not more than 10 titles. The document should be submitted for recordation along with the required fee and the required cover page as furnished by the Copyright Office. The document, once recorded, will be returned to the sender with a certificate of recordation. A copy of the original document can be submitted instead of the original if accompanied by a sworn or official certification that the copy is a true copy of the original.

Under the Copyright Act, certificates of acknowledgment of transfers of copyright ownership (which includes mortgages) executed in the United States or elsewhere are considered prima facie evidence of the transfer.

The Recordation of Loans in Local Jurisdictions

One federal court has held that federal recordation is necessary to preserve a security interest in copyright mortgages and preempts state recordation systems. In the 1990 decision of *Peregrine Entertainment v. Capitol Federal Savings and Loan Association of Denver,* a district court of California held that a creditor bank's security interest in a film company's copyrights were unperfected because the bank failed to record its mortgage in the Copyright Office. Therefore, it is still generally considered desirable for maximum security that the mortgagee comply with both federal and state recordation law.

In a 1992 submission to Congress, the American Bar Association and the Copyright Office pointed out that it is unclear as to what extent the federal Copyright Act preempts the field in order to make state recordation unnecessary (although a persuasive argument can be made that there is such preemption). This concern was in connection with the then-pending Copyright Reform Act of 1993, which was never passed. One reason for compliance with state law is that the foreclosure of a copyright mortgage under court decisions is currently recognized as a matter for state law. When foreclosure of a copyright mortgage is sought and an independent ground of federal jurisdiction is available, such as diversity of citizenship of the parties, a federal court may accept jurisdiction over the controversy and apply state law to the foreclosure of a federally recorded mortgage.

State filing procedures are simplified in the music-centered states of New York, California, and Tennessee. Each state applies the Uniform Commercial Code, which recognizes mortgages on intangible property, such as copyrights. The UCC specifies that where national registration is available, as in copyrights, a state filing of a financial statement is not necessary nor is it effective protection for a lender unless accompanied by recordation in the U.S. Copyright Office.

In 1990, a federal district court ruling confirmed this status as a preemption of the Uniform Commercial Code, citing the need for national uniformity and the value of eliminating the expense involved in carrying out searches in numerous state jurisdictions with the concomitant risk of missing something along the way.

Sale of Property upon Default

In rare instances it may become necessary to sell the copyright in order to repay a loan. In such a case, consideration must be given to whether there should be a public or a private sale. In some security agreements, it is expressly provided that in the event of a breach or default by the mortgagor, at the mortgagee's option the copyrights can be sold at either a private or a public sale after a reasonable notice to the mortgagor. The usual practice is to advertise the sale in trade papers such as *Billboard,* with the mortgagee reserving the right to bid at the sale. In bidding, the mortgagee may take credit for all or part of the indebtedness against the purchase price.

In the mid-1970s the Union Planters Bank of Memphis, Tennessee, tried to auction off the mortgage it held on the East Memphis music catalog, whose owner, Stax Records, had defaulted. Before the auction a number of potential buyers made inquiries, but none made the required minimum bid to match the bank's *upset price* (the minimum price at which bids would be accepted in the auction). Accordingly, the bank became the owner and administrator of the catalog, pending exploration of other sale possibilities. The upset price reported was about $2 million, representing at least that amount loaned upon such security.

Some modern mortgage agreements, instead of specifying the various remedies of the mortgagee in the event of a default, merely adopt by reference the "remedies of a secured party under the Uniform Commercial Code." This law, adopted with some variation by all 50 states, sets forth in detail the sale procedures to be followed.

Exclusive State Recordation for Certain Rights

Part of a music publisher's general assets given as security for a loan may include certain assets that relate to copyright and yet are not statutory copyrights. One of these assets is known as *incomplete compositions*—works in progress for which no copyright registration has been obtained. Another asset is compositions to be written in the future under exclusive songwriter agreements. These common law copyrights and rights to future works are not protected under federal law; the only recordation procedure available for such rights is under state law.

Exclusive Writer Contracts

In evaluating an exclusive writer contract as an asset to secure payment of a loan, inspection of the contract must be made to determine whether there is any restriction on assignment in the event of foreclosure. Since the relationship between an exclusive writer and his or her publisher may be deemed highly personal, the contract should be expressly assignable if a lender is to be protected. In some instances, if the exclusive writer has a good relationship with his or her publisher, the writer may consent to a limited assignability in order to qualify the publisher for a loan that may also accrue to the writer's benefit.

The lender must also determine whether, as is frequently the case, there are unrecouped advances by the publisher to the writer. Such unrecouped advances constitute a valuable and well-defined asset if the writer's royalty statements show a consistent earnings history, since it is then clear that the advances can be charged against future earnings of the writer. On the other hand, without an earnings history, the advances should be largely disregarded because advances to writers are not ordinarily considered to be personal loans and are customarily recoupable only out of royalties otherwise due from the publisher to the writer.

Conditions on the Administration of a Loan

It would be a foolish business practice for a lender to forbid, out of a sense of extreme caution, any use of copyrights that are security for the loan, during the term of a loan. Such a prohibition might lead to the deterioration in value over an extended period of nonexploitation.

Just as in most business loans the trade reputation and skill of the borrower must be considered along with an analysis of his or her assets, so also the business skill of a music business borrower must be duly weighed. Even if the borrower is regarded as reputable and skillful, the lender is likely to stipulate that certain conditions in the conduct of the music business must be adhered to as long as the loan is outstanding. For example:

- ▶ No license shall be granted that extends beyond the term of the security agreement unless the specific written consent of the mortgagee is first obtained, except with respect to the continued clearance of public performance rights through ASCAP or BMI and except for nonexclusive phonograph record mechanical reproduction licenses.
- ▶ Any phonograph record mechanical reproduction license that is to extend beyond the term of the mortgage shall be issued at not less than the statutory rate for compulsory licenses, subject only to customary record club and budget record discounts.
- ▶ No license shall be granted or agency relationship created that involves the payment of money advances recoupable from earnings unless the full advance is applied upon receipt against the loan.
- ▶ No new version or arrangement can be made during the term of the mortgage unless the copyright is obtained by the mortgagor at its expense and the copyright is expressly made subject to the terms and provisions of the mortgage.
- ▶ No new lyric writer, composer, or arranger may be given any participation or claim of participation in rights or earnings of any of the mortgaged property, except on customary terms in the ordinary course of business, without the specific written consent of the mortgagee.

- All songwriter and composer royalties that may become due during the term of the security agreement shall be promptly segregated in a special bank account when collected, and shall be promptly remitted, together with required royalty statements, when contractually due. In the event that the borrower receives a claim of nonpayment or other breach in respect of such obligations or payment, written notice shall be promptly served upon the mortgagee.
- The provisions of the paragraph above shall also apply to royalties due under other agreements such as with a foreign original publisher whose composition is subpublished by the mortgagor.
- The mortgagee shall be promptly notified in writing of any claim by a third party that any of the mortgaged property infringes another work or lacks the required originality for a valid copyright.
- No infringement action shall be brought by or with the consent of the mortgagor without the written consent of the mortgagee.
- The services of a particular individual as general manager of the mortgagor shall continue during the term of the security agreement unless the mortgagee in writing shall approve his or her replacement.

Outstanding Advances at the Time of a Loan

The prospective lender should bear in mind that it is a well-established custom in the music industry for a music publisher to seek advances against future royalties. Advances not only finance the business but also assure proper exploitation by the party that makes the advances. These advances also ease the problem of delay in the collection of income, especially in fields such as foreign subpublishing.

In the past, advances from foreign subpublishers were less important than advances from the performing rights organizations. Both ASCAP and BMI have, however, as a general policy, discontinued making advances, except in emergency situations, although SESAC continues to make them. The Harry Fox Agency, which functions as a collection agent for mechanical royalties payable by record companies, does not make advances to music publishers either. By the same token, record companies do not make advances against mechanical income that arises from the sale of records. However, record companies may give advances against artist royalties to induce artist-writers to give mechanical licenses at a discount rate for so-called controlled compositions (see Chapter 2, page 21). Other instances of possible unrecouped advances occur in the case of prior grants of foreign subpublishing rights, print rights, and video and DVD licenses.

There are two types of advances—specific and general. A specific advance is recoupable only from the earnings of specified musical works or a single work. A general advance is usually recoupable from the earnings of the entire catalog. Even a general advance is not a general obligation. It bears no interest, it is a debit against a specific earnings account, and it does not ordinarily continue in effect beyond the term of the applicable agreement.

If advances exist at the time a loan is applied for, prudent business practice of the lender dictates that they be given due weight in determining the size of the loan as well as whether the borrower should be required to reduce the amount of the loan proceeds. At the same time, some credit rating value should be given to a publisher regarding the publisher's right to recoup advances from future writer royalties.

The Appraiser's Report and Representations of the Borrower

Most major music business loans and all Pullman securitization projects require expert business and legal analysis from accountants and attorneys who specialize in the field. However, even the experts must be given an accurate description of the property to be reviewed. The primary source of this information is the borrower. This information is subject to verification through various sources, such as the performing rights organizations, the Harry Fox Agency, and the Copyright Office. Here is a basic list of items or representations that a music publisher may be required to supply to a potential lender.

- Identification of the copyrights by title, author, composer, copyright registration number, and date of registration. Footnote details should be given if the balance of the current copyright term is not owned by the publisher or if the publisher has less than full ownership.
- A typical songwriter agreement and a footnote designation of any songwriter agreement with terms less favorable to the publisher.
- A representation that all songwriter royalty accounts are current unless otherwise stated.
- In the case of songs originating with a foreign or other third-party publisher, a representative subpublishing agreement and a specification of less favorable agreements and noncurrent royalty accounts.
- For any song where the borrower owns less than 100 percent of the U.S. rights, a designation of who has administrative rights and the responsibility to pay songwriter royalties.
- Copies of royalty statements from the performing rights societies of which the publisher is a member and from the Harry Fox Agency (last 5 years).
- A summary of all advances currently outstanding against the publisher's account.
- A summary of each unrecouped advance given by the publisher against songwriters, other publishers, or other third-party accounts and a designation of whether the advance is general or specific.
- A summary of miscellaneous income over the last 5 years (i.e., from commercial jingles, printed music uses, foreign licensees).
- A summary of all music deriving from or used in motion picture scores or musical plays.

- A list of exclusive writer contracts, showing the names of writers, the duration of exclusivity, and obligations for future salary payments or advances.
- For copyrights originating before 1978: a list of renewal copyright rights obtained from authors or their statutory successors (i.e., widows and children)—both copyrights presently in the renewal term and copyrights in their original term—showing the grantor, the title of the song, and the effective date of the renewal copyright period; whether any obligations were incurred over and above standard writer royalties; whether life insurance has been obtained or is obtainable on the grantor's life; and whether a notice of termination has been received for the 19-year extended period after the 56 years of copyright or the 20-year extension after the 75th year of the copyright.
- The cost of acquisition of any portion of the catalog acquired from other publishers and the amortization of such acquisition cost.
- A schedule of major physical assets such as recording equipment, studio, and real estate, together with the date and cost of acquisition.
- A schedule of master recordings owned or controlled by the publisher and the royalty arrangements involved.
- An inventory of printed goods on hand.
- A salary schedule of the publisher's personnel.
- A schedule of all rents and the duration of all leases.
- A schedule of the publisher's stockholders and outstanding stock as well as any pension or profit-sharing plans.
- A schedule of all liens and other encumbrances, both recorded and unrecorded.

Using this information, an expert appraiser can advise the prospective mortgagee regarding the potential future earnings and the resale value of the catalog involved.

The Bankruptcy of the Borrower

The voluntary or involuntary bankruptcy of a publisher has far-reaching consequences for potential creditors. Under the SGA contract, and under many other writer or subpublication agreements as well, the contract terminates and the copyright is subject to recapture in the event of bankruptcy. If such a provision is enforceable, the songs become worthless to the potential creditor of a bankrupt publisher. However, to the extent that such agreements are executory (which is the case when both parties have not performed their obligations), these termination provisions are likely to be invalid. Under Section 541(c) of the Bankruptcy Code, any provision in a contract expressly prohibiting any assignment is invalid with respect to an assignment that benefits the estate. Therefore, if the value of the bankrupt party's estate is increased owing to the continued ownership of compositions subject to these termination provisions, the compositions remain a part of the bankrupt party's estate.

Under copyright law, exclusive licenses and assignments of copyrights are transfers of ownership and therefore, under bankruptcy law, fully executed rather than executory, even though the assignee (the publisher) may have ongoing future royalty obligations. By contrast, nonexclusive licenses are likely to be executory. As a result, a bankruptcy trustee or assignee must assume the obligations under a nonexclusive license in order to continue deriving its benefits.

In the case of *In Re Waterson, Berlin & Snyder Co.*, 48 F.2d 704 (2d Cir. 1931), the court held that the sale of copyrights by a trustee in bankruptcy did not destroy a contractual obligation to pay future royalties to writers. This continuing obligation means that the purchaser at a bankruptcy sale, including the lender, cannot acquire copyrights free of future royalty obligations.

Finally, the federal Bankruptcy Code gives the trustee in bankruptcy (often the same as the debtor in possession) the ability to void certain transactions between the debtor and other persons which occurred prior to the filing for bankruptcy, the most important of which is the ability to void "preferences." The basic elements of a preference, as set forth in Section 547 of the Bankruptcy Code, are (1) a transfer of an interest in property (2) to or for the benefit of the debtor (3) for or on account of an antecedent debt (4) made while the debtor is insolvent (5) made within 90 days before the bankruptcy filing (one year if the creditor is an "insider" (6) which enables the creditor to receive more than he or she would have received in a liquidation of the debtor if the transfer had not occurred. The subject is a complicated one, but the general concept is not—namely not to permit the assets of the debtor available to other creditors to be depleted on the eve of bankruptcy by a transfer to a creditor which fits within the various criteria. The risks of preferences must always be taken into account when a lender structures a loan.

29

Printed Music

The business of music is not limited to supplying music to the listening public. There are millions of people who use printed music—in homes, schools, and a variety of entertainment venues. A recent survey sponsored by the International Music Products Association (NAMM) found that active music making takes place in half the homes of America. Whether the music makers are amateur or professional, they rely upon printed music in varying degrees. The aggregate earnings for sale of printed music in the year 2000 as reported by the National Music Publishers' Association was $316.05 million, a 5 percent increase over sales in 1999.

The NAMM survey stated:

> Printed music covers a very broad body of work, from simple popular tunes to full orchestral works; sale prices vary with the complexity of the work. These works may be published individually as sheet music, or in a wide variety of collections or folios. The works may be prepared, published and/or distributed by the original music publisher or its authorized (that is, licensed) print agent.

The market for printed music is related to and dependent upon the popularity of the instruments upon which the music will be performed. Table 29-1 gives 2001 sales figures for the most popular instruments.

Despite the fact that state and local budget cuts throughout the United States have resulted in a severe cutback in formal music education in public schools, music continues to be a vital part of most preschool and elementary programs, and extracurricular music activities in high school and college, from choral groups and marching bands to full concert orchestras, abound. In the United States, the Music Teachers National Association is comprised of 24,000 independent and collegiate music teachers. The National Association for Music Education has 90,000 members, including university faculty and researchers, college students preparing to enter the music teaching field, and active music teachers.

For all music makers—students, professionals, and amateurs—printed music is a vital resource.

Table 29-1

Sales of Musical Instruments in 2001

Instrument	No. of Units Sold	Dollar Totals ($millions, rounded up)
Electric guitar	895,110	$481.18
Acoustic guitar	847,388	$441.1
Woodwinds	365,220	$326.88
Brass	235,600	$236.79
Drum kits	186,732	$134.5
Strings	127,500	$63
Turntables	91,000	$13
Digital pianos	80,2000	$152
Keyboard synthesizers	64,418	$0.9
Vertical pianos	50,923	$173.7
Grand pianos	28,064	$378.9

Source: Paul Majeski, *The Music Trade.*

To meet the demand for multiple voice and instrument combinations, the number of different publications of the same song may exceed 40. Arrangements of popular music are often revised to satisfy the most recent taste of the public (for example, in the arrangement style of a recent hit recording). Similarly, classical and semiclassical music arrangements are modified from time to time to include different instrumentation and voices. The price and availability of a particular selection depend on what the music will be used for. To take just one category, music for piano, the types available are methods and studies, collections (folio), teaching and recital pieces, duets, two pianos, and solos (easy, regular, and intermediate). There are numerous printed editions of the single selection "Rhapsody in Blue," ranging from a full symphonic orchestra score with a list price of $85 to an organ solo of the theme selling for $3.95. A piece that is available in a wide range of individual printed forms will appear in folios, which are softcover collections, and in song books or albums. These may have a list price as high as $45 for the hardcover illustrated editions. A full symphonic orchestration of a major piece may cost as much as $75.

While there are exceptions for top hits, sheet music sales of most popular compositions are either small or nonexistent. A print order of 1,000 copies is not infrequent and many dance and rap songs never appear in sheet music form at all. If printed, popular songs are ordinarily released as piano-vocal sheet music or in folio format until they become accepted as standard hits.

EDUCATIONAL MUSIC

"Educational music" is music intended to be sold in schools, colleges, institutions, or industrial plants for performance by amateur musical groups. Included are solo or group arrangements of classical, semiclassical, and popular music deemed suitable for vocal or instrumental renditions.

Writer Royalties

Songwriter contracts in the field of popular music include specific royalties for various categories of printed editions. The rate for sheet music usually ranges between 8 and 12 cents per copy, although somewhat higher rates can be negotiated for established standard tunes or show or film titles, and 10 percent of the wholesale price for folios. The Popular Songwriters Contract used by the Songwriters Guild of America contains provisions for royalties to be paid on a sliding scale, from a minimum of 10 percent of the wholesale price for the first 200,000 copies to a minimum of 15 percent of wholesale price on copies sold in excess of 500,000. In practice, however, sliding scale royalties are rarely used, and many publishers simply compute the writer's share of royalties as 50 percent of their own share, which is 20 percent of receipts on sheet music and 10 to 12.5 percent on folios. The 50 percent computation is also used for sheet music that is downloaded from Internet sites (see below, page 289).

When a song is included in a folio or other collection, the Guild's contract, as well as many others, appropriately notes that the stated royalty must be prorated among all of the copyrighted songs in the compilation. Thus, in a folio of 10 copyrighted songs licensed at an aggregate of 10 percent royalty, each individual copyrighted song earns 1 percent.

Print Publishers

In today's market, the field for preparing, printing, and distributing folios is dominated by three large firms—Hal Leonard Publishing Corporation, Music Sales Corp, and Warner Brothers Publishing—all of which offer exclusive or nonexclusive services to other publishers. Even giant EMI, with hundreds of thousands of copyrights, elects to issue its printed music under licensing arrangements with Hal Leonard.

Print publishers operate either as licensees or selling agents. Licensee arrangements generally provide for payment to the music publisher of a negotiated royalty. The print publisher bears all costs of preparation and printing, as well as the risks of unsold inventory. Under the selling agent arrangement, which is less common, the music publisher pays the expense of preparation and printing and is entitled to the sales receipts less a commission to the agent.

When the print publisher is a licensee, the writer's share is fixed at 50 percent of royalties received, the same as for mechanical royalties. When the print publisher is a selling agent, most standard agreements specify that the rates are the same as when the music publisher is also the print publisher.

Royalties on Licensee Arrangements

Some typical rates, which are usually paid on net sales, are as follows:

- ▶ Educational band arrangements, choral and orchestra arrangements: 12$^1/_2$ percent of retail selling price

- ▸ Individual or separately printed copies of easy piano solos, guitar solos, and organ solos (piano-vocal, regular sheet music, not included in this category): 15 percent of the retail selling price
- ▸ Folios: A pro-rata portion of 12.5 percent of the retail selling price
- ▸ For regular piano-vocal copies: There may be payment of a stated amount, such as 60 cents per copy sold, or a percentage of the suggested retail list price, such as 20 percent

Sometimes, licensees will offer an advance to the music publisher, to be recoupable out of royalties on sales.

Selling Agent Agreements

As previously noted, folios are also issued through selling agents who are paid a commission for their services, with the costs of printing and preparation of editions charged to the account of the music publisher. The commissions charged are about 20 to 30 percent of the amounts received from sales.

Emphasizing its role as agent rather than licensee, one firm offers special procedures for exclusive selling-agent rights to an entire catalog for a period of years. All bills for printing by outside printers are rendered, and all sales invoices are issued, in the name of the song publisher at the address of the selling agent. Checks from jobbers and dealers in payment for printed editions are drawn directly to the order of the song publisher and these checks are transmitted monthly to the song publisher, together with statements showing the number of copies sold and the agent's bill for services rendered.

Term

The minimum term of the nonexclusive or exclusive licensee or sales agent agreements ranges from 1 to 5 years. The contracts frequently provide for automatic extensions from year to year, unless either party gives a written notice of termination prior to the anniversary date. A licensee-distributor will often be granted the right to sell off accumulated inventory on hand at the termination date subject to its rendering statements and paying royalties in accordance with the agreement between the parties. For protection, the publisher will limit this sell-off period—perhaps to 6 months, for example. Implicit in this arrangement is the condition that no additional printing will occur within the sell-off period, and it is desirable that a sworn statement of inventory be obtained at the commencement of the sell-off period. Such periods may vary with the particular product. For example, the sell-off period for sheet music and personality folios may be limited to 6 to 12 months, but may be extended to 18 months for mixed folios. If royalties have been prepaid on all inventory, the sell-off period may be unlimited.

Specialty Folios

Frequently, a *personality folio* is published in conjunction with a best-selling record of a recording artist or a group. The folio will include all the compositions on the record, whether or not they were written by the artist, together with likenesses or photographs of the artist and venues at which the artist performed, and a biography of the artist. The title of the folio is often the name of the recording artist and the title of the album, for example, *Garth Brooks's The Chase* or *Madonna's Erotica*. A personality folio may feature the works of one artist, but with selections from several albums, or may also include compositions written but not recorded by the featured star. Personality folios normally require written permission from the artist for the use of his or her name, likeness, and biography.

Some folios consist of the songs from a successful musical (e.g., *Chicago, Guys and Dolls,* or *The Music Man*), or from a best-selling motion picture soundtrack album (e.g., *Moulin Rouge* and *Sleepless in Seattle*). As with personality folios, this type of folio may include logo, artwork, and descriptive materials from the show or film, photographs of the performers and sets, and other items that make the folio valuable as a souvenir.

The distributor-licensee of such folios will pay the customary royalties of about 12.5 percent of the suggested retail selling price, pro-rata, to the licensing music publishers; an additional royalty of about 5 percent for the featured personality or materials is required.

Notice of Copyright

Since the United States joined the Berne Convention in 1989, the absence of a copyright notice on printed copies of music does not invalidate the copyright. When licensing print versions of words or music, however, it is highly desirable to require that the printed product carry the name of the copyright owner, the date of copyright, the copyright symbol or word, and the phrase "Used by permission." The inclusion of such notice has the practical advantage of advising potential cover artists and other users of the name and identity of the true owner. It also avoids certain defenses that might otherwise be available to infringers as to imposition of attorneys' fees and statutory damages. For more information on the advantages of including a complete copyright notice, see Chapter 10, page 87.

Fakebooks

An illegal, unauthorized compilation of the simple melody line and chord symbols for multiple tunes is called a *fakebook* (not named to call attention to their illegal status but because performing musicians can use them to play songs they haven't memorized). The most well known of the illegal fakebooks is a three-volume collection ironically called the *Real Book,* which contains thousands of jazz standards. The illegal printers and distributors of fakebooks pay no royalties to the composers and publishers of the songs contained in the fakebook. In effect, the fakebook replaces and substitutes for folios and sheet music, depriving writers and publishers of royalties and profits. Such lost revenues can be extensive: assuming a retail price of $3.95 for the sheet music of a popular song, a legal compilation containing the music for 1,000 songs would sell for over $3,500. An illegal fakebook with 1,000 songs may be sold for as little as $35.

The bargain price to the user and the profit to the illicit printer and distributor make fakebooks difficult to control. However, substantial awards of damages under the Copyright Act have been made against fakebook printers and distributors, and dealers who sell them are also held liable. Fakebook activities are punishable under Section 506 of the Copyright Act, either as misdemeanors or, when there are large sums involved and/or repeated offenses, by imprisonment.

To combat the proliferation of fakebooks, many legitimate music publishers, including Hal Leonard and Warner, now produce low-priced legal fakebooks which contain extensive collections of legitimately compiled songs, both for favorites from different genres and for specific categories, which are fully licensed by the appropriate publishers and which sell for as little as $30.

Return Privileges and Reserves

The granting by distributors of *return privileges* to jobbers or dealers means that they may return unsold copies to the seller. Most songs are popular hits on the charts for a limited period, and sheet music of those songs is likely to sell only during that period. Return privileges may ensure that the jobber or dealer will stock sufficient copies to be able to satisfy the public demand during the peak popularity of the song.

To protect themselves from the negative effects of returns, licensees commonly maintain reserves to avoid overpayment of royalties. The reserve quantity, whether or not it has been sold, is treated as if has not been sold, and therefore royalties are not paid. Suppose, for example, a distributor has sold 1,000 copies of the sheet music for a song but the reserve clause specifies that 25 percent of net sales will be held as reserves against returns for the first quarter of an annual accounting period. The distributor would pay royalties to the music publisher only on 750 copies. Typical reserves are as high as 50 percent for the first quarter period of sales, diminishing to 25 percent for the second quarter, 15 percent for the third quarter, and no reserves for the fourth quarter. Another way to ensure that dealers carry sufficient stock to meet peak demands is to offer steep discounts if the dealer stocks the product in large quantities *without* return privileges.

Discounts

The basic discount structure for sales on daily orders for jobbers is 50 to 55 percent of the retail price. For retail dealers, the discounts on daily orders range from 40 to 50 percent of retail, although only 33.3 percent is offered on educational editions. Discounts for qualifying stock orders (large semiannual orders) are higher, ranging from 55 percent to, in a few cases, 60 percent to jobbers and from 45 to 55 percent to dealers. Companies that order semiannually are also given dating advantages affecting return privileges ranging from 90 days for domestic to 120 days for foreign.

Discount ratings are often based on volume and regularity, whether or not the company orders on a daily or stock basis. Additional discounts are also sometimes offered when a dealer is willing to buy and display "new issues"—new printed editions—in specific music categories. The new-issue discount may be as much as an extra 10 percent of the normal discounted figure.

Subpublishing Deals

Like sound recordings, popular printed music is not exported but licensed for printing to foreign subpublishers. In some instances print licensees will obtain worldwide printing rights and will produce folios that can be sold throughout the world. One prominent licensee prints for the world in the United States and exports quantities of folios for foreign distribution to international distributors. Under the terms of the licensee printing arrangement with subpublishers, the foreign subpublisher agrees to pay the U.S. publisher a royalty, commonly a minimum of 10 percent of the retail price, which is usually divided equally between the U.S. writer and publisher.

Since administering the collection of mechanical license fees and performance fees is, as a rule, more lucrative than the handling of printed editions, some U.S. publishers encourage printing in a foreign country by providing that the subpublisher's share of mechanical royalties and performance fees will be lower for unprinted songs than for those that are printed. The question of whether a folio publication, as distinguished from sheet music, satisfies the "print" requirement should be covered in the agreement with the subpublisher.

The Internet: Digital Sales and Distribution

The digital age has ushered in a renaissance in the sales and distribution of popular sheet music and music folios, as well as provided new opportunities for individual artists and groups to transcribe and print their own sheet music. One Internet site, sheetmusicdirect.com, which is a joint venture started by Hal Leonard and Music Sales, offers downloadable selections that can be printed on home computers and/or mail-order sales of 366,000 titles, a selection which dwarfs even the largest bricks-and-mortar wholesalers (50,000 titles) and big-city retailers (at best 10,000). There are numerous competitors. One competitor, musicnotes.com, offers 15,000 digital sheet music titles and over 250,000 music books, single sheets, and other nondigital products. Prices for downloadable, single-selection sheet music range from free (for music in the public domain) to about $5.

The files that can be downloaded from sheetmusicdirect.com are prepared using a music notation software package called Sibelius, a program that makes it possible for users to create a digital file in one of several ways: inputting the score manually using a computer keyboard in conjunction with a MIDI keyboard, generating the score from a MIDI file, playing it manually, or scanning an already printed score. Sibelius, which supports a wide range of notations, is an interactive program, which means that composers and musicians can edit their work while it is still in digital form. Digital sheet music can be published on CDs, delivered via the Internet, or sent to printers specializing in the production of top-quality, color-enhanced folios.

Part Four

Other Aspects
of the Music Business

30

Privacy and Publicity Rights

The music and record industries thrive on publicity. Sales of records are stimulated by the use of a top artist's name or portrait on an album jacket. The use of an artist's name and likeness on sheet music and song folios is a valuable marketing device. In addition, television and radio commercials often use an artist's name or voice in advertising products. Hotels, resorts, and amusement parks frequently announce, by name and photograph, the personal appearance of top artists or make other similar associations between artists and merchandise. Items such as T-shirts, buttons, and posters featuring recording artists' likeness are valuable tie-ins with record sales. Although most of these uses are eagerly sought by artists and the industry and may be permissible by virtue of the operative contractual provisions, careful consideration must be given in each instance to the individual's right to control and benefit from the so-called rights of privacy and publicity.

The Right of Privacy

The right of privacy, or the personal right "to be let alone," is a relatively new Anglo-American legal concept. Impetus to the development of this right is largely attributed to a *Harvard Law Review* article by Samuel D. Warren and Louis D. Brandeis, published in 1890. They wrote:

> The press is overstepping in every direction the obvious bounds of propriety and of decency. Gossip is no longer the resource of the idle and of the vicious, but has become a trade, which is pursued with industry as well as effrontery. To satisfy a prurient taste the details of sexual relations are spread broadcast in the columns of the daily papers. To occupy the indolent, column upon column is filled with idle gossip, which can only be procured by intrusion upon the domestic circle. The intensity and complexity of life, attendant upon advancing civilization, have rendered necessary

some retreat from the world, and man, under the refining influence of culture, has become more sensitive to publicity, so that solitude and privacy have become more essential to the individual; but modern enterprises and inventions have, through invasions upon his privacy, subjected him to mental pain and distress, far greater than could be inflicted by mere bodily injury.

Warren and Brandeis sought recognition of a separate right distinct from defamation, contract, or property rights. At first there was some hesitation in legal circles to endorse this right of privacy. The highest court of the first state to directly confront the concept, New York, rejected the notion that there existed a separate legal right of privacy in that state. Reacting to this decision, the New York legislature enacted a statute that today is found in Sections 50 and 51 of the Civil Rights Law. This statute makes it a misdemeanor for a person, firm, or corporation to use for "advertising purposes, or for the purpose of trade, the name, portrait or picture of any living person" without first obtaining written consent. The statute also permits suit for injunctive relief as well as damages, including, in some cases, punitive damages.

As time went by, other states—including Oklahoma, Utah, Virginia, and California—adopted acts similar to New York's. Today the right of privacy is recognized either by statute or through judicial decision in all but a few jurisdictions in the United States. Furthermore, the U.S. Supreme Court has said that an independent right of privacy is guaranteed by the Constitution against certain governmental interference.

The Right of Privacy and Freedom of the Press

The constitutional guarantees of freedom of speech and the press may be raised in opposition to a claim for invasion of privacy. Under the Supreme Court's holdings, the right of privacy cannot be asserted to prohibit the publication of matters that are "newsworthy." In other words, matters of public interest are allowed, even if the report is false, unless there is proof that the defendant published the report with knowledge of its falsity or in reckless disregard of its truth. This doctrine applies to an individual who is a "public figure" as well as an individual who may have been thrust into an event of public interest. A performing artist may well be viewed as a "public figure" in connection with his or her public activities. In addition, news functions or informative presentations are not considered to be limited to newspapers; magazines, newsreels, radio, television, and books have received this privilege as well.

Generally, the defense of freedom of speech or press would not apply to certain types of commercial speech, for example, an advertisement using the endorsement of a public figure, such as a celebrity. A defense of *express waiver* may be asserted—in other words, that the individual consented to the use. Under certain statutes, this consent must be in writing. Other defenses may stress that the use was incidental or insignificant, such as the mere mention of a celebrity's name in a film or book, or that the use was not for purposes of "advertising" or "trade" in jurisdictions where this type of use is prohibited by statute.

The Right of Publicity

The music and record industries' concern in their daily operations is how the exploitation of a personality is affected by the individual's right to privacy on the one hand and right of publicity on the other. In most instances, the primary concern of an artist is to obtain publicity and have his or her name and vocal or visual likeness recognized by the public. The artist does not seek privacy as much as control over and benefit from the commercial use of his or her name, photograph, and likeness. Some jurisdictions have recognized the legitimacy of this right of publicity and have granted it recognition either by statute or by case law. This right, which protects the ability of an individual to control and profit from the publicity values that the artist has achieved, is similar in theory to the exclusive right of a commercial enterprise to the benefits that goodwill and secondary meaning of its name produce. In those cases in which pure privacy theory might be unsuccessfully invoked, such as when the artist with a celebrity status may be considered a public figure, the right of publicity may nevertheless be successfully asserted.

This concept is generally credited as having grown from the 1986 case of *Original Appalachian Artworks, Inc. v. Topps Chewing Gum, Inc.,* 642 F. Supp. 1031, which dealt with baseball cards. In that case, a chewing gum manufacturer had entered into agreements with ballplayers for the exclusive right, for a limited time, to use the ballplayers' likenesses on baseball cards. Subsequently, another gum manufacturer obtained similar rights from the same ballplayers. The first gum manufacturer sued the second to protect its exclusive rights in the photographs. The defendant argued that the action was in privacy, that privacy actions were personal and not assignable, and that only the ballplayers had the legal standing to sue. The late Judge Jerome Frank said:

> In addition to and independent of that right of privacy . . . a man
> has a right in the publicity value of his photograph, i.e., the right
> to grant the exclusive privilege of publishing his picture . . . .
> This right might be called a "right of publicity." For it is common
> knowledge that many prominent persons (especially actors and
> ballplayers) far from having their feelings bruised through public
> exposure of their likenesses would feel sorely deprived if they no
> longer received money for authorizing advertisements.

Thus, the court recognized the right of publicity and distinguished this right from the pure privacy theory. This was also significant because, without a contrary statute, the right of privacy is a personal right that terminates on the death of the individual. In New York, any right of publicity also terminates on death of the individual. Therefore, the right of publicity cannot be transferred to heirs. However, the majority of states (such as California) hold that the right survives death; as a precondition in such cases, though, the courts generally require that the right must have been exploited during the lifetime of the celebrity, for example, by the licensing of merchandising rights.

In right of publicity cases, the unauthorized use of a celebrity's name or likeness in connection with the dissemination of news or information of public interest is usually held to be privileged under the constitutional guarantees of the freedom of speech and of the press. This treatment is similar to that accorded in right of privacy cases. The constitutional privilege would not ordinarily apply where the unauthorized "use" is for commercial exploitation.

A number of issues come into play when dealing with issues of rights of publicity concerning celebrity names and likenesses, including free speech and the purpose of the use of the name and/or likeness (for example, has the name/image been used for purely commercial purposes, say to sell a product?). In 1999, Dustin Hoffman sued *Los Angeles Magazine* for publishing, without his authorization, a digitally altered image of him as the Tootsie character in the film of the same name in an article in *Los Angeles Magazine* entitled "Grand Illusions." The article contained pictures of clothing designed by fashion designers who were among the magazine's cover advertisers, and included a photo of Hoffman's head taken from *Tootsie* digitally superimposed on the body of a model who was wearing a gown designed by Richard Tyler and shoes by Ralph Lauren (neither was worn by Hoffman in the movie). Hoffman was originally awarded $3 million by a U.S. district court on the grounds that the magazine's "free speech" was commercial in nature. However, this verdict was reversed on appeal, with the Circuit Court of Appeals holding that the article was not "commercial," which would have been excluded from First Amendment protection. Furthermore, since the article stated, more than once, that the photographs had been digitally altered, there was no misrepresentation that the actor had actually posed in that manner or approved the use and no clear and convincing evidence of actual malice. The court noted that if the same altered photo had been used in a Ralph Lauren advertisement, the result might have been different (*Hoffman v. Capital Cities/ABC*, 255 F.3d 1180 [9th Cir. 2001]).

The Use of Name or Likeness for Trade or Advertising

In those jurisdictions that recognize that the individual has the right to control the use of his or her name or likeness, whether under a right of publicity or a right of privacy, the individual is protected against the unauthorized commercial use of his or her name or likeness, such as in an advertisement on T-shirts or in posters endorsing a commercial product.

As noted above, under a New York statute it is a criminal misdemeanor and the basis for an action for injunction and damages to use the name, portrait, or picture, for advertising or trade purposes, of any living person without written consent or, if a minor, the consent of the minor's parent or guardian. At the same time, this statute indicates that it shall not be construed to prevent the use of the "name, portrait or picture of any author, composer or artist in connection with his literary, musical or artistic productions which he has sold or disposed of with such name, portrait, or picture used in connection therewith." Consequently, the name of a composer can be used without written consent in connection with an authorized record of the author's composition.

Although California courts have recognized a right of privacy under the common law, the California legislature has enacted a statute dealing with the use of a person's name, photograph, or likeness for purposes of advertising products or services or for purposes of solicitation of purchases of products or services. Under this statute, any person who knowingly makes such use without the injured person's prior consent or, if a minor, the prior consent of a parent or guardian, is liable for any damages sustained by the injured person. In addition, the person violating this law is liable to the injured party for no less than $300. The statute provides, however, that the "use of a name, photograph, or likeness in connection with any news, public affairs or sports broadcast or account, or political campaign shall not constitute a use for purposes of advertising or solicitation."

In *White v. Samsung Electronics America,* 971 F.2d 1395 (9th Cir. 1992), a federal court of appeals applying California case law ruled that TV star Vanna White could protect herself even when there was no use of name, voice, signature, or likeness. The case involved a robot dressed in White's style with hair in her style and standing before a Wheel of Fortune, which further tied the robot to Vanna White. This evocation of the star's image was held to be a violation of rights without reliance on the California statute itself. Many other jurisdictions, as well as a strong dissenting opinion in the California federal appeals court, consider this to be an extreme holding. Moreover, this case is significant because Vanna White resides in California, as do many other stars, and the ruling further stated that the star's place of domicile determines the applicable law, regardless of where the advertising is shown.

California and Tennessee have both passed special legislation affecting unauthorized posthumous exercise of rights of publicity for commercial purposes for periods of 50 years and 10 years, respectively, after death. However, with respect to California decedents, it is essential to note that there are specific registration requirements and statutory filing fees if recovery is to be sought from such uses.

In contrast to New York practice, most states that recognize the individual's right to control the use of his or her name or likeness do not require written consent to the use of such name or picture. Such consent may be oral or may be established by the custom of the business involved.

Privacy Contract Clauses

Contracts in the fields of music and records often seek to prevent problems with the right of privacy or the right of publicity by including specific provisions regarding the use of name, image, or biographical material. Exclusive recording contracts between an artist and a record company usually state that the record company has the sole right to use and authorize others to use the artist's name, signature, likeness, and biographical material in connection with the artist's services under the agreement. This not only grants the required consent to the record company but may also serve as the basis for prohibiting another record company from similar use. Some record contracts also provide for the record company to handle "merchandising rights" in an artist's name and likeness. This covers such situations as the licensing of posters, T-shirts, buttons, and similar items, frequently on a basis that the artist will receive 50 percent of the company's net receipts.

Under the form of agreement developed by the American Federation of Musicians between a musician and a booking agent, the agent is granted rights to use the musician's name and likeness, and the right to authorize others to make such use, for advertising and publicity.

Careful drafting is necessary to properly delineate the rights that are to be transferred from the artist to the contracting company. In cases involving merchandising rights to the character of Count Dracula as portrayed by Bela Lugosi, and the commercial rights to the names and likenesses of Laurel and Hardy, the courts were called on to decide whether, under certain types of grant clauses, the performers had transferred their entire exclusive merchandising rights. In both instances the courts held that they had not and that the film companies had acquired only the right to use their name and likenesses in connection with specific films for which the performers had rendered their services. Where the contract is silent with respect to these rights, the courts may find that the rights remain with the artist.

Similarly, a divergence between the use authorized by the artist and the actual use made of his or her name, likeness, or biographical material may lead to a privacy suit. A slight variation in use may be insufficient to be actionable.

Works in the Public Domain

Reliance on the right of privacy was unsuccessful in preventing the publication of uncopyrighted works of Mark Twain under his name. The same theory was also rejected in the use of uncopyrighted Russian music with accurate composer credits given to Khatchaturian, Prokofiev, and Shostakovich. When a work is unprotected by copyright, there is no obligation to drop author credit; in fact, failing to give credit would appear to be more objectionable.

False attribution of a writer as author of a work not written entirely by that person may itself be held to be an invasion of the right of privacy. Such a writer would justifiably complain against an unfair appropriation of his or her reputation and possible damage to the reputation by a false author's credit. This frequently occurs in stage works where the writer wants to avoid unfavorable reviews by critics.

When a name or likeness is considered part of the public domain, such as the face of George Washington or a recording of Alexander Graham Bell's voice, it is considered a valuable part of cultural history. One judge said of attempts to extend rights of publicity into what should be public domain "as harmful as underprotecting [intellectual property]. Creativity is impossible without a rich public domain."

Remedies for the Invasion of Privacy

There are three types of relief granted by courts in cases where the right of privacy has been found to have been invaded. Courts may grant damages, issue injunctions prohibiting such conduct, and impose criminal penalties against the defendant.

Criminal penalties, where available, are rarely imposed. In New York, Virginia, Utah, and Oklahoma, a violation of the privacy statute is a misdemeanor. Yet the vast majority of cases brought under a statute such as New York's are civil actions.

Generally, a plaintiff in a privacy action is seeking redress in compensatory damages and, for certain abuses where malice is shown, punitive damages. There may be a damage award for mental pain and suffering, without proof by the plaintiff of actual monetary losses. In right-of-publicity cases, the measure of damages may be what the misappropriated right is worth rather than actual damages.

31

The Protection of Ideas and Titles

Hank Ballard, the originator of the twist, receives no royalties from other individuals who have profited from that dance. Chubby Checker, who became synonymous with the twist in the public eye and reaped huge financial rewards, never paid a dime to Ballard for copying the dance. Similarly, a rival network was able to copy the idea of the superstrong *Six Million Dollar Man* in a counterpart program entitled *The Bionic Woman* without fear of penalty.

Ideas themselves are not copyrightable and are ordinarily free for the taking due to the belief that society benefits from their free dissemination. Courts do, however, protect the manner in which ideas are expressed. For example, while a song lyric about aliens from Mars cannot be copied, another writer is free to pen a different lyric concerning Martian invaders.

The courts also give copyright owners the exclusive right to develop copyrighted material for further exploitation. For instance, a song such as "Frosty, the Snowman" can be developed into a storybook only with the consent of the copyright owner, and a novel can be dramatized only with the permission of its copyright owner (usually the author). The reproduction of a doll or other three-dimensional form based on a distinctive character in story or song—such as Superman, Spider-Man, or Alvin and the Chipmunks—is also an exclusive right stemming from copyright. and is separate and apart from the dialogue of the characters in the story.

The legal bases for the protection of the development of such characters are a mixture of copyright law (for artistic, written, or three-dimensional reproduction of a fictional character) and principles governing unfair competition. The latter principle has been applied to prevent the misappropriation by one person of the results of another individual's labors.

Compensation for Ideas

Ideas themselves are safeguarded when disclosed privately under circumstances indicating a mutual understanding, express or implied, that there will be remuneration if they are used. In one case, the plaintiff had submitted to the secretary of a movie producer, orally and by a short outline in writing, the idea for a motion picture on the life of Floyd Collins, who had been trapped and had died in a cave after extensive rescue efforts. The plaintiff alleged that he had made it clear he was to be paid if the idea was used and the secretary had agreed. The defendant film producer subsequently made a motion picture on the life of Collins. The appellate court in California found, on the basis of the plaintiff's allegations, a claimed implied contract to pay for the plaintiff's services that would result in liability if, after a full trial, it was proved that there actually was such an understanding between the parties and that the synopsis as delivered by the plaintiff, in reliance on such an agreement, was the basis of the resulting film. This ruling was made despite the fact that the story was in the public domain, having been fully explored in the press.

In another breach of contract case, a California court held that the movie *Coming to America* was based on a two-page treatment by columnist Art Buchwald entitled "It's a Crude, Crude World," and that Buchwald and his producer, Alain Bernheim, were entitled to $150,000 and $750,000, respectively, for their contributions.

In the absence of an express or implied contract to pay, the courts have sometimes held a defendant liable for the use of a plaintiff's idea on the theory that otherwise the defendant would be unjustly enriched. This can result when the situation is similar to a contract relationship but essential elements of contractual agreement are lacking. For example, if an agent promises to pay, without authorization, for an idea accepted on behalf of a defendant, the defendant may be held liable if he or she uses the idea.

Some courts protect ideas on the grounds of a breach of a confidential relationship. This may occur, for example, with regard to secret ideas disclosed in an employer-employee relationship. A court has held that where there was a confidential relationship and the plaintiff disclosed to the defendant a little-known song in the public domain discovered by the plaintiff, the defendant could not exploit the song.

Issues of Concreteness and Originality

While it is sometimes stated that a plaintiff must prove that his or her idea was novel and original and that it was reduced to concrete form, the facts necessary for such proof may vary widely. For example, the combination of three old ideas has been held to constitute a novel and original idea.

It is generally accepted that an idea need not be reduced to writing to be considered "concrete." To some courts, a concrete idea is one that has been developed to the point of availability for use. A concrete idea is sometimes explained as being different from an abstract idea and as having the status of property.

If an idea is reduced to writing it may be protected by copyright on the basis of being considered an "original work . . . of authorship fixed in [a] tangible medium of expression" under the standards of Section 102 of the Copyright Act. This protection extends from fixation. The written expression can be submitted for registration as an unpublished work in the Copyright Office. Similarly, the recording of an idea can also be regarded as fixed and protected by copyright and may be registered as an unpublished work.

A further method employed by songwriters or record producers to establish the creation and date of origin of a work is to enclose their material in carefully sealed envelopes and to mail the material to themselves by registered mail, which, when received, remains unopened. This approach may be more effective than registration in maintaining the privacy of the idea, but is less reliable than an official registration.

In all cases, for their protection, informed songwriters, music publishers, and record producers should maintain complete and up-to-date records indicating when and to whom proposals were submitted, including files of all letters accompanying enclosures.

The Consideration of Unsolicited Ideas

Bearing in mind the potential litigation that may result from the disclosure of ideas, some companies, including music publishers and record companies, have adopted a policy of not considering unsolicited ideas. In this way lawsuits and attorneys' fees can clearly be avoided. If possible, the incoming material should be routed to persons, such as the comptroller, who have no responsibility for creative endeavors. The material should be handled by form replies and returned. While it can be argued that valuable ideas may be lost through this practice, professionals in the field can be trusted to supply most marketable ideas.

Some companies refuse to review an idea unless the submitter signs a release. One form of release makes the company and its officers the sole arbiter of the novelty, usability, and value of the idea. Since the company's obligations are so indefinite, there is some doubt as to the legal enforceability of this type of release.

Another form of release provides that the parties will mutually agree on the value of an idea that is used, but if they disagree, the maximum value of the idea is fixed at a certain sum, such as $500 or $1,000, or the release may provide for a fixed sum, say $500, if the idea is used. This type of release is probably more enforceable than a release under which the company and its officers have complete discretion.

As a word of caution, however, it should be recognized that even the release form is to the benefit of the company, not the submitter.

The Use of Titles

Titles are not subject to copyright protection. For example, the title "Stardust" is not protected by the Copyright Act. Titles have long been protected by the doctrine of unfair competition, which will be applied to titles that have achieved a secondary meaning in the eyes of the public as being associated with particular works. Most titles do not have a secondary meaning. A casual check of the ASCAP or BMI indexes or of the Copyright Office records will reveal numerous instances of title duplications. Indirectly, some copyright protection of titles can be accomplished by inserting them into the body of the song lyric.

Secondary meaning is more easily achieved when a title is fanciful and uses arbitrarily selected word groupings rather than generally descriptive or frequently used phrases. For example, "My Only Love" or "Yours Sincerely" are general phrases that probably could not be preempted. On the other hand, "Begin the Beguine" is a fanciful, unique title. It is also possible that even a geographic description not otherwise capable of being a trademark, such as "Oklahoma" or "South Pacific" might, over the years, establish such solid public perception of them as Rodgers and Hammerstein works that they acquire secondary meaning.

A secondary meaning is not necessarily permanent. Since unfair competition is not a copyright concept, there is no fixed period of exclusive protection and no easily determined date when the protection ceases and the title is in the public domain. The determining factor is failure to use or exploit for a sufficient period of time to constitute abandonment. "Information Please" was a valuable title during its use on radio, but if not for the almanac using the title *Information Please,* it might be considered abandoned today and therefore available for anyone. Public identification does not necessarily mean that the title is associated with public success. The play *Slightly Scandalous* had a short life and was a commercial failure, but it nevertheless had sufficient secondary meaning to serve as the basis for an injunction against a motion picture of the same name.

Music is an essential ingredient of, and sister field to, motion pictures. It is common for a major motion picture to popularize a theme song from the movie with the same title. Many a film trades on the established goodwill of a well-known song title. Irving Berlin's "White Christmas," first sung by Bing Crosby in the film *Holiday Inn,* went on to be a great song success and was even used in another film entitled *White Christmas.* Likewise, the film originally identified with the biography *The Jane Froman Story* was released, finally, under the title *With a Song in My Heart.* The publisher of the relatively new success at the time, "Young at Heart," was paid $15,000 for a synchronization license and title use for a Warner Bros. picture of the same name. In addition, a popular song known as "Ode to Billy Joe" was featured in the music and story line of a film with that title.

Song titles are frequently used as the titles of record albums, as a natural identification of the type of music in the album, although the title song is often only one-tenth of the contents of the record. "Love Story," a composition from the popular film of the same title, was the title of a number of albums issued by different record companies. Rarely is the publisher paid a premium for such title use, but in one case, where the song was omitted from the record, a special royalty was paid. It is arguable that, on the same theory that a motion picture producer pays for the use of a song title for a motion picture, a record company should make a special payment for the right to use a song title as the title of an album.

32

Names and Trademarks

One cannot overemphasize the value of names in the music industry. The tremendous variety in names of artists, record companies, and music publishers ranges from names that simply identify, such as the Harry Connick Jr. Orchestra, Sony Records, and the Famous Music Corporation, to such fanciful names as the Backstreet Boys, Pearl Jam, the Spice Girls, and the Dixie Chicks. The names of record companies and music publishers are relatively insignificant in terms of their influence on consumer purchases in popular music. Consumers don't go to music stores and request a "Dwarf Music song" or an "Acuff-Rose Music song." They purchase recordings by artist name. They will ask for Korn (on Sony/Epic) or Sheryl Crow (on Universal/A&M) or Bruce Springsteen (Columbia).

The goodwill attached to names in the music business is even more important in music industry circles. A dealer or jobber is more likely to stock and feature a new record released by a successful and established record label or artist than a record by a new firm or artist. An artist may favor a recording agreement with Sony Records over one with a lesser label. A writer may prefer to enter a contract with Warner/Chappell Music than with a less well-known publisher.

In the field of classical (sometimes called "serious") and educational music publishing, the names of established publishers tend to have greater value than the names of those in popular music. Purchasers of classical music rely on and respect the editorial selection and quality standards of well-known classical music publishers, whereas in the popular music field, printed sales usually depend on prior popular music recordings to stimulate consumer interest. Similarly, the consumer seeking a classical music recording may be influenced by the reputation of the record company on whose label the recording is released; certain labels have achieved a reputation for both technical and artistic quality.

The selection, protection, and development of names and trademarks are complex matters. The names and trademarks must be distinctive enough that property rights accrue to the proper persons or firms. For product identification they should not infringe on other persons' or firms' rights in names or trademarks previously used. Close similarity can lead to confusion concerning product, credit problems, misdirection of mail and telephone calls, and legal entanglements.

Copyrightability

There is no protection for brand names, trademarks, slogans, and other short phrases or expressions under the Copyright Act, nor may familiar symbols or designs qualify for copyright registration in and of themselves. Legal protection of a name, slogan, phrase, or symbol must generally come from common law, the law of unfair competition, and registration under federal trademark law or the trademark laws of the individual states.

The Copyright Act does provide that copyright can be obtained in "pictorial, graphic and sculptural works." In order to be copyrightable, a work must include an appreciable amount of original text or pictorial materials. Consequently, copyright may apply to qualifying prints, advertisements, and labels used in connection with the sale or advertisement of articles of merchandise. For example, a record label named Mountainview in conjunction with a photograph of Mount Vesuvius might seek copyright protection, in addition to protection under trademark law. The copyright protection would, however, not extend to the name separate and apart from the pictorial matter.

Trademarks and Service Marks

There are two types of marks that can be registered in the U.S. Patent and Trademark Office in Washington, D.C. The *trademark* distinguishes a product and identifies its origins: for example, the RCA Victor name and the logo of a dog with a phonograph. The *service mark* is used in the sale or advertising of services to identify the services of one person and distinguish them from the services of others: for example, Jay-Z. In some cases the identical mark may be used as both a trademark and a service mark by the same business, such as one selling musical instruments and rendering repair services under the same mark.

While service marks are often incorrectly referred to as trademarks, there are usually no important legal consequences resulting from the use of the incorrect terminology. Unless indicated otherwise, the word "trademark" as used in this chapter should be considered to include "service mark."

Differentiating Between Copyrights and Trademarks

There is a tendency among people in the music business to refer to "copyright" when they mean exclusive rights that are available only through trademark protection or through rules of law relating to unfair competition. A simple distinction between copyright and trademarks is that copyright protects the *fixed expression* of literary, artistic, and musical works of authorship, whereas trademarks and service marks serve as *badges of identification* that protect the goodwill attached to a particular product or service and safeguard the public from confusion as to the source or identity of the products or services involved. Other differences between copyright and trademarks are outlined in Table 32-1.

Table 32-1

Differences Between Copyrights and Trademarks

Copyright	**Trademark**
▶ The duration is ordinarily limited to the life of the author plus 70 years.	▶ There is an unlimited number of successive 10-year terms.*
▶ The certificate is issued by the government without prior search for conflicting claims or prior notice to the public.	▶ The certificate is issued by the government only after a search for conflicting marks, notice to the public of the pending application, and an opportunity for objections to be filed.
▶ Notice of copyright may be used from the first publication.	▶ Notice indicating registered federal trademark is not permitted until after registration.
▶ Statutory protection begins at fixation in a copy.	
▶ Registration of copyright is permitted for unpublished or published music at any time during the term of copyright protection.	▶ Common law protection begins at use.
	▶ The registration of trademark is not achieved (even if application has been previously filed) until after proven use in interstate commerce or in commerce between a state and a foreign country.
▶ Originality is required for a valid copyright.	
▶ Copyright is fully assignable.	
▶ The licensee of a copyright need not be supervised by the owner of copyright.	▶ Originality or novelty is not essential for a valid trademark. Identification with product or service is significant.
▶ Under the Copyright Act of 1909, duration was limited to the original 28-year term plus one 28-year renewal, since extended for works fixed before 1978 to a total of 95 years.	▶ Trademark is assignable only with the goodwill of the business in which the mark is used.
▶ Under the 1909 Act, the statutory protection of unpublished compositions was conditioned on registration; prior to registration there was common law protection.	▶ The licensee of the trademark must be under the owner's supervision and control to ensure that the product's identity, quality, and character are preserved.

*Prior to the Trademark Law Revision Act of 1988, successive 20-year terms were applicable.

The Selection of a Name

Choosing and registering a name for a record label or band can be a complex and time-consuming task. Not only must the name be appropriate for the label or group, it must not conflict with an already-registered name belonging to another entity. Within the music industry, the stories are numerous and legendary regarding the sources of inspiration for new names. For instance, the historic record label Stax is a combination of the names of its two founders, Jim Stewart and Estelle Axton. Laura Nyro's firm, Tuna Fish Music, memorializes her favorite sandwich. Certain names represent an attempt to present a consolidated trade image. For example, Screen-Gems-EMI Music indicates an identification with its original parent company, Capitol-EMI. BMG Classics is a label owned by BMG Entertainment. Warner Bros. Music was a change of name from the former Music Publishers Holding Company, purchased by Warner Bros. Pictures in 1929. Then in the late 1980s Warner Bros. Music acquired Chappell Music and became Warner/Chappell Music. Before their sale in 1986, CBS had two publishing firms, April Music and Blackwood Music; the initial letters of their names provided an easy identification as to which was the ASCAP-affiliated firm and which was the BMI-affiliated firm.

There are various ways to go about selecting names for corporations or trademarks. A choice may be made from different categories, just as the U.S. Weather Bureau uses male and female names in alphabetical order to denote successive hurricanes, and the U.S. Navy uses the names of fish to differentiate among submarines. Music publishers may be named after fruits (Apple Music), birds (Thrush Music), or geographic locations (Broadway Music). Dictionaries, atlases, maps, and even telephone books are other sources of inspiration. Some fairly common devices that have been used include spelling a name backward (Patti Page's EGAP Music), using a child's name (Alice, Marie), combining the names of a husband and wife (Marydan), joining the syllables of partners' names (Franstan), or using the founder's name (Johnny Cash's House of Cash).

Many record companies are identified with parent firms such as Warner and Universal. Others, such as Elektra and Epic, are unique to themselves. Some common names, such as London, Capitol, and King, have their own special history and position. In general, however, a common name is less desirable for new companies for several reasons. A common name may be confused with the names of other companies in related or unrelated fields and consequently may subject the new company to a possible lawsuit on the grounds of trademark infringement or unfair competition. In addition, different rules of trademark registration apply to common names. And, finally, the previous use of a common name may present a bar to the incorporation of a new firm.

The selection of musicians' names, like the selection of actors' names, can be an art. Some highly successful artists—among them Janet Jackson, Garth Brooks, Whitney Houston, and Barbra Streisand—have kept their own names. However, popular music abounds with highly imaginative names. A review of

Billboard's charts reveals such names as LL Kool J, Eminem, Goo Goo Dolls, 'N Sync, and Madonna.

Prior and Conflicting Company Names and Marks

In the initial enthusiasm of starting a new business, a music publisher or record company will frequently be annoyed when its chosen name is rejected by the nameless bureaucrat who passes on proposed incorporation documents for a new company. Each of the 50 states has its own corporate registration procedures. In the music-oriented states of New York, California, and Tennessee, it is usually the Department of State that refuses to accept a name it regards as too similar to other existing corporate names. Although such a rejection may be frustrating, it should be appreciated as an early warning of a possible conflict.

In music publishing, all major performing rights organizations—ASCAP, BMI, and SESAC—should be consulted before a new publisher name is adopted. The many thousands of names already on file should not be duplicated because important performance credits may be lost due to confusion of names. In response to telephone or letter inquiry, both ASCAP and BMI provide specific advice as to the availability of a name. In fact, it is the practice to reserve on request, for a limited period, a name determined to be available, in order to allow time to organize the new company.

The annual editions issued by music trade papers, such as the *Billboard International Buyer's Guide,* and industry reference books, such as the *Recording Industry Sourcebook,* also list publishers and record company labels and names.

Search Organizations and Services

Listings in trade publications, telephone books, the Internet, and other information sources noted previously are not necessarily complete, and in some cases a new company may want to hire professional help rather than makeng its own search. Of course, a trademark attorney has expertise in arranging for a search and interpreting the results, and this expertise is significant in giving assurance to a proposed trademark user. Trademark search organizations are listed in the Yellow Pages of telephone directories. Two of the better-known ones are:

- ▶ Thomson & Thomson, which has offices throughout the United States, as well as in Canada, Japan, and several European countries (Web site: www.thomson-thomson.com). The company's ISS (Identical Screening Searches) Online gives exact trademark matches in over 200 countries.
- ▶ CCH CORSEARCH (Commerce Clearing House Trademark Research Corporation merged with CORSEARCH in 2000) (Web site: www.corsearch.com).

Both companies issue prompt reports on trademarks registered with the U.S. Patent and Trademark Office in Washington, D.C. On request, they also report on trademarks registered with the office of the state secretary's office in one or more designated states. Such reports may also be expanded to include similar names in telephone directories. Affiliates and associates of these firms in Washington, D.C., conduct similar research in the trademark records and the Copyright Office records to supplement their own music industry trade directories and their own files and resource material. Such a report can sometimes be used in a defensive stage rather than in searching for a new name. Thus, if an investment has already been made in a name and a claim is asserted by a third party that the name is unduly similar to its prior name, a search may reveal many other uses of the name, indicating that it should be regarded as public property available for further use.

The U.S. Patent and Trademark Office does not offer a search service, but its files are available for a personal search in the public search library of the Patent and Trademark Office, located on the second floor of the South Tower Building, 2900 Crystal Drive, Arlington, VA 22202, or at the Patent Office's Web site, www.uspto.gov. There are also approximately 75 patent and trademark depository libraries throughout the United States in which a search can also be conducted. These libraries have CD-ROMs containing the trademark database of registered and pending trademarks.

Primary sources of information used by trademark attorneys which are also available to the public are the annually issued *Trademark Register of the United States* and the *Compu-Mark Directory of U.S. Trademarks,* which list all registered names and marks.

The trademark classes of interest to the music industry are International Class 15 (musical instruments), International Class 16 (paper goods and printed matter), and International Class 9 (records, tapes, CDs, etc.). A complete list of all classes may be found at the Trademark Office Web site.

Because it is frequently difficult for a layperson to determine whether a proposed name might be a trademark infringement, if there is any doubt, it is prudent to consult an attorney specializing in trademark law.

Trademark and Name Infringement

One form of trademark infringement is covered by state laws against unfair competition. The passing off or the attempt to pass off on the public the goods or business of one person as the goods or business of another, or the conduct of a trade or business in such a manner that there is an express or implied representation to that effect, is fraud. There may also be unfair competition by misappropriation as well as by misrepresentation even in the absence of fraudulent intent. In a number of states, as well as under federal law (18 USC Section 2321) it is a criminal offense to infringe, imitate, or counterfeit trademarks or to sell goods under such marks. Under the terms of some statutes, the offender is also subject to a penalty recoverable in a civil or quasi-criminal action. Offenders must be found guilty of a fraudulent or criminal intent in order for the offense to constitute a violation of the statutes.

Until 1996, when the Federal Anti-Dilution Act was signed into law, the right of a trademark owner to obtain injunctive relief against an infringer rested on proving that the person or company, which was in competition with the trademark owner, had used a similar or identical trademark to the one already registered, and that such use was likely to cause "confusion" on the part of consumers. Under the 1996 Act, the owner of a "famous" mark, whether or not it is registered, may seek relief against the commercial use of the mark in interstate commerce on the grounds that such use constitutes "dilution," but the owner of the famous mark must prove actual dilution, not just a "likelihood of confusion" as in the case of other trademark infringement claims. Whether a name or mark is sufficiently "famous" is measured by seven factors, none of which is essential or determinative by itself, but only as a part of the comprehensive examination of the factors as a group:

- Degree of acquired or inherent distinctiveness of the name
- Duration and extent of use of the name in connection with the claimant's goods or service
- Duration and extent of advertising and publicity of the name by claimant
- Geographical extent of the area in which the name is used
- The channels of trade for the good or services with which the name is used
- The degree of recognition of the name in the trading area and channels of trade used by the claimant and the alleged infringer
- Whether the mark was registered on the *Principal Register* (see below, "The Advantages of Registration")

Dilution of a famous name occurs when an infringing use undermines the strong positive association consumers have with the name and the owner of the name. An example of dilution would be a recording by studio artists of a so-called "tribute" to Barbra Streisand that consisted of instrumental versions of songs made famous by the star. Another would be to present a line of fancy gloves using the name of Michael Jackson, a famous wearer of gloves. An example of tarnishing (or degrading or bringing ridicule) would be to use a famous name for a pornographic magazine or Web site. The ice cream name Cherry Garcia is a registered trademark of the estate of Jerry Garcia, but if the ice cream maker had used the name without authorization, it would probably be considered an example of dilution under the Act. Two uses of famous trademarks are entirely legal: in comparative advertising, when the advertiser is identifying a competing product by name, and in news reporting and commentary.

Domain names are like federally registered trademarks in that once a domain name has been registered, the name cannot legally be used for another Web site. However, although registration of a domain name is protection against use of that name for a different site, it is not legal protection against other forms of infringement, and conventional trademark registration procedures should also be followed.

Domain names are obtained by applying for registration with Network Solutions, Inc. (now owned by VeriSign), or another name registry authorized by the Internet Corporation for Assigned Names and Numbers (ICANN), a global non-profit private-sector coordinating body. The most popular domain name extensions are .com, .org, .net, but new extensions, such as .biz, .info, and .name, are approved from time to time to handle the load.

If the owner of a trademark believes that someone is infringing on that trademark by using it as part of a domain name, there are several actions that the owner may bring: a federal lawsuit under the Anti-Cybersquatting Consumer Protection Act; an administrative proceeding under the Uniform Domain Name Dispute Resolution Policy (UDRP) adopted by ICANN; or a lawsuit brought in a state with an anti-cybersquatting statute, such as California. Because UDRP proceedings generally bring a faster resolution than the other two methods, they have been popular among musical artists. To prevail in a UDRP proceeding, the claimant must prove that:

1. The domain name is the same or confusingly similar to a trademark in which the claimant has rights.
2. The alleged infringing party has no rights or legitimate interests in the domain name.
3. The domain name was registered and used in bad faith.

Madonna and Jethro Tull are among the artists who have regained their trademarks from cybersquatters using the UDRP.

Names of Artists

Although unique names for artists abound in the music field, some artists may be surprised to find that their flight of imagination in coining a name is not unique. Even in the situation where the artist wants to use his or her given name, caution should be exercised where the name is common. For example, there are probably numerous women named Amy Grant and Anita Baker and men named Barry White and Michael Jackson, but if any of them is intent on breaking into the music field, he or she would be well advised to choose a different professional name.

Before launching a public career, it is prudent to check with artist unions regarding the name desired. The American Federation of Television and Radio Artists, the union for performers on radio, television, and records, can provide information about similar names of performers on its roster. The American Guild of Variety Artists (AGVA), the union for performers in night clubs and cabarets, will search its roster and report on possible conflicts in the use of a name as well.

The Registration of Names

ASCAP, BMI, and SESAC should each be consulted concerning prior uses of a name by their affiliated music publishers. If a proposed name is confusingly similar to other names, they may refuse to accept a new member or affiliate. In the area of records, the American Federation of Musicians enters into written union agreements with any record company using union musicians. The AFM maintains extensive lists of and data concerning record companies and record labels for use in union negotiations and for contract enforcement regarding pay and working conditions. Record producers or companies may file with the union a proposed record company or record label name; in response to inquiries, the union advises as to possible conflicting usage. All communications should be directed to the national office of the American Federation of Musicians.

A corporate name must have government approval before a company can be incorporated under that name. As indicated above, a proposed name must be cleared by the particular state in which incorporation is desired. A given state does not require a search of the names incorporated in other states. But each state does cross-check proposed corporate names, no matter what the business. As a result, the Whiz Bang Music Corporation may fail to get clearance in a state that has previously granted such name clearance for, say, a hat company. If the party is still interested in that particular name, despite the rejection by the state secretary's office, clearance may be granted in some instances by obtaining waivers from prior users in the state.

Most states have specific procedures for obtaining corporate name clearance. A good source for information on state procedures is the U.S. Small Business Administration Web site. Go to www.sba.gov and, in the search box, type in "business names." You can then click on "SBA: Business Names," which will allow you to access those state Web sites that provide Internet information on how to register corporate names. In one state, New York, the first step is to send a letter to the New York State Department of State, Division of Corporations, State Records and Uniform Commercial Code, 41 State Street, Albany, NY 12231, requesting information as to the availability of a desired corporate name and enclosing a $5 fee for each name you wish to have checked. If the name does not conflict with one already in existence according to the state's files, the applicant can reserve the name for 60 days by sending in a completed Application for Reservation of Name (go to the office's Web site, www.dos.state.ny.us), together with the statutory filing fee of $20, while the Certificate of Incorporation is being prepared. Two further extensions of 60 days each may be granted upon application for an Extension of Reservation of Name.

The Registration of Marks

Under the U.S. trademark law, provision is made for the registration of a trademark, which distinguishes a product and identifies its origins. Provision is also made for the registration of a service mark, which is used in the sale or advertising of services to identify the services of one person and distinguish them from the services of others. There is no statutory basis for the registration of trade or commercial names used merely to identify a business entity, but the name may be registered as a mark if it is also used as a trademark or service mark.

No time limit exists within which an application for registration should be filed. An application may be filed in three situations:

1. When the mark has already been used in interstate commerce or in commerce between a state and a foreign country
2. When there is a bona fide intention to use the mark in interstate commerce or in commerce between a state and a foreign country, but registration will not be issued until use is made and proved
3. Under certain international treaties, whereby an applicant may file based on an application or registration in a qualifying foreign country

This last use in relation to goods or products means that the mark has been affixed to goods or their tags, labels, displays, or containers, and the product has been sold or shipped in such commerce. When the mark is used in relation to a service, it denotes the sale or advertising of services rendered in such commerce.

Once a mark has been registered, a registrant should give public notice of the registration by using, in conjunction with the mark, the words "Registered in U.S. Patent and Trademark Office" or "Reg. U.S. Pat. and TM. Off.," or the letter R enclosed in a circle: ®. In suits for infringement under the Trademark Act of 1946, commonly known as the Lanham Act, failure to give such notice of registration prevents the registrant from recovering profits or damages unless the defendant had actual notice of the registration. It is legally improper to use this notice before the issuance of a registration and certificate. The impropriety may be a cause for refusal of registration and may result in fraud sanctions under the Lanham Act.

A complete application for the registration of a trademark or service mark consists of (1) a written application, (2) a drawing of the mark, (3) three specimens or facsimiles of the mark as used in commerce, which for service marks would include copies of advertisements, and (4) the filing fee of $325 per class. Forms for the registration of trademarks or service marks can be obtained on-line from the U.S. Patent and Trademark Office (PTO) (www.uspto.gov) or by calling the Trademark Assistance Center at (703) 308-9000. An applicant may file his or her own application, but in most instances it is wise to appoint an attorney for that purpose.

Before the Patent and Trademark Office issues a certificate of registration, the mark is published in the *Official Gazette,* a weekly PTO publication, which is also available on-line. The purpose of this publication is to allow anyone to object to the registration of the mark by filing an opposition to registration with the PTO within 30 days of publication. In an opposition proceeding, the prevailing party is the one that can prove prior use of the mark. If the mark is not opposed, the PTO generally issues a certificate of registration about 12 weeks after publication in the *Official Gazette.*

Anyone who claims rights in a mark may use the TM or S designation (for trademark or service mark) with the mark to alert the public to the claim. No registration or pending registration is necessary. The claim may or may not be valid. When a registration has been issued, the TM or S can be replaced by the symbol ® or words denoting registration.

A registration issued by the Patent and Trademark Office on or after November 16, 1989, the effective date of the Trademark Law Revision Act of 1988, remains in force for 10 years from the date of registration and may be renewed by filing a renewal application for additional 10-year periods, provided the mark is in use in commerce when the renewal application is filed. Registrations that were issued before November 16, 1989, have a 20-year original term and may be renewed for additional 10-year periods.

Trademark and service mark registrants must avoid official cancellation for nonuse of the mark. This requires the filing of an affidavit of use of the mark immediately after the fifth year of use of the mark following the date of registration and again during the ninth year following the date of registration. The latter may be combined with a renewal application.

The Advantages of Registration

Under the Lanham Act, there is provision for registration on either of two registers, the *Principal Register* and the *Supplemental Register.* To qualify for registration on the *Principal Register,* a mark must be arbitrary, fanciful, or in some other way "distinctive," as opposed to a descriptive or common name. Other marks that are capable of distinguishing the applicant's products can be registered on the *Supplemental Register.*

It is not necessary for the owner of a trademark to register the mark; the common law protects trademark rights. However, registration results in certain advantages. Registration on the *Principal Register* places the public on constructive notice of the registrant's claim to ownership. Registration also creates certain presumptions of ownership, of validity of the trademark, and of the exclusive right to use the mark on the goods or for the services for which the mark is registered. Registrants are given the right to sue in federal court, the right in certain cases to prevent importation of goods bearing an infringing mark, and also the benefit of incontestability on filing an affidavit showing continuous use of the mark for a 5-year period as indicated above.

Registration on the *Supplemental Register* does not give constructive notice to the public or presumptive evidence of ownership, validity, the exclusive right to the mark, or the right to prevent importation of goods carrying an infringing mark. Nor does it confer the benefit of incontestability. However, it does give the right to sue in federal court and the lawful right to use the notice of registration, which may be helpful in preventing infringement.

Trademark Registration at Home and Abroad

The registration of trademarks can be made under state laws as well as under the federal law. Usually a federal registration is considered to give sufficient protection to the trademark without the need for additional registrations under state laws. Of course, registration only under state laws is not as strong as federal registration. Registration under federal law will suffice as a holding pattern covering all states until use commences within a given state, whereas a state registration is strictly limited to its own borders.

The diverse nature of trademark laws in foreign countries makes it essential that those who wish to protect their marks abroad seek the advice of experts. In virtually all foreign countries a trademark need not have been used before it may be registered, and a registration may be used to bar the importation into the country of products to which the mark is affixed. There have been cases in which individuals registered the names and marks of world-renowned corporations and subsequently blocked the efforts of those companies to register their marks until financial settlements were made.

In the case of the music industry, if a record company proposes to license its product to be released in a foreign country on its own label, it is important that trademark registrations for the label be obtained in the licensed territory. The terms of certificates of registration in foreign countries differ in accordance with the laws of each country. In the absence of registration, the legal protection of the label (trademark) license may be jeopardized. It is also prudent to have proper trademark license agreements, which must be recorded in many countries and, in many cases, approved by governmental authorities.

The advice of trademark experts should be obtained in the complicated and technical field of foreign trademarks and licenses. Certain law firms in the United States and foreign countries specialize in foreign trademark registrations.

The Ownership of Rights in an Artist's Name

In the field of music, numerous parties may claim the right to use and participate in the benefits from the use of an artist's or group's name, including record companies and managers, and, in the case of a group, the different members of the group.

A record company usually has the exclusive right, by contract, to use and exploit an artist's name in connection with recordings made during the term of the exclusive recording contract. In addition, the company, after the expiration of the contract, has the continued right under the original contract to use the artist's name to identify, advertise, and promote the product previously made.

When popular group names such as the Ink Spots, Buffalo Springfield, Pink Floyd, and the Byrds become the subject of disputes among former members of the group, concepts of partnership property law become applicable to resolve the disputes.

Sometimes a performer changes names along the way, and questions arise as to whether the right to use the former name also encompasses the new name. For example, Tiny Tim was formerly known as Darry Dover. A record company was barred by a court from attempting to use Tiny Tim's current name and "unique style, appearance, and personality" to identify, advertise, and promote records made when he was identified as Darry Dover. However, some artist contracts specifically provide for the right to use names by which the artist may be known either now or in the future. Such a clause might have led to a different result in the Tiny Tim controversy.

The unauthorized use of a name may arouse the interest of the Federal Trade Commission or local criminal authorities interested in protecting the consumer from fraudulent or deceptive practices. A record company may be exposed if the title of a recording misrepresents the contents of the recording; for example, a recording containing performances by artists "in the style of" Bob Dylan is titled "A Tribute to Bob Dylan," or a recording containing songs made popular by Frank Sinatra but not sung by Sinatra is titled "The Best of Sinatra." To avoid confusion on the part of the consumer—and possible legal action—there should be visible disclaimers and/or appropriate and visible subtitles that make clear what the contents of such recordings are.

A Record Company's Rights in a Name

As indicated above, in order for the record company to protect its investment in recordings and promotion, the typical artist's contract specifies that the record company has the exclusive right to use the artist's name on and in connection with the recordings made under the agreement, for the duration of the agreement. Sometimes this right is limited to use in connection with the recordings of the particular artist. More often the record company obtains the right to exploit the name for its own institutional advertising purposes, even without reference to specific recordings of the artist.

The typical contract forbids the artist from using his or her name during its term to advertise or promote records made by other persons or firms. This restriction seems natural and justified. However, if the artist is likely to produce records of other artists, he or she may seek to exclude such activities from the restriction.

Group Members' Rights in a Name

Most popular music groups have a highly informal arrangement among the individual members. The groups are often born in a spirit of great mutual enthusiasm and optimism, and rarely do they have the business acumen or exercise the caution to require the drafting and execution of a formal partnership agreement. Yet the typical popular music group is a partnership, no matter how informal the arrangement. When the group splits up, dissolves, or looks for substitutions, it must cope with principles of partnership law with regard to the asset of the group name.

When Buffalo Springfield broke up, the drummer formed a new group under that name. The other original members objected to the new group, labeling it "phony" in a statement to the public. The drummer then obtained a temporary restraining order by a court against such statements, asserting his right as a partner to use the group name. However, another court later dissolved the temporary restraining order on the grounds that the other partners, even though no longer active, had the right to protect the name as a partnership asset by insisting on its use as identification of only the original group.

In their early days as a band, the Beatles had a drummer other than Ringo Starr. Although the Beatles were reorganized with the approval of the various members, the original drummer was not barred from referring to his "original" Beatles membership in connection with his new recordings.

One of the smoother transitions from a group to a solo name can be found in the divorce of soloist Diana Ross from the group known as the Supremes. For a considerable period of time before she left the group, with the cooperation of the Supremes' record company, Ross's name preceded the group name so that the public came to identify her as a solo artist. After the separation, both Diana Ross and the remainder of the group—still called the Supremes—continued to enjoy popular success.

Doing Business Under an Assumed Name

It is not always essential to form a corporation to do business under an assumed name. In the early stages, and continuing indefinitely in many cases, a person or a group of persons may choose to do business under an assumed company name. Thus, a business made up of one or more individuals may decide to select a convenient name, such as the Ace Music Company, or the Jeff Tracy Music Associates, or the Gladstone-Black Company. When this is done, however, the business entity should comply with state requirements for doing business under an assumed name before trying to open a bank account or cash checks under that name. In New York, for example, this requires filing a sworn statement identifying the actual persons behind the new name.

An advantage of registering under the state statutes relating to doing business under an assumed name is that it may help to establish a priority of use in the event that groups with conflicting names are formed later.

33

Agents and Managers

Agents and managers in the music business generally represent performing artists. Except in the case of composers and lyricists who write for the stage, screen, or television, and who may have agents, songwriters generally feel no need for a representative. On the other hand, songwriters usually have a music publisher (sometimes their own company) whose function is to promote and exploit works by endeavoring to secure performances, recordings, and synchronization uses, as well as to administer foreign and other rights. When a recording artist is also a songwriter, as is often the case, or when publishing rights are linked with dramatic rights, as in the case of show and film music, the artist is more likely to use a manager.

The Roles of Agents and Managers

The term *personal representative* is used to encompass both agents and managers, but the two play quite different roles. An *agent* finds or receives offers of employment and usually negotiates the terms of the contract. An agent works on a commission basis, normally 10 to 15 percent of the artist's earnings for a given engagement. The rate depends on state regulation, the particular talent union involved, and the duration of the engagement negotiated.

The largest general talent agencies in the music area are the William Morris Agency, International Creative Management (ICM), Creative Artists Agency (CAA), and The Firm. There are many other firms, such as Monterey Peninsula Artists, Associated Booking, and Artist Group International, to name a few, which are not as large as the big four but which have impressive rosters. The major agencies have numerous clients in various entertainment fields and extensive staffs to represent them, sometimes with offices in the leading entertainment centers in the United States and abroad. Agents are constantly breaking away from the larger agencies and moving elsewhere. For example, ICM co-CEO James Wiatt defected to William Morris in 1999; "superagent" Mike Ovitz left CAA (which he co-founded) to work for Disney in 1997 and shortly thereafter left Disney to form Artist Management Group in 1998, whose assets were subsequently sold to The Firm, founded in 1997 by Jeff Kwatinetz and Michael Green, themselves former agents at the Gallin-Morency talent management agency.

In contrast to the talent agencies specializing in securing employment for their clients, *personal managers* are responsible for day-to-day career development and personal advice and guidance. They also plan the long-range direction of the artist's career. Because of the broader nature of their responsibilities, managers usually have a much smaller number of clients than agents. Their responsibilities include:

- ▶ Choosing literary, artistic, and musical materials
- ▶ Supervising publicity, public relations, and advertising campaigns
- ▶ Adopting the proper format for the best presentation of the artist's talents
- ▶ Selecting booking agents to secure engagements for the artist
- ▶ Determining (in conjunction with the booking agent) the types of employment most beneficial to the artist's career
- ▶ Selecting and supervising the artist's accountants and attorneys
- ▶ Overseeing the design and maintenance of the artist's Web site

Personal managers generally do not travel with the artists they represent. Instead, road managers are engaged at the artist's expense; their job is to handle, under the manager's supervision, the numerous day-to-day business matters on the road, such as transportation, hotels, and collections, as well as stage, sound, and lighting needs. Personal managers may also serve as buffers to insulate the artist from requests for endorsements and appearances, as well as for charitable gifts, appearances, and the like. In addition, managers play important roles in the artist's relationships with the record label to which the artist is signed, including being involved in the selection of songs to be recorded and the choice of sides to be released. They also supervise the relationship with the artist's booking agency to obtain the maximum benefits for the artist, and sometimes they assist in the selection of music publishers for songs the artist writes.

Managers receive commissions of between 15 and 25 percent of the artist's gross earnings, plus reimbursement for travel and other out-of-pocket expenses. Commissions payable to the manager are usually in addition to booking agent's commissions. Many management agreements, especially those with new artists, provide for commissions which start low, when the artist needs every available penny, but escalate as the artist's earnings increase.

Although many personal managers give financial advice as a part of their functions, successful artists usually engage a business manager for bookkeeping and tax planning, as well as to assist in investment decisions and personal financial planning. This person will often be an accountant or a tax attorney. The business manager customarily collects the artist's earnings, pays the manager and other people working for the artist, manages the artist's investments, and sees to the filing of all tax returns. Business managers' fees range from 2 to 6 percent of the artist's gross income, although sometimes a monthly or annual flat fee is arranged.

Exclusive Representation

Agents and managers almost invariably function as exclusive representatives of their clients in their respective fields of endeavor. This enables them to develop the artist's career without being concerned that some other agent or manager will arrange conflicting or overlapping engagements. Exclusivity also assures the personal representatives that they will be compensated for their time and effort in building an artist's career. Because of this exclusivity, they are entitled to commissions even on earnings that do not result from their direct efforts, such as an opportunity presented by a friend or colleague of the artist. This is justified by the fact that their efforts serve to generate visibility for the artist that may lead to these other opportunities.

In situations in which an agent specializes in a particular area or areas and has no interest or ability in fields outside of those areas, the artist may limit the representative's commissions to his or her areas of expertise. Although a recording artist is normally represented for personal appearances, television shows, films, stage, and recording contracts by the same agent, it is conceivable that one or more of these fields would be excluded, especially by a more suc-cessful artist who wants to retain control and avoid commissions. For example, some artists negotiate the exclusion of booking agent commissions in specific high-paying venues such as Atlantic City and Las Vegas and work solely through their managers or in-house staff in those excluded areas.

In the field of classical music, concert artists are frequently represented by personal managers who also serve as booking agents for combined fees. Firms active in this area include ICM (International Creative Management) Artists, which represents cellist Yo-Yo Ma and pianist Emanuel Ax, and International Management Group (IMG) Artsts, which has offices in New York, London, Kuala Lumpur, and Paris and represents violinist Itzhak Perlman and soprano Kiri Te Kanawa. Some concert agents also act as an employer, for example, for a community concert touring series, in which case commissions are waived.

The Management Contract

A standard management contract provides for an initial term between 1 and 3 years, plus options (exercisable by the manager) to extend the term to a total of 5 years or the duration of a recording agreement secured during the term, whichever is longer. A management contract may provide for early termination if an achievement plateau is not reached, in either earnings or some other accomplishment, such as the artist obtaining a major label record contract or a significant tour. This clause is often referred to as a "kick-out clause." Generally, a manager will have 6 months to 1 year to obtain an offer from a major record label or label with national distribution, with a 1- to 3-month extension if the manager is actively engaged in bona fide negotiations for such a deal. When a management agreement is terminated, the manager's obligation to give advice and counsel ends. However, almost every management agreement provides that management commissions continue after the end of the term on the artist's earnings under contracts or engagements entered into or performed during the term as well as all "substitutions, modifications and extensions by options or otherwise" of those contracts. For example, a recording artist with a former manager who participated in an early career decision to sign with a certain record company may be obliged to pay that manager commissions as long as royalties still flow from that record contract. In addition, if there is no hiatus (for example, an interim contract with another label before resuming relations with the first record company), the manager may have a claim that recordings made after the end of the manager's term are under an extension of, or substitution for, the original contract.

Under such contract provisions, an artist may end up paying commissions to a manager for years after their relationship has terminated. To remedy this situation, a so-called phase-out or "sunset" clause is frequently negotiated as part of the management contract. Under this type of clause, the manager may receive, for example, full commissions for the first 2 years after the expiration or termination of the management contract, half-commissions for the next 2 years, and no commissions thereafter. The phase-out can occur over any negotiated length of time and with any decreasing percentage increments.

The term *commissionable income* in a management agreement includes the artist's gross income in whatever form (royalties, bonuses, and stock) earned by the artist as a result of the artist's activities in the entertainment field, and both *gross income* and *entertainment field* should be clearly defined in the contract.

Recording costs, video production costs, tour support from the record company, and sound and lights during touring are generally excluded from gross income on which management commissions are calculated. Occasionally, booking agent fees are also excluded. The theory behind allowing these exclusions is that these monies merely pass through the artist's hands to third parties and thus should not be commissionable. The exclusion of recording costs can make a big difference. For example, if the artist has a $200,000 recording fund and $150,000 is spent on recording costs, this leaves $50,000 for the artist. However, if the manager were to take a 20 percent commission on the whole fund ($200,000), the commission would be $40,000, leaving only $10,000 for the artist. If recording costs were excluded from the same gross income, the manager could only commission the remaining $50,000, in which case the manager would receive $10,000, leaving $40,000 for the artist. Managers generally will agree to exclude recording costs from gross income, as well as at least some of the other categories mentioned above.

Managers may also waive or defer commissions for weeks in which the artist has not achieved a certain level of income. This is sometimes referred to as a "bread-and-butter clause": the manager will not earn (or will defer) commissions while the artist is simply trying to put food on the table.

Generally, managers are reimbursed for out-of-pocket expenses incurred on behalf of the artist, such as long-distance phone calls, faxes, postage, messengers, and travel expenses. The artist should limit the manager's ability to incur excessive expenses. For example, the contract may stipulate that the manager cannot incur a single expense of $500 (or $1,000 or some other specific amount) in total expenses during a single month without the artist's prior written approval.

Most managers seek a broad power of attorney to sign all contracts on the artist's behalf, endorse checks payable to the artist, and engage third parties (such as agents, accountants, and public relations firms) to work for the artist. Insofar as possible, the artist should try to put limits on such broad powers. For example, an artist may limit the manager's power to sign engagement contracts to so-called one-nighters, the reasoning being that offers by promoters for one-night engagements do not stay open long, and if the artist is not available to sign the agreement, the opportunity may be lost. Other approaches are to require the manager to consult with the artist or to seek the artist's approval before committing him or her to an engagement. However, consultation is considerably weaker than the right of approval. As a compromise, the artist may retain a right of approval that is not to be withheld unreasonably.

In most cases, if a member of an artist group leaves, he or she is still bound to the manager, whether the departing member continues as a solo artist or with another group. A group artist should make sure that a departing member will not be bound to the manager for longer than the term of the initial (pre-departure) management contract. In other words, the term of the management contract should not start running anew for a departing member. Additionally, if new members join the group, they are likely to be required to enter into the same management contract as the existing one between the artist group and the manager.

The manager's ability to assign a management contract should be limited to assignments to an entity in which the original manager has an ownership or a controlling interest. In addition, a "key man clause" may be added, providing, for example, that if the manager is not involved in the day-to-day management of the artist, then the artist may terminate the management contract.

The close and often difficult relationship between artists and managers during the years of active management makes it desirable that the parties involved be sure of their compatibility before entering into binding contracts. The negotiation of a complete management agreement—one that deals with most of the areas mentioned above, with the assistance of attorneys experienced in the field—is perhaps one way to ascertain whether this compatibility exists. Simply stated, if the prospective manager and the artist cannot reach a working agreement in their initial negotiation, it is best for both concerned to avoid entering into a long-term contract.

Abuses by Agents and Managers

Although most agents and managers are ethical, the relationship with the artist does open the possibility of certain forms of abuse, each of which should be specifically recited in the management contract as a cause for termination. Any of the following actions on the part of the manager is cause for termination:

▶ Withholding monies from the artist through theft, embezzlement, misappropriation, forgery, fraud, or other dishonest conduct
▶ Entering into an arrangement with a third party for the services of an artist whereby compensation is paid directly to the agent, under terms not disclosed to the artist, with the intent to provide additional compensation to the manager
▶ Improperly representing the artist without the artist's authorization
▶ Commingling monies belonging to different artists

Regulation of Agents and Managers

While all states regulate employment agencies by statute, many states do not so regulate managers. Managers take the position that their services are outside the scope of state laws that govern employment agencies, and indeed most management agreements specifically disclaim any obligation to seek or obtain employment, even though this is exactly what many managers do.

Among states that regulate agents and managers, California, with its ties to the entertainment industry, is probably the leader. California statutes specifically govern talent and literary agents and control fees and the duration of the contracts with such agents. Under California's Talent Agencies Act (California Labor Code section 1700), agents and managers who are in the "occupation of procuring employment" for artists must obtain a license. There has been considerable debate as to what amount of "procurement" is necessary to violate the act. In 1999, in *Park v. Deftones,* 71 C.A. 4th 1465 (1999), the Deftones were able to undo their contract with a former unlicensed manager by arguing he had violated the statute by booking live engagements. In the 1996 case of *Anita Baker v. Sherwin Bush,* the California labor commissioner upheld the hearing officer's finding of fact that the unlicensed manager was not merely a "conduit" for employment offers that came to him, but was actively engaged in promoting employment opportunities, and that therefore his management agreement was unenforceable even though it contained the usual exculpatory language about not being required to seek employment. The act, which is under the jurisdiction of the California Labor Commission, attempts to protect artists from unscrupulous managers. Its licensing process involves, among other things, the submission of affidavits by "at least two reputable residents who have known or been associated with, the applicant for two years" which state "that the applicant is a person of good moral character" as well as the posting of a $10,000 bond, which is intended to confirm the manager's creditworthiness. After the application has been submitted, the labor commissioner may "cause an investigation to be made as to the character and responsibility of the applicant" (Sections 1700.6(d), 1700.15, 1700.7).

All disputes between artists and managers are decided by the California labor commissioner. An unlicensed manager who is found guilty of violating its provisions can face both the termination of the contract and the restitution to the artist of all commissions paid. There are no criminal penalties.

New York State regulates theatrical employment agencies by statute under its General Business Law. In New York, agents who seek engagements for performing artists can charge a maximum commission of 10 percent.

In the 1991 case of *PPX Enterprises v. A Tribe Called Quest*, PPX had contracted with the well-known rap group A Tribe Called Quest to obtain a recording agreement for them. PPX was not the group's manager, nor was it a licensed employment agent. Although PPX secured a recording agreement, the group refused to pay PPX its 15 percent fee. The court held that the group's commission agreement with PPX was unenforceable, and the group did not have to pay PPX because it was neither an agent nor a manager. Note that nearly every professional management contract has a provision that states (usually in bold type) that the artist confirms that he or she fully understands that the manager is not an employment agency and has not represented that he will seek employment opportunities for the artist.

Unions such as the American Federation of Musicians (AFM), the American Federation of Television and Radio Artists (AFTRA), and the American Guild of Variety Artists (AGVA) regulate agents. Only AGVA attempts to regulate managers, whereas all three unions supervise agents by granting them franchise certificates; union members are barred from dealing with agents who lack such certificates. Subjects of regulation include maximum commission rates, duration of the contract, and conflicts of interest. AFTRA and AFM disseminate approved forms of agreements between artists and representatives under which an artist is afforded an opportunity to terminate if the agency has not offered a designated number of engagements.

Similarly, AGVA, which operates in the area of musical performance in nightclubs, cabarets, theaters, and other areas of live entertainment, limits its members' contracts with agents to those agents who are franchised by AGVA. The representative of the authorized agents is the Artists' Representatives Association (ARA).

Trade Organizations for Personal Managers

Two major professional organizations exist for personal managers: the National Conference of Personal Managers (NCOPM), formerly the Conference of Personal Managers, and the Music Managers Forum (MMF). Many leading managers belong to NCOPM, which operates an eastern division and a western division in addition to the national office. The NCOPM is actively involved in lobbying Congress on issues affecting managers and the artists they represent. Members of this organization adhere to its code of ethics and business practices. Benefits of membership include newsletters, an information library, publicity, and the right to use the NCOPM standard management contract. (For more information, visit their Web site, www.ncopm.com.)

The MMF was originally formed as the International Manager's Forum in 1993 in New York to provide monthly forums for managers to discuss the various issues that affect them as well as to further their interests and those of the artists they represent in all aspects of the music industry. The organization has approximately 60 members in cities across the country as well as chapters in Canada, the U.K. and Australia. The MMF publishes a newsletter featuring information on the organization's activities. (For more information, visit the Web site of Music Managers Forum-US: www.mmf-us.org.)

Competition for Personal Managers

For years personal managers have viewed with alarm the increasing number of attorneys, accountants, business managers, and even publicists undertaking functions formerly performed by personal managers. For example, it has been recognized that the complexities of negotiating a complicated agreement between a record company and an artist require the services of skilled attorneys. If the attorney is a strong negotiator and commands substantial fees, often on a contingent basis, the more sophisticated artist may question the rationale of having a manager as well. Similar problems occur where the functions of accountants, business managers, or publicists tend to overlap with those of a manager.

When another professional replaces a personal manager, the artist should beware of potential conflicts of interest. The artist should be especially cautious when the artist's attorney is also a stockholder or officer in the manager's company or an employee of the artist's manager. In such an instance the artist should seek separate counsel. Although opportunities and temptations are ever-present, a lawyer should not simultaneously negotiate contracts for an artist while serving as that artist's manager. Nevertheless, a growing number of attorneys are assuming the role of personal manager and charging for their services on the same commission basis. While this scenario sometimes works, attorneys are often ill-suited to fill these dual roles. While they may be better at negotiating the record deal once it is achieved, finding such a deal often requires skills not taught in law school.

Because record companies routinely reject unsolicited materials, including demo tapes of unknown artists seeking record deals, many attorneys in the entertainment industry have undertaken the practice known as "shopping." Attorneys who "shop" record deals for artists have varying fee arrangements for such activities. Some attorneys favor an hourly wage ranging from $150 to $350. Often the attorney will request a nonreturnable advance retainer, which can range from $1,500 to $5,000 and which is applied against a contingency fee.

Other attorneys either opt for prepayment of expenses or for a percentage of a record deal (usually 10 to 15 percent of net advances and royalties). Fee arrangements between the attorney and artist may include any combination or all of the preceding elements.

The attorney's role as a shopper primarily involves contacts with key record company personnel. In agreeing to pay advance retainers and contingency fees, the artist is essentially purchasing the attorney's access to those who may be in a position to offer a record deal. Consequently, shopping is inherently prone to ethical abuses. Unscrupulous attorneys may even offer shopping services in return for front money, even though they do not believe their efforts will be successful. Such attorneys may not even make sincere efforts to shop the artist for fear of damaging their own credibility with record company personnel. Accordingly, shopping for record deals may be a more appropriate activity for personal managers. Note, however, there are many highly reputable attorneys with excellent shopping contacts.

Sometimes an attorney will get a contractual understanding that his or her legal services will also be used in the event that a contract results or that such services are included in a contingent fee arrangement. More often, a shopper's contract, whether with an attorney or another party, is a contingent-fee percentage deal and attorney's fees are not included. The applicable percentage can vary from 10 to 20 percent; the higher rate is justified as replacing what a personal manager would have received for the same services. The base on which this negotiated percentage is applied varies from:

- ▶ Any and all advances and earned royalties exceeding such advances for the full contract life and for so long as royalties are paid
- ▶ Any and all initial recording costs and net cash advances for the first album
- ▶ Only the initial net cash advance without reference to the recording costs paid by the label but not retained by the artist
- ▶ A combination of any of the above together with "best efforts" to use the shopper as producer or as executive producer of all songs recorded on first album or first two albums
- ▶ A combination of the above but with escalated percentages based on the amount of initial or otherwise qualifying advance payment, such as 10 percent on an amount of $10,000 or less, 15 percent on $15,000 or more, and 2 percent for amounts of $25,000 or more

There is also a major issue to be settled as to the length of time the exclusive shopper's status applies. A nonexclusive shopper's deal is less desirable since possible disputes may result as to who obtained the deal. Most term contracts further provide that for a reasonable period, such as 6 months after expiration of the allowed period, any resulting contract with a label that had entered into negotiations during the allowed term shall be considered still under the contract. A fair provision is to give up to a 90-day extension at the normal end of term if negotiations are then in progress with a qualifying label and full details of such party and offer are disclosed.

When referring to a "record deal" as a qualification for the shopper's fee, caution should be exercised to define what the parameters are of a deal which qualifies. For example, must it be with one of the five majors (Universal, WEA, EMI, BMG, Sony); or an independent label distributed by one of the five major labels; or an independent label with other national distribution; or an independent label with regional distribution; or any label capable of undertaking a "commercial release"; or any label that will finance two or more record sides? The artist should also consider minimum financial requirements (advances and royalties).

Artists should keep in mind that a shopper is often the only way to directly submit a demo to a major label. For example, the *Arista Records Submission Guidelines* clearly state that the company accepts unsolicited materials from an artist or songwriter *only* if the artist is represented by a lawyer, manager, or music publisher. The demo must not be more than four songs in length and must be accompanied by a letter to a specific A&R person. The guidelines also state that the demo should be submitted to the proper A&R person for the particular style of music.

Relationships Between Artists and Personal Representatives

From time to time, there are changes in agency personnel. As indicated above, two agencies will merge; or a well-known agent who has handled a particular motion picture or recording star will move from one agency to another or will establish a new agency; or a recognized personal manager will join a larger talent organization.

The artist who appreciates the greater attention and facilities that may accompany such a change may be happy with the new arrangements. On the other hand, an artist who enjoys being the stellar attraction of a small organization may be dissatisfied with being a small fish in a big pond. Artists who have developed close personal relations with an individual representative who has moved on to another agency or firm or formed his or her own business may be disgruntled unless they can follow their representative to their new connection. This is understandable because the manager-artist relationship is by nature extremely close.

Courts appreciate the significance of a personal relationship, and as a result they sometimes stretch in favor of the artist who is objecting to a material change in the basic relationship with his or her manager and wants to terminate the management agreement. Nevertheless, the courts must respect the intentions of the parties as revealed by their agreement. Thus, in the case of the contract with a large talent agency, where the relationship is not necessarily very personal, the court may be unwilling to relieve the artist of his or her contractual obligations if no specific provision has been made in the agreement. It is up to the artist to have provided in the agreement for such contingencies.

Some union agreements protect the artist in this area by requiring the talent agency to name several key individuals who will actually service the artist. Some artists will designate their own particular key person with whom they anticipate a close working relationship. Other union agreements permit termination of an agency agreement in the event of a merger of the agency with another agency.

The termination of an artist's relationship with an agency will apply only to new contracts not previously handled by the agency. There is a continuing right to commissions on earnings under contracts and engagements secured by the agency. In a 1992 case, *Watts v. Columbia Artists Management Inc.*, a New York county court held that Columbia Artists Management was due commissions from pianist Andre Watts for engagements scheduled before termination of the contract.

Notices and Payments

Most agreements negotiated by managers or agents provide that all notices and payments shall be made through the office of the manager or agent. This protects both the artist and the personal representative. Representatives can spot-check the artist's royalty receipts in order to ensure that royalty accountings are rendered in a timely fashion and are generally in order. They can also calculate and receive their appropriate commissions. Insofar as the record company is concerned, it may confer with the representative rather than with the artist on such matters, especially where the artist is frequently on tour or not known to attend to business.

34

Taxation in the Music Business

Accountants and attorneys in the tax field often advise clients of the truism that "tax avoidance is not tax evasion." The U.S. Supreme Court has expressed its approval of tax avoidance as the act of an informed taxpayer who takes advantage by legal means of the right to decrease the amount of taxes he or she would otherwise have to pay. Tax savings may be achieved through depreciation allowances, certain charitable contributions, the transfer of rights in copyrights to a child or other person in a lower tax bracket, and the deduction of permissible business and professional expenses.

Capital Gains

The tax laws treat long-term capital gains more favorably than ordinary income. At this time, a favorable 20 percent rate applies to long-term gains and a rate of 28 percent applies to short-term capital gains. In general, an asset must be held for at least 18 months for gain to be long-term. For those in the 15 percent tax bracket, the capital gains rate is 10 percent. For assets acquired after December 31, 2000, and held for at least 5 years, the top rate drops to 18 percent. Obviously, this compares favorably with ordinary income tax brackets, which can be over 30 percent. In addition, capital losses may be used to offset capital gains plus $3,000 of ordinary income. Moreover, unused capital losses can be carried over to later years.

A musical composition or similar property is not considered a "capital asset" if it is held by a taxpayer whose personal efforts created such property. This applies not only to authors and composers but also to persons who receive rights in copyrighted works as donees by virtue of gifts or trusts. It does not include purchasers or heirs, and under the present tax laws, sales by them can qualify as capital gains if there are gains after depreciation recapture. By an amendment to the Internal Revenue Code, Congress provided that if there was a sale of property for a consideration in excess of its depreciated value, the amount of depreciation taken must be recognized as ordinary income. For example, if a spouse inherited a copyright at a value of $20,000, depreciated it by $4,000 so that its basis was $16,000, and then sold it for $25,000, the first $4,000 of gain would be considered ordinary income (to offset the ordinary deduction from ordinary income for depreciation taken in prior years); the remaining gain of $5,000 would qualify as capital gain.

Note the word "gain" in the term *capital gain*. There is no tax whatsoever on the basic cost recouped by the sale. For instance, disregarding the factor of allowable depreciation (which is discussed later), a music publisher that acquires a copyright for $15,000 and resells it a year later for $20,000 is not taxed on the $15,000 cost and pays tax at capital gain rates only on the $5,000 profit. In general, the cost basis allowed to be recovered, in the case of a sale by anyone other than the author, is the sum of the costs incurred in obtaining the copyright, less any depreciation taken on such costs; any excess over such depreciated cost is treated as ordinary income. Any additional gain is treated as capital gain.

With regard to deceased authors, if a copyright is sold by the estate or a person deriving rights through the estate, a capital gain may generally be claimed. For inherited property the basis is usually the fair market value at the date of death. If a federal estate tax return has to be filed, the basis will be the fair market value at the date of death, or if elected by the estate, a date 6 months later. In the event that a federal estate tax return need not be filed, the basis will be the value at the date of death used for the payment of state inheritance taxes. This basis is used for both capital gain and depreciation purposes.

For situations involving an inheritance from an heir of the author, or the formula for increasing the basis for estate taxes paid on any appreciation in value, it is suggested that attorneys or accountants be consulted for appropriate advice.

Generally, in the case of gifts of property, the donee retains the donor's basis. If the donee sells for an amount less than his or her basis, resulting in a loss, then the donee is required to adopt the fair market value of the property at the date of the gift, which may reduce the loss for tax purposes. If the donee sells for an amount in excess of his or her basis, the excess is subject to capital gain treatment if otherwise qualified; but where the donor was the author, capital gain treatment would not be available.

Considerable difficulty was encountered in the past in determining the type of sale that qualifies for capital gain treatment. This difficulty existed because copyright was regarded as an indivisible entity for copyright purposes despite its various component elements such as motion picture rights, performance rights, mechanical rights, and publication rights, all of which make up what has been called a "bundle of rights." It was questionable whether the sale of particular rights would qualify for capital gain treatment for tax purposes. However, in *Hedwig et al. v. United States*, a 1952 case involving the film rights to *Forever Amber*, the court determined that for capital gain tax purposes there is nothing inherent in the nature of a copyright that prevents separate sales of each of the parts comprising the whole. This position is reinforced by the Copyright Act of 1976, which explicitly recognizes the divisibility of the various exclusive rights that comprise a copyright and provides that any of such exclusive rights may be transferred and owned separately.

Where the purchase price is a percentage of future earnings (akin to a royalty), the sale of rights by one music publisher to another is sufficient for capital gain treatment if the sale is full and final and the purchase price is not merely an anticipation of future income, such as an advance against future royalties. If the transaction qualifies as a so-called installment sale, the seller will report gains only as payments are actually received. Local state consequences must also be considered.

No capital gain advantages are available to persons or firms that hold properties "primarily for sale to customers in the ordinary course of . . . business." Music publishers are normally licensors, not sellers, of copyrights and thus are excluded from the category of taxpayers who are required to pay taxes at ordinary income rates on amounts received from the sale of their catalog. It is a rare instance when the heirs of authors seek capital gain treatment. This situation may be in large part the result of a tradition against outright sale by authors' surviving spouses and children; they honor the authors' decision to keep a continuing royalty interest and forgo the attraction of an outright sale that may prove to be improvident. An author's heirs must bear in mind that the right to receive a substantial sum yearly in royalties over the remaining life of a copyright carries with it the obligation to pay income tax at ordinary rates, except as the copyright may be depreciated. The effect of depreciation is discussed below.

Estate and Gift Taxes

Musical assets of artists pass on to heirs in two forms: (1) gifts within their lifetime, testamentary under a will or in the absence of a will ("intestate") and under state statute, and (2) statutory rights of renewal and termination to designated statutory heirs regardless of any contrary terms of a will except when the copyright statute makes the executor or next of kin the statutory heir in absence of a widow, child, or grandchild (see Chapter 11). Before the major estate tax changes of 2001, the amount of music business gifts and testamentary or intestate transfers that was exempt from taxation was $675,000, and the rate of taxation on amounts exceeding $675,000 ranged from 37 to 55 percent. In 2002, the exemption was raised to $1 million, with the highest applicable tax rate being 50 percent. Between 2002 and 2010, the exemption will be increased in annual increments, and the maximum rate of taxation similarly decreased. In 2009 the exemption will be $3.5 million and the highest tax rate will be 45 percent. Unless Congress acts in the meantime, in 2010 these changes will lapse and the situation will be as it was in 2001.

With reference to statutory rights of renewal and termination, as discussed in Chapter 11, no estate transfer tax ever applied. These valuable rights come to the beneficiary tax free in all cases.

The gift tax under the 2001 revision allows tax-free gifts of up to $11,000 annually for any of an unlimited number of recipients, which can be doubled to $22,000 when the gift is jointly given by husband and wife. Even gifts in excess of these exempted amounts can be without tax implications if a gift tax return is filed and the aggregate lifetime amount of all such gifts is not in excess of the applicable exemption.

Depreciation and Amortization

A Treasury Department publication that specifies that copyrights are subject to depreciation states, "The purpose of depreciation is to let you recover your investment over the useful life of the property." Because a copyright is recognized to be an intangible asset of diminishing value, a portion of receipts from licenses or other uses of the copyright may be considered to be not ordinary income but a payment to replace lost value.

Unlike capital gain, depreciation is available to authors and composers as well as to music publishers. However, in practical effect, the depreciation allowance for original authors and the original publisher is negligible. Freelance, self-employed composers, lyricists, and recording artists are entitled to current tax-year deductions for qualifying business expenses. This avoids the limitation on depreciation write-offs which would be duplicative of expense write-offs. However, such expenses cannot exceed income related to the expense and are not available to the nonprofessional. The right to depreciate is applicable not only to purchasers of copyrights but also to estates, heirs, and trusts. This right is substantial in respect to purchases and can be substantial for heirs of writers as well. The depreciable value is generally "stepped up" to the fair market value of the copyright at the date of death of the last owner, or 6 months later if the estate was subject to federal estate tax, providing that there was a valid election by the executor or administrator to value the estate at the later date.

When a donee takes over a predecessor's asset valuation basis, the donee assumes both the basis and the accumulated depreciation of the former owner. Thus, in determining the amount of depreciation to be recaptured as ordinary income in the event of a sale, depreciation taken by both the seller and the prior owners (whose basis was assumed) must be considered.

As an example of the application of depreciation, let's assume a purchase by a music publisher of a copyright for $10,000. The music publisher would determine, after consultation with an accountant and attorney, the period over which the cost would be depreciated for tax purposes. If the period is 10 years, the $10,000 cost would normally be depreciated on a straight-line basis in 10 equal installments of $1,000 each so that the publisher would have an allowance of $1,000 per year against taxable earnings. In effect, at the end of 10 years, the publisher would have recaptured the basic investment and would be in a position to replenish the catalog by the purchase of another song. A record company is in a similar position with regard to the depreciation of the costs of its master recordings.

Prior to 1990, the tax laws as interpreted by the Internal Revenue Service singled out copyrights and other intangibles by requiring that depreciation must be computed on a straight-line basis and disallowing the use of alternative methods available to other property owners. This meant that the cost for tax purposes (less projected salvage value at the end of the depreciation period) could only be depreciated in equal installments over the depreciation period. In the event that a copyright became valueless in any year before the end of the depreciation period, the unrecovered cost (or other basis for depreciation) might be deducted in that year.

A 1994 Internal Revenue Service training manual for music industry audits states that the flow-of-income approach can be used to amortize record masters unless the 3-year safe-harbor alternative is used. ("Safe harbor" is discussed in the following section.) Under the income-forecast method, an estimate is made of the total amount of income that is to be received over the economic life of the asset. The depreciable basis of the assets is written down each year in the same proportion that the receipts for a particular year bear to the total anticipated receipts, so the years with the greatest proportion of receipts bear the greatest proportion of depreciation, and there is a closer match between expenses and income. The IRS manual states that demo records can be treated either as current expense fully deductible in the year of expenditure or as research and development expense to be amortized over 60 or more months.

Where the safe-harbor approach is not applicable, it is probable that a flow-of-income method is now required for noncorporate producers, as well as S corporations and personal holding companies. For these taxpayers, expenses for the production of a film, sound recording, book, or similar property that are otherwise eligible are deductible on a prorated basis over the years in which the income is received. The law defines the terms *film* and *sound recording* but does not define either *book* or *similar property*. Nevertheless, the Senate Committee Report on the Tax Reform Act of 1976 mandates the use of the flow-of-income method for a musical copyright on the theory that it is "similar property." Thus noncorporate producers are definitely required to use the flow-of-income method to depreciate record master costs and would appear to be required to use this method for musical copyrights as well. Corporate producers have the option of depreciating on either a straight-line basis or a flow-of-income basis.

Depreciation of items used in a taxpayer's music business activities, including electronic equipment such as synthesizers and other studio equipment, must be spread out on a depreciation schedule based on the allowable useful life of the property. However, the cost of Section 179 qualifying business equipment can be deducted in the year the equipment is purchased and first used, up to a limit of $25,000 in 2003.

Tax Treatment of Record Masters

It is well recognized in the record industry that the overwhelming majority of new recordings have a useful commercial life of less than 1 year from the date of release. This is primarily due to the fact that most popular recordings do not reach the break-even point of recovering their cost and are discontinued for lack of popularity. However, there are evergreens in the record field just as there are standards in the music publishing field. Vintage recordings of Duke Ellington, Hank Williams, The Rolling Stones, and the Beatles continue to have regular sales long after their original cost was recouped. These vintage recordings would have been fully depreciated many years ago, but when they are transferred to a new owner, the valuation of the sale creates a new basis for depreciation.

In cases in which it is mandated that the flow-of-income approach is to be used, there is no question whether to treat recording costs as current expenses to be deducted from current income before computing taxable income or to capitalize them and depreciate them over time. The flow-of-income basis is mandated for noncorporate taxpayers only; corporate taxpayers have an option of using either a straight-line depreciation method or a flow-of-income depreciation method.

The flow-of-income approach has caused problems. It requires complicated estimates and results in long delays in recovering expenses. To alleviate this inequity, the Internal Revenue Service has adopted a 3-year safe-harbor rule that can be elected by any individual creator (or by any corporation or partnership owned at least 95 percent by an individual alone or together with close family members). This safe harbor allows a rapid depreciation and amortization of costs, at the rate of 50 percent in the first year and 25 percent in each of the 2 successive years, provided that it applies to all creative costs incurred in the tax year in question. Some tax filers who are eligible for the flow-of-income or the safe-harbor approach may also be eligible to deduct against current income expenses to acquire qualifying property under Section 179. However, this course should be carefully considered, as it may, among other ramifications, reduce or eliminate the taxpayer's eligibility to claim an earned income credit.

In some instances it may suit the tax-planning needs of a record company to depreciate recording costs over time rather than deduct them as a current expense. This occurs typically when there are considerable startup costs and little current income but there are expectations of greater income in the future. Increased current profits can thereby be shown because there are fewer current expenses to be deducted, and the deductions are preserved for later years when they are able to offset greater income. Even a depreciation basis does not prejudice the right of the company to take a write-off of the undepreciated costs in the year when the record itself is discontinued from the company catalog and its inventory of such discontinued records is sold as scrap. However, most smaller companies seek maximum current deductions in order to decrease their taxes immediately and conserve their cash.

It should be remembered that the treatment of recording costs will affect the tax results applicable to gain on the sales of masters. When depreciation has been taken, the gains equal to the depreciation are considered as ordinary income and the remaining balance as capital gain if the master is a capital asset in the hands of the seller. The tax benefit rule is equally applicable when an expense other than depreciation is deducted. If, for example, the cost of producing a master recording is written off in the year of production and the master is later sold, to the extent of the original write-off, the gain is considered ordinary income and the remaining balance is considered capital gain, provided that the master is a capital asset of the seller.

Charitable Contributions

Charitable gifts of appreciated property—such as a library of unreleased masters or a valuable copyright—given to a qualifying charitable organization can sometimes provide tax benefits to the donor. In certain cases, a donor can deduct the fair market value of a gift, as determined by an expert appraiser, from his or her taxable income. In contrast to a sale, a donor need not worry about finding a purchaser willing and able to pay the appraised value of the property.

The tax laws impose several limitations on the tax benefits of gifts of appreciated property. Unfortunately, these tax benefits are largely unavailable to the composer or lyricist who created the subject of the gift or to the donee of the composer or lyricist who seeks to make a charitable gift. In this case, the taxpayer can only deduct the original cost of creation, which is usually negligible. This limitation, however, is not ordinarily applicable to publishers or heirs.

Income tax deductions for the charitable contributions of individuals are restricted to 50 percent of adjusted gross income, subject, however, to a ceiling of 30 percent with certain carryover rights on the excess if a sale of a property would have resulted in a long-term capital gain. For corporations, the percentage restriction is 10 percent of taxable income, subject to certain adjustments. There may be a further limitation on the benefits of a charitable contribution with respect to the calculation of the alternative minimum tax. In calculating this tax, a taxpayer who is subject to such tax and who has made a charitable contribution of appreciated property must reduce the amount of the contribution by the amount of the untaxed appreciation.

Deductions for Home Used as Office or Studio

Many freelance vocalists and musicians require extensive rehearsals, coaching, and practice to maintain their income-producing skills. They often carry on these activities in their home. The Internal Revenue Service has strict limitations concerning the deduction of operating and depreciation expenses allocable to the portion of a home used for business purposes where the use is on an exclusive and regular basis as a principal place of business, as a place for seeing business clients, or as a separate business structure.

In 1997, Congress reacted to a 1993 Supreme Court ruling that had tightened the meaning of "principal place of business." The new law relaxed the requirements for a deductible home office as of December 31, 1998, so that it would qualify if used for administrative or management activities of any trade or business if there was no other fixed location to perform such duties. In other respects it continued the two basic tests: (1) the importance of activities performed at each place of business and (2) the time spent at each place.

Several steps can be taken to protect the home office deduction.

- ▶ Perform most work activities at home and document them.
- ▶ Document all business meetings at home.
- ▶ Move the home office into a separate structure, such as a garage, and do not mix business and personal matters in the same space.
- ▶ Prove that the employer requires a home office, for example, by a letter. If the taxpayer is an employee, he or she must also show that the home office is being used for the "convenience" of the taxpayer's employer.

Items such as heat, electricity, insurance, and rent, or in the case of home ownership, taxes, mortgage interest, and depreciation, may be deducted on an allocated basis. If all rooms at home are approximately the same size, the business portion of office or studio-in-home expenses can be computed by the ratio of the number of rooms used for business purposes to the total number of rooms. Thus, in a 10-room dwelling of roughly equal size where one room is set aside for business purposes, 10 percent of the dwelling expenses are for business purposes. In other instances, the ratio is the number of square feet in the business space to the total square feet: for example, 330 square feet divided by 3,300 square feet, or 10 percent.

The home office deduction cannot be more than the total gross income from the business use of the home, after deduction of business expenses other than home expenses. However, any balance remaining can be carried forward to future years. Only household expenses and repairs that benefit the business space are deductible. The cost of painting another room would, for instance, not be deductible, although part of the cost of painting the outside of the house may be deductible. Lawn care and landscaping costs are not deductible. Small businesses can also deduct up to $25,000 of the cost of new qualifying business equipment.

Shifting Taxable Income to Persons in Lower Tax Brackets

Many a successful parent would like to avoid additional income at his or her current high tax rate by shifting the income to a child or other dependent in a lower tax bracket. Although this cannot be done with ordinary personal service income, it is perfectly legal in the case of music royalties. While the mere reallocation of actual or anticipated income within a family group is not permissible, it is considered proper to make a bona fide gift or transfer of copyright, since the conveyance is then not of income but of property capable of producing income. However, any unearned income of a child under age 14 can be subject to socalled kiddie tax.

An IRS ruling makes it attractive for a company owner to grant minority interests to children or other relatives while still living instead of through a will. This can reduce eventual estate taxes as well as the current income tax of the original parent owner. Such exemptions for gifts are currently $11,000 a year per recipient for each donor, but for community property of husband and wife a joint annual gift of $22,000 per child is allowed.

Where there is a direct transfer to a beneficiary, there can be no strings attached, such as a right of recapture after college graduation. The assignment cannot be hazy; it is best to document it fully by written notice to the publisher, by registration of copyright assignment, if any, and perhaps even by the appointment of a bank or other institution to collect and distribute the monies. Properly accomplished, it is clear that the income tax is chargeable to the new owner of the income-producing property and not to the assignor, although the assignor may be liable for gift taxes if the gift does not come within the statutory exemptions to which the donor may be entitled.

Some successful songwriters have established trust funds for their children without including ASCAP or BMI performance monies. The divisibility of copyright is accepted for tax purposes. No capital gain on resale can eventually be claimed by the child or trustee who received the gift from the songwriter because, under tax law, a donee of an author or composer is treated the same as the donor and is therefore barred from the benefit of capital gains.

When an aged person, such as a parent, is dependent on a successful songwriter for support, consideration may be given to shifting income by a transfer of copyright or of the property right to a royalty contract. There can be a direct conveyance to the parent, provided that there is no obligation to return the property in the future; it is reasonable to expect that the parent will express appreciation by a bequest back to the assignor. By virtue of the trust or conveyance, the assignor is relieved of taxes on the income. Taxes paid by the dependent are likely to be lower than those that would be payable by the assignor if the income were attributable to him or her.

In determining whether to shift income to the dependent, the grantor must consider the possible loss of a dependency deduction on his or her own tax return if the dependent's income increases beyond certain limits. For example, assigning property that produces sufficient income to a widowed parent over 65 to cover 50 percent or more of his or her living expenses may cause the grantor to lose the deduction for the dependent. Nevertheless, the assignment can result in a tax saving at the donor's top tax bracket.

Shifting Income from One Year to Other Years

On either a fiscal or calendar year, benefit may be obtained by deferring the receipt and reporting of income to a future date, despite the loss of use of the money until its receipt. One reason for this is the continued availability of monies that would otherwise have to be paid as taxes. Another reason may be the expectation that there will be lower earnings in future years and therefore the deferred income will be reported at a lower tax rate. Some writers, publishers, and record artists contract for delays in payments of royalties until a subsequent year.

In each case of income deferral, the question of "constructive receipt" arises. This problem is present if the taxpayer waives receipt of monies to which he or she is entitled in the tax year or delays cashing a check that is in his or her hands before the end of the current tax year. The element of subterfuge involved can be avoided by a forthright provision in a royalty agreement designed to accomplish the same benefit.

A typical acceptable provision, in the instance of a recording artist, provides that the royalties payable in any one year may not exceed a stated maximum, and that any excess is accumulated for disbursement in future years when the current earnings do not reach the earnings ceiling. Other contracts, such as that between a show music writer and a music publisher, or an exclusive service contract between a songwriter and publisher for the services of the writer, may call for an annual minimum guaranteed payment to the writer on the understanding that the publisher can withhold earnings in excess of a ceiling figure fixed in the agreement. At the end of the term of the agreement, the accumulated amount withheld, if any, is disbursed over a stated number of years at an annual figure set forth in the contract.

When this method of income deferral is used, it is required that the funds being held by the publisher or the recording company remain in the business and be subject to the risk of the business. A contractual provision whereby the person liable for the payment of the deferred amount places the funds in escrow or in trust, or in some other manner earmarks the funds and removes them from the possible claims of creditors, destroys the advantage sought, and results in a constructive receipt of the funds by the person entitled to them.

Deferral of Income Through Retirement Plans

The Internal Revenue Code permits the deferral of a limited amount of such income without the previously described risk by the device of a retirement plan. For self-employed individuals, this can be a Keogh plan, an individual retirement account (IRA), a simplified employee pension (SEP), a deferred salary plan, or a Roth IRA.

There are two general types of Keogh plans: defined-benefit plans and defined-contribution plans. Most persons have a defined-contribution plan, the two main types of which are a money-purchase plan and a profit-sharing plan. Under a money-purchase plan, the participant agrees to put a certain minimum percentage of self-employed income into the account each year. Most Keogh plan holders who receive income from freelancing and who do not have employees, such as self-employed songwriters, have a money-purchase plan. Where the holder has employees, it is likely that a profit-sharing plan will be used.

Under either type of defined-contribution plan, contributions can equal up to 25 percent of earned income, or $40,000, whichever is lower. For this purpose, earned income consists of net earnings from self-employment less the Keogh contribution; this, in effect, limits the contribution to 20 percent of the net earnings from self-employment before the Keogh contribution to a money-purchase plan. Under a money-purchase plan, the full amount of the contribution is deductible for tax purposes from gross income in the computation of adjusted gross income. Under a profit-sharing plan, the deduction from gross income for tax purposes is technically limited to 15 percent of the net earnings from self-employment, less the Keogh contribution, thus restricting the deduction to 13.0435 percent.

The effect of the use of the Keogh plan is virtually the same as if the writer had arranged for the deferment of the payment of the amount contributed to the plan. However, by using the plan, the writer removes the funds from the risk of the publisher's or recording company's business. The writer effectively pays no current tax on the contribution, earns interest on the contribution (no interest is earned when funds are left with the publisher), and pays no tax on the interest until it is withdrawn.

In a situation where income is deferred by contractual arrangements, the contract has to provide in advance how much is to be paid (or deferred) each year. Under the Keogh plan, annual determinations may be made as to how much to "defer" by making the contribution, so long as the limitations are observed. Contracts providing for deferments stipulate the time and amount of payout. Payouts under the Keogh plan are generally not permitted to begin before age 59 without penalty (except in case of total disability), and in any event must begin no later than April 1 of the year when the participant reaches the age of 70 years and 6 months. If not fully withdrawn by that year, the plan must provide for ultimate payout over a period that does not extend beyond the life expectancy of the participant, or the joint lives of the participant and his or her beneficiary, as computed in accordance with Internal Revenue Service regulations. Since, by virtue of having taken the deduction at the time of contribution, the self-employed individual has not paid tax in the earlier year, the entire amount drawn later, including the interest earned, is subject to tax.

A word of caution is required with respect to employees. In all probability, a self-employed composer or recording artist does not have employees, but if he or she does, and then adopts a Keogh plan, the plan usually must provide benefits for all full-time employees whose period of employment extends to 1 year or more and who are at least 21 years old.

Employed workers, as well as self-employed workers, may establish an individual retirement account (IRA), which, as in the case of a Keogh plan, permits the deferral, for income tax purposes, of a certain amount of income and the future earnings, such as interest, on such deferred income. To be eligible, neither the individual nor the spouse can be covered by an employer retirement plan unless the adjusted gross income is under $54,000 if married or under

$34,000 if single. Only a partial tax deduction is permitted if the adjusted gross income is between $54,000 and $64,000 if married or between $34,000 and $44,000 if single. Where there is ineligibility for all or partial deductions for IRAs, nondeductible contributions are still allowed.

Under an IRA plan a worker can make deductible contributions of up to $3,000 of earned income annually, which amount might rise to $6,000 if the worker had an unemployed spouse. If earnings were less than $3,000, the contribution can be made for up to the full amount earned. A self-employed person may contribute to both an IRA and a Keogh plan, but after the age of 70 years and 6 months he or she may no longer contribute to the IRA plan.

In the instance where an individual is both employed, being, for instance, a member of a band, and self-employed, operating as a songwriter who receives royalties from ASCAP and a music publisher, that individual may establish and contribute to both an IRA and a Keogh plan. If both the participant and spouse work, each may establish an IRA and contribute up to $3,000 annually; the couple's total IRA annual contribution might thus total $6,000.

Under an IRA, as in the case of a Keogh plan, distributions to the participant may begin at the age of 59 years and 6 months without penalty but need not begin before the age of 70 years and 6 months. If the amount in the plan is not fully withdrawn in that year, the withdrawal must extend over a period not longer than the life expectancy of the participant or the joint lives of the participant and the participant's beneficiary, as computed in accordance with Internal Revenue Service regulations. All amounts withdrawn from IRAs are subject to income tax at the time of withdrawal, with the exception of amounts contributed where no deduction was previously claimed.

Keogh plan distributions are treated in the same manner as IRA distributions for income tax purposes, except that certain favorable tax provisions apply to lump-sum Keogh distributions.

Where an individual is employed, there are other retirement plans that might be considered. One is the simplified employee pension (SEP) plan, set up by an employer, which is designed to give employers an easy way to make payments toward their employees' pension plans.

Another retirement plan is the Section 401(k), or deferred-salary plan, established by an employer or a self-employed individual, which permits individual contributions to be made on a pretax basis.

Finally, the Taxpayer Relief Act of 1997 established the Roth IRA for contributions up to $3,000 a year, or $6,000 for a couple, for qualifying taxpayers whose adjusted gross income is within certain limits. This is known as a "back-loaded IRA" because the contribution when initially made is not deductible and must use after-tax earnings, although certain of the distributions can be tax-free and all the earnings are tax-deferred. This means that funds can grow tax-deferred and, for example, be withdrawn up to $10,000 tax-free for the purchase of a first home or can be used for individual or family college expenses with taxation when withdrawn at ordinary income rates for the earnings accumulation portion. Otherwise, Roth IRA withdrawals must be deferred until the age of 59 years and 6 months; withdrawals made before that age are subject to a 10 percent penalty.

The Tax Implications of Type of Business Organization

The way a business is organized—sole proprietorship, partnership, C corporation, S corporation, limited liability company—has tax implications.

S CORPORATIONS

An *S corporation* is a regular (C) corporation where the stockholders have made an election to treat its income and losses as if they were the stockholders' direct income and losses, rather than those of the corporation. For tax purposes, it is as if the corporation were a partnership or a sole proprietorship. Through use of an S corporation, a stockholder can achieve the limited liability afforded by a corporation and also avoid the double taxation of corporations, first on the corporation's profits and second upon stockholder dividends.

The tax treatment is particularly beneficial in the case of new businesses expected to lose money at their beginning. A shareholder is entitled to take tax losses that may be offset against income from other sources.

An S corporation must have one class of stock with no more than 75 shareholders, and all of its shareholders must agree to the S status. Shareholders who work for the corporation are treated as employees for Social Security tax payments. They do not pay self-employment tax on their salary income or other receipts from the corporation.

THE LIMITED LIABILITY COMPANY

Limited liability companies(LLCs) are another business organization option now available in many states, including New York and California. They combine many of the features of both limited partnerships and corporations. Unlike a limited partnership, which prohibits a limited partner from actively participating in the business, the LLC allows its members to participate in management without jeopardizing limited liability. An LLC, much like an S corporation, offers flow-through taxation of its members.

The LLC form raises potential federal and state security law issues. Specifically, if a membership interest in an LLC is determined to be a "security," registration requirements, fraud liability, and disclosure obligations may come into play. To date, no court has found the requisite level of "member passivity" (one test among others) to reach this conclusion. However, in the case of producers or musical recording or performance groups, these issues may arise if there is a change in the ownership of the LLC. To prevent this from happening, the operating agreement should recognize that each member's interest may be altered by decisions beyond the member's control but it is nevertheless the intent that ownership interests be exempt from public securities laws. The operating agreement should expressly state that membership interests are for the member's own account and not intended for resale.

Family-Owned Businesses

Many songwriters and some independent publishers operate as family-owned businesses. As such, there is a possible estate tax benefit under the Taxpayer Relief Act of 1997. Recognizing that it is undesirable to force a sale of all or part of a family business in order to pay estate taxes, the 1997 Taxpayer Relief Act excludes such businesses from estate tax if the value of the business exceeds 50 percent of the entire estate value (with certain adjustments). A further requirement is that the decedent be a U.S. citizen or legal resident and that the executor of the estate enter into an agreement that the exclusion will be waived if the family heirs to the business do not materially participate for at least 10 years or otherwise dispose of the business. A qualifying family business must have been owned by the decedent or members of the family for at least 5 of the 8 years preceding death and those members must have materially participated in the business operation. It is a further condition that not over 35 percent of the income of the business was in the category of personal holding company income. This determination involves careful analysis of what portion of the income came from, for example, concert income of a popular artist or producer or a composer-songwriter's current income. In some instances, careful management can reduce such percentages by spreading the source of such funds among members of a band, guest artists, etc.

Corporations and the Personal
Holding Company Designation

A *personal holding company* is defined as a corporation a majority of whose stock is held, directly or indirectly, during the last half of the year, by not more than five persons and at least 60 percent of whose gross income is the result of the creative activity of its principal shareholders. This type of income includes, among other types of receipts, the income from copyright and other royalties. The income of a personal holding company is subject to regular corporate tax rates, and its undistributed income is taxed at 39.1 percent. The total tax bite can be enormous.

Even if a corporation is not classified as a personal holding company, the accumulated income, to the extent that it exceeds $250,000 ($150,000 if it is a service corporation in the field of performing arts) and is not required for the reasonable needs of the business, may be subject to certain surtaxes.

There are actions that can be taken to avoid personal holding company surtaxes, as well as ways to take advantage of federal, state, and city tax laws as they relate to the various corporate forms of organization. Anyone in the music business considering incorporating as a technique for reducing taxes should explore all options carefully with attorneys and accountants before making a decision.

Royalties as Income

Royalties are taxed on the same basis as ordinary income. Consequently, comparative calculations are advisable to determine whether there is a sufficient tax advantage to warrant the use of one of the tax-saving devices discussed above.

Foreign Royalties Subject Only to U.S. Tax

By reciprocal treaties with many countries, U.S. taxpayers are exempt from foreign income tax on royalties earned abroad. For example, the treaty between the United States and the United Kingdom provides for a tax exemption in the country of source of income, and taxation in the country of residence, with respect to royalties from copyrights and like property. This exemption, however, does not apply if the taxpayer has a permanent establishment in the country that is the source of income and the royalties are directly associated with the business operations carried on by the permanent establishment.

Most publishers and record companies are aware of the necessity of filing nonresident tax exemption claims with foreign governments, either directly or through foreign subpublishers or agents. Authors and composers encounter this necessity only when they deal directly with foreign music or record companies, instead of in the customary manner through a U.S. firm. Reciprocal treaties are designed to avoid double taxation and the inconvenience of having to file for refunds of moneys withheld at the source. (Treaties are not uniform; specific reference should be made to the particular treaty when a question arises. Treaties are supplied by the Superintendent of Documents, U.S. Government Printing Office, Washington, DC 20005.) The National Music Publishers Association has maintained a list of foreign countries from which copyright royalties may be paid free of withholding taxes or at reduced withholding taxes. Notable among such countries are Australia, Belgium, Canada, France, Germany, Italy, the Netherlands, and the U.K.

Regarding royalties earned in a foreign country in which the recipient maintains a permanent establishment (so that the tax treaty would not be applicable) or earned in a country with which the United States does not have a tax treaty, it is probable that the source country will impose a tax on the income there derived and that the United States will also tax that income. Some or all of the adverse effects of that double taxation can be ameliorated by the appropriate use of the foreign tax credit in the U.S. tax return.

Retention of Tax-Related Documents

It is generally recommended that supporting records be retained for possible audit for at least 6 years, despite the fact that the IRS can only assess tax for a particular year for 3 years after a return for the applicable year was filed or due to be filed. However, this period is extended to 6 years if there is a 25 percent or more deficiency in gross income reports, and in the absence of a filing, there is no time limit. For purposes of capital gain or depreciation, the period of retaining basic historic accounting information is necessarily extended to the period for which the basic cost is established.

Audit Procedures

In 1994. the Internal Revenue Service under its Market Segment Specialization Program (MSSP) prepared a training manual concerning music business audits, and in 1995, issued a manual concerning Form 1040 issues. Both manuals are available on-line at www.irs.gov.

The 1994 manual describes the functions of various participants in the industry and offers information that should be noted by an IRS auditor reviewing the returns of such individuals. For example, it states:

> There is extensive bartering activity in the industry. It occurs in the form of swap-outs (advertising for cars, advertising for tickets, etc.). . . . There are many checks and balances in the industry on income reporting, but some activities, such as playing small clubs for the door receipts, love offerings at concerts and churches, and concession sales at small locations, present situations where income may go unreported.

Some relevant points from the 1994 manual for specific categories are as follows:

SONGWRITERS

- ▶ A review is required of office-in-home expenses where the premises are not exclusively used for business.
- ▶ A vacation home or other such place claimed as a required "place to think" is not allowable.
- ▶ Travel expenses "in many cases, include personal expenses."
- ▶ With regard to related returns, partnerships and corporations may be formed to seek to shift income between entities for beneficial tax treatment, which, although allowable, must be cross-checked to get a true income picture.

MUSIC PUBLISHERS

- ▶ "Related returns" may include separate publishing entities to conform to the requirements of performing rights societies. If the songwriter is a shareholder, issues with regard to royalty advances may warrant examination.

LIVE PERFORMERS

> The single most common audit adjustment is disallowance of personal expenses being claimed as business deductions. "Stars"

frequently take the position that since they are in the limelight all the time, virtually everything they do is "business" and is part of the image-making and maintaining process.

Examples given of nonallowable deductions are home improvements, vacation homes, and boats, as well as failure to distinguish stage clothes from street clothes. The position taken by the IRS is that peripheral business benefits from an activity do not convert personal expenses to business expenses.

With regard to the support personnel for a star, two deductions are not allowed, one for the reimbursement of "away-from-home" expenses paid by the featured artist and the other by the support personnel who have already been reimbursed.

VIDEO AND RECORD PRODUCERS

▶ Determine if the producer has the opportunity for other types of income, such as studio rental, talent scouting, writing, etc. Question the producer about any label deals, pressing and distribution deals, agreements with other producers on joint production arrangements.

▶ Watch for reimbursements to producers from record companies for out-of-pocket expenses.

▶ With regard to "custom sessions," described as vanity deals where a prospective artist pays cash for the studio and production services involved, unreported income should be sought out.

▶ Past examinations have shown that some producers will purchase expensive gifts, such as autos, for artists as incentives . . . without Form 1099 being issued to the recipient.

▶ The cost of record masters should be amortized unless the 3-year safe-harbor alternative is used. This is defined as allowing depreciation and amortization of costs at 50 percent in the first year and 25 percent in each of the next 2 years.

▶ Payment of employment taxes for engineers, musicians, arrangers, backup vocalists, etc., whether freelancers or staff members, should be checked.

▶ Avoidance of self-employment taxes on producer royalties by placement on Schedule E or on face of 1040 forms should also be checked.

▶ Related income sources such as songwriting, publishing, and performing should be compared. Some producers use a corporate form for one function and Schedule C for other business activities, and for a general audit all should be reviewed at once.

MANAGERS

▶ Make sure that expenses claimed are not refunded by the artist.

▶ Some expenses may be capital in nature, requiring safe harbor or amortization and depreciation.

▶ Compare the related returns of the manager in other functions, such as music publisher or for merchandising and souvenir sales.

35

Record Clubs and Premiums

Approximately 17 million Americans belong to record clubs. Total club and mail-order sales in 1997 were about $1.5 billion, with close to 80 percent attributable to sales by record clubs. It is estimated that of the total record consumer group, those who rely exclusively on club sources are only 3 percent of the total consumer group and those who buy from a club as well as retail outlets constitute 14 percent of all record-buying consumers.

In the field of general record club activity, there are two major record clubs. The largest is Columbia House, with about 14 million members. Until 2002, when Blackstone Capital Partners purchased a majority stake for $450 million, it was jointly owned by Time Warner and Sony.

The second major record club is BMG Direct Marketing, with 8 million members. BMG, which was formerly the RCA Record Club and is now an affiliate of the German firm Bertelsmann A.G., also operates the BMG Music Service, the BMG Compact Disc Club, and the International Preview Society, which handles classical recordings.

The major record clubs handle the catalogs of various record companies, as well as the basic catalogs of their mother companies. Both major record clubs obtain their product from other labels on a nonexclusive basis.

Membership Plans

Record clubs offer various purchasing plans to attract prospective members. For example, new members are usually offered a certain number of records free or for a nominal charge, subject to handling costs. Members then must purchase a given number of records at the regular price within a given number of years, such as six selections within 2 years. One BMG Web site offer in 2002 was for 7 free introductory CDs, with an obligation to purchase one (at the minimum price of $14.98 in 2002) within a year; once the obligation was met, the consumer would receive 4 additional free CDs. It should be noted, however, that shipping and handling charges apply even to the "free" CDs.

Both BMG and Columbia House have relied on a negative option under which record club members receive a monthly featured selection unless they have declined such receipt by a specific date. However, Columbia House Record Club has established an alternative plan that eliminates the negative option of automatic shipment. This plan requires a commitment to buy six selections at regular club prices over a 2-year period and offers the member the right to cancel membership at any time after meeting that obligation. Further, no unrequested selections are sent to members.

With the advent of e-mail offers, members now not only have the opportunity to listen to samples of selected items but, in the case of BMG, also have the benefit of chat rooms for discussions among members. Record club members are also given access to CD samplers in order to audition new recordings. Further, Internet access offers both the customary array of informative magazines targeted by music category and Web sites with over 16,000 music selections.

Record clubs target buyers 30 years old and over, approximately 10 years older than the median age of record store buyers. According to the Recording Industry Association of America, a large percentage of music consumers is over the age of 25, with the fastest-growing segment over 45. However, record stores still cater to teenage buyers by blaring new releases, scaring off adult buyers. Record clubs allow adult buyers to avoid all the hassles of record stores, malls, and parking lots by purchasing music in the convenience of their own homes. In 1999, Columbia House negotiated a long-term agreement allowing Columbia House's members to download single selections and make custom CDs using CDNow's facilities.

Outside-Label Agreements

In their contractual agreements with outside labels, both BMG and Columbia House normally provide that the licensed product will bear the original label and jacket when sold through the club. All record club product, however, bears the club's bar code and is not subject to returns through conventional stores.

Royalties payable by Columbia House to the outside labels are about 9.5 percent of the regular club price (less a charge allocated to the record container), based on 85 percent of the records sold and not returned; the royalty for soundtrack, original-cast, and classical albums is typically about 12 percent. Other clubs pay a similar royalty. Traditionally, clubs do not pay royalties on "bonus" or "free" records distributed to members. However, clubs will sometimes accept a limitation on the number of bonus or free records approved for distribution. Limitations require that free records will not exceed a set percentage of the records sold; the clubs will pay royalties on any bonus CDs that exceed such limitations. In some contracts, such royalties will be at a lower rate than that applicable to regular club sales.

Ordinarily the Columbia House and BMG clubs take master tapes from outside labels on a nonexclusive basis and press records based on the tapes.

Advances against royalties to become due to the label are customarily negotiated upon commencement of the term, and the duration of the term is for a limited number of years. The operation is thus similar to that of a foreign licensee of an outside label. The clubs pay, as in the case of foreign licensees, mechanical copyright license fees and payments on sales that become due to the Music Performance Trust Fund and the Special Payments Fund established through the American Federation of Musicians.

Artist Royalties

A fairly standard agreement with U.S. artists provides that the artist receives one-half of his or her standard royalty rate on sales through clubs and that no royalties are payable on bonus or free records. The bonus and free-record clauses tend to match similar provisions in agreements between clubs and record companies.

Reduced artist royalties further serve to attract record clubs operating outside of the United States. It is common for foreign licensees to place U.S. records in clubs on the basis of lower royalties payable to the U.S. licensors, as compared to the royalty rates on traditional sales.

Popular recording artists who fear that a record club will flood club members with free or bonus records, for which royalties will not be payable, may get a contract provision stipulating that the number of records of the artist given away by a club cannot exceed the number sold. Record companies can achieve similar protection in their agreements with the clubs. For their part, record clubs contend that, in the United States at least, free or bonus goods serve as an incentive to make purchases and that club distribution does not "cannibalize" sales through retail stores and other outlets. They also argue that the clubs make it possible for smaller record companies to compete with the majors, at least in their distribution channel, thereby making them more effective in acquiring and retaining new artists.

Foreign Record Clubs

There are record clubs in most of the principal territories of the world, including Australia, Austria, Belgium, Canada, Denmark, England, Finland, France, Germany, Japan, the Netherlands, Sweden, and Switzerland. In 1996 club sales in the United Kingdom were 10 percent of total record turnover. Germany's direct-mail market was at 16.5 percent in 1997 and was slightly more in 1994. Prior to its acquisition by Universal, PolyGram formed a direct-marketing division, consolidating its Dial Record Club (France), its 2-million-member Britannia Music (United Kingdom), and its Italian, Dutch, and German companies, giving it a base membership of well over 3 million members. With the increasing availability and popularity of the Internet and the numerous Web sites maintained by retailers that all offer product, club sales are likely to diminish in the future rather than grow.

Foreign licensees with their own record clubs or arrangements with third-party record clubs will seek the right to release a licensor's recordings through such channels. Some licensors may refuse to permit sales through record clubs without prior approval. Licensees frequently request the right to pay reduced royalty rates on club sales, contending that they themselves receive a limited licensing royalty from clubs owned and operated by third parties. If the licensee operates its own record club, it will assert that the high cost of advertising and large amounts of uncollectable monies mandate a reduced royalty rate on club sales. The rates will be the subject of bargaining and are usually one-half of the rates applicable to regular retail sales.

Mechanical License Fees

Throughout their history of operations in the United States, the major record clubs have relied on an industry-accepted practice of reduced mechanical license royalty rates. The assumed rate (payable quarterly) was placed at 75 percent of the standard rate paid by the originating record label. In 1990, music publishers unsuccessfully challenged this practice, claiming that club sales in the absence of written confirmation of such reduced rate constituted an infringement. The court dismissed the action on the grounds that acceptance and negotiation of royalty payments at the assumed rate, without restrictive endorsement or other effective notice of protest, ratified an implied license for use of copyrighted songs and created an implied license for future periods. (The case in question, *Wixen Music Publishing, Inc. et al. v. CBS Records dba Columbia House Records,* is unpublished.) Furthermore, even if a rare publisher were to object, any co-owner of the song in question could be the source of a binding, nonexclusive license if the co-owner did not join in a rejection of such rate.

The Harry Fox Agency, which represents many publishers, has balked at waiving royalties on free or bonus records and normally collects such royalties from record clubs. The Harry Fox Agency will accept the 75 percent rate provided that it does not reduce the royalty below 75 percent of the statutory compulsory mechanical license rate, regardless of lesser negotiated licenses with originating labels. A 1999 dispute arose as to whether this 75 percent rate should continue as an industrywide custom without formal regulation beyond merely incorporating the issuing label's terms of license minus 25 percent. The Harry Fox Agency claims that in a digital age, auditing and accounting procedures are more efficiently handled with specific licensees, whereas the clubs counter that a changeover is costly and unnecessary in the face of established cooperation between accounting staffs.

Premiums

A premium offer may arise when a business such as a supermarket or a tire company sells records at an unusually low price in order to encourage patronage for its regular products. This is a promotional plan that frequently involves a guarantee to the record company of a substantial number of sales.

Since the price paid to the record company is low, it must keep its costs at a reduced level. The margin of profit on each record is small, but a premium transaction entails large volume and low distribution expenses. In connection with a premium offer, the record company will seek low mechanical license rates from the music publishers and will have to evaluate the royalty rates that must be paid to the performing artists. Some agreements with artists provide for no royalties in the case of premium sales; others may establish reduced royalty rates. Where the artist agreement does not provide for low royalty rates, the record company may have to negotiate with the artist, stressing the promotional exposure and publicity value as well as the volume of sales, which may result in sizable royalty payments even at a lower royalty rate.

36

Music Videos

The creation, distribution, and broadcast of a music video is now considered an essential aspect of the promotion of a new record. The release of most major label popular records is accompanied by a music video, usually a 3- to 5-minute visualization of a song featuring visual and audio performances by the artist who recorded it. Videos aired on MTV, the 24-hour cable music channel, or its sister channel, VH-1, as well as on other cable and regular TV music channels, clearly generate increased sales. One study shows that videos played in music retail stores are even more influential marketing tools than MTV. Record companies frequently pay movie theaters and restaurants to display music videos in their establishments, as well. Although music videos were initially seen primarily as promotional tools rather than as forms of commercial entertainment, the record company policy of granting free licenses to networks and programs is no longer necessarily the case. In recent years, for instance, MTV has had to negotiate multimillion-dollar payments with a number of major record companies for rights to selected video clips for periods ranging from 1 week to 30 days.

MTV and VH-1, both owned by Viacom's MTV Networks, continue to be the dominant video programmers. MTV, the first 24-hour music channel, now reaches 79 million homes. In an attempt to maintain the interest of its target audience of 12- to 34-year-olds, executives have chosen to cut back on the number of nonmusic programs that had begun to dominate MTV's format. The 16-year-old channel has recently added such shows as *The Cut, BIOrhythm,* and *Fanatic,* all of which focus on music and recording artists. These recent changes have seen a substantial increase in ratings and profit for the MTV Networks.

VH-1 began as the stepchild of MTV when it began airing in 1985 in an effort by MTV to ward off competition. The programming began with little or no direction and a sparse audience. But since 1994 format changes similar to those of its parent company have made VH-1 a viable alternative to MTV, reaching over 68 million homes by the end of 1999. VH-1 has focused on the 18- to 49-year-old audience, a slightly older demographic than MTV targets.

With a mix of adult-oriented video rotations and shows such as *Pop-Up Video* and *Behind the Music*, VH-1 has become the preferred channel for this coveted consumer group.

However, a number of channels serving specialized markets, both musically and geographically, now provide viable options to both the consumer and the industry. Country Music Television (CMT) and Black Entertainment Television (BET) focus on specific musical genres, while The Box, the only all-request video channel, allows the viewer to choose from up to 200 current videos of all genres. Sessions@aol.com also offers songs, videos, and other features to the on-line consumer. Such competitive programming has forced MTV Networks to adapt format and content in order to maintain its majority audience share.

However, the dominant strength of the two MTV services was such that the Justice Department commenced an investigation in late 1999 of possible anti-trust violations in their dealings with music companies. In connection with this investigation, an MTV executive stated, "We took exclusive rights to only 4 of the more than 1,000 videos used this year."

Today, music videos are also a part of a growing commercial market. The exploitation of music videos has resulted in revenues derived from exhibition on network, cable, and local television, viewings in commercial clubs, plays on video jukeboxes, and the sale of videocassettes and videodiscs for home use. All major record companies now deliver long-form music videos (such as concert films) and short-form music video compilations of their artists directly to music retailers and video distributors for home sale.

Video Technology

Although the technology for storing and replaying video images continues to advance, some familiar problems still exist. When home video was first intro-duced, consumers were faced with the dilemma of which of two incompatible systems to invest in, Betamax or VHS. Similarly, software producers were required to invest in one or both of these technologies, resulting in general market resistance and delay. Today, new competitive clashes exist, as between the laser disc (LD) and digital versatile disc (DVD). Sales for the laser disc, a 12-inch video disc with a 120-minute capacity (60 minutes per side) are steadily declining as the market for DVD expands. Only one company, Pioneer, offers a dual DVD/LD player that continues to be popular on the market. However, trends clearly suggest that the laser disc will soon be outdated; major retail chains such as Tower and Virgin favor DVD and have ceased offering laser discs.

Introduced on the market in 1997, DVD has quickly become a format of choice for home video viewers. One year after their release into the marketplace in 1997, nearly 600,000 DVD players had been sold. (By way of comparison, only 320,000 CD players were sold the first year after they were introduced, and 515,000 VCRs were sold in the same time span.) It is estimated that by the end of 2002, over 1.1 billion DVD movies and music videos had been shipped. The total number of DVD players sold to U.S. consumers through 2002 is estimated at 43.7 million, in nearly 33 million households. The advantages of DVDs over CDs are similar to the advantages of CDs over LPs and tapes: increased storage capacity and superior audiovisual qualities. In addition, the majority of DVD releases feature surround-sound capabilities. Like CDs, DVDs are 5 $\frac{1}{2}$ inches in diameter. Originally designed to store 128 minutes of digital video, DVDs with double that capacity are now available. The latest entries in the disc market, which are based on what is known as blue-laser technology, have even greater storage capacities, up to 5 times that of the original DVDs, but they are unlikely to make a dent in the home consumer market in the near future.

Video Licensing

New video technology presents new licensing opportunities and challenges, requiring a combination of past licensing practices. For instance, conventional audio CDs use mechanical reproduction licensing, which in the United States is on a statutory basis (see Chapter 15, page 153). However, visual materials require fully negotiated synchronization licenses; where lyrics or music are presented on screen in place of printed materials, a special form of synchronization license is required.

In addition, a "fixing fee" is evolving for video use; this is a fixed, nonrecoupable initial payment, which is often supplemented by an advance against royalties. The royalty structure itself can sometimes be analogized to "double statutory," which is a shorthand device used for requesting just over 16 cents, or simply negotiated fresh from a standpoint of between 8.5 cents and 16 cents per song per unit.

Meanwhile, for major-budget feature films, video uses are usually negotiated at significant fixed sums of as much as $7,500 to $12,500 worldwide. Whether this buyout includes foreign sales, for which different collection procedures apply, has not yet been tested. A rare alternative is a rollover advance in which the fixed sum constitutes an advance for the first 50,000 or other stated number of units upon either manufacture or sale, as negotiable, with additional advances for each successive plateau.

Advances in technology have led to "future-technology clauses" because some firms are concerned about broad licenses for all potential new technology and refuse to license or issue short-term licenses without options other than to negotiate in good faith consistent with then-existing industry standards to secure their rights as advanced technology becomes available. These clauses, however, cannot be limited to any medium or they will be strictly limited to the designated medium. For example, in *Subfilms, Ltd. v. MGM/UA Home Video, Inc.*, 988 F.2d 122 (9th Cir. 1993), the court held that a future-technology clause limited to theatrical and television rights did not encompass the right to distribute in videocassettes.

Audiovisual Rights

Music videos involve contractual rights and obligations among record companies, artists, producers, music publishers, and others. Perhaps to a lesser extent, other software programming may be concerned with all or some of the same entities, persons, or factors as well. Insofar as music videos and other software programming are audiovisual motion picture productions, the legal and contractual principles and standards involved in such technology are similar to those discussed in Chapter 23, "Music for Motion Pictures," and in Chapter 24, "Licensing Recordings for Motion Pictures."

Record manufacturers engaged in video programming, whether in the form of music videos or other software, have enlarged the scope of their operations to include filmmaking and its attendant problems. The increasing length of record company-artist contracts bears witness to this phenomenon, as record companies, artists, and producers attempt to cover contractually the multiplying complexities of the record and film business.

The music video's success in promotional and commercial markets has impelled record companies to strive vigorously to obtain video rights from artists. These rights have become key issues in contractual negotiations. In support of their claims to video rights, record companies contend that audiovisual products offer strong competition to traditional audio sound carriers—records, tapes, and CDs—for the future consumer home market.

For years record companies included language in their artist contracts permitting them to use recordings in audiovisual form and restricting artists from appearing in audiovisual media for other companies. One agreement provided that the artist's recording might be used exclusively "in any medium and by any means whatsoever, including but not limited to audiovisual records, motion pictures, television or any medium or devices now or hereafter known, and to utilize photographs, drawings, and pictorial animation in connection therewith." Another agreement defined a record or phonograph record as a "film, video tape, or similar device which embodies the artist's audio performance with a visual rendition of the artist's performance, i.e., a sight and sound device."

Today, recording agreements contain separate definitions for videos and their uses. One form defines video recordings to include "videocassettes, videodiscs, and new media video recordings that enable a program to be perceived visually . . . when used in combination or as a part of a piece of electronic, mechanical or other apparatus." The same agreement also defines the terms videocassette, videodisc, and home video use.

While music videos are primarily 3- to 5-minute clips, like those used by MTV, the typical definitions of records or phonograph records or video recordings contain no time or length limitations. As defined, an artist would be disqualified from performing in films or videotapes of live concerts, full-length feature films or documentaries, or film television programs in which an artist visually performs only a single song. For example, a record company could require consent for one of its artists' participation in a Woodstock-type concert film or possibly even in a feature-length film that contains concert footage of an artist under contract to the company, such as *Detroit Rock City*. The record company could refuse consent or, theoretically, might even condition approval on its being granted the right to distribute the film theatrically, on television, and in videocassettes for home use. This could be extremely detrimental to an artist who seeks and treasures film appearances.

Artists may therefore try to limit the definition of a record or video recording to audiovisual productions of a short duration, to audiovisual productions of one or two songs, or to copies to be marketed to the public for home use only. A common issue is whether there can be any commercial exploitation of audiovisual products without the express consent of the artist. While artists may agree to promotional uses of music videos, they may refuse to allow commercial exploitation without their prior written approval. Some companies may accept this restriction, but others will resist strongly. A new artist may find it very difficult to obtain the right to approve commercial uses of music videos.

Some record companies have acquiesced to limiting their rights to audiovisual performances of sound recordings produced under the recording artist agreement. Even in these cases, though, the record company would probably retain exclusive control over the video exploitation rights for promotional purposes and for home video sales.

Although it is common for a record company to have the exclusive right to make music videos for their artists, more often than not the record company will not be obligated to finance and produce such videos. This is similar to the record company's lack of specific obligations to carry out and finance promotional activities in support of phonograph records. However, unlike most new artists, established artists do obtain commitments from record companies to produce music videos, typically on a per-record basis. Because of the substantial costs of producing a music video, a record company will generally agree to create one for a new or less-established artist only after a record appears to be a commercial success. Some independent record companies are even starting to direct funds that were formerly devoted to independent promotion into video production.

Artists ordinarily have no rights to produce and finance a music video independently in the absence of the record company's consent, despite the record company's lack of any obligation to grant such approval or to produce a music video itself. But artists may attempt to protect themselves by reserving video rights, subject to granting the record company a right of first refusal, for a limited period of time, to produce and exploit the music video. Under the right of first refusal, the record company would have the prerogative of matching offers of third parties. The record company might also be granted the right of first negotiation, which would entitle it to be approached first and negotiated with before any third parties.

Alternatively, the artist and record company may agree that neither party shall have the exclusive right to produce and exploit a music video, prohibiting them from making a music video without mutual approval. This serves to delay their negotiations for control of music video rights until a future time when it may be easier to assess the appropriateness of any particular course of action.

The record company ordinarily acquires the entire ownership interest in the videotapes and other physical materials, as well as the copyright in the audiovisual work itself, including the visual images and the accompanying sounds. A motion picture or other audiovisual work such as a music video is generally deemed eligible for the © copyright notice. It is not qualified for the copyright notice applicable to sound recordings.

In the case of most artists, the agreement between a record company and the artist is an employment contract. The copyright in the audiovisual work, at least to the extent of an artist's contributions, thus belongs to the record company as a work for hire under the 1976 Copyright Act. The act grants work-for-hire status to one "specially ordered or commissioned for use ... as a part of a motion picture or other audiovisual work," where the parties have expressly agreed in writing "that the work shall be considered a work made for hire." In the case of a work for hire, the record company is the "author" for copyright purposes, as well as the owner of the video. The Copyright Act provides that for works made for hire the copyright will endure for a term of 95 years from the year of its first publication, or a term of 120 years from the year of its creation, whichever expires first. The record company, as "author," could not have its rights terminated by others under the termination provisions of the act. In any event there would be protection against termination under such provisions accorded to a music video as a derivative work. Whether or not a record company owns the audiovisual work, as a work for hire or otherwise, a record company will demand that the artist grant it all exploitation rights in a music video. This will include not only promotional uses and home video sales but also licensing to third parties for broadcast or exhibition over free, pay, or cable television and in nightclubs.

While the main emphasis of record labels is on promoting their product, the major labels are increasingly requesting fees for the broadcast of their music videos on television and for their showings in nightclubs. For television usage, fees usually range up to $100, with some instances of larger payments for exclusive broadcast rights for a certain period of time. Some major labels have entered into license agreements with music video library agencies, such as Rockamerica. These agencies license music videos to nightclubs and may also license to colleges, restaurants, and retail stores. Typically, license fees paid by nightclubs range from about $3 to $9 per video clip per month.

Production Costs and Their Recoupment

Under most artist agreements, a record company advances production costs of music videos produced under the contracts. These costs may range anywhere from $25,000 to over $1 million, with the amounts usually below $100,000. Only artists who guarantee multiplatinum success will warrant costs near or exceeding the $1 million mark; rapper-actor Will Smith released the most expensive video to date, with production costs nearing $2 million.

Whether the music video is considered a promotional or a commercial vehicle largely influences the method for recoupment of production costs by the record company. Unlike most other record promotion expenses, which are borne entirely by the record company, the companies commonly insist on a form of recoupment that involves the artist. Under most label contracts, the record company becomes entitled to recoup a certain percentage of the video production costs out of the artist's record royalties, or out of the artist's share of the video income, or both. In most cases income derived by record companies from the exploitation of music videos is still insignificant in today's market. Accordingly, record companies look to the artist's record royalties for the recoupment of from 50 to 75 percent, and sometimes more, of the video production costs. At times the percentages are reduced if the underlying album achieves a high plateau of sales.

Typically, video production costs are also recoupable from the artist's share of net video receipts from the commercial exploitation of the music video. The usual artist participation is 50 percent of such net video receipts. These net receipts are defined as the gross receipts from commercial exploitation, less video production costs, distribution fees and expenses, and payments to third parties. In lieu of payment to the artist of a portion of the net video receipts, a less common approach is to pay a royalty to the artist on units of videocassettes and videodiscs sold. This royalty is from 10 to 25 percent of the wholesale selling price.

One creative way employed by popular artists to subsidize the production costs of music videos has been corporate sponsorship. This may include the subsidization of the artist's music videos in exchange for featuring the product subtly in the video itself (e.g., the sponsor's beer bottle on the star's keyboard), with the cooperation and participation of the record company.

Musical Composition Licenses

Ownership interests in musical compositions contained in a music video are generally held by the music publisher of those compositions. In some cases the music publisher is an affiliate of the record company. The essential rights required to produce and exploit a music video are the right to couple the music in timed relation to the visual images (the *synchronization right*), the right to publicly perform the composition as a part of the video, the right to make copies of the composition as included in the video, and the right to distribute to the public copies of the composition as integrated into the music video.

There are also compositions written, owned, or controlled by the recording artist and embodied in music videos (known as *controlled compositions*). In this instance, record companies will demand the issuance of free synchronization licenses as well as free licenses for the other essential rights referred to above.

Publishers and artists ordinarily agree on the promotional uses of music videos because they stand to benefit from the performance royalties resulting from the exhibition of the music video as well as from the added exposure the video provides for the song. When music videos are shown, provisions for payment will vary. In justification of free licenses, the record company may contend that the songwriting artist does not lose a fee entirely since license fees are deductible in calculating the artist's share of net video receipts, and the artist's share is thereby increased if there is no deduction of license fees. Some record companies will provide for a fee, royalty, or other payment for the use of a controlled composition. This fixing fee may initially be set forth in the contract or may be deferred until industry standards have further evolved. At issue is the form of payment: Should there be a flat one-time fee, a per-copy remuneration, or a combination of both? Record companies usually choose to waive such fees for promotional videos.

Where compositions are not controlled, there are differing approaches to their licensing by the copyright proprietors or their representatives. Independent publishers may be willing to give free synchronization and other licenses for strictly promotional usages, although there is no uniformity. With regard to commercial use, compensation is a certain requirement. While record companies favor a complete flat-fee buyout of rights, many publishers demand a flat fee plus per-copy payment.

Trade Paper Coverage of Music Videos

Music videos are reported in detail by *Billboard*. *Billboard*'s weekly Video Monitor lists the most-played clips on BET, CMT, MTV, and VH-1. *Billboard* also publishes a weekly chart called The Clip List, showing a sampling of playlists submitted by selected national and local music video outlets.

In addition to *Billboard*, a few specialized publications cover the video field. For example, *CVC Report: The Music Video Programming Guide*, issued twice monthly except in January and August, focuses on chart action and station playlists. Its charts are based on more than 100 reporting outlets and are presented as a general Top 50 list combining all music formats, and a Top 20 list for each specific genre of pop, R&B/rap, rock/alternative, and "club land" videos. *CVC* backs up the charts with individual playlists of TV and cable stations along with valuable personnel identification, such as program managers, producers, and music coordinators. In addition, its Contact Update column furnishes addresses, telephone and fax numbers, and suggested contact times for promotional reviews of new music videos as well as previews of videos in production.

37

Demonstration Records in the Electronic Age

The demonstration record, or demo, is the key means of showcasing a new song or artist. A songwriter/artist may play a demo for a record company to generate interest in a recording contract or to a music publisher to convince them that the song is worth publishing. In turn, a publisher may use a demo to convince a record company's A&R personnel to record a song. In addition, demos are often presented directly to recording artists and producers who are seeking new material. And, finally, demos can be used to present a musical product to people unable to read music in a readily accessible form.

The better the quality of a demo, the more likely it is to attract favorable attention to an artist, group, or song. In the past, publishers generally wanted to hear only studio-produced demos recorded under the supervision of the publisher's professional manager or, on occasion, supervised for the publisher by the writer. They also wanted written arrangements to be in place, rather than impromptu or "head" arrangements, and insisted on having a say in the selection of musicians and instrumentation.

Technological advances in the digital age mean that an artist's first recording—whether produced in an independent studio or a sophisticated home studio—is often of master quality. Such demos may be acquired by a record company as a master recording for the production of phonograph records or offered by the artist directly to consumers via the Internet. Writer artists can market their own products directly and distribute them either via downloading or through mail-order response to an Internet offering.

Production Methods

Recording studios were once rated by the number of tracks available and the width of the tape used. Tape width ranged from $1/4$-inch to 2-inch tape and the number of tracks from 2 to 48. The greater the number of tracks and width of the tape, the higher the quality and the greater the cost of recording time. However, because digital reproduction is so clear, an 8-track digital system can achieve results that are equal to or better than those obtained by a system based on a 24-track analog tape recorder, and at a fraction of the cost. The steadily decreasing cost of digital gear means that artists who would not in the past have had access to high-quality audio equipment now have the opportunity to purchase their own systems. The digital storage and reproduction of music has enhanced the artist's ability to record, through clearer, cheaper, and more accessible innovations. With the advent of digital recording technologies, the old ways of recording have disappeared nearly as fast as vinyl records did when CDs came on the scene.

Because most digital audio recording systems feature random access, the songwriter can edit his or her production in ways that would be impractical or impossible in analog recording. The editing capabilities include tuning a recorded vocal or instrumental line; changing the tempo of the song, even dramatically, without the "Alvin and the Chipmunks" effect resulting when a tape is simply speeded up or slowed down; moving pieces of a performance by tiny increments of time, to change the "feel" or to compensate for timing errors on the part of the performers; copying repeated vocal parts to other locations; and changing the location of lines, verses, chorus, etc.

Smaller studios specializing in the production of demos often charge from $25 to $75 per hour for their facilities, which include an audio engineer/computer operator. A programmer, typically a keyboard player with a strong knowledge of synthesizers, creates the music bed, or "track." In the hip-hop and rap worlds, this track is generally called the beats. The beats/track are usually printed to a hard drive on a digital audio workstation (DAW). A DAW can be a garden-variety PC or Mac with some specialized hardware and software, or it can be a dedicated piece of hardware that only does music. Once the songwriter and the programmer are satisfied with the instrumental track, vocalists, and sometimes additional instrumentalists, are called in. When the recording and mix are finished, the demo is printed to a 2-track master, also known as a stereo master, generally on an audio CD. This master is the property of the songwriter. Demo studios typically charge from $5 to $10 for a cassette copy of a master and from $10 to $20 for a CD copy. Songwriters who need multiple copies typically make themselves on their own computers or in their home studios. They may also have copies made at one of the many "dupe houses," which specialize in making such copies quickly and cheaply.

Studios used for making demos have singers and musicians on call for such work at rates averaging $50 to $100 dollars per song for each artist, although the best vocalists get up to $300 per song. Good programmers, who often create all or most of a music track via MIDI and loops, are in great demand, as are accurate and fast singers who can knock out a good lead vocal, a track of ad-libs, and several harmony or background vocal tracks in a few hours. People who play only "real" instruments, such as guitar, bass, drums, or a horn, generally get very little work.

The making of demos is in the nature of bread-and-butter work, and there are fine singers and musicians who are available for demo sessions when they are not otherwise employed. Some of the vocalists and musicians are under exclusive recording contracts with record companies, but their contracts are not usually construed as prohibiting performance on demos, which are not for commercial release.

Doing It Yourself

An alternative to renting time in an expensive studio is home recording. To record a high-quality, three-song demo in an old analog studio might range between $5,000 and $10,000 in rental fees. Today, artists can *purchase* digital multitrack equipment for less, and the number of home studios in the United States has dramatically increased in recent years. Companies such as Tascam and Alesis, with their competing modular digital multitrack (MDM) recorders, have set the standards for the industry.

Today, many demos produced in home studios are recorded and mixed digitally on DAWs (see above). Although DAW recording can be done without a tape component or together with one of the multitrack digital systems such as Tascam's DA-98 or Alesis's ADAT LX-20, increasingly the trend is to use hard-disk recorders, dispensing with digital tape altogether. Alternatively, after being edited on a DAW, the tracks can be transferred to a DAT. This process allows editing flexibility not available on a direct to DAT system, which is another alternative.

Whatever system is used, the home studio gives the artist greater flexibility in recording without the time pressures connected with hourly recording studio rates.

CD-Rs and MiniDiscs

A *CD-recordable (CD-R)* drive allows users to record top-quality digital audio files to CDs which can be played on home or portable computers. CD-Rs may be burned on stand-alone units or on digital audio workstations equipped with CD-R drives or CD-Audio recording software. *Minidiscs* were introduced in 1991 by Sony as a disc-based digital medium for recording and listening to consumer audio with near-CD quality. One major difference between minidiscs and tape and CDs, apart from size, is that Minidisc content is re-recordable: tracks can be edited, moved, deleted, and replaced. When Minidiscs were first introduced, their audio quality was inferior to that of CDs, and some professional studios recommended that musicians not use them for masters. Although the sound has improved since they were first introduced, and many units feature MIDI control, the Minidisc format has never achieved the market share envisioned by its developer, and Minidiscs are still more likely to be used by consumers than by musicians who want to record masters in their home studios.

Drum Machines and Synthesizers

Important components of contemporary music technology are drum machines and synthesizers. Drum machines, which feature superb sound clarity, can replace live drummers for most demos, except perhaps for heavy metal, "roots" rock and roll, and acoustic music. The availability of music synthesizers and MIDI computer technology has permitted even economically produced demos to sound sophisticated and complex. Using the great flexibility of synthesizers, many musicians with good musical ideas are able to construct elaborate arrangements. The resultant product can sound as if it was recorded at a multitrack studio session lasting many hours.

Cost Factors

The final costs of producing a high-quality demo vary considerably, depending on a number of factors: the number of musicians involved, whether the arrangements are impromptu or prepared, whether a home studio or a professional studio is used, the sophistication of the equipment, and so on. For a demo made at a studio, the cost could be as low as several hundred dollars for a song that includes four or five musicians and a professional singer, or as high as $1,000 per song for a demo requiring more musicians and taking longer to produce.

Payment to musicians and vocalists for demos is customarily at a lower rate than the regular union scale for commercial recordings, and the AFM scale rates for demo sessions are lower than the scale rates for a commercial session. The AFM requires that the full commercial scale be paid if a demo is used as a final master for release by a record company. Vocalists on demo dates are subject to AFTRA regulation, which relies on the local chapter to decide on demo scale and whether subsequent use as a commercial record requires only the difference or a full commercial scale.

A demo may be of high enough quality to be released by a record company, and many publishers investing in high-end demos are looking to achieve such quality. When there is any possibility that the demo may actually be released commercially, caution should be exercised in using artists who have exclusive recording commitments unless advance waivers are obtained.

The Assumption of Demo Expenses

If a music publisher makes or authorizes the making of a basic, relatively inexpensive demo, the publisher usually assumes the entire cost. Sometimes the cost of making a demo is paid for by the songwriter prior to placing his or her song with a publisher; and as a condition of the assignment of the copyright by the songwriter to the publisher, the latter is required to repay the cost. In either instance, the monies paid by the publisher for demos are treated as publisher expenses, as in the case of advertising or promoting a recording. Some publishers require songwriters to agree that anywhere from half to all of the cost of making a demo shall be considered an advance against writer royalties, although only partial recoupment by the publisher is common. If agreed to by the writer, it is in his or her interest to limit the recoupment of the cost to royalties on the song in the demo, rather than allowing the cost to be charged generally against the writer's royalties from all songs placed with the publisher. Writers will contend that the cost of making a demo is in the nature of promotional expenses, since it is an essential first step in promoting a song, and that no promotional expenses should be charged to the writer. On the other hand, publishers may point out that the writer's performance fees are untouched and may argue that the recoupment of only one-half or more of the cost of making a demo from mechanical royalties is fair and equitable.

Subsidized Demos

A record company, music publisher, or producer can become sufficiently attracted by a rough demo to be willing to finance a better-quality, more expensive recording. As a result, the company or producer may enter into an exclusive demonstration recording artist agreement, which provides for limited funding for the express purpose of financing a quality demo. The record company, publisher, or producer may believe in the potential of the song or the artist enough to underwrite the expense of that recording but be unwilling to extend such financing without a written agreement granting specific rights.

The subsidizing party may request the right of first refusal to acquire the subsidized demo, including the song and the artist. It will then have a certain period of time after the completion of the demo to sign the artist or songwriter on the basis of terms already negotiated or to be negotiated in good faith during the first-refusal period. No other entity will be able to negotiate for the product until the first-refusal period has expired. The subsidizing party may also request a right of last refusal, which gives it a further option, for a period stated, to match any offer obtained from another record company. In defense against such an impediment to free negotiations, it is desirable for the artist to obtain the right to purchase the demo at its full cost when the first refusal period expires, so that the artist can be free from any last-refusal obligation.

The subsidizing party may also require that the demo cost be recouped from the first proceeds of a deal made with the completed subsidized demo, whether the deal is with a record company (including possibly the subsidizing party) or otherwise. The recoupment may be drawn from any advances or royalties earned by the music or artist, in the form of music publisher, producer, songwriter, or recording artist receipts. The subsidizing party, as part of the negotiations, may seek the right to participate in producer, writer, publisher, and artist earnings over and above recoupment.

A demo subsidy deal should be prepared in writing with clearly defined terms. It should include such items as a budget detailing all authorized expenditures for studio, musicians, and equipment. Many subsidized demos involve previously approved recording budgets of as much as $15,000 covering a basic two or three selections. The right of restricted ownership of the sound recording copyright in the demo should be expressed in the document, as should the description of the restriction (usually not for any unauthorized use other than for audition). Rights of first and last refusal as well as rights of recoupment should be expressed as well, including how long a demo will be "shopped" and whether the subsidizing party has a further right to recoup its investment if a later deal is made with a third party involving the subsidized demo.

A cautious investor will insist on the submission of invoices before each installment is paid, whereas a sophisticated demo producer may insist on a demo fund with retention of any saved amounts as a producer or artist fee for the demo itself. All participants in the demo session should be required to sign their consents to allow the conversion of the demo to a record master that can be commercially released, subject only to appropriate union scale, pension, and welfare payments.

Occasionally a record studio will subsidize the production of a demo by providing studio time and facilities. Like any other subsidizing party, it will expect recoupment of its investment and possible participation in the earnings of the producer, writer, publisher, and artist.

A demonstration recording agreement gives the artist an opportunity to submit a quality demo for maximum showcasing of talent and also gives the record company a chance to hear a product under conditions similar to what would be delivered under a full-budget deal. Such deals restrict the bargaining power of the artist, but that disadvantage is often outweighed by the fact that the financing party has as much interest as the artist does in shopping the demo and may provide backing for multiple auditions.

The Submission of Demos

Aspiring recording artists often face the dilemma of how to get their demo records considered by A&R people. The simple answer is to find a manager or producer who is respected in the industry to make the submission for them. This is easier said than done because it is often like putting the cart before the horse: managers and producers with a track record of success are usually available only after the artist has surmounted substantial initial hurdles. One effective way for artists to distribute their demos to these often-elusive industry professionals is to showcase themselves at one of the many annual trade shows. In addition to offering the artist the opportunity to perform live for industry personnel, the trade shows are an excellent place for artists to hand out demos to any interested individuals. Even artists who do not earn a showcase slot can benefit from attending these conferences. Often the record companies have booths where A&R staff will listen to demos on the spot and offer comments and criticisms.

Because of the difficulty that artists experience in reaching A&R, a new breed of music industry representative has emerged—the shopper. Shoppers are often attorneys willing to make the submission on a personal presentation basis or producers seeking to make an early tie-in with potential talent for a combined package. (See Chapter 33, page 325, for a more detailed discussion of shoppers.)

The Independent Demo

As mentioned at the beginning of the chapter, more and more artists are making independent demos, often of master quality. If the goal is to make a demo master that is a salable product for use in retail stores, it pays to get a bar code. Distributors and retailers do not want to carry a product that cannot be processed through bar code procedure for inventory and other purposes. Bar code numbers are assigned through the Uniform Code Council (Web site: uc-council.org). The processing fee is based on annual sales. If a company's annual sales are under $2 million, the fee is $500.

In addition, a record release number is necessary. It can be based on any letters or numbers and gets printed on inserts, inscribed on stampers, marked for identification on master tapes, and is often used in computer entries of inventory where bar codes do not operate. An example of such a release number picked at random would be MWK-0005.

Pressing and packaging services are often advertised in *Billboard* and other trade journals. An example of a leading supplier of such services is Disc Makers, which claims to be "America's Number 1 Manufacturer for the Independent Music Industry" (Web site: www.discmakers.com). Disc Makers offers a free package of valuable information materials, including a list of names and addresses of available distributors, suggestions for independent music publicity, and a useful *Guide to Master Tape Preparation*. The latter can be downloaded from their Web site. In addition, they will send their own illustrated catalog of available services and packages for production of CD, CD-ROM, cassette, and vinyl product.

38

Payola

As commonly used in the music industry, the term *payola* refers to the unauthorized payment of money, services, or other valuable considerations to broadcasting station personnel (usually disc jockeys, record librarians, or program directors) in return for their broadcast use of a particular record or song. Under the Federal Communications Act of 1934, as amended, since 1960 payola has been a federal crime carrying a sentence of up to $10,000 in fines, or imprisonment of up to 1 year, or both. It is not an offense, however, if the payment is disclosed to the station as well as to the independent or other program producer or person for whom the program is produced or supplied.

Where the station licensee has knowledge of the payment, it must inform the public by means of an announcement on the program involved. The station cannot willingly remain in ignorance of such payment while its employees supplement their income by payola. Section 317 of the Communications Act of 1934 provides that radio executives must exercise "reasonable diligence" in supervising their employees.

The Incentive to Engage in Payola

The obvious incentive for engaging in payola is to increase the sales of records and the performances and other uses of a song by creating the public illusion of their spontaneous and genuine promotion. Payola is a crutch on which a promotion person with a second-rate product or insufficient contacts or ability may be tempted to lean. And when a record company representative or musician doesn't ante up the expected payment to a disc jockey or other station employee used to getting payola, they may bottle up and keep a record from the public ear, no matter how good it is.

Contacts and promotion are recognized as essential and legitimate factors in the success of a recording in the popular music industry. An excellent song or record is worthless without public exposure. One witness in the first congressional hearings on payola said, "Until the public actually hears your product, you can't tell whether you have a hit or not." The editorial work of a music publisher must be supplemented by the vital work of joining with the record company in convincing disc jockeys and video programmers to play a particular record and song. This is a function of music publishers' and record companies' promotion departments.

It is not unusual for personnel in the broadcasting and music industries to have mutual interests and good rapport. Music and record company promotion people often achieve a "friend of the family" status with one another and with broadcasting personnel that may be expressed by tips on employment opportunities and other favors. Disc jockeys sometimes help music promoters by calling attention to new songs and master recordings from their local area or an up-and-coming "regional breakout" of records or songs. There are other areas of constructive cooperation as well, like promoting charities sponsored by the record industry, such as the T. J. Martell Foundation for Leukemia, Cancer and AIDS Research, and attending industry functions. In addition, many radio and video programmers are invited to record company staff conventions at which the talents of their artists are displayed and the artists personally meet the programmers.

It becomes a matter of degree as to when gifts and entertainment at theaters, restaurants, nightclubs, and other arenas cross the line between the realm of normal business socializing and enter the area of payola through implication of a promise of airplay.

Commercial Bribery

Although the relationships of music publishers and songwriters to record company personnel are not subject to the federal payola statute, they may constitute another type of payola. Such relations, as well as those in broadcasting station payola situations, are subject to the commercial bribery laws in effect in many states when they involve the payment of money or other valuable consideration to an employee behind the back of his or her employer.

Payola in the sense of pay-for-play, or "plugging," has been with the music industry for many years. In 1916, the Music Publishers Protective Association noted that publishers were paying as much as $400,000 a year to artists to plug their songs. The publishers agreed to levy a fine of $5,000 on any member who continued the practice. However, the agreement was unenforced and ineffective. In the late 1930s, a group of publishers retained the late Joseph V. McKee, attorney and one-time acting mayor of New York City, to work with the Federal Trade Commission in obtaining a code outlawing payola. This move also failed.

Publishing Interests and Payola

It does not constitute payola when a recording star who is not a writer acquires a financial publishing interest in a song that may be suitable for his or her recording. This situation is similar to the ownership of music publishing firms by record companies that may be motivated to record songs in their publishing catalog. In fact, some record firms make special incentive payments to their A&R people who obtain publishing rights to material recorded.

Payola and Trade Papers

Payola has also been offered with respect to record charts in trade papers. A prominent trade paper research director once reported that he personally turned down a bribe of $3,000 to put a song on the charts, and that he had to discharge two employees in his department who received valuable gifts from record manufacturers. Former *Billboard* publisher Hal B. Cook has advocated an independent audit of industry rating systems, stating: "If charts are unduly influenced by economic considerations, a false market condition is created."

At one time there was a suspicion that record retailers were taking bribes in order to report falsely inflated sales figures in order to influence record charts. However, *Billboard*'s adoption of data processing through Broadcast Data System and SoundScan appears to have stopped this practice.

How Payola Works

The 1959 report of the congressional subcommittee investigating payola stated:

> The subcommittee held 19 days of hearings on "payola" and related unfair and deceptive practices. . . . Fifty-seven witnesses were heard; they included disc jockeys and other programming personnel, network and licensee executive personnel, phonograph record manufacturers and distributors, independent data processors, trade paper representatives, songwriters and publishers, and members of the subcommittee staff. Testimony appears to indicate that the selection of much of the music heard on the air may have been influenced by payments of money, gifts, etc., to programming personnel. In some instances, these payments were rationalized as licensing fees and consultation fees.

Testimony revealed that although the motivation for payola was universal, the practices were multifaceted. Automobiles and television sets were given to disc jockeys as gifts. Weekly or monthly checks were remitted. Stipulated payments based on the number of records sold in an area were made. "Cut-ins" (a portion of revenues) on publishing rights were arranged.

After its extensive study of payola in the music broadcasting business, the congressional committee successfully introduced a number of amendments to the law in 1960, making payola a federal crime. In recommending these amendments, the committee offered numerous examples of situations that would be affected by the amendments.

▶ A record distributor supplies copies of records to a radio station or disc jockey for broadcast purposes. No announcement is required unless the supplier furnishes more copies of a particular recording than are necessary. Thus, should the record supplier furnish 50 or 100 copies of the same release, with an agreement by the station, express or implied, that the record will be used on a broadcast, an announcement is required because consideration beyond the matter used on the broadcast has been received.

▶ An announcement is required for the same reason if the payment to the station or disc jockey is in the form of cash or other property, including stock.

▶ Several distributors supply a new station, or a station that has changed its program format (e.g., from rock and roll to popular music), with a substantial number of different record releases. No announcement is required under Section 317 of the U.S. Criminal Code where the records are furnished for broadcast purposes only; nor does the public interest require an announcement in these circumstances. The station would have received the same material over a period of time had it previously been on the air or followed this program format.

▶ Records are furnished to a radio station or disc jockey in consideration of the special plugging of the record supplier or performing talent beyond an identification reasonably related to the use of the record on the program. If the disc jockey states, "This is my favorite new record, and is sure to become a hit; so don't overlook it," and it is understood that some such statement is made in return for the record and would not otherwise have been made, an announcement is required. It does not appear that in those circumstances, the identification is reasonably related to the use of the record on that program. On the other hand, no announcement is required if a disc jockey states: "Listen to this latest release of performer 'X,' a new singing sensation," and such an advertisement is customarily part of the disc jockey's program format regardless of whether or not the particular record had been purchased by the station or furnished free of charge. It would appear that the identification by the disc jockey is reasonably related to the use of the record on that particular program.

▶ Free books or theater tickets are furnished to a book or drama critic of a station. When the books or plays are reviewed on the air, no announcement is required. On the other hand, if 40 tickets are given to the station with the understanding, express or implied, that the play will be reviewed on the air, an announcement is required. There has been a payment beyond the furnishing of a property or service for use on or in connection with a broadcast.

▶ A well-known performer appears as a guest artist on a program at union scale because the performer likes the show, although the performer normally commands a much higher fee. No announcement is required.

Despite the widespread publicity that the federal payola law of 1960 received, payola has continued. In 1986, then Senator Al Gore launched a Senate investigation of the record business, stating that the practice of giving gifts in exchange for air time "has again reared its ugly head" and noting that a great deal of money, as well as drugs and prostitution, was involved. It was indicated that indirect payola had become a common occurrence because of the record companies' having hired some 200 "independent promoters" who were to use their own devices when promoting records, without direct instructions or control by the record companies that hired them. According to *The Wall Street Journal,* some $80 million a year was being spent for this function. The cost of the individual record promotion necessary for Top 20 chart status was quoted at somewhere between $150,000 and $250,000. As a result of the investigation and Senate hearings, the direct engagement of independent promoters by record companies was drastically curtailed.

Because payola is a federal crime, it may someday be used as a basis for civil or criminal RICO litigation. The Racketeer-Influenced and Corrupt Organizations statute was used in the 1990 federal prosecution of record promoter Joe Isgro; the government indictment elevated the payola misdemeanor charge into mail fraud to qualify for RICO status. The case, which alleged the use of multiple independent promoters engaged by Isgro on behalf of client record labels to buy airplay on key stations, was ultimately dismissed owing to procedural defects. However, a 1995 court of appeals decision overturned the procedural dismissal and authorized reinstatement of the case for trial. The charges involved defrauding record companies, making undisclosed payments of cash and cocaine to radio station personnel, and racketeering. (Procedural complications resulted in a final dismissal.)

The pattern established in the Isgro case is likely to be repeated in similar situations. Likewise, in civil actions under RICO, a station owner who can claim that an employee received illegal payments could sue for triple damages under this statute.

Payola also concerns the Federal Trade Commission, which is charged with regulation of competition in supplying of goods in interstate commerce under Section 5 of the Federal Trade Commission Act. Under that section, unfair or deceptive acts or practices, as well as unfair competition, are declared unlawful. The FTC construed payola as a violation of Section 5 and investigated numerous record manufacturers and distributors. As a result, many such companies entered into consent decrees under which they agree to cease and desist from payola practices. Violations of the decree will usually subject the companies to penalties, in contrast to the warnings likely to be meted out to companies not parties to a decree.

Yet another blow to the practice of payola was administered by the Internal Revenue Service, which initiated its own investigation after having been apprised of evidence indicating the possibility that disc jockeys and other persons were understating taxable income. As a result, firms making payola payments were not allowed to deduct such bribery expenses from their income, and they also became subject to audit by the tax authorities.

Recently there has been Congressional interest in station owners like Clear Channel Communications, which owns, programs, or sells air time for 1,200 radio stations owned in the United States and which has equity interests in some 240 radio stations internationally. Its subsidiary Clear Channel Entertainment, formerly SFX Entertainment, is the world's largest producer and promoter of life entertainment. Clear Channel thus has the means to promote those artists whose concerts they are investing in. Concentration of radio station ownership has magnified these problems. Until 1996, FCC regulations stipulated that a single company could own no more than two broadcast stations in any one market and no more than 40 total. When these caps were lifted by the Telecommunications Act of 1996, the result was rampant consolidation. Today, four radio stations control access to 63 percent of the 41 million listeners of the Contemporary Hit Radio/Top 40 format. *The Wall Street Journal* quotes record labels as saying they pay independent contractors (promoters) between $200 and $300,000 per song and sometimes up to $1 million. This breaks down to $500 to $2000 each time a station adds a song to its playlist for the week.

39

Trade Practice Regulations

The Federal Trade Commission and the Department of Justice enforce statutes designed to foster and promote the maintenance of fair competitive conditions in interstate commerce in the interest of protecting industry, trade, and the public. The stated goal of the FTC is "working for consumer protection and a competitive marketplace." For example, MTV plays a dominant role in the presentation of music videos to cable viewers through MTV, VH-1, and The Box. In late 1999 the Department of Justice began looking into possible antitrust violations on the part of MTV in their dealings with the music companies that supply the videos. The FTC has intervened to bar the practice of giving payola to broadcasting station personnel in order to achieve a preferred position in the exposure of records and musical compositions over the air to the public.

Payola is only one of the many abuses that have been called to the attention of the FTC. A substantial number of complaints relate to discrimination between retail outlets and chain stores regarding prices, services, and facilities. Other complaints deal with misrepresentation and deception by various members of the music industry engaged in the manufacture, distribution, and sale of recordings.

The FTC has adopted a procedure to clarify and define practices that violate the statutes it enforces in order to encourage voluntary compliance with the laws on the part of the industry. This procedure includes trade practice hearings at which all members of the industry and other interested parties are offered an opportunity to present views, information, and suggestions regarding the establishment of rules designed to furnish guidance in the requirements of the applicable laws. Following the consideration of these comments and suggestions, the FTC publishes trade practice rules for the industry. Those rules which outline practices that violate the statutes administered by the FTC are discussed below.

Discriminatory Price Differential Practices

There is a prohibition against discriminatory price differential practices where the effect may substantially lessen competition, or create a monopoly, or injure, destroy, or prevent competition with a competitor or its customers. The rule bars both secret and open direct and indirect rebates, refunds, discounts, credits, or other forms of price differential to purchasers of goods of similar grade and quality.

For example, in June 2002, in a final resolution of a case involving alleged price fixing of recordings of the Three Tenors World Cup concerts, the FTC ordered Vivendi Universal S.A. (PolyGram, Decca, UMG, and Universal) to "cease and desist" any activities designed to "fix, raise, or stabilize price levels" in connection with U.S. sales of any audio or video product. It was also barred from entering into agreements designed to withhold from the market any "truthful" advertising and promotion of such products. The original complaint, which was brought against Vivendi and Warner (Warner later entered into a voluntary consent order to refrain from further such activities), charged that these companies, in an effort to maximize sales of the Three Tenors 1998 World Cup Concert, had acquired the rights to the first two concerts and subsequently agreed not to discount or advertise the 1990 and 1994 concerts for a "moratorium period" lasting 2 1/2 months after the release of the 1998 album and video. The effect of this agreement, said the FTC, was to unreasonably restrain competition, increase prices, and injure consumers.

In another proceeding, the FTC found that it would be unlawful price discrimination if "free goods" were supplied to some but not to all customers. However, it is not the intent of the FTC rulings to prohibit price differentials that legitimately reflect differences in the cost of manufacture, sale, or delivery resulting from differing methods or production or different quantities of products to be sold or delivered to customers in different functional categories. For example, it is legitimate to grant a lower price to wholesalers than to retailers on goods intended for distribution to retailers.

While there appears to be no dispute about the *right* to fix different prices for retailers, rack jobbers, and wholesalers, there can be factual disputes regarding which functional category a given purchaser falls into. Although there is little argument about the functions of a distributor, the first link in the chain of distribution headed by manufacturers, some distributors simultaneously operate as rack jobbers on the side and service locations that undersell their regular dealer customers. There are even distributors who own one-stops. The rack jobber, as commonly understood, services supermarkets, variety stores, drug stores, and other busy retail outlets, whereas the one-stop stocks the records of many manufacturers so that jukebox operators and small dealers can buy everything they need at one location instead of having to contact a number of distributors. Retailers in competition with the rack locations assert that in reality all risk and control are vested in the rack jobbers and that they should therefore be regarded as retailers.

In 1994, the FTC conducted hearings regarding opposition to the resale of used CDs. This developed into a general inquiry into the fixing of CD price levels and whether there was any concerted activity among otherwise competing labels. The descriptive legal phrase for this is *conscious parallelism* where, although not an active conspiracy involving face-to-face meetings or correspondence, memoranda, and agreements between competitors, there is an effort to match price levels other than for purely competitive purposes. The same pricing as a result of exercise of independent good-faith business judgment is allowed, but in the absence of such exercise of independent judgment, the conclusion may be that conscious parallelism exists. The question will always be one of fact.

A variation on illegal conspiracy to fix prices occurs when otherwise competitive labels agree among themselves on a uniform credit discount for prompt cash payment of outstanding invoices, a practice that is almost the same as uniform price fixing. In contrast, a trade association agreement, or even an informal agreement between otherwise competing labels, to exchange credit quality information as to prospective or actual customers is allowed. In the music industry, as elsewhere, this exchange of good or bad or intermediate credit history is a valuable self-protection in furtherance of honest competition.

Proportional Equality in Advertising, Promotional Allowances, or Facilities

The FTC requires proportional equality in the treatment of competing customers in the supplying of advertising or promotional allowances, marketing services, or facilities. Where the allowance, service, or facility offered to certain customers was not suitable to other, similarly situated customers, an equivalent alternative allowance, service, or facility must be offered. For example, the FTC considers it a violation of fair practices if racks, browsers, bins, displays, special packaging, and other similar services and facilities are supplied to certain customers but not made known and available on proportionally equal terms to all competing customers. A similar conclusion applies to preferential treatment in cooperative advertising allowances, to the furnishing of free merchandise with the proviso that it be used for advertising or that the proceeds of its sale be used for advertising purposes, and to the granting of allowances for advertising based on a fixed percentage of a customer's purchases.

Price Fixing, Tie-in Sales, and Other Deceptive Practices

In the early 1990s a CD price war was initiated by several discount retailers, including Best Buy, Circuit City, and Target. To nip that practice in the bud, the five major label groups (Warner Music Group, Sony Music Entertainment, EMI Recorded Music, BMG Entertainment, and Universal Music Group), which now control about 85 percent of CDs sold in the United States, withheld advertising subsidies to retailers who continued to advertise CDs below a minimum amount set by the labels. The FTC determined that these activities were in violation of existing antitrust statutes, and in 2000, the big five agreed voluntarily to stop the practice. In a related proceeding, the attorney generals of 43 states brought a lawsuit against the five majors as well as the retailers Tower Records, Music Land,

and Trans World Entertainment, claiming that an artificially high price had been fixed for CDs purchased between January 1, 1995, and December 22, 2000. This was settled in early 2003 when the defendants agreed to establish a $67.4 million fund to distribute among purchasers of CDs during the period in question, plus an additional $75.7 million in CDs to be given to nonprofit organizations and schools and libraries. However, if the number of claimants to the $67.4 million turns out to be so large that the award per claimant would drop below $5, everything will go to the nonprofit organizations.

Also prohibited are tie-in sales that involve the coerced purchase of one product as a prerequisite to the purchase of other products. A tie-in would occur if a store were required to order 100 singles for every 20 albums of a particular artist or to purchase a minimum of 10 new releases of a designated new artist in order to get a standard discount on established charted album artists.

Companies may not sell products or fix prices on the condition that the purchaser agree not to offer the products of competitors. For example, a record company cannot put a particular store on its blacklist if that store seeks to handle the product of a competitor label. Similarly, a record label may not refuse to sell the work of a particular artist who refuses to extend his or her contract with that record label.

The FTC also has the right to require companies to desist from advertising and sales practices that mislead or deceive consumers. For example, a record that does not have two distinctly separate modulations derived from an original live recording for which a minimum of two separate channels were employed cannot be advertised as a "stereo" recording. However, the words may be used with a monaural recording having two separate modulations provided there is clear disclosure that the recording was originally monaural and was altered to simulate stereophonic reproduction.

The FTC regulates deceptive practices involving misuse of names of featured performing artists, misrepresentation of the contents of recordings, and deception involving reissues, new titles, and date or origination.

In 2001, the U.S. Department of Justice launched an antitrust investigation involving the activities of two of the largest on-line subscription services, Pressplay (formed by Sony and Universal) and MusicNet (formed by Warner, BMG, and EMI). The contention is that the record companies which own the services, through their cross-licensing agreements, effectively freeze out third-party subscription services, leaving independent record companies no choice but to distribute through either MusicNet or Pressplay. At issue is whether the inherent right of companies to license their own recordings is being used to throttle competition in on-line subscription services.

Sound-Alike Recordings

With the crackdown on record piracy, there was an accompanying growth in what have been called *sound-alike recordings*, recordings of hit songs by artists other than the original artist where the expectation is that the recording features the original artist.

Although it is established that sound recording copyright does not protect against a sound-alike imitation by another artist, the Federal Trade Commission is alert to unfair trade practices that might otherwise occur in sound-alike situations. The FTC will issue warnings and/or take action when names and likenesses of the performers are used to deceive consumers into the belief that the record offered for sale is the original version by the original artist. For example, the FTC requires that "tribute" recordings (for example, "A Tribute to Frank Sinatra" or to Tommy Dorsey or to Elvis Presley) which print the name of the original artist in large letters and/or include a picture of the original artist— must prominently display a disclaimer stating that "This is not an original artist recording" as well as a disclosure of the name of the actual performer.

In 1980, the FTC issued a special guide concerning the use of endorsements and testimonials in advertising. The guide outlines the requirements for accuracy in advertising and promotion. For example, if a critic says that a recording is "technically great, but artistically inadequate" and the promotional quotation merely reads that the recording is "great," the promoter has violated FTC requirements. Similarly, if an artist records as a sideman early in his or her career and later becomes a superstar, record companies cannot market the early recordings with the superstar advertised as a "featured artist." Even consumer endorsements used in promotion are subject to the commission guidelines. A consumer cannot be paid for a favorable endorsement unless full disclosure of the payment is made.

40

Work Permits for Foreign Artists

American artists such as Pearl Jam and R.E.M. have conducted successful tours of Europe or Africa, and European artists such as the Rolling Stones and U2 have achieved tremendous acceptance in the United States. While other segments of the music industry have lately shown substantial weakness, the global touring business (dominated by Clear Channel Entertainment; see page 371) has mushroomed from $1 billion 5 years ago to almost $5 billion today.

Underlying the exchange of artists and their performance in foreign countries is a world of red tape and procedures involving international policy issues of job security for native artists and preserving balances of trade.

For a foreign artist who wants to perform or record in the United States, there is a complicated process that often involves alien employment certification preliminary to the issuance of a temporary work visa. An understanding of the procedures, rules, and overlapping authority of the U.S. State Department, the Immigration and Naturalization Service (INS), and in some circumstances the U.S. Department of Labor is essential to any concert producer, booking agent, record company, and television or film producer who wants to import musical talent from other countries.

Types of Work Visas

There are three categories of temporary work visas available to foreign artists: O, P, and H-2B. The O status is available to those individuals of "extraordinary ability in the sciences, arts, education, business, or athletics." P-1 visas are available to artists, entertainers, and athletes who perform as part of a group that has received international recognition as outstanding for a substantial period of time; P-2, to artists or entertainers who perform individually or with a group pursuant to a reciprocal exchange program between U.S. and foreign organizations; and P-3 to "culturally unique" individuals or organizations coming to America to express their art form. The claim of O or P status must be accompanied by supporting documentation. In 2001 there were 85,310 entries allowed on P and O temporary visas. To quality for H-2B status, the entertainer must get a certification from the Department of Labor that there are no comparably qualified persons available for the employment, and that the pay and other facets of such employment satisfy prevailing standards. This discussion will be limited to the O and P categories as they deal more specifically with the field of music.

The Proper Petitioner and Petitions

Although vitally interested, the foreign musician or musical group is only the beneficiary of the alien employment certification and the immigration petition, and not the proper party to act as the official petitioner. The petitioner must be in the category of the "importing employer" or an agent. The petitioner need not be a U.S. resident or citizen.

Petitions are commonly filed by booking agencies, concert promoters, and the like, who are deemed to have the proper status for such filings. It is best to assure that the petitioner's status and relationship to the beneficiaries will be continued throughout the U.S. engagement for which application is made. If the relationship is not continued, a new petitioner must file a new application. For example, although a Boston concert promoter may be an appropriate petitioner for a single appearance in that city, if a six-city tour is planned, there will have to be six different petitioners, one for each city. It is far better for the booking agency handling the entire tour to be the single petitioner. If a tour is part of a record promotion, the record company as employer, though only indirectly involved in specific concert appearances, can be the petitioner for the entire tour as well as for employment at a record studio. It is more usual to have a general agency (e.g., William Morris Agency, Associated Booking Corporation) serve as petitioner representing an interested party in all facets of U.S. employment.

The services of foreign entertainers are restricted to the activity, area, and employer specified in the petition. A new petition is required for further engagements, or if there is a change of employer or area of performance. An exception, where the performer is already in the United States, is an appearance without compensation on a charity show, for which no musician or other performer receives any compensation or reimbursement of expenses. When there are changes in the itinerary of an O or P entertainer beneficiary within the time period of the original itinerary, it is common simply to notify the INS office that handled the original petitions by submitting a letter of notification, preferably either in person or by certified mail, return receipt requested. Any new or separate engagement on other media, such as television or radio, requires a new petition.

An O or P status petitioner may petition directly to the INS and need not obtain an application from the Department of Labor. Even if the artist is as well established as Elton John, Cecile Bartoli, or the Vienna Philharmonic, it is important to buttress the claim of extraordinary ability or of outstanding international recognition (the basis for an O or P petition, respectively) with all the supporting proof available. The following extract from the applicable INS regulations indicates the criteria involved in the determination of extraordinary ability:

> Whether the alien has been nominated for or has been the recipient of significant national or international awards in the particular field, such as an Academy Award, an Emmy, a Grammy, or a Director's Guild Award, or at least three of the following forms of documentation that the alien: (1) has or will perform a lead or starring role in productions or events that have a distinguished reputation; (2) has achieved national or international recognition for achievements; (3) has performed a lead, starring, or critical role for organizations and establishments that have a distinguished reputation; (4) has a record of major commercial or critically acclaimed successes; (5) has received significant recognition for achievements from organizations, critics, government agencies, or other recognized experts in the field in which the alien is engaged; (6) has commanded or now commands a high salary or other substantial remuneration for services in relation to others in the field; (7) other comparable evidence.

The criteria determining outstanding international recognition are:

> Whether the alien group has been nominated or has received significant international awards or prizes for outstanding achievement in its field, or by three of the following types of documentation that establish that the entertainment group has: (1) performed or will perform as a starring or leading entertainment group in productions or events that have a distinguished reputation; (2) achieved international recognition and acclaim for outstanding achievements in its field as evidenced by reviews in major newspapers, trade journals, magazines, or other published material; (3) performed and will perform services as a leading or starring group for organizations and establishments that have a distinguished reputation; (4) acquired a record of major commercial or critically acclaimed successes; (5) achieved significant recognition for achievements from organizations, critics, government agencies, or other recognized experts in the field; or (6) commanded or now commands a high salary or other substantial remuneration for services compared to others similarly situated in the field.

Types of Petitions and Accompanying Documents

When an entire orchestra, band, or other group with a single itinerary requests a temporary work visa, it is desirable to file petitions in group form rather than individually. One reason for this is that the $130 filing fee covers all members of the group. More importantly, it avoids duplication of effort, and eliminates the risk that processing delays on one group member's petition may hold up others whose petitions have already been approved. If there is a change in group personnel and group qualification before the commencement of a tour, the original petition may be amended. However, a change in personnel after initial entry into the United States usually requires a new petition and new filing fee. The new petition should be sent to the same INS processing center as the previous petition with a copy of the original petition, approval notice, and all supporting documentation, and should make reference to the file number and the date of the earlier approval.

It is to be assumed that a group known and regularly appearing under a group name is an entity and that the qualifications are the group's rather than those of individual members. In fact, the petition should use the group name in the space for "name of beneficiary"; individual member names can be attached on an accompanying schedule showing names, citizenships, birth dates, places of birth, and current addresses.

If the artists are already in the United States, forms must be filed to allow them to change status, for example, from visitor to temporary worker, or to extend their stay. To change status, the artist or artists must file Form I-506, along with the entry permit he or she was given on arrival, known as the I-94 form. Artists wishing to extend their stay within the same visa status must each file Form I-539 with their I-94 form. H-2B artists must file with the Department of Labor seeking certification, then file Form I-797, the approval notice of the initial petition, along with the I-94 form. All material to be filed should be submitted together with the O, P, or H-2B petitions to the INS.

Petitions for either an O or P visa should be accompanied by documentary proof of professional standing. This may be in the form of record or concert reviews or hit charts. It is also advisable to have letters of endorsement from recognized experts in the applicant's field of music, such as critics, concert promoters, recognized artists, publishers, or record company personnel, or a certificate of membership in a select professional society. Such endorsements should be in the English language or accompanied by an English translation made by a translator who submits a certificate of competency to translate and a notarized statement of the accuracy of the translation.

Before a foreign artist can be approved for a work permit with an O or P petition, a consultation requirement must be met, usually at the U.S. Consul where the artist resides. However, the INS usually gives the U.S. labor organization whose membership of musicians or of vocalists would normally offer the services covered by the petition a 15-day period within which to submit a written advisory opinion on the application.

In cases in which the petitioner has determined that expedited consultation procedures are required to accommodate tight scheduling of a production, the petitioner can submit a special $1,000 fee, which theoretically expedites the process so that an answer is given within 15 days. However, following the terrorist event of September 11, 2002, major delays in responses to all applications, even those accompanied by the special fee, are routine. Nonexpedited applications are frequently delayed for two or three months; petitioners submitting expedited applications must pass a new security check, and there is no assurance of a 15-day response.

All documents accompanying a petition for a work permit must be submitted in duplicate. If the return of documents is desired, this must be explicitly requested, and two photocopies must accompany the originals when submitted.

Where to File Petitions

The two governmental departments normally concerned with the foreign artist's entry under the P and O procedures are the INS and the U.S. Department of State. The INS is the primary agency concerned with the foreign artist's employment petitions in the United States.

The INS maintains 37 district offices spread throughout the United States, plus four district offices in foreign countries (Italy, Mexico, the Philippines, and Germany). There are also four regional service centers where most applications and petitions are processed. They are in Vermont, Texas, California, and Nebraska. While forms can be obtained from the INS district offices, they should be submitted to the appropriate regional service center by mail. Any regional center can handle all territorial employment included in the itinerary of an artist, so long as the petition at least partially involves employment in the territory of the district office.

It is neither necessary nor desirable to send multiple petitions to a number of regional service centers. In fact, it is sometimes better to select one regional service center in preference to another. Factors to consider include the possibility of faster service and familiarity with entertainment industry problems. Since all dealings with these remote adjudication centers are required to be by mail or telephone only, geographical proximity to the parties or their attorney is not crucial. An experienced immigration attorney can give valuable assistance in selecting the best INS office with which to file, in situations in which there is a choice.

A matter of convenience to all parties concerned is the use of telegrams by the regional adjudication centers to confirm entry approval to petitioners as well as to notify U.S. consular offices abroad so that they may process visa applications. Such notification, which can be extremely valuable when time is of the essence and any delays will be costly, can be obtained simply by noting "Cable Requested" on the top of the forms.

Personal appearance by the petitioner is strongly discouraged, and all requests for expedited consideration must now be made by overnight or same-day mail with a request for cable notification and documentation of the urgency of the case. Attorneys will not be given information about the status of a pending case unless they have filed a special notice of appearance on INS Form G-28, signed by the petitioner.

When requested by a petitioner residing abroad, the State Department is primarily involved with handling requests for information, forms, the processing of papers in foreign countries through the various U.S. consular offices, and the issuance of visas where approved. The actual approval is handled by the Department of Labor and INS, as noted above.

Artist's or Group's Accompanying Personnel

Performing artists attract ticket buyers and high fees on the basis of their individual reputations and talent. However, few major artists are truly a solo entity. They usually depend on backup musicians, accompanists, road managers, publicity agents, sound technicians, and, in some instances, even special hairdressers, valets, or maids. When applying for work visas in the United States, the unique and special talent of the major artist often does not extend to members of his or her entourage. The hairdresser, so essential to an artist in London, might be replaced in the United States by an equally qualified American. A bass player or pianist who wants to accompany a well-known artist overseas may be regarded by an AFM union representative as merely a competitor of an equally competent U.S. musician.

In one petition application for a foreign orchestra that used electronic instruments and equipment, a sound technician was recognized as a uniquely qualified member of the group despite having basic technical skills generally on the same level as those of U.S. technicians in the same field. However, in this case, the orchestra itself was using special sound equipment designed by this individual. The equipment had to be continually repaired, and rearranged to fit different concert halls, for which functions the equipment designer had special training and experience that was not interchangeable with that of other technicians who did not have such familiarity with the orchestra or equipment. In contrast, the work visa for the road manager was not approved. Although he was familiar with the personal whims and needs of the orchestra personnel as to dining, accommodations, and travel, his function was deemed not so exceptional that it could not be performed by a U.S. citizen without special and extensive training, and the petition was not approved.

In the end, decisions regarding the issuance of work permits are highly subjective, and supporting affidavits and explanations must clearly delineate the unique qualities of accompanying personnel.

Rejection and the Right of Appeal

In the fast-moving world of musical entertainment, a frequent concern in the employment of foreign artists is undue delay in clearing them for an engagement. Delays may force a prospective employer to find substitute artists to fill a concert hall or other place of engagement. Rarely will an employer be able to wait for the extended time involved in new applications or appeals. Unfortunately, since 2001, security procedures have increased delays in clearing foreign artists.

In the event of a refusal to admit, the petitioning artist can appeal or reapply. The regulations of the INS require that the petitioner must be notified of the reasons for such denial and of the right to appeal. With regard to the O and P petitions, regulations further require that if a projected adverse decision is based upon evidence not submitted by the petitioner, that is, third-party evidence, the petitioner must be so notified and invited to rebut that evidence. (Third parties, for example, unions, critics, or experts in the related entertainment field, are frequently consulted by the adjudicating officer of the INS in order to obtain an advisory opinion regarding the qualifications of the petitioner and the nature of the services to be performed.) Advisory opinions are sometimes given orally in the interest of expeditious handling of applications. For purposes of appeal from a rejected petition, even an oral opinion is subject to review by a petitioner because the opinion must be confirmed in writing within 15 days from the date when it was requested.

By statute, O and P petitions are automatically denied on certain grounds, such as insanity, chronic alcoholism, narcotics addiction, and conviction of trafficking in narcotics.

Union Comity

Although not required by law or regulation, it is advisable for foreign artists on a U.S. tour to consult the applicable U.S. union as to its requirements. For example, the AFM for the United States and Canada have reciprocally agreed to assist musicians in obtaining work permits in either country. Canadian musicians, who are members of the AFM for the United States and Canada jointly, must pay a "work dues equivalent" to certain AFM locals where the artist's services are performed, which charge its U.S. members similarly. These dues may run as high as 5 percent of wage scale in some instances. (These dues are not charged to foreign musicians who are not from Canada.)

The AFM Canadian office services all work permits of Canadian or U.S. AFM members for cross-border engagements. Its administrative fee for this service is $20 (Canadian) for regular services and $25 (Canadian) if given less then a 35-day advance notice before engagement. The Canadian work permit is called a Temporary Employment Authorization (IMM-1120); the U.S. form for similar engagements is called a Class P-2. The cost of a work permit for musicians with U.S. citizenship to work in Canada is $110 (U.S.) per petition, plus a $5 "user fee" if the group is driving a commercial vehicle across the border or is importing merchandise for sale; for Canadian musicians to work in the United States, the fee is $150 (Canadian) for single musicians and $450 for multiple entry of 2 to 14 musicians traveling and entering the United States as a unit.

Where unions have approved an exchange, both countries are expected to abide by the category and hours of employment specific to the union rules in the place of performance. Although such a "trade" of work is sometimes arranged through a booking agency, the international unions themselves may at times informally facilitate such an exchange and thereby clear the way for the U.S. union to advise the applicable government office of no objection to the permit. International union arrangements with the union in a foreign artist's home country often cover membership status in the United States as well. Nonunion members can be required to join the U.S. union after 30 days from the commencement of employment in a "union shop."

Multiple Entries into the United States plus Extensions

Performing artists may interrupt a U.S. tour to perform in other countries before returning to the United States. This interruption does not require duplicate work clearances because multiple-entry permission is available. In such cases, the foreign musician should ask the U.S. consul for a multiple-entry visa. When the artist arrives in the United States, the artist's visa (INS Form I-94) will indicate the duration approved by INS and whether multiple entries are permitted. Artists with O visas can receive a stay of up to 3 years initially and may be granted extensions, in 1-year increments, in order to permit that individual to continue to complete the same event or activity. Artists with P visas may be granted a stay of up to 5 years, with extensions up to another 5 years in 1-year increments in order to permit the artist to complete the same event.

Applications for extensions are made to INS on Form I-539. In addition, the petitioner must request an extension of the validity of the initial petition on Form I-129B. The two are considered separately although filed together. A denial of an extension of a stay is not appealable; a denial of extension of the petition is. If the petition is extended but the stay is not, the artist may go to another country, such as Canada, and ask the U.S. consul there for a new visa based on the extended petition. If new engagements are involved, a new I-129B petition must also be filed with the INS.

Taxation

Compensation for a foreign artist's personal appearances in the United States is subject to the income taxes of either the United States, the country of origin of the artist, or both. Artists from some countries—Canada, France, Germany, Sweden, and the United Kingdom—can avoid U.S. withholding taxes (currently 30 percent) on their U.S. earnings because of the existence of treaties between the United States and those countries called Conventions for the Avoidance of Double Taxation. Artists from nontreaty countries are subject to full U.S. tax on their earnings from appearances in the United States. Artists are required to obtain tax clearance or an exemption certificate from the IRS district director before departure from the United States.

Eligibility under double-taxation treaties requires the filing of proof with the IRS district director that the artist qualifies as a taxpayer in the artist's country of origin. For instance, U.K. taxpayers obtain such a certificate from the Financial Intermediaries and Claims Office in Nottingham. When an artist fails to file timely exemption status, application for a refund upon later qualification may be applicable.

Taxation on compensation received by U.S. artists performing in other countries varies from country to country.

41

Sources of Information

It is important for people in the music business to keep informed of news and developments in the industry. A prime source of information is the trade press. In addition, there exists a large network of publications, archives, organizations, research services, and reference materials that provide information on all aspects of the music industry. The Internet now serves to link these sources and to provide an unprecedented range of news and information to both interested browsers and industry professionals.

Trade Press

Two of the leading weekly trade publications that concentrate on the music industry are *Billboard* and *College Music Journal New Music Report (CMJ)*. To keep abreast of developments in the business, songwriters, performers, publishers, and record companies read at least one of these magazines.

Billboard, probably the most widely read trade publication in the industry, covers domestic and international artists, sales, radio programming, and marketing and industry news, and includes weekly reviews of new singles and albums. *Billboard* tracks the airplay and sales success of albums and singles/tracks in numerous genres. The weekly magazine also features a reviews and previews section, which describes promising new recordings. The most outstanding of the week's releases—those which the editors feel "deserve special attention on the basis of musical merit and/or chart potential"—are reviewed in the "Spotlights" section; those which are predicted to hit the top half of the chart in their respective genre are chosen as "Picks"; and those highly recommended because of their musical merit regardless of their chart potential are labeled "Critics' Choices."

The range of musical formats and genres in contemporary music is indicated by the many charts in a typical issue of *Billboard* or *CMJ*. For example, the following is a partial listing of the "top" and "hot" charts featured in *Billboard* in one week in the fall of 2002:

- ▶ Bluegrass Albums
- ▶ Blues
- ▶ Contemporary Christian
- ▶ Country Albums, Country Singles and Tracks
- ▶ Dance Music (subdivided into Club Play, Breakouts, Maxi-Single Albums, and Electronic Albums)
- ▶ Gospel
- ▶ Latin Albums (subdivided into Latin Pop, Tropical/Salsa, and Regional Mexican), Latin Tracks
- ▶ World (including Australia, Argentina, Canada, Denmark, France, Germany, Italy, Japan, the Netherlands, New Zealand, Norway, Portugal, Spain, Sweden, U.K.

There were also charts headed Top Music Videos, Top DVD Sales, Top VHS Sales, Top Video Rentals, Heatseekers, Top Independent Albums, Top Internet Album Sales, Top Pop Catalog, and Top Soundtracks. In any given week, there may be charts for reggae, jazz, kid audio, and others.

The Billboard Hot 100 lists the week's most popular singles or tracks by title, name of artist, name of producer, and record label name and number. Also indicated are the number of weeks a record has been on the chart, its standing in each of the two previous weeks, the availability of video clips, the names of its writers, publisher, and sheet music supplier, and the publisher's affiliation with ASCAP or BMI. Songs registering the greatest airplay and sales gains for the past week are marked by a red circle around the number of their standing on the chart. Each song certified as a 500,000 -unit shipment (gold) by the Recording Industry Association of America (RIAA) is accompanied by a black bullet; songs with shipments of 1 million (platinum) are marked with a black triangle.

Billboard ranks albums in a separate chart entitled The Billboard 200, which lists the 200 best-selling albums in the United States in order. The numbers of those recordings that registered the greatest sales gains during the week are circled; RIAA-certified gold albums (500,000 shipped) are marked with a bullet; and RIAA-certified platinum albums (1 million shipped) are marked with a triangle. Albums with a net shipment of 10 million (diamond) are marked with a black diamond.

Billboard's formula for determining a recording's position on the Hot 100 includes both sales and airplay data. Before 1991, airplay figures were obtained from weekly playlists supplied by the various radio stations and sales figures were based on manually obtained reports from retail outlets. Currently, the airplay part of the formula is calculated on the basis of data supplied by Broadcast Data Systems (BDS), which electronically monitors hundreds of radio stations 24 hours a day 7 days week to determine the number of times a song has been played in a given time period. These figures are combined with listener data (the estimated number of different people who listen to a particular station during that same time period) to come up with a reliable estimate of a song's actual popularity with radio listeners. Weekly sales figures are obtained from SoundScan, which combines point-of-sale entries from thousands of record outlets using bar-code scans with data from on-line and mail-order retailers. Although it is impossible for SoundScan to provide completely accurate totals (Christian music, for example, racks up a percentage of its sales at conventions, and some independent retailers have not installed the equipment that generates the computerized reports), the SoundScan numbers are used throughout the industry to gauge the success of recordings.

In addition to reviews and charts, *Billboard* contains coverage of international news and lists the best international sellers in designated markets. A typical issue of *Billboard* also reports changes in artist affiliations with record companies, shifts in record company personnel, special sales promotions, news of new and impending legislation and government investigations, meetings of distributors, discussions of publishing and record company business developments, and acquisitions and mergers of publishing and record companies.

Billboard issues annual directories that include valuable information about record manufacturers, music publishers, record wholesalers, and firms engaged in services and supplies for the music industry. The *Billboard* directories are international in scope, and are a great aid to U.S. record companies and publishers who want to familiarize themselves with their counterparts in foreign countries. For example, the *Billboard International Buyer's Guide* lists record and video companies, music publishers, music industry distributors and suppliers, equipment manufacturers, and sources of music industry services. Other directories include the *Billboard International Talent & Touring Directory*, the *Billboard Record Retailing Directory*, *The Radio Power Book*, *The Nashville 615/ Country Music Sourcebook*, and the *International Latin Music Buyer's Guide*.

Billboard also publishes *Amusement Business* (www.amusementbusiness.com), the "international newsweekly for sports and mass entertainment," which covers musical and theatrical entertainment, carnivals, circuses, and variety and specialty acts. It reports on all aspects of live musical entertainment, from jazz to symphony and from country to ragtime. It includes valuable directory and chart materials as well. *Airplay Monitor*, also published by *Billboard*, charts and analyzes radio airplay of music. This magazine helps fill the void left by the *Gavin Report*, a popular trade magazine also charting airplay that stopped printing in 2001.

Unlike *Billboard*, *CMJ* focuses primarily on independent artists and labels and is often used by new artists to identify alternative outlets, such as college, noncommercial, and alternative radio stations. Like *Billboard*, *CMJ* contains both album reviews and popularity charts, but while *Billboard* charts track both record sales and commercial airplay, *CMJ* weekly charts focus on airplay. *CMJ* charts include Top 20, Beat Box (hip-hop and urban), Triple A (adult album alternative), Loud Rock, Jazz, New World, RPM (electronic music), and Internet Broadcast. *CMJ* does not chart pop singles, but its Core College Radio and Commercial Alternative Cuts charts list singles in the alternative music category. Each chart lists in green print the records that received a "significant increase in airplay." Additionally, a green triangle indicates the records that have experienced the "greatest chart movement" and a heart indicates the "most requested titles." Table 41-1 illustrates the difference in focus between *Billboard* and *CMJ*.

Table 41-1

Top Albums Listed by *Billboard* and *CMJ*, week of September 26, 2002

Chart Position	*Billboard*	*CMJ*
1	*Home* Dixie Chicks Monument/Columbia	*One Beat* Sleater-Kinney Kill Rock Stars
2	*Let Go* Avril Lavigne Arista	*Kill The Moonlight* Spoon Merge
3	*The Eminem Show* Eminem WEB/Aftermath	*Turn On The Bright Lights* Interpol Matador
4	*Nellyville* Nelly Fo' Reel/Universal	*Songs For The Deaf* Queens of the Stone Age Interscope
5	*Unleashed* Toby Keith Dreamworks (Nashville)	*A Rush Of Blood To The Head* Coldplay Capitol
6	*The Rising* Bruce Springsteen Columbia	*Trust* Low Kranky
7	*Come Away With Me* Norah Jones Blue Note	*Now You Know* Doug Martsch Warner Bros.
8	*A Rush Of Blood To The Head* Coldplay Capitol	*Lost In Space* Aimee Mann Superego

CMJ provides a listing of new releases from various alternative record companies. Further, *CMJ* convenes its annual *CMJ* Music Marathon & Musicfest, an alternative music convention that showcases new artists and provides industry information to executives and to fans.

In addition to *Billboard* and *CMJ*, there are a number of other trade publications that provide valuable information to industry professionals.

▶ *Radio & Records (R&R)* is a weekly in-depth trade paper targeted to radio programmers and executives, but with significant coverage of the music industry. *R&R* furnishes extensive and detailed information on the current music programming of leading radio stations throughout the United States, subdivided by region and by music format. Unlike the *Billboard* charts, which give weight to both store sales and airplay information, or *CMJ*, which gives some consideration to sales, *R&R* does not use sales information. Its top singles chart is titled CHR, an abbreviation for Contemporary Hit Radio. It includes the top 40 songs in the country based on national airplay and also shows the standing of each song in the previous two weeks. The chart identifies a rising chart status by a black circle around the number on the chart. A song that has concurrent airplay on 60 percent of the reporting stations is highlighted by the word "Breaker." It designates songs as "Most Added" to station playlists and "Hottest" to indicate those receiving the heaviest airplay reports. *R&R* also lists a limited number of top-played records in Australia, Canada, and the United Kingdom, based on foreign sources. At *R&R's* Web site, www.radioandrecords.com, there is a link to *The Green Book of Songs by Subject,* now in its 5th edition, which has over 86,000 song listings, 1,500 labels, and 9,100 artists, and cross-references songs and albums by subject and concept.

▶ *Urban Network* (www.urbannetwork.com) is a trade magazine focusing on urban music, including such genres as rap, hip-hop, R&B, and gospel. All aspects of the industry are covered, including extensive radio playlists and charts, record reviews, industry news, video charts, and "clip of the week," as well as artist profiles and album sales distinguished by U.S. region.

▶ *New on the Charts* (www.newonthecharts.com) is a monthly information service sold by subscription only to professionals in the music industry. Sometimes called "the tip sheet," it supplies the names, addresses, and telephone numbers of producers, publishers, booking agents, record labels, and personal managers associated with entries on the *Billboard* Top 100 Pop and Top 50 Urban and Country charts. It also lists each month's label, publisher, booking agency, and management signings, as well as film and TV projects currently in production that need music.

▶ The *A&R Registry* (www.musicregistry.com) published every two months by the Music Business Registry, offers a nearly complete list of U.S.-

based record labels, and those in Toronto, along with the relevant executives and A&R support staffs. Contact information, including addresses, phone numbers, fax numbers, and e-mail, is also given.

▶ *Pollstar* (www.pollstar.com) is a weekly guide for music industry professionals in the field of concert, club, theater, and other live entertainment venues. It furnishes tour itineraries, box office results, contact directories, news items, and artist, agency, and manager profiles.

Government Institutions

The U.S. Copyright Office files became particularly valuable as a result of the physical destruction of buildings in Europe during World War II and the resulting loss of important copyright records. News came from Finland that its great composer Jan Sibelius had insufficient data to furnish his advisers and was thus unable to keep abreast of the uses of his extensive catalog in the United States. The Copyright Office, as a gesture of goodwill, made a complete analysis of his approximately 800 works registered at any time in the United States, setting forth the dates of original and renewal registrations, the history of any assignments, and the original recordings indicated by Notices of Use on file. This gift required 200 hours of work. The Copyright Office made a similar study of about 3,000 musical compositions of German origin, replacing catalog information that had been destroyed in wartime.

Today, the facilities of the Copyright Office are available for such research services at a service charge of $75 per hour. When a search is requested, all known basic facts should be sent to the office. These should be assembled on a search request form furnished by the Copyright Office. An estimate of the hours and charges will be furnished upon receipt of the request form.

In addition to its search services, the Copyright Office can be of value in furnishing copies of missing songs that have been filed with a copyright registration. A copy of unpublished manuscripts and published songs will be supplied, provided that the copy request is authorized in writing by the copyright owner or the owner's agent, the request is made by an attorney for use in a court proceeding, or there is a court order requiring such a copy.

All pre-1978 registrations are recorded on index cards. Entries from January 1, 1978, to the present, as well as those pre-1978 works for which registration has been renewed since January 1, 1978, are recorded electronically and published on the Internet (lcweb.loc.gov/copyright). Entries from 1891 through 1978 are published in the *Catalog of Copyright Entries,* which is on file in larger public libraries, available for inspection on microfiche in the Search Room of the Copyright Office and in the Library of Congress, and available for sale to the public. Entries from 1979 through 1982 are available only on microfiche. The only way to search for registrations made since 1982, outside of the Library of Congress itself, is by using the Internet to access the electronic catalog. The electronic catalog will continue to be published in eight parts, among which are separate parts for performing arts (which includes musical works), sound recordings, and renewals. Unpublished as well as published materials are included in all parts except renewals. The catalog is indexed by copyright registration number, title of the work, claimant's name, and in the case of sound recordings, the names of principal performers. The appropriate use of the catalog can satisfy simply and inexpensively many requests for information regarding copyrighted material.

As noted above, songs registered before January 1, 1978, will be added to the electronic database only when the registration is renewed. For example, under the terms of the Copyright Renewal Act of 1992 the renewal of copyright for works published between January 1, 1964, and December 31, 1977, is optional. Thus a song registered in 1976 whose renewal registration is due in the year 2004 will not be added unless and until it is renewed on that date. For works under copyright protection on or after January 1, 1978, registration may be made at any time during the period of protection.

The Copyright Office assembles important federal and state court decisions regarding copyrights and related subjects in the field of intellectual property; these are published in a series of bulletins entitled *Decisions of the United States Courts Involving Copyright*. The Copyright Office also issues gratis a series of individual circulars explaining various aspects of domestic and international copyright protection. For information on ordering these documents, as well as copyright registration listings, go to the following Web site: www.copyright.gov/circs/circo2.

Many searches are accomplished using the services of private firms. A prominent firm such as Thomson & Thomson charges varying rates depending on the type of report requested and how soon it is needed.

1. *Full U.S. copyright search.* Search for the copyright ownership of a specified property, such as a motion picture, literary work, television program, screenplay, or song. The search is based on a search of U.S. Copyright Office records, on-line databases, and Thomson & Thomson's propriety sources and includes:

   ▸ Information revealing underlying and derivative works
   ▸ Copyright registration and renewal data
   ▸ A summary of assignments and other recorded instruments
   ▸ Biographical information on the authors

2. *Original or unexploited work search.* Full U.S. copyright search coverage for original screenplays or unexploited works that do not involve a derivative or underlying work.

3. *U.S. copyright screening search.* A search of the U.S. Copyright Office records for registration and renewal data and a listing of recorded documents for a particular work.

Another excellent government source of information is the Archive of Folk Culture. In 1928, the Library of Congress Music Division established a national repository for documentary manuscripts and sound recordings of American folk music. In 1981, its official name was changed from the Archive of Folk Song to the Archive of Folk Culture. Since its establishment, over 30,000 hours of recordings containing more than 300,000 items of folk songs, folk music, folk tales, oral history, and other types of folklore have been sent to the Library of Congress, primarily from the United States. These records include traditional sea chanteys, authentic cowboy songs, songs of the Mormons, ballads of the Civil War, Anglo-American songs and ballads, Negro work songs and spirituals, fiddle and banjo tunes, songs of many Indian tribes, as well as folk songs and music from Brazil, Mexico, Morocco, Puerto Rico, and Venezuela.

A catalog listing the entire series of recordings available from the Library of Congress may be obtained from the Archive of Folk Culture, Library of Congress, Washington, DC 20540; Web site: http://lcweb.loc.gov/folklife/archive.html. The archive has available extensive field notes, many textual transcriptions, and some musical transcriptions, in folders and bound volumes, for supplementary information about the recordings. It has also compiled about 200 bibliographies and other reference lists covering many areas and subjects in the field of folklore and folk music; an inventory of the bibliographies and lists is available upon request.

In January of 2003 the Library of Congress announced the first annual selection of 50 recordings to the National Recording Registry, a special collection of historically important recordings encompassing music (from a variety of genres, including folk music, opera, rock, jazz, and rap) famous radio broadcasts (including Welles's *War of the Worlds* and Eisenhower's D-Day address), and other audio milestones.

The Smithsonian Institution, a nonprofit organization, is in the unique position not only to record but also to keep in print valuable archival music. Its mission as a curator is to keep alive a record of music from around the world that reflects our varied history and culture. Among its collections is the historic Folkways label, acquired in 1987, and the additional labels of Cook, Dyer-Bennett, Fast Folk, Monitor, and Paredon. Folkways has approximately 30,000 musical performances, ranging from folk, jazz, blues, classical, the spoken word, and native oral traditions to sounds from nature and children's recordings. Its music comes from around the world, from the Americas, Africa, Asia, Europe, and the Caribbean.

The Smithsonian provides a full description of its musical operations at its Web site (http://www.folkways.si.edu). Folkways also distributes its music via Liquid Audio (www.liquidaudio.com), avoiding the typical mail-order process. These sites include music, video clips, liner notes, and, for special releases, educational audiotapes, musical instructional videos, video anthologies, and books.

Yet another program that disseminates music is Smithsonian Productions, which has produced many radio and television programs. These include the radio series *Jazz Smithsonian,* a multiyear series on public radio, featuring performances by the Smithsonian Jazz Masterworks Orchestra, and *Folk Masters,* another public radio series that aired for several years and showcased perform-ances by top artists in traditional music. The Peabody Award–winning radio series, *Black Radio: Telling It Like It Was,* included many examples of African-American music from the middle and latter parts of the 20th century. In 1998, Smithsonian Productions coproduced the public radio series *Remembering Slavery,* with a companion book and audiotape set. In 1999, it joined forces with PBS and the Filmmakers Collaborative of Boston to present a four-part television series entitled *The Mississippi River Song.* The project also included a seven-part public radio series, a companion book, and a two-CD set from Folkways Recordings.

Information can also be obtained from the Center for Black Music (CBM) Library and Archives, a research facility dedicated to the collection and preser-vation of all genres of African-American music—popular, jazz, and classical—from all regions. Located at Columbia College in Chicago, CBM has an impres-sive Web site at www.cbmr.org.

Music Organizations

Because the music business is based on vast catalogs of millions of titles, each with its own history of legal title and licensing history, it is ideally suited to the modern database operation that these organizations have adopted. ASCAP, BMI, and the Harry Fox Agency are important sources of information regarding the history, ownership, and rights under copyright of musical works. ASCAP and BMI maintain index departments that supply information to the industry and to the public concerning millions of old and more recent compositions. All new copyright registrations in the U.S. Copyright Office are entered into their indexes. ASCAP offers its song index information through the ASCAP Clearance Express (ACE) on-line service (www.ascap.com/ace/ace.html); BMI through its HyperRepertoire databank (http://repertoire.bmi.com/startpage.asp).

The Harry Fox Agency also has a large database with information about the songs that it represents, including their composers and how to license them. This information is accessible by the public in the "Songfile" component of the Harry Fox Web site (www.harryfox.com). In addition, the Web site has tools for publisher members allowing them to access information about their songs, accounts, and licensing activity.

The various performance right societies throughout the world have an umbrella organization in International Confederation of Societies of Authors and Composers (CISAC). CISAC has set up a global system to enable world-wide identification of musical works, the World Information Database (WID), which is currently administered by ASCAP, on an interim basis, on behalf of all CISAC members. As of early 2003, some 50 societies had on-line access to the WID and another 70 had received hard copies. The WID is subsidized by contributions of CISAC member societies in proportion to their size and revenues. The standard used for this identification incorporates essential data from all member societies that identifies song title, composer(s), author(s), and publisher(s), as well as territory affiliated and originating society for each of the millions of songs in the database. Each work is assigned a unique identifying number, an International Standard Work Code. The WID is different from the databases that can be searched by the public (e.g., ASCAP's World Works List) in that it includes confidential data and can thus be accessed only by password.

The WID system will be invaluable in expediting accounting between participating societies and distributions to qualifying members. The stated goal is to eventually have 80 percent of the world's music copyright repertoire identified and on-line.

Another important standard was announced in February of 2003 by IFPI and RIAA: the Global Release Identifier (GRid) system designed to enable copyright owners to track digitally distributed music. The GRid identifier is the electronic analog to the Universal Product Code affixed to CDs, and it complements, rather than replaces, other identifiers such as the International Standard Recording Code (ISRC) now used for tracks in any format. The IFPI will administer the system, which will be open to record companies, distributors, licensed online music services, and retailers.

The many performing rights societies, through their membership with CISAC, have organized a central information center through Switzerland's SUISA for general cross-checking of all repertoires. Similarly, Norway's Nordisk Copyright Bureau has accepted the role of central research source for various societies involved in mechanical licensing. This is a major step toward erasing the infamous "black box" problem of unallocated monies due to absence of identification of the owner. In addition, individual members of the Harry Fox Agency, ASCAP, BMI, or SESAC are able to request access to their respective private economic data.

Professional Research Services

When it is necessary to locate the owners of musical copyrights in connection with prospective motion picture, television, stage, and record productions, ASCAP, BMI, the Harry Fox Agency, and unions and trade organizations may be helpful. The U.S. Copyright Office can be helpful. Where an initial request for information produces unsatisfactory results, or where the inquirer does not have the staff, time, or expertise to make his or her own inquiries, professional services may be employed. The same services may also be sought where expertise is needed for the investigation of outstanding licenses.

In addition to Thomson & Thomson, there are several on-line firms advertising discount copyright searches and negotiating. For example, at the time of this writing, a site named Lawmart.com was offering title searches for $279. Other firms who will perform these services include the Copyright Clearance Center, Inc. (www.copyright.com) and the Art Law Center (www.artlaws.com).

Reference Materials

There are a number of reference books and manuals that can be used to supplement the aforementioned sources of information.

Joel Whitburn's Record Research releases a series of books prepared under license from *Billboard* magazine detailing the history of all *Billboard* chart action for singles and albums. Organized alphabetically by artist name and also by song title, Whitburn's publications furnish valuable research and programming material as well as incidental facts concerning both the recordings and the artists. Further information is available at www.recordresearch.com.

Billboard Books publishes a number of useful sources that provide record charts, reference materials, and how-to guides. Books such as *Top Pop Singles, Top Pop Albums, Billboard's Top 10 Charts,* and *The Billboard Book of Number One Hits* are chart-based books that span 40 years of popular music. Billboard's reference titles include *This Business of Artist Management, This Business of Music Marketing and Promotion,* and *The Encyclopedia of Record Producers.* Finally, such sources as *How to Be a Working Musician, The Real Deal: How to Get Signed to a Record Label from A to Z,* and *Start and Run Your Own Record Label* are guides for both amateurs and professionals in the music industry. Billboard also publishes the *AudArena Stadium and Facility Buyer's International Guide,* an annually updated catalog of concert and performance venues across the country.

Other important print sources are the massive 29-volume 2001 edition of *The New Grove Dictionary of Music and Musicians* (third edition) and the *Encyclopedia of Popular Music in the World. The New Grove Dictionary* is an extremely thorough reference to all genres of music, including classical, popular, and jazz. Entries include information on musical forms, citations and institutions, terms and definitions, instruments, composers and performers, as well as musical history. The *Encyclopedia of Popular Music in the World* is a three-volume source covering the music industry, social and cultural contexts, various musical genres, and the music of various countries and world regions. While it is considerably less thorough than the *Encyclopedia of Popular Music,* its global focus makes it a valuable resource.

The Copyright Society of the U.S.A., which is hosted and maintained by the Duke University School of Law, is of special interest to anyone interested in the music business. Their functions, news, and valuable suggested on-line copyright resources and links are available at http:law.duke.edu/copyright/html/research.

International Trade Shows and Associations

A number of domestic and international trade shows, associations, and societies offer a wealth of information as well as prime networking opportunities for those in the record industry.

Since 1967, the International Music and Publishing Market, commonly known as MIDEM, has held an annual international trade show for music business participants including publishers, record companies, artists, managers, performance rights societies, and equipment manufacturers and suppliers. Held in Cannes, France, at the end of January, the five-day networking event features conferences and concerts showcasing new and established international artists.

Throughout the year, *Billboard* magazine organizes and sponsors trade meetings in the United States as well as abroad. The subject matter ranges from such diverse topics as music videos at the annual *Billboard* Film & TV Music Conference, to music programming and international music business trade at *Billboard*'s annual Dance Music Summit. Other *Billboard*-sponsored events include the *Billboard* Music and Money Symposium and the *Billboard* Latin Conference and Awards.

The International Association for the Study of Popular Music is a nonprofit organization headquartered in Bay City, Michigan. Started in 1981 by musicians, music teachers, researchers, and journalists, its aim was to pool information about popular music otherwise neglected in academic circles and cultural administration. The association continues to organize conferences, symposia, and meetings to exchange information and ideas on various topics at regional and international levels. In addition, it publishes two newsletters, *The Review of Popular Music* and *Popular Music Perspectives,* the latter covering its biannual international conferences.

42

Technology and Music

In 1945, Zechariah Chafee Jr., professor of law at Harvard University and a leading First Amendment scholar, wrote in the *Columbia Law Review* that

> Copyright is the Cinderella of the law. Her rich older sisters
> Franchises and Patents, long crowded her into the chimney
> corner. Suddenly the fairy godmother, Invention, endowed her
> with mechanical and electrical devices as magical as the pumpkin
> coach and the mice footmen. Now she whirls through the mad
> mazes of a glamorous ball.

Indeed, thanks to such technological innovations as television, video, satellite broadcasting, and increasingly sophisticated sound systems, the music industry has danced frequently and happily all the way to the bank, rewarded for decades with enormous profit growth figures. When technology raised the specter of new unauthorized uses, such as record rental shops or home copying, legislative changes were enacted to protect the flow of royalties. Today, technological advances revolve around the Internet. The relationship between the Internet and the music industry promises (or threatens) to bring about a revolution in music marketing and distribution. As the on-line consumer base expands, so too do the capabilities of computer programming. Internet users can receive music without leaving the home, send music to others, communicate with others who are listening to the same music, make customized compilations, and access information about music that they are listening to.

As digital transmission has grown in capacity and popularity, major corporations have been forced to take heed, both to obtain protection against rampant infringement and to exploit the new technology themselves. Similarly, music business establishments and trade associations such as ASCAP, BMI, SESAC, NMPA, and RIAA have expanded their watch on technology in order to maintain and expand their profit base. Given our society's growing demand for immediate gratification, downloading is becoming increasingly popular not only for savvy users, but also for pirates. Cinderella may still be at the ball, but the mazes are more complicated than ever, and she needs both a guide and a bodyguard.

The Market for Internet Music

Just how popular have Internet distribution and streaming become, and how popular will they be in the future? Jupiter Media Metrix forecasts a $5.5 billion music market with an estimated 210.8 million on-line user base by 2006. While some observers believe that the industry will inevitably change over to direct distribution but that the change will be gradual, others believe that there will be a rapid, radical shift. They point to the almost overnight switch from vinyl LPs to CDs as an indicator of how fast a technological development can sweep through the industry. They believe that digital distribution will level the playing field between independent and major record labels, since on-line distribution affords even the smallest record labels the opportunity to reach as wide an audience as a major record label. The prospect of direct foreign sales makes on-line retail particularly attractive to smaller labels that cannot afford their own international setup.

Dissenters point to the modest start of on-line distribution and seem to feel that until the major labels fully embrace this technology, it will not become the norm. Although a 1998 study by Jupiter Communications entitled "Music Industry and the Internet: Usage, Retail & Digital Distribution" recommended that labels should "proactively adopt digital distribution as a means of delivering music," the major labels have responded cautiously to Internet distribution. They are not willing either to relinquish copyright control of their biggest artists to potential on-line piracy or to upset relationships with traditional middle retailers. However, despite their initial reluctance, most major labels have become increasingly involved in on-line distribution as the number of on-line buyers continues to grow (see below, page 404). In 2002, on-line record sales were reported at about $1 billion, and according to Media Metrix, on-line download sales had reached $29 million.

Internet music distribution operates in two ways. Users can make on-line purchases from such sites as Amazon.com—with the completed order being delivered by mail—or download music directly from the Web. However, although the delivery of music through garden-variety mail-order systems has been relatively straightforward, the direct downloading of music via the Internet has been a tumultuous affair for the industry from the very start.

During the 1990s, a number of Web sites, including N2K's Music Boulevard and CDnow.com, began selling CDs via the Internet. As early as 1997, CDNow's annual revenues were $16 million, a 33 percent share of the new market. In 1998, CDNow acquired Music Boulevard and its revenues climbed to $98.5 million (though they suffered an overall operating loss of $120 million the same year). Amazon.com, a major on-line bookseller, added mail-order music to its inventory in 1998. By 1999, Amazon had become the top music seller on-line, and in 2001, it had cornered 65 percent of the on-line music market. Currently, five "bricks-and-clicks" operations—Barnes and Noble, Best Buy, Tower, CDNow (purchased by Bertelsmann in 1999), and CDBaby.com (which came on the scene in 1998)—are Amazon.com's major competitors.

An on-line distributor of CDs of independent artists, CDBaby retains a minimal download fee of $4 per CD sold, regardless of sale price. By mid-2002, CDBaby was carrying titles by 22,000 artists and selling 4,000 albums a week, and was the second largest retailer of independent music on the Web, after Amazon. Like CDBaby, MP3.com allows independent artists to sell CDs through their Web site, though MP3.com takes a much larger cut—50 percent.

Many thousands of independent artists and record labels have taken advantage of e-commerce software packages with the goal of selling their CDs through their own Web sites. Three major artists who have used the Internet to economic advantage are Prince, Todd Rundgren, and David Bowie. Prince (www.npgmusicclub.com) has continued selling the majority of his CDs over the Internet since breaking with his label, Time Warner, in 1996. Todd Rundgren's Web site, www.tr-i.com, for Todd Rundgren-Interactive, offers different paid subscriber packages, which are combinations of on-line music, mail-order CDs, books, and videos, and Rundgren claims that both he and his subscribers are benefiting financially. When David Bowie made his single "Telling Lies" available in September 1996 for download, free of charge, for one week, the song was downloaded 450,000 times to users in 87 countries. In 1999, Bowie, a committed Internet advocate, arranged with 50 participating U.S. retail Web sites for a two-week advance to have 10 songs on his forthcoming Virgin album available for digital downloading in the North American market. The media barrage sent his new album to the Top 5 charts in several European markets within a week of its official release. As of this writing Bowie's Subscription Internet Community "BowieNet" features an online radio utilizing RealNetworks technology to stream audio to its members. There are also numerous less famous artists taking advantage of the Internet to circumvent the recording industry and sell directly to the consumer. For a partial list of the independent artists utilizing the Internet, check out The World Wide Web Independent Music Directory at www.indiemusic.com.

Starting Your Own Music Web Site

Peter Spellman points out in his work "The Self-Promoting Musician" that constructing a Web site can cost an artist anywhere from nothing to over $1,000 a year. Options for bands looking to save money include encouraging Web-savvy fans to develop fan sites, or searching for students in art schools with graphic design or new media programs who want to expand their portfolios and will work for relatively low rates. The essential components for constructing a Web site of your own are: (1) a computer and modem, (2) an HTML editor program, (3) graphics software (to get your page noticed), (4) a domain name, and (5) a host. Some services, such as Geocities (www.geocities.com) or Bandhost (www.bandhost.com), will host your site for free, but they will not allow you to use your own domain name. Some services you definitely want included in a domain name hosting account are RealAudio and/or MP3 streaming, CGI capabilities, multiple pop 3 e-mail accounts, and FTP access to your account. See Chapter 33, page 310, for information on domain names.

Downloading Music and Video Files via the Internet

At the time of this writing, there are several technological formats for compressing music so that it can be easily downloaded from the Internet. Two examples are MPEG (which stands for Moving Picture Experts Group, a family of standards used for coding audiovisual information—e.g., movies, video, music—into a digitally compressed format) and RealAudio (with available software for Microsoft, Macintosh, and Unix environments).

The best-known compression format is MPEG Audio Layer–3 (aka MP3). Originally intended for digital video, it has been adopted by the computing community as the standard for audio file compression and transmission over the Internet. This technology allows a data reduction of 1:12 (around 64 kbits per second per audio channel) while maintaining a high level of audio quality. Any selection of recorded music can be transformed into an MP3 file with the use of an encoder, sometimes called a "ripper," which can be downloaded from several different Web sites. Once the music has been compressed into an MP3 file, it can be posted on a Web site for downloading or distributed as an e-mail attachment. Users can also purchase software that records MP3 files onto a CD-R (recordable compact disc), a process that is called "burning."

To play back MP3 files, the user must have special decoding software, most of which is widely available for downloading free of charge. Winamp and Musicmatch are popular for Windows users; Macintosh users can try Macamp. The Real Player Plus G2 from RealNetworks supports MP3, as well as streaming RealAudio and RealVideo. In addition to playing MP3 files on computers, there is now special hardware that allows listeners to enjoy digital music away from the computer. A mere sampling of the ever-expanding list includes RIO PMP300 and RIO 500 by Diamond Multimedia, Nomad by Creative Labs, and iPod by Macintosh.

Apple's digital media software (QuickTime 6) for both Mac and Windows-based computers allows the user to create, play, and stream audio and video content over the Internet. With QuickTime 6, the user can create professional-quality MPEG-4 audio and video files that can be played back not only by QuickTime 6, but by any other MPEG-4–compliant player. Microsoft Windows XP Media Center Edition allows the user to watch DVD movies or home movies, listen to music, view slideshows, and even watch and digitally record live television programs.

One of the first companies to take advantage of the new technology was the Internet Underground Music Archive (IUMA). Started in 1993 by two college students as a database of songs of unknown bands that paid IUMA to promote their music, by 1998 IUMA was getting 250,000 hits per day. Not long after came Good Noise, one of the first companies to sell MP3 files on-line for consumers to download.

FROM MP3.COM TO KAZAA

In 2000, MP3.com put 45,000 copyrighted CDs onto its Web site and allowed users to download them in MP3 format, using a service called MyMp3.com, if the users showed proof of purchase of the CD, either by purchasing it at a partner site or by having the actual CD inserted into the user's computer and read by an MP3.com program. Within weeks, the RIAA brought suit against MP3.com for copyright infringement and won an injunction that forced the service to remove the CDs from its site. MP3.com defended itself by saying that the consumers downloading the files were simply "time-shifting" (that is, transferring music from one medium to another for the convenience of playing it at a later time), an action which was made legal under the Audio Home Recording Act of 1992. However, MP3.com lost, because time shifting was not the issue, but rather the ownership of the music on MP3.com's database. The judge in the case ruled that creation of the database was infringement. MP3.com was later sued by the individual record companies as well, and ended up settling for around $150 million in past damages, though the law would have allowed for up to $3.6 billion in damages. Vivendi Universal acquired MP3.com in 2002, and the site now offers (for sale) 1.6 million downloadable songs from over 250,000 artists.

Napster began in 1999 as a project for a computer programming class of an 18-year-old Northeastern University student. Napster was organized as a search engine and proprietary software which allowed users to search for music files by title among the music files of other users within its network and, communicating directly with those users (peer-to-peer file sharing), download those music files to their own computer. Napster became wildly popular with college students and, as the broadband user base increased, with the Internet community as a whole. At its peak in February 2001, Napster had over 26 million users, downloading hundreds of thousands of song titles.

In April 2001, the big five record companies, along with several individual artists such as Metallica, sued Napster for enabling copyright infringement. Napster defended itself by arguing that consumers had a right to make noncommercial copies of their records under the Audio Home Recording Act, and that, in addition, it fell within the safe-harbor provisions of the Digital Millennium Copyright Act and could not be liable for the illegal file swapping of its users. The court issued a preliminary injunction, demanding that Napster remove songs that the plaintiffs identified as their own. Unable to meet the requirement that it filter these titles out of its network, Napster shut down service. It also settled with the National Music Publisher's Association, which had filed a suit similar to that of the record companies, for around $26 million.

In May 2002, a month before Napster sought Chapter 11 protection against creditors, Bertelsmann made an offer to buy the company for $8 million contingent upon a bankruptcy proceeding creating a shield against creditor claims. The business rationale was that the continuing value of the trademark and the customer list would enable Bertelsmann to develop a lawful subscription service based on Napster's former customer list. The sale was blocked by the bankruptcy court after challenges that Bertelsmann's $80 million creditor claim made the deal too close for comfort due to lack of an arm's-length negotiation between Napster and Bertelsmann. After Bertelsmann withdrew from further negotiations, Napster's Web site displayed the simple statement "Napster was here," a declaration of final defeat.

Within days of Napster turning off its service, its millions of users began flocking to clone services such as AudioGalaxy, Morpheus, Aimster, Grokster, and KaZaA. According to Jupiter Media Metrix, from March 2001 to August 2001 the number of unique users to these clone sites increased 492 percent, from 1.2 million to 6.9 million. The most popular of these was KaZaA: by the end of 2002, its software had been downloaded over 37 million times, allowing users access to copyrighted music, motion pictures, and television shows.

The music industry (RIAA, NMPA, and various recording and motion picture companies) brought suit against all these services on the grounds of copyright infringement, with varying degrees of success. In fall 2002, RIAA and NMPA had forced a settlement with Audiogalaxy whereby the service agreed to obtain the permission of copyright holders for any music used on their network and to pay back damages. In December 2002, a judge granted a preliminary injunction against Madster (née Aimster, but forced to changed its name after losing a suit brought by AOL charging that the name violated AOL's AIM trademark), ordering the service to block all infringing files from its network. At the end of the year no action had yet been taken in a suit brought in a Los Angeles court against Morpheus, Grokster, and KaZaA. The KaZaA case is complicated by the fact that Sharman Networks, the distributor of the file-swapping program, is not based in the United States.

Streaming

Streaming involves transmitting audio and/or video content via the Internet in a compressed, digitized format that is temporarily stored in the computer's random access memory, making it available for listening and viewing purposes; streamed content cannot be downloaded. Streaming is used to transmit radio programs and television programs, and has gained popularity among Internet music providers who have begun to recognize the vast marketing and promotional possibilities of presenting music for listening pleasure only.

Web radio has developed into a major force. In 1996, only three Internet radio stations were in operation. By 1999, that number was up to 185, and in 2002, the BRS Radio-Directory listed over 5,000 radio stations broadcasting online, with 364 being Internet-only channels. In April 2002, one Internet radio site (Spinner.com) reported broadcasting over 22 million songs each week with over 375,000 songs in rotation on over 150 music channels. In mid-2002 their service was registering 1.5 million listeners monthly. Measurecast.com, a site that tracks audience data for Webcasters, tracked data for over 1,300 stations. Just one of those broadcasters, Live365.com, claims to offer a choice of 12,000 on-line radio stations featuring different types of music, from Goth to UK Garage. Jupiter Media Metrix estimated that over 20 percent of Americans over the age of 12 have listened to Web radio. According to CNN, nearly 25 million Americans were dialing up Internet radio daily. Webcasters under the Clear Channel Broadcasting Company were the most popular, receiving almost 1 million visitors monthly. Whether and to what extent Webcasting can be under FCC regulation is an important issue under current consideration. For information on small Webcaster licensing, see Chapter 7, page 67.

The Record Companies and the Internet

Initially, the record industry was slow to react to the new technology. Even as millions of Internet users flocked to early file-swapping networks and later to MP3 megasites like MP3.com, the record companies were still only dabbling in the formats as promotional tools. For example, in 1999, Atlantic allowed those who purchased the Sugar Ray CD "Sugar Ray" on CDNow to download a previously unreleased Internet-only live track as well. They were happy to see orders rise 70 percent while the download was available. Similar experiments were conducted with Tori Amos, the Beastie Boys, and others.

As stated earlier, a major reason for the initial hesitancy of the record industry to embrace the new technology was that they were not willing either to risk losing copyright control of their major artists to potential on-line piracy or to upset relationships with traditional retailers. The late nineties saw a series of shifting alliances between record, Internet, and technology companies as the industry worked toward the goal of exploiting the new technology without losing control or revenue in the process. Determining a viable means to this end was made even more complicated by the extraordinary amount of corporate consolidation that occurred during the late 1990s. For example, at one point, Time Warner and Sony announced that their joint music venture, Columbia House, would team up with CDNow to act as a channel for digital releases. Not long after, the deal became a casualty of the AOL-Time Warner merger.

During the years 2001–2002, the major labels tried various strategies to make the delivery of legal on-line music a financially successful enterprise. In 2001, AOL-Time Warner joined with BMG, EMI, and RealNetworks to launch MusicNet. By spring of 2002, MusicNet (www.real.com) had 40,000 subscribers to its on-line distribution service, and it claimed to offer approximately 80,000 tracks. A monthly subscription of $9.95 allowed users to download (but not burn to CD-R) 100 tracks and stream 100 tracks per month, and downloaded files were programmed to expire after 30 days unless renewed.

Currently, there are a number of on-line alternatives to the peer-to-peer file sharing services, and they all offer similar pricing: $9 or $10 per month for listening access to the site's catalog of on-line songs and about 99 cents to download a song and copy it onto a CD. Two of the largest sites are PressPlay, the result of collaboration between Sony and Universal, and MusicNet, created by Warner, Bertelsmann, and EMI and currently sold by RealNetworks and AOL. Three other relatively popular sites are MusicNow (formerly Full Audio), RealOne, and MusicPass. In February 2003, AOL announced the launch of its own on-line music service, making over 250,000 titles available to its 27 million members. A number of the services offer "tethered" downloads: customers can copy the files to more than one computer (for example, a desktop and a laptop), but cannot copy the files to a disc or send them to anyone else. These services are to be distinguished from Internet radio services like MusicMatch's Radio MX (where listeners can select the artist they want to listen to but not the song) and "pure" Internet radio. Subscribers to MusicMatch pay from $2.95 to $4.95 a month, depending on what option they choose.

Satellite Radio

In 2001, XM became the first company to begin offering a digital audio radio service whereby radio signals were beamed from stations on the ground to satellites, then directly to special receivers in cars or homes. With an XM receiver, users tuned in to any program from a participating broadcaster or content provider (71 music channels and 29 talk/sports/news channels, 30 of them commercial-free, for a monthly fee of $9.95)—no matter where they were in the United States—could hear CD-quality audio. The target market was huge, and included people who are constantly on the road or commute every day by automobile and listeners who live in areas able to receive only a few FM stations. (Without satellite radio, any one program targeting a niche market, for example, lovers of Broadway show tunes, can reach only an extremely limited audience; with satradio, every aficionado of show tunes in the United States could, theoretically, tune in, making it economically feasible to broadcast such programs.) XM receivers quickly became one of the fastest-selling electronics products of all time, and by the end of the first quarter in 2002, the company had 76,000 subscribers. XM claimed that it would have 350,000 subscribers by 2003.

At the end of 2002, Sirius Satellite Radio was XM's sole competition. Like XM, its network cost about $1.5 billion to construct. Sirius's price was closer to $13 a month, but all its music programs (it offered 100 channels, 60 music and 40 sports, news, and entertainment) were commercial-free. As of October 2002, Sirius had over 16,000 subscribers.

Digital broadcasts simultaneous with analog conventional broadcasts are operated by 15 of the top 20 U.S. broadcasters (including Clear Channel and Viacom) by means of "sideband" transmissions bracketing the host analog signal through proprietary coding and power techniques of iBand. The claimed advantage of this parallel broadcast is elimination of interference and noise such as occurs in a moving vehicle going over bridges, through tunnels, and other locations that interfere with analog broadcasts. The technology was originally developed by Lucent.

Security on the Internet

As Internet technology has developed, so has the demand for more advanced security systems. (The protection of literary and artistic rights through technical devices is not a recent concept. For years, pay-TV channels have, with varying degrees of success, tried to enforce limited access by scrambling their signals.) As on-line retail activity continues to rise, the success of the Internet as a profitable business vehicle hinges upon both security of payment systems and the protection of exclusive rights. Legitimate companies all try to prevent on-line theft by using some system, such as Liquid Audio, that protects content as well as tracking the playing, storing, and distribution of digital music. Liquid Audio permission sets include playback periods, export and CD-R burn permissions, and play-counts. Eventually, technological devices for copyright security and enforcement, implemented within the digital media economy, will nurture a healthy growth of e-commerce while protecting the owners of intellectual property, suppliers of equipment, and the consumer.

The two primary means of protecting data are watermarking and encryption.

Watermarking involves embedding data into a digital file—the watermark—which cannot be removed without damaging the file and which can contain copyright and royalty tracking information. One piece of watermark data may be a mark that identifies the recipient of the file, so that illegal copies can be tracked back to the infringer (fingerprinting). Watermarking is also used for *data authentication,* so that any modification of a file can be detected.

Encryption is the process of encoding digital files such that only the intended receiver has the decryption key or so that decryption can be accomplished only when a secure agent in a device in the possession of the receiver recognizes the user's formula.

Critics feel that these security devices may never be fully effective against computer hackers, who seem to always be one step ahead. This argument may have merit, given some recent developments. According to *Replication News* (now *Media Line*), Internet hackers have organized to develop ways to defeat the anti-copying protection in DVD players and have set up a number of Web sites that offer the information to users. A variety of software programs available on the Internet allow users to disable copy protection. In addition, there are hardware options that can be used to defeat security devices.

Policing the Internet

Internet piracy—downloading and copying music without paying the copyright holders—is rampant, and the pace has accelerated as the software used to compress and decompress files has become more sophisticated, speed of transmission and accessibility to the Internet have increased, and file-sharing programs have proliferated. Additionally, on-line violations are extremely difficult and tedious to track.

The development of portable MP3 players has been a major concern of groups such as the RIAA and IFPI, who are committed to stamping out Internet piracy. These groups feel that since the MP3 format is the overwhelming choice of Internet pirates, hardware that plays MP3 files, such as the MPMan and the palm-sized Rio, developed by Diamond Multimedia Systems, have simply fueled the flames of Internet piracy.

In *RIAA v. Diamond Multimedia Systems, Inc.*, 180 F.3d 1072 (9th Cir. 1998), the RIAA sought an injunction against the sale of the Rio, claiming that this device encouraged users to download pirated music and would thus replace the sale of CDs. The case turned on whether or not the Audio Home Recording Act of 1992, which was passed to protect artists from copyright infringement involving digital recording devices, included the MP3 player. Under that act, all digital recording devices must include a serial copy management system (SCMS). However, the act provided for an exemption for computer equipment. The court of appeals determined that since MP3 players are primarily used for playback purposes, they fall within the exemption.

In 1997, RIAA joined 12 record companies in copyright infringement lawsuits against three Internet music archive sites that offered MP3 compressed titles, seeking restraining orders and temporary injunctions. The cases were settled on January 21, 1998; the defendants were required to pay $100,000 for each infringed sound recording, but the RIAA agreed to forgo payment provided that the defendants not repeat the offense.

In December 1998, 160 organizations—including the RIAA, the five major labels, and technology companies such as Liquid Audio, America Online, Lucent Technologies, AT&T, RealNetworks, Toshiba, and Matsushita—instituted the Secure Digital Music Initiative (SDMI). The goal of the SDMI was to encourage the development of technological devices and formulas designed to deter Internet piracy. In 1999, the SDMI rolled out a plan called the Portable Device Specification system, whereby creators of copyrighted music files would gradually begin adding watermarks to these files, and makers of playback devices would add components to equipment that would detect these watermarks. In the fall of 2000, SDMI encoded and watermarked some audio files and challenged hackers to crack the code. When a professor at Princeton did just that, and threatened to publish the SDMI watermark code, which had not yet been universally instituted, RIAA threatened to sue him. Although RIAA did not pursue the suit, the incident was a major setback for the entire initiative, and most observers believe that SDMI is not the answer.

By 2002, many CD manufacturers, including Vivendi and BMG, had introduced CDs that were encrypted with a code that made computer CD drives malfunction when users attempted to make copies. These early attempts at encryption were prone to malfunctions in audio CD players, and many of the CDs simply did not play at all on PC or Mac computer drives.

The current status of SDMI as of this writing is aptly summarized by RIAA vice president and associate director of antipiracy Frank Creighton, "The real goal is to minimize the problem. . . . We're not so naive as to be sitting here telling you it will all go away."

The RIAA has taken a pro-active approach to one major source of cyberpiracy: college campuses. Students often have access to their colleges' powerful computer systems, and a great deal of infringing activity takes place on campus. The RIAA has implemented an educational program called Sound-byting. According to Mark Mooradian, senior analyst at Jupiter Communications, "There is a real educational initiative that needs to be taken by the music industry to teach people that music has value that needs to be paid for." Numerous universities and other institutions are working with the RIAA to identify and curtail the activities of students who are using the institutional Internet to upload and distribute illegally copied "new media." The IFPI has said that 99 percent of music on the Internet is pirated. Despite those who suggest that piracy might benefit the recording industry by helping customers sample songs before buying albums, many studies, most recently one by Jupiter Media Metrix, have shown that consumers who download pirated songs show a decrease in their level of music spending. According to the RIAA, piracy creates a loss of $300 million per year to the U.S. recording industry.

Internet Effect on Performance Rights Organizations

As with all other digital technologies, streaming can rob the copyright holder of performance rights. All three of the U.S. performance rights organizations (ASCAP, BMI, and SESAC) contend that songwriters and publishers fully deserve performance royalties for audio streaming in the same manner as regular radio broadcast. FCC-licensed stations that are extending their programming to include simultaneous digital delivery anticipate that such claims will be approved and are already putting in place the necessary means to compute such royalties.

In 1998, ASCAP developed RateCalc to solve the difficult problem of licensing music over the Internet. RateCalc allows Internet music users to calculate their ASCAP licensing fees while on-line. The ASCAP RateCalc procedure asks the potential Internet site licensee to give good-faith estimates of user revenue coming from subscriber fees, connect charges, etc., plus revenue from advertisers and sponsors or program suppliers, even if in barter form, but deducting any agency commissions. The questionnaire also asks for estimated or actual site visits and estimated or actual total music usage and ASCAP music uses. RateCalc uses these figures, in two separate equations, to calculate two fees. Both are compared to the minimum annual fee of $264, and whichever is the largest is the quoted license fee.

ASCAP has also introduced ACE, an on-line service that provides information about a particular song. The user simply enters the title of the song and is then given the writer(s) and publisher(s) of the song. Each song in the ASCAP directory is given a title code (T-code), which allows the user to differentiate between two songs with the same title.

In June 2002, BMI announced a licensing agreement with Cellus USA that will reportedly cover the public performance rights, in connection with wireless networks, on behalf of its members. Current "short message services" (SMS) for wireless telephones provided by Cellus USA include: ringtones, downloadable logos, and picture messages that consumers can send to themselves or others. BMI's HyperRepertoire service (discussed in Chapter 14) is a song database that allows the user to search for information on writers or publishers by song title, publisher, or writer's name.

Copyright Legislation

The first federal statute to expressly address the digital music revolution was the Audio Home Recording Act of 1992. It was followed in 1995 by a second statute, the misnamed Digital Performance Right in Sound Recordings (DPRSR) Act. This legislation was intended to assure hardware manufacturers as well as tape and CD-R suppliers that they would be immune from copyright infringement lawsuits if they honored statutory license fees based on their gross receipts. The legislation was endorsed by the copyright and record industries, including the RIAA, AFM, AFTRA, ASCAP, BMI, and the Songwriters Guild of America.

When it comes to other aspects of digital sound recording distribution, including downloading via CDNow, MP3.com, etc., the DPRSR Act uses the same "voluntary" or arbitration procedures as set out for performances but at the special reproduction rates so negotiated or set, calculated on each song and each unit of reproduction. The act calls it "digital phonograph delivery" (DPD) as distinguished from subscription or other performance without downloading capacity. Of special note is the recognition that a controlled-composition rate is inapplicable except for an artist contract wherein the artist was contractually obligated before June 22, 1995, and where the controlled-composition rate contract was entered into by an artist who retained administrative or ownership rights after the songs in question were recorded.

It is obvious that these exceptions recognize a need not to detract from contractual rights previously owned by a record company and contractual negotiations freely entered into by an artist/owner of music publishing rights. It is a limited victory for the music publisher group.

Under the Copyright Act of 1976, an individual cannot be convicted of criminal copyright infringement unless he or she willfully infringes a copyright "for purposes of commercial advantage or private financial gain." In *United States v. LaMacchia*, 871 F. Supp. 535 (D. Mass. 1994), the defendant, a graduate student attending MIT, solicited users of a bulletin board system to submit copies of copyrighted computer software programs for posting on the system and then encouraged users to download the copies illegally. Because there was no evidence that LaMacchia had profited in any way from the act, the district court dismissed the charges. Congress attempted to address this problem in the No Electronic Theft Act (NET Act), signed on December 16, 1997 (Public Law 105-147), which added a definition for the term *financial gain* to include the receipt (or expectation of receipt) of anything of value, including other copyrighted works. Further, this act also criminalizes the electronic reproduction or distribution of copyrighted works by electronic means, if more than $1,000 in total retail value during any 180-day period is involved.

Signing the Digital Millennium Copyright Act (DMCA) of 1998 brought the United States into compliance with two important World Intellectual Property Organization treaties dealing with issues related to copyright in a digital environment, including protecting the use of technological measures designed to control unauthorized copying, transmission, and use of copyrighted products and making it illegal to circumvent those measures. One way to prevent unauthorized access to music on the Internet is to prohibit the manufacturing of technologies or products used to defeat such security devices as watermarking and encryption. Such preventive measures stop illegal circumvention at the source, a method superior to measures which target only isolated illegal acts. The treaties further target the deliberate alteration or deletion of copyright management information.

At the same time that the DMCA prescribed measures against illegal copying of digital files, it created certain "safe harbors" for Internet service providers (ISPs). On-line service providers falling into one of the following safe harbors would be subject only to carefully proscribed injunctive remedies and would be exempt from any monetary damages. Some examples of safe harbors are the following:

- ► Where the service provider acts as a "mere conduit" for an infringing transmission
- ► Where the service provider has unknowingly stored infringing material and has received no financial benefit and responds "expeditiously" to remove the infringing material
- ► Where the provider has unknowingly linked users to sites containing infringing material and responds "expeditiously" to remove the infringing material

In order to qualify for these safe harbors, the service provider must inform users that it will terminate the services of repeat infringers and must accept and accommodate any "standard" technological security devices used by the copyright owners to identify and protect the copyright owner's rights.

Sound Quality

Companies involved in developing the latest technologies in music are constantly searching for ways to improve sound quality. The two formats that developers hope will replace the compact disc just as the compac disc has virtually replaced the vinyl record are DVD-Audio and Super Audio CD (SACD).

DVD-Audio is a digital format designed to provide audio quality that surpasses the quality of conventional CDs as well as DVD video. These "advanced audio" discs are available from EMI/Capitol, Warner/Rhino, and Chesky Records (among others). Many DVD-Audio discs include DVD-Video components (regional codes) making them compatible with DVD-Video players. Although DVD-Audio discs can be played on conventional DVD players, the best results can be obtained only with players programmed for DVD-Audio. The SACD currently offers three density layer variations; one of these (the "hybrid disc") allows playback on conventional CD players, but, as with DVD-Audio, obtaining the highest fidelity requires a SACD player. With the SACD format, Sony and Philips employ content protection of an invisible watermark variation: Pit Signal Processing-Physical Disc Mark (PSP-PDM). It is very difficult for anyone to write this watermark on a recordable disk, yet playback is allowed only when the PSP watermark is found. In mid-2002, ABKCO announced the SACD release of "The Rolling Stones Remastered" series encompassing 22 albums which were originally recorded between 1963 and 1970.

Licensing Issues

MULTIMEDIA

Music is an integral part of most types of interactive CD-ROMs, which range from educational to entertainment. Over the last decade, for example, video games have increasingly relied on the use of well-known copyrighted music to enhance the experience for players.

The use of music on multimedia CD-ROMs has created new issues for licensing. There are three basic ways of licensing music on interactive CD-ROMs, depending on the circumstances.

1. A flat fee is usually charged for works where relatively few copies will be made and none will be sold. This method is often used for promotional CD-ROMs or for corporate training videos.
2. For video games that are for sale or that will be mass-produced, a royalty system is most often employed. The copyright owner will charge a royalty based upon the sales of the work containing the music.
3. In instances where there is more than one song involved in the work (some CD-ROMs can have thousands of songs), music copyright owners will typically request a royalty that is prorated among the number of copyrighted musical selections in the work.

MIDI Files

A musical instrument digital interface (MIDI) file is created by entering notes with a MIDI device (controller) and can only be played back on a synthesizer, synthesizer software (e.g., Microsoft GS Wavetable Synth [windows] and Midi Jukebox [Mac]) or a computer sound card. The Copyright Office states that MIDI files are indistinguishable from other sound or phonogram recordings, and so a MIDI file license is determinied by calculating the applicable statutory mechanical rate.

The Future

Over the past decade, advances in technology have made it theoretically possible to fully integrate customized cable television and satellite radio programming; activities made possible through Internet access, including Web radio and television, music, and videos; video games; and telephone service. Ultimately, convergence may make it possible to reach into the homes of all citizens, providing them the opportunity to use, purchase, and interact with any and all types of "information" and to become an active participant in the whole chain of content creation, manufacturing, marketing, promotion, exhibition, distribution, and even sales.

At the same time that changes in devices used by consumers have moved the communications industry closer to technological convergence, there have been significant mergers among companies that control the communications media. Three recent examples of corporate consolidation were the 1996 merger of Disney with ABC, the 1998 takeover of WebTV by Microsoft, and the megamerger of AOL and Time-Warner in early 2000. In the world of radio broadcasting, since passage of the 1996 Telecommunications Act mandated deregulation of the industry, consolidation has been rampant. According to the Future of Music Coalition (www.futureofmusic.org), in late fall 2002, ten parent companies controlled two-thirds of both market and revenue and two—Clear Channel and Viacom—had a 42 percent market share and 45 percent of industry revenues. Many observers believe that the overall effect of these concurrent trends on the broadcast music industry has been negative, leading to increasing homogeneity of formats and reduced access of musicians to radio. In September 2002, the FCC announced plans to conduct an open review of current ownership rules.

As technology continues to advance, bringing music to people in ways not dreamed of even a decade ago, issues and problems will emerge that even the keenest of imaginations might not have predicted. Issues that were touched on only briefly in the last edition of this book have come to the fore and new issues have emerged.

If legislation is passed requiring encoding of music owners' identities and royalty provisions in whatever medium the music appears, the traditional rights of bargaining for individual uses will be permanently diluted. The encoding of

CDs, for example, will allow cheaper and more efficient logging of broadcast uses than the logging techniques of ASCAP and BMI, and may ultimately lead to music being treated as a public utility with standardized rates.

Expired copyrights, once in the public domain, will be easily identified through the use of new data banks and encoding devices, making users better aware of the economic benefits of using public domain music at the expense of copyrighted music. On the plus side for artists and record companies, the long lag between broadcast uses of music and the payment of fees due for performance rights will be shortened considerably when identification of broadcast uses is done through encoding devices, and, in general, the collection of royalties will be expedited. Encoding will also make it easier to identify infringing sampling. Satellite broadcast techniques have transcended historic national boundaries, making obsolete licenses issued on an exclusive territorial basis.

The dramatic growth of the Internet and digital technology creates some interesting scenarios for the future. If anyone can simply download a favorite song (after listening to the song for free), will the need for music stores be eliminated? As the price of computer-connected recording hardware and recordable media continues to drop, and increasing numbers of people are able to burn their own CDs directly off of the Internet, where will traditional record stores and CD replicators fit in? What will be the effect on royalty rates of the elimination of packaging for music that is downloaded? As pointed out elsewhere in the book, overall record sales are declining worldwide. Will the new technology, which allows Internet users to sample the latest release of an artist before making a purchase, increase consumer satisfaction and thus boost sales? Finally, does the increasing availability and sophistication of affordable recording equipment presage the demise of the traditional record company? An artist who owns a high-quality digital recording studio can now do his or her own recording, offer the song to millions of consumers over the Internet, and, theoretically, take care of promotion and marketing through a Web site—all without the aid of a record company.

In the face of the challenges brought by digital-age technology it is perhaps too easy to become like Chicken Little and cry in in dismay, "The sky is falling." The sky is not falling. The prospect of unlicensed digital bootlegging or free offerings from unsigned acts is no more insurmountable an obstacle to industry success than were home taping, rental shops, photocopying, and other music reprography in the past. Where there is a challenge, there are creative minds working to meet the challenge. If free music is offered, record sales may be lost, but new advertising revenue streams will be gained. If valuable archival recordings are slipped onto Web sites by illegal hackers, investigators and enforcement agencies will develop some new form of technology to find and punish the interlopers. If consumers demand do-it-yourself compilations, licensed intermediate retailers will arrange for a fair redistribution of revenues.

A cry like "The sky is falling" can arouse panic only in those who aren't alert to what is *really* going on around them. That is hardly the case with the music industry. The concerned industry members who generate millions of words of comments in *Billboard* and other trade papers and in convention gatherings and lectures are wide awake. They see the problems clearly, but at the same time they see the opportunities and accept the challenges.

CHAPTER 1: SUBJECT MATTER AND SCOPE OF COPYRIGHT

§101. Definitions[2]

Except as otherwise provided in this title, as used in this title, the following terms and their variant forms mean the following:

An "anonymous work" is a work on the copies or phonorecords of which no natural person is identified as author.

An "architectural work" is the design of a building as embodied in any tangible medium of expression, including a building, architectural plans, or drawings. The work includes the overall form as well as the arrangement and composition of spaces and elements in the design, but does not include individual standard features.[3]

"Audiovisual works" are works that consist of a series of related images which are intrinsically intended to be shown by the use of machines or devices such as projectors, viewers, or electronic equipment, together with accompanying sounds, if any, regardless of the nature of the material objects, such as films or tapes, in which the works are embodied.

The "Berne Convention" is the Convention for the Protection of Literary and Artistic Works, signed at Berne, Switzerland, on September 9, 1886, and all acts, protocols, and revisions thereto.[4]

The "best edition" of a work is the edition, published in the United States at any time before the date of deposit, that the Library of Congress determines to be most suitable for its purposes.

A person's "children" are that person's immediate offspring, whether legitimate or not, and any children legally adopted by that person.

A "collective work" is a work, such as a periodical issue, anthology, or

---

*The superscript numbers in the text refer to endnote numbers that appear in the Copyright Act. Because the material in this appendix has been excerpted, in some cases the numbers are not consecutive.

encyclopedia, in which a number of contributions, constituting separate and independent works in themselves, are assembled into a collective whole.

A "compilation" is a work formed by the collection and assembling of preexisting materials or of data that are selected, coordinated, or arranged in such a way that the resulting work as a whole constitutes an original work of authorship. The term "compilation" includes collective works.

"Copies" are material objects, other than phonorecords, in which a work is fixed by any method now known or later developed, and from which the work can be perceived, reproduced, or otherwise communicated, either directly or with the aid of a machine or device. The term "copies" includes the material object, other than a phonorecord, in which the work is first fixed.

"Copyright owner", with respect to any one of the exclusive rights comprised in a copyright, refers to the owner of that particular right.

A work is "created" when it is fixed in a copy or phonorecord for the first time; where a work is prepared over a period of time, the portion of it that has been fixed at any particular time constitutes the work as of that time, and where the work has been prepared in different versions, each version constitutes a separate work.

A "derivative work" is a work based upon one or more preexisting works, such as a translation, musical arrangement, dramatization, fictionalization, motion picture version, sound recording, art reproduction, abridgment, condensation, or any other form in which a work may be recast, transformed, or adapted. A work consisting of editorial revisions, annotations, elaborations, or other modifications, which, as a whole, represent an original work of authorship, is a "derivative work".

A "device", "machine", or "process" is one now known or later developed.

A "digital transmission" is a transmission in whole or in part in a digital or other non-analog format.[5]

To "display" a work means to show a copy of it, either directly or by means of a film, slide, television image, or any other device or process or, in the case of a motion picture or other audiovisual work, to show individual images nonsequentially.

An "establishment" is a store, shop, or any similar place of business pen to the general public for the primary purpose of selling goods or services in which the majority of the gross square feet of space that is nonresidential is used for that purpose, and in which nondramatic musical works are performed publicly.[6]

A "food service or drinking establishment" is a restaurant, inn, bar, tavern, or any other similar place of business in which the public or patrons assemble for the primary purpose of being served food or drink, in which the majority of the gross square feet of space that is nonresidential is used for that purpose, and in which nondramatic musical works are performed publicly.[7]

The term "financial gain" includes receipt, or expectation of receipt, of anything of value, including the receipt of other copyrighted works.[8]

A work is "fixed" in a tangible medium of expression when its embodiment in a copy or phonorecord, by or under the authority of the author, is sufficiently permanent or stable to permit it to be perceived, reproduced, or otherwise communicated for a period of more than transitory duration. A work consisting of sounds, images, or both, that are being transmitted, is "fixed" for purposes of this title if a fixation of the work is being made simultaneously with its transmission.

The "Geneva Phonograms Convention" is the Convention for the Protection of Producers of Phonograms Against Unauthorized Duplication of Their Phonograms, concluded at Geneva, Switzerland, on October 29, 1971.[9]

The "gross square feet of space" of an establishment means the entire interior space of that establishment, and any adjoining outdoor space used to serve patrons, whether on a seasonal basis or otherwise.[10]

The terms "including" and "such as" are illustrative and not limitative.

An "international agreement" is—

(1) the Universal Copyright Convention;

(2) the Geneva Phonograms Convention;

(3) the Berne Convention;

(4) the WTO Agreement;

(5) the WIPO Copyright Treaty;[11]

(6) the WIPO Performances and Phonograms Treaty;[12] and

(7) any other copyright treaty to which the United States is a party.[13]

A "joint work" is a work prepared by two or more authors with the intention that their contributions be merged into inseparable or interdependent parts of a unitary whole.

"Literary works" are works, other than audiovisual works, expressed in words, numbers, or other verbal or numerical symbols or indicia, regardless of the nature of the material objects, such as books, periodicals, manuscripts, phonorecords, film, tapes, disks, or cards, in which they are embodied.

"Motion pictures" are audiovisual works consisting of a series of related images which, when shown in succession, impart an impression of motion, together with accompanying sounds, if any.

To "perform" a work means to recite, render, play, dance, or act it, either directly or by means of any device or process or, in the case of a motion picture or other audiovisual work, to show its images in any sequence or to make the sounds accompanying it audible.

A "performing rights society" is an association, corporation, or other entity that licenses the public performance of nondramatic musical works on behalf of copyright owners of such works, such as the American Society of Composers, Authors and Publishers (ASCAP), Broadcast Music, Inc. (BMI), nd SESAC, Inc.[14]

"Phonorecords" are material objects in which sounds, other than those accompanying a motion picture or other audiovisual work, are fixed by any method now known or later developed, and from which the sounds can be perceived, reproduced, or otherwise communicated, either directly or with the aid of a machine or device. The term "phonorecords" includes the material object in which the sounds are first fixed.

"Pictorial, graphic, and sculptural works" include two-dimensional and three-dimensional works of fine, graphic, and applied art, photographs, prints and art reproductions, maps, globes, charts, diagrams, models, and technical drawings, including architectural plans. Such works shall include works of artistic craftsmanship insofar as their form but not their mechanical or utilitarian aspects are concerned; the design of a useful article, as defined in this section, shall be considered a pictorial, graphic, or sculptural work only if, and only to the extent that, such design incorporates pictorial, graphic, or sculptural features that can be identified separately from, and are capable of existing independently of, the utilitarian aspects of the article.[15]

For purposes of section 513, a "proprietor" is an individual, corporation, partnership, or other entity, as the case may be, that owns an establishment or a food service or drinking establishment, except that no owner or operator of a radio or television station licensed by the Federal Communications Commission, cable system or satellite carrier, cable or satellite carrier service or programmer, provider of online services or network access or the operator of facilities therefor, telecommunications company, or any other such audio or audiovisual service or programmer now known or as may be developed in the future, commercial subscription music service, or owner or operator of any other transmission service, shall under any circumstances be deemed to be a proprietor.[16]

A "pseudonymous work" is a work on the copies or phonorecords of which the author is identified under a fictitious name.

"Publication" is the distribution of copies or phonorecords of a work to the public by sale or other transfer of ownership, or by rental, lease, or lending. The offering to distribute copies or phonorecords to a group of persons for purposes of further distribution, public performance, or public display, constitutes publication. A public performance or display of a work does not of itself constitute publication.

To perform or display a work "publicly" means

(1) to perform or display it at a place open to the public or at any place where a substantial number of persons outside of a normal circle of a family and its social acquaintances is gathered; or

(2) to transmit or otherwise communicate a performance or display of the work to a place specified by clause (1) or to the public, by means of any device or process, whether the members of the public capable of receiving the performance or display receive it in the same place or in separate places and at the same time or at different times.

"Registration", for purposes of sections 205(c)(2), 405, 406, 410(d), 411, 412, and 506(e), means a registration of a claim in the original or the renewed and extended term of copyright.[17]

"Sound recordings" are works that result from the fixation of a series of musical, spoken, or other sounds, but not including the sounds accompanying a motion picture or other audiovisual work, regardless of the nature of the material objects, such as disks, tapes, or other phonorecords, in which they are embodied.

"State" includes the District of Columbia and the Commonwealth of Puerto Rico, and any territories to which this title is made applicable by an Act of Congress.

A "transfer of copyright ownership" is an assignment, mortgage, exclusive license, or any other conveyance, alienation, or hypothecation of a copyright or of any of the exclusive rights comprised in a copyright, whether or not it is limited in time or place of effect, but not including a nonexclusive license.

A "transmission program" is a body of material that, as an aggregate, has been produced for the sole purpose of transmission to the public in sequence and as a unit.

To "transmit" a performance or display is to communicate it by any device or process whereby images or sounds are received beyond the place from which they are sent.

A "treaty party" is a country or intergovernmental organization other than the United States that is a party to an international agreement.[18]

The "United States", when used in a geographical sense, comprises the several States, the District of Columbia and the Commonwealth of Puerto Rico, and the organized territories under the jurisdiction of the United States Government.

For purposes of section 411, a work is a "United States work" only if—
(1) in the case of a published work, the work is first published—
    (A) in the United States;
    (B) simultaneously in the United States and another treaty party or parties, whose law grants a term of copyright protection that is the same as or longer than the term provided in the United States;
    (C) simultaneously in the United States and a foreign nation that is not a treaty party; or
    (D) in a foreign nation that is not a treaty party, and all of the authors of the work are nationals, domiciliaries, or habitual residents of, or in the case of an audiovisual work legal entities with headquarters in, the United States;
(2) in the case of an unpublished work, all the authors of the work are nationals, domiciliaries, or habitual residents of the United States, or, in the case of an unpublished audiovisual work, all the authors are legal entities with headquarters in the United States; or
(3) in the case of a pictorial, graphic, or sculptural work incorporated in a building or structure, the building or structure is located in the United States.[19]

A "useful article" is an article having an intrinsic utilitarian function that is not merely to portray the appearance of the article or to convey information. An article that is normally a part of a useful article is considered a "useful article".

The author's "widow" or "widower" is the author's surviving spouse under the law of the author's domicile at the time of his or her death, whether or not the spouse has later remarried.

The "WIPO Copyright Treaty" is the WIPO Copyright Treaty concluded at Geneva, Switzerland, on December 20, 1996.[20]

The "WIPO Performances and Phonograms Treaty" is the WIPO Performances and Phonograms Treaty concluded at Geneva, Switzerland, on December 20, 1996.[21]

. . .

A "work made for hire" is—

(1) a work prepared by an employee within the scope of his or her employment; or

(2) a work specially ordered or commissioned for use as a contribution to a collective work, as a part of a motion picture or other audiovisual work, as a translation, as a supplementary work, as a compilation, as an instructional text, as a test, as answer material for a test, or as an atlas, if the parties expressly agree in a written instrument signed by them that the work shall be considered a work made for hire. For the purpose of the foregoing sentence, a "supplementary work" is a work prepared for publication as a secondary adjunct to a work by another author for the purpose of introducing, concluding, illustrating, explaining, revising, commenting upon, or assisting in the use of the other work, such as forewords, afterwords, pictorial illustrations, maps, charts, tables, editorial notes, musical arrangements, answer material for tests, bibliographies, appendixes, and indexes, and an "instructional text" is a literary, pictorial, or graphic work prepared for publication and with the purpose of use in systematic instructional activities.

In determining whether any work is eligible to be considered a work made for hire under paragraph (2), neither the amendment contained in section 1011(d) of the Intellectual Property and Communications Omnibus Reform Act of 1999, as enacted by section 1000(a)(9) of Public Law 106-113, nor the deletion of the words added by that amendment—

(A) shall be considered or otherwise given any legal significance, or

(B) shall be interpreted to indicate congressional approval or disapproval of, or acquiescence in, any judicial determination, by the courts or the Copyright Office. Paragraph (2) shall be interpreted as if both section 2(a)(1) of the Work Made For Hire and Copyright Corrections Act of 2000 and section 1011(d) of the Intellectual Property and Communications Omnibus Reform Act of 1999, as enacted by section 1000(a)(9) of Public Law 106-113, were never enacted, and without regard to any inaction or awareness by the Congress at any time of any judicial determinations.[23]

The terms "WTO Agreement" and "WTO member country" have the meanings given those terms in paragraphs (9) and (10), respectively, of section 2 of the Uruguay Round Agreements Act.[24]

A "computer program" is a set of statements or instructions to be used directly or indirectly in a computer in order to bring about a certain result.[25]

§102. Subject Matter of Copyright

In general[26]

(a) Copyright protection subsists, in accordance with this title, in original works of authorship fixed in any tangible medium of expression, now known or later developed, from which they can be perceived, reproduced, or otherwise communicated, either directly or with the aid of a machine or device. Works of authorship include the following categories:

    (1) literary works;

    (2) musical works, including any accompanying words;

    (3) dramatic works, including any accompanying music;

    (4) pantomimes and choreographic works;

    (5) pictorial, graphic, and sculptural works;

    (6) motion pictures and other audiovisual works;

    (7) sound recordings; and

    (8) architectural works.

(b) In no case does copyright protection for an original work of authorship extend to any idea, procedure, process, system, method of operation, concept, principle, or discovery, regardless of the form in which it is described, explained, illustrated, or embodied in such work.

§103. Subject Matter of Copyright: Compilations and Derivative Works

(a) The subject matter of copyright as specified by section 102 includes compilations and derivative works, but protection for a work employing preexisting material in which copyright subsists does not extend to any part of the work in which such material has been used unlawfully.

(b) The copyright in a compilation or derivative work extends only to the material contributed by the author of such work, as distinguished from the preexisting material employed in the work, and does not imply any exclusive right in the preexisting material. The copyright in such work is independent of, and does not affect or enlarge the scope, duration, ownership, or subsistence of, any copyright protection in the preexisting material.

§104. Subject matter of copyright: National origin[27]

(a) Unpublished Works.—The works specified by sections 102 and 103, while unpublished, are subject to protection under this title without regard to the nationality or domicile of the author.

(b) Published Works.—The works specified by sections 102 and 103, when published, are subject to protection under this title if—

(1) on the date of first publication, one or more of the authors is a national or domiciliary of the United States, or is a national, domiciliary, or sovereign authority of a treaty party, or is a stateless person, wherever that person may be domiciled; or

(2) the work is first published in the United States or in a foreign nation that, on the date of first publication, is a treaty party; or

(3) the work is a sound recording that was first fixed in a treaty party; or

(4) the work is a pictorial, graphic, or sculptural work that is incorporated in a building or other structure, or an architectural work that is embodied in a building and the building or structure is located in the United States or a treaty party; or

(5) the work is first published by the United Nations or any of its specialized agencies, or by the Organization of American States; or

(6) the work comes within the scope of a Presidential proclamation. Whenever the President finds that a particular foreign nation extends, to works by authors who are nationals or domiciliaries of the United States or to works that are first published in the United States, copyright protection on substantially the same basis as that on which the foreign nation extends protection to works of its own nationals and domiciliaries and works first published in that nation, the President may by proclamation extend protection under this title to works of which one or more of the authors is, on the date of first publication, a national, domiciliary, or sovereign authority of that nation, or which was first published in that nation. The President may revise, suspend, or revoke any such proclamation or impose any conditions or limitations on protection under a proclamation.

For purposes of paragraph (2), a work that is published in the United States or a treaty party within 30 days after publication in a foreign nation that is not a treaty party shall be considered to be first published in the United States or such treaty party, as the case may be.

(c) Effect of Berne Convention.—No right or interest in a work eligible for protection under this title may be claimed by virtue of, or in reliance upon, the provisions of the Berne Convention, or the adherence of the United States thereto. Any rights in a work eligible for protection under this title that derive from this title, other Federal or State statutes, or the common law, shall not be expanded or reduced by virtue of, or in reliance upon, the provisions of the Berne Convention, or the adherence of the United States thereto.

(d) Effect of Phonograms Treaties.—Notwithstanding the provisions of subsection (b), no works other than sound recordings shall be eligible for protection under this title solely by virtue of the adherence of the United States to the Geneva Phonograms Convention or the WIPO Performances and Phonograms Treaty.[28]

. . .

§105. Subject Matter of Copyright: United States Government Works[35]

Copyright protection under this title is not available for any work of the United States Government, but the United States Government is not precluded from receiving and holding copyrights transferred to it by assignment, bequest, or otherwise.

§106. Exclusive rights in copyrighted works[36]

Subject to sections 107 through 121, the owner of copyright under this title has the exclusive rights to do and to authorize any of the following:

(1) to reproduce the copyrighted work in copies or phonorecords;

(2) to prepare derivative works based upon the copyrighted work;

(3) to distribute copies or phonorecords of the copyrighted work to the public by sale or other transfer of ownership, or by rental, lease, or lending;

(4) in the case of literary, musical, dramatic, and choreographic works, pantomimes, and motion pictures and other audiovisual works, to perform the copyrighted work publicly;

(5) in the case of literary, musical, dramatic, and choreographic works, pantomimes, and pictorial, graphic, or sculptural works, including the individual images of a motion picture or other audiovisual work, to display the copyrighted work publicly; and

(6) in the case of sound recordings, to perform the copyrighted work publicly by means of a digital audio transmission.

. . .

§107. Limitations on Exclusive Rights: Fair Use

Notwithstanding the provisions of sections 106 and 106A, the fair use of a copyrighted work, including such use by reproduction in copies or phonorecords or by any other means specified by that section, for purposes such as criticism, comment, news reporting, teaching (including multiple copies for classroom use), scholarship, or research, is not an infringement of copyright. In determining whether the use made of a work in any particular case is a fair use the factors to be considered shall include-

(1) the purpose and character of the use, including whether such use is of a commercial nature or is for nonprofit educational purposes;

(2) the nature of the copyrighted work;

(3) the amount and substantiality of the portion used in relation to the copyrighted work as a whole; and

(4) the effect of the use upon the potential market for or value of the copyrighted work.

The fact that a work is unpublished shall not itself bar a finding of fair use if such finding is made upon consideration of all the above factors.

. . .

§109. Limitations on Exclusive Rights: Effect of Transfer of Particular Copy or Phonorecord[40]

(a) Notwithstanding the provisions of section 106(3), the owner of a particular copy or phonorecord lawfully made under this title, or any person authorized by such owner, is entitled, without the authority of the copyright owner, to sell or otherwise dispose of the possession of that copy or phono-record. Notwithstanding the preceding sentence, copies or phonorecords of works subject to restored copyright under section 104A that are manufactured before the date of restoration of copyright or, with respect to reliance parties, before publication or service of notice under section 104A(e), may be sold or otherwise disposed of without the authorization of the owner of the restored copyright for purposes of direct or indirect commercial advantage only during the 12-month period beginning on-

(1) the date of the publication in the Federal Register of the notice of intent filed with the Copyright Office under section 104A(d)(2)(A), or
(2) the date of the receipt of actual notice served under section 104A(d)(2)(B), whichever occurs first.

(b)(1)(A) Notwithstanding the provisions of subsection (a), unless authorized by the owners of copyright in the sound recording or the owner of copyright in a computer program (including any tape, disk, or other medium embodying such program), and in the case of a sound recording in the musical works embodied therein, neither the owner of a particular phonorecord nor any person in possession of a particular copy of a computer program (including any tape, disk, or other medium embodying such program), may, for the purposes of direct or indirect commercial advantage, dispose of, or authorize the disposal of, the pos-session of that phonorecord or computer program (including any tape, disk, or other medium embodying such program) by rental, lease, or lending, or by any other act or practice in the nature of rental, lease, or lending. Nothing in the preceding sentence shall apply to the rental, lease, or lending of a phonorecord for nonprofit purposes by a non-profit library or nonprofit educational institution. The transfer of pos-session of a lawfully made copy of a computer program by a nonprofit educational institution to another nonprofit educational institution or to faculty, staff, and students does not constitute rental, lease, or lending for direct or indirect commercial purposes under this subsection.

(B) This subsection does not apply to—

(i) a computer program which is embodied in a machine or product and which cannot be copied during the ordinary opera-tion or use of the machine or product; or
(ii) a computer program embodied in or used in conjunction with a limited purpose computer that is designed for playing video games and may be designed for other purposes.

. . .

§110. Limitations on Exclusive Rights: Exemption of Certain Performances and Displays[41]

Notwithstanding the provisions of section 106, the following are not infringements of copyright:

(1) performance or display of a work by instructors or pupils in the course of face-to-face teaching activities of a nonprofit educational institution, in a classroom or similar place devoted to instruction, unless, in the case of a motion picture or other audiovisual work, the performance, or the display of individual images, is given by means of a copy that was not lawfully made under this title, and that the person responsible for the performance knew or had reason to believe was not lawfully made;

(2) performance of a nondramatic literary or musical work or display of a work, by or in the course of a transmission, if—

(A) the performance or display is a regular part of the systematic instructional activities of a governmental body or a nonprofit educational institution; and

(B) the performance or display is directly related and of material assistance to the teaching content of the transmission; and

(C) the transmission is made primarily for—

(i) reception in classrooms or similar places normally devoted to instruction, or

(ii) reception by persons to whom the transmission is directed because their disabilities or other special circumstances prevent their attendance in classrooms or similar places normally devoted to instruction, or

(iii) reception by officers or employees of governmental bodies as a part of their official duties or employment;

(3) performance of a nondramatic literary or musical work or of a dramatico-musical work of a religious nature, or display of a work, in the course of services at a place of worship or other religious assembly;

(4) performance of a nondramatic literary or musical work otherwise than in a transmission to the public, without any purpose of direct or indirect commercial advantage and without payment of any fee or other compensation for the performance to any of its performers, promoters, or organizers, if—

(A) there is no direct or indirect admission charge; or

(B) the proceeds, after deducting the reasonable costs of producing the performance, are used exclusively for educational, religious, or charitable purposes and not for private financial gain, except where the copyright owner has served notice of objection to the performance under the following conditions;

(i) the notice shall be in writing and signed by the copyright owner or such owner's duly authorized agent; and

(ii) the notice shall be served on the person responsible for the performance at least seven days before the date of the performance, and shall state the reasons for the objection; and

(iii) the notice shall comply, in form, content, and manner of service, with requirements that the Register of Copyrights shall prescribe by regulation;

. . .

(6) performance of a nondramatic musical work by a governmental body or a nonprofit agricultural or horticultural organization, in the course of an annual agricultural or horticultural fair or exhibition conducted by such body or organization; the exemption provided by this clause shall extend to any liability for copyright infringement that would otherwise be imposed on such body or organization, under doctrines of vicarious liability or related infringement, for a performance by a concessionnaire, business establishment, or other person at such fair or exhibition, but shall not excuse any such person from liability for the performance;

(7) performance of a nondramatic musical work by a vending establishment open to the public at large without any direct or indirect admission charge, where the sole purpose of the performance is to promote the retail sale of copies or phonorecords of the work, or of the audiovisual or other devices utilized in such performance, and the performance is not transmitted beyond the place where the establishment is located and is within the immediate area where the sale is occurring;

(8) performance of a nondramatic literary work, by or in the course of a transmission specifically designed for and primarily directed to blind or other handicapped persons who are unable to read normal printed material as a result of their handicap, or deaf or other handicapped persons who are unable to hear the aural signals accompanying a transmission of visual signals, if the performance is made without any purpose of direct or indirect commercial advantage and its transmission is made through the facilities of: (i) a governmental body; or (ii) a noncommercial educational broadcast station (as defined in section 397 of title 47); or (iii) a radio subcarrier authorization (as defined in 47 CFR 73.293-73.295 and 73.593-73.595); or (iv) a cable system (as defined in section 111 (f));

. . .

§114. Scope of Exclusive Rights in Sound Recordings[46]

(a) The exclusive rights of the owner of copyright in a sound recording are limited to the rights specified by clauses (1), (2), (3) and (6) of section 106, and do not include any right of performance under section 106(4).

(b) The exclusive right of the owner of copyright in a sound recording under clause (1) of section 106 is limited to the right to duplicate the sound recording in the form of phonorecords or copies that directly or indirectly recapture the actual sounds fixed in the recording. The exclusive right of the owner of copyright in a sound recording under clause (2) of section 106 is limited to the right to prepare a derivative work in which the actual sounds fixed in the sound recording are rearranged, remixed, or otherwise altered in sequence or quality. The exclusive rights of the owner of copyright in a sound recording under clauses (1) and (2) of section 106 do not extend to the making or duplication of another sound recording that consists entirely of an independent fixation of other sounds, even though such sounds imitate or simulate those in the copyrighted sound recording. The exclusive rights of the owner of copyright in a sound recording under clauses (1), (2), and (3) of section 106 do not apply to sound recordings included in educational television and radio programs (as defined in section 397 of title 47) distributed or transmitted by or through public broadcasting entities (as defined by section 118(g)): Provided, That copies or phonorecords of said programs are not commercially distributed by or through public broadcasting entities to the general public.

(c) This section does not limit or impair the exclusive right to perform publicly, by means of a phonorecord, any of the works specified by section 106(4).

. . .

§115. Scope of Exclusive Rights in Nondramatic Musical Works: Compulsory License for Making and Distributing Phonorecords[49]

In the case of nondramatic musical works, the exclusive rights provided by clauses (1) and (3) of section 106, to make and to distribute phonorecords of such works, are subject to compulsory licensing under the conditions specified by this section.

(a) Availability and Scope of Compulsory License.—

(1) When phonorecords of a nondramatic musical work have been distributed to the public in the United States under the authority of the copyright owner, any other person, including those who make phonorecords or digital phonorecord deliveries, may, by complying with the provisions of this section, obtain a compulsory license to make and distribute phonorecords of the work. A person may obtain a compulsory license only if his or her primary purpose in making phonorecords is to distribute them to the public for private use, including by means of a digital phonorecord delivery. A person may not obtain a compulsory license for use of the work in the making of phonorecords duplicating a sound recording fixed by another, unless:

(i) such sound recording was fixed lawfully; and
(ii) the making of the phonorecords was authorized by the owner of copyright in the sound recording or, if the sound recording was fixed before February 15, 1972, by any person who fixed the sound

recording pursuant to an express license from the owner of the copyright in the musical work or pursuant to a valid compulsory license for use of such work in a sound recording.

(2) A compulsory license includes the privilege of making a musical arrangement of the work to the extent necessary to conform it to the style or manner of interpretation of the performance involved, but the arrangement shall not change the basic melody or fundamental character of the work, and shall not be subject to protection as a derivative work under this title, except with the express consent of the copyright owner.

(b) Notice of Intention to Obtain Compulsory License.—

(1) Any person who wishes to obtain a compulsory license under this section shall, before or within thirty days after making, and before distributing any phonorecords of the work, serve notice of intention to do so on the copyright owner. If the registration or other public records of the Copyright Office do not identify the copyright owner and include an address at which notice can be served, it shall be sufficient to file the notice of intention in the Copyright Office. The notice shall comply, in form, content, and manner of service, with requirements that the Register of Copyrights shall prescribe by regulation.

(2) Failure to serve or file the notice required by clause (1) forecloses the possibility of a compulsory license and, in the absence of a negotiated license, renders the making and distribution of phonorecords actionable as acts of infringement under section 501 and fully subject to the remedies provided by sections 502 through 506 and 509.

. . .

§116. Negotiated Licenses for Public Performances by Means of Coin-Operated Phonorecord Players[52]

(a) Applicability of Section.—This section applies to any nondramatic musical work embodied in a phonorecord.

(b) Negotiated Licenses.—

(1) Authority for negotiations.—Any owners of copyright in works to which this section applies and any operators of coin-operated phonorecord players may negotiate and agree upon the terms and rates of royalty payments for the performance of such works and the proportionate division of fees paid among copyright owners, and may designate common agents to negotiate, agree to, pay, or receive such royalty payments.

(2) Arbitration.—Parties not subject to such a negotiation, may determine, by arbitration in accordance with the provisions of chapter 8, the terms and rates and the division of fees described in paragraph (1).

(c) License Agreements Superior to Copyright Arbitration Royalty Panel Determinations.—License agreements between one or more copyright owners

and one or more operators of coin-operated phonorecord players, which are negotiated in accordance with subsection (b), shall
be given effect in lieu of any otherwise applicable determination by a copyright arbitration royalty panel.

(d) Definitions.—As used in this section, the following terms mean the following:

(1) A "coin-operated phonorecord player" is a machine or device that-

(A) is employed solely for the performance of nondramatic musical works by means of phonorecords upon being activated by the insertion of coins, currency, tokens, or other monetary units or their equivalent;

(B) is located in an establishment making no direct or indirect charge for admission;

(C) is accompanied by a list which is comprised of the titles of all the musical works available for performance on it, and is affixed to the phonorecord player or posted in the establishment in a prominent position where it can be readily examined by the public; and

(D) affords a choice of works available for performance and permits the choice to be made by the patrons of the establishment in which it is located.

(2) An "operator" is any person who, alone or jointly with others-

(A) owns a coin-operated phonorecord player;

(B) has the power to make a coin-operated phonorecord player available for placement in an establishment for purposes of public performance; or

(C) has the power to exercise primary control over the selection of the musical works made available for public performance on a coin-operated phonorecord player.

. . .

ENDNOTES

2. The Audio Home Recording Act of 1992 amended section 101 by inserting "Except as otherwise provided in this title," at the beginning of the first sentence. Pub. L. No. 102-563, 106 Stat. 4237, 4248. The Berne Convention Implementation Act of 1988 amended section 101 by adding a definition for "Berne Convention work." Pub. L. No. 100-568, 102 Stat. 2853, 2854. . . .

3. In 1990, the Architectural Works Copyright Protection Act amended section 101 by adding the definition for "architectural work." Pub. L. No. 101-650, 104 Stat. 5089, 5133. That Act states that the definition is applicable to "any architectural work that, on the date of the enactment of this Act, is unconstructed and embodied in unpublished plans or drawings, except that protection for such architectural work under title 17, United States Code, by virtue of the amendments made by this title, shall terminate on December 31, 2002, unless the work is constructed by that date."

4. The Berne Convention Implementation Act of 1988 amended section 101 by adding the definition of "Berne Convention." Pub. L. No. 100-568, 102 Stat. 2853, 2854.

5. The Digital Performance Right in Sound Recordings Act of 1995 amended section 101 by adding the definition of "digital transmission." Pub. L. No.104-39, 109 Stat. 336, 348.

6. The Fairness in Music Licensing Act of 1998 amended section 101 by adding the definition of "establishment." Pub. L. No. 105-298, 112 Stat. 2827, 2833.

7. The Fairness in Music Licensing Act of 1998 amended section 101 by adding the definition of "food service or drinking establishment." Pub. L. No. 105-298, 112 Stat. 2827, 2833.

8. In 1997, the No Electronic Theft (NET) Act amended section 101 by adding the definition for "financial gain." Pub. L. No. 105-147, 111 Stat. 2678.

9. The WIPO Copyright and Performances and Phonograms Treaties Implementation Act of 1998 amended section 101 by adding the definition of "Geneva Phonograms Convention." Pub. L. No. 105-304, 112 Stat. 2860, 2861.

10. The Fairness in Music Licensing Act of 1998 amended section 101 by adding the definition of "gross square feet of space." Pub. L. No. 105-298, 112 Stat. 2827, 2833.

11. The WIPO Copyright and Performances and Phonograms Treaties Implementation Act of 1998 requires that paragraph (5) of the definition of "international agreement" take effect upon entry into force of the WIPO Copyright Treaty with respect to the United States. Pub. L. No. 105-304, 112 Stat. 2860, 2877.

12. The WIPO Copyright and Performances and Phonograms Treaties Implementation Act of 1998 requires that paragraph (6) of the definition of "international agreement" take effect upon entry into force of the WIPO Performances and Phonograms Treaty with respect to the United States. Pub. L. No. 105-304, 112 Stat. 2860, 2877.

13. The WIPO Copyright and Performances and Phonograms Treaties Implementation Act of 1998 amended section 101 by adding the definition of "international agreement." Pub. L. No. 105-304, 112 Stat. 2860, 2861.

14. The Fairness in Music Licensing Act of 1998 amended section 101 by adding the definition of "performing rights society." Pub. L. No. 105-298, 112 Stat. 2827, 2833.

15. The Berne Convention Implementation Act of 1988 amended the definition of "Pictorial, graphic, and sculptural works". . . . Pub. L. No. 100-568, 102 Stat. 2853, 2854.

16. The Fairness in Music Licensing Act of 1998 amended section 101 by adding the definition of "proprietor." Pub. L. No. 105-298, 112 Stat. 2827, 2833. . . .

17. The Copyright Renewal Act of 1992 amended section 101 by adding the definition of "registration." Pub. L. No. 102-307, 106 Stat. 264, 266.

18. The WIPO Copyright and Performances and Phonograms Treaties Implementation Act of 1998 amended section 101 by adding the definition of "treaty party." Pub. L. No. 105-304, 112 Stat. 2860, 2861.

19. The Berne Convention Implementation Act of 1988 amended section 101 by adding the definition of "country of origin" of a Berne Convention work, for purposes of section 411. Pub. L. No. 100-568, 102 Stat. 2853, 2854. . . .

20. The WIPO Copyright and Performances and Phonograms Treaties Implementation Act of 1998 amended section 101 by adding the definition of "WIPO Copyright Treaty." Pub. L. No. 105-304, 112 Stat. 2860, 2861. . . .

21. The WIPO Copyright and Performances and Phonograms Treaties Implementation Act of 1998 amended section 101 by adding the definition of "WIPO Performances and Phonograms Treaty." Pub. L. No. 105-304, 112 Stat. 2860, 2862. . . .

23. The Satellite Home Viewer Improvement Act of 1999 amended the definition of "a work made for hire" by inserting "as a sound recording" after "audiovisual work." Pub.

L. No. 106-113, 113 Stat. 1501, app. I at 1501A-544. The Work Made for Hire and Copyright Corrections Act of 2000 amended the definition of "work made for hire" by deleting "as a sound recording" after "audiovisual work." Pub. L. No. 106-379, 114 Stat. 1444. . . .

24. The WIPO Copyright and Performances and Phonograms Treaties Implementation Act of 1998 amended section 101 by adding the definitions of "WTO Agreement" and "WTO member country," thereby transferring those definitions to section 101 from section 104A. Pub. L. No. 105-304, 112 Stat. 2860, 2862.

25. In 1980, the definition of "computer program" was added to section 101. Pub. L. No. 96-517, 94 Stat. 3015, 3028.

26. In 1990, the Architectural Works Copyright Protection Act amended subsection 102(a) by adding at the end thereof paragraph (8). Pub. L. No. 101-650, 104 Stat. 5089, 5133.

27. The Berne Convention Implementation Act of 1988 amended section 104(b) by redesignating paragraph (4) as paragraph (5), by inserting after paragraph (3) a new paragraph (4) and by adding subsection (c) at the end. Pub. L. No. 100-568, 102 Stat. 2853, 2855. . . .

28. The WIPO Copyright and Performances and Phonograms Treaties Implementation Act of 1998 requires that subsection (d), regarding the effect of phonograms treaties, take effect upon entry into force of the WIPO Performances and Phonograms Treaty with respect to the United States. Pub. L. No. 105-304, 112 Stat. 2860, 2877.

. . .

35. In 1968, the Standard Reference Data Act provided an exception to Section 105, Pub. L. No. 90-396, 82 Stat. 339. Section 6 of that act amended title 15 of the United States Code by authorizing the Secretary of Commerce, at 15 U.S.C. 290e, to secure copyright and renewal thereof on behalf of the United States as author or proprietor "in all or any part of any standard reference data which he prepares or makes available under this chapter," and to "authorize the reproduction and publication thereof by others.". . .

36. The Digital Performance Right in Sound Recordings Act of 1995 amended section 106 by adding paragraph (6). Pub. L. No. 104-39, 109 Stat. 336. In 1999, a technical amendment substituted "121" for "120." Pub. L. No. 106-44, 113 Stat. 221, 222.

. . .

40. The Record Rental Amendment of 1984 amended section 109 by . . . inserting a new subsection (b) after subsection (a). Pub. L. No. 98-450, 98 Stat. 1727. Section 4(b) of the Act states that the provisions of section 109(b), as added by section 2 of the Act, "shall not affect the right of an owner of a particular phonorecord of a sound recording, who acquired such ownership before [October 4, 1984], to dispose of the possession of that particular phonorecord on or after such date of enactment in any manner permitted by section 109 of title 17, United States Code, as in effect on the day before the date of the enactment of this Act." Pub. L. No. 98-450, 98 Stat. 1727, 1728. . . .

41. *Editor's note:* This endnote lists the changes made in Section 110 as a result of the Extension of Record Rental Amendment, the Technical Corrections to the Satellite Home Viewer Act, and The Fairness in Music Licensing Act of 1998. For the complete citation, see the Copyright Act.

46. *Editor's note:* Endnote 46 lists the changes made in Section 114 as a result of The Digital Performance Right in Sound Recordings Act of 1995 and the Digital Millennium Copyright Act of 1998. For a complete citation, see the Copyright Act.

. . .

49. *Editor's note:* Endnote 49 lists the changes made in Section 115 as a result of The Record Rental Amendment of 1984 and The Digital Performance Right in Sound Recordings Act of 1995. For the complete citation, see the Copyright Act.

52. The Berne Convention Implementation Act of 1988 added section 116A. Pub. L. No. 100-568, 102 Stat. 2853, 2855. The Copyright Royalty Tribunal Reform Act of 1993 . . . substituted, where appropriate, "Librarian of Congress" or "copyright arbitration royalty panel" for "Copyright Royalty Tribunal.". . .

CHAPTER 2: COPYRIGHT OWNERSHIP AND TRANSFER

§201. Ownership of Copyright[1]

(a) Initial Ownership.—Copyright in a work protected under this title vests initially in the author or authors of the work. The authors of a joint work are coowner of copyright in the work.

(b) Works Made for Hire.—In the case of a work made for hire, the employer or other person for whom the work was prepared is considered the author for purposes of this title, and, unless the parties have expressly agreed otherwise in a written instrument signed by them, owns all of the rights comprised in the copyright.

(c) Contributions to Collective Works.—Copyright in each separate contribution to a collective work is distinct from copyright in the collective work as a whole, and vests initially in the author of the contribution. In the absence of an express transfer of the copyright or of any rights under it, the owner of copyright in the collective work is presumed to have acquired only the privilege of reproducing and distributing the contribution as part of that particular collective work, any revision of that collective work, and any later collective work in the same series.

(d) Transfer of Ownership.—

(1) The ownership of a copyright may be transferred in whole or in part by any means of conveyance or by operation of law, and may be bequeathed by will or pass as personal property by the applicable laws of intestate succession.

(2) Any of the exclusive rights comprised in a copyright, including any subdivision of any of the rights specified by section 106, may be transferred as provided by clause (1) and owned separately. The owner of any particular exclusive right is entitled, to the extent of that right, to all of the protection and remedies accorded to the copyright owner by this title.

(e) Involuntary Transfer.—When an individual author's ownership of a copyright, or of any of the exclusive rights under a copyright, has not previously been transferred voluntarily by that individual author, no action by any governmental body or other official or organization purporting to seize, expropriate, transfer, or exercise rights of ownership with respect to the copyright, or any of the exclusive rights under a copyright, shall be given effect under this title, except as provided under title 11.[2]

§202. Ownership of Copyright As Distinct from Ownership of Material Object

Ownership of a copyright, or of any of the exclusive rights under a copyright, is distinct from ownership of any material object in which the work is embodied. Transfer of ownership of any material object, including the copy or phonorecord in which the work is first fixed, does not of itself convey any rights in the copyrighted work embodied in the object; nor, in the absence of an agreement, does transfer of ownership of a copyright or of any exclusive rights under a copyright convey property rights in any material object.

§203. Termination of Transfers and Licenses Granted by the Author[3]

(a) Conditions for Termination.—In the case of any work other than a work made for hire, the exclusive or nonexclusive grant of a transfer or license of copyright or of any right under a copyright, executed by the author on or after January 1, 1978, otherwise than by will, is subject to termination under the following conditions:

(1) In the case of a grant executed by one author, termination of the grant may be effected by that author or, if the author is dead, by the person or persons who, under clause (2) of this subsection, own and are entitled to exercise a total of more than one-half of that author's termination interest. In the case of a grant executed by two or more authors of a joint work, termination of the grant may be effected by a majority of the authors who executed it; if any of such authors is dead, the termination interest of any such author may be exercised as a unit by the person or persons who, under clause (2) of this subsection, own and are entitled to exercise a total of more than one-half of that author's interest.

(2) Where an author is dead, his or her termination interest is owned, and may be exercised, as follows:

(A) the widow or widower owns the author's entire termination interest unless there are any surviving children or grandchildren of the author, in which case the widow or widower owns one-half of the author's interest;

(B) the author's surviving children, and the surviving children of any dead child of the author, own the author's entire termination interest unless there is a widow or widower, in which case the ownership of one-half of the author's interest is divided among them;

(C) the rights of the author's children and grandchildren are in all cases divided among them and exercised on a per stirpes basis according to the number of such author's children represented; the share of the children of a dead child in a termination interest can be exercised only by the action of a majority of them.

(D) In the event that the author's widow or widower, children, and grandchildren are not living, the author's executor, administrator, personal representative, or trustee shall own the author's entire termination interest.

(3) Termination of the grant may be effected at any time during a period of five years beginning at the end of thirty-five years from the date of execution of the grant; or, if the grant covers the right of publication of the work, the period begins at the end of thirty-five years from the date of publication of the work under the grant or at the end of forty years from the date of execution of the grant, whichever term ends earlier.

(4) The termination shall be effected by serving an advance notice in writing, signed by the number and proportion of owners of termination interests required under clauses (1) and (2) of this subsection, or by their duly authorized agents, upon the grantee or the grantee's successor in title.

(A) The notice shall state the effective date of the termination, which shall fall within the five-year period specified by clause (3) of this subsection, and the notice shall be served not less than two or more than ten years before that date. A copy of the notice shall be recorded in the Copyright Office before the effective date of termination, as a condition to its taking effect.

(B) The notice shall comply, in form, content, and manner of service, with requirements that the Register of Copyrights shall prescribe by regulation.

(5) Termination of the grant may be effected notwithstanding any agreement to the contrary, including an agreement to make a will or to make any future grant.

(b) Effect of Termination.—Upon the effective date of termination, all rights under this title that were covered by the terminated grants revert to the author, authors, and other persons owning termination interests under clauses (1) and (2) of subsection (a), including those owners who did not join in signing the notice of termination under clause (4) of subsection (a), but with the following limitations:

(1) A derivative work prepared under authority of the grant before its termination may continue to be utilized under the terms of the grant after its termination, but this privilege does not extend to the preparation after the termination of other derivative works based upon the copyrighted work covered by the terminated grant.

(2) The future rights that will revert upon termination of the grant become vested on the date the notice of termination has been served as provided by clause (4) of subsection (a). The rights vest in the author, authors, and other persons named in, and in the proportionate shares provided by, clauses (1) and (2) of subsection (a).

(3) Subject to the provisions of clause (4) of this subsection, a further grant, or agreement to make a further grant, of any right covered by a terminated grant is valid only if it is signed by the same number and proportion of the owners, in whom the right has vested under clause (2) of this subsection, as are required to terminate the grant under clauses (1) and (2) of subsection (a). Such further grant or agreement is effective with respect to all of the persons in whom the right it covers has vested under clause (2) of this subsection, including those who did not join in signing it. If any person dies after rights under a terminated grant have vested in him or her, that person's legal representatives, legatees, or heirs at law represent him or her for purposes of this clause.

(4) A further grant, or agreement to make a further grant, of any right covered by a terminated grant is valid only if it is made after the effective date of the termination. As an exception, however, an agreement for such a further grant may be made between the persons provided by clause (3) of this subsection and the original grantee or such grantee's successor in title, after the notice of termination has been served as provided by clause (4) of subsection (a).

(5) Termination of a grant under this section affects only those rights covered by the grants that arise under this title, and in no way affects rights arising under any other Federal, State, or foreign laws.

(6) Unless and until termination is effected under this section, the grant, if it does not provide otherwise, continues in effect for the term of copyright provided by this title.

§204. Execution of transfers of Copyright Ownership

(a) A transfer of copyright ownership, other than by operation of law, is not valid unless an instrument of conveyance, or a note or memorandum of the transfer, is in writing and signed by the owner of the rights conveyed or such owner's duly authorized agent.

(b) A certificate of acknowledgment is not required for the validity of a transfer, but is prima facie evidence of the execution of the transfer if-

(1) in the case of a transfer executed in the United States, the certificate is issued by a person authorized to administer oaths within the United States; or

(2) in the case of a transfer executed in a foreign country, the certificate is issued by a diplomatic or consular officer of the United States, or by a person authorized to administer oaths whose authority is proved by a certificate of such an officer.

§205. Recordation of transfers and other documents[4]

(a) Conditions for Recordation.—Any transfer of copyright ownership or other document pertaining to a copyright may be recorded in the Copyright

Office if the document filed for recordation bears the actual signature of the person who executed it, or if it is accompanied by a sworn or official certification that it is a true copy of the original, signed document.

(b) Certificate of Recordation.—The Register of Copyrights shall, upon receipt of a document as provided by subsection (a) and of the fee provided by section 708, record the document and return it with a certificate of recordation.

(c) Recordation as Constructive Notice.—Recordation of a document in the Copyright Office gives all persons constructive notice of the facts stated in the recorded document, but only if-

(1) the document, or material attached to it, specifically identifies the work to which it pertains so that, after the document is indexed by the Register of Copyrights, it would be revealed by a reasonable search under the title or registration number of the work; and

(2) registration has been made for the work.

(d) Priority Between Conflicting Transfers.—As between two conflicting transfers, the one executed first prevails if it is recorded, in the manner required to give constructive notice under subsection (c), within one month after its execution in the United States or within two months after its execution outside the United States, or at any time before recordation in such manner of the later transfer. Otherwise the later transfer prevails if recorded first in such manner, and if taken in good faith, for valuable consideration or on the basis of a binding promise to pay royalties, and without notice of the earlier transfer.

(e) Priority Between Conflicting Transfer of Ownership and Nonexclusive License.—A nonexclusive license, whether recorded or not, prevails over a conflicting transfer of copyright ownership if the license is evidenced by a written instrument signed by the owner of the rights licensed or such owner's duly authorized agent, and if

(1) the license was taken before execution of the transfer; or

(2) the license was taken in good faith before recordation of the transfer and without notice of it.

ENDNOTES

1. In 1978, section 201(e) was amended by deleting the period at the end and adding, "except as provided under title 11."

2. Title 11 of the United States Code is entitled "Bankruptcy."

3. In 1998, the Sonny Bono Copyright Term Extension Act amended section 203 by deleting "by his widow or her widower and his or her grandchildren" from the first sentence in paragraph (2) of subsection (a) and by adding subparagraph (D) to paragraph (2). Pub. L. No. 105-298, 112 Stat. 2827, 2829.

4. The Berne Convention Implementation Act of 1988 amended section 205 by deleting subsection (d) and redesignating subsections (e) and (f) as subsections (d) and (e), respectively. Pub. L. No. 100-568, 102 Stat. 2853, 2857.

CHAPTER 3: DURATION OF COPYRIGHT[1]

§301. Preemption with Respect to Other Laws[2]

(a) On and after January 1, 1978, all legal or equitable rights that are equivalent to any of the exclusive rights within the general scope of copyright as specified by section 106 in works of authorship that are fixed in a tangible medium of expression and come within the subject matter of copyright as specified by sections 102 and 103, whether created before or after that date and whether published or unpublished, are governed exclusively by this title. Thereafter, no person is entitled to any such right or equivalent right in any such work under the common law or statutes of any State.

(b) Nothing in this title annuls or limits any rights or remedies under the common law or statutes of any State with respect to—

(1) subject matter that does not come within the subject matter of copyright as specified by sections 102 and 103, including works of authorship not fixed in any tangible medium of expression; or

(2) any cause of action arising from undertakings commenced before January 1, 1978;

(3) activities violating legal or equitable rights that are not equivalent to any of the exclusive rights within the general scope of copyright as specified by section 106; or

(4) State and local landmarks, historic preservation, zoning, or building codes, relating to architectural works protected under section 102(a)(8).

(c) With respect to sound recordings fixed before February 15, 1972, any rights or remedies under the common law or statutes of any State shall not be annulled or limited by this title until February 15, 2067. The preemptive provisions of subsection (a) shall apply to any such rights and remedies pertaining to any cause of action arising from undertakings commenced on and after February 15, 2067. Notwithstanding the provisions of section 303, no sound recording fixed before February 15, 1972, shall be subject to copyright under this title before, on, or after February 15, 2067.

(d) Nothing in this title annuls or limits any rights or remedies under any other Federal statute.

(e) The scope of Federal preemption under this section is not affected by the adherence of the United States to the Berne Convention or the satisfaction of obligations of the United States thereunder.

(f)(1) On or after the effective date set forth in section 610(a) of the Visual Artists Rights Act of 1990, all legal or equitable rights that are equivalent to any of the rights conferred by section 106A with respect to works of visual art to which the rights conferred by section 106A apply are governed exclusively by section 106A and section 113(d) and the provisions of this title relating to such sections. Thereafter, no person is entitled to any such right or equivalent right in any work of visual art under the common law or statutes of any State.[3]

(2) Nothing in paragraph (1) annuls or limits any rights or remedies under the common law or statutes of any State with respect to—

(A) any cause of action from undertakings commenced before the effective date set forth in section 610(a) of the Visual Artists Rights Act of 1990;

(B) activities violating legal or equitable rights that are not equivalent to any of the rights conferred by section 106A with respect to works of visual art; or

(C) activities violating legal or equitable rights which extend beyond the life of the author.

§302. Duration of Copyright: Works Created on or after January 1, 1978[4]

(a) In General.—Copyright in a work created on or after January 1, 1978, subsists from its creation and, except as provided by the following subsections, endures for a term consisting of the life of the author and 70 years after the author's death.

(b) Joint Works.—In the case of a joint work prepared by two or more authors who did not work for hire, the copyright endures for a term consisting of the life of the last surviving author and 70 years after such last surviving author's death.

(c) Anonymous Works, Pseudonymous Works, and Works Made for Hire.—In the case of an anonymous work, a pseudonymous work, or a work made for hire, the copyright endures for a term of 95 years from the year of its first publication, or a term of 120 years from the year of its creation, whichever expires first. If, before the end of such term, the identity of one or more of the authors of an anonymous or pseudonymous work is revealed in the records of a registration made for that work under subsections (a) or (d) f section 408, or in the records provided by this subsection, the copyright in the work endures for the term specified by subsection (a) or (b), based on the life of the author or authors whose identity has been revealed. Any person having an interest in the copyright in an anonymous or pseudonymous work may at any time record, in records to be maintained by the Copyright Office for that purpose, a statement identifying one or more authors of the work; the statement shall also identify the person filing it, the nature of that person's interest, the source of the information recorded, and the particular work affected, and shall comply in form and content with requirements that the Register of Copyrights shall prescribe by regulation.

(d) Records Relating to Death of Authors.—Any person having an interest in a copyright may at any time record in the Copyright Office a statement of the date of death of the author of the copyrighted work, or a statement that the author is still living on a particular date. The statement shall identify the person filing it, the nature of that person's interest, and the source of the information recorded, and shall comply in form and content with requirements that the Register of Copyrights shall prescribe by regulation. The Register shall maintain current records of information relating to the death of authors of copyrighted works, based on such recorded statements and, to the extent the Register considers practicable, on data contained in any of the records of the Copyright Office or in other reference sources.

(e) Presumption as to Author's Death.—After a period of 95 years from the year of first publication of a work, or a period of 120 years from the year of its creation, whichever expires first, any person who obtains from the Copyright Office a certified report that the records provided by subsection (d) disclose nothing to indicate that the author of the work is living, or died less than 70 years before, is entitled to the benefit of a presumption that the author has been dead for at least 70 years. Reliance in good faith upon this presumption shall be a complete defense to any action for infringement under this title.

§303. Duration of Copyright: Works Created but Not Published or Copyrighted Before January 1, 1978[5]

(a) Copyright in a work created before January 1, 1978, but not theretofore in the public domain or copyrighted, subsists from January 1, 1978, and endures for the term provided by section 302. In no case, however, shall the term of copyright in such a work expire before December 31, 2002; and, if the work is published on or before December 31, 2002, the term of copyright shall not expire before December 31, 2047.

(b) The distribution before January 1, 1978, of a phonorecord shall not for any purpose constitute a publication of the musical work embodied therein.

§304. Duration of Copyright: Subsisting Copyrights[6]

(a) Copyrights in Their First Term on January 1, 1978.—

(1)(A) Any copyright, in the first term of which is subsisting on January 1, 1978, shall endure for 28 years from the date it was originally secured.

(B) In the case of—

(i) any posthumous work or of any periodical, cyclopedic, or other composite work upon which the copyright was originally secured by the proprietor thereof, or

(ii) any work copyrighted by a corporate body (otherwise than as assignee or licensee of the individual author) or by an employer for whom such work is made for hire, the proprietor of such copyright shall be entitled to a renewal and extension of the copyright in such work for the further term of 67 years.

(C) In the case of any other copyrighted work, including a contribution by an individual author to a periodical or to a cyclopedic or other composite work—

(i) the author of such work, if the author is still living,

(ii) the widow, widower, or children of the author, if the author is not living,

(iii) the author's executors, if such author, widow, widower, or children are not living, or

(iv) the author's next of kin, in the absence of a will of the author,

shall be entitled to a renewal and extension of the copyright in such work for a further term of 67 years.

(2)(A) At the expiration of the original term of copyright in a work specified in paragraph (1)(B) of this subsection, the copyright shall endure for a renewed and extended further term of 67 years, which—

(i) if an application to register a claim to such further term has been made to the Copyright Office within 1 year before the expiration of the original term of copyright, and the claim is registered, shall vest, upon the beginning of such further term, in the proprietor of the copyright who is entitled to claim the renewal of copyright at the time the application is made; or

(ii) if no such application is made or the claim pursuant to such application is not registered, shall vest, upon the beginning of such further term, in the person or entity that was the proprietor of the copyright as of the last day of the original term of copyright.

(B) At the expiration of the original term of copyright in a work specified in paragraph (1)(C) of this subsection, the copyright shall endure for a renewed and extended further term of 67 years, which—

(i) if an application to register a claim to such further term has been made to the Copyright Office within 1 year before the expiration of the original term of copyright, and the claim is registered, shall vest, upon the beginning of such further term, in any person who is entitled under paragraph (1)(C) to the renewal and extension of the copyright at the time the application is made; or

(ii) if no such application is made or the claim pursuant to such application is not registered, shall vest, upon the beginning of such further term, in any person entitled under paragraph (1)(C), as of the last day of the original term of copyright, to the renewal and extension of the copyright.

(3)(A) An application to register a claim to the renewed and extended term of copyright in a work may be made to the Copyright Office—

(i) within 1 year before the expiration of the original term of copyright by any person entitled under paragraph (1)(B) or (C) to such further term of 67 years; and

(ii) at any time during the renewed and extended term by any person in whom such further term vested, under paragraph (2) (A) or (B), or by any successor or assign of such person, if the application is made in the name of such person.

(B) Such an application is not a condition of the renewal and extension of the copyright in a work for a further term of 67 years.

(4)(A) If an application to register a claim to the renewed and extended term of copyright in a work is not made within 1 year before the expiration of the original term of copyright in a work, or if the claim pursuant to such application is not registered, then a derivative work prepared under authority of a grant of a transfer or license of the copyright that is made before the expiration of the original term of copyright may continue to be used under the terms of the grant during the renewed and extended term of copyright without infringing the copyright, except that such use does not extend to the preparation during such renewed and extended term of other derivative works based upon the copyrighted work covered by such grant.

(B) If an application to register a claim to the renewed and extended term of copyright in a work is made within 1 year before its expiration, and the claim is registered, the certificate of such registration shall constitute prima facie evidence as to the validity of the copyright during its renewed and extended term and of the facts stated in the certificate. The evidentiary weight to be accorded the certificates of a registration of a renewed and extended term of copyright made after the end of that 1-year period shall be within the discretion of the court.

(b) Copyrights in Their Renewal Term at the Time of the Effective Date of the Sonny Bono Copyright Term Extension Act.[7]—Any copyright still in its renewal term at the time that the Sonny Bono Copyright Term Extension Act becomes effective shall have a copyright term of 95 years from the date copyright was originally secured.[8]

(c) Termination of Transfers and Licenses Covering Extended Renewal Term. —In the case of any copyright subsisting in either its first or renewal term on January 1, 1978, other than a copyright in a work made for hire, the exclusive or nonexclusive grant of a transfer or license of the renewal copyright or any right under it, executed before January 1, 1978, by any of the persons designated by subsection (a)(1)(C) of this section, otherwise than by will, is subject to termination under the following conditions:

(1) In the case of a grant executed by a person or persons other than the author, termination of the grant may be effected by the surviving person or persons who executed it. In the case of a grant executed by one or more of the authors of the work, termination of the grant may be effected, to the extent of a particular author's share in the ownership of the renewal copyright, by the author who executed it or, if such author is dead, by the person or persons who, under clause (2) of this

subsection, own and are entitled to exercise a total of more than one-half of that author's termination interest.

(2) Where an author is dead, his or her termination interest is owned, and may be exercised, as follows:

(A) the widow or widower owns the author's entire termination interest unless there are any surviving children or grandchildren of the author, in which case the widow or widower owns one-half of the author's interest;

(B) the author's surviving children, and the surviving children of any dead child of the author, own the author's entire termination interest unless there is a widow or widower, in which case the ownership of one-half of the author's interest is divided among them;

(C) the rights of the author's children and grandchildren are in all cases divided among them and exercised on a per stirpes basis according to the number of such author's children represented; the share of the children of a dead child in a termination interest can be exercised only by the action of a majority of them.

(D) In the event that the author's widow or widower, children, and grandchildren are not living, the author's executor, administrator, personal representative, or trustee shall own the author's entire termination interest.

(3) Termination of the grant may be effected at any time during a period of five years beginning at the end of fifty-six years from the date copyright was originally secured, or beginning on January 1, 1978, whichever is later.

(4) The termination shall be effected by serving an advance notice in writing upon the grantee or the grantee's successor in title. In the case of a grant executed by a person or persons other than the author, the notice shall be signed by all of those entitled to terminate the grant under clause (1) of this subsection, or by their duly authorized agents. In the case of a grant executed by one or more of the authors of the work, the notice as to any one author's share shall be signed by that author or his or her duly authorized agent or, if that author is dead, by the number and proportion of the owners of his or her termination interest required under clauses (1) and (2) of this subsection, or by their duly authorized agents.

(A) The notice shall state the effective date of the termination, which shall fall within the five-year period specified by clause (3) of this subsection, or, in the case of a termination under subsection (d), within the five-year period specified by subsection (d)(2), and the notice shall be served not less than two or more than ten years before that date. A copy of the notice shall be recorded in the Copyright Office before the effective date of termination, as a condition to its taking effect.

(B) The notice shall comply, in form, content, and manner of service, with requirements that the Register of Copyrights shall prescribe by regulation.

(5) Termination of the grant may be effected notwithstanding any agreement to the contrary, including an agreement to make a will or to make any future grant.

(6) In the case of a grant executed by a person or persons other than the author, all rights under this title that were covered by the terminated grant revert, upon the effective date of termination, to all of those entitled to terminate the grant under clause (1) of this subsection. In the case of a grant executed by one or more of the authors of the work, all of a particular author's rights under this title that were covered by the terminated grant revert, upon the effective date of termination, to that author or, if that author is dead, to the persons owning his or her termination interest under clause (2) of this subsection, including those owners who did not join in signing the notice of termination under clause (4) of this subsection. In all cases the reversion of rights is subject to the following limitations:

(A) A derivative work prepared under authority of the grant before its termination may continue to be utilized under the terms of the grant after its termination, but this privilege does not extend to the preparation after the termination of other derivative works based upon the copyrighted work covered by the terminated grant.

(B) The future rights that will revert upon termination of the grant become vested on the date the notice of termination has been served as provided by clause (4) of this subsection.

(C) Where the author's rights revert to two or more persons under clause (2) of this subsection, they shall vest in those persons in the proportionate shares provided by that clause. In such a case, and subject to the provisions of subclause (D) of this clause, a further grant, or agreement to make a further grant, of a particular author's share with respect to any right covered by a terminated grant is valid only if it is signed by the same number and proportion of the owners, in whom the right has vested under this clause, as are required to terminate the grant under clause (2) of this subsection. Such further grant or agreement is effective with respect to all of the persons in whom the right it covers has vested under this subclause, including those who did not join in signing it. If any person dies after rights under a terminated grant have vested in him or her, that person's legal representatives, legatees, or heirs at law represent him or her for purposes of this subclause.

(D) A further grant, or agreement to make a further grant, of any right covered by a terminated grant is valid only if it is made after the effective date of the termination. As an exception, however, an agreement for such a further grant may be made between the author or any of the persons provided by the first sentence of clause (6) of this subsection, or between the persons provided by subclause (C) of this clause, and the original grantee or such grantee's successor in title, after the notice of termination has been served as provided by clause (4) of this subsection.

(E) Termination of a grant under this subsection affects only those rights covered by the grant that arise under this title, and in no way affects rights arising under any other Federal, State, or foreign laws.

(F) Unless and until termination is effected under this subsection, the grant, if it does not provide otherwise, continues in effect for the remainder of the extended renewal term.

(d) Termination Rights Provided in Subsection (c) Which Have Expired on or Before the Effective Date of the Sonny Bono Copyright Term Extension Act.—In the case of any copyright other than a work made for hire, subsisting in its renewal term on the effective date of the Sonny Bono Copyright Term Extension Act[9] for which the termination right provided in subsection (c) has expired by such date, where the author or owner of the termination right has not previously exercised such termination right, the exclusive or nonexclusive grant of a transfer or license of the renewal copyright or any right under it, executed before January 1, 1978, by any of the persons designated in subsection (a)(1)(C) of this section, other than by will, is subject to termination under the following conditions:

(1) The conditions specified in subsections (c) (1), (2), (4), (5), and (6) of this section apply to terminations of the last 20 years of copyright term as provided by the amendments made by the Sonny Bono Copyright Term Extension Act.

(2) Termination of the grant may be effected at any time during a period of 5 years beginning at the end of 75 years from the date copyright was originally secured.

§305. Duration of Copyright: Terminal date

All terms of copyright provided by sections 302 through 304 run to the end of the calendar year in which they would otherwise expire.

Endnotes

1. *Editor's note:* Endnote 1 refers to Private Law 92-60, 85 Stat. 857, effective December 15, 1971, which gave the works of Mary Baker Eddy an unprecedented extension of duration of copyright but was found to be unconstitutional in 1987 because it violates the Establishment Clause of the first Amendment.

2. *Editor's note:* Endnote 2 lists changes made in Section 301 as a result of The Berne Convention Implementation Act of 1988, the Architectural Works Copyright Protection Act, the Visual Artists Rights Act of 1990, and the Sonny Bono Copyright Term Extension Act.

3. The Visual Artists Rights Act of 1990, which added subsection (f), states, "Subject to subsection (b) and except as provided in subsection (c), this title and the amendments made by this title take effect 6 months after the date of the enactment of this Act."...

4. In 1998, the Sonny Bono Copyright Term Extension Act amended section 302 by substituting "70" for "fifty," "95" for "seventy-five" and "120" for "one hundred" each place they appeared. Pub. L. No. 105-298, 112 Stat. 2827.

5. In 1997, section 303 was amended by adding subsection (b). Pub. L. No. 105-80, 111 Stat. 1529, 1534. In 1998, the Sonny Bono Copyright Term Extension Act amended section 303 by substituting "December 31, 2047" for "December 31, 2027." Pub. L. No. 105-298, 112 Stat. 2827.

6. The Copyright Renewal Act of 1992 amended section 304 by substituting a new subsection (a) and by making a conforming amendment in the matter preceding paragraph (1) of subsection (c). Pub. L. No. 102-307, 106 Stat. 264. The Act, as amended by the Sonny Bono Copyright Term Extension Act, states that the renewal and extension of a copyright for a further term of 67 years "shall have the same effect with respect to any grant, before the effective date of the Sonny Bono Copyright Term Extension Act [October 27, 1998], of a transfer or license of the further term as did the renewal of a copyright before the effective date of the Sonny Bono Copyright Term Extension Act [October 27, 1998] under the law in effect at the time of such grant." The Act also states that the 1992 amendments "shall apply only to those copyrights secured between January 1, 1964, and December 31, 1977. Copyrights secured before January 1, 1964, shall be governed by the provisions of section 304(a) of title 17, United States Code, as in effect on the day before . . .[enactment on June 26, 1992], except each reference to forty-seven years in such provisions shall be deemed to be 67 years." Pub. L. No. 102-307, 106 Stat. 264, 266, as amended by the Sonny Bono Copyright Term Extension Act, Pub. L. No. 105-298, 112 Stat. 2827, 2828. . . .

7. A series of nine Acts of Congress extended until December 31, 1976, previously renewed copyrights in which the renewal term would otherwise have expired between September 19, 1962 and December 31, 1976. The last of these enactments is Pub. L. No. 93-573, 88 Stat. 1873, enacted December 31, 1974, which cites the eight earlier acts. See also section 102 of the Transitional and Supplementary Provisions of the Copyright Act of 1976, in Part I of the Appendix. Pub. L. No. 94-553, 90 Stat. 2541.

8. The effective date of the Sonny Bono Copyright Term Extension Act is October 27, 1998.

9. See endnote 8, supra.

CHAPTER 4: COPYRIGHT NOTICE, DEPOSIT, AND REGISTRATION

§401. Notice of Copyright: Visually Perceptible Copies[1]

(a) General Provisions.—Whenever a work protected under this title is published in the United States or elsewhere by authority of the copyright owner, a notice of copyright as provided by this section may be placed on publicly distributed copies from which the work can be visually perceived, either directly or with the aid of a machine or device.

(b) Form of Notice.—If a notice appears on the copies, it shall consist of the following three elements:

(1) the symbol © (the letter C in a circle), or the word "Copyright", or the abbreviation "Copr."; and

(2) the year of first publication of the work; in the case of compilations or derivative works incorporating previously published material, the year date of first publication of the compilation or derivative work is sufficient. The year date may be omitted where a pictorial, graphic, or sculptural work, with accompanying text matter, if any, is reproduced in or on greeting cards, postcards, stationery, jewelry, dolls, toys, or any useful articles; and

(3) the name of the owner of copyright in the work, or an abbreviation by which the name can be recognized, or a generally known alternative designation of the owner.

(c) Position of Notice.—The notice shall be affixed to the copies in such manner and location as to give reasonable notice of the claim of copyright. The Register of Copyrights shall prescribe by regulation, as examples, specific methods of affixation and positions of the notice on various types of works that will satisfy this requirement, but these specifications shall not be considered exhaustive.

(d) Evidentiary Weight of Notice.—If a notice of copyright in the form and position specified by this section appears on the published copy or copies to which a defendant in a copyright infringement suit had access, then no weight shall be given to such a defendant's interposition of a defense based on innocent infringement in mitigation of actual or statutory damages, except as provided in the last sentence of section 504(c)(2).

§402. Notice of Copyright: Phonorecords of Sound Recordings[2]

(a) General Provisions.—Whenever a sound recording protected under this title is published in the United States or elsewhere by authority of the copyright owner, a notice of copyright as provided by this section may be placed on publicly distributed phonorecords of the sound recording.

(b) Form of Notice.—If a notice appears on the phonorecords, it shall consist of the following three elements:

(1) the symbol ℗ (the letter P in a circle); and

(2) the year of first publication of the sound recording; and

(3) the name of the owner of copyright in the sound recording, or an abbreviation by which the name can be recognized, or a generally known alternative designation of the owner; if the producer of the sound recording is named on the phonorecord labels or containers, and if no other name appears in conjunction with the notice, the producer's name shall be considered a part of the notice.

(c) Position of Notice.—The notice shall be placed on the surface of the phonorecord, or on the phonorecord label or container, in such manner and location as to give reasonable notice of the claim of copyright.

(d) Evidentiary Weight of Notice.—If a notice of copyright in the form and position specified by this section appears on the published phonorecord or phonorecords to which a defendant in a copyright infringement suit had access, then no weight shall be given to such a defendant's interposition of a defense based on innocent infringement in mitigation of actual or statutory damages, except as provided in the last sentence of section 504(c)(2).

§403. Notice of Copyright: Publications Incorporating United States Government works[3]

Sections 401(d) and 402(d) shall not apply to a work published in copies or phonorecords consisting predominantly of one or more works of the United States Government unless the notice of copyright appearing on the published copies or phonorecords to which a defendant in the copyright infringement suit had access includes a statement identifying, either affirmatively or negatively, those portions of the copies or phonorecords embodying any work or works protected under this title.

§404. Notice of Copyright: Contributions to Collective Works[4]

(a) A separate contribution to a collective work may bear its own notice of copyright, as provided by sections 401 through 403. However, a single notice applicable to the collective work as a whole is sufficient to invoke the provisions of section 401(d) or 402(d), as applicable with respect to the separate contributions it contains (not including advertisements inserted on behalf of persons other than the owner of copyright in the collective work), regardless of the ownership of copyright in the contributions and whether or not they have been previously published.

(b) With respect to copies and phonorecords publicly distributed by authority of the copyright owner before the effective date of the Berne Convention Implementation Act of 1988, where the person named in a single notice applicable to a collective work as a whole is not the owner of copyright in a separate contribution that does not bear its own notice, the case is governed by the provisions of section 406(a).

§405. Notice of Copyright: Omission of Notice on Certain Copies and Phonorecords[5]

(a) Effect of Omission on Copyright.—With respect to copies and phonorecords publicly distributed by authority of the copyright owner before the effective date of the Berne Convention Implementation Act of 1988, the omission of the copyright notice described in sections 401 through 403 from copies or phonorecords publicly distributed by authority of the copyright owner does not invalidate the copyright in a work if—

(1) the notice has been omitted from no more than a relatively small number of copies or phonorecords distributed to the public; or

(2) registration for the work has been made before or is made within five years after the publication without notice, and a reasonable effort is made to add notice to all copies or phonorecords that are distributed to the public in the United States after the omission has been discovered; or

(3) the notice has been omitted in violation of an express requirement in writing that, as a condition of the copyright owner's authorization of the public distribution of copies or phonorecords, they bear the prescribed notice.

(b) Effect of Omission on Innocent Infringers.—Any person who innocently infringes a copyright, in reliance upon an authorized copy or phonorecord from which the copyright notice has been omitted and which was publicly distributed by authority of the copyright owner before the effective date of the Berne Convention Implementation Act of 1988, incurs no liability for actual or statutory damages under section 504 for any infringing acts committed before receiving actual notice that registration for the work has been made under section 408, if such person proves that he or she was misled by the omission of notice. In a suit for infringement in such a case the court may allow or disallow recovery of any of the infringer's profits attributable to the infringement, and may enjoin the continuation of the infringing undertaking or may require, as a condition for permitting the continuation of the infringing undertaking, that the infringer pay the copyright owner a reasonable license fee in an amount and on terms fixed by the court.

(c) Removal of Notice.—Protection under this title is not affected by the removal, destruction, or obliteration of the notice, without the authorization of the copyright owner, from any publicly distributed copies or phonorecords.

§406. Notice of Copyright: Error in Name or Date on Certain Copies and Phonorecords[6]

(a) Error in Name.—With respect to copies and phonorecords publicly distributed by authority of the copyright owner before the effective date of the Berne Convention Implementation Act of 1988, where the person named in the copyright notice on copies or phonorecords publicly distributed by authority of the copyright owner is not the owner of copyright, the validity and ownership of the copyright are not affected. In such a case, however, any person who innocently begins an undertaking that infringes the copyright has a complete defense to any action for such infringement if such person proves that he or she was misled by the notice and began the undertaking in good faith under a purported transfer or license from the person named therein, unless before the undertaking was begun—

(1) registration for the work had been made in the name of the owner of copyright; or

(2) a document executed by the person named in the notice and showing the ownership of the copyright had been recorded.

The person named in the notice is liable to account to the copyright owner for all receipts from transfers or licenses purportedly made under the copyright by the person named in the notice.

(b) Error in Date.—When the year date in the notice on copies or phonorecords distributed before the effective date of the Berne Convention Implementation Act of 1988 by authority of the copyright owner is earlier than the year in which publication first occurred, any period computed from the year of first publication under section 302 is to be computed from the year in the notice. Where the year date is more than one year later than the year in which publication first occurred, the work is considered to have been published without any notice and is governed by the provisions of section 405.

(c) Omission of Name or Date.—Where copies or phonorecords publicly distributed before the effective date of the Berne Convention Implementation Act of 1988 by authority of the copyright owner contain no name or no date that could reasonably be considered a part of the notice, the work is considered to have been published without any notice and is governed by the provisions of section 405 as in effect on the day before the effective date of the Berne Convention Implementation Act of 1988.

§407. Deposit of Copies or Phonorecords for Library of Congress[7]

(a) Except as provided by subsection (c), and subject to the provisions of subsection (e), the owner of copyright or of the exclusive right of publication in a work published in the United States shall deposit, within three months after the date of such publication-

(1) two complete copies of the best edition; or

(2) if the work is a sound recording, two complete phonorecords of the best edition, together with any printed or other visually perceptible material published with such phonorecords.

Neither the deposit requirements of this subsection nor the acquisition provisions of subsection (e) are conditions of copyright protection.

(b) The required copies or phonorecords shall be deposited in the Copyright Office for the use or disposition of the Library of Congress. The Register of Copyrights shall, when requested by the depositor and upon payment of the fee prescribed by section 708, issue a receipt for the deposit.

(c) The Register of Copyrights may by regulation exempt any categories of material from the deposit requirements of this section, or require deposit of only one copy or phonorecord with respect to any categories. Such regulations shall provide either for complete exemption from the deposit requirements of this section, or for alternative forms of deposit aimed at providing a satisfactory archival record of a work without imposing practical or financial hardships on the depositor, where the individual author is the owner of copyright in a pictorial, graphic, or sculptural work and (i) less than five copies of the work have been published, or (ii) the work has been published in a limited edition consisting of numbered copies, the monetary value of which would make the mandatory deposit of two copies of the best edition of the work burdensome, unfair, or unreasonable.

(d) At any time after publication of a work as provided by subsection(a), the Register of Copyrights may make written demand for the required deposit on any of the persons obligated to make the deposit under subsection (a). Unless deposit is made within three months after the demand is received, the person or persons on whom the demand was made are liable—

(1) to a fine of not more than $250 for each work; and

(2) to pay into a specially designated fund in the Library of Congress the total retail price of the copies or phonorecords demanded, or, if no retail price has been fixed, the reasonable cost to the Library of Congress of acquiring them; and

(3) to pay a fine of $2,500, in addition to any fine or liability imposed under clauses (1) and (2), if such person willfully or repeatedly fails or refuses to comply with such a demand.

(e) With respect to transmission programs that have been fixed and transmitted to the public in the United States but have not been published, the Register of Copyrights shall, after consulting with the Librarian of Congress and other interested organizations and officials, establish regulations governing the acquisition, through deposit or otherwise, of copies or phonorecords of such programs for the collections of the Library of Congress.

(1) The Librarian of Congress shall be permitted, under the standards and conditions set forth in such regulations, to make a fixation of a transmission program directly from a transmission to the public, and to reproduce one copy or phonorecord from such fixation for archival purposes.

(2) Such regulations shall also provide standards and procedures by which the Register of Copyrights may make written demand, upon the owner of the right of transmission in the United States, for the deposit of a copy or phonorecord of a specific transmission program. Such deposit may, at the option of the owner of the right of transmission in the United States, be accomplished by gift, by loan for purposes of reproduction, or by sale at a price not to exceed the cost of reproducing and supplying the copy or phonorecord. The regulations established under this clause shall provide reasonable periods of not less than three months for compliance with a demand, and shall allow for extensions of such periods and adjustments in the scope of the demand or the methods for fulfilling it, as reasonably warranted by the circumstances. Willful failure or refusal to comply with the conditions prescribed by such regulations shall subject the owner of the right of transmission in

the United States to liability for an amount, not to exceed the cost of reproducing and supplying the copy or phonorecord in question, to be paid into a specially designated fund in the Library of Congress.

(3) Nothing in this subsection shall be construed to require the making or retention, for purposes of deposit, of any copy or phonorecord of an unpublished transmission program, the transmission of which occurs before the receipt of a specific written demand as provided by clause (2).

(4) No activity undertaken in compliance with regulations prescribed under clauses (1) and (2) of this subsection shall result in liability if intended solely to assist in the acquisition of copies or phonorecords under this subsection.

§408. Copyright Registration in General[8]

(a) Registration Permissive.—At any time during the subsistence of the first term of copyright in any published or unpublished work in which the copyright was secured before January 1, 1978, and during the subsistence of any copyright secured on or after that date, the owner of copyright or of any exclusive right in the work may obtain registration of the copyright claim by delivering to the Copyright Office the deposit specified by this section, together with the application and fee specified by sections 409 and 708. Such registration is not a condition of copyright protection.

(b) Deposit for Copyright Registration.—Except as provided by subsection (c), the material deposited for registration shall include-

(1) in the case of an unpublished work, one complete copy or phonorecord;

(2) in the case of a published work, two complete copies or phonorecords of the best edition;

(3) in the case of a work first published outside the United States, one complete copy or phonorecord as so published;

(4) in the case of a contribution to a collective work, one complete copy or phonorecord of the best edition of the collective work.

Copies or phonorecords deposited for the Library of Congress under section 407 may be used to satisfy the deposit provisions of this section, if they are accompanied by the prescribed application and fee, and by any additional identifying material that the Register may, by regulation, require. The Register shall also prescribe regulations establishing requirements under which copies or phonorecords acquired for the Library of Congress under subsection (e) of section 407, otherwise than by deposit, may be used to satisfy the deposit provisions of this section.

(c) Administrative Classification and Optional Deposit.—

(1) The Register of Copyrights is authorized to specify by regulation the administrative classes into which works are to be placed for purposes of deposit and registration, and the nature of the copies or phonorecords to

be deposited in the various classes specified. The regulations may require or permit, for particular classes, the deposit of identifying material instead of copies or phonorecords, the deposit of only one copy or phonorecord where two would normally be required, or a single registration for a group of related works. This administrative classification of works has no significance with respect to the subject matter of copyright or the exclusive rights provided by this title.

(2) Without prejudice to the general authority provided under clause (1), the Register of Copyrights shall establish regulations specifically permitting a single registration for a group of works by the same individual author, all first published as contributions to periodicals, including newspapers, within a twelve-month period, on the basis of a single deposit, application, and registration fee, under the following conditions-

(A) if the deposit consists of one copy of the entire issue of the periodical, or of the entire section in the case of a newspaper, in which each contribution was first published; and

(B) if the application identifies each work separately, including the periodical containing it and its date of first publication.

(3) As an alternative to separate renewal registrations under subsection (a) of section 304, a single renewal registration may be made for a group of works by the same individual author, all first published as contributions to periodicals, including newspapers, upon the filing of a single application and fee, under all of the following conditions:

(A) the renewal claimant or claimants, and the basis of claim or claims under section 304(a), is the same for each of the works; and

(B) the works were all copyrighted upon their first publication, either through separate copyright notice and registration or by virtue of a general copyright notice in the periodical issue as a whole; and

(C) the renewal application and fee are received not more than twenty-eight or less than twenty-seven years after the thirty-first day of December of the calendar year in which all of the works were first published; and

(D) the renewal application identifies each work separately, including the periodical containing it and its date of first publication.

(d) Corrections and Amplifications.—The Register may also establish, by regulation, formal procedures for the filing of an application for supplementary registration, to correct an error in a copyright registration or to amplify the information given in a registration. Such application shall be accompanied by the fee provided by section 708, and shall clearly identify the registration to be corrected or amplified. The information contained in a supplementary registration augments but does not supersede that contained in the earlier registration.

(e) Published Edition of Previously Registered Work.—Registration for the first published edition of a work previously registered in unpublished form may be made even though the work as published is substantially the same as the unpublished version.

§409. Application for Copyright Registration[9]

The application for copyright registration shall be made on a form prescribed by the Register of Copyrights and shall include-

(1) the name and address of the copyright claimant;

(2) in the case of a work other than an anonymous or pseudonymous work, the name and nationality or domicile of the author or authors, and, if one or more of the authors is dead, the dates of their deaths;

(3) if the work is anonymous or pseudonymous, the nationality or domicile of the author or authors;

(4) in the case of a work made for hire, a statement to this effect;

(5) if the copyright claimant is not the author, a brief statement of how the claimant obtained ownership of the copyright;

(6) the title of the work, together with any previous or alternative titles under which the work can be identified;

(7) the year in which creation of the work was completed;

(8) if the work has been published, the date and nation of its first publication;

(9) in the case of a compilation or derivative work, an identification of any preexisting work or works that it is based on or incorporates, and a brief, general statement of the additional material covered by the copyright claim being registered;

(10) in the case of a published work containing material of which copies are required by section 601 to be manufactured in the United States, the names of the persons or organizations who performed the processes specified by subsection (c) of section 601 with respect to that material, and the places where those processes were performed; and

(11) any other information regarded by the Register of Copyrights as bearing upon the preparation or identification of the work or the existence, ownership, or duration of the copyright.

If an application is submitted for the renewed and extended term provided for in section 304(a)(3)(A) and an original term registration has not been made, the Register may request information with respect to the existence, ownership, or duration of the copyright for the original term.

. . .

ENDNOTES

1–7. *Editor's Note:* Endnotes 1 through 7 list changes made in Sections 401, 402, 403, 404, 405, 406, and 407 as a result of the Berne Convention Implementation Act of 1988. For a complete citation, see the Copyright Act.

8. *Editor's Note:* Endnote 8 lists changes made in Section 408 as a result of The Berne Convention Implementation Act of 1988 and the Copyright Renewal Act of 1992. For a complete citation, see the Copyright Act.

9. The Copyright Renewal Act of 1992 amended section 409 by adding the last sentence. Pub. L. No. 102-307, 106 Stat. 264, 266.

CHAPTER 5: COPYRIGHT INFRINGEMENT AND REMEDIES[1,2]

§501. Infringement of Copyright[3]

(a) Anyone who violates any of the exclusive rights of the copyright owner as provided by sections 106 through 121 or of the author as provided in section 106A(a), or who imports copies or phonorecords into the United States in violation of section 602, is an infringer of the copyright or right of the author, as the case may be. For purposes of this chapter (other than section 506), any reference to copyright shall be deemed to include the rights conferred by section 106A(a). As used in this subsection, the term "anyone" includes any State, any instrumentality of a State, and any officer or employee of a State or instrumentality of a State acting in his or her official capacity. Any State, and any such instrumentality, officer, or employee, shall be subject to the provisions of this title in the same manner and to the same extent as any nongovernmental entity.

(b) The legal or beneficial owner of an exclusive right under a copyright is entitled, subject to the requirements of section 411, to institute an action for any infringement of that particular right committed while he or she is the owner of it. The court may require such owner to serve written notice of the action with a copy of the complaint upon any person shown, by the records of the Copyright Office or otherwise, to have or claim an interest in the copyright, and shall require that such notice be served upon any person whose interest is likely to be affected by a decision in the case. The court may require the joinder, and shall permit the intervention, of any person having or claiming an interest in the copyright.

(c) For any secondary transmission by a cable system that embodies a performance or a display of a work which is actionable as an act of infringement under subsection (c) of section 111, a television broadcast station holding a copyright or other license to transmit or perform the same version of that work shall, for purposes of subsection (b) of this section, be treated as a legal or beneficial owner if such secondary transmission occurs within the local service area of that television station.

(d) For any secondary transmission by a cable system that is actionable as an act of infringement pursuant to section 111(c)(3), the following shall also have standing to sue: (i) the primary transmitter whose transmission has been altered by the cable system; and (ii) any broadcast station within whose local service area the secondary transmission occurs.

(e) With respect to any secondary transmission that is made by a satellite carrier of a performance or display of a work embodied in a primary transmission and is actionable as an act of infringement under section 119(a)(5), a network station holding a copyright or other license to transmit or perform the same version of that work shall, for purposes of subsection (b) of this section, be treated as a legal or beneficial owner if such secondary transmission occurs within the local service area of that station.

(f)(1) With respect to any secondary transmission that is made by a satellite carrier of a performance or display of a work embodied in a primary transmission and is actionable as an act of infringement under section 122, a television broadcast station holding a copyright or other license to transmit or perform the same version of that work shall, for purposes of subsection (b) of this section, be treated as a legal or beneficial owner if such secondary transmission occurs within the local market of that station.

(2) A television broadcast station may file a civil action against any satellite carrier that has refused to carry television broadcast signals, as required under section 122(a)(2), to enforce that television broadcast station's rights under section 338(a) of the Communications Act of 1934.

§502. Remedies for Infringement: Injunctions

(a) Any court having jurisdiction of a civil action arising under this title may, subject to the provisions of section 1498 of title 28, grant temporary and final injunctions on such terms as it may deem reasonable to prevent or restrain infringement of a copyright.

(b) Any such injunction may be served anywhere in the United States on the person enjoined; it shall be operative throughout the United States and shall be enforceable, by proceedings in contempt or otherwise, by any United States court having jurisdiction of that person. The clerk of the court granting the injunction shall, when requested by any other court in which enforcement of the injunction is sought, transmit promptly to the other court a certified copy of all the papers in the case on file in such clerk's office.

§503. Remedies for Infringement: Impounding and Disposition of Infringing Articles

(a) At any time while an action under this title is pending, the court may order the impounding, on such terms as it may deem reasonable, of all copies or phonorecords claimed to have been made or used in violation of the copyright owner's exclusive rights, and of all plates, molds, matrices, masters, tapes, film negatives, or other articles by means of which such copies or phonorecords may be reproduced.

(b) As part of a final judgment or decree, the court may order the destruction or other reasonable disposition of all copies or phonorecords found to have been made or used in violation of the copyright owner's exclusive rights, and of all plates, molds, matrices, masters, tapes, film negatives, or other articles by means of which such copies or phonorecords may be reproduced.

§504. Remedies for Infringement: Damages and Profits[4]

(a) In General.—Except as otherwise provided by this title, an infringer of copyright is liable for either—

(1) the copyright owner's actual damages and any additional profits of the infringer, as provided by subsection (b); or

(2) statutory damages, as provided by subsection (c).

(b) Actual Damages and Profits.—The copyright owner is entitled to recover the actual damages suffered by him or her as a result of the infringement, and any profits of the infringer that are attributable to the infringement and are not taken into account in computing the actual damages. In establishing the infringer's profits, the copyright owner is required to present proof only of the infringer's gross revenue, and the infringer is required to prove his or her deductible expenses and the elements of profit attributable to factors other than the copyrighted work.

(c) Statutory Damages.—

(1) Except as provided by clause (2) of this subsection, the copyright owner may elect, at any time before final judgment is rendered, to recover, instead of actual damages and profits, an award of statutory damages for all infringements involved in the action, with respect to any one work, for which any one infringer is liable individually, or for which any two or more infringers are liable jointly and severally, in a sum of not less than $750 or more than $30,000 as the court considers just. For the purposes of this subsection, all the parts of a compilation or derivative work constitute one work.

(2) In a case where the copyright owner sustains the burden of proving, and the court finds, that infringement was committed willfully, the court in its discretion may increase the award of statutory damages to a sum of not more than $150,000. In a case where the infringer sustains the burden of proving, and the court finds, that such infringer was not aware and had no reason to believe that his or her acts constituted an infringement of copyright, the court in its discretion may reduce the award of statutory damages to a sum of not less than $200. The court shall remit statutory damages in any case where an infringer believed and had reasonable grounds for believing that his or her use of the copyrighted work was a fair use under section 107, if the infringer was: (i) an employee or agent of a nonprofit educational institution, library, or archives acting within the scope of his or her employment who, or such institution, library, or archives itself, which infringed by reproducing the work in copies or phonorecords; or (ii) a public broadcasting entity which or a person who, as a regular part of the nonprofit activities of a public broadcasting entity (as defined in subsection (g) of section 118) infringed by performing a published nondramatic literary work or by reproducing a transmission program embodying a performance of such a work.

(d) Additional Damages in Certain Cases.—In any case in which the court finds that a defendant proprietor of an establishment who claims as a defense that its activities were exempt under section 110(5) did not have reasonable grounds to believe that its use of a copyrighted work was exempt under such section, the plaintiff shall be entitled to, in addition to any award of damages under this section, an additional award of two times the amount of the license fee that the proprietor of the establishment concerned should have paid the plaintiff for such use during the preceding period of up to 3 years.

§505. Remedies for Infringement: Costs and Attorney's Fees

In any civil action under this title, the court in its discretion may allow the recovery of full costs by or against any party other than the United States or an officer thereof. Except as otherwise provided by this title, the court may also award a reasonable attorney's fee to the prevailing party as part of the costs.

§506. Criminal Offenses[5]

(a) Criminal Infringement.—Any person who infringes a copyright willfully either—

> (1) for purposes of commercial advantage or private financial gain, or
> (2) by the reproduction or distribution, including by electronic means, during any 180-day period, of 1 or more copies or phonorecords of 1 or more copyrighted works, which have a total retail value of more than $1,000,

shall be punished as provided under section 2319 of title 18, United States Code. For purposes of this subsection, evidence of reproduction or distribution of a copyrighted work, by itself, shall not be sufficient to establish willful infringement.

(b) Forfeiture and Destruction.—When any person is convicted of any violation of subsection (a), the court in its judgment of conviction shall, in addition to the penalty therein prescribed, order the forfeiture and destruction or other disposition of all infringing copies or phonorecords and all implements, devices, or equipment used in the manufacture of such infringing copies or phonorecords.

(c) Fraudulent Copyright Notice.—Any person who, with fraudulent intent, places on any article a notice of copyright or words of the same purport that such person knows to be false, or who, with fraudulent intent, publicly distributes or imports for public distribution any article bearing such notice or words that such person knows to be false, shall be fined not more than $2,500.

(d) Fraudulent Removal of Copyright Notice.—Any person who, with fraudulent intent, removes or alters any notice of copyright appearing on a copy of a copyrighted work shall be fined not more than $2,500.

(e) False Representation.—Any person who knowingly makes a false representation of a material fact in the application for copyright registration provided for by section 409, or in any written statement filed in connection with the application, shall be fined not more than $2,500.

(f) Rights of Attribution and Integrity.-Nothing in this section applies to infringement of the rights conferred by section 106A(a).

§507. Limitations on Actions[6]

(a) Criminal Proceedings.—Except as expressly provided otherwise in this title, no criminal proceeding shall be maintained under the provisions of this title unless it is commenced within 5 years after the cause of action arose.

(b) Civil Actions.—No civil action shall be maintained under the provisions of this title unless it is commenced within three years after the claim accrued.
. . .

§512. Limitations on Liability Relating to Material Online[9]

(a) Transitory Digital Network Communications.—A service provider shall not be liable for monetary relief, or, except as provided in subsection (j), for injunctive or other equitable relief, for infringement of copyright by reason of the provider's transmitting, routing, or providing connections for, material through a system or network controlled or operated by or for the service provider, or by reason of the intermediate and transient storage of that material in the course of such transmitting, routing, or providing connections, if—

> (1) the transmission of the material was initiated by or at the direction of a person other than the service provider;
>
> (2) the transmission, routing, provision of connections, or storage is carried out through an automatic technical process without selection of the material by the service provider;
>
> (3) the service provider does not select the recipients of the material except as an automatic response to the request of another person;
>
> (4) no copy of the material made by the service provider in the course of such intermediate or transient storage is maintained on the system or network in a manner ordinarily accessible to anyone other than anticipated recipients, and no such copy is maintained on the system or network in a manner ordinarily accessible to such anticipated recipients for a longer period than is reasonably necessary for the transmission, routing, or provision of connections; and
>
> (5) the material is transmitted through the system or network without modification of its content.

(b) System Caching.—

> (1) Limitation on Liability.—A service provider shall not be liable for monetary relief, or, except as provided in subsection (j), for injunctive or other equitable relief, for infringement of copyright by reason of the intermediate and temporary storage of material on a system or network controlled or operated by or for the service provider in a case in which—

(A) the material is made available online by a person other than the service provider;

(B) the material is transmitted from the person described in subparagraph (A) through the system or network to a person other than the person described in subparagraph (A) at the direction of that other person; and

(C) the storage is carried out through an automatic technical process for the purpose of making the material available to users of the system or network who, after the material is transmitted as described in subparagraph (B), request access to the material from the person described in subparagraph (A), if the conditions set forth in paragraph (2) are met.

(2) Conditions.—The conditions referred to in paragraph (1) are that—

(A) the material described in paragraph (1) is transmitted to the subsequent users described in paragraph (1)(C) without modification to its content from the manner in which the material was transmitted from the person described in paragraph (1)(A);

(B) the service provider described in paragraph (1) complies with rules concerning the refreshing, reloading, or other updating of the material when specified by the person making the material available online in accordance with a generally accepted industry standard data communications protocol for the system or network through which that person makes the material available, except that this subparagraph applies only if those rules are not used by the person described in paragraph (1)(A) to prevent or unreasonably impair the intermediate storage to which this subsection applies;

(C) the service provider does not interfere with the ability of technology associated with the material to return to the person described in paragraph (1)(A) the information that would have been available to that person if the material had been obtained by the subsequent users described in paragraph (1)(C) directly from that person, except that this subparagraph applies only if that technology—

(i) does not significantly interfere with the performance of the provider's system or network or with the intermediate storage of the material;

(ii) is consistent with generally accepted industry standard communications protocols; and

(iii) does not extract information from the provider's system or network other than the information that would have been available to the person described in paragraph (1)(A) if the subsequent users had gained access to the material directly from that person;

(D) if the person described in paragraph (1)(A) has in effect a condition that a person must meet prior to having access to the material, such as a condition based on payment of a fee or provision of a password or other information, the service provider permits access to the stored material in significant part only to users of its system or network that have met those conditions and only in accordance with those conditions; and

(E) if the person described in paragraph (1)(A) makes that material available online without the authorization of the copyright owner of the material, the service provider responds expeditiously to remove, or disable access to, the material that is claimed to be infringing upon notification of claimed infringement as described in subsection (c)(3), except that this subparagraph applies only if—

(i) the material has previously been removed from the originating site or access to it has been disabled, or a court has ordered that the material be removed from the originating site or that access to the material on the originating site be disabled; and

(ii) the party giving the notification includes in the notification a statement confirming that the material has been removed from the originating site or access to it has been disabled or that a court has ordered that the material be removed from the originating site or that access to the material on the originating site be disabled.

(c) Information Residing on Systems or Networks at Direction of Users.-

(1) In General.—A service provider shall not be liable for monetary relief, or, except as provided in subsection (j), for injunctive or other equitable relief, for infringement of copyright by reason of the storage at the direction of a user of material that resides on a system or network controlled or operated by or for the service provider, if the service provider—

(A)(i) does not have actual knowledge that the material or an activity using the material on the system or network is infringing;

(ii) in the absence of such actual knowledge, is not aware of facts or circumstances from which infringing activity is apparent; or

(iii) upon obtaining such knowledge or awareness, acts expeditiously to remove, or disable access to, the material;

(B) does not receive a financial benefit directly attributable to the infringing activity, in a case in which the service provider has the right and ability to control such activity; and

(C) upon notification of claimed infringement as described in paragraph (3), responds expeditiously to remove, or disable access to, the material that is claimed to be infringing or to be the subject of infringing activity.

(2) Designated Agent.—The limitations on liability established in this subsection apply to a service provider only if the service provider has designated an agent to receive notifications of claimed infringement described in paragraph (3), by making available through its service, including on its website in a location accessible to the public,

and by providing to the Copyright Office, substantially the following information:

    (A) the name, address, phone number, and electronic mail address of the agent.

    (B) other contact information which the Register of Copyrights may deem appropriate.

The Register of Copyrights shall maintain a current directory of agents available to the public for inspection, including through the Internet, in both electronic and hard copy formats, and may require payment of a fee by service providers to cover the costs of maintaining the directory.

    (3) Elements of Notification.—

    (A) To be effective under this subsection, a notification of claimed infringement must be a written communication provided to the designated agent of a service provider that includes substantially the following:

        (i) A physical or electronic signature of a person authorized to act on behalf of the owner of an exclusive right that is allegedly infringed.

        (ii) Identification of the copyrighted work claimed to have been infringed, or, if multiple copyrighted works at a single online site are covered by a single notification, a representative list of such works at that site.

        (iii) Identification of the material that is claimed to be infringing or to be the subject of infringing activity and that is to be removed or access to which is to be disabled, and information reasonably sufficient to permit the service provider to locate the material.

        (iv) Information reasonably sufficient to permit the service provider to contact the complaining party, such as an address, telephone number, and, if available, an electronic mail address at which the complaining party may be contacted.

        (v) A statement that the complaining party has a good faith belief that use of the material in the manner complained of is not authorized by the copyright owner, its agent, or the law.

        (vi) A statement that the information in the notification is accurate, and under penalty of perjury, that the complaining party is authorized to act on behalf of the owner of an exclusive right that is allegedly infringed.

    (B)(i) Subject to clause (ii), a notification from a copyright owner or from a person authorized to act on behalf of the copyright owner that fails to comply substantially with the provisions of subparagraph (A) shall not be considered under paragraph (1)(A) in determining whether a service provider has actual knowledge or is aware of facts or circumstances from which infringing activity is apparent.

(ii) In a case in which the notification that is provided to the service provider's designated agent fails to comply substantially with all the provisions of subparagraph (A) but substantially complies with clauses (ii), (iii), and (iv) of subparagraph (A), clause (i) of this subparagraph applies only if the service provider promptly attempts to contact the person making the notification or takes other reasonable steps to assist in the receipt of notification that substantially complies with all the provisions of subparagraph (A).

(d) Information Location Tools.—A service provider shall not be liable for monetary relief, or, except as provided in subsection (j), for injunctive or other equitable relief, for infringement of copyright by reason of the provider referring or linking users to an online location containing infringing material or infringing activity, by using information location tools, including a directory, index, reference, pointer, or hypertext link, if the service provider—

(1)(A) does not have actual knowledge that the material or activity is infringing;

(B) in the absence of such actual knowledge, is not aware of facts or circumstances from which infringing activity is apparent; or

(C) upon obtaining such knowledge or awareness, acts expeditiously to remove, or disable access to, the material;

(2) does not receive a financial benefit directly attributable to the infringing activity, in a case in which the service provider has the right and ability to control such activity; and

(3) upon notification of claimed infringement as described in subsection (c)(3), responds expeditiously to remove, or disable access to, the material that is claimed to be infringing or to be the subject of infringing activity, except that, for purposes of this paragraph, the information described in subsection (c)(3)(A)(iii) shall be identification of the reference or link, to material or activity claimed to be infringing, that is to be removed or access to which is to be disabled, and information reasonably sufficient to permit the service provider to locate that reference or link.

(e) Limitation on Liability of Nonprofit Educational Institutions.—

(1) When a public or other nonprofit institution of higher education is a service provider, and when a faculty member or graduate student who is an employee of such institution is performing a teaching or research function, for the purposes of subsections (a) and (b) such faculty member or graduate student shall be considered to be a person other than the institution, and for the purposes of subsections (c) and (d) such faculty member's or graduate student's knowledge or awareness of his or her infringing activities shall not be attributed to the nstitution, if—

(A) such faculty member's or graduate student's infringing activities do not involve the provision of online access to instructional materials that are or were required or recommended, within the preceding 3-year period, for a course taught at the institution by such faculty member or graduate student;

(B) the institution has not, within the preceding 3-year period, received more than 2 notifications described in subsection (c)(3) of claimed infringement by such faculty member or graduate student, and such notifications of claimed infringement were not actionable under subsection (f); and

(C) the institution provides to all users of its system or network informational materials that accurately describe, and promote compliance with, the laws of the United States relating to copyright.

(2) For the purposes of this subsection, the limitations on injunctive relief contained in subsections (j)(2) and (j)(3), but not those in (j)(1), shall apply.

(f) Misrepresentations.—Any person who knowingly materially misrepresents under this section—

(1) that material or activity is infringing, or

(2) that material or activity was removed or disabled by mistake or misidentification,

shall be liable for any damages, including costs and attorneys' fees, incurred by the alleged infringer, by any copyright owner or copyright owner's authorized licensee, or by a service provider, who is injured by such misrepresentation, as the result of the service provider relying upon such misrepresentation in removing or disabling access to the material or activity claimed to be infringing, or in replacing the removed material or ceasing to disable access to it.

(g) Replacement of Removed or Disabled Material and Limitation on Other Liability.—

(1) No Liability for Taking Down Generally.—subject to paragraph (2), a service provider shall not be liable to any person for any claim based on the service provider's good faith disabling of access to, or removal of, material or activity claimed to be infringing or based on facts or circumstances from which infringing activity is apparent, regardless of whether the material or activity is ultimately determined to be infringing.

(2) Exception.—Paragraph (1) shall not apply with respect to material residing at the direction of a subscriber of the service provider on a system or network controlled or operated by or for the service provider that is removed, or to which access is disabled by the service provider, pursuant to a notice provided under subsection (c)(1)(C), unless the service provider—

(A) takes reasonable steps promptly to notify the subscriber that it has removed or disabled access to the material;

(B) upon receipt of a counter notification described in paragraph (3), promptly provides the person who provided the notification under subsection (c)(1)(C) with a copy of the counter notification, and informs that person that it will re-place the removed material or cease disabling access to it in 10 business days; and

(C) replaces the removed material and ceases disabling access to it not less than 10, nor more than 14, business days following receipt of the counter notice, unless its designated agent first receives notice from the person who submitted the notification under subsection (c)(1)(C) that such person has filed an action seeking a court order to restrain the subscriber from engaging in infringing activity relating to the material on the service provider's system or network.

(3) Contents of Counter Notification.—To be effective under this subsection, a counter notification must be a written communication provided to the service provider's designated agent that includes substantially the following:

(A) A physical or electronic signature of the subscriber.

(B) Identification of the material that has been removed or to which access has been disabled and the location at which the material appeared before it was removed or access to it was disabled.

(C) A statement under penalty of perjury that the subscriber has a good faith belief that the material was removed or disabled as a result of mistake or misidentification of the material to be removed or disabled.

(D) The subscriber's name, address, and telephone number, and a statement that the subscriber consents to the jurisdiction of Federal District Court for the judicial district in which the address is located, or if the subscriber's address is outside of the United States, for any judicial district in which the service provider may be found, and that the subscriber will accept service of process from the person who provided notification under subsection (c)(1)(C) or an agent of such person.

(4) Limitation on Other Liability.—A service provider's compliance with paragraph (2) shall not subject the service provider to liability for copyright infringement with respect to the material identified in the notice provided under subsection (c)(1)(C).

. . .

(i) Conditions for Eligibility.—

(1) Accommodation of Technology.—The limitations on liability established by this section shall apply to a service provider only if the service provider—

(A) has adopted and reasonably implemented, and informs subscribers and account holders of the service provider's system or network of, a policy that provides for the termination in appropriate circumstances of subscribers and account holders of the service provider's system or network who are repeat infringers; and

(B) accommodates and does not interfere with standard technical measures.

(2) Definition.—As used in this subsection, the term "standard technical measures" means technical measures that are used by copyright owners to identify or protect copyrighted works and—

(A) have been developed pursuant to a broad consensus of copyright owners and service providers in an open, fair, voluntary, multi-industry standards process;

(B) are available to any person on reasonable and nondiscriminatory terms; and

(C) do not impose substantial costs on service providers or substantial burdens on their systems or networks.

(j) Injunctions.—The following rules shall apply in the case of any application for an injunction under section 502 against a service provider that is not subject to monetary remedies under this section:

(1) Scope of Relief.—

(A) With respect to conduct other than that which qualifies for the limitation on remedies set forth in subsection (a), the court may grant injunctive relief with respect to a service provider only in one or more of the following forms:

(i) An order restraining the service provider from providing access to infringing material or activity residing at a particular online site on the provider's system or network.

(ii) An order restraining the service provider from providing access to a subscriber or account holder of the service provider's system or network who is engaging in infringing activity and s identified in the order, by terminating the accounts of the subscriber or account holder that are specified in the order.

(iii) Such other injunctive relief as the court may consider necessary to prevent or restrain infringement of copyrighted material specified in the order of the court at a particular online location, if such relief is the least burdensome to the service provider among the forms of relief comparably effective for that purpose.

(B) If the service provider qualifies for the limitation on remedies described in subsection (a), the court may only grant injunctive relief in one or both of the following forms:

(i) An order restraining the service provider from providing access to a subscriber or account holder of the service provider's system or network who is using the provider's service to engage in infringing activity and is identified in the order, by terminating the accounts of the subscriber or account holder that are specified in the order.

(ii) An order restraining the service provider from providing access, by taking reasonable steps specified in the order to block access, to a specific, identified, online location outside the United States.

(2) Considerations.—The court, in considering the relevant criteria for injunctive relief under applicable law, shall consider-

(A) whether such an injunction, either alone or in combination with other such injunctions issued against the same service provider under this subsection, would significantly burden either the provider or the operation of the provider's system or network;

(B) the magnitude of the harm likely to be suffered by the copyright owner in the digital network environment if steps are not taken to prevent or restrain the infringement;

(C) whether implementation of such an injunction would be technically feasible and effective, and would not interfere with access to noninfringing material at other online locations; and

(D) whether other less burdensome and comparably effective means of preventing or restraining access to the infringing material are available.

(3) Notice and Ex Parte Orders.—Injunctive relief under this subsection shall be available only after notice to the service provider and an opportunity for the service provider to appear are provided, except for orders ensuring the preservation of evidence or other orders having no material adverse effect on the operation of the service provider's communications network.

(k) Definitions.—

(1) Service Provider.—

(A) As used in subsection (a), the term "service provider" means an entity offering the transmission, routing, or providing of connections for digital online communications, between or among points specified by a user, of material of the user's choosing, without modification to the content of the material as sent or received.

(B) As used in this section, other than subsection (a), the term "service provider" means a provider of online services or network access, or the operator of facilities therefor, and includes an entity described in subparagraph (A).

(2) Monetary Relief.—As used in this section, the term "monetary relief" means damages, costs, attorneys' fees, and any other form of monetary payment.

(l) Other Defenses Not Affected.—The failure of a service provider's conduct to qualify for limitation of liability under this section shall not bear adversely upon the consideration of a defense by the service provider that the service provider's conduct is not infringing under this title or any other defense.

(m) Protection of Privacy.—Nothing in this section shall be construed to condition the applicability of subsections (a) through (d) on—

(1) a service provider monitoring its service or affirmatively seeking facts indicating infringing activity, except to the extent consistent with

a standard technical measure complying with the provisions of subsection (i); or

(2) a service provider gaining access to, removing, or disabling access to material in cases in which such conduct is prohibited by law.

(n) Construction.-Subsections (a), (b), (c), and (d) describe separate and distinct functions for purposes of applying this section. Whether a service provider qualifies for the limitation on liability in any one of those subsections shall be based solely on the criteria in that subsection, and shall not affect a determination of whether that service provider qualifies for the limitations on liability under any other such subsection.

§513. Determination of Reasonable License Fees for Individual Proprietors[10]

In the case of any performing rights society subject to a consent decree which provides for the determination of reasonable license rates or fees to be charged by the performing rights society, notwithstanding the provisions of that consent decree, an individual proprietor who owns or operates fewer than 7 non-publicly traded establishments in which nondramatic musical works are performed publicly and who claims that any license agreement offered by that performing rights society is unreasonable in its license rate or fee as to that individual proprietor, shall be entitled to determination of a reasonable license rate or fee as follows:

(1) The individual proprietor may commence such proceeding for determination of a reasonable license rate or fee by filing an application in the applicable district court under paragraph (2) that a rate disagreement exists and by serving a copy of the application on the performing rights society. Such proceeding shall commence in the applicable district court within 90 days after the service of such copy, except that such 90-day requirement shall be subject to the administrative requirements of the court.

(2) The proceeding under paragraph (1) shall be held, at the individual proprietor's election, in the judicial district of the district court with jurisdiction over the applicable consent decree or in that place of holding court of a district court that is the seat of the Federal circuit (other than the Court of Appeals for the Federal Circuit) in which the proprietor's establishment is located.

(3) Such proceeding shall be held before the judge of the court with jurisdiction over the consent decree governing the performing rights society. At the discretion of the court, the proceeding shall be held before a special master or magistrate judge appointed by such judge. Should that consent decree provide for the appointment of an advisor or advisors to the court for any purpose, any such advisor shall be the special master so named by the court.

(4) In any such proceeding, the industry rate shall be presumed to have been reasonable at the time it was agreed to or determined by the court. Such

presumption shall in no way affect a determination of whether the rate is being correctly applied to the individual proprietor.

(5) Pending the completion of such proceeding, the individual proprietor shall have the right to perform publicly the copyrighted musical compositions in the repertoire of the performing rights society by paying an interim license rate or fee into an interest bearing escrow account with the clerk of the court, subject to retroactive adjustment when a final rate or fee has been determined, in an amount equal to the industry rate, or, in the absence of an industry rate, the amount of the most recent license rate or fee agreed to by the parties.

(6) Any decision rendered in such proceeding by a special master or magistrate judge named under paragraph (3) shall be reviewed by the judge of the court with jurisdiction over the consent decree governing the performing rights society. Such proceeding, including such review, shall be concluded within 6 months after its commencement.

(7) Any such final determination shall be binding only as to the individual proprietor commencing the proceeding, and shall not be applicable to any other proprietor or any other performing rights society, and the performing rights society shall be relieved of any obligation of nondiscrimination among similarly situated music users that may be imposed by the consent decree governing its operations.

(8) An individual proprietor may not bring more than one proceeding provided for in this section for the determination of a reasonable license rate or fee under any license agreement with respect to any one performing rights society.

(9) For purposes of this section, the term "industry rate" means the license fee a performing rights society has agreed to with, or which has been determined by the court for, a significant segment of the music user industry to which the individual proprietor belongs.

ENDNOTES

1. Concerning the liability of the United States Government for copyright infringement, see 28 U.S.C. 1498. Title 28 of the United States Code is entitled "Judiciary and Judicial Procedure."

2. In 1998, two sections 512 were enacted into law. On October 17, 1998, the Fairness in Music Licensing Act of 1998 was enacted. This Act amended Chapter 5 to add section 512, entitled "Determination of reasonable license fees for individual proprietors," Pub. L. No. 105-298, 112 Stat. 2827, 2831. On October 28, 1998, the Online Copyright Infringement Liability Limitation Act was enacted. This Act amended Chapter 5 to add section 512, entitled "Limitations on liability relating to material online," Pub. L. No. 105-304, 112 Stat. 2860, 2877. In 1999, a technical correction was enacted to redesignate the section 512 that was entitled "Determination of reasonable license fees for individual proprietors" as section 513. . . .

3. *Editor's note:* Endnote 3 lists the changes made to Section 501 as a result of the Berne Convention Implementation Act of 1988, the Satellite Home Viewer Act of 1988, the

Satellite Home Viewer Improvement Act of 1999, the Copyright Remedy Clarification Act of 1990, and the Visual Artists Rights Act of 1990. For the complete citation, see the Copyright Act.

4. *Editor's note:* Endnote 4 lists the changes made to Section 504 as a result of the Berne Convention Implementation Act of 1988 and the Digital Theft Deterrence and Copyright Damages Improvement Act of 1999. For the complete citation, see the Copyright Act.

5. *Editor's note:* Endnote 5 lists the changes made to Section 506 as a result of the Piracy and Counterfeiting Amendments Act of 1982, the Visual Artists Rights Act of 1990, and the No Electronic Theft (NET) Act of 1997. The latter also directed the United States Sentencing Commission to "ensure that the applicable guideline range for a defendant convicted of a crime against intellectual property . . . is sufficiently stringent to deter such a crime" and to "ensure that the guidelines provide for consideration of the retail value and quantity of the items with respect to which the crime against intellectual property was committed.". . .

6. In 1997, the No Electronic Theft (NET) Act amended section 507(a) by inserting "5" in lieu of "three." Pub. L. No. 105-147, 111 Stat. 2678.

9,10. See Endnote 2.

CHAPTER 10: SUBCHAPTER A—DEFINITIONS[1]

§1001. Definitions

As used in this chapter, the following terms have the following meanings:

(1) A "digital audio copied recording" is a reproduction in a digital recording format of a digital musical recording, whether that reproduction is made directly from another digital musical recording or indirectly from a transmission.

(2) A "digital audio interface device" is any machine or device that is designed specifically to communicate digital audio information and related interface data to a digital audio recording device through a nonprofessional interface.

(3) A "digital audio recording device" is any machine or device of a type commonly distributed to individuals for use by individuals, whether or not included with or as part of some other machine or device, the digital recording function of which is designed or marketed for the primary purpose of, and that is capable of, making a digital audio copied recording for private use, except for-

(A) professional model products, and

(B) dictation machines, answering machines, and other audio recording equipment that is designed and marketed primarily for the creation of sound recordings resulting from the fixation of nonmusical sounds.

(4)[Digital Audio Recording Medium]—

(A) A "digital audio recording medium" is any material object in a form commonly distributed for use by individuals, that is primarily marketed or most commonly used by consumers for the purpose of making digital audio copied recordings by use of a digital audio recording device.

(B) Such term does not include any material object-

(i) that embodies a sound recording at the time it is first distributed by the importer or manufacturer; or

(ii) that is primarily marketed and most commonly used by consumers either for the purpose of making copies of motion pictures or other audiovisual works or for the purpose of making copies of nonmusical literary works, including computer programs or data bases.

(5) [Digital Musical Recording]—

(A) A "digital musical recording" is a material object—

(i) in which are fixed, in a digital recording format, only sounds, and material, statements, or instructions incidental to those fixed sounds, if any, and

(ii) from which the sounds and material can be perceived, reproduced, or otherwise communicated, either directly or with the aid of a machine or device.

(B) A "digital musical recording" does not include a material object-

(i) in which the fixed sounds consist entirely of spoken word recordings, or

(ii) in which one or more computer programs are fixed, except that a digital musical recording may contain statements or instructions constituting the fixed sounds and incidental material, and statements or instructions to be used directly or indirectly in order to bring about the perception, reproduction, or communication of the fixed sounds and incidental material.

(C) For purposes of this paragraph—

(i) a "spoken word recording" is a sound recording in which are fixed only a series of spoken words, except that the spoken words may be accompanied by incidental musical or other sounds, and

(ii) the term "incidental" means related to and relatively minor by comparison.

(6) "Distribute" means to sell, lease, or assign a product to consumers in the United States, or to sell, lease, or assign a product in the United States or ultimate transfer to consumers in the United States.

(7) An "interested copyright party" is—

(A) the owner of the exclusive right under section 106(1) of this title to reproduce a sound recording of a musical work that has been embodied in a digital musical recording or analog musical recording lawfully made under this title that has been distributed;

(B) the legal or beneficial owner of, or the person that controls, the right to reproduce in a digital musical recording or analog musical recording a musical work that has been embodied in a digital musical recording or analog musical recording lawfully made under this title that has been distributed;

(C) a featured recording artist who performs on a sound recording that has been distributed; or

(D) any association or other organization-

(i) representing persons specified in subparagraph (A), (B), or (C), or

(ii) engaged in licensing rights in musical works to music users on behalf of writers and publishers.

(8) To "manufacture" means to produce or assemble a product in the United States. A "manufacturer" is a person who manufactures.

(9) A "music publisher" is a person that is authorized to license the reproduction of a particular musical work in a sound recording.

(10) A "professional model product" is an audio recording device that is designed, manufactured, marketed, and intended for use by recording professionals in the ordinary course of a lawful business, in accordance with such requirements as the Secretary of Commerce shall establish by regulation.

(11) The term "serial copying" means the duplication in a digital format of a copyrighted musical work or sound recording from a digital reproduction of a digital musical recording. The term "digital reproduction of a digital musical recording" does not include a digital musical recording as distributed, by authority of the copyright owner, for ultimate sale to consumers.

(12) The "transfer price" of a digital audio recording device or a digital audio recording medium-

(A) is, subject to subparagraph (B)—

(i) in the case of an imported product, the actual entered value at United States Customs (exclusive of any freight, insurance, and applicable duty), and

(ii) in the case of a domestic product, the manufacturer's transfer price (FOB the manufacturer, and exclusive of any direct sales taxes or excise taxes incurred in connection with the sale); and

(B) shall, in a case in which the transferor and transferee are related entities or within a single entity, not be less than a reasonable arms-length price under the principles of the regulations adopted pursuant to section 482 of the Internal Revenue Code of 1986, or any successor provision to such section.

(13) A "writer" is the composer or lyricist of a particular musical work.

CHAPTER 10: SUBCHAPTER B—COPYING CONTROLS

§1002. Incorporation of Copying Controls

(a) Prohibition on Importation, Manufacture, and Distribution.—No person shall import, manufacture, or distribute any digital audio recording device or digital audio interface device that does not conform to—

(1) the Serial Copy Management System;

(2) a system that has the same functional characteristics as the Serial

Copy Management System and requires that copyright and generation status information be accurately sent, received, and acted upon between devices using the system's method of serial copying regulation and devices using the Serial Copy Management System; or

(3) any other system certified by the Secretary of Commerce as prohibiting unauthorized serial copying.

(b) Development of Verification Procedure.—The Secretary of Commerce shall establish a procedure to verify, upon the petition of an interested party, that a system meets the standards set forth in subsection (a)(2).

(c) Prohibition on Circumvention of the System.—No person shall import, manufacture, or distribute any device, or offer or perform any service, the primary purpose or effect of which is to avoid, bypass, remove, deactivate, or otherwise circumvent any program or circuit which implements, in whole or in part, a system described in subsection (a).

(d) Encoding of Information on Digital Musical Recordings.—

(1) Prohibition on encoding inaccurate information.—No person shall encode a digital musical recording of a sound recording with inaccurate information relating to the category code, copyright status, or generation status of the source material for the recording.

(2) Encoding of copyright status not required.—Nothing in this chapter requires any person engaged in the importation or manufacture of digital musical recordings to encode any such digital musical recording with respect to its copyright status.

(e) Information Accompanying Transmission in Digital Format.—Any person who transmits or otherwise communicates to the public any sound recording in digital format is not required under this chapter to transmit or otherwise communicate the information relating to the copyright status of the sound recording. Any such person who does transmit or otherwise communicate such copyright status information shall transmit or communicate such information accurately.

CHAPTER 10: SUBCHAPTER C—ROYALTY PAYMENTS

§1003. Obligation to Make Royalty Payments

(a) Prohibition on Importation and Manufacture.—No person shall import into and distribute, or manufacture and distribute, any digital audio recording device or digital audio recording medium unless such person records the notice specified by this section and subsequently deposits the statements of account and applicable royalty payments for such device or medium specified in section 1004.

(b) Filing of Notice.—The importer or manufacturer of any digital audio recording device or digital audio recording medium, within a product category or utilizing a technology with respect to which such manufacturer or importer has not previously filed a notice under this subsection, shall file with the Register of Copyrights a notice with respect to such device or medium, in such form and content as the Register shall prescribe by regulation.

(c) Filing of Quarterly and Annual Statements of Account.—

(1) Generally.—Any importer or manufacturer that distributes any digital audio recording device or digital audio recording medium that it manufactured or imported shall file with the Register of Copyrights, in such form and content as the Register shall prescribe by -regulation, such quarterly and annual statements of account with respect to such distribution as the Register shall prescribe by regulation.

(2) Certification, verification, and confidentiality.—Each such statement shall be certified as accurate by an authorized officer or principal of the importer or manufacturer. The Register shall issue regulations to provide for the verification and audit of such statements and to protect the confidentiality of the information contained in such statements. Such regulations shall provide for the disclosure, in confidence, of such statements to interested copyright parties.

(3) Royalty Payments.—Each such statement shall be accompanied by the royalty payments specified in section 1004.

1004. Royalty Payments[2]

(a) Digital Audio Recording Devices.—

(1) Amount of payment.—The royalty payment due under section 1003 for each digital audio recording device imported into and distributed in the United States, or manufactured and distributed in the United States, shall be 2 percent of the transfer price. Only the first person to manufacture and distribute or import and distribute such device shall be required to pay the royalty with respect to such device.

(2) Calculation for devices distributed with other devices.—With respect to a digital audio recording device first distributed in combination with one or more devices, either as a physically integrated unit or as separate components, the royalty payment shall be calculated as follows:

(A) If the digital audio recording device and such other devices are part of a physically integrated unit, the royalty payment shall be based on the transfer price of the unit, but shall be reduced by any royalty payment made on any digital audio recording device included within the unit that was not first distributed in combination with the unit.

(B) If the digital audio recording device is not part of a physically integrated unit and substantially similar devices have been distributed separately at any time during the preceding 4 calendar quarters, the royalty payment shall be based on the average transfer price of such devices during those 4 quarters.

(C) If the digital audio recording device is not part of a physically integrated unit and substantially similar devices have not been distributed separately at any time during the preceding 4 calendar quarters, the royalty payment shall be based on a constructed price reflecting the proportional value of such device to the combination as a whole.

(3) Limits on royalties.—Notwithstanding paragraph (1) or (2), the amount of the royalty payment for each digital audio recording device shall not be less than $1 nor more than the royalty maximum. The royalty maximum shall be $8 per device, except that in the case of a physically integrated unit containing more than 1 digital audio recording device, the royalty maximum for such unit shall be $12. During the 6th year after the effective date of this chapter, and not more than once each year thereafter, any interested copyright party may petition the Librarian of Congress to increase the royalty maximum and, if more than 20 percent of the royalty payments are at the relevant royalty maximum, the Librarian of Congress shall prospectively increase such royalty maximum with the goal of having no more than 10 percent of such payments at the new royalty maximum; however the amount of any such increase as a percentage of the royalty maximum shall in no event exceed the percentage increase in the Consumer Price Index during the period under review.

(b) Digital Audio Recording Media.—The royalty payment due under section 1003 for each digital audio recording medium imported into and distributed in the United States, or manufactured and distributed in the United States, shall be 3 percent of the transfer price. Only the first person to manufacture and distribute or import and distribute such medium shall be required to pay the royalty with respect to such medium.

§1005. Deposit of Royalty Payments and Deduction of Expenses[3]

The Register of Copyrights shall receive all royalty payments deposited under this chapter and, after deducting the reasonable costs incurred by the Copyright Office under this chapter, shall deposit the balance in the Treasury of the United States as offsetting receipts, in such manner as the Secretary of the Treasury directs. All funds held by the Secretary of the Treasury shall be invested in interest-bearing United States securities for later distribution with interest under section 1007. The Register may, in the Register's discretion, 4 years after the close of any calendar year, close out the royalty payments account for that calendar year, and may treat any funds remaining in such account and any subsequent deposits that would otherwise be attributable to that calendar year as attributable to the succeeding calendar year.

§1006. Entitlement to Royalty Payments[4]

(a) Interested Copyright Parties.—The royalty payments deposited pursuant to section 1005 shall, in accordance with the procedures specified in section 1007, be distributed to any interested copyright party—

(1) whose musical work or sound recording has been-

(A) embodied in a digital musical recording or an analog musical recording lawfully made under this title that has been distributed, and

(B) distributed in the form of digital musical recordings or analog musical recordings or disseminated to the public in transmissions, during the period to which such payments pertain; and

(2) who has filed a claim under section 1007.

(b) Allocation of Royalty Payments to Groups.—The royalty payments shall be divided into 2 funds as follows:

(1) The sound recordings fund.—66 2/3 percent of the royalty payments shall be allocated to the Sound Recordings Fund. 2 5/8 percent of the royalty payments allocated to the Sound Recordings Fund shall be placed in an escrow account managed by an independent administrator jointly appointed by the interested copyright parties described in section 1001(7)(A) and the American Federation of Musicians (or any successor entity) to be distributed to nonfeatured musicians (whether or not members of the American Federation of Musicians or any successor entity) who have performed on sound recordings distributed in the United States. 1 3/8 percent of the royalty payments allocated to the Sound Recordings Fund shall be placed in an escrow account managed by an independent administrator jointly appointed by the interested copyright parties described in section 1001(7)(A) and the American Federation of Television and Radio Artists (or any successor entity) to be distributed to nonfeatured vocalists (whether or not members of the American Federation of Television and Radio Artists or any successor entity) who have performed on sound recordings distributed in the United States. 40 percent of the remaining royalty payments in the Sound Recordings Fund shall be distributed to the interested copyright parties described in section 1001(7)(C), and 60 percent of such remaining royalty payments shall be distributed to the interested copyright parties described in section 1001(7)(A).

(2) The musical works fund.—

(A) 33 1/3 percent of the royalty payments shall be allocated to the Musical Works Fund for distribution to interested copyright parties described in section 1001(7)(B).

(B)[Music Publishers and Writers—]

(i)Music publishers shall be entitled to 50 percent of the royalty payments allocated to the Musical Works Fund.

(ii) Writers shall be entitled to the other 50 percent of the royalty payments allocated to the Musical Works Fund.

(c) Allocation of Royalty Payments Within Groups.—If all interested copyright parties within a group specified in subsection (b) do not agree on a voluntary proposal for the distribution of the royalty payments within each group, the Librarian of Congress shall convene a copyright arbitration royalty panel which shall, pursuant to the procedures specified under section 1007(c), allocate royalty payments under this section based on the extent to which, during the relevant period—

(1) for the Sound Recordings Fund, each sound recording was distributed in the form of digital musical recordings or analog musical recordings; and

(2) for the Musical Works Fund, each musical work was distributed in the form of digital musical recordings or analog musical recordings or disseminated to the public in transmissions.

§1007. Procedures for Dstributing Royalty Payments[5]

(a) Filing of Claims and Negotiations.—

(1) Filing of claims.—During the first 2 months of each calendar year after calendar year 1992, every interested copyright party seeking to receive royalty payments to which such party is entitled under section 1006 shall file with the Librarian of Congress a claim for payments collected during the preceding year in such form and manner as the Librarian of Congress shall prescribe by regulation.

(2) Negotiations.—Notwithstanding any provision of the antitrust laws, for purposes of this section interested copyright parties within each group specified in section 1006(b) may agree among themselves to the proportionate division of royalty payments, may lump their claims together and file them jointly or as a single claim, or may designate a common agent, including any organization described in section 1001(7)(D), to negotiate or receive payment on their behalf; except that no agreement under this subsection may modify the allocation of royalties specified in section 1006(b).

(b) Distribution of Payments in the Absence of a Dispute.—After the period established for the filing of claims under subsection (a), in each year after 1992, the Librarian of Congress shall determine whether there exists a controversy concerning the distribution of royalty payments under section 1006(c). If the Librarian of Congress determines that no such controversy exists, the Librarian of Congress shall, within 30 days after such determination, authorize the distribution of the royalty payments as set forth in the agreements regarding the distribution of royalty payments entered into pursuant to subsection (a), after deducting its reasonable administrative costs under this section.

(c) Resolution of Disputes.—If the Librarian of Congress finds the existence of a controversy, the Librarian shall, pursuant to chapter 8 of this title, convene a copyright arbitration royalty panel to determine the distribution of royalty payments. During the pendency of such a proceeding, the Librarian of Congress shall withhold from distribution an amount sufficient to satisfy all claims with respect to which a controversy exists, but shall, to the extent feasible, authorize the distribution of any amounts that are not in controversy. The Librarian of Congress shall, before authorizing the distribution of such royalty payments, deduct the reasonable administrative costs incurred by the Librarian under this section.

CHAPTER 10: SUBCHAPTER D—PROHIBITION ON CERTAIN INFRINGEMENT ACTIONS, REMEDIES, AND ARBITRATION

§1008. Prohibition on Certain Infringement Actions

No action may be brought under this title alleging infringement of copyright based on the manufacture, importation, or distribution of a digital audio recording device, a digital audio recording medium, an analog recording device, or an analog recording medium, or based on the noncommercial use by a consumer of such a device or medium for making digital musical recordings or analog musical recordings.

. . .

ENDNOTES

1. The Audio Home Recording Act of 1992 added chapter 10, entitled "Digital Audio Recording Devices and Media," to title 17. Pub. L. No. 102-563, 106 Stat. 4237.

2. The Copyright Royalty Tribunal Reform Act of 1993 amended section 1004(a)(3) by substituting "Librarian of Congress" in lieu of "Copyright Royalty Tribunal," where appropriate. Pub. L. No. 103-198, 107 Stat. 2304, 2312.

3. The Copyright Royalty Tribunal Reform Act of 1993 amended section 1005 by striking the last sentence which began "The Register shall submit to the Copyright Royalty Tribunal." Pub. L. No. 103-198, 107 Stat. 2304, 2312.

4. The Copyright Royalty Tribunal Reform Act of 1993 amended section 1006(c) by substituting "Librarian of Congress" in lieu of "Copyright Royalty Tribunal," where appropriate. Pub. L. No. 103-198, 107 Stat. 2304, 2312. In 1997, section 1006(b)(1) was amended to insert "Federation of Television" in lieu of "Federation Television" wherever it appeared. Pub. L. No. 105-80, 111 Stat. 1529, 1535.

5. The Copyright Royalty Tribunal Reform Act of 1993 amended section 1007 by substituting "Librarian of Congress" in lieu of "Copyright Royalty Tribunal" or "Tribunal," where appropriate, by amending the first sentence in subsection (c) and by inserting "the reasonable administrative costs incurred by the Librarian" in the last sentence of subsection (c), in lieu of "its reasonable administrative costs." Pub. L. No. 103-198, 107 Stat. 2304, 2312. . . .

The following list of government bodies, trade associations, private companies, and other organizations are of special interest to anyone who is or wants to be part of the music industry. The Web sites of most of the groups listed have sections of interest to nonsubscribing visitors.

GOVERNMENT ORGANIZATIONS: UNITED STATES

Library of Congress (www.loc.gov)

In addition to a link to the U.S. Copyright Office (www.copyright.gov), which has the full text of the Copyright Law in both pdf and text format, the Library of Congress Web site is a treasure trove of links to sites of interest for artists and consumers alike. Three of primary interest are:

- ▶ Motion Picture and Television Reading Room (www.loc.gov/rr/mopic). This site provides on-line access to hundreds of films and videos in the public domain.
- ▶ Archive of Folk Culture Collections (www.loc.gov/folklife). The Archive of Folk Culture provides on-line access to recordings in a number of genres, including some very specialized niches, such as Northern California Folk Music from the Thirties and Hispano Music and Culture of the Northern Rio Grande.
- ▶ National Recording Preservation Board (www.loc.gov/rr/record/nrpb). The NRPB, mandated by the National Recording Preservation Act of 2000, is an advisory group bringing together a number of professional organizations (including ASCAP, AFM, BMI, RIAA, and SESAC, among others) and experts concerned with the preservation of recorded music. On this site is a link to the Recorded Sound Reference Center, which provides access to its collection to those doing research leading to a publicly available work, such as a book, article, thesis, radio/film/television production, or public performance. The Reference Center has over 2 million items encompassing audio formats from cylinders to CDs.

Library of Congress
101 Independence Avenue S.E.
Washington, DC 20559-6000
Tel: 202 707 5840, fax: 202 707 2371

National Endowment for the Arts (http://arts.endow.gov/ or www.nea.gov)

The NEA was created in 1965 by Congress to provide national recognition and support to significant projects of artistic excellence. In conjunction with the International Association of Jazz Educators (IAJE; www.iaje.org), the NEA gives annual awards to three living jazz masters on the basis of nominations from the public, including the jazz community. Biographies, discographies, and streaming audio and video presentations on present and past American Jazz Masters are available at the IAJE Web site.

1100 Pennsylvania Avenue NW
Washington DC 20506
Tel: 202 682 5400; fax: 202 682 5677;
e-mail: webmgr@arts.endow.gov

United States Patent and Trademark Office (www.uspto.gov)

The USPTO Web site provides a link to the Trademark Electronic Search System database, which contains data on all registered trademarks. It also offers extensive descriptions of the process of choosing a trademark, patent, or domain name.

General Information Services Division
Crystal Plaza 3, Room 2C02
Washington, DC 20231
Tel: 800 786 9199; e-mail: usptoinfo@uspto.gov
(use Web site to access specific e-mail forms)

INTERNATIONAL ORGANIZATIONS

International Confederation of Societies of Authors and Composers (CISAC) (www.cisac.org)

The mission of CISAC, which counts 199 member societies from 13 countries representing over 2 million creators of intellectual property, is to work toward maximum international recognition of creators' rights. CISAC's Web site has links to information about such important in-process international standards as the International Standard Musical Work Code, the musical Works Information Database (WID), and the International Standard Audio-visual Number.

CISAC Secretariat General
20-26 Boulevard du Parc
92200 Neuilly/sur/Siene
France
Phone: +33 (0)1-55-62-08-50; fax: + 33 (0)1-55-62-08-60;
e-mail:cisac@cisac.org

International Federation of Phonographic Producers (IFPI) (www.ifpi.org)

IFPI's membership is comprised of 1,500 record producers and distributors in 74 countries. It has national groups in 46 countries. IFPI coordinates international strategies in the areas of antipiracy enforcement and digital technologies, and is the ISO-appointed international registration authority for the International Standard Recording Code.

IFPI Secretariat
54 Regent Street
London W1B 5RE
Tel: 44 (0)20 7878 7900; fax: 44 (0)20 7878 7950;
e-mail: info@ifpi.org

IFPI European Office
Square de Meeûs 19
1050 Brussels
Belgium
Tel: 32 2 511 9208; fax: 32 2 502 3077;
e-mail: euroinfo@ifpi.rog

IFPI Latin America
806 Douglas Road, Suite 625
Coral Gables, FL 33134
Tel: 1 9301 567 0861; fax: 1 305 567 0871;
e-mail: alugo@ifpi

World Intellectual Property Organizations (WIPO) (www.wipo.org)

The roots of WIPO can be traced back to 1893, when the Paris Convention and the Berne Convention merged to form the United International Bureaux for the Protection of Intellectual Property (BIRPI). In 1960, BIRPI moved to Geneva, and in 1970 changed its name to the World Intellectual Property Organization. Today, WIPO has 179 member nations (representing 90 percent of the world's people's) and is a specialized agency of the United Nations system of organizations. Under WIPO's Digital Agenda, the organization is engaged in on-going policy making as a response to the "confluence of the Internet, digital technologies, and the intellectual property system." A key element of the Digital Agenda is the need for effective on-line systems to resolve disputes. The WIPO Web site has links to several virtual exhibitions, including Music in the Digital Age, which features a tour of a virtual sound recording studio.

WIPO
34 Chemin de Columbettes
Geneva, Switzerland
Tel: (4) 1 22 338 91 11

WIPO-U.S.
2 United Nations Plaza Suite 2525
New York, NY 10017
Tel: 212 963-6813

International ISWC (International Standard Musical Work Code) Agency (www.iswc.org)

The International ISWC Agency, which is appointed by the International Standards Organization (ISO), is responsible for maintainence and administration of the International Standard Musical Work Code, which is a unique, permanent, and internationally recognized reference number for the identification of musical works. The ISWC number is a part of CISAC's Common Information System.

Address: See CISAC, above

PERFORMANCE AND MECHANICAL RIGHTS LICENSING ORGANIZATIONS

ASCAP (The American Society of Composers, Authors and Publishers) (www.ascap.com)

ASCAP is a membership organization of over 145,000 U.S. composers, songwriters, and publishers. ASCAP licenses and distributes royalties for the nondramatic public performance of its members' copyrighted works. Nonmembers can use the ASCAP Web site to download numerous license forms, including those related to Internet and radio uses. The ASCAP Foundation (www.ascapfoundation.org) sponsors programs and activities which serve the entire music community; funds numerous scholarships awarded to students in arts programs in high school and college; gives awards to outstanding composers, songwriters, and conductors; and runs Save the Music, a program which provides musical instruments, sheet music, band arrangements, and method books to schools nationwide.

ASCAP Headquarters
One Lincoln Plaza
New York, NY 10023
Tel: (212) 621-6000; fax: (212) 724-9064;
e-mail: info@ascap.com

ASCAP Los Angeles
7920 W. Sunset Boulevard, Third Floor
Los Angeles, CA 90046
Tel: (323) 883-1000; fax: (323) 883-1049

ASCAP London
8 Cork Street
London W1X1PB
Tel: 011-44-207-439-0909; fax: 011-44-207-434-0073

ASCAP Nashville
Two Music Square West
Nashville, TN 37203
Tel: (615) 742-5000; fax: (615) 742-5020

ASCAP Miami
420 Lincoln Rd, Ste. 385
Miami Beach, FL 33139
Tel: (305) 673-3446; fax: (305) 673-2446

ASCAP Chicago
1608 N Milwaukee, Ste. 1007
Chicago, IL 60647
Tel: (773) 394-4286; fax (773) 394-5639

ASCAP Puerto Rico
654 Ave. Muñoz Rivera
IBM Plaza Ste. 1101 B
Hato Rey, PR 00918
Tel: (787) 281-0782; fax. (787) 767-2805

ASCAP Membership—Atlanta
PMB 400
541 Tenth Street NW
Atlanta, GA 30318
Tel: (404) 351-1224; fax: (404) 351-1252

ASCAP Licensing—Atlanta
2690 Cumberland Parkway, Suite 490
Atlanta, GA 30339
Tel: 1-800-505-4052

Broadcast Music Inc. (www.bmi.com)

BMI collects license fees on behalf of about 300,000 composers, songwriters, and music publishers for the public performance of the 4.5 million works in its repertoire, including airplay, The BMI Foundation (www.bmifoundation.org)

is a not-for-profit company dedicated to encouraging the creation, performance, and study of music through awards, grants, scholarships, internships, and commissions. Visitors to their Web site do not need to be members to search the BMI Repertoire (http://repertoire.bmi.com), a database with information on all compositions registered with BMI. Users can search by artist, title, composer, even publisher.

BMI Headquarters
320 West 57th Street
New York, NY 10019-3790
(212) 586-2000

BMI Nashville
10 Music Square East
Nashville, TN 37203-4399
Tel: (615) 401-2000

BMI Los Angeles
8730 Sunset Blvd., 3d Floor West
West Hollywood, CA 90069-2211
Tel: (310) 659-9109

BMI London
84 Harley House
Marylebone Rd
London NW1 5HN, England
Tel: 0 11 44 207486 2036

BMI Miami
5201 Blue Lagoon Drive, Suite 310
Miami, FL 33126
Tel: 305 266-3636

BMI Atlanta
P.O. Box 19199
Atlanta, GA 31126
Tel: (404) 261-5151

BMI Puerto Rico
255 Ponce de Leon
East Wing, Suite A-262
BankTrust Plaza
Hato Rey, Puerto Rico 00917
Tel: (787) 754-6490

The Canadian Musical Reproduction Rights Agency Limited (CMRRA) (www.cmrra.ca)

CMRRA collects fees for the reproduction rights—in CDs, cassettes, films, TV programs, and other audiovisual productions—to compositions owned by its members. All the forms necessary to register a work with CMRRA can be downloaded from their site.

CMRRA
56 Wellesley Street W. #320
Toronto, Ontario M5S 2S3
Canada
Tel: 416 926 1966; fax: 416-926-7521

Harry Fox Agency (www.nmpa.org/hfa.html)

The Harry Fox Agency (HFA), which issues licenses and collects and distributes royalties for the mechanical reproduction of U.S. music publishers' copyrights, maintains a Web site jointly with the National Music Publishers' Association. The site has numerous useful links, including one to FLADEM (Federation of Latin American Music Publishers) and a site called CapitolConnect, which makes it easy for users to follow the status of pending legislation and Congressional hearings on issues of importance to the music industry.

Harry Fox
711 Third Avenue
New York, NY 10017
Tel: 212 834 0100;
e-mail: clientrelations@harryfox.com

SESAC (Society of European Stage Authors and Composers) (www.sesac.com)

SESAC, Inc., is a performing rights organization with headquarters in Nashville and offices in New York, Los Angeles, and London. SESAC is smaller than ASCAP or BMI, but claims to offer a more personalized relationship with its members. The Web site has links to SESAC's *Focus* magazine.

SESAC Headquarters
55 Music Square East
Nashville, TN 37203
Tel: 615 320 0055; fax:615 329 9627

SESAC New York
152 West 57th ST, 57th Floor
New York, NY 10019
Tel: 212 586 3450; fax: 212-489-5699

SESAC Los Angeles
501 Santa Monica Blvd, Ste. 450
Santa Monica, CA 90401-2430
Tel: 310 393 9671; fax: 310 393 6497

SESAC International
6 Kenrick Place
London W1H 3FF England
Tel: 0 20 7486 9994; fax: 0 20 7486 9929

Société du Droit de Reproduction des Auteurs (SODRAC) (www.sodrac.com)

SODRAC is a reproduction rights society that collects royalties from producers of sound and video recordings, radio broadcasters, and educational institutions for reproduction of copyrighted works in Canada and abroad.

SODRAC
759, Carre Victoria Square
Suite 420, Montreal, PQ H2Y 2J7
Tel: 514 845 3268; fax: 514 845 3401

UNIONS

American Federation of Musicians (www.afm.org)

The AFM represents over 250 local unions in the United States and Canada. Their Web site, which bills itself as the on-line community for musicians, offers numerous services for members, such as a comprehensive listing of auditions. Nonmembers have access to current press releases.

1501 Broadway, Ste. 600
New York, NY 10036
Tel: 212-869-1330; fax: 212-764-6134;
e-mail: info@afm.org

American Federation of Television and Radio Artists (www.aftra.org)

AFTRA is an 80,000-member national labor organization affiliated with the AFL-CIO. It represents its members in a number of areas, including: news and broadcasting, entertainment programming, the recording business, and recorded commericals. In February of 2003, AFTRA and the Screen Actors Guild (www.sag.org) announced a proposed consolidation of their two unions. AFTRA's Web site, under Resources/Related Links, has one of the best sets of links on the Web to important sources of information on and services related to the music industry.

AFTRA Headquarters
260 Madison Avenue
New York, NY 10016
Tel: 212-532-0800; fax: 212-545-1238;
e-mail: aftra@aftra.org

American Guild of Musical Artists (www.musicalartists.org)

AGMA is a national AFL-CIO union representing soloists, choristers, dancers, choreographers, stage managers, and stage directors.

AGMA
1430 Broadway, 14th Floor
New York, NY 10018
Tel: 212 265 3687; fax: 212 262 9088;
e-mail: AGMA@musicalartists.org

Trade Associations and Affiliates

Academy of Country Music (www.acmcountry.com)

The Academy of Country Music sponsors the annual Academy of Country Music Awards. At this time of this writing, their Web site was under construction.

Academy of Country Music
4100 Alameda Ave., Ste. 208
Hollywood, CA 91505
Tel: 818 842 8400; fax 818 842 8535;
e-mail: academyoffice@aol.com

Association of Independent Music Publishers (AIMP) (www.aimp.org)

The primary goal of AIMP, whose membership includes independent music publishers as well as publishers affiliated with record labels or motion picture television production companies, is to educate and inform local music publishers about current industry trends and practices through monthly meetings, forums, and workshops.

AIMP New York
156 West 56th Street, Ste. 1803
New York, NY 10019
Tel: 212 582 7622; fax: 212 582 8273;
e-mail (membership info): NYjoin@aimp.org

AIMP California
P.O. Box 1561
Burbank, CA 91507-1561
Tel: 818 842 6257;
e-mail (info):info@aimp.org, membership info: LAjoin@aimp.org

Audio Engineering Society (www.aes.org)

The Audio Engineering Society is a professional society devoted exclusively to audio engineering. For a $20 annual membership, students can have access to the on-line version of the *Journal of the Audio Engineering Society.*

> Audio Engineering Society
> 60 East 42d Street, Room 2520
> New York, NY 10165-2520

Chorus America (www.chorusamerica.org)

Founded in 1977, Chorus America has 1,200 individual, chorus, and corporate members. To accomplish its mission, which is to promote the practice and appreciation of choral music in the United States, Chorus America provides information, publications, conferences, training programs, networking, and awards. Visitors to the the Web site can access a complete list of choral groups in the United States, by state, group, or member name.

> Chorus America
> 1156 15th Street NW, Ste. 310
> Washington, DC 20005
> Tel: 202 331 7577; e-mail: service@chorusamerica.org

Country Music Association (www.cmaworld.com)

Founded in 1958, CMA has over 6,000 members in 43 countries. CMA hosts the annual Country Music Awards and operates the Country Music Hall of Fame and Museum in Nashville. The Web site offers an up-to-date list of international country music festivals.

> Country Music Association
> One Music Circle South
> Nashville, Tennessee 37203
> Tel: 615 244 2840; fax: 615 726-0314

Gospel Music Association (www.gospelmusic.org)

Founded in 1964, the Gospel Music Association is an umbrella organization whose membership is open not only to those who make their living as country music artists or entrepreneurs but to anyone interested in gospel music. There is a special membership rate for students. GMA sponsors the annual Dove Awards, Gospel Music Week, Seminar in the Rockies, and the Academy of Gospel Music Arts. The Web site offers links to all these programs, as well as free access to the GMA magazine, *GMA Today.* The site also offers a list of Christian bookstores, searchable by city and state.

Gospel Music Association
1205 Division Street
Nashville, TN 37203
Tel: 615 242 0303; fax: 615 254 9755

International Bluegrass Music Association (www.ibma.org)

The IBMA Web site has a link to www.discoverbluegrass.com, which allows users to search for bluegrass resources by category (e.g., festivals), state, organization, or name.

International Bluegrass Music Association
2 Music Circle South, Ste. 100
Nashville, TN 37203
Tel: 615 256 3222, 888 4384262; fax: 615 256 0450;
e-mail: info@ibma.org

International Recording Media Association (IRMA) (www.recordingmedia.org)

IRMA's membership includes all facets of the recording industry, including raw materials providers, manufacturers, replicators, duplicators, packagers, copyright holders, and related industries. Their Web site provides a link to the IRMA Online International Source Directory of the major supppliers of products and services to all areas of the audio/video/data industry, as well as to their Anti-Piracy Certification/Compliance program for the manufacturers of CDs, DVDs, and CD-ROMS.

IRMA
182 Nassau St., Ste. 204
Princeton, NJ 08542
Tel: 609 279 1700; fax: 609 279 1999;
e-mail: info@recordingmedia.org

Music Managers Forum (www.mmf-us.org)

MMF provides monthly forums for managers to discuss the various issues that affect them as well as to further their interests and those of the artists they represent in all aspects of the music industry. MMF, which has approximately 60 members in cities across the country as well as chapters in Canada, the U.K., and Australia, publishes a newsletter featuring information on the organization's activities and legislative updates.

MMF
PO Box 444,
Village Station, New York, NY 10014-0444,
(212) 213-8787

Music Publishers' Association (www.mpa.org)

Founded in 1895, MPA is the oldest music trade association in the United States. In addition to serving as a forum for 55 member publishers on issues of importance to music publishing, it provides up-to-date news on legislation and regulations affecting the industry and keeps members informed of the latest technology and systems being used for engraving, printing, distribution, and licensing. MPA maintains the *Music Publishers Directory*.

> Music Publishers Association
> PMB 246
> 1562 First Avenue
> New York, NY 10028
> Tel and fax: 212 327 4044;
> e-mail: Mpa-admin@mpa.org

The National Academy of Television Arts and Sciences (www.emmyonline.org)

The National Academy of Television Arts and Sciences Web site has four main links: to its home page, to chapter news and regional Emmy awards, to a database listing of jobs in the television industry, and to national student television awards. The www.emmyonline.org/national page offers numerous options for visitors, including access to current and archival information on the Emmy Awards and to on-line issues of *Television Quarterly*.

> Emmy Awards
> 111 West 57th Street, Suite 600
> New York, NY 10019
> Tel: 212-586-8424; fax: 212-246-8129;
> e-mail: natashq@aol.com

National Association of Broadcasters (www.nab.org)

NAB represents the interests of free, over-the-air television and radio broadcasters. Their Web site offers many resources to nonmembers, including, on the Research and Information page, a link to radio-locator.com (formerly the MIT list of radio stations on the Internet), which is a fully searchable database (by city or ZIP, call letters, streaming format, and country) of over 10,000 radio station Web pages and over 2,500 audio streams from stations in the United States and around the world.

> National Association of Broadcasters
> 1771 N Street, NW
> Washington, DC 20036
> Tel: 202 429 5300; fax: 202 429 4199;
> e-mail: nab@nab.org

National Conference of Personal Managers (www.ncopm.com)

NCOPM is an organization "committed to the advancement of personal managers and their clients." A list of personal managers who are members of NCOPM can be accessed via their Web site.

> NCOPM
> c/o Clinton Ford Billups
> PO Box 357, Riverton, CT 06065
> e-mail: cfbproductions@earthlink.net

National Music Publishers Association (NMPA) (www.nmpa.org)

See above, under Performance and Mechanical Rights Licensing Organizations, The Harry Fox Agency.

Nashville Songwriters Association International (www.nashvillesongwriters.com)

NSAI sponsors the annual Tin Pan South songwriters festival, and condusts numerous symposiums and workshops for its members.

> NSAI
> 1701 West End Avenue, 3d floor
> Nashville, TN 37203
> Tel: 615-256-3354; fax: 615-256-0034;
> e-mail (general inquiries: nsai:nashvillesongwriters.com

Recording Industry Association of America (RIAA)(www.riaa.com)

According to RIAA, a trade group that represents the U.S. recording industry, its membership accounts for about 90 percent "of all legitimate sound recordings produced and sold in the United States." RIAA has been in the forefront of national and international antipiracy efforts and counts as part of its mission protection of First Amendment rights of artists. The RIAA certifies gold, platinum, multiplatimum, and diamond record sales awards.

> RIAA
> 1330 Connecticut Avenue NW, Ste. 300
> Washington, DC 20036
> Tel: 202 775 0101; fax: 202 775 7253;
> e-mail: click on About Us/Contact Us at the Web site.

INDUSTRY SERVICE ORGANIZATIONS

BZ/Rights & Permissions (www.bzrights.com)

In addition to its function as a comprehensive rights clearance service, BZ/Rights & Permissions handles U.S. Copyright Office searches for clients, publishes the *Mini-Encyclopedia of Public Domain Songs,* and offers a consulting service for companies that want to do their own clearances.

> BZ/Rights and Permissions
> 121 West 27th Street, Ste. 901
> New York, NY 10001
> Tel: 212 924 3000; fax: 212 924 2525;
> e-mail: info@bzrights.com

CCH CORSEARCH (cch-corsearch.com)

CCH CORSEARCH offers numerous search services, including North American trademark availability, corporate name availability (including dbas), copyright clearance searches, and domain name searches, as well as on-going infringement watches.

> CCH CORSEARCH
> 233 Spring Street
> New York, NY 10013
> Tel (customer service): 800-732-7241;
> e-mail: info@cch-corsearch.com

Jukebox License Office (www.jukeboxlicense.com)

The Jukebox License Office, which licenses jukebox operators to play all music in the ASCAP, BMI, and SESAC repertoire, offers two rate structures, one for members of the Amusement and Music Operators Association (www.amoa.com; 800-937-2662) and one for nonmembers.

> Jukebox License Office
> 1700 Hayes Street, Suite 201
> Nashville, TN 37203-3014
> Tel: 800-955-5853, 615-320-4000; fax: 615-320-4004;
> e-mail: information@jukeboxlicense.com

Public Domain Music Works (www.pubdomain.com)

For a monthly subscription, members can search 10,000 public domain works by title, genre, composer, keyword, lyric, or any word or phrase. The Web site also offers copyright searches, as well as sheet music for thousands of public domain titles.

> Public Domain Music Works
> PO Box 3102
> Margate, NJ 08402
> Tel: 609-822-9401, 800-827-9401; fax: 609-822-1638;
> e-mail: info@pubdomain.com

Thomson & Thomson (www.thomson-thomson.com)

Thomson & Thomson is one of the most highly regarded trademark and copyright search and watch services in the world. The IP (intellectual property) section of the T&T Web site is an excellent source for recent and archived articles on copyright and trademark issues, both national and international.

> Thomson & Thomson
> 500 Victory Road
> North Quincy, MA 02171
> Tel: 800-692-8833;
> email: support@t-t.com

EDUCATIONAL GROUPS

Smithsonian Folkways Recordings (www.folkways.si.edu)

The two catalogs available for download in pdf format at the Folkways Web site are A World of Sound (Folkways releases from 1948–1987, and Cook, Dyer-Bennet, Fast Folk, Monitor releases) and Smithsonian Folkways (Folkways releases post-1987).

> e-mail: webster@folkways.si.edu

International Association for Jazz Education (www.iaje.org)

IAJA, a nonprofit organization dedicated to the continued growth of jazz and jazz education worldwide, has over 8,000 members in 35 countries. Among the activities sponsored by IAJA are on-line jazz education (Jazz OLE), publication of the *Jazz Education Journal* (with full-text retrieval of articles offered on-line), and the IAJA Annual Conference. Their award-winning Web site provides numerous links to sites of interest to jazz aficionados.

> IAJA
> 2803 Claflin Road
> Manhattan, KS 66502
> Tel: 785 776 8744; fax 785 776 6190;
> e-mail: info@iaje.org

JazzReach Performing Arts & Education Association, Inc. (www.jazzreach.org)

JazzReach is a nonprofit group that produces multimedia educational outreach programs for young people, both in schools and, in conjunction with the Fresh Air Fund, in camps.

> Jazz Reach
> 217 Dean Street
> Brooklyn, NY 11217
> Tel: (718) 625 5188;
> e-mail: info@jazzreach.org

Music Teachers National Association (www.mtna.org)

Founded in 1876, MTNA has 24,000 mebers, who are independent and collegiate teachers of all instruments, including voice. MTNA publishes *The American Music Teacher* and the *MTNA Newsletter,* and, under the auspices of the MTNA Foundation, gives grants and awards to students to pursue continuing education opportunities,

> MTNA National Headquarters
> 441 Vine Street, Ste. 505
> Cincinnati, OH 45202-2811
> Tel: 513-421-1420, 888-512-5278; fax: 513-421-2503;
> e-mail: mtnanet@mtna.org

The National Association for Music Educaiton (www.menc.org)

Formerly Music Educators National Conference, MENC changed its name in 1998. Its 90,000 members are active music teachers, university faculty and researchers, high school honor society members, and MusicFriends (MusicFriends can be reached via MENC's Web site or by going to www.musicfriends.org).

> MENC
> 1806 Robert Fulton Drive
> Reston, VA 20191
> Tel: 800-336-3768, 703-860-4000; fax: 703-860-1531

PUBLICATIONS AND DIRECTORIES

Billboard (www.billboard.com)

Billboard's Web site offers numerous services for nonsubscribers, including access to the *Billboard* charts and the *Billboard* tour database. All the *Billboard* directories can be purchased via billboard.com. Visitors can also subscribe to a free newsletter.

> Billboard
> 770 Broadway
> New York, NY 10003
> 646 654 4400

The Music Business Registry (www.musicregistry.com)

Use the Music Business Registry Web site to order any of their directories, for example, their A&R Registry of the A&R staff of all major and indie labels in New York, Los Angeles, Nashville, Toronto, and London. The site also offers an up-to-date calendar of events, with links to the various sponsors, and current articles on the state of the industry.

Music Business Registry
7510 Sunset Boulevard, #1041
Los Angeles, CA 90046-3400
Tel: 818-995-7458; fax: 818-995-7459;
e-mail: info@musicregistry.com

The Network (www.thenetworkmag.com)

The *Network* magazine Web site offers links to various subscription-only journals, including *Urban Inspired,* a gospel music trade publication. Nonsubscriber visitors to the site have access to weekly chart, new release, airplay, and sales data.

New On The Charts (www.newonthecharts.com)

A subscription-only service for music industry professionals (songwriters, e.g., must have at least one song recorded and commercially released nationally) that offers up-to-date listings of charted recordings, music videos, signings, and international deals.

Radio and Internet Newsletter (RAIN) (www.kurthanson.com)

RAIN offers a free daily newsletter with commentary on key issues affecting radio and the Internet.

119 West Hubbard, Ste. 4E
Chicago, IL 60610
Tel: 312 527 3879;
e-mail: kurt@kurthanson.com

Record Research Inc. (www.recordresearch.com)

A complete on-line catalog of books with Billboard chart data on every record every charted, as well books on pop and rock, country, and R&B.

Record Research
Dept. N
PO Box 200
Menomonee Falls, WI 53052-0200
Tel: 414-251-5408; fax: 414-251-9452;
e-mail: books@recordresearch.com

MUSIC TRADE SHOWS

Midem (www.midem.com)

For 38 years, Midem has hosted the largest international trade show in the music industry. The Web site offers detailed information about each year's show, as well as links to Midem partners, including a link to *Music and Media,* a European trade journal for the music and broadcast industries which also publishes a free newsletter.

Reed Midem Organization
125 Park Avenue, 24th Floor
New York, NY 10017
Tel: 212 370 7470; fax: 212 370 7471;
e-mail: midem@aol.com

South by Southwest (www.sxsw.com)

The SXSW Web site is primarily devoted to coverage of the South by Southwest Music and Media Conference and Festival (annually since 1987), but it also offers link to news stories of interest to the music industry, updated daily.

South by Southwest
PO Box 4999
Austin, TX 78765
Tel: 512 467 7979; fax: 512 451 0754;
e-mail: sxsw@sxsw.com

MISCELLANEOUS

The Blues Foundation (www.blues.org)

The Blues Foundation sponsors the Annual Blues Hall of Fame inductions, the Handy Awards, the International Blues Challenge, and Blues in the Schools. Their Web site offers links to these programs, as well as access to the full text of articles from current and past newsletters.

Blues Foundation
49 Union Ave
Memphis, TN 38103
Tel: 901 527 2583; fax 901 529 4030;
e-mail: bluesinfo@blues.org

Bug Music (www.bugmusic.com)

Bug Music, which has branches in Hollywood, Nashville, New York, London, and Munich, combines the functions of music publisher and independent music administrator. The company does not own the copyrights to the songs written by its clients, but actively engages in promoting those songs.

Bug Music
6777 Hollywood Blvd.
Hollywood, CA 90028
Tel 323 466-4352 Fax 323 466-2366

Digital Media Association (DiMA) (www.digmedia.org)

Founded in 1998, DiMA is an alliance of companies that develop and deploy technologies to perform, promote, and market music and video content on the Web and through other digital networks. Members include new media—RealNetworks, Liquid Audio, Listen.com; e-commerce—CDNow, Tower Online, EMusic.com; and Webcasters—MTVi, NetRadio, Echo Networks.

> DiMA
> 1120 Connecticut Avenue NW
> Washington, D.C. 20036
> Tel: 202 715 0590; fax: 202 715 0591;
> e-mail: jpotter@digmedia.org

Future of Music Coalition (www.futureofmusic.org)

The Future of Music Coalition, which hosts an annual Policy Summit (keynote speakers in 2003 included Sen. Russ Feingold and FCC Commissioner Jonathan Adelstein), is a nonprofit organization whose mission is to disseminate information to the media, policymakers, and the public about music/technology issues.

> Future of Music Coalition
> c/o Michael Bracy
> 1615 L Street NW, Ste. 520
> Washington, DC 20036
> Tel: 202 429 8855; fax: 202 429 8857

Internet Underground Music Archive (www.iuma.com)

IUMA's stated mission is to bring new artists and fans together via its Web site, which offers Real Audio sampling of music, MP3 downloads, and IUMA Radio. Site visitors can also interact with artists through e-mail and message boards.

Pollstar (www.pollstar.com)

Pollstar magazine, with branches in Fresno, California, and in London, covers the concert and tour industry. Nonsubscribing visitors to their Web site have access to the Tours du Jour links to current and future tours of over 50 top artists and groups.

> Pollstar
> 4697 W. Jacquelyn Avenue
> Fresno, CA 93722-6413
> Tel: 559 271 7900; fax: 559 271 77979;
> e-mail: webmaster@pollstar.com

Rhythm and Blues Foundation (www.rhythm-n-blues.org)

The Rhythm and Blues Foundation, a nonprofit organization dedicated to the historical and cultural preservation of rhythm and blues music, sponsors the Annual Pioneer Awards and administers the Motown Universal Music Group Fund and the Benjamin B. Gordy Fuqua Fund. Visitors to the site can sign up for a free subscription to their quarterly newsletter.

> Rhythm and Blues Foundation
> 1555 Connecticut Avenue NW, Ste. 401
> Washington, DC 20036-1111
> Tel: 202.588.5566; fax: 202.588.5549; e-mail link provided on the site

Spinner (www.spinner.com)

Spinner is a free Internet radio service that gives listeners access to over 175 stations with ability to save links to as many as 40 of them and offers on-line artist information and station charts.

The World Wide Web Independent Music Directory (www.indiemusic.com)

One of the main functions of the Independent Music Directory is to nurture the growth of independent music, and the site offers links to the Web sites and music of hundreds of independent artists and bands, as well as links to e-zines and independent labels.

ON-LINE MUSIC SERVICES

The roster of sites that offer on-line music other than radio can change overnight, as can their pricing structures and what you get for the different options (e.g., downloads for listening only, downloads for listening and playing, burning capabilities, and extras such as PressPlays's audio versions of archived *Billboard* charts. Some of the best known of these sites are eMusic (www.emusic.com), MusicNow (www.music.fullaudio.com), PressPlay (www.pressplay.com), and Rhapsody (www.listen.com). The MusicNet site (www.musicnet.com) provides links to MusicNet on AOL (open to AOL subscribers only) and to RealOne.

Contract Checklists

The following checklists are intended as a general guide to the areas that should be covered when negotiating contracts of the following types:

- ▶ Demo Shopping Agreement
- ▶ Demo Subsidy Deal
- ▶ Distribution Agreement Between Record Label (Owner) and Distributor
- ▶ Exclusive Artist Agreement
- ▶ Exclusive Songwriter Contract
- ▶ Foreign Subpublishing Agreement
- ▶ Home Video/DVD Reproduction of Song
- ▶ Live Concert Appearances
- ▶ Master Use License for Film or TV Show
- ▶ Mechanical Reproduction License
- ▶ Personal Manager
- ▶ Single-Song Contract

In all cases, the points listed for each type of contract are intended only as a review of basic "deal points." *Anyone contemplating entering into a long-term contract is strongly urged to consult with experienced professional managers, attorneys, and accountants.*

NEGOTIATION CHECKLIST:
DEMO SHOPPING AGREEMENT

☐ Names, addresses of artist and entity doing shopping (producer or shopper)

☐ Delivery date of completed demo

☐ Party responsible for initial payment of costs

    ☐ Recoupment of costs

    ☐ From first proceeds?

☐ From proceeds allocated to artist or to producer or shopper in shares advanced by each?

☐ Negotiations/ultimate approval on any resulting contract

    ☐ Joint approval? Solely determined by artist? Solely determined by shopper? Determined by shopper subject to meeting stated criteria?

    ☐ Waiver of right to object if: deal with a major label, an independent label distributed by a major label, any label distributed nationally, any nationally distributed label which has prior album on *Billboard* chart, any regionally distributed label

☐ Expiration (return of rights to artist) terms

    ☐ Rights revert after stated number of months without successful negotiations

    ☐ Elapse of stated number of months while offer is in process of being negotiated triggers an additional stated period if necessary to conclude negotiations (e.g., one month, two months, or three months)

    ☐ Continuing rights to have a private-label release subject to stated artist and producer royalties if parties fail to obtain a satisfactory customary release within the stated period

☐ Compensation to producer or shopper

    ☐ Advance payment in cash?

    ☐ Percentage based on any net advance obtained from purchaser?

    ☐ Continuing percentage on royalties for all recordings made under contract obtained by shopper?

    ☐ Limited participation to one, two, three, or other number of albums and/or recordings made for resulting label?

NEGOTIATION CHECKLIST:
DEMO SUBSIDY DEAL

❐ Amount of budget or demo recording fund to be financed

❐ Number of songs to be delivered in demo form

❐ Identification of artist(s), producer, and essential sidemen

❐ Date of recording and date of intended delivery to financing party (label, publisher, or independent investor)

❐ Timetable for decision of financing party on whether to proceed to next stage—master recording under exclusive artist contract

❐ Right of first refusal vs. preset recording contract

    ❐ Terms of artist contract if preset as part of demo deal

    ❐ Timetable under right of first refusal on best available terms: how long before must accept or reject

    ❐ If rejected, are revised terms to be brought back to financing party for second consideration before proceeding with third-party submission

❐ Role of financing party

    ❐ Right or not to check production terms

    ❐ Credit or not as "executive producer"

❐ Right of financing party to recoup costs of demo if resultant delivery to a third party after rejection by financing party

NEGOTIATION CHECKLIST:
DISTRIBUTION AGREEMENT BETWEEN INDEPENDENT LABEL (OWNER) AND MAJOR LABEL (DISTRIBUTOR)

DISTRIBUTOR'S RESPONSIBILITIES

❐ Warehousing

❐ Solicitation and servicing of sales orders

❐ Maintaining consigned inventory quantities

❐ Ensuring customer creditworthiness (i.e., approval policies, etc.)

❐ Returns (designation as saleable or damaged)

❐ Reporting of sales and returns: frequency and structure (e.g., monthly reports of units sold and dollars; weekly regional reports of units sold)

❐ Guarantee to Owner of inclusion in Distributor's "new release" notices

❐ Manufacturing terms on behalf of Owner, e.g., credit on favorable terms

❐ Provision of desk/office space for Owner at Distributor's offices.

❐ Inclusion of Owner in Distributor's advertising, sales programs, industry conventions, etc.

❐ Administration of payments of mechanical royalties

❐ Extending Credit for Owner's Manufacturing costs

MAJOR LABEL (OWNER) RESPONSIBILITIES

❐ Number and frequency of new albums delivered to Distributor

❐ Manufacture and delivery of inventory

❐ Payment of copyright and artist royalties

❐ Ultimate payment for returns (damaged, obsolete, etc.)

❐ Use of Distributor's credit and bar codes on product

❐ Responsibilities for marketing and promotion.

❐ Advances (Distributor to Owner): nature and details of all advances, procedure for unrecouped advances, etc.

    ❐ Following execution of agreement

    ❐ Following delivery of manufacturing parts

    ❐ Any additional advances

DISTRIBUTION FEE (OWNER TO DISTRIBUTOR)

❐ Calculation of basic fee: percentage of net sales (after deductions from gross sales)

❐ Less discounts (e.g., for fast cash payment)/free goods/reserves

❐ Less costs of shipping, handling, packing, manufacturing

❐ Less costs of processing returns

CREDIT TERMS

❐ Deferred charges (without interest for period of deferral)

❐ Time frame for balance of payments due

MISCELLANEOUS

❐ New major artists: good-faith discussions of possible co-funding (additional advances, special royalties, etc.)

❐ Key man clauses

    ❐ Participation of named management person essential to agreement

    ❐ Termination clause in the event that named person fails to be engaged in full-time active management of Owner

❐ Right of first refusal of Distributor in the event of a sale of all or any part of Owner's stock or assets

❐ Costs of promotional materials (photos, art, promotional posters, etc., for each artist; special window displays, Internet banners, video promotions)

    ❐ Owner? Distributor? Shared? Designated party for each?

❐ Territory

    ❐ World?

    ❐ If some territories excluded, Owner's right to move in after prior-commmitment agreements terminate

❐ Audit rights and limitations

NEGOTIATION CHECKLIST:
EXCLUSIVE ARTIST AGREEMENT

❑ Artist or group: official name(s); address(es) to which notices are to be sent

❑ Record company: name and address

❑ Contract period of recording obligation: measured by specified time period or by number of satisfactory albums?

❑ Options: conditions of exercise; number of possible terms

❑ Minimum and maximum number of recorded sides during each term.

❑ Advances

    ❑ Signing advance

    ❑ Per-album advance: specification of installments and how computed (e.g., if measured by amount of royalties earned on prior releases, provide formula including percentage of U.S. royalties, minimum and maximum figures)

❑ Royalties

    ❑ Accounted for quarterly, semiannually, annually

    ❑ Payments due after close of accounting period within: 45 days, 60 days, 90 days

    ❑ Computation of U.S. royalties: wholesale or retail price basis; computed on all sales or on specific percentage; reserves against returned goods

    ❑ Escalation clauses: upon exercise of options; increased percentages for stated volume-level plateaus

    ❑ Foreign royalties: percentage of U.S. rate

❑ Audit rights: within what period of time after accounting statements

❑ Recording costs as advances against royalties: clear statement of what constitutes a recording cost (e.g., are independent promotion costs included?)

❑ Video costs: recoupable in full from record royalties or partly recoupable

❑ Merchandising: assignment of rights; revenue split

❑ Song publishing

    ❑ Assignment of rights

    ❑ Waiver of controlled composition rate in return for co-ownership

- ❏ Group issues
    - ❏ Restriction or not on leaving member rights to move to other label
    - ❏ Selection of replacement
- ❏ Merchandising rights or restrictions: i.e., T shirts, books
    - ❏ Income split
- ❏ Song publishing rights
    - ❏ Granted to what entity (e.g., record label affiliate)
    - ❏ Terms
    - ❏ If reserved or otherwise unavailable, is there a controlled composition reduced rate?

NEGOTIATION CHECKLIST:
EXCLUSIVE SONGWRITER CONTRACT

- ❏ Name and address of writer
- ❏ Name and base address of publisher
- ❏ Scope of assignment: copublishing deal or full publisher assignment
- ❏ Employment status of writer: salaried employee with regular hours or independent contractor
- ❏ Advances
    - ❏ Time frame: Schedule of advance payments
    - ❏ Advances are/are not tied into a record artist deal
- ❏ "Delivery" requirements: minimum recorded and released songs in each stated term; definition of satisfactory "delivery"
- ❏ Duration: stated time period; tied to delivery requirements; a combination thereof
- ❏ Exercise of options
    - ❏ Revised advance terms in exercised option periods (e.g., carry-forward of unrecouped prior advances)
- ❏ Royalties for full publisher contract, percentage
- ❏ Royalties for copublishing deal: percentage of split, administrative charge before calculating split
- ❏ Charges or not for demo records against writer royalties, percentage
- ❏ Controlled composition clauses: publisher/copublisher to honor
- ❏ Accounting periods: quarterly, semiannual, annual
- ❏ Payment after accounting within 45, 60, 90 days
- ❏ Audit: rights can be exercised for what period of years?
- ❏ Foreign retention of part of gross at-source earnings by appointed foreign subpublisher who is/is not affiliate of U.S. publisher
- ❏ Expiration of period of contract
    - ❏ Return of songs at stated time following expiration
    - ❏ Retention of copyrights for length of copyright or for specified number of years after expiration
- ❏ Return of unexploited copyrights tied to failure to obtain recording, film use, etc.; time allowed before required return

NEGOTIATION CHECKLIST:
FOREIGN SUBPUBLISHING AGREEMENT

❐ Names and permanent addresses of U.S. entity and subpublisher

❐ Song list or catalog designation

❐ Territory covered

❐ Term of administration rights

    ❐ Rights to collect "pipeline" delayed receipts after end of term

❐ Percent of receipts kept as service fee before balance remitted to publisher

❐ Revised percentage, if applicable, for local cover records obtained in territory

❐ Sub-subpublisher (if any)

    ❐ Territories involved

    ❐ Fees: In addition to subpublisher fee or included in basic fee calculation (at-source computation)

❐ Option periods/terms for exercise of options

NEGOTIATION CHECKLIST:
HOME VIDEO/DVD
REPRODUCTION OF SONG

- ❑ Identify song licensor by name and address as well as song title and songwriter name or names and artist
- ❑ Identify manufacturer of video/DVD by name and address and title and nature of program, film, etc.
- ❑ Duration of intended use
- ❑ Nature of intended use: featured vocal or instrumental, background vocal or instrumental
- ❑ Territory of sale: U.S., North America, World
- ❑ Duration of licensed use and terms of option to extend, if any
- ❑ Advances: when paid and against what royalty rate
- ❑ Rollover advance payable at outset and again after stated sales plateaus (e.g., 50,000, 100,000, etc. units sold)
- ❑ Flat-fee buyout for single payment without continuing royalty
- ❑ Accouting periods: monthly, quarterly, semiannual
- ❑ Payments due: within 45 days, 60 days, 90 days, 330 days
- ❑ Inventory sell-off period
- ❑ Right to audit: length of time after statement rendered

NEGOTIATION CHECKLIST:
LIVE CONCERT APPEARANCES

- ❏ Date and place of engagement
- ❏ Type of venue
    - ❏ Stadium, night club, cabaret, etc.
    - ❏ Indoor or outdoor
- ❏ Rain date (for outdoor venue)
- ❏ Capacity of venue: number of seats, standing room
- ❏ Sound and light equipment: supplied by whom, run by whom during concert
- ❏ Nature of performance: opening act, feature act
- ❏ Duration of performance
- ❏ Payment
    - ❏ Amount and type (e.g., flat payment or advance against ticket sales)
    - ❏ When due, in what installments
    - ❏ How paid (e.g., if deposit, with whom)
- ❏ Expenses: costs assumed by what party
- ❏ Provision of time for rehearsal and sound check time if required and dressing room description and required refreshments, etc.
- ❏ Publicity and advertising provisions and materials and any specifics as to billing in ads and posters.
- ❏ Exclusivity provisions for promoter: territory and for how long before and after scheduled date?
- ❏ Option for return engagement
- ❏ Merchandising
    - ❏ Items to be sold (T-shirts, books, records, videos)
    - ❏ Facilities (kiosks, booths)
    - ❏ Division of revenues
- ❏ Insurance
    - ❏ Type: personal injury, property damage, etc.
    - ❏ Obtained by whom
- ❏ Union jurisdiction (e.g., AGMA for vocalist, AFM for musician)

NEGOTIATION CHECKLIST:
MASTER USE LICENSE
FOR FILM OR TV SHOW

❐ Identify master by song title, artist, and record release date
and number

❐ Identify licensor of master and licensee/user by name and address

❐ Identify film title or TV show title

❐ Nature of intended use

   ❐ Featured vocal or instrumental, background vocal
   or instrumental

   ❐ Opening or closing theme

   ❐ One or multiple uses in same show

❐ Duration of intended use

❐ Fee calculation

   ❐ Flat fee or advance against continuing royalty

   ❐ Inclusion or not of video/DVD rights

   ❐ "Most favored" basis or not (i.e., no higher fee to other
   masters in same show)

❐ Fee amount

❐ Territory: U.S., North America, World

❐ Credits

   ❐ Content

   ❐ Front end or closing

NEGOTIATION CHECKLIST:
MECHANICAL REPRODUCTION LICENSE

- ❏ Type of use: album or single
- ❏ If album, type of album: one artist or compilation
- ❏ Medley: permitted or not; split terms
- ❏ Territory: U.S., North America, World
- ❏ Rate: Full statutory, 75% of statutory, some other percentage?
- ❏ Accounting periods: monthly, quarterly, semiannual
- ❏ Payments due: within 45 days, 60 days, 90 days
- ❏ Specification of credits to be printed on label and/or jacket (e.g., publisher, songwriter, performance rights society)
- ❏ Use or not of song title as album title
- ❏ Duration of recording

NEGOTIATION CHECKLIST:
PERSONAL MANAGER

☐ Identification of signatories: artist and address; group names and addresses; manager's name and base office address

☐ Scope

    ☐ Exclusive for all areas and territories of entertainment business

    ☐ If not full exclusive, specific exclusions (e.g., "film and acting services"; "outside of North America")

☐ Duration

    ☐ Basic duration

    ☐ Early termination rights or not (e.g., artist can terminate early in case of failure to achieve a stated level of activity [e.g., gross earnings within stated time] or stated form of record contract [e.g., album release on major label, nationally distributed label, or any label]

    ☐ Options or not to manager to extend contract term for successive option periods; exercise of options on what specific conditions (e.g., stated prior gross earnings; continuation as recording contract artist)

☐ Manager's fees

    ☐ Basic rate; applicable to full gross earnings or after stated deductions for travel, accompaniment, booking agent?

    ☐ Escalation/waiver/reduction/deferment clauses: escalation at certain weekly or monthly gross receipt plateaus; de-escalated below such plateaus; deferred below a specified low weekly earnings amount

☐ Power of attorney

    ☐ Type of agreements manager is entitled to act for artist under power of attorney (e.g., any and all agreements or only as specified [e.g., only for one-night engagements])

    ☐ Prior notice requirements

    ☐ Limit or not on amount of weekly expenditures manager can sign off on.

☐ Bar sale or assignment of contract by manager except to firm in which he continues as a key person

☐ "Sunset provision": after expiration of term and exercised options, manager's commissions on continuing sources or royalties are reduced or eliminated

NEGOTIATION CHECKLIST:
SINGLE-SONG CONTRACT

❏ Name and address(es) of songwriter(s)

❏ Name and base address of publisher

❏ Shares when more than one writer signatory

❏ Employment status: song written on assignment from publisher—employer or as independent writer(s)?

❏ Advances: when paid

❏ Demo costs chargeable in whole/in part against writer royalties?

❏ Royalties

    ❏ What percentage of receipts (usually 50 percent)

    ❏ Foreign earnings: subject/not subject to publisher-affiliated foreign firm retaining stated share before computing writer royalty on net receipts in U.S.

❏ Cross-collateralization or not with earnings/advances against royalties with other songs by same writer with same publisher

❏ Accounting periods: quarterly, semiannual, annual

❏ Payment after accounting within 45, 60, 90 days

❏ Audit: rights can be exercised for what period of years

❏ Writer/publisher rights:

    ❏ Does publisher have right to change title of song and/or revise lyrics

    ❏ Is publisher required to get approval for jingle license and/or film synchronization license?

❏ Return of song rights tied to failure to get record released, film use, etc.; time allowed before required return

Index

Univision, 139
Unix, 401
Unpublished works, copyright protection for, 59, 88–91
Unsolicited ideas, 302
Upper-level bonus payment, 147
Upset price, 277
"Up, Up and Away," 147, 253
Urban Network, 390
Uruguay Round Agreements Act (URAA), 8, 71, 116
USAlliance Federal Credit Union, 148
Usher, 27
U2, 377

Values, currency, 46–47
Vanguard Recording Society, Inc. v. Kweskin, 12–13
VCRs, 6
VeriSign, 311
Versions
    local, 212
    new, of works, 121–122
VH-1, 351–352, 358, 372
Viacom, 133, 351, 405, 412
Vicarious liability, 190–191
Video files, downloading of, 401–403
Video licensing, 353
Video Monitor, 358
Video producers, and tax audits, 345
Video rights, 22–23
Videos
    film, 230–231
    music, 351–358
Video technology, 352–353
Vienna Philharmonic, 378
Virgin Records, 266, 400
Visas, work, 377–378
Vivendi, 407–408
Vivendi Universal, 402
Vivendi Universal S.A., 373
Vivian Beaumont Theater, 245
Volt, 267

Waits, Tom, 254
The Wall Street Journal, 117, 371
Wal-Mart, 5
Waring, Fred, 129
Warner, 11, 39, 65, 112, 210, 256, 265, 267, 307, 373, 375, 405
Warner Bros. Music, 183, 307
Warner Bros. Pictures, 303, 307
Warner Bros. Publications, 186
Warner Bros. Records, 39, 63
Warner Brothers Network, 139
Warner Brothers Publishing, 285, 288
Warner/Chappell Music, Inc., 112, 208, 222, 236, 256, 263, 304, 307
Warner Group, 265
Warner Music Group, 374–375
Warner/Rhino, 411
Warning stickers, 77–79
Warranties, 251–252
Warren, Samuel D., 293–294
War of the Worlds, 393
Washington, George, 299
Washington state law, 77
Watermarking, 406

Waters, John, 243
Waters, Muddy, 30
Waterson et al., 111
Watts, Andre, 328
Watts v. Columbia Artists Management, Inc., 328
The Way We Were, 238
WEA, 327
Webber, Andrew Lloyd, 166, 188, 193, 238
Web site, music, starting own, 400–401
WebTV, 412
Weinstein brothers, 244
Welles, Orson, 393
West Side Story, 232
Wexler, Jerry, 30, 267
W. G. Slantz, 135
"When the Red, Red Robin Comes Bob, Bob Bobbin' Along," 111–112, 129–130
Whitburn, Joel, 396
White, Barry, 311
White, Vanna, 297
White Christmas, 303
"White Christmas," 226, 303
White v. Samsung Electronics America, 297
"Whoomp! There It Is!," 198
"Who's Sorry Now," 108, 111, 112, 130
Wiatt, James, 318
Wild spots, 50
William Morris Agency, 318, 378
Williams, Hank, 334
Winamp, 401
Windows, 401, 412
Windows 95, 250
Windows XP, 250
Windows XP Media Center Edition, 401
Windswept Pacific, 257
WIPO Copyright Treaty, 205
WIPO Phonograms and Performances Treaty, 205
"Witchcraft," 238
Wither, Bill, 247
With a Song in My Heart, 303
Wixen Music Publishing, Inc. et al. v. CBS Records dba Columbia House Records, 349
Wonder, Stevie, 27, 223
Woods, Harry, 111–112
Woodstock, 355
Woods v. Bourne Co., 111–112, 129–130
Word Catalog, 256
Work permits, for foreign artists, 377–385
Works created by natural persons after December 31, 1977, 105
Works for hire, 24, 105, 176–181, 227–228, 356
Works in public domain, 106, 115–116, 118–121, 298–299
World economy, performance monies and, 133, 134
World Information Database (WID), 394–395
World Intellectual Property Organization (WIPO), 8, 67, 203, 204–205, 410

World market for music, 207
World Trade Organization (WTO), 8, 143–144, 203
The World Wide Web Independent Music Directory, 400
Writer(s)
    exclusive, contracts for, 277–278
    local, royalties of, 212–213
    as publisher, 222–225
    theater, rights of, 238–241
Writer agreements, exclusive, 173
Writer awards, of performing rights organizations, 149
Writer-publisher joint firms, 223
Writer royalties, 285
Writer's interest in co-ownership, 185–186
Writer's share, of mechanical fees, 160
Writing show, 243

XM, 405

Yankwich, Leon R., 127
Years, shifting income between, 337–338
Yellow Pages, 308
"You'd be So Nice to Come Home To," 250
"Young at Heart," 303
"Your Cheatin' Heart," 256

Zappa, Frank, 77, 199
Ziegfeld Follies, 238
Zomba Music, 255, 256, 266
ZZ Top, 85–86